STILL ACTING GAY:

Male Homosexuality in Modern Drama

John M. Clum

ST. MARTIN'S GRIFFIN

NEW YORK

First published in 1992 by Columbia University Press

ISBN 0-312-22384-6

Library of Congress Cataloging-in-Publication Data

Clum, John M.
    [Acting Gay]
    Still acting gay : male homosexuality in modern drama / John M.
    Clum.
       p. cm.
    Originally published: Acting gay. Rev. ed. New York : Columbia
University Press, © 1994, in series: Between men—between women.
    Includes biographical references and index.
    ISBN 0-312-22384-6
    1. American drama—20th century—History and criticism.
2. Homosexuality and literature—History—20th century. 3. English
drama—20th century—History and criticism. 4. Gay men's writings,
American—History and criticism. 5. Gay men's writings, English—
History and criticism. 6. Gay men in literature. I. Title.

PS338.H66 C58 2000
812'.509353—dc21

                                                           00-021499

Composition by Westchester Book Composition

First St. Martin's Griffin edition: May 2000

10 9 8 7 6 5 4 3 2 1

Because the prosecution has held that McKinney and Henderson lured Shepard to McKinney's truck by pretending to be gay themselves, the defense asked the Fireside staff if the men were "acting gay." The witnesses didn't think so, even after defense attorney Jason Tangeman tried to make it more specific by asking, "Did they fluctuate their voices?"

Report on trial of Aaron McKinney, murderer of Matthew Shepard,
aol Gay Community News, October 28, 1999

There really weren't scenes like that in the movie where I had to "act gay." Everyone in the movie just assumes Oscar's gay.

Matthew Perry, *The Advocate*, November 9, 1999.

For Walter S. Melion
Without whom. . .

CONTENTS

PREFACE TO *STILL* ACTING GAY

"Do I act gay?" Billy (Sean Hayes), in Tommy O'Haver's delightful self-described film "trifle," *Billy's Hollywood Screen Kiss* (1998), asks repeatedly. We know Billy *is* gay because Billy has told us in the first line of the film that he is gay and that his gayness will dominate the narrative. Yet Billy is self-conscious about "acting" gay. In part the film is about Billy's lack of "gaydar," his inability to see that the object of his affection, puppy-dog-cute Gabriel (Brad Rowe), is in the process of coming out. Gabriel clearly is deciding how much he wants to act gay (queer theorists would tell us that there is no such thing as "being," only "acting," or performing, gayness, or anything else), but Billy is not the best of role models. If someone does not tell Billy straight out (no pun intended) that he is gay, as Billy tells us himself, Billy seems clueless. Yet anyone with the slightest gaydar would know about Gabriel (gay-briel?), who signals his gayness every way he can and flirts quite outrageously. Billy worries about "acting gay" because he is hung up on his gayness, on memories of childhood and adolescent angst and rejection. He wants Gabriel to be as angst-ridden as he is. Their fumbling attempt at getting into bed together would be fine for two sixteen-year-olds, as it is in the lovely "first time" scene in the film of Jonathan Harvey's *Beautiful Thing,* but Billy and Gabriel are grown men and Gabriel loses interest. Within twenty-four hours Gabriel finds what he wants, "I think I know what I'm supposed to have," a humpy underwear model who is not angst ridden.

"Do I act gay?" Billy means, "Do I show stereotypical signs of gayness?" "Do I unwittingly perform actions characteristic of gay men?" In his meaning, it is a silly question. We may not choose to be attracted to members of the same sex, but, to a large extent, we choose our signs of gayness, our gay "act." Leather or drag, camp or jock, or some combination with different elements dominant in different contexts. Does Billy act gay? Since he tells us he's gay in the first line of the film, we will see everything he does as acting gay. Sean Hayes, who plays Billy, is the sort of actor one would hire to play a stereotypical gay character. He's slender, cute, sweet, with a very expressive face and a high tenor voice. The object of his affection, Gabriel, played by the amateurish Brad Rowe, may not be stereotypically gay, whatever that means, but he is so flirtatious with Billy, so busy with his eyes, that he has to be gay. Is Rowe the actor trying too hard to act gay when he is supposed to be doing the opposite? Does he think he's just acting cute?

Paradoxically, Sean Hayes plays his own games about being and acting gay. On the *Billy's Hollywood Screen Kiss* website, both Hayes and Rowe claim to be heterosexuals. They may well be, but we all know the official Hollywood mythology: There are no gay actors, only gay roles. In typical Hollywood style, these straight guys show their coolness by having no problem playing gay guys. The corporate thinking seems to be that an openly gay actor playing a gay character would be too threatening to a few million people. The gay media supports this canard by making *Out Magazine* cover boys of straight actors who "courageously" play gay parts. On the website for the NBC sitcom, *Will and Grace*, on which Sean Hayes plays a gay character, Hayes claims that he likes to keep his sexuality a mystery. Now there's a coy one—straights can think he's straight; gays can think he's gay. Something for everyone. On *Will and Grace* Hayes plays a more flamboyant version of his Billy, a real queen who is always surprised when people think he's gay, the foil to the "straight looking and acting" Will. This is the new formula for the late nineties. In addition to a straight woman with a gay male sidekick, we have a "straight looking and acting" gay man with a flamboyantly gay sidekick. The same formula is repeated in the film comedy, *Kiss Me Guido* (1997), where "straight looking and acting" gay man, Warren, has a flamboyantly gay sidekick, Terry, played by the divo of independent gay films, Craig Chester. In *Kiss Me Guido,* supposedly straight would-be actor Frankie learns to bond with his gay roommate by acting a gay role in a terrible off-off-Broadway drama. Acting gay, or at least acting same sex desire, leads to an ambiguous loving, potentially sexual relationship between Frankie and Warren. Coming out into the world of theater is for Frankie at least accepting gay people and the validity of same sex desire.

There are many ways of acting gay. We all choose some acts and reject others. *Billy's Hollywood Screen Kiss* offers three generations of gay style: a grand old queen (played by cult film auteur Paul Barthel); a forty-ish serious type, a survivor of the AIDS holocaust (Richard Ganoung, who starred in the AIDS era classic, *Parting Glances*); and a younger generation not quite sure how to act. At a recent gay pride festival, I ran into a friend of mine, a successful investment banker, dressed in leather at the COMMAND booth. I asked him where the crinoline booth was. Briefly we had acted for each other. His leather is a means of acting out some of his fantasies and his sense of himself when he is out of his business suit. My quip was an expression of my gay act, the older generation queen always ready with the camp *riposte,* the expression of the social world I came out into around the time of *The Boys in the Band.* When my partner was told our friend had gotten into leather, his automatic response was "Italian leather?" He thinks of acting gay in terms of a different sort of fashion statement than our leather clad friend. Leather is the other side of female drag, an attire that symbolizes an extreme masculinity and erases dreaded signs of effeminacy. But it's all drag. Choosing one act is rejecting another, but the choice and rejection may be transitory. A leather queen on Saturday night might be camping it up in designer clothes at Sunday brunch. Who wants to be a one trick pony? Hollywood's Billy is old fashioned enough to think that being gay might be a result of inheriting "the show tune gene," but show tunes, themselves vehicles for flamboyant performance, are another medium of expression for an older generation of gay men, not a cause of gayness.

Most gay people know queer theorist Judith Butler is right when she says gender is an act. I am aware of that every day as I walk across the Duke quad and watch the performances of young straight men and straight women trying to get the attention of the same men. Language is reduced to a few safe exchanges in the lowest possible voice. Many young women now talk in an ugly throaty voice to be "one of the boys." Femininity is out for men and women. Gay men can free themselves from these acts, though not all gay men want to, but they then have to choose another one or more acts: drama queen, butch gay Republican, leather queen, pretty boy (not totally a matter of choice), gym boy, angry queer, earnest queer theorist, half of an assimilated middle-class gay couple. Calling these "performances" does not mean they don't have meaning for the performers. God knows, "performance" is a better word than "lifestyle"—only our opponents think there is *a* gay lifestyle. I prefer plain "style" and aspire to having some of same. We do what is comfortable for us—"natural," to use an unfashionable word.

What does "gay" mean anyway? Desiring and having sex with partners of the same sex? A lot of people do that and deny their gayness. Gay critic Alan Sinfield is correct in writing that the gay subculture "is fraught with the contradictions of its own history and of its crucial positioning in the prevailing sex-gender system; it is divided by hierarchies of class, age, education, and ethnicity that occur in society at large."[1] At best, gayness asserts "a political and legal unity of interests between subjects variously categorized as perverse/ sick/mad/queer/contagious and so on."[2] But gayness is itself an endangered state. Writers talk of the "post-gay" era, and there is some validity in this. Post-and anti-gay critics claim that gay culture at the end of the century has become the culture of ultimate narcissism. As novelist John Weir quips, "If gay men ruled America, there would be tax credits for joining a gym."[3] It can also be a culture of self-congratulation. At a time of great social inequity, poverty, and civil wars, gay popular culture presents visions of gay men as the ultimate martyrs, even as Christ, as in Terrence McNally's *Corpus Christi*. We've been through homophobia and we're still here. And we're all young with washboard stomachs and great pecs. To believe these canards is to lose those attributes our history taught us—irony and an understanding of performativity. They also deny the reality of aging when one of the most important questions for us now is how we age gracefully and happily in a youth-dominated culture. There's little for a middle-aged queen in *Out Magazine* and its ilk.

Our enemies on the right and the queer theorists, the vestiges of sixties gay radicalism, both live to fight the same losing battles against assimilation. Lesbian and gay couples are living together in domestic arrangements, joining churches and civic organizations not hostile to them, and adopting children (in some enlightened states). I sit in our Unitarian church on Sunday mornings surrounded by same sex couples with their children, often from previous marriages, whose very existence argues for fluidity of desire. We're not just hairdressers and interior decorators anymore, but lawyers, doctors, stock brokers, and auto mechanics. Most people do not bat an eye. Yes, we have enemies, but there are also racists and antisemites in our beloved country, and folks eager to blow me up simply because I'm an American. Moreover, my experience in England and parts of Europe convince me that, despite remaining anti-sodomy laws, there is more freedom for lesbians and gay men here, in the United States, than in other Western countries (not to mention non-Western countries). This is not to say that we do not have battles yet to wage. Taking our battle to the streets does not seem useful. Against whom should we fight? Disney likes us, which ultimately is more important than the fact that nasty old Jesse Helms and his clones hate us. Who has more power in our society? Yes, it is horrible that young Matthew Shepard was brutally murdered by a couple of young, screwed up losers, but the good news is that most Americans felt the grotesque savagery perpetrated on that young man was awful.

Gay men may also be forgetting that gayness is an expression of particular historical circumstances. The gays we see on television and in film are middle-class products of urban societies. The 1997 film *Delta* suggests how different their expressions of gayness might be if they were from a small southern town or, perhaps, from Vietnam. Our current sense of sexual identity, a product of what Alan Sinfield calls metropolitan culture will change, perhaps, into something more radically transformative of society. When I dealt with my sexuality, and I dealt with it different ways during my twenties (gayness, repression, a stab at heterosexual marriage, gayness), I felt that my choice was between "being" gay or "acting" straight. For me, whatever I was going to be was connected with my desire for a stable, nurturing, loving relationship. I also felt, as many gay men did in my generation, that being gay tied me to Culture in meaningful ways. As gay film critic Richard Dyer described us:

> Queerness brought with it artistic sensitivity—it gave you the capacity to appreciate and respond to culture. It was a compensation for having been born or made queer.... It also made you doubly "different"—queer and cultured. And how splendid to be different! Even if you were awful.[4]

It was the well-established involvement of gays in culture, as well as a relatively unhostile environment, that led so many gay men into theater. Now those cultural institutions that were so important to me and my friends (opera, theater, etc.) seem as alien to young gay folk as they do to their straight counterparts. *Billy's Hollywood Screen Kiss* suggests that this relationship of queerness and culture hasn't totally changed, but culture is now L.A., not Lincoln Center or the Village, and Mecca for gay culture is West Hollywood (if you are under thirty and good-looking).

Now many of our cultural gurus argue for sexual fluidity. If the sex itself is the most important thing, why worry about gay or straight? I know married men my age who were satisfied with occasional trips to the baths to take care of their desire for men—they did not believe love between men was possible, but sex certainly was and it was more exciting to think of that sex as separate from love or commitment, which they got from their wives. Now such variety is even less problematic. For those in the middle of the Kinsey scale, why specialize? Why worry about gay or straight? The polymorphous perversity celebrated by Joe Orton is, for those folks, the wave of the future. Gay organizations now have loads of initials to spell out "gay, lesbian, queer, bisexual, transgendered"—so many labels argue for no labels at all. I heard rock star Michael Stipe say in an interview that he wasn't bisexual, but sexual, which seemed a sensible self-definition. Stipe was one of the producers of Todd Haynes's intriguing film celebration of seventies glam rock, *Velvet Goldmine* (1998), which saw these rock stars as sexual revolutionaries in believing one chose one's sexual style like one chose one's costume. Since two of the three leading characters were more conventionally homosexual than "sexual," the film argued against its own premise, but Haynes was most fascinated with the protean glitter star, Brian, who could change personae at will. Coupled middle-aged gay men like me are no threat to the social order. We want spousal benefits to go with our dual mortgages. We would like the same legal rights and privileges as married heterosexuals. However much the religious right may want to deny us what they have, we're not enemies of marriage. We're upholding a coupled society. Are the young people I see interested in monogamy or rigid categories of sexuality? For many, the answer is no. A new age is dawning as we cross Bill Clinton's bridge into the twenty-first century. On the MTV series *Undressed* the primary anxiety for some of its lesbian and gay characters is the possible bisexuality of their partners.

So what does *Still Acting Gay* mean beyond a clever title my editor and I cooked up over Chardonnay in a Chelsea bar? I'm still acting gay in the way I enjoy, being camp in my old(er) queen way, working on a drama faculty, loving opera and musical theater, going to antiques fairs, doing gourmet cooking, reading *The Advocate*. But gay drama, as it was six years ago, when the last edition of this book was published, may be a thing of the past, partly because being gay is intrinsically less problematic and because many of us are part of a larger fabric of social relations. There are still gay ghettos and stories of those ghettos—West Hollywood, Chelsea, Boy's Town in Chicago—but living there is now a choice, not a necessity for many men. Many of us prefer a social world that isn't all gay. We continue to march in Pride Parades, but who's on the sidelines throwing rocks? As I reread what I wrote in 1991 and 1993, I realize that a lot of it is now history—gay history as well as theater history.

I began the first edition of *Acting Gay* with a quote from playwright Lanford Wilson: "The theater is the only public forum a gay writer has." As the millennium approaches, theater no longer is the only medium in which we are visibly present in narratives we write. We're everywhere in the media. We're almost a necessity playing the new Ethel Mertzes, the sidekicks of zany straight women, on television sitcoms and hit film comedies, often written and produced by gay men. At the beginning of the fall 1999 television season, media watchers noted that there would be seventeen television series with recurring gay characters. MTV's candid *Undressed,* in which same-sex couples actually kiss and get into bed together, just like the straight couples, suggests that many teenagers—at least the ones who watch MTV—are not as homophobic as their elders. In the 1999 film, *American Beauty,* the gay couple is the only happy marriage we see in this dark vision of suburbia (like Jack Straw and Peter Ochello in Tennessee Williams's *Cat on a Hot Tin Roof*). We're the subjects of serious, gay-created films. Gay writers and pundits are on chat shows. There are celebrated openly gay rock stars. Which is to say that gay men no longer need to go to the theater to see ourselves and our lives and that gay dramatic writers no longer see the theater as the only medium open to us. Most of our successful plays are quickly turned into movies. Meanwhile, at least in 1999, there were precious few plays opening in New York and London that focussed on gay characters. With something as intelligent and candid as *Queer as Folk* playing on British television, who needs to go to the theater?

For those of us who have been toiling in the vineyard of gay theater for the past few decades, this raises the question of what gay theater can and should do in an era in which serious drama is seldom Broadway fare (even the highly praised *Angels in America* lost money in its Broadway run). Serious drama is now off-Broadway at best. But drama is no longer a New York monopoly. The most moving productions of *Angels in America* and Terrence McNally's *Love! Valour! Compassion!* that I have seen were produced in a 100 seat non-equity theater in Baltimore, Maryland. Gay drama is still produced in small, adventurous theaters all across America; from Theatre Rhinoceros in San Francisco, to Bailiwick Repertory in Chicago, to AXIS Theater in Baltimore; to Actor's Express in Atlanta, to Manbites Dog Theater in Durham, North Carolina, to Theater on the Square in Indianapolis, and places in between because gay men are still a core audience for theater. Bill Kaiser's *Purple Circuit Newsletter,* a boon to those of us in gay theater, lists scores of gay theatrical productions in every issue. The bad news is nobody's making any money. John Dunn's DIALOGUS Play Service and Publishing, which supported many of us as playwrights, had to close its doors. Can good theater survive for long as a totally unremunerative enterprise?

One can look at this book as a history and a challenge. It is a testament to the importance of gay playwrights in the history of American and British theater. I do not discuss writers like Oscar Wilde, about whom reams have been written in recent years, including Moises Kaufmann's brilliant theater piece, *Gross Indecency: The Three Trials of Oscar Wilde*; two plays by distinguished straight British playwrights (David Hare's *The Judas Kiss* and Tom Stoppard's *The Invention of Love*); and a high budget film (*Wilde*). Nor do I discuss popular British playwrights of the thirties, forties, and fifties, Terrence Rattigan and Somerset Maugham who sometimes chafed under the restrictions against dramatizing "the love that dare not speak its name."[5] If I don't mention John van Druten, who wrote Broadway adaptations like *I Remember Mama* and *I Am a Camera* and, more importantly, penned that hilarious allegory of fifties gay culture, *Bell, Book, and Candle*; or Arthur Laurents, whose *The Enclave* was ahead of its time, to say the least (I do mention them in my reading list), I cover enough drama to show that the tradition of what can be called gay drama has been central to twentieth-century theater, though critics once called it "superficial."

While the body of work discussed in the ensuing chapters is varied, there are common threads. In describing what she calls "second generation AIDS drama," Therese Jones says that the creators of these works "share with us the exhilarating and empowering fusion of carnival—a festive perception of the world that succeeds moments of natural and social crisis, consecrates inventive freedom, and liberates from establishes truths—and the politics of representation—the assertion of subjectivity and foregrounding of individual experience."[6] I would assert that this description applies to the best of gay drama from Jean Cocteau to Tennessee Williams to Tony Kushner and beyond. Our best playwrights have always seen realism as a trap—as the least theatrical of the modes of dramatic representation and the one on which the values of mainstream society are most indelibly inscribed. Our playwrights have developed a dramatic medium that allows space for, in ascending order of importance: *display,* of the male body and of queer theatricality; *polemic,* some assertion of where we will not compromise with the mainstream; *self-examination* of ourselves as individuals and members of what is called the gay community; *transformation* through theatricality and irony of the representational and narrative forms which maintain our oppression; and *celebration* of our courage, resistance, and difference.

At times in our drama, one or more of these elements becomes exaggerated. What seems to draw large gay audiences are plays whose principal function is to serve as a pretext for guys taking their clothes off. Ronnie Larson's *Making Porn* and its spin-offs; the Los Angeles production, *Naked Boys Singing*; or silly fluff like *Cute Boys in Their Underpants* or *Two Guys in a Bed on a Cold Winter Night* seem to exist only so that we can see the guys' peepees. Would *Love! Valour! Compassion!,* a fine play, have made it onto Broadway and into so many theaters across the country if the cast had remained clothed? I write in Chapter I about how the naked gay penis is equated for many in the audience, straight and gay, with gay male sexuality. However, there's no danger in male nudity for a gay audience. It's merely display. We're men, after all, and have that male desire to see what we desire. Of course, that nudity is also a provocation to those who find genitalia threatening. Display alone turns drama into an elaborate striptease. Nor does polemic make interesting drama. Drama, after all, is more interesting when it raises questions rather than answer them.

> No one cares what you think as a gay man, duck. That wasn't the question. What do you think as a member of the human race?

In Terrence McNally's *Love! Valour! Compassion!* the bitter John Jeckyll poses this question to his weekend date, a young Latino who defines himself both as a person of color and as a gay man. John's question crystallizes a problem for gay dramatists. The mirror gay drama holds up to contemporary gay culture may include, amidst the self-congratulation, an unintentional critique of the narcissism and self-righteousness we can demonstrate. Only by showing how our experience connects with others in our society can we create a drama that offers a vision of America in which we are responsible citizens. We should be exploding repressive categories, not reinforcing them. In the final chapter, I focus on plays that do this kind of work.

For our enemies, gay theater is an enemy they can conquer. Perhaps those of us in theater should be delighted someone still finds theater dangerous, but we're an easy target. The so-called Christian right can't stop NBC from having gay characters on its sitcoms or Disney giving gay employees domestic partnership rights, but they can stop local government funding of theaters and other arts organizations.

In 1993, as a response to a local production in Cobb County, Georgia, of Terrence McNally's *Lips Together, Teeth Apart,* which has no gay characters, but deals compassionately with the homophobia of four heterosexuals who are visiting Fire Island, the County Council passed a proclamation condemning "the gay lifestyle." When they realized that passing a resolution banning the funding of art that promoted such a "lifestyle" would quickly die in a court challenge, the Council decided to ban all government funding of the arts. These actions were repeated in Mecklenburg County, North Carolina, after a theater in Charlotte produced *Angels in America.* Other theaters in Jesse Helms's home state pulled productions of the benign musical *La Cage aux Folles* after the religious right threatened to make the productions a political issue. These groups couldn't stop the film version of *La Cage aux Folles, The Birdcage,* from being a hit at their movie theaters, but they can scare theaters working on slim financial margins. Lest we think this sort of thing only happens south of the Mason-Dixon line, remember the threats against the theater, actors, and audience from so-called Christian groups when Terrence McNally's *Corpus Christi* was announced by the Manhattan Theater Club. These groups realize that theater possesses a power and greater danger than that of celluloid and the electronic media. The relationship between live performer and audience is a potent one.

Bringing this book, first written in 1991 and updated a couple of years later, into the present, has not been difficult, but I am grateful for the opportunity of doing it. The original text represents my thinking at a specific moment in gay history and in the history of American and British theater. This is not a rewrite, but I have revised my comments on some writers and plays. There are still statements in the book that are, from the viewpoint of the year 2000, anachronisms.

I wrote this book when AIDS was the focal point of gay politics and a devastating reality for gay men. AIDS is now, for gay men, a controllable condition instead of an immediate death sentence. The nightmare of AIDS persists, however, as a disease of the poor around the world and in our own cities. Organizations created to serve the gay community now have expanded their outreach. AIDS is still a presence in gay drama as it is in our lives, but it is no longer necessarily linked to pathos.

Nor is AIDS the focus of our political activity as it was at the beginning of the nineties. We're now fighting for the full rights of citizenship. While federal, state, and local governments, seemingly the most conservative secular institutions in our society, are slow to move in many areas, a significant number of corporations and institutions recognize our right to be honest and proud about who we are. Such corporations and institutions also recognize the validity of our partnerships. The religious right is still screaming, but more and more Americans realize that government has no right legislating what goes on between consenting adults in the bedroom. The Internet is the new mode of communication and information, and major Internet providers have gay "channels" and chat rooms. Duke University, where I work, has a lesbian-gay-bisexual email list that features lively discussion, sometimes heated, between students, faculty, and staff on subjects of mutual concern. It is unlikely such a wide range of people would ever gather in the same room for such a debate.

The greatest change in gay drama in the past five years is that playwrights no longer feel the need to see gayness as a problem to be explained. Homosexual desire is a presence and gay characters don't have to talk about why they're gay. Insofar as homosexuality and/or homophobia underlie the action of a play, they do so as part of a larger social critique.

Since I wrote *Acting Gay,* I have changed my thinking on Tennessee Williams. I now see his insistence on presenting homosexuality in the virulently anti-homosexual Cold War era as being far more significant and revolutionary than the cautious way in which he staged it. I have to thank David Savran's fine book, *Communists, Cowboys and Queers* for enriching my thinking on Williams. Queerness is indeed all over Williams's texts and few writers of his time can claim such a revolutionary stance toward sexual desire and behavior. My published work on Williams since *Acting Gay* is infused with my current thinking on gay and straight America's greatest playwright.[7] The bulk of my revisions in this edition are in the Williams section.

In *La Cage aux Folles,* Albin/Zaza sings "I Am What I Am." I have to sing that to those who complain that *Acting Gay* isn't theoretical enough. I was trained in a different era and theater, not theory, is my passion and my language. I overheard a graduate student say about my relationship with theory to another graduate student, "He's read the stuff, but he just doesn't seem to *care.*" Exactly! For better or worse, this book represents the way I think about theater and gay politics. I can only hope it also represents those subjects fairly and accurately.

Baltimore and Durham, 2000

ACKNOWLEDGMENTS

Acting Gay was originally Richard Mohr's idea and his editorial acumen is evident here in many ways. The book grew out of an essay I wrote for *Theater Journal* that forms the basis of Chapter five. Thanks to Sue-Ellen Case for inviting me to write that. An earlier version of my discussion of *Love! Valour! Compassion!* in Chapter eight appeared in *Terrence McNally: A Casebook*, edited by Toby Silverman Zinman (Garland, 1997).

I am grateful to my wonderful editor at St. Martin's, Michael Flamini, for making this updated version possible. I also want to offer continued thanks to my first editor at Columbia University Press, Ann Miller, for her help on the first versions and her faith in the project over the years. Also, thanks to my original production editor, Anne McCoy, and my original, knowledgeable copyeditors, Janet Boulton and Leslie Bialler, who caught my errors of fact as well as style. I am lucky, too, to have as superb a production editor as Alan Bradshaw at St. Martin's.

Thanks, too, to the colleagues and friends who help me shape my ideas: the one and only Robert Patrick, Samuel Adamson, John Cannon, Jonathan Cullen, Gregory J. Tomso, Stephen Holden, Don Shewey, Clifford Hindley, Anthony Lyn, Godfrey Hamilton, Mark Pinkosh, and, of course, Bob West.

Thanks to the playwrights who have been helpful in supplying me with scripts of their plays and, often, helpful discussions: Neal Bell, Tony Kushner, Chay Yew, Craig Lucas, Joe Calarco, Steve Murray, and Naomi Wallace. I am also grateful to agents George Lane, Gilbert Parker, and Carl Mulert.

Thanks also to former department chairs David Ball and Stanley Fish for enabling my work on the first version, and to my current colleague, chairperson, and friend, Richard Riddell, for his help and support with all my work over the past seven years. Thanks to my assistant, Kevin Poole, for covering for me while I wrote the additional chapters and for his insights. Thanks, too, to all my colleagues in drama at Duke, particularly Dale and Phyllis Randall, Jody McAuliffe, Erin Cressida Wilson, and Jeff Storer. I could not ask for a more supportive environment in which to work. Special thanks to friend and colleague Jon Dominic Rossini for all his help.

The dedication remains to my partner of fifteen years, Walter Melion, whose presence in my life makes my work possible and my acting gay more, well, gay.

★

INTRODUCTION

In these pages I seek to interpret the central works of what I call gay male drama, written by twentieth century English and American playwrights. Gay American playwright Lanford Wilson has said, "The theater is really the only public forum a gay writer has."[1] While this is not as true as it was a decade ago, theater in this century has been a particularly important voice in gay culture and has often acted as its mirror. As Alan Sinfield puts it, "Theater has been a particular site for the formation of dissident sexual identities."[2] The plays I discuss in these pages reflect transformations in the way gay men see themselves and in the roles they play in twentieth century American and British society.

The history of homosexuality in drama records a series of moves back and forth from the unspoken to the spoken, from the unseen to the seen. Homosexual desire is affirmed in Marlowe, acknowledged in Jonson, and explored in Shakespeare. It is at least suggested in comedies of the Restoration. For most of the history of theater, the gay playwright's unspoken compact with producers and audiences entailed keeping his homosexuality offstage or presenting homosexuality in a coded manner so that heterosexuals in the audience need not notice it. With a few forays farther back in time, *Acting Gay* primarily focusses on plays written in the United States and Great Britain since 1930. The story of male homosexuality in modern drama actually goes back almost to the invention of the term "homosexual." Andre Gide's *Saul* was written shortly after he met Oscar Wilde in the mid-1890s. Laurence Senelick's superbly annotated anthology, *Lovesick: Modern Plays of Same-Sex Love, 1894–1925,* documents gay drama in France, Germany, Russia, England, and the United States. I begin with the history of the silences and the codes used in the presentation of homosexuality in the dramas of the thirties, forties, and fifties, which mirror the changing position of gay men offstage. Play-wrights like Tennessee Williams were able to create rich, powerful drama out of their sense of difference even when that difference, though a wellspring of their genius, could not be given positive voice.

In the past twenty years, homosexuality in drama has moved from shame-filled hints and indirection to proud assertion. Heterosexism, which used to be upheld as the norm, is driven offstage in a comforting fantasy not fully enacted outside the theater.[3] Short lists of openly gay playwrights on this side of the Atlantic: Jon Robin Baitz, Robert Chesley, Christopher Durang, Harvey Fierstein, William Hoffman, Albert Innaurato, Larry Kramer, Tony Kushner, Craig Lucas, Terrence McNally, Robert Patrick, Guillermo Reyes, Paul Rudnick, Nicky Silver, Doric Wilson, Lanford Wilson, Chay Yew—and in Great Britain: Andrew Alty, Kevin Elyot, Jonathan Harvey—attest to the vitality and centrality of contemporary gay drama.

Alan Sinfield observes that "Representations in theatre helped to estab-lish, consolidate and challenge notions of lesbians and gay men which were held by both them and the society at large."[4] This sense of two worlds, the ever changing, so-called "gay community" and mainstream society that has marginalized us in various ways over the past century, is crucial to my ar-gument.

The term *gay drama* refers to two kinds of plays written for two types of audiences. One type is the post-Stonewall play that is written primarily for gay audiences and speaks to our shared experience. Such works, from the plays of Robert Patrick in the 1960s to Robert Chesley and Doric Wilson in the early 1980s, are purposely "coterie" plays, not intended for an outside audience. Now an openly gay play like Tony Kushner's *Angels in America* or Terrence McNally's *Love! Valour! Compassion!* may open in a more main-stream theater, even move to Broadway, because the gay audience for such a play is numerous and visible and the mainstream press will not automatically decry it as they would have a generation ago (see Chapter Four). Still, the audience for such a play is primarily a gay one. If one wants to study a body of work that reflects the attitudes and language of the out-of-the-closet, polit-icized New York gay man at a certain period over the past thirty-five years, these "inside" plays provide a more reliable gauge than what we see in com-mercial films or television sitcoms.

However, a couple of generations back, when gay people were sup-posed to be invisible, the gay playwrights who achieved the greatest exposure, through both stage production and publication, were those who, for a com-bination of personal, artistic, and economic reasons, chose to write for the Broadway theater, at the time the only game in town, and who, as a result, had to mediate between the closeted gay and straight members of their audi-ence. In a similar fashion, they had to mediate between their own vision and political stance as homosexuals[5] in an oppressive time and the often conservative, heterosexist attitudes of most of their audience. It took courage to allow "the love that dare not speak its name" the faintest whisper.

If homosexuality was mentioned, it was usually in a heterosexual, heterosexist voice, in melodramas by heterosexual playwrights that exploited taboos about homosexuality while presenting homosexual stereotypes. These plays tell one little about the real experience of homosexuals between 1930 and 1960, but much about the official view of homosexuals. They place homosexuals within the conventions of the dominant genre of mid-twentieth century British and American drama, the realistic "problem play," in which a social or psychological aberration that threatens a community is introduced only to be, in the end, expunged. In the history of this genre, homosexuality is usually presented as "the problem" that must be solved or eliminated by the final curtain. In general, the history of representations of homosexuals and homosexual desire is one of integration into, compromises with, and extensions of this dramatic form, which has transmitted and affirmed the values of its audiences for more than a century. In Part 2, I will show how two such commercial "problem plays," Mordaunt Shairp's *The Green Bay Tree* (1933)[6] and Robert Anderson's *Tea and Sympathy* (1953), distilled the homosexual stereotypes of their respective times and described the limited roles gay men were allowed in their societies. Since the realistic problem play has, to a great extent, been appropriated by television, I include discussions of a few of television's attempts to dramatize the "problem" of homosexuality in the 1980s.

A tradition of cross-fertilization between British and American drama makes their pairing a natural, if not seamless, subject. Most of the plays discussed in this volume have been produced in both Great Britain and the United States. American-born playwright Martin Sherman lives and writes in London where his gay plays *Bent* (1979) and *A Madhouse in Goa* (1989) received their premieres. Londoner Noel Coward wrote *Design for Living* (1933) for Broadway. Many of the British plays discussed in this volume have been produced in New York and in regional and university theaters across the country. American plays like Harvey Fierstein's *Torch Song Trilogy* (1980) and Larry Kramer's *The Normal Heart* (1985) have been produced successfully in London, where Tony Kushner's *Angels in America* received its first major production. I do not presume that the gay cultures of Great Britain and the United States share an identity. Indeed some of the most successful British gay plays are received here, in the United States, with some bafflement. The differences in reception reflect basic differences in gay identity and self-perception in the two countries.

This book is divided into four sections. The two chapters of Part I, "Bodies and Taboos," center on the presentation of the physical aspects of homosexuality and their relationship to the norms of the segment of society represented by their audience. The first chapter focusses on three commonly staged visual images of homosexuality: men kissing, male nudity, and drag. The second chapter is a discussion of a group of early AIDS dramas that exemplify the difference between mainstream "outside" drama, which presents the gay man and the Person With AIDS as problems that invade "normal" society, and "inside" gay drama, which focusses on the adjustment of the Person With AIDS to his changed sense of himself, his past, and his possibilities. I place these plays in the context of the nineteenth-century play that is the paradigm in popular drama of representations between sexual freedom and illness—*La Dame aux Camelias* by Alexandre Dumas.

Part 2, "Codes and Closets," is a survey of dramas written between 1930 and 1968 that, in various ways, opened up a space for homosexual characters while, paradoxically, maintaining the closet. These plays are either "problem plays" by heterosexual playwrights or plays by homosexual playwrights that cautiously, as they must, introduce homosexuality in a coded or elliptical manner.

Part 3, "Staging 'A Culture That Isn't Just Sexual,'" focusses on drama written between the mid-1960s and the mid-1990s in which homosexuality is directly presented Chapter 5 treats plays that present incidents or figures central to gay history or gay culture. Chapters 6 and 7 discuss dramas of Post-Stonewall gay life.

Part 4, "From Insularity to Engagement," new to this edition, places recent British and American gay drama in the context of where we are now politically and suggests possibilities for gay drama in the future.

We know now that the history of gay playwrights in America is at least a century old, that our most successful turn-of-the-century playwright, Clyde Fitch, was homosexual and probably was, at one time, a lover of Oscar Wilde. George Kelly, one of the most successful playwrights of the twenties and thirties, lived with the same man for decades.[7] It would have been inconceivable for these men, working in the commercial theatre, to write gay characters, gay drama. Gay men are now, as the century ends, very much in the spotlight, but we still face catcalls as well as applause. Nonetheless, we are onstage for good. For many of us, the issue now is to be seen as legitimate members of a large and varied cast, not leading players in dramas that deny, denigrate, or threaten our very existence or in dramas that place us in a parallel universe to that occupied by our fellow citizens.

PART 1

BODIES AND TABOOS

CHAPTER ONE

SEEING GAY

"I saw! I know! You disgust me. . . ."
BLANCHE DUBOIS, IN TENNESSEE WILLIAMS,
A Streetcar Named Desire

The history of the representation of homosexual desire onstage is a series of moves from nothing, to innuendo and gesture, to discussion without any physical signs of attraction or affection, to, finally, showing. The continuing shock value of open demonstrations of homosexual affection or desire shows not only the continuity of heterosexism but also the theatrical principle that bodies contain the greatest potential danger for a contemporary audience, and theater's power stems from its danger.

An emphasis on the centrality of the physical aspect of drama is particularly crucial to a discussion of gay drama, for what might be seen in gay drama is what is usually, for much of the mainstream theatrical audience, unseen. Even speculation about what it would be like to see a homosexual act or, worse, an expression of gay love, is commonly kept locked in a cerebral closet.

What is "seen" in gay drama can be frighteningly erotic or erotically frightening to some members of the audience, and what Martin Esslin rightly calls "the profoundly erotic nature" of performed drama will be central to this discussion.[1] As Herbert Blau asserts, "The erotic capacity of theater is not of secondary importance. It is right there, in the bodies."[2]

Don Shewey has written provocatively about the erotic relationship between audience and actor in live theater: "Apart from the erotic desire aroused by performers we find sexually attractive, our desire is provoked by a curiosity about people very different from ourselves."[3] What happens when a man or woman in the audience sees attractive actors perform a frightening, alien act of physical intimacy for which the audience member may have words, but which he or she has never seen? This question defines not only the erotics of gay drama but also its politics.

The act an audience sees may have been created by one or a number of writers of the dramatic text that is the produced play: actors, director, playwright, designers. Any student of theater knows that the play the audience sees and hears has been "written" by a number of people other than the author, as well as by the social and physical conditions of performance. A gay director might find a homosexual subtext in a heterosexual drama, just as a heterosexual director can, even unwittingly, eliminate the homoeroticism of a gay script. A gay actor might find a gay subtext to a script, while a homophobic actor, or an actor fearful of what playing a gay character could do to his career, might turn a gay character into a stereotype or remove all traces of homosexual desire from his character.

Moreover, the composition of the audience itself writes a great part of the play. It affects both the erotic dynamics of the production—how the audience views representations of gay sexuality and the extent to which the audience feels, resists, or simply does not respond to the erotics of the spectacle—and the politics of the production. Herbert Blau notes: "Gathered in the audience—which elicits thought to the degree that it resists definition—are issues of representation, repression, otherness, the politics of the unconscious, ideology, and power."[4]

The history of the homosexual in drama is the history of the shifts in the dominant society's perception of "repression, otherness, the politics of the unconscious, ideology, and power." These are the very issues central to gay drama. But in an audience of both heterosexuals and homosexuals, these issues will be seen from different points of view, as in fact they will also be seen from different points of view by liberated, politicized, homosexuals and conservative, closeted homosexuals. Much of what follows in this study explores the erotic and political dynamics of the relationship of performed work to its audience—and the way playwrights, directors, and actors manipulate these dynamics.

SHAKESPEARE'S GAY MERCHANT

A case in point is William Shakespeare's *The Merchant of Venice* (1596), as directed by Bill Alexander for the Royal Shakespeare Company in 1987.[5] At the end of scene 1, in which Antonio has promised to find Bassanio money so that he can join the ranks of Portia's suitors, Antonio embraces Bassanio and kisses him passionately. Bassanio pushes Antonio away, the two men look at each other in silence for a moment, then Bassanio runs off, leaving Antonio alone and again melancholy.

This short scene, lasting little more than fifteen seconds, presents what has become a common contemporary interpretation of the Antonio-Bassanio relationship. The older Antonio still loves his young former ephebe, Bassanio, who now, for reasons of sexual inclination, romantic love, financial need, appetite, or a combination of all four, has eyes only for Portia: hence Antonio's melancholy. Antonio, having given Bassanio his body sexually, will now have to "lend my body for his wealth" (V,i,249).[6] Antonio's kiss provides the motivation for his generosity and sacrifice. Portia's knowledge of Antonio's love for Bassanio complicates her late actions, including her welcome of Antonio into Belmont and her acceptance of his bond supporting Bassanio's fidelity:

> ANTONIO: I dare be bound again,
> My soul upon the forfeit, that your lord
> Will never more break faith advisedly.
> PORTIA: Then you shall be his surety. (V,i,254)

This final challenge of Portia's is delivered in this production with a clear understanding of what Antonio has been to Bassanio, but it is now his soul that is his surety, not his body or his wealth, as his relationship with Bassanio will now be purely spiritual. One wonders though whether the callow Bassanio is capable of a spiritual relationship with man or woman.

In speaking of Bill Alexander's production of *The Merchant of Venice*, I invoke a contemporary "play" that ignores recent historical writings about the use of terms of love between men in Elizabethan society.[7] Alexander's interpretation of relationships between men, building on the word *love*, is decidedly "contemporary," but since he is working with contemporary actors playing before a contemporary audience, one with whom the actor shares a contemporary sense of the meanings of the words he is speaking, this approach is wholly valid. Alexander's production of *The Merchant of Venice* is a "gay play." The title character is homosexual, and his love for Bassanio becomes a dominant, though unspoken and unwritten force in the play.

Presenting a homosexual dimension to the relationship between Antonio and Bassanio also allows the actors to explore the complex relations of homosociality and homosexuality in the male groupings in the play and the ways in which the men's relationships marginalize the women to whom they proclaim love.[8] Sexual or not, love between men is in Shakespeare's Venice and Belmont more powerful than male-female love. (Indeed, Bassanio's love for Portia and Lorenzo's for Jessica seem to have more to do with money than with love. Antonio could afford not to be married.)

In Alexander's production, there is irony, too, in the relationship of Antonio's homosexuality to his virulent anti-Semitism. The final image is of

Antonio silently dangling a necklace with a cross on it over Jessica's head. Jessica had dropped the necklace, and Antonio mockingly returns it to her. Antonio demonstrates that for him Jessica cannot "pass" as Christian. Yet at the end, after the members of mainstream society have exited, both Jessica and Antonio are left onstage, isolated from that society to which the Jew and the homosexual can be only partially connected.

A gay critic can argue with this *Merchant of Venice* for its lack of a historical understanding of homosexuality,[9] though the thoughtful interpretations of the script's sexual and anti-Semitic politics that infused Alexander's production are more interesting than the pretty noninterpretations of the 1989 Peter Hall production. Alexander's presentation of the Antonio-Bassanio relationship at least puts the merchant of Venice somewhere near the center of the play named after him.

The challenge of Alexander's production was in what the audience saw, not in what they heard, emphasizing the centrality of seeing to the theatrical experience. As Herbert Blau notes: "The words fly up and the body remains below, in its seeming legibility, and we still tend to preserve, along with the carnal authenticity of the actor, the primacy of the visual. Thus we think of the audience, first, as coming to *see* a play."[10] This primacy of the visual is all too often lost in drama criticism. Antonio's kiss, performed in Bill Alexander's *Merchant of Venice*, may not have been indicated or justified by a traditional reading of Shakespeare's words, but the fact remains that it had more theatrical power as a seen action than it would have if it had been described or celebrated in a hundred lines of verse.

In the remainder of this chapter, I want to examine three ways in which homosexuality can be figured visually in ways variously shocking and affirming to differing interpretive communities in the same audience:[11] kissing, frontal nudity, and drag.

KISSING SCENES

The relationship of body to word, action to dialogue, and actor to audience in gay drama, as well as the threat of gay physicality to some members of the audience, can be seen in two gay sex scenes in plays by Martin Sherman, a respected gay playwright who has succeeded in the commercial theater with a minimum of artistic or political compromise.

Sherman's *Bent*, the 1979 drama of the persecution of gays in Nazi Germany and a theatrical rallying cry for gay men, has become so central to contemporary drama that it even appears in a leading anthology for "Introduction to Drama" courses as the quintessential gay drama (albeit with an apologetic prefatory note).[12]

Bent contains one of the most celebrated sex scenes in contemporary drama. Two men, prisoners at Dachau in 1936, standing at attention under the scrutiny of guards, forbidden to move, much less touch each other, talk each other to orgasm. In a kind of gay version of the love duet from *Tristan und Isolde* without the music, a homosexual act is confined to words:

> HORST: I'm kissing you.
> MAX: Burning.
> HORST: Kissing your eyes.
> MAX: Hot.
> HORST: Kissing your lips.
> MAX: Yes.
> HORST: Mouth.
> MAX: Yes.
> HORST: Inside your mouth.
> MAX: Yes.
> HORST: Neck.
> MAX: Yes.
> HORST: Down.
> MAX: Yes.
> HORST: Down . . .
> MAX: Yes . . .
> . . . . . .
> HORST: Do you feel me inside you?
> MAX: I want you inside me.
> HORST: Feel . . .
> MAX: I have you inside me.
> HORST: Inside.
> MAX: Strong.
> HORST: Do you feel me thrust . . . ?[13]

After the event one of the men proclaims: "We were real. We were human. We made love. They're not going to kill us" (p. 129). In my experience seeing various productions of this play with various audiences, the response to this scene is usually enthusiastic applause. The audience is won over by the erotically charged dialogue and the virtuosity of acting the scene requires. Though the language is graphically sexual, the audience sees nothing but two fully clothed men standing at attention, looking straight ahead. Gay men (and women) can read the scene as an enactment of the duplicity gays historically have had to stage in their own lives and can enjoy a verbal eroticism seldom presented so candidly in mainstream drama. Heterosexuals can be comforted that homosexual sex has been safely restricted to words, that their restrictions, like the Nazis', have been maintained by the enactment.

In the original London and New York productions, audiences did not have to deal with knowledge that the actors who spoke these lines were doing any more than "acting" homosexual desire. Richard Gere's Broadway run in

Bent coincided with the first run of his film *American Gigolo*, in which he played a hustler who "didn't do fags." And ten years ago Ian McKellen, who starred in the original 1979 London production, was not openly homosexual. The audience *saw* no homosexuality in that scene from *Bent*. Casting is one of the most important signs in drama, and it has been a tradition to cast what we might call "openly heterosexual" actors in leading homosexual roles as a way of defusing the threatening aspects of the play for a mainstream audience.[14] In the 1990 London revival starring McKellen and Michael Cashman, both now openly and politically active gay actors, performances of *Bent* were even more affirming experiences for gay men and more richly challenging, perhaps more threatening, for their fellow audience members (and, given the strictures of Section 28,[15] the National Theatre revival of *Bent* was nothing less than an act of defiance).

Sherman's *A Madhouse in Goa* (1989)[16] reverses the tactic of *Bent* by presenting a simulated homosexual act onstage that is belied and complicated by the language used during the act. In *A Madhouse in Goa*, an extremely uptight young Jewish American travels alone and miserable around the world after his graduation from college, trying unsuccessfully to conquer his self-hatred and his grief at losing his first love. David, our central character, is now—1965—at a small inn on Corfu where, in the central scene of the play, he is ravished by a handsome young Greek waiter whose English seems to be limited to pop lyrics:

> COSTOS: [sings] 'In the jingle-jangle morning, I'll come following you.'
> *He speaks in a murmur as he explores* DAVID's *body.*
> Do you feel the jingle-jangle? You come following through under the board-walks? What a day for a daydream. All my thoughts are far away. Do you believe in magic? Homeward bound, I'm homeward bound. . . .
> DAVID: Oh . . .
> COSTOS: These boots are made for walking . . .
> DAVID: Ohh . . .
> COSTOS: California dreamin' on a winter's day . . .
> DAVID: Ohhh!
> [David has an orgasm.][17]

In the 1989 London production, David's throes of orgasm at this point were most convincingly portrayed by Rupert Graves, a young actor who is known for his convincing enactments of homosexual desire. On the night I saw the play, despite the fact that the act of manual sex was hidden under a blanket, the result of this scene was not the jubilant applause that usually greets the words-only sex scene in *Bent*, but the noisy, extremely dramatic exit of a couple from the third row of the stalls. First the husband stormed out in a fit of moral outrage or, most likely, homosexual panic. Then the wife stalked up the aisle while audibly holding forth on the disgusting waste of money she had been forced to witness. Another, unplanned scene had been added to the play by this couple, one that demonstrated the danger of bodies over words as the scene onstage dramatized the growing gulf between word and act even in moments of intimacy (where, some might say, words are always irrelevant). It was seeing what is usually unseen and, for many, taboo that inspired the demonstration of outrage. One of my London students said in class that he shouldn't have had that scene "forced on" him, an interesting and apt turn of phrase that well defines the position of passivity in which an audience places itself, a position that is noticed only when an audience member is threatened with something he or she does not want to face—like embodied homosexuality.

The two scenes from Martin Sherman's plays demonstrate the difference between verbalizing homosexual desire and enacting it physically through what might be called, now with a double entendre, homosexual acts. These acts, whether created by playwright, director, or actors, are calculated to "force themselves" and the homosexual desire they represent on a mainstream audience without losing or totally alienating that audience. In a society that still does not tolerate any overt sign of affection between men, a gay audience will see them as affirming while heterosexual members of the audience will be confronted by that which their laws and mores have kept relatively invisible.

The only sex act in Harvey Fierstein's *Torch Song Trilogy* (1981), the most commercially successful "gay play," is a hilarious mockery of backroom anal sex performed by one fully clothed actor. There is virtually no kissing between lovers. Fierstein knows well that bodies are far more threatening than words.

Sexual desire is not the only dimension of the homosexual experience, but it is the core of that experience. It is sexual desire and acting upon that desire that puts the homosexual into conflict with dominant power structures. It is where we must begin. How does one dramatize homosexual desire? Can one represent desire without words? One can "force on" an audience sexual acts, kissing, embracing, looking. Or one can enact those opposites which have also been central to the experience of many homosexuals: *not* looking, *not* kissing, *not* embracing. Or one can enact the cause of these negations: heterosexism, which can be dramatized by acts of brutality, acts that sometimes result from the negation of one's homosexual desire.

One of the more interesting aspects of homophobia is, as Richard Mohr points out: "People in general find gay love—kisses of parting at the train station and the like—sicker even than gay sex."[18] The sight of two men kissing each other on the lips can evoke enormous fear and hostility in some audience members. Anyone who sat in a movie theater when Peter Finch and Murray Head kissed in *Sunday, Bloody Sunday* (1971), or when Michael Caine and Christopher Reeve kissed in *Deathtrap* (1982), or when Harry Hamlin and Michael Ontkean kissed in *Making Love* (1982), will remember the audible, hostile response such images provoked. Everyone knows that sex between men happens, but the sight of two men kissing is often seen as a transgression of the gender order, taken by many to be "natural."[19] A kiss is a sign of affection, of love, not merely of lust. A kiss, to paraphrase the old song, isn't just a kiss. Hence its theatrical power.

In the 1990 film *Longtime Companion*, written by gay playwright Craig Lucas, a group of gay friends watch together as a television soap opera, appropriately titled "Other People," presents a kiss between two male lovers (the scene has been written by one of the characters). The camera cuts from the televised kiss to the reaction of the gay friends, to the window of an appliance store where a battery of television screens offer the image of two handsome men kissing. The kiss is a triumph for the gay men, though a qualified one, as AIDS has begun to take its toll on their society. The only viewers we see are two women who watch the kiss curiously through the store window, but we hear, in the same shot, the whoop of delight of an unseen group of gay men (is it the writer and his friends or an offscreen group of men who can see the television sets through the store window or a surrogate for the gay men in the audience?). The missing audience is that of straight men. Like much of the film, the scene is about performance and audience, as it shows the power of that kiss on writers, actors, and audiences, except the audience that would treat the kiss with the greatest fear and hostility—heterosexual men.

It is often recorded in psychological studies of homosexuality and homophobia that young men will perform all sorts of sexual experimentation with each other except kissing, for kissing would define their actions as homosexual. The same is true of prisoners, military men, and male prostitutes. The homosexual act that defines the actor as homosexual is the kiss on the lips.[20] C. A. Tripp, in *The Homosexual Matrix*, still one of the classic studies of homosexuality and heterosexism, writes:

> Part of what needs to be accounted for is the fact that murder, graft, and a host of violent crimes, though strongly taboo, fail to stir the intensely personalized emotions that can still be aroused by the homosexual. A main reason seems to be that homosexuality can touch people, can involve them vicariously, in ways that serious offenses do not. Its individual actions include components common in everyone's behavior, here seen in a violational context. Thus, for most people, one of the most disturbing images in homosexuality is that of two men kissing, for it is easily imagined and sharply at odds with what is expected.[21]

The kiss is an act that brings alien homosexual desire into the realm of the known and thus asserts a threatening parity between homosexual and heterosexual desire.

"Embedded" in the meaning of kissing scenes in drama is the question of whom the audience sees kissing. A heterosexist audience not only experiences the inevitable tension between actor (real person) and character (fictional creation) but adds to that experience the iconic reading of the kissing men as homosexuals and nothing but homosexuals. There may be, for some, sentimental stirrings evoked by the kiss. Others in the audience may admire the courage of the actors, who usually take great pains to establish their heterosexual credentials in their Playbill biographies. (Indeed, the number of actors who feel compelled to mention in the program the women to whom they are married or engaged or with whom they are cohabiting—irrelevant information at best—is a sign of the current fear in the theater of being taken as gay or, as a corollary assumption, HIV positive). In *Longtime Companion*, the lead actor on a soap opera, now thrown into an onscreen gay romance by the script, is terrified of what will happen to his career. He has been so successful in keeping his own gayness secret that even the gay writer of the soap opera thinks he's straight.

Some members of an audience watching a male-male kiss will lose track of characters and actors and see in the kiss not a moment in a drama, but a generic homosexual act: "Two men kissing!" A kiss between two men, then, can be used to unleash the force of the audience's gut response to homosexuality. The history of male-male kissing scenes in American drama shows that playwrights are always aware of their power and either exploit or try to defuse their shock value.

At the climactic moment of Arthur Miller's 1955 play, *A View from the Bridge*, Brooklyn longshoreman Eddie Carbone pins his wife's cousin, Rodolpho, to the wall and kisses him on the mouth, an action that on the Broadway stage in 1955 was far more shocking than it would be in a revival. Miller and his colleagues used this shock tactic not only to support the pathology of the central character but also to echo the shock of broken taboos central to Greek tragedy.

Eddie has raised his niece, Catherine, and, as Catherine has grown up, he has become so infatuated with her that he can no longer have sexual relations with his wife. Partly to placate his rightfully suspicious wife, Eddie has brought her two cousins over from Sicily illegally and gotten them jobs on the waterfront. Rodolpho, the younger cousin, a thin, blond, somewhat androgynous young man, becomes increasingly involved with Eddie's beloved Catherine, and this attachment puts Eddie into an Othello-like jealous rage against Rodolpho.

Paradoxically, Eddie's jealousy emerges as the suspicion that Rodolpho is homosexual and merely exploiting Catherine to get his American citizenship. Such a suspicion supports jealousy of Rodolpho while denying that he could be a sexual threat:

> EDDIE: I'm tellin' you sump'm, wait a minute. Please. . . . I'm tryin' to
> bring out my thoughts here. Couple of nights ago my niece brings out a

dress which it's too small for her, because she shot up like a light this last year. He takes the dress, lays it on the table, he cuts it up; one-two-three, he makes a new dress. I mean he looked so sweet there, like an angel—you could kiss him he was so sweet.[22]

To Eddie, Rodolpho's effeminacy "ain't right" because it isn't masculine, yet it is a threat to his possession of Catherine. It also "ain't right" because it places Rodolpho in the feminine position of sexual passivity: "you could kiss him he was so sweet." Though this remark is a common ("Aye, madam, it is common") means of describing an effeminate man, one that denies him even the supposed sexual aggressiveness of the homosexual, it also hints at the possibility that Rodolpho's effeminacy might really be attractive to Eddie.

Rodolpho's transgression of stereotypical masculinity makes him, to Eddie, homosexual, though Eddie has no words for that. He doesn't need those words. The script assumes that effeminacy and homosexuality are so linked in an audience's mind that mention of one implies the other.

Rodolpho is given many of the attributes of the fifties homosexual stereotype—he is thin and blond, has a high voice, enjoys women's company, and needs his burly older brother to fight his battles for him—but of course Rodolpho is not *really* homosexual. Homosexuals are usually invisible—or dead—in fifties drama, even when they are invoked, and Miller seems as frightened of mentioning the word, of invoking more than a hint, as Eddie is.

Eddie's kiss is meant to be a brutal humiliation and exposure of Rodolpho's lack of manhood, which of course is synonymous with homosexuality:

> RODOLPHO: She'll be my wife. That is what I want. My wife!
> EDDIE: But what're you gonna be?
> RODOLPHO: I show you what I be.
> EDDIE: Come on, show me! What're you gonna be? Show me!
> RODOLPHO *flies at him in attack.* EDDIE *pins his arms, laughing, and suddenly kisses him.* (p. 63)

All Eddie Carbone's sexual problems are expressed in that kiss: his thwarted desire for his eighteen-year-old niece, his shame at not being able to perform sexually with his wife, his terror of Rodolfo's challenge to his notions of manhood, and his attraction to Rodolpho. It is an act demonstrating the vulnerability of Eddie's sense of his masculinity; it is also a brutal act, but much of Arthur Miller's writing exists to vindicate crass patriarchal brutality.[23]

To prevent Rodolpho from marrying Catherine, Eddie betrays him and his brother Marco to the immigration authorities. Miller, true to form, sees all this nastiness as *Eddie's* "tragedy." At the end of the play, Alfieri, the lawyer who has served as a kind of Greek chorus, praises Eddie's "purity":

> But the truth is holy, and even as I know how wrong he was, and his death useless, I tremble, for I confess that something perversely pure calls to me from his memory—not purely good, but himself purely, for he allowed himself to be wholly known and for that I think I will love him more than all my sensible clients. (p. 86)

The words in which Miller tries to gift-wrap Eddie's brutality can soften the blow only if Eddie's action can be justified. What would justify that action? Rodolpho's homosexuality, of course. The play argues that it is all right for a young man not to be macho; it does not argue for his right to be what he is accused of being. The kiss is a nasty mockery of an unspeakable—and unactable—reality that the play, by implication, decries as much as Eddie does. It is a negation, on Eddie's part and on Miller's, of even the possibility of the reality the kiss mocks. We shall see in chapter 4 how typical Miller's tactics are of the American drama of his time.

Miller is writing his "modern" form of Greek tragedy in *A View from the Bridge*, complete with quasi-chorus. The hint of homosexuality is his counterpart to the horrible violation of taboos in Greek tragedy—like incest (also hinted at) or eating one's children.

Miller's attitude toward homosexuality can be attributed in part to the time and place of his plays and audience; it may also mirror the attitude of a well-meaning liberal of the forties and fifties. In his quasi-autobiographical play, *After the Fall* (1964), the insecure, beautiful singer, Maggie, is "for Negroes and Puerto Ricans and truck drivers,"[24] but violently against "fags." In one of their final feuds, Maggie accuses her husband:

> MAGGIE: Fags wear pants like that; I told you. They attract each other with their asses.
> QUENTIN: You calling me a fag now?
> MAGGIE, *very drunk*: Just I've known fags and some of them didn't even know themselves that they were. . . . And I didn't know if you knew about that.
> QUENTIN: That's a hell of a way to reassure yourself, Maggie. (p. 99)

Maggie's accusation is taken as the last word in cruelty, the ultimate castrating comment. Fags aren't men and therefore can't satisfy the sex goddess. Of course, in Maggie's reasoning, any man who does not show sexual interest in her is a "fag." Miller turns Maggie's homophobia against her. Is this possible because the heterosexist taunts are coming from a woman? In the recent, highly successful London production, Maggie was played by a black actress, so it was possible to give Maggie's antigay epithets a more nuanced reading. However it is seen, the "fags" in *After the Fall* are totally in Maggie's imagination. They do not visibly exist onstage any more than they existed in *A View from the Bridge*.

Eddie's kiss indicated, paradoxically, a feared but invisible, unthinkable homosexuality. Commercial gay works make gay characters more visible, but they are often cautious, even contradictory, in their use of the kiss. At the highly melodramatic conclusion of the first act of Mart Crowley's *The Boys in the Band* (1968),[25] the heterosexual Alan, in a fit of outrage, gay bashes the effeminate Emory while screaming a catalogue of homophobic epithets. As the two are separated, Harold, the guest of honor at the ill-fated birthday party, arrives and is kissed passionately by the hustler who has been bought as a birthday present. Crowley is quite aware of the shock value of this moment for many in his audience and exploits that value. The kiss is presented not as something gay men would naturally do but as something outrageous, more outrageous than the violence that preceded it (and for some audience members, Alan's violent attack would be "natural," justified). Because of Alan's presence, the self-hating homosexual characters see the kiss through heterosexist eyes—that is, the eyes of most of the audience. Harold's laughter at his "present" becomes sinister, bizarre, and the freakshow aspect of the play is reinforced.

In the film of Harvey Fierstein's *Torch Song Trilogy* (1988), the only onscreen passionate kiss is between Arnold's present and past lovers, Alan and Ed. In other words, the kiss is not connected to the love the film nominally affirms, but to betrayal. A male-male kiss is still unacceptable.

Lanford Wilson, whose plays are challenges to many American taboos, created a far more affirming kissing scene in his *Fifth of July*.[26] In 1980, Wilson revised his 1978 off-Broadway success for Broadway, with its larger, more diverse, and more conservative audience. The central character in *Fifth of July*, Ken Talley, lost the use of his legs in Vietnam and is terrified of going back to teaching because of how the students will look at him. Ken is also a homosexual, who has, because of his fears about his handicaps, a troubled relationship with his extremely intact lover, Jed. *Fifth of July* is one of the few commercially successful "gay plays" in which homosexuality is not the, or even a, problem for the leading characters or the people around them, and Ken and Jed's relationship is no more fraught than those of the heterosexual characters in the play. If homosexuality isn't a problem, how is it spoken about in drama presented before a Broadway audience for whom homosexuality, if it is anything at all, is a problem? More difficult: how does one *show* homosexuality in a nonproblematic way? Wilson's answer was a kissing scene.

If Lanford Wilson traded in stereotypes, Ken's paraplegia would be a physical manifestation of the moral, emotional, spiritual handicap of homosexuality. But Jed, who spends most of the play shirtless and in cutoffs, is

physically as healthy a specimen as one can envision. That potential stereotype, then, is canceled out. Of course, part of showing anything onstage involves casting, and if, as was the case, Ken is played successively by William
Hurt, Christopher Reeve, and Richard Thomas, both the handicap and the
homosexuality are made palatable, unthreatening, by being in some sense
erased. Superman a queer paraplegic?

Wilson, however, did not want Ken and Jed's homosexuality so easily
ignored. To make sure the audience must deal with it, he wrote in a passionate
kiss between Ken and Jed. In the original production at the Circle Repertory
Company in the heart of Greenwich Village, that kiss came as a rather matter-
of-fact event fifteen minutes into the play.

Wilson and his director, Marshall Mason, wanted to keep the kiss in
the Broadway production, but they knew it was likely to evoke a response
that would disrupt the play for a few moments (titters and macho noises).
During the preview process, in which a play is revised on the basis of audience
reaction, the kissing scene was moved to a number of different places, and
audience reaction was gauged. Finally Wilson and Mason decided to put it at
the beginning of the play, when an audience is still settling in. The idea was
to get the response out of the way at the very outset rather than court the
possibility of audience outbursts later on. At the rise of the curtain, Ken is
seated at a desk (no sign yet of his artificial legs or crutches). Jed enters,
crosses to Ken, and, after two lines, they kiss. Their physical relationship is
established unambiguously.

Wilson knew that the sight of two men kissing was as potentially
shocking in 1980 as it had been in 1955 when *A View from the Bridge* was
first produced. The hostile response of some audience members had to be
anticipated and accommodated without seriously compromising Wilson's desire to present, without problematizing, gay lovers. But the kiss is crucial in
making gayness onstage more than a safe matter of words. The kiss in *Fifth
of July* defines, affirms, and challenges. Its shock value is used to serve a
purpose opposite to that of the kiss in *A View from the Bridge*. But an uneasy
compromise had to be made with the audience, which became a factor in
shaping the dramatic text.

THE GAY BODY

In John Guare's 1990 success, *Six Degrees of Separation*,[27] the major theatrical shock comes when Ouisa Kittredge, an affluent upper-middle-class New
York housewife, opens the guest-bedroom door and discovers that her house
guest, who she thinks is Sidney Poitier's son, is in bed with a male hustler.
She—and the audience (from a safe distance; the bedroom is veiled by
scrims)—see not the usual bodies properly hidden under the covers, but two
men engaging rather energetically in an act of oral sex. This would be enough

to make clear that Ouisa's house has been invaded by an outrageous, alien sexuality. However, for the next three or four minutes, the naked hustler chases the housewife around the living room and lunges at her husband, Flan.

In one sense the scene is farcical: Ouisa screams "He has a gun! He has a knife!" which is obviously untrue (the hustler is adorned only with socks), but expressing fear in phallic symbolism, however comic, may be the most appropriate response for Ouisa. In another sense, Guare has presented an image that is most unsettling, not just to Ouisa, but to most of his audience, who watches not just a naked man but the naked body of an aggressive gay man. The hustler's last words are a furious "Fuck you" directed to the husband as he grabs the lapels of Flan's bathrobe. In this circumstance "Fuck you" is not just an epithet: it is a sexual threat.

The Kittredge's house guest, a young black man who appeared on their doorstep the previous night claiming to be a friend of their children, is not who he claims to be. His Brooks Brothers shirt is not a genuine sign of class, but a borrowed, perhaps stolen, prop. Paul is a feared unknown—a gay black stranger, an alien who brings into the Kittredge house and sexless marriage a threatening, alien sexuality.[28]

Why did John Guare feel that such a barrage of frontal nudity, in addition to the simulated sex act, was crucial to this moment in his play? What is the threat of that naked body and in what ways does that body read as gay?

Like the male-male kiss, male nudity can cause audience members to lose sight of character and actor and see only an iconic phallic presence. Moreover, nudity creates self-consciousness as audience members focus momentarily on their own responses. That moment briefly changes the dynamics of theater, as the audience fragments into different interpretive communities and the dramatic illusion is lost in favor of a real physical presence.

What the audience sees as the hustler runs around the room is a naked male body, which to some extent takes precedence over the character the actor is playing. At one performance, a friend of mine overheard a woman sitting nearby comment, as the hustler ran around the stage, "I didn't know they flapped like that." Anatomical curiosity took precedence over focus on character or dramatic action in a reaction that is probably not uncommon. Indeed, there is no character except a nameless generic hustler, and the audience doesn't even know the man is a hustler until they are told so later. There is simply a nude male actor up there, but what does he figure? The audience sees what is usually unseen onstage, the penis, in this case attached to a man who refuses to be clothed; he remains nude throughout the scene and uses his nudity as a tool of aggression. Clearly he is unafraid of being seen, and even likes it, as does the mysterious Paul, who tells Ouisa, "It gives me a thrill to be looked at" (p. 38).

The character—and actor—insist upon being viewed, which in itself is a challenge to traditional gender roles. In her book on the male nude, Margaret

Walters asserts, "There is still a rigid division between the sex that looks and the sex that is looked at."[29] Of course, men are supposed to be the lookers, not the objects of the gaze. Thus the willfully nude male is placing himself in the passive position of object of the gaze. But our hustler can hardly said to be passive, as he chases the Kittredges around the living room with only his nakedness as a weapon.

The real, physical presence of the nude body and the audience's awareness that the actor knows he is being seen is what makes theatrical nudity so powerful. The audience member is not an unseen (by the object of their gaze) voyeur, but a seen, known, though (usually) anonymous onlooker. And many people do not know how to look at the penis, do not think they should look. Yet the actor willingly and knowingly displays it to us. There is a personal transaction in such a scene onstage unlike that of a nude scene in a film. As Barbara Freedman defines it:

> What do we mean when we say that someone or something is theatrical? What we mean is that such a person is aware that she is seen, reflects that awareness, and so deflects our look. We refer to a fractured reciprocity whereby beholder and beheld reverse positions in a way that renders a steady position of spectatorship impossible.[30]

The notion of the "gay body" as some kind of "third sex," neither male nor female, has long since been discarded. The gay body is, indeed, no different from the straight body (for all one knows, the naked actor who played the hustler could have been heterosexual). The homosexual act had to be displayed in some way to indicate that this is the body of a homosexual. Or is it? Does engaging in a homosexual act for money make a man a homosexual? Many hustlers would say no. The enactment and the male body raise the issue of what is a homosexual, or at least they explode the myth of the distinctly marked homosexual body. Yet that naked body does come to figure the homosexual body.

Margaret Walters maintains that, for complex reasons, in modern Western culture "the exposed body is emotionally charged and potentially subversive."[31] Once the notion of subversiveness is introduced to a discussion of the male body, we are on our way toward a linking of that body with homosexuality. The unclad body emphasizes the physical equivalence of gay and straight men; but the nakedness, the forcing of the gaze and narcissistic enjoyment of that gaze, the forbidden freedom of the uncovered penis, and the assumption that viewing the penis is a pleasurable act all represent, not male sexuality, but gay sexuality. Hence the proliferation of nude men in mainstream drama about homosexuals and in mainstream gay drama. The danger in the willfully nude male body is homosexuality.

John Guare is a heterosexual playwright focusing on the point of view of upper-middle-class, heterosexual New Yorkers. The only passion expressed is voiced by the young men with whom the mysterious black, Paul, has slept. Trent Conway, the young man who taught Paul how to ingratiate himself with Trent's rich New York friends tells one of his peers: "Paul stayed with me for three months. We went through the address book letter by letter. Paul vanished with the L's. He took the address book with him. Well, he's already been in all your houses. Maybe I will meet him again. I sure would like to" (p. 79). Rick, the young actor Paul conned, tells the audience: "We took a carriage ride in the park and he asked me if he could fuck me and I had never done anything like that and he did and it was fantastic. It was the greatest night I ever had and before we got home he kissed me on the mouth and he vanished" (p. 91).

Sexual passion in Guare's play is homosexual passion, forbidden but fascinating, rendering even nominally straight men, like Rick, sexually passive. "I didn't come here to be *this*," Rick says, before committing suicide. *This* is not homosexual, but sexually passive, unmanned. (That Rick feels compelled to kill himself puts *Six Degrees of Separation* back into the dramatic conventions of dramas of the forties and fifties.)

The uncovered penis, the naked male body, figures the power of what Paul represents—sexual chaos, mystery, the unknown, homosexuality. *Six Degrees of Separation* was an enormous success in New York, selling out even after its move from the small Mitzi E. Newhouse Theatre to the cavernous Vivian Beaumont. It is a mainstream play, written by a playwright who proclaims his heterosexuality in both program blurb and dust jacket and written for the white, upper-middle-class audience it depicts (it takes place in an elegant apartment overlooking Central Park, a few blocks from the Lincoln Center theater in which it was performed). In the world of Guare's play, blackness provokes a mixture of liberal guilt and uncertainty, but gayness provokes chaos. The phallus still has the same power it had in Greek and Roman theater, but nowadays that power is tied not to sexual potency and fertility but to homosexual pleasure.

In *Six Degrees of Separation*, Guare is appropriating what has become almost a convention of both mainstream and coterie gay drama, male nudity. The sight of the nude man as a scopular object, the viewing of the male nude as a pleasurable activity, is a common element of gay theater. Gay men do not react with shock at the sight of a naked man any more than heterosexual men react with shock at the sight of a naked woman. One question is the extent to which the nudity in *Six Degrees of Separation*, like the nudity in the sixties musical *Hair* or in Peter Shaffer's highly successful *Equus* (1973), is responsible for the play's considerable commercial success. The titillation of watching the forbidden is one of theater's traditional attractions.

Classical American gay drama—works by Tennessee Williams and William Inge—were "daring" because the man was presented as the object of the gaze. Stanley Kowalski, in undershirt, gaudy bowling shirt, and silk pajama pants, exists to be looked at, and the women in Williams' *A Streetcar*

Named Desire (1947) look and respond. Even Blanche's denigration of Stanley is tied to an appreciation of his physical presence: "A man like that is someone to go out with—once—twice—three times when the devil is in you."[32] The women look and the man is looked at ; this pattern is central to Williams' work. Maggie the Cat, walking around in her slip in Williams' *Cat on a Hot Tin Roof* (1955), may be erotically charged for some members of the audience, but she isn't really the object of the gaze. Brick is. Maggie looks at him and comments on his beauty: "I wish you would lose your looks. If you did it would make the martyrdom of Saint Maggie a little more bearable. But no such goddamn luck. I actually believe you've gotten better looking since you went on the bottle."[33]

Brick certainly isn't the only male character in Williams to be the object of the gaze: there are, among others, Val Xavier in *Orpheus Descending* (1957) and Chance Wayne in *Sweet Bird of Youth* (1959). William Inge follows the same pattern: it is the hunky man who upsets households and communities in *Picnic* (1953) and *Come Back, Little Sheba* (1949). Straight men could fantasize about the sexual attractiveness and power these male characters had, and women in the audience could identify with the women in the play, but gay men knew what these plays were about. Inge and Williams wrote sexual fantasies that celebrate male beauty and sexual attractiveness by reversing the usual roles of seer and seen, placing the point of view in the eyes of the female characters. The plays may have been—should have been—somewhat unsettling, but in the fifties the men kept their pants on.

When gay drama "came out" off Broadway in the seventies, nudity became almost a convention, as female nudity became a convention for the movies. Liberation meant the freedom to look at naked men onstage and to admit that that was pleasurable. Robert Patrick's work is full of men taking their clothes off, though Patrick often satirizes the narcissism and exploitation involved in New York gay culture. In *T Shirts* (1978), three gay men undress and group together to watch their reflection on the television screen:

> TOM: When there's light just on you, you reflect real bright in the TV screen.
> KINK: We really do look just like three pretty little Maxfield Parrish nudes.
> TOM: Even Marvin's pretty.
> MARVIN: Isn't it nice? I discovered it the other day.
> *They admire themselves, TOM especially, try two or three different poses.*[34]

As the handsome, young Tom continues to pose nude, long after his older companions have put their clothes back on, Patrick satirizes a world in which the handsome stranger becomes not merely the object of displaced sexual fantasy, as in Williams and Inge, but a real sexual possibility, the handsome young gay who will get ahead through his looks and sexual availability. When one of the older, less good-looking characters comments glibly that looks aren't everything, Tom quickly rejoins: "Yes, they are. Don't give me that tired shit. They are so. If you've got looks, you can get anything else. And if you don't, there isn't anything else worth having. I'm sick of that crap. Looks *are* everything" (p. 38). Yet the world Tom's looks allow him to enter will also exploit him: "When a society's only values are good looks and money, sooner or later people are going to wind up exchanging one for the other," and the result is "a conglomerate as heartless as Con Ed" (p. 35). Marvin, who offers this social wisdom, also admits, "If I had the slightest chance of getting in on any of it, you wouldn't hear a peep from me!" (p. 35).

Like most commercial playwrights, Patrick has it both ways in *T Shirts*, both titillating and criticizing his New York gay audience. He satirizes a society that puts undue value on looks, but he buys into that society by offering looks for money, by offering the sight of the naked Tom to his audience. He defuses Marvin's analysis of his culture by having Marvin admit, "The only reason I'm reactionary is because I get no reactions" (p. 35).

Patrick's *Mercy Drop* (1973, published 1979), not only moved toward a climactic nude scene but featured on the cover of the published version a production shot featuring a nude young man (the actor Kevin Breslin as Johnny).[35] Clearly the sight of the nude male was considered as integral part of reading the published text as it was of seeing the produced play.

In *Mercy Drop*, as in much other gay drama, being the object of the gaze empowers:

> JOHNNY: I was thinking I was naked and helpless and small and alone behind locked doors in an uncaring city in the arms of a strong and hungry meat-eating animal—and there was nowhere to go and no one to call and nothing that I could do—but one thing—and I did it!
> JOHNNY *spins in* MARVIN's *arms and stands tall and gorgeous.*
> JOHNNY: I spun in your arms and stood tall and proud and I said: "I am Venus, Aphrodite, Cytherea, Kypris, the foam-born, goddess of love and beauty, and I have been trapped these fifteen years in this boy's body—and you and your touch have freed me—for this you shall forevermore be my poet and my puppet, my favorite, fop and fool."
> JOHNNY *stands radiant. Suddenly he flings* MARVIN *to the ground.*
> JOHNNY: And you knelt! You Knelt!
> MARVIN: And I was conquered.[36]

Johnny's empowerment comes from his celebration of his own nakedness, which fully reveals his androgyny. The slender, "girlishly beautiful" (p. 5) adolescent with long hair and soft face also has a large penis. He comes to see himself not as the passive boy, not even as the classical passive boy, the subservient Ganymede, but as the powerful Venus, whom men worshiped and served. Johnny moves from masculine passivity to feminine power as Marvin kneels before him in worship and submission and also in preparation for oral sex. Johnny's naked body is the most vivid image of what he represents in the play. At the same time the presentation of that image onstage and the use of that image to market the published text represents another aspect of gay culture in the seventies, the marketing of the heretofore forbidden image of the male nude as object of desire.[37]

Such combined exploitation and exploration of the metaphoric possibilities of the male nude became a convention of gay theater in the era between Stonewall and the age of AIDS (as we shall see later, AIDS playwrights like Robert Chesley use the nude body in very different ways). By 1980, gay drama had moved into mainstream venues, where nudity provided shock value for part of the audience as it provided the expected titillation for the gay clientele.

In the first scene of Martin Sherman's *Bent* (1979), Max, suffering from a hangover, is surprised and mystified when a blond, naked man emerges from his bedroom. Wolf is Max's trick from the night before, his naked body the sign of Max's sexual promiscuity. But Wolf is also the first victim of the Nazis: by the end of the scene he has been shot and his throat has been cut. As his nudity represents the most visibly overt sexuality in the play, so his murder is the first bloody action. Wolf embodies both the threatened gay sexuality and the brutal physical violence of the Nazis.

Why does Wolf have to appear naked? Why not in underpants or a jock strap? The answer is that they would cover the focal penis, which figures homosexual desire and the promiscuous gay underworld in which Max lives at the beginning of the play. For some in the audience it represents the sexual freedom a criminally repressive society will destroy; for others it represents an alien, threatening sexuality.

At the beginning of the second act of Terrence McNally's oft-rewritten *The Lisbon Traviata* (1985), Stephen, the unhappy opera queen, comes into his apartment early in the morning and confronts the naked body of his partner's new lover. Stephen's passion is almost entirely displaced onto opera, particularly the cult of Maria Callas. "Opera is about us, our life and death passions—we all love, we're all going to die. Maria understood that,"[38] Stephen tells the naked Paul. The irony of the scene is in the talk of and music of opera juxtaposed with the physical reality of the naked Paul. McNally's opera queens do not live in the world of physical reality but of camp fantasy. The displacement of their emotions onto opera and dead divas cuts them off from real life-and-death passions. The naked male body is in many ways the opposite of the opulent, sentimental fantasy of Maria Callas: performed opera is about transcendence of the flesh. What Stephen and his fellow opera queen, Mendy, have in common with Callas is that, like her, they live in unhappy isolation. Pleasure in male sexuality, represented by Paul's nakedness, is replaced by the sentimentalizing of opera's version of (male-created) feminine passion.

The gay Spanish filmmaker Pedro Almodóvar's use of actor Antonio Banderas is a case study in how nudity can figure gayness. In two of Almodóvar's films, *La Ley del Deseo (Law of Desire)* (1987) and *Átame (Tie Me*

Up, Tie Me Down) (1990), the handsome young Banderas plays a psychopath, brutally and sometimes murderously trying to possess fully the object of his infatuation (the two characters are different in class and sexual orientation but identical in motivation and even in their penchant for home repair). In *Law of Desire*, Banderas, who plays a gay man obsessed with a gay film director, appears partially clad or naked in many of his scenes, the object of the gaze. His desire to possess the filmmaker is presented as murderous pathology but also feminine, a gay male version of Glenn Close's character, Alex, in the film *Fatal Attraction* (1987).

In *Tie Me Up, Tie Me Down*, he is, except for one shot of him from overhead as part of a fragment image of a sex scene, fully clothed, while the leading lady is often nude or seminude. Though his character is equally possessive and pathological, he is presented neutrally. Almodóvar seems to think making the nude Banderas the passive object of the gaze changes his sexuality, makes him more passive, feminine, like the nude willing victim in *Tie Me Up*. It is also clear that the film is a (failed) attempt at reaching a mass audience larger than that for the overtly gay *Law of Desire* and that male nudity would be scary for members of the former audience and a turn-on for the latter.

Like men kissing, male nudity still has shock value for many in a "mainstream" audience, while it offers long forbidden pleasure to gay men.

DRAG

When the audience entered Stratford-upon-Avon's Swan Theatre for the 1989 production by Danny Boyle for the Royal Shakespeare Company of Ben Jonson's seldom performed *Epicoene, or the Silent Woman*,[39] they saw clothes strewn about the stage. When Clerimont and his page entered half clad, the audience realized that the clothes strewn about the stage were not so much the signs of a sloppy master and servant as of sexual urgency. The page was indeed Clerimont's "ingle." But the youth, reversing Elizabethan convention, was embodied by a young woman, not a boy. As the Elizabethan theater defused the danger of embodying a heterosexual relationship by casting boys as women,[40] this production began by defusing the contemporary horror of pederasty by casting an androgynous young woman as the boy. The audience could see the idea of the sexual relationship of Clerimont and his "ingle" without dealing with a literal embodiment of a potentially shocking relationship.

A viewer might think that Boyle was buying in to the old, inaccurate cliche of male-male sexual relationships as a parody of male-female relationships. However, it became clear when Epicoene, the title character, appeared, that Boyle was playing a much more elaborate game with his audience's assumptions about sex and homosexuality. The androgynous young man who played Epicoene (not a regular member of the RSC but cast for this role only) was quite intentionally the most beautiful "woman" on the stage, though no effort was made to disguise his obviously masculine voice, thus underscoring once again the gap between body and word. The program listed the actor, John Hannah, as "Hannah John," but the voice let the audience in on the joke before the end of act 3.

What was being presented here? First, the misogyny in Jonson's script was underscored by this beautiful transvestite surrounded by grotesque women. One might ask whether the production was commenting on the misogyny in Jonson's script or reinforcing it, but one could not avoid noticing the way in which the production confounded its presentation of the unfortunate, ancient mixture of gender and homosexuality by ending with Dauphine Eugenie, the architect of Epicoene's disguise, rolling around on the floor with the now unwigged and unfrocked Epicoene, clearly masculine and clearly Dauphine Eugenie's "ingle." With the kiss of Dauphine Eugenie and his half-clad male lover, the joke on old Morose was turned into a joke on the audience—and also a challenge to it. Homosexual desire and transvestism have been untied, and one has, in the embrace of the two young men, the only nongrotesque presentation of sexuality in the play.

Clearly the creators of this production of *Epicoene* were mindful of the mainstream audience, gradually exposing to them the text they saw in Jonson's script, a text that saw the world of the play as a network of misogyny and homosexual desire. The production mocked the misogyny in Jonson's play while celebrating the homosexual desire with which the misogyny maintains an unstable relationship. To a mainstream audience member, this might have seemed a subversive production. It not only subverted, as farce traditionally does, patriarchal authority and sexuality but subverted as well the heterosexual norm that farce traditionally upholds.

This production of *Epicoene*, then, had two characters in drag: a woman dressed as a boy and a man dressed as a woman, which is a modification and expansion of the central joke in Jonson's dark comedy. It is difficult to imagine the erotics of *Epicoene* in Jonson's theater, in which boys played all the parts: "Its mannish women no less than its 'ingles' and its 'manikins' were boys, of course, whose undeveloped or precocious sexuality would have lent an edge to its audience's attention—satiric, paedophilic, what you will—inseparable from Jonson's textual emphasis on Jonson's cross-gendered comic types."[41] At the least, the erotics of performance were different from, or complicated, the erotics of the script. Having a woman play the "ingle" as a "trouser role" in 1989 ties the scene to another tradition in theater (in the late seventeenth and eighteenth centuries, trouser roles allowed women to display more of their bodies than traditional women's roles, thus truly reversing the erotics of the scripted situation), while it defuses the danger of the pederastic relationship, which is taboo on stage and off. Epicoene himself is another matter. In this 1989 production, the man in drag playing *Epicoene* brought into the production the politics of drag and its relationship to homosexuality.

The fact is that, unlike kissing scenes and the uncovered penis, drag may figure homosexuality but is not, for a heterosexist audience, transgressive. It merely underscores the connection between homosexuality and effeminacy. The Harvey Fierstein-Jerry Herman musical, *La Cage aux Folles* (1983), was a hit despite its lead characters' being a homosexual couple, because one of the gay men spent most of the show in a dress and was almost completely woman-identified. The musical was about a middle-aged married couple whose son is about to get married to the wrong girl. Gay men could take the drag queen's song, "I Am What I Am," as a song of gay pride, but the heterosexual audience saw a reinforcement of the usual stereotypes of gay couples ("Who's the man and who's the woman?").

Fierstein's *Torch Song Trilogy* (1981) reinforces the same stereotypes. The leading character is a drag queen who aspires to being the ideal Jewish mother. Arnold's values are those of the typical Wednesday-matinee audience. With his overweight body and gravelly voice, Arnold is an unusual drag queen, a textbook example of what Richard Dyer calls *inbetweenism*[42], which he sees as a dwindling species: "Once the E.R.A. and gay civil rights bills have been passed, me and mine will find ourselves swept under the carpets like the blacks done to Amos, Andy, and Aunt Jemina."[43]

The powerful final scene in *Epicoene* offered the unmasking of the young page in drag and the embrace that followed. The drag was merely part of a nasty trick, not an expression of the gender identification of the character. The putting on of drag by the central character in *La Cage aux Folles*, "with a rare combination of girlish excitement and manly restraint" (how in between can you get?), is moving from the humdrum male life to a glamorous fantasy world as it is a move from aging to eternal youth: "So when my spirits start to sag/ I hustle out my highest drag/ And put a little more mascara on."[44]

Drag defuses the threat of homosexuality. Albin's "big switch" to the glamorous Zaza is fulfillment of the wish "to be someone who's anyone other than me." As the audience watches Albin don his drag, they see a middle-aged man become a expensively, garishly dressed caricature of a woman—a living example of inbetweenism. Moreover, drag is merely "dressing up." In Albin's song, we see him "put on" a costume in no physical way connected to his "real self." It is a theatrical act placed within the context of theater.[45]

Moreover, drag places Albin's homosexuality and his thirty-year relationship with his partner in a familiar pattern. The dress of one character— and the playing out of that character's wifely and maternal feelings—equates the "marriage" with heterosexual marriages. In his liner notes for the original cast album, Harvey Fierstein writes: "Here, amidst the age-old triangle of mother, father, and child, we found our justification, our universality, our reason to create." In making Albin a devoted mother, Fierstein denies his maleness and, in a central way, his homosexuality. Drag makes homosexuality safe.

Still, drag can be more than a reinforcement of a stereotype of the effeminate homosexual; it can be a defiance of rigid definitions of sexual identity. Here is where "La Cagelles," the chorus of the musical *La Cage aux Folles*, complicated the audience's response. The singing, dancing drag artists were so convincing in their gaudy, often revealing costumes, one could not spot the one or two women in the chorus until the curtain call. To confuse gender more, offstage women's voices were mixed into the sound of the chorus the audience saw. Drag here was not caricature—as it was for Albin—but convincing imitation.

While the use of drag in *La Cage aux Folles* shows the slipperiness of gender definitions, it never unties the link of homosexuality to effeminacy. Albin's lover was not a drag artist but was always played by an actor whose heterosexuality was never in doubt. The presence of Gene Barry, television's Bat Masterson, as a homosexual kept things safe for the suburban audiences. Homosexuals wear dresses—or act like they should wear dresses. Categories are kept intact.

In the 1988 Broadway hit, *M. Butterfly*, drag, ironically, denied the homosexuality of a seventeen-year affair between two men. The audience is to believe that a French diplomat, Rene Gallimard, conducted his affair with a Chinese transvestite totally believing that women's clothes covered a woman's body. At one point Gallimard allows that his belief might have willfully erased the shadow of a doubt: "Did I not undress her because I knew, somewhere deep down, what I would find? Perhaps. Happiness is so rare that our mind can turn somersaults to protect it."[46] Here and elsewhere, David Henry Hwang, the playwright, turns not-very-convincing rhetorical somersaults to keep his homosexual affair heterosexual, to keep the focus on the way Western men see Asians and the way men project their own fantasies onto women. Hwang has his characters spell everything out for the audience; this is not the most interesting way to write a play, but it keeps the audience from drawing its own conclusions. When a judge asks the transvestite how he could fool his lover for so long, the man answers: "One, because when he finally met his fantasy woman, he wanted more than anything to believe that she was, in fact, a woman. And second, I am an Oriental. And being an Oriental, I could never be completely a man" (p. 83).

Hwang displaces the usual heterosexist baggage of effeminacy onto Asians and exploits Western disdain for Asians. When Song undresses in front of Gallimard and offers himself—as a man—to his lover of seventeen years, Gallimard answers: "I'm a man who loved a woman created by a man. Everything else—simply falls short" (p. 90). The plodding literalness of Hwang's play also keeps it heterosexual. If the play acknowledged the subtext that Gallimard loved a man in woman's clothing, it would have had more complexity. Taking Gallimard's assertions at face value, as the play expects its audiences to do, is like accepting the denials of "outed" gay performers.

Hwang's play is most interesting for what it shows about the taste of Broadway audiences. Homosexuality is hinted at but safely displaced; so a play managed to be about the long-term romance of two men while denying that it is about that at all. The white man is safely heterosexual, duped by a wily drag queen who he thought all along was a woman. There are strong similarities between *M. Butterfly* and *Six Degrees of Separation* (1990), the next serious American drama to be a commercial success. Both are about nonwhite homosexual con men who dupe upper-middle-class whites. In both, the nonwhite gay man is there to provide a catalyst for a commentary on the heterosexual, white experience. The homosexual is basically a crafty actor who gains acceptance, even love, by conning heterosexuals. The homosexual is not who or what he seems. Drag in *M. Butterfly* is a means of commenting on Gallimard's patriarchal view of women and Asians. Yet the homosexual is still a man in a dress.

In performance, Song changes from drag into western men's clothing onstage, an act that usually elicits applause from the audience. What are they applauding? A man's ability to wear men's clothing? The convincing nature of the female masquerade Song enacted during the first two acts? Or the fact that this man has finally moved into gender-appropriate clothing?

It is only in his afterword to the published text that Hwang acknowledges that his play could have a different meaning for homosexuals. But that meaning, as he sees it, has to do only with the way "Rice Queens" (Caucasian gay men who are attracted to Asian men) treat their Asian lovers, who inevitably, for reasons of racial self-hatred, see themselves as "the women" in the relationship.

The work of serious gay theater artists over the past forty years has defied the sort of formulations drag has represented in the commercial theater. In recent years some of their work has developed a wide, mainstream audience. Charles Busch's *Vampire Lesbians of Sodom* ran for years off Broadway, and Charles Ludlam's *The Mystery of Irma Vep* has become a staple of professional theaters across the country and was recently produced in London. Ludlam's play is an example of how drag can be used to confound the very formulations of which it inevitably becomes part.

In *The Mystery of Irma Vep*, each of the two actors plays male and female characters in a quasi-Victorian "penny dreadful" that travesties the sex roles central to Gothic romance. What becomes clear in performance is that both the male and female characters are "drag" enactments, cartoons of the ways in which the characters play out their sex roles. The title character, Irma Vep, is another character in disguise, but when "Irma" is unmasked, the other character is not sure which of the characters played by the actor playing "Irma" has been revealed:

> LADY ENID (*Reaches up and rips off* IRMA'*s face, which is a rubber mask, revealing the other player*): Edgar?
> JANE: No, Jane!
> LADY ENID: Jane! You?[47]

This metatheatrical moment owes its success, as do a number of inside jokes in the play, to the multiple, role-within-role-playing that is a great deal of the fun of *The Mystery of Irma Vep*, but it also underscores the fluidity of gender the role-playing asserts. Irma could be Edgar or Jane who, after all, are embodied by one actor. Edgar and Jane, like Irma, are disguises. In Stan Wojewodski's 1991 production at Center Stage in Baltimore, "Irma" was played by the actor who plays Edgar and Jane, but not with the rubber mask the script calls for. Instead, the actor is in drag, including a pillbox hat and veil, but without a wig (the actor's own short hair was clearly visible).[48] Enid's misperception that Irma was Edgar was the audience's as well. Gender role playing became all the more complicated.

In serious works, like writer Neil Bartlett's and composer Nicholas Bloomfield's musical theater piece *Sarrasine* (1990), it can be part of a deconstruction of gender and of the relationship between erotic desire and art.

In choosing Honore de Balzac's 1830 story *Sarrasine* for his theater piece, Bartlett is also paying homage to the work of literary theory that inspires such a pluralistic reading, Ronald Barthes' elaborate analysis, *S/Z*.[49]

In Bartlett's free adaptation of Balzac's story, it is the present and the elegant Mme. de Rochefide has come to Venice to hire the famed singer Zambinella to sing for her. De Rochefide had heard Zambinella sing once, when she was nineteen years old and has been ever since obsessed with the purity of that voice and fascinated with the castrato's sexual ambiguity: "She was dressed as a woman, but everyone said, 'You know he's not a man.' . . . And I remember thinking that is too beautiful to be a man."[50] Mme. de Rochefide's use of *that* to free La Zambinella from conventional gender definitions connects to her fascination with what she sees as the purity and perfection of the eunuch artist.

La Zambinella appears first as a two-hundred-and-fifty-year-old eunuch: "His face and body are ruined, sexless." His body is covered by a "shapeless gown made from what looks like an old theatre curtain." With his theatrical bearing, full makeup and rings on every finger, he is the incarnation of the aging diva. When La Zambinella finally speaks, however, it is in the crass language of a cynical showgirl: "I don't care if everybody is waiting they can wait all fucking night I'm not doing it right?" This first incarnation of the aging castrato was played by the famous drag queen Bette Bourne,

founder of the performing group "Bloolips." Soon, two more versions of La
Zambinella join Ms. Bourne: Zambinella as the young diva, as he appeared
to the young French nobleman Sarrasine in Balzac's story (played by a man,
Francois Testory). This second incarnation is the most ambiguous. Testory
changes from gown to showgirl costume, to spangled g-string, to an
eighteenth-century Italian aristocratic boy's outfit. Testory represents Zambinella as protean object of desire. Finally, we see Zambinella as a worldly wise
chanteuse (played by singer Beverly Klein). Bourne usually speaks and sings
in English; Testory, in Italian; Klein, in French. These three embodiments of
Zambinella appear together for most of the musical play. Together they represent the complex, illusive castrato.

The Zambinellas present Mme. de Rochefide with the score of an opera
based on the story of Sarrasine and demand that she participate with them in
its enactment. As three performers play Zambinella, Mme. de Rochefide plays
herself and the young nobleman Sarrasine, who falls in love with Zambinella
and abducts her but discovers that she is a man and is killed by henchmen of
Zambinella's protector, the Cardinal.

The various stories collected in *Sarrasine* center on the primary
transaction of theater, performance for money. Zambinella was castrated for
money, performs for money, and receives money from his lovers. He remembers his lovers by counting the rings they gave him as payment for his
sexual favors. Mme. de Rochefide pays for this final performance of Zambinella. Yet within these transactions, beauty is created and loved is inspired. The story of Sarrasine is also one of erotic desire and gender.
Sarrasine became enamored of what he thought was a beautiful woman. In
the Balzac story, he screams at the person he now sees as a sham woman:
"Monster! You who can give life to nothing. For me, you have wiped
women from the earth."[51] Bartlett's Sarrasine is twice removed from the audience. He is enacted by Mme. de Rochefide's reading of his lines, and he
is seen through Sarrasine's descriptions and reactions. Sarrasine is the audience member who falls in love with a performance—a perfect musical
performance and a performance of feminity. Zambinella is masculine and
feminine, though neither male nor female. He/she is protean, enlarged and
freed by his/her gender ambiguity. Bartlett says that "the castrato is sex itself, the ultimate sexual myth. Straight men, gay men, women—everyone
fell in love with the castrato."[52]

In Balzac's story, Zambinella admits to being heartless, unable to love.
In Bartlett's work, Zambinella may not be able to experience love, but he/she,
the artist, can dream it: "I dream of it every night and when I dream I can
see love . . . I want it. I ache for it. For loves different to any you have every
known; loves stronger than any you could every imagine." Sarrasine's love is
destroyed when he discovers that Zambinella does not fit his gender definitions; she is a monster or an "illusion." She is denied reality. But Bartlett's
musical play celebrates illusions, dreams, art as the sites of love. Like many

works of gay theater, it echoes Blanche DuBois's proclamation, "I don't want realism. I want magic!"

> If your dreams aren't dreams of Love,
> How will you live
> When you're awake?

In waking life, though, power comes from being unknowable, unattainable. At the end, Mme. de Rochefide says: "No one will have known me. I am proud of that." The "perfect," unknowable Zambinella has, for her, provided moments of beauty and inspired dreams of love.

In Bartlett's piece of theater magic, the young, nineteenth-century sculptor is given the body and voice of a middle-aged woman. The castrato is given male and female bodies, masculine and feminine characteristics. Zambinella's female drag created the illusion of a woman, but hides that fact that he is a man. His male costume creates the illusion of a man, but hides his lack of male genitalia. Drag, then, is not feminine apparel hiding a male body. It is another question mark in a work that offers no stable answers. *Sarrasine*, like Zambinella, is fascinating, yet ultimately impossible to establish clearly. It shows the way drag, traditionally used to parody women and reinforce gay sterotypes, can be used to unmoor seemingly fixed gender categories.

"I SAW! I KNOW!"

The epigraph for this chapter is Blanche DuBois' response to seeing her husband, Allan Grey, in bed with another man: "I saw! I know! You disgust me. . . ."[53] "Seeing" a homosexual act for Blanche is "disgusting." For Ouisa, in *Six Degrees of Separation* (1990), seeing is terrifying, a prelude to what she thinks will be a violent attack and robbery. But between *A Streetcar Named Desire* (1947) and *Six Degrees*, "seeing" has moved from an act recounted in exposition to an act seen by the audience. The kiss in *A View from the Bridge* was shocking in 1955, but it was not an enactment of homosexual desire, which still could not be shown onstage. However cautiously or elliptically presented, as in *Fifth of July* (1978), the enactment of homosexuality is more than words. Like homosexuality itself—indeed, like sexuality—it is a matter of bodies and seeing, and it is here that a discussion of gay drama must begin. However, before the kissing scenes, the nudity, and the drag, there was a history of coded representation of homosexuality that reinforced a sense of identity and community for the homosexuals in the audience while maintaining the heterosexists' sanctions, taboos, and superstitions about homosexuality and homosexuals.

CHAPTER TWO

AIDS DRAMA: DISPLACING *CAMILLE*

"I have lived for love and now I am dying of it."
MARGUERITE GAUTIER, IN ALEXANDRE DUMAS, FILS,
La Dame aux Camélias

"Something bad is happening.
Something very bad is happening.
Something stinks—
Something immoral—
Something so bad that words
Have lost their meaning."
DR. CHARLOTTE, IN WILLIAM FINN, *Falsettoland*

AIDS drama would seem to be more likely material for the final chapter of a narrative of gay drama to the present. I want, however, to resist the reinforcement of AIDS eschatology; the gay community is very much alive. More to the point, it is in AIDS drama and AIDS discourse that we see most clearly the continuation of nineteenth-century constructions and metaphors of disease and what Paula Treichler calls "the myth of the homosexual body." Gay AIDS dramas dismantle the misapprehensions about AIDS while affirming the Person With AIDS. They also, in the process, deconstruct oppressive constructions of homosexuality that have been perpetuated by popular dramatic representations.

ACTING AIDS

During a rehearsal of a play of mine, an actor playing a character who is HIV-positive asked me whether it would be all right if he had the makeup people paint some Kaposi's sarcoma lesions on his hands so that the audience could see his "condition." Without the signs of an AIDS-related disease, how could he show anything? AIDS itself is invisible, known only by its effects—physical, psychological, and social. HIV-positive status, too often equated in our society with full-blown AIDS, is yet more invisible, a dormant virus that will rouse at a signal from an unseen alarm clock.

My young actor faced the problem of acting AIDS. Enactments of AIDS and people with AIDS reflect the ways in which AIDS is, to use Paula A. Treichler's term, "an epidemic of signification." But the signification of AIDS is fraught with complexities. Ironically, we cannot depict AIDS: we can depict only the symptoms of those diseases the immunovirus allows to infect and ravage a person. We can show more easily the social and political status of the Person With AIDS. AIDS itself is invisible, unactable.

Is the very fact of the body of a Person With AIDS the most powerful theatrical sign of the condition? In London in 1990, a theater company heralded its presentation of *Hamlet* starring a Person With AIDS in the title role. What did *Hamlet*, more about social and political corruption and disease than about physical disease, have to do with AIDS? How was acting *Hamlet* a political statement for a Person With AIDS? Was it not the same statement of courage and artistic devotion in the face of almost insurmountable difficulties that it was when Ian Charleson, dying of HIV-related infections, perilously played Hamlet at the National Theater the year before? The difference is that Charleson's condition was not known outside the theatrical community until his death. For most of his audience, the fact of AIDS was not one of the signs of Charleson's performance. The second *Hamlet* was more about performing with AIDS than it was about Hamlet.

Acting the part of a Person With AIDS focuses the audience's attention on the body and the person's drastically altered relationship to his body. It also focuses attention on the person's altered relationship to society. AIDS discourse not only reflects a horror of physicality but also reinforces the political dimension of the physical. It takes us back to the body of the person infected with the virus and to the problematic body of the homosexual as well. "Whatever else it may be," Paula Treichler writes, "AIDS is a story, or multiple stories, read to a surprising extent from a text that does not exist: the body of the male homosexual."[1] For Simon Watney, AIDS is "embodied as an exemplary and admonitory drama, relayed between the image of the miraculous authority of clinical medicine and the faces and bodies of individuals who clearly disclose the stigmata of their guilt. The principal target of this sadistically punitive gaze is the body of the homosexual."[2] And the signs—the debilitation, the lesions—become in this drama evidence of the moral and physical "disease" of homosexuality. Who is the audience for what Simon Watney calls "the spectacle of AIDS"? Those already inclined to marginal-ize—or worse—the homosexual, whose sexual activities have been brought out of the closet for this spectacle of retribution. Who is the author? The same audience whose ignorance, prejudice, and power are reinforced by this drama.

The body of the AIDS patient, then, becomes a principal player in a moral allegory as primal as *Everyman*. AIDS is not disease, but retribution. The lesions caused by Kaposi's sarcoma are signs of corruption. Therefore the Person With AIDS should be isolated but not offered any of the benefits of society: compassion, government support for medical treatment. But he also should be used as the sign for the inevitable result of "giving in" to homo-sexual desire.

What separates drama from literature is the need for the body, though, as I pointed out in the first chapter, the body depicting the gay man needn't be a "homosexual body." Thus the very impossibility of fixing the homosexual body is dramatized by having a heterosexual play a homosexual. Enacting the diseased body is equally difficult, thus the physical problem of AIDS drama, which has its antecedents in earlier dramatizations of disease.

In Robert Chesley's play *Hold*, Dog imagines his dead lover and rem-inisces with him while slowly taking off all his clothes and revealing that he is "exotically spotted with a considerable number of Karposi's Sarcoma le-sions."[3] It is likely that Chesley, the most intensely physical of gay play-wrights, wanted the part played by an actor with KS rather than one with lesions painted by a makeup person, which forces the audience to come to terms with the physical reality and disfigurement of the AIDS-related disease, the sign of AIDS itself. What is left for the central character in *Hold* is the naked body, signed with lesions, the physical embodiment of the remembered passion of a lover whose mind was ravaged by an opportunistic infection. Dog is painfully aware that his partner is now a figment of his imagination, seen but not physically felt: "I wish you were really here, Lad. Your *body*, living. And your mind. . . . I wish I weren't just imagining the warmth of your belly against my back, your arms around me, your cock bobbing against my butt" (p. 156). What is most missed is touch, which cannot be fully remembered or fantasized. Yet to the audience, the naked body of the lover is as real as Dog's body. The theatrical experience is different from that of the central, imagining character; it is actually more physical.

The vividness and physical intensity of Chesley's play center on the vision of two naked men, which becomes not an overture to desire but the unveiling of the site of memory, grief, and affirmation. In the published text of his AIDS plays, Chesley does not let his readers escape the physical reality of AIDS; the photograph of Chesley on the last page (159) of the published text shows him shirtless, exposing the numerous lesions that mark his body, even circling the tattoo on his arm that is a playful, more willful ornament.

This photograph is in contrast with the picture on the back cover of Chesley, dressed in leather jacket and Levis, cigarette in hand, posed against the corner of a brick wall as if he were on sexual display. To his right, around the corner, is a bare, lightly painted, well-lit expanse of wall. To his immediate left, in the shadows, is a wall decorated with appropriate graffiti. A dark, shadowy figure painted on the wall seems about to strike Chesley. To its left are the words "The Undead." The two photos, both built on what should be provocative, celebratory displays of the body, offer another drama of AIDS that figure Chesley's lament for the sexually liberated past.

Chesley's AIDS plays focus on physicality and fantasy, on memories of a Whitmanesque fantasy world of men communing in a "holy madness" of sex, which is an act of "breaking down walls": "Our spirits were enthralled with the dream of breaking down *all* walls between *all* men. So many men, so little time—remember? Fuck a guy, find his beauty and touch it, share."[4]

Chesley's plays reflect their author's changing responses to the AIDS crisis. *Night Sweat* (1984), which was the first full-length AIDS play, is an angry fantasy of a world in which sex is death. Gay men who have lost all hope go to the Coup de Grâce Club to be killed while enacting their favorite sexual fantasy. Sex is possible with other infected men, but in the Coup de Grâce Club the oppressive equation sex = death dominates absolutely. The only escapes from the fatal "ultimate experience" are hope, love, and a renewed desire to live. Richard, the despairing principal character, is saved from the "ultimate experience" by being forced to reaffirm life and sex as a vital element of life:

> RICHARD: But I'm going to die!
> TOM: Yes, yes. But meanwhile you're going to live! Live until the very *moment* you die! (Tom *embraces* RICHARD.) And make love! Make love in every possible, safe and sensible way! Enjoy it all, from the most delicate cruising to the heaviest S & M trips.[5]

The title, *Night Sweat*, bridges past sex and present disease, as Chesley's play affirms sexual liberty and celebration in the face of AIDS. It celebrates the possibility of a present ecstasy, and it does so through vivid enactment of sexual acts that begin as manifestations of both Eros and Thanatos but later are expressions of love. The play ends with a celebratory dance that defies sexual norms and gender definitions as it defies death.

Few playwrights in the history of drama have experienced or depicted the world as sensually as has Robert Chesley. Even at their saddest, his plays have an erotic charge that is missing in the more discursive AIDS plays—one might say in most drama. Chesley wants to restore sensuality; first in defiance of AIDS, later as a way of experiencing AIDS. His plays are about physicality as they move from life celebration to masturbatory fantasy to memory.

Lanford Wilson's *A Poster of the Cosmos* (1988) can be compared with Chesley's work in its intense sense of the physicality of AIDS, as well as in its psychological and spiritual dimension. Like the Dog plays, *A Poster of the Cosmos* is written in the past tense. The life and experience of the speaker of this extended monologue are far from the upper-middle class inhabited by most characters in gay drama. Tom is a baker, his shirt still covered with flour as he sits in a police station and tells of the events that led to his arrest.

Tom has lived for three years with Johnny, and he remembers vividly Johnny's physicality, his energy, his twitching, his hyperactivity. It is clear throughout the monologue that Tom inhabits a nonreflective, physical world: "I'm your kinna guy, fellas, I won't think about it. We do what we do, we do what's gotta be done."[6]

The audience, like the unseen police, are led to believe that Tom's confession will be about murdering the already dying Johnny, racked with pain, but Tom's confession is far less conventional. After Johnny died in Tom's arms, Tom "cut a place on his cheek where he used to dig and on his chest where he used to gouge out these red marks and in his hair. And when the blood came I licked it off him" (p. 75). Tom, who has tested negative, hopes the ingestion of his lover's blood will kill him, but the act is also the ultimate physical communion—literally sharing the loved one's blood and his infection. Wilson uses "came," the past tense of "come," to suggest the sexual dimension of Tom's act and the way in which AIDS forces sex into the past and into associations with infection. Unlike Chesley's plays, *A Poster of the Cosmos* is presented totally through words—exposition—but at its center is a vivid, harrowing physical image, a reverse vampirism in which receiving blood of a loved one is deadly.

The title of Wilson's play not only refers to the defunct soccer team Johnny loved but testifies to the elusiveness of even the most concrete language. The title contains physical reality one step removed—a picture of a soccer team—as Tom's narration, his words, both express and belie the physical power of his act, which is for much of the play misunderstood by the audience. The word *Cosmos* is both specific-physical and universal-metaphysical, the dual worlds of the love Tom feels for Johnny.

The denouement of much AIDS drama is often a symbolic enactment of the disappearance of the body, as if acting the effects of the condition would somehow be unbearable or sacrilegious. Yet enacting disappearance places the Person With AIDS, rather than his adversaries, in the position of being the "problem" of traditional realistic drama—the problem that has to be removed by the final curtain. Ironically, even in gay drama the Person With AIDS is often "expunged," a victim of the inexpressibility of AIDS, the fear of disfigurement and death, and the exigencies of post-Ibsen drama.

At the end of William Hoffman's play *As Is* (1985), the white hospital curtain is pulled around the bed that now contains Rich, the Person With AIDS, and his partner, Saul. This act hides not only the sexual act that is the resolution of the play but also the body of the Person With AIDS. The rest of Rich's story is narrative, told by the hospice worker. The Person With AIDS disappears from the stage at the end of Andy Kirby's *Compromised Immunity* (1985), leaving his male nurse to narrate the lessons learned while holding a scarf—a remnant of the now-invisible object. Jean Claude van It-allie's *Ancient Boys* (1989) has its central character enact a ritual suicide that is also a disappearance: "*He slips into the see-through pyramid, and, from the inside, pulls the last piece into place. He puts a crystal on his forehead. We see him on his back, his arms folded across his chest. The lights fade on him.*"[7]

In the play *Andre's Mother* (1988), by Terrence McNally, the final ceremony for Andre's friends and family is releasing his soul, now represented by white balloons: "When you let go, it means you're letting his soul ascend to Heaven. That you're willing to let go."[8]

Ironically, disappearance is often what the character with AIDS wants, an escape from being seen with the visible signs of the disease, a horror especially for men for whom appearance has been crucial. Rich, in Hoffman's *As Is*, tells Saul: "What's so hot about living when you're covered with lesions and you're coming down with a new infection every day? . . . If it gets too bad, I want to be able to quietly disappear."[9] The beautiful Peter, in Richard Greenberg's *Eastern Standard* (1988), tells his sister that he has decided "to diminish without witnesses."[10] Disappearance is the only way to have a glamorous farewell, or at least a farewell that preserves the memory of one's glamour. There are no beautiful death scenes (*pace* Larry Kramer), as in *La Dame aux Camélias*, only an absence, a closing of the curtain, a fade out of the lights—or an ascending white balloon.

EQUATIONS

In writing about AIDS drama, one is writing about drama's relation to disease, particularly communicable, sexually transmitted disease. And realistic drama's relation to disease is a reflection of a society's relation to disease, expressed in language that is not only a tool for healing the body but also a means of policing the body. In his superb study, *Disease and Representation: Images of Illness from Madness to AIDS,* Sander L. Gilman maintains: "The social reality of disease is constructed on the basis of specific ideological needs and structured along the categories of representation accepted within that ideology."[11] Therefore, "the infected individual is never value neutral" (p. 7). Medical historian Charles Rosenberg has written, "The desire to explain sickness and death in terms of volition, of acts done or left undone—is ancient and powerful."[12]

Since realistic drama is usually postulated on some scheme of moral, social or psychological cause and effect, diseases in drama tend to have moral, social, or psychological causes, thus mirroring society's tendency to link disease and morality. It is not surprising, then, that causality becomes central to AIDS drama, as it is central to much of AIDS discourse, in which the cause of AIDS becomes not the retrovirus but the mode of transmission: nonprocreative, transgressive sex. Homosexuality and AIDS have been not merely joined into a causal relationship in the minds of many people but actually equated, as Allan M. Brandt points out:

> Now AIDS threatened heterosexuals with homosexual contamination. In this context, homosexuality—not a virus, causes AIDS. Therefore homosexuality itself is feared as if it were a communicable, lethal disease. After a generation of work to strike homosexuality from the psychiatric, diagnostic manuals, it had suddenly reappeared as an infectious, terminal disease.[13]

This is not surprising, since homosexuality has been linked to metaphors of disease for more than a century and, because of that link, has been feared as something "catching."

The connection between homosexuality and disease, tied to the move of homosexual acts into the realm of medical discourse in the late nineteenth century,[14] is a corollary to a more general linking of sexual promiscuity with disease that was evident in nineteenth-century literature about syphilis. Brandt has written exhaustively and powerfully about the ways in which "venereal disease became a metaphor for late Victorian anxieties about sexuality, contagion, and social organization"[15] These Victorian anxieties are precursors of AIDS hysteria in the late twentieth century; the infection has been the focal point of right-wing sexual hysteria, justification for a return to the "old ways" and "traditional family values," which are seen as charms to ward off evil homosexual spirits and as the only true vaccination against AIDS/homosexuality.[16] This shibboleth moves AIDS into the discourse of family as well as of morality and medicine, and since American drama is essentially domestic, AIDS drama places its characters into the discourse of family values.

Thus AIDS entwines us in a series of equations:

> AIDS = homosexuality
> AIDS = disease
> Homosexuality = disease
> Homosexuality = AIDS
> Nonmarital, uncontrolled sex = disease
> Transgression of family values = disease

The Person With AIDS also becomes linked in a causal relationship to his sexual past, particularly to the "liberated" gay past. The unabashed enjoyment of erotic pleasure that was the focus of gay life for many in the sixties and seventies has been presented by our enemies as a Sodom (literally as well as figuratively) for which gay men are being punished, a notion underscored by the human penchant for simplicity in causal explanations. Even for those, like Susan Sontag, who do not believe such canards, the past becomes fearful territory:

> The fear of AIDS imposes on an act whose ideal is an experience of pure presentness (and a creation of the future) a relation to the past to be ignored at one's peril. Sex no longer withdraws its partners, if only for a moment, from the social. It cannot be considered just a coupling: it is a chain, a chain of transmission, from the past.[17]

But for many gay men, the past was a time of unabashed enjoyment of erotic pleasure. To denigrate that past is to denigrate a way of life, an ethos. For the generation that lived through the erotic age, finding a meaningful present in an age in which sex has become not only deeroticized but terrifying involves retrieving and affirming the past and purging it of the stigma of guilt, sin, and corruption with which AIDS and heterosexism have stained it.[18]

For a society that sees AIDS as a moral disease, the cure is a return to what Julia Kristeva calls "the Law of the Father," a discourse and a set of values that reinstate patriarchy. Society must be purged of its problem, which is sexual transgression, and the "proper" patriarchal, heterosexist order must be restored. AIDS plays, like many gay plays, ask whether, within the framework of realistic drama, it is possible for a new order to be established that replaces the Law of the Father with an order that allows the gay man place and power. Can the Law of the Father be seen as the "problem" and thus expunged? Can realistic drama, with its dependence on causality, allow space for a celebration of the past?

"MARGUERITE IS ILL"

In mainstream popular drama, particularly television drama, the gay Person With AIDS is heir to the fate of the nineteenth-century "fallen woman," doomed to the punishment of fatal disease. I offer an extended reading of Alexandre Dumas, fils' dramatization of his novel *La Dame aux Camélias* (1852) because this ever-popular play demonstrates how realistic drama has, from its beginnings in the mid-nineteenth century, placed sexually active characters within the realm of disease as well as that of the normative discourse of sexual morality. *La Dame aux Camélias* reveals how a popular drama can seem to be opening a space for a character who lives outside of conventional sexual morality while proving that such a space is impossible.

La Dame aux Camélias has also achieved status as a camp classic, a position confirmed by Giuseppe Verdi's opera *La Traviata* (1853), by the Garbo film version, *Camille* (1936), and by Charles Ludlam's celebrated travesty version onstage. The 1990 revival of this central work by Ludlam, who died recently of AIDS-related infections, must have inspired at least some members of the audience to see the play as an AIDS narrative: it has always been easy to read *La Dame aux Camélias* as a gay narrative.

Dumas' heroine, the doomed courtesan Marguerite Gautier, is the ancestor of the gay character with AIDS in mainstream drama. Her ancestor among "fallen woman" is the sinister creature called Marwood in eighteenth-century bourgeois drama, whose goal was the corruption and destruction of male and female innocence.[19] Marwood was a female Satan, despairing and destroying. Marguerite, suffering the ravages of her sexuality and the disease that figures her behavior, becomes a relatively passive figure, more to be pitied than condemned.

Marguerite, in living for "love," lives for pleasure, behavior that is presented as symptomatic of a social and moral disease that leads to actual, physical disease. The beautiful, available body of the courtesan is a site of attraction and pleasure but also a site of corruption and disease. The woman is passive, but so is the man, lured by the beauty and sexual freedom of the woman. The only active roles are those of denial and renunciation.

To see women and sex this way is to see them through the eyes of patriarchal morality. Marguerite must please austere father figures, including a very fatherly God. Ultimately, it is her acceptance of their authority and judgment that allows her to be seen as a sympathetic victim rather than as a social outcast who deserves her suffering. It is her understanding of her responsibility for her disease that makes the death scene "the ultimate tearjerker," to use Charles Ludlam's term.

Marguerite may have originally found the life of a courtesan an escape from her impoverished existence as a poor embroideress, but now it is an addiction, an illness: "If I were to begin to take care of myself, my dear man, I should die. Don't you see that it is only the feverish life I live that keeps me alive?"[20] Marguerite's life is "feverish," diseased, but to lose the disease is to lose her life. The disease is linked to a life outside the economy and ethos of the middle class—a life of pleasure, of spending money without earning it, of sex without love, a life of the senses—but Marguerite articulates her society's estimation of the physical and spiritual price she pays for moving outside the dominant economy: "because in the midst of this restless existence of ours, our senses live, but our hearts are stifled" (p. 133).

In the novel on which the play is based, Dumas replaces biological with moral causality, presenting the disease as a metaphor for Marguerite's "nature" but also as the cause of her compulsions: "Her illness, subdued but far from conquered, continued to stir in her those feverish desires which are almost invariably a result of consumptive disorders."[21]

Dumas obsesses on the ravaged body of Marguerite. Her coughing blood and wasting away are not enough: he is compelled to exhume her rotting corpse a year later: "A foul odor emerged, despite the aromatic herbs with which it had been strewn. . . . The eyes were simply two holes, the lips had gone, and the white teeth were clenched. The long, dry, black hair was stuck over the temples and partly veiled the green hollows of the cheeks."[22] These details of decomposition are not unique to Marguerite, of course, but the effect of such a description of the dead courtesan's face is to link her real and metaphoric "illness" with ugliness and disfiguration. Dumas thus figures Marguerite's illness not as consumption but as syphilis, a disfiguring, deadly venereal disease. In his book, *Disease and Representation: Images of Illness from Madness to AIDS*, Sander L. Gilman displays the title-page illustration of a mid-nineteenth-century French edition of a poem, "Syphilis." A young man is kneeling, holding the left hand of a well-dressed courtesan. A bouquet of flowers lies at her feet. In her right hand, the courtesan holds a mask up to her face. The mask is of a beautiful woman; the face is a rotting death's head. Gilman uses the illustration to show how, by the nineteenth century, vice and disease are equated and become linked to the courtesan: "The female is seen as the source of pollution, but also as the outsider, the prostitute, the socially deviant individual."[23] The picture could be an illustration of the meeting of Marguerite and Armand.

In both novel and drama, Marguerite's disease is not the only double bind that traps her: she is also caught in an impossible nexus of forbidden promiscuity and forbidden monogamous love. She renounces her beloved Armand and returns to her former life in a noble sacrifice to his father, so that he can ensure the successful marriage of his chaste daughter, Armand's sister. Her sacrificial move back to promiscuity is a move back to the city and to her disease. The Marguerites of the world cannot be allowed to infect family life. Marguerite's disease becomes dangerous—to herself and others—when she falls in love and becomes a threat to middle-class life. She stepped out of place and out of line. In speaking of Violetta Valery, Verdi's operatic version of Marguerite Gautier, Catherine Clément writes:

> She is sucked into unmarked swamps, interstices that are neither bourgeois, nor workingclass, nor noble. Places of circulation where women get stuck in the mud; ones they will never get out of. The family's son can take a spin there, he will get out just fine, having seen life; but the woman never gets out. . . . Because she wanted to leave, Violetta must pay the required price, her life itself.[24]

No one has to tell Marguerite this. She knows it. Old Duval need only give the right cues for Marguerite herself to articulate society's "wisdom": "And so, whatever she may do, the woman, once she has fallen can never rise again. God may forgive her, perhaps, the world never. What man would wish to make her his wife, what child to call her mother. It is all true, what you have told me" (pp. 140–141).

Marguerite's redemption can come only through sacrifice. She is allowed neither promiscuity nor monogamy, and since chastity is not her choice, her fate is death. And she takes on the judgment of such agents of society as wealthy old men with chaste daughters. But the agents of power in her world are seen not only as right and just but also as merciful. Old Duval forgives Marguerite—from a distance. The courtesan keeps to her place outside the structure of the middle-class family, in her own subculture, where she is both contained and expendable. Nature and God will mete out the inevitable punishment.

The play, like the novel, was thought to be a "true picture" of life in the Parisian fast lane, the demimonde. Everyone knew the identity of the prototypes of the characters. The authority of history, of real names and events, validates the moral scheme of the fiction. However, the events of realistic drama obey not nature and God but the old Duvals who are their representatives. The mores of society allow Marguerite no escape from either the disease of hedonism or the attendant disease of consumption. The only noble act allowed her is renunciation, but still she must die, a fact she accepts nobly: "I have lived for love and now I am dying of it" (p. 163). She has lived for sex, which previously she carefully separated from love, but she dies from love for Armand. Or she dies because of her return to sexual activity, the "feverish" life. But consumption is not a venereal disease, though here it is a potent code for one, a respectable, contagious disease figuring the results of pollution of body and spirit. And she knows her death is "God's will": "Believe me, God sees more clearly than we do" (p. 163). What is it God sees? Marguerite's harsh self-judgments prefigure the expressions of internalized heterosexism voiced by gay characters in pre-Stonewall plays like Mart Crowley's *The Boys in the Band* (1968).

The myth enacted here lives on through AIDS discourse.[25] The pleasure ghetto of gay life infects the middle class through AIDS, perhaps even infecting innocent heterosexuals and children if it is not contained. AIDS, homosexuality, and nonprocreative sexuality are equated as diseases and spreaders of disease.[26] Austere father figures like Jerry Falwell can "hate the sin but love the sinner"—if from a distance. The libertine must keep her or his place, must not infect. And the source of sexual infection, pollution, is feminine, or worse, homosexual. Sander L. Gilman points out how AIDS discourse modifies the traditional gendering of venereal disease: "The male is not only the sufferer, but also the source of his own pollution. Here we have the conflation of the male and female images traditionally associated with sexually transmitted diseases such as syphilis."[27]

The "truth" of *La Dame aux Camélias* resembles what Simon Watney describes as the commonly accepted "truth" of AIDS, which "resolutely insists that the point of emergence of the virus should be identified as its cause. Epidemiology is thus replaced by a moral etiology of disease that can only conceive homosexual desire through a medicalized metaphor of contagion."[28]

Marguerite Gautier's rotting face is the figure for her sexual behavior, itself diseased, "feverish," and potentially infectious. Her disease is both the cause of her behavior and its effect. But, from our point of view, Marguerite's illness can also be seen as her internalization of the judgments of her society. The truly subversive figure would have at least a sense of irony about her expressions of the justness of her own doom. Charles Ludlam, who loved Garbo's *Camille* and had one of his greatest successes as Marguerite, could justify the tears shed over the lady by his belief that, "At the heart of the dramatic event lies the spirit of masochism."[29] Masochism, however, is also a pathological state all too often identified with gay men.

Onstage Marguerite's disease is signified by a cough, an occasional fainting spell, and words, as if any more overtly physical tokens of her illness would be unbearable, improper. The disease loses its vivid embodiment and its figurative relationship with syphilis but not its equation with her "feverish" sexual behavior.

THE VIEW FROM OUTSIDE

There are two ways in which AIDS dramas may try to revise or explode the connected sets of equal signs that constitute a certain kind of AIDS discourse. A well-meaning mainstream work, written for a predominantly heterosexual audience, may present a compendium of the facts while insisting on the pre-eminent qualities of love and compassion that can burst the bonds of prejudice. Gay AIDS drama defies the moral causalities and upholds the value of the liberated life before AIDS.

In mainstream popular drama, however well-meaning, AIDS and people with AIDS are ground into the mill of the problem play, and the Person With AIDS, not the virus or the social problems the person faces, is the problem. The Person With AIDS, in other words, must carry, as he too often does, the baggage of nineteenth-century causalities. I devote this section to television dramas because it is on television that we see most clearly that mainstream mixture of well-intentioned liberalism, shaped by the industry's sense of public values, and popular thinking about homosexuals and homosexuality. Television is, for our time, the major purveyor of middlebrow, "outside" drama.

The 1980s ended on prime-time television with a New Year's Eve re-run of a made-for-television biography of Liberace, who died of AIDS in 1987. Somehow this combination of ostentatious wealth, showbiz glitz, and AIDS more aptly encapsulated the decade than the network executives, to whom I don't attribute much sense of irony, could have envisioned. In a sweet but bizarre scene, after we have suffered with Liberace through his unhappy liaison with a cynical cokehead, Scott Thorsen, who "outed" Liberace by suing him for palimony, we find the pianist at his pool with another beautiful young man, this time an intense brunet (brunets tend to be intense and steadfast in

TV's version of gay life). Staring at the Speedo-clad youth posing beside his pool, Liberace claims to find his "personality" attractive, and with a clasping of hands, they vow "friendship." The young man accompanies Liberace through his illness and vows to keep his secret from the world. We are to assume that this friendship between Liberace and the youth is just that, that Liberace has not infected his young friend. In good television morality, the wages of sex is disease, and love between men must remain, in the age of AIDS as before, asexual (even when the young man looks magnificent lounging by one's pool in a Speedo and is on salary).

In one of the teleplay's final moments, Victor Garber's eerie facsimile of Liberace is gaunt, wasted, slumped in the back seat of a limousine; his devoted chauffeur companion eyes him protectively through the rear-view mirror. *Liberace: Behind the Music* did not judge its subject: after all, Liberace was a product of television. Instead it made him the object of pity, the pathetic lonely man who looked for love in the wrong places. In the final scenes, he is allowed chaste love, but only when his death is imminent. This is, in other words, *La Dame aux Camélias* revisited; as camp, in its own way, as Ludlam's *Camille*, but endearingly ignorant of its own silliness.

An Early Frost, written by Ron Cowen, is the best-known AIDS drama, having appeared on network television in 1985 and been distributed on videotape. It is, as one would expect of prime-time commercial television, an "outside view," however well-meaning as an effort to present gay men with AIDS in a compassionate way. As such, it demonstrates both the virtues and the limitations of television's appropriation of nineteenth-century problem drama. However well-written and well-intentioned, *An Early Frost* yet manages to keep in place all the discursive connections that entrap AIDS and people with AIDS. The teleplay is a celebration of traditional sex roles and of middle-American marriage, which is briefly threatened but eventually re-affirmed. The way in which the teleplay seems to question but ultimately upholds established values is an object lesson on the relationship of television "realism" to any social problem that stretches "traditional family values."

Under the title of *An Early Frost*, we see the "normal" routine of the Pierson family, who live in that generic television house we have seen continuously since "Father Knows Best" in the fifties, though one is never clear exactly where the Piersons live. We know only that it is a plane ride away from Chicago, thus a safe distance from "urban problems" like homosexuality. It could be a suburb, a town, or a small city. Of course, geography is irrelevant. The Piersons live in Televisionland.

Within this world, gender and family roles are clearly delineated. Nick, the macho father, runs a lumberyard with his son-in-law, who has taken the role of the oldest son in the family business and home. In his spare time, Nick fiddles with the car. In the living room, his wife, Kathy, gives piano lessons— though she seems to know only one piece of music—thus having a career that allows her to express her "feminine sensitivity" without leaving the home.

Social life and rituals center in the living room, with bridge games and anniversary parties bringing together this family, which includes a daughter and a son-in-law and the wife's mother, who gives the wife a matrilineal support group to compensate for her pathologically stolid husband. Traditional values are upheld but are not based on any visible ethnicity, religion, or social group. Gender roles are acted out: husband gets up before dawn to work out; wife cans vegetables, demonstrating her link to a traditional past, despite her cigarette smoking, her music, and her slacks.

Yet casting complicates the typical picture somewhat: Gena Rowlands and Ben Gazzara, with their barrage of Actors Studio mannerisms and urban accents, hardly seem comfortable as the people-next-door. Moreover, Rowlands played a lesbian in an earlier TV film, *A Question of Love* (1978). Middle America needn't make a complete identification with these folks; the casting says "serious drama," not television "real life." And Kathy's "artiness" (she is a graduate of a music conservatory who married and settled down instead of pursuing a career) makes her a bit suspect on Main Street: "Don't worry, folks, the Piersons aren't People Like Us."

The doorbell rings at the Pierson's twenty-fifth-anniversary party, heralding the arrival of the problem-play's mysterious visitor, the disrupter of the family pattern, the prodigal son, Michael (not the butch diminutive "Mike," like his father's "Nick," but "Michael"). On this family visit, Michael announces that he has just been made junior partner in his law firm: the Ivy League education the family gave their son has begun to pay off. When his mother asks whether Michael has met any nice girls, his answer is coyly evasive: "Well, I haven't been a monk."

In the next sequence we see "the problem" that will upset the Pierson household: Michael's Chicago home life and his diagnosis of AIDS, which will be presented not as Michael's problem but as his parents'. Michael wakes up in a beautiful lakefront high-rise condo straight out of *Metropolitan Home*. It is contemporary and cold, not the least "homey." This is the generic yuppie apartment of television and film—beautiful, sterile, and vulnerable to threat from outside. Michael is awakened by his handsome lover, Peter, who holds out Michael's cup of morning coffee and playfully rouses Michael for his day at work. Can it be a coincidence that Peter's plain-colored open-necked sport shirt and slacks resemble the outfits Michael's mother wears?

Michael and Peter are television's version of an acceptable gay couple.[30] Michael is the "straight" homosexual: handsome, charming, sensitive, and totally devoid of effeminacy. He is also painfully aware that his homosexuality does not fit into his own personal vision of the American dream. His gay life is a secret at work and with his family. Peter is the male counterpart of the girl a mother dreams of for her son. He is handsome and nurturing, he does the wifely jobs of shopping and cooking, and he succeeds, most of the time, in laughing off Michael's closeted behavior. While Michael is a lawyer, Peter, openly gay, runs a chic boutique that sells merry-go-round horses, jukeboxes, and other camp items, presumably to other very rich urban gays. He sells a form of nostalgia, but in a contemporary, sterile store disconnected from the roots of the nostalgia. Michael and Peter have it all—looks, money, success, marriage, vacations in Hawaii—but the setting shows that something is missing. According to the narrative, what is most missing is real membership in Michael's family circle, something Peter wants and Michael dreads. When Peter asks Michael whether he has told his family about their relationship, Michael counters: "I don't talk about sex with my family and they don't talk about sex with me." Michael understands well how the typical middle-American family will read his relationship with Peter.

In the urban fast lane, the wages of sex is death. Michael was sexually active before he met Peter, and Peter has had a few flings when Michael was overbusy at the law firm. Michael now has *pneumocystis carinii*, a rare pneumonia that has become a calling card of full-blown AIDS. The diagnosis of AIDS is disclosed at the hospital by a kindly doctor who presents the objective, but compassionate, medical view and accepts the relationship of Michael and Peter, who is sitting at Michael's side as a good spouse should be. Later, in spite of an ignorant hospital worker who leaves Michael's food outside his door, and ambulance drivers who refuse to take him to the hospital, it is made clear that the medical establishment is, as usual on television, knowledgeable, kind, tolerant, and supportive. Hospital rooms are big enough for a basketball game. This is an OK place to leave your son, an important factor as the teleplay progresses.

When Michael returns home, a guilt-ridden Peter confesses to his flings. This is the only time the invisible "gay scene" of bars and nonmonogamous sex is invoked, and Michael responds with all the wrath of the wronged wife. Peter has betrayed their relationship. He has also given Michael an easy reason for his illness: "You're sorry. And I have AIDS."

After breaking up with Peter, Michael returns to his family, and the real play, set in the locus of the traditional family, begins. The problem has now come home and must be faced. Michael tells his parents that he has AIDS and that he is gay, as if the two facts were necessarily equated. Significantly, he tells them at night, outside the house. The reactions to the information underscore the differences and problems in what we might see as an already dysfunctional family. Dad rears back to punch his son; Mom steps in to protect.

It is clear from their reactions that the fact of Michael's homosexuality is far more upsetting than his terminal illness and that the narrative must provide some explanation for this nonviral "problem." Michael is blessed with a set of parents straight out of Freud: doting mother and distant father. Thus Michael can be blamed for his immorality and his parents can be blamed for not raising him properly. In addition, Michael's pregnant sister starts acting out her own little psychodrama against her mother and refuses to see Michael (he might infect her unborn baby). Michael's mother and her mother seem to be the only healthy, caring people. For the first three-quarters of the teleplay, Mother knows best and must work out a solution to the problem of holding her family together. Her real mission is to get all members of the family to do the right thing. When asked by Michael whether she approves of his gayness, she responds: "No. The thing is, you're my son. I wouldn't let anything in the world separate us." Family is all.

In an abortive attempt at reconciliation, Michael goes to visit his father in the lumberyard and tells him that he is "ashamed" (of his sexuality? of AIDS?). But shame is not enough for Nick, who feels that his son is now a stranger. All Nick has to offer is disapproval and dismissal. But when Michael convulses from an attack of toxoplasmosis, Nick can carry his son down the stairs and into the hospital, though he won't visit him there.

While recovering in the hospital from his second opportunistic infection, Michael has come to terms with both his illness and his sexuality through his friendship with a real queen, and a nonupper-middle-class one at that, a former chef named Victor. At first, Michael is revolted by Victor, who not only displays the very visible signs of Kaposi's sarcoma and chemotherapy but also exhibits the flagrant signs of stereotypical Hollywood homosexuality: effeminacy, an irreverent, self-protective wit, campiness, and a fondness for Susan Hayward movies. Michael's first response to Victor mirrors Nick's sullen, macho response to Michael's homosexuality. Coming to terms with Victor is coming to terms with his own difference.

When Peter makes a surprise appearance at the Pierson household and is invited by Michael's mother to stay a few days, Nick glowers. Peter may be Michael's loving partner, but he also represents an alien world. When Michael's mother notes that Michael's first apartment was more like a closet than a home (truer than she knows) Michael and Peter are reduced to a fit of giggling that brings them closer together but further alienates Nick, who never laughs.

The women love Peter (of course!), but disapproving Dad must have a middle-of-the-night confrontation with this interloper—the Father and the Other. We're back in the haunts of Camille. Ultimately, Peter, like Marguerite, bows to the power of the Law of the Father. He shows Nick a picture of him and Michael on a fishing trip (see, Dad, we're just normal guys), then tells Nick that Michael will need his father's strength and stolidity if he is to fight his illness. Peter can take over the mother's nurturing role, but he cannot do the macho bit. The scene between the father and Peter, as played by Ben Gazzara and D. W. Moffett, is a duet between burly bass and countertenor on the verge of tears. Peter may be sweet, but he's not the man Michael's father is. The narrative is moving toward its inevitable reinforcement of the Law of the Father.

Michael realizes that his place is with Peter, who loves him and will take care of him, but by the time Michael talks of returning to Peter in Chicago, he is already harboring thoughts of suicide, the aftermath of the death of his friend Victor. Victor is alone and lonely, as movie and television queens always are and are supposed to be, and Victor, tidily, dies off camera. There is no more space for him in the world of television than a brief moment of pity. Michael, realizing not only his own future but also his difference, goes into a fit of suicidal despair.

Michael is saved from suicide by his father, and the climax of the play is his fight with his father: "I'm not the man you wanted me to be. Well, I don't give a damn what you think anymore, because I'm a better man than you'll ever be, you son of a bitch." This classically Oedipal moment leads to his father's loving embrace and the admission that he doesn't want his son to die. Michael has received enough lessons in manhood from his father to put up the good fight. Ultimately the family rifts are healed not by the mother's intervention but by the father's action and his hypermasculinity. Mother is literally pushed aside in the scene of father-son reconciliation. It was his son's feminine shame and coward-ice that most bothered Nick, it turns out, not merely his homosexuality, which might be forgiven if not accepted, would Michael only act like a man. In this drama of sexual stereotypes, Michael-the-homosexual is allowed the best of fa-ther and mother. He needs his father's strength but needs also the "feminine" sensitivity to admit to Peter that he loves him. The marriage of Michael and Pe-ter may be a better one than that of Nick and Kathy, but television can only sug-gest this when AIDS dooms such a union.

At the end of *An Early Frost*, the family is healed. Michael can play duets with his mother (the same piece, now four hands), sister can embrace Michael, and Mom and Dad can stand arm in arm as Michael's taxi leaves to take him back to Chicago and Peter and AIDS-related infections. The drama is resolved for the Pierson family by Michael's leaving the scene. The inter-ruption of their family pattern has been disposed of, lovingly and affirmingly, but disposed of nonetheless, in the manner of realistic drama. Michael is driven around the corner on a rainy night as an ominous rumble is heard on the sound track. He has gone back to the world he belongs in, and the family is no longer disrupted. Mom and Dad stand side by side on their front lawn. Michael has disappeared from the scene, and their "family values" have been upheld: they will lose their son, but everything they stand for will have been vindicated.

What is affirmed ultimately in *An Early Frost* are the values and au-thority of television itself: tolerance, love, marriage, and family. While those values at first seem feminine, they must be tied to masculine toughness and action: father still knows best. Homosexuals are to be accepted, but they don't live on the tree-lined streets of Televisionland: they live in cities, with all the other serious social problems that deserve tolerance and distance. Michael, his homosexuality, his AIDS, have all been seen from the point of view of Tele-visionland. Michael's own point of view is less and less the focus as the teleplay progresses: he and AIDS get pushed literally out of the picture. What the family has to go through is far more important because more typical. Television knew how to handle the problem so that everyone Felt Good at the end and so that the authorized point of view—that of the TV Couple arm in arm on their front lawn, secure in their rightness—triumphed.

In *Our Sons* (aired in May 1991),[31] the mothers of a gay couple are single, working women; Audrey (Julie Andrews), a successful executive living in a beautiful beachfront house in San Diego, California, and LuAnne (Ann Margret), a waitress in a Fayetteville, Arkansas, bar who lives in a mobile home with an American flag hanging in front. The focus of the telefilm is on the relationships that these women from different sides of the tracks forge with the only men in their lives, their gay sons.

LuAnne threw Donald (played by Željko Ivanck), her seventeen-year-old son, out of their home when she discovered he was gay. He is now twenty-eight, has somehow become a successful architect, and is dying of AIDS-related diseases. His devoted lover is James (Hugh Grant), Audrey's son, a composer and cocktail pianist-singer. Unlike LuAnne, Audrey has always claimed to accept her son's homosexuality, though, as he tells her, "We would need spiked boots, Mother, you and I, to step over what has been swept under the rug since I was eighteen years old. Mountains." Audrey has never faced her disappointment that James is gay, never accepted Donald as James' partner, never faced her anxiety about the possibility that James may be infected. James, as uptight a WASP as his mother, will not be tested for HIV antibodies.

Through Audrey's mediation, a favor to her son, there is a reconciliation between LuAnne and Donald: LuAnne admits that she was wrong and Donald forgives her. Before Donald dies, and through LuAnne's candor, Audrey comes to realize that she needs to accept James fully. Homosexuality and AIDS have again been equated, though the script makes clear it is wrong to accept middle-American hatred of homosexuals and the attitude that gays bring AIDS on themselves. It is equally wrong to settle for liberal tolerance, for loving someone "in spite of" his sexual orientation. The script's heart is in the right place, but the ending is a peculiarly Oedipal one. LuAnne takes her son's coffin back to Arkansas, thus signaling her acceptance of his life and her willingness to be honest with her friends about her "queer" son. Audrey and James are now a couple.

James had complained at the beginning of the film that Audrey accepted James' sexuality when he was unattached but never accepted his relationship with Donald. Before Donald dies, LuAnne shows him a picture he drew as a child of a castle. LuAnne remembers that they pledged to live in that castle, which would be "full of magic." Both mothers wanted exclusive relationships with their sons, a demand the film in no way judges. At the end, Audrey gets her wish. If James is HIV-positive, and the script hints that he is, Audrey can care for him:

> JAMES: I might need you.
> AUDREY: Oh, God, I hope so.

There is no hint that James might find another partner. While the dialogue has moved Audrey to an acceptance of James' life and his right to a loving relationship with another man, the action moves him out of other men's beds and back into mother's arms. The one song we hear James sing is "Someone to Watch Over Me." At the end, as he and his mother stand together, the tune plays again on the soundtrack. The "Someone" is clearly Mother. Michael, in *An Early Frost*, at least got to go home to his lover.

There is camp fun in seeing Julie Andrews arrive at an Arkansas trailer park in a limousine and in seeing Andrews and Ann Margret square off. Hugh Grant was imported from England to play James, probably as a sop to gay audiences (Grant was one of the stars of the 1987 film version of E. M. Forster's novel *Maurice*), but while his character, as befits Julie Andrews' son, is very stiff-upper-lip British, he was directed to play James in an American accent, which emphasizes the incredibility of his character. The commercials for various vaginal ointments made clear that the advertisers saw *Our Sons* as a "women's film," ignoring the buying power of the gay viewer, a group advertising agencies never think of targeting. The film sees AIDS and homosexuality from a mother's point of view, not from a gay man's. From the *New York Times'* usual patriarchal position, television critic John J. O'Connor wrote:

> "Our Sons," then, might be expected to leave the gay community reasonably pleased. Perhaps even a little gratitude would be in store. Don't count on it. Many homosexuals today are not about to be satisfied with occasional crumbs from the groaning board of popular culture. They are fed up with seeing their very existences viewed primarily as "controversial." Even the occasionally more sensitive films use distancing ploys, exploring not the lives of homosexuals but the anguished fretting of their parents or friends.[32]

O'Connor grudgingly acknowledged a valid anger. In the most popular of popular cultures, AIDS and the homosexual have become inextricably entwined, as they have in the most hateful heterosexist expressions during the past decade. The daring move would be for television to dramatize the lives of male homosexuals who are not HIV-positive, who cannot be thrust into a pre-Stonewall world and discourse by AIDS. But the captains of the television and advertising industries do not see the gay viewing audience as reliable potential consumers of their products. Lesbians and gay men remain outside the mainstream.

RAPPROCHEMENT

In the mid-eighties AIDS was the focus of most gay drama, as the diverse population known as the "gay community" began to be unified in its attention to an epidemic that ravaged lovers, friends, neighbors, and acquaintances. Gay drama about AIDS to some extent dispenses with the Law of the Father, or at least with the father, and with the dismissive resolutions of conventional problem plays. The voice of the straight world is now the sibling or caregiver. In both William Hoffman's *As Is* (1985) and Larry Kramer's *The Normal Heart* (1985), a gay character must come to terms with his older brother as father surrogate, as the voice of society. For Ned in *The Normal Heart*, his brother represents the exclusivity and judgments of the straight male: "You can only find room to call yourself normal,"[33] but Ned's brother apologizes, accepting the errors of vision he and the straight world he represents share. In *As Is*, Rich's straight brother cries for forgiveness from Rich. The old judgments of parents are gone, and siblings must accept the new law of love and compassion.

Andy Kirby's *Compromised Immunity*, a 1985 production of London's estimable Gay Sweatshop,[34] effects a rapprochement between the dominant "straight" world and that of a gay Person With AIDS. In the fashion of popular British drama à la Peter Shaffer, the play alternates scenes with narration, here split between the two protagonists as they forge a friendship. Peter Dennett, a young heterosexual nurse, is assigned to his East London teaching hospital's first AIDS patient, a feisty thirty-six-year-old civil servant, Gerry Grimond. Gerry at first treats Peter with a combination of wariness and hostility:

> GERRY: You know nothing about AIDS!
> PETER: Stick around and teach me then. And if you want my sympathy, you'll have to start treating me like another human being. Imagine I'm gay if it makes it any easier.[35]

But Peter has his own prejudices. In explaining why Gerry was nasty to the female nurses, he demonstrates his acceptance of stereotypes:

> PETER: Homosexuals don't get on with women, sexual rivals you see. You're both after men.
> GERRY: So you don't get on with lesbians then?
> PETER: I don't even know any.
> GERRY: You work with at least two. . . . It might help if you stopped pontificating about what gays are and are not and do and do not prefer. (p. 56)

The play explores the AIDS = homosexuality equation from within. Peter's problem is not dealing with the hospital's first AIDS patient: it is dealing with a homosexual. Gerry's problem with AIDS is not merely medical: it has weakened his resistance to shame, which is "how you feel about how other people feel about what you are" (p. 60). "It took years to build up a resistance to the way people treated me as gay and now that's as compromised as my physical immunity" (p. 61).

Despite the fears of his girlfriend, who doesn't like Peter dealing with an AIDS patient, and against his own professional ambitions, Peter continues to treat Gerry, whose depression leads him to attempt suicide. Peter realizes that treating Gerry has a spiritual as well as a medical dimension. He tries unsuccessfully to spur the conscience of Gerry's estranged lover. At a gay disco, he meets a young man and convinces him to become Gerry's friend. That young man, Ian, reconnects Gerry to his gay friends and, thus, to life. "Do you know why I'm still here? Because they are coming, because some of the doors I shut have started opening again. I'm gay and I'm dying. I know I said being gay doesn't matter any more. But it does. Ian helped me realize that" (p. 77). Peter cannot cure Gerry, but he has helped Gerry reclaim his identity and his life. Gerry has taught Peter "about being more than an ill person" (p. 79). A rapprochement has been effected between the straight world, its medical discourse and authority, and the world of the gay man with AIDS.

Unlike the angrier American plays, Kirby's *Compromised Immunity* is optimistic—even sentimental—about productive professional and personal relationships between people with AIDS and the heterosexuals who take care of them. The play is more focused on forging links between the gay and straight communities than on providing a critique of the medical and political Establishment's responsibility for the AIDS crisis. Is it that in an Englishman's eyes Peter and Gerry are linked by class loyalties that transcend other rifts? Would the play be different if Gerry were upper-middle class and the hospital was in Queen's Square or Harley Street?

Broadway's people with AIDS are upper-middle class, which is a logical result of the demographics of the "legitimate" theater. They, too, are integrated into the dominant society with surprising, if not particularly convincing, ease.

Richard Greenberg's *Eastern Standard* (1988) is a masterfully written contemporary comedy, celebrated by mainstream heterosexual drama critics as an accurate picture of contemporary life for New York City yuppies. The title reinforces the sense of typicality and authority Greenberg's play invests in its characters. In the world of *Eastern Standard*, gay men and straight men and women are united by education and class in ways that make their differences in sexual orientation relatively unimportant. Straight Stephen confides his relational failures to his gay friend, Drew, for whom Stephen sometimes finds male blind dates. Phoebe's handsome brother, Peter, is also gay. Most of the play explores the new romances of Stephen and Phoebe, and Peter and Drew on the sands of the Hamptons.

Peter has AIDS, which he announces to his sister with a death sentence, "I'm going to die soon."[36] For beautiful, vain Peter, who can make such an announcement over lunch at a chic restaurant, dealing with AIDS, like everything else, is dealing with an image problem: "Nobody ever looked at me without thinking I'd live forever" (p. 21), and Peter would rather disappear from the scene, put himself "in the hands of strangers who'll never have seen me as anything but a bag of bones and lesions" (p. 63). He doesn't want his conservative mother (there is no father to worry about) to know that he has AIDS (and is gay) because: "My mother has a certain way of seeing me. . . . I rely on it" (p. 50).

Peter has, we are told, "slept with the entire free world." The link between this hyperbolic promiscuity and his AIDS is never directly made, but he describes his past life to straight Stephen in a way that makes it sound both attractive and superficial:

> You'd see someone, you'd find him early; and you didn't think—is he going to like me, is he smart, will we have anything to talk about? No, you thought: there's my evening. And the glitter in his eyes, taking you in as if you were a newly discovered continent. And it might last an hour, or sometimes a day, or some amazing times a month, but it never got stale, because the minute you felt yourself start to become boring, you'd just click away—scarcely even saying goodbye. And never—never—any regret, because there was always someone else who'd fall in love with you a few minutes away. (p. 69)

Peter's description of his past, the longest set speech in the play, is an example of a convention of AIDS dramas, the "aria of reminiscence," in which the Character With AIDS celebrates his past promiscuity or laments the impersonality of the urban gay lifestyle. Jean Claude van Itallie's *Ancient Boys* (1989) offers a vivid example of a more mournful reminiscence, as two friends lament the separation of love and desire in their society:

> REUBEN: If I ever slept with anybody I'm close to, it'll be you. I love you. But I don't sleep with my friends. I just sleep with—not even men—with parts of men: thighs in denim, an ass in chaps, a big chest . . .
> LUKE: Ditto. Ditto. I've tried to get away from all that by vowing I'm not sleeping with anybody I don't have a feeling for. So I end up not sleeping with anybody.[37]

Peter's description of his past in Greenberg's *Eastern Standard* is less poignant, less judgmental. Yet in a play about finding and celebrating the possibility of loving relationships, the aria sings of an empty, vain world, earning straight Stephen's response: "I'm sorry—but it sounds awful." The apology allows Stephen a liberal stance, but the judgment is only conditionally rebutted: "Once in a while it was."

Peter spends much of the play eluding Drew's romantic overtures, as he wants to elude the shame of the spectacle of his AIDS, his disfigurement. But miraculously, between scenes, Drew commits to caring for Peter, and Peter, who has never had a serious relationship in his life, accepts Drew's love. In a self-reflexive moment, Drew and Peter present the "moral" of *Eastern Standard*, the grace of dealing with "unmet expectations":

> PETER: I was looking for an escape. And you'd sort of hoped for a lover without complications.
> DREW: These utopian scenarios tend to fall apart in the second act. The strong among us adjust. (p. 104)

And Drew swears his version of "till death do us part":

> PETER: When are you going to leave me?
> DREW: When you aren't there anymore. (p. 105)

At the finale of the play, the two couples drink a champagne toast "to couples," as they prepare to go back to the city and the compromised life.

It may seem odd to compare this sweet yuppie romance with the classic "tearjerker," *Camille*, but Peter, the beautiful libertine, is miraculously converted to romantic love and a gay "marriage" that is qualified by his fatal illness. His past is presented both as a vision of erotic freedom and of heartlessness. Peter and Drew are redeemed, too, by living outside of the gay world, which is only presented as promiscuous sex unsupported by any social or cultural life or sense of identity. Membership in the upper-middle class dissolves all other differences, and the norms and values of that class are never challenged even by those who transgress them. Popular drama has not come far since *La Dame aux Camélias* opened in 1852.

REDEEMING THE PAST

Gay AIDS dramas, though different in style and focus, tend to share two crucial elements: a reaffirmation of the pasts of the characters, and the affirmation of a radically changed present that not only vindicates but celebrates gayness. In many ways, William M. Hoffman's *As Is* (1985) is the paradigmatic AIDS drama in its reflection of a changed world. *As Is* is not only about dealing with an ominous, conditional present but about forging new links to the past, as Saul and Rich live through personal revolutions:

> RICH: Remember Sunday afternoons blitzed on beer?
> SAUL: And suddenly it's Sunday night and you're getting fucked in the second-floor window of the Hotel Christopher and you're being cheered on by a mob of hundreds of men.[38]

The litany of "Remember" is replaced by "I used to" as Saul and Rich continue their celebration of their sexual past:

> SAUL: God, I used to love promiscuous sex.
> RICH: Not "promiscuous," Saul, nondirective, noncommitted, nonauthoritarian—
> SAUL: Free, wild, rampant—
> RICH: Hot, sweaty, steamy, smelly—
> SAUL: Juicy, funky, hunky—
> RICH: Sex.
> SAUL: Sex. God, I miss it. (p. 521)

Saul and Rich merge as their memories of the past merge, and during the course of *As Is*, past and present intertwine as Saul and Rich go backwards and forwards through their relationship. The play opens with the division of the spoils after their separation and ends with the couple climbing into bed together to reconsummate their reforged relationship. This movement from divorce to consummation, both forward and reverse, underscores what AIDS has done to time and memory.

Rich and Saul are a marriage of WASP and Jew, poet with a hunger for freedom and loyal homebody. They are, as the division of spoils demonstrates, affluent, another dream gay couple whose world was one of tasteful but grand consumption. Even their professions, photographer and poet-caterer, represent the affluent urban world of expensive furniture, art, and parties. This was the traditional "gay world" about to be changed by AIDS, governed by hedonism, consumption, and above all by taste. Thus the postseparation negotiations over who gets the cobalt glass, the Barcelona chair, and the Cadmus drawings, remnants of a marriage lost when Rich left steadfast, domestic, kvetching Saul for a feckless, beautiful young man, a muse for his poetry. When Rich visits Saul to divide their possessions, he has AIDS and has been rejected by his new lover, the clients on whom his catering business depends, friends, and family:

> SAUL: You'll stay here with me.
> RICH: Till death do us part.
> SAUL: I love you. (p. 514)

Rich may mock "Till death do us part," but this crucial but oft-forgotten marriage vow is exactly what he and Saul forge during the course of the play, even overcoming their fear of sex to find some way of sharing physical intimacy. Saul will take Rich "as is": "I'll be here for you no matter what happens" (p. 548). Without denigrating the past, Saul and Rich affirm the devotion and commitment of a loving, caring relationship. Like Drew and Peter in *Eastern Standard,* Saul and Rich forge their new life together in a qualified world, a far cry from the carefree past that they can neither relive nor forget.

As Rich and Saul move from divorce to remarriage, they move forward from memories of their voluptuous past to memories of that moment when the nightmare touched their lives:

> SAUL: I was at the St. Marks baths soaking in a hot tub when I first heard about AIDS. It was how many years ago? My friend Brian—remember him—was soaking, too, and he told me about a mutual friend who had died the week before. It was "bizarre," he said. (p. 522)

Saul's reminiscence is followed by another litany, this time of "The first time . . ." stories of AIDS touching people's lives. The nameless characters who recount their tales place Rich and Saul in a larger perspective: a Person With AIDS and his lover. Later, when Rich recounts the story of his life as a gay man, from closeted adolescence to coming out to his relationship with Saul and the "shallow, callow and selfish" Chet, we see his life as the typical experience of a New York gay man celebrating his physicality. One night as he runs through lower Manhattan, training for the New York marathon, his joy becomes religious: "I'm running and telling God I didn't know he was that good or that big, thank you Jesus, thanks, thanks. . . . The next morning I woke up with the flu and stayed in bed for a couple of days and felt much better. But my throat stayed a little sore and my glands were a little swollen" (p. 523).

If the present is not sickness, as it is for Rich, it is the fear that consumes Saul, particularly when he goes to the old night spots: "They remind me of accounts of Europe during the Black Plague: coupling in the dark, dancing till you drop. The New Wave is the corpse look" (p. 509).

At the end of the play, after Saul denies Rich the pills that would allow him to commit suicide (controlling the way one dies seems to some the only control left), Rich accepts his present, dependent relationship with Saul and envisions not only the ultimate future after death but an immediate future as a poet. With that, he and Saul negotiate the consummation of their remarriage in the limited privacy of Rich's hospital room.

As Is is not only a play about coming to terms with disease and with one's love for a partner but also a play about coming to terms with one's past without guilt or regret. Sexual promiscuity is not lamented as a probable cause of Rich's contracting AIDS but is celebrated, its loss lamented. AIDS is lamented, but Rich learns to celebrate the life he has left. Sex is not merely equated with death but is reintegrated into Rich and Saul's relationship. The play is also about proving depth of commitment and concern, thus confounding notions of superficiality and fecklessness.

As Saul brings Rich the pills that could kill him, he has an epiphany-like vision in a puddle outside a Greenwich Village sex shop: "In this dirty little puddle was a reflection of the red neon sign. It was beautiful. And the whole street was shining with the most incredible colors. They kept changing as the different signs blinked on and off. . . . I don't know how long I stood there. A phrase came to me head: 'The Lord taketh and the Lord giveth' " (p. 548).

Saul can see beauty and a reason to live in a puddle, and Rich can revive his need to write. Art will no longer come from the form of a beautiful youth but out of a compromised world. And love will not be the search for a muse but the realization that people must love each other "as is."

The final move toward reconsummation of their relationship in Rich's hospital bed is the triumph of desire, now qualified and modified, in the new world. Rich's body is now far from the perfect object of desire: "I have Kaposi's sarcoma, a hitherto rare form of skin cancer. It's spreading. I have just begun chemotherapy. It nauseates me. I expect my hair will fall out. I also have a fungal infection of the throat called candidiasis, or thrush. My life expectancy is . . ." (p. 542). Sex will now be something different from the wild celebration of the past. Now careful, frightening, but affirming their commitment.

While Hoffman uses the affirmation of the past as one element in re-fashioning life in the age of AIDS, Robert Chesley is more insistent on the justification and celebration of past eroticism. Yet Chesley's best-known play, *Jerker*, or *The Helping Hand: A Pornographic Elegy with Redeeming Social Value and a Hymn to the Queer Men of San Francisco in Twenty Telephone Calls, Many of Them Dirty* (1986), finds little space for the present. Nor does it find space for a larger social context for its characters, who live in problematically hermetic worlds.

Jerker uses the AIDS-age phenomenon of telephone sex to underscore the alienation from their past and from each other that gay men now experience. J. R., a handicapped Vietnam veteran, calls Bert, a businessman whom he has seen in bars, and they share masturbatory fantasies. While the physical isolation and separateness of the characters and the solitary practice of masturbation are poignant reminders of the reduction of eroticism in the age of AIDS, the scenes celebrate the power of sexual fantasy to join these men, whose experience is described by Edmund White in his essay, "Esthetics and Loss":

> Onanism—singular or in groups—has replaced intercourse. This solitude is precisely a recollection of adolescence. Unloved, the body releases its old sad song, but it also builds fantasies, rerunning idealized movies of past realities, fashioning new images out of thin air.[39]

J. R. and Bert's fantasies are of adolescence, of sexual play between brothers in a rural setting, an idealized past of physical pleasure without regret, fear, or disease. But even this shared fantasy cannot fend off the plague. First Bert cries over the death of a friend, and his anger and grief lead to the first nonsexual conversation, as Bert vents his anger over denigrations of the past:

> But, you know, everyone's putting it down nowadays. 'The party's over! The party's over!' Well, fuck it all *no! That wasn't just a party!* It was more: a *lot* more, at least to some of us, and it was *connected* to other parts of our lives, *deep* parts, *deep* connections. I'm not going to deny that drugs were part of it, and I *know* for some guys it was—or turned out to be— hell. But that's not the whole story. For me, for a *lot* of guys, it was . . . *living*; and it was *loving*.[40]

J. R.'s past also includes Vietnam, the cause of the crutches that lean against his wall. Vietnam, which maimed him physically, taught him "what immoral means": compared with Vietnam, sexual activity is "all that is *good*— really, truly *basically* good. Something in me *knows* that, knows that it's just the exact opposite of the evil I've seen" (p. 475).

In *Jerker* the only bearable erotic fantasy is of sex before AIDS. As J. R. and Bert fantasize a pure, outdoor adolescence, a rural idyll, another friend's masturbatory fantasies have to be in the pre-AIDS past: "He can't even fantasize what he wants to do with another man unless it's before . . . all this" (p. 476). Bert asks the central question for men terrified of AIDS and robbed of their past, "What does that leave us, huh?," and J. R.'s response affirms the saving emotions that remain: "Loving can't be killed: it's stronger" (p. 476). Yet Chesley wants to affirm that the sexual encounters of the past were also love—that love isn't only disembodied feeling. Bert recounts in considerable detail a sexual encounter he had in 1979, before the plague. The value of Bert's memory is not only the present sexual pleasure it gives him and J. R. but the affirmation it offers: "Getting me to remember—that it was love. And . . . a virus can't change that" (p. 483).

A virus can change the present and the future, however. Bert gets sick, and in the final scenes of the play, J. R. can reach only Bert's answering machine, which plays a Judy Garland song that now takes on ironic significance:

> So as long as you've begun it,
> And you know you shouldn't have done it . . .
> Oh, do it again—(p. 490)

The voice of Judy Garland, whose death was a catalyst for the Stonewall riot, sings a song about forbidden sex. The lyric that once meant sex that was naughty—wrong—now hints at sex that is literally deadly. Always a song of defiance, it now affirms sex even in the face of death.

Both the power and the poignancy of *Jerker* are contained in the fact that J. R. never gets to give Bert the loving comfort he offers. Finally, when

Bert is only a voice on his answering machine, J. R. gives his phone number. J. R. likes "anonymous encounters." He is writing "a history, a history of love among strangers" (p. 479), and anonymous encounters are what he wants to affirm. "And *nobody* can say it's without meaning: just that both parties have voluntarily chosen to limit the *medium* for meaning—limit it to what's good, limit it to sex" (p. 479).

At the end, speaking to Bert's answering machine, J. R. proclaims his love for Bert, but Bert and J. R. never have the embrace or the assurances of Hoffman's lovers. The world they celebrate also isolates because it offers no liberating vision of the present or the future. The sexual freedom decried as a cause of the spread of the AIDS virus is celebrated as it must be to offer the gay man anything but guilt, regret, and a rejection of his own experience. But there are limitations to the fantasies Bert and J. R. offer each other.

The attitude of the characters in *Jerker* mirrors that of Ghee in Harvey Fierstein's *Safe Sex* (1987): the enemy is "now": "We can never touch as before. We can never be as before. 'Now' will always define us. Different times. Too late."[41] *Safe Sex*, the centerpiece play of the trilogy of the same name, has two lovers precariously balanced on a giant seesaw. Mead wants to hold Ghee, who is obsessed with his Safe Sex list of do's and don'ts. Of course, any move of one partner toward the other upsets the precarious balance of the seesaw and sends both crashing to the ground. Human connection, at least for gay men, cannot stay aloft in the age of AIDS. In a lengthy monologue, Ghee compares "then" when "We had great sex, but argued politics," with "now," when "we enjoy politics but argue sex" (p. 56).

In the first play of the *Safe Sex* trilogy, *Manny and Jake*, Manny is haunted by the fact that he is a carrier, that sex with him is deadly. He can only lament the past: "A moment of silence for what we used to do and how it felt" (p. 12). Manny's lament becomes a litany as he sits static throughout the play in a lotus position, echoing and expanding his own mantra: "A moment of silence for, what can't be done. Another for what can't be undone. A moment of silence for letting go of dreams. And one for stifled lives. For loss. For want. And a toast to those who can change. Who have changed. Who want to change and not forget" (p. 21).

Manny cannot forget nor can he change. His obsession with loss and with his own status as "carrier" has rendered him immobile, unfeeling. But sex to him was nothing but physical satisfaction: "Separation was my only rule" (p. 17). AIDS has enforced the separation without the physical gratification. When Jake offers him affection, solace, and comfort, Manny rejects him—and his own humanity:

> JAKE: People shouldn't be alone.
> MANNY: I'm not people anymore. (p. 23)

Ghee, in *Safe Sex*, is spared the same isolation by Mead's insistence that they embrace. By moving together toward the center of the seesaw, they maintain balance, stay aloft. One—two—can embrace, love safely, even "now." Fierstein's toast is for people who can "change and not forget."

"TILL DEATH DO US PART"

To "change and not forget"—the phrase is the epitome of what is essential to survival and growth in AIDS drama. Change is moving toward an affirmation of love, a physical and spiritual embrace that overcomes the internalized homophobia and fears of commitment that were the crippling detritus of the past. AIDS drama may not be erotic, but it is unabashedly romantic, even at its most violent.

It is a tragic irony that AIDS can validate gay relationships by showing the sacrifice and devotion of the caring partner toward his lover. In *An Early Frost*, Michael can go "home" to his lover, Peter, because their love has been tested by Michael's illness. In *As Is*, Rich realizes that Saul's domesticity and kvetching are what he needs now, not Chet's beauty and fecklessness.

The question in AIDS drama is, "Will you still love me when I'm deathly ill and covered with lesions?"

> RICH: But what happens when it gets worse? It's gonna get worse.
> SAUL: I'll be here for you no matter what happens.
> RICH: Will you?
> SAUL: I promise. (*As Is*, p. 548)

> PETER: When are you going to leave me?
> DREW (*turns to him; simply*): When you aren't there anymore. (*Eastern Standard*, p. 105).

The sign of moral failure is to give up on a relationship, as Gerry's lover, Hugh, does in Kirby's *Compromised Immunity*, or as Chet does to Rich in *As Is*.

A discussion of Larry Kramer's *The Normal Heart*, which ends with a deathbed marriage, brings us back full circle to problems of AIDS discourse discussed earlier in the chapter.

The Normal Heart, a thinly veiled *drama à clef*, chronicles Kramer's own battles with the closety Gay Men's Health Crisis, which reflected the New York gay community's resistance to giving up on promiscuity as the primary tenet of gay liberation despite the ravages of the AIDS epidemic, and his battles with the indifference of Mayor Koch's administration. Throughout the play Kramer's message of sexual abstinence is shouted, as it was emblazoned throughout Kramer's editorials and letters during the eighties. Ned

Weeks, Kramer's character in the play, is a contemporary, gay Cassandra, whose dire but accurate prophesies are scorned by his fellow gays: "After years of liberation, you have helped make sex dirty again for us—terrible and forbidden."[42]

The Normal Heart ends not with Ned's dismissal from the Gay Men's Health Crisis, which he founded, but with his marriage to the dying Felix. Interwoven with scenes depicting the political battle over AIDS are scenes chronicling Ned and Felix's romance.

Ned meets Felix when he goes to the *New York Times* to challenge gay reporters to cover the AIDS story, which is being buried on the back pages if treated at all. Felix is a fashion writer who tries to keep closeted on the heterosexist *Times* but who writes about "gay designers and gay discos and gay chefs and gay rock stars and gay photographers and gay models and gay celebrities and gay everything. I just don't call them gay" (p. 41). While Felix is not eager to "come out" at the *Times*, he is eager to establish a relationship with Ned.

Kramer uses the Ned-Felix relationship to show what was wrong with gay relationships in the age of liberation and how old, self-destructive behavior patterns doom current partners. On their "first date," Felix reminds Ned that they had sex in the baths years before and that Ned rejected any further contact, "I really am not in the market for a lover," a line he repeats on this date with Felix. Felix, the "strong" partner in this conventional dramatic gay relationship, responds with the lesson Ned must learn if he is to bring his political platform into his own life: "Men do not just naturally not love—they learn not to" (p. 53). They learn from the heterosexist world in which they are raised, but the message is reinforced by the promiscuous urban gay world in which sex is "okay as long as we treat each other like whores" (p. 53).

Ned is instantaneously cured of the neuroses that had him running "after people who didn't want me and away from people who do" (p. 49), and he and Felix move in together. But there can be no happily-ever-after in Kramer's jeremiad. Ned and Felix must pay for their promiscuous past even though Felix, like Marguerite Gautier, judges his past actions in a way consonant with society's judgment: "I sometimes make mistakes and look for love in the wrong places" (p. 53). Looking for love in the baths is extremely naive, but one shouldn't die for such romantic idealism. Yet die Felix must, for Kramer is intent to show that true love is as doomed by the AIDS virus as are the constantly shifting liaisons of the leaders of the Gay Men's Health Crisis.

Kramer gives Felix a death scene that Dumas or Giuseppe Verdi would have admired. After Felix dispenses some final bits of wisdom and advice, he and Ned are married by a doctor in the presence of Ned's now-apologetic brother. There can be no love relationship, only a deathbed marriage. Gay men are once again doomed to be alone. "È strano!"

Kramer has trapped himself in his own rhetoric. There is no space for resolution of the crisis that obsesses him, no space for the love that could be a counter to the promiscuity he excoriates as not only exploitative and destructive—as he presented it in his novel *Faggots* (1978)—but now also deadly. We can feel pathos for the death of the sweet, handsome, noble Felix (played, by the way, by D. W. Moffett, who a few months later would play Peter in *An Early Frost*), but who or what is at fault? Kramer, too, confuses the mode of transmission with the virus itself. In doing so, he buys into all the destructive confusion of AIDS discourse. Anger isn't enough.

Kramer's political confusion is expressed not only in the text of the play but also in the texts that form the play's setting. However naturalistic the script seems, Kramer has set his play within walls on which are painted statistics that are also accusations: of indifference or worse on the part of Mayor Koch and the city government, of the federal government, and of the *New York Times*. Moderate gay groups, like the Gay Men's Health Crisis, are damned by inference in the longest passage, filling an entire wall, which describes the futile AIDS strategy of polite cooperation and "backstairs diplomacy" with Washington officials. This strategy is likened to the one the American Jewish Committee followed during the Holocaust, when more radical action against a seemingly indifferent American government might have saved more European Jews. Raising the specter of the Holocaust clarifies Kramer's politics. Is AIDS being used, through design or negligence, as a "final solution" for homosexuals in America? If so, then radical action is the only possible response and protection, and that action can be effective only if gay men are willing to "come out." But surely this argument could be presented without turning the attack so completely against the gay community. An effective call to arms does not divide, it unites, something Kramer himself realized in 1987: "In reading over my collected diatribes of the past years, I realized I am still unable to resolve this fundamental problem—how to inspire you without punishing you."[43] As we shall see, Kramer found a more effective, more focused vehicle for his anger than the theatrical diatribe.

INTO THE STREETS

> Principal dramatic form of the decade (owing to AIDS):
> the memorial service.
>> "THEATER: THE BEST OF THE '80's,"
>> *Village Voice*, JANUARY 2, 1990

In an article in the October 1989 issue of *American Theatre*, Alisa Solomon writes:

> Recently, AIDS has fallen off as a central subject for new drama. It's no
> wonder. When, for instance, spectacle and public ritual are so movingly

combined in the image and action of the Names Project Quilt, conventional theatre seems redundant—at best a pale imitation of the formal, mass expressions that help give shape to real grief and anger. Time and again the spirited protesters of ACT UP have demonstrated that the theatre of AIDS is in the streets.[44]

That Solomon's article on ACT UP (the AIDS Coalition to Unleash Power) was printed in the best chronicle of the current state of American drama gives credence to her argument. From the vantage point of the early nineties, AIDS drama looks like it has run its course. Its apex was reached in 1985, that strange banner year for gay men.

1985 was the year the AIDS crisis allowed a space for gay men on television. On "Dynasty," Steven Carrington fell in love with Luke, who thanked the Carrington family for letting him sit at their table, a symbolic moment that suggested that gay men, hats in hand, might find a place in America's living rooms and cultural consciousness. It was the year Laura Z. Hobson's novel *Consenting Adult* (1975) was moved from the world of New York Jewish intelligentsia to Televisionland and Marlo Thomas. It was the year of the most daring of television dramas, *Welcome Home, Bobby*, in which a teenage boy, who had been having an affair with an older man, made clear to his family that his sexual partners were going be his choice. In these television programs, as in *An Early Frost*, the young gay man battled his strong father while a noble mother mediated. The son won, but his days in Televisionland were numbered.

Television had another vision that year, one that drastically revised the public image of AIDS and of gay men for middle America. "Dynasty" viewers were not only watching handsome blond Steven go through fits of ambivalence over his sensitive brunet lover, Luke, but they also saw the ravaged remains of Rock Hudson as he carried on, in and around the stable, with Steven's stepmother. It took an actor to focus America's attention on AIDS. Even the actor in the White House, who refused to mention AIDS for the first five years of the epidemic, had to acknowledge his friend's death.

Hudson's death also gave his *Giant* costar, Elizabeth Taylor, a new role as spokesperson for the American Foundation for AIDS Research, which was established with a grant from the ailing Hudson. In a brilliant piece of gallows humor, the late Stephen Chapot described sitting in the balcony with three other Persons With AIDS, watching the spectacle of an AIDS fundraiser featuring Elizabeth Taylor. Chapot's essay is a stunning piece, exposing the absurdity of a spectacular Hollywood benefit performance, another kind of AIDS theater:

> The show is everything you would expect from this town in a crisis. No one mentions the word AIDS until twenty-five minutes into the show, and when it comes, it's mentioned by the director of the AIDS Project. Someone snick-

ers. "She dresses like my old aunt." They present an award to a man in a wheelchair who has brought his own oxygen. This is an audience that gives a man a standing ovation for dying in public. . . .

When Taylor does make her appearance, she promises "to spend the rest of my life fighting AIDS." I chuckle, "So will I, honey, so will I."[45]

1985 was also the year in which Robert Chesley's *Jerker* takes place, and in which William Hoffman's *As Is* and Larry Kramer's *The Normal Heart*, the most commercially successful AIDS plays, received major New York productions. *As Is* moved from the Circle Repertory Theatre in Greenwich Village to Broadway and then on to a lugubrious television production (1986). *The Normal Heart* earned the record of being the longest-running production at Joseph Papp's New York Shakespeare Festival, and rumors spread that Barbra Streisand would produce a film version.

Two years later, AIDS as theater had transformed itself radically. In San Francisco, activist Cleve Jones, while recuperating from stab wounds inflicted by fag bashers who had seen him "come out" on TV's "60 Minutes," devised the idea of the AIDS quilt. His panel, the first panel of the quilt, would be a memorial to his friend, actor Marvin Feldman. In October of 1987, almost two thousand panels of the AIDS quilt were displayed on the Mall in Washington, D.C. In a moving ceremony, the names of the people celebrated by quilt panels were read out. Among the readers was playwright Harvey Fierstein and producer Joseph Papp. The ceremony, the reading of names, and the unveiling of the giant pattern of tributes was one form of AIDS theater. The sense of communion that comes from being in an audience, of sharing an event—that sense that theater shares with religion—is a crucial part of the experience of the quilt. It is not like looking at a painting, or a quilt on display in a crafts gallery or museum. The communal viewing of the quilt, the sharing of the emotions it evokes, is central to the experience.[46]

A more lively form of AIDS theater was the brainchild of Larry Kramer, whose rage led him from editorial vituperation, to the Gay Men's Health Crisis, to *The Normal Heart*, to a chaotic farce about the First Family of the eighties, *Just Say No* (1988), an attempt to parody what was already absurd, to founding ACT UP, which has proved that the protests and street theater of the sixties can be useful in the conservative eighties and nineties.

Just Say No was a testament to the limitations of theater as an effective expression of Kramer's anger. A bizarre farce, with characters who clearly represent the Reagans and Mayor Koch, the play was more an exercise in what we now call "outing" (exposing closeted homosexuals who are supporting oppression of other gays) than focused drama. Kramer's introduction to the published version of *Just Say No* is far clearer than the play itself, showing that during the AIDS crisis, Kramer grew as an essayist, while his ability to form a coherent drama dwindled. It is not surprising that the next Larry Kramer production to appear at the New York Shakespeare Festival (in the summer of 1990) was *Unnatural Acts*, a theater piece based on excerpts from the essays collected in his *Reports From the Holocaust*, with, as a curtain raiser, a fifteen-minute dance-theater piece performed to selections from the speeches of Jesse Helms.[47]

By the time *Unnatural Acts* was produced (1990), Kramer would be better known as AIDS polemicist and activist than as playwright. ACT UP grew out of a speech Kramer gave on March 10, 1987. Two weeks later, ACT UP had its first demonstration on Wall Street, replete, significantly, with props built in the shops of the New York Public Theater. Kramer describes the public demonstrations of ACT UP as theater: "Each action is like an enormous show. We're divided into committees, doing banners, logistics, media, just like a producer would hire people for scenery, costumes, publicity."[48]

The purpose of the production is to garner the largest audience possible through doing something so theatrical that the media cannot resist covering it. In his history of the tragic farce of the American medical and pharmaceutical Establishment's handling of AIDS, Bruce Nussbaum credits ACT UP with providing the impetus for forcing the National Institutes of Health and corporations like Burroughs-Wellcome to act with a modicum of competence and responsibility.[49] Now there are ACT UP chapters all over the country, even in the front yard of Burroughs-Wellcome and Jesse Helms, Raleigh-Durham, North Carolina.[50]

ACT UP demonstrations dramatize the AIDS crisis through vivid theatrical metaphors played out where decisions are made—on Wall Street, in the headquarters of drug companies, and at medical conventions. In doing so, they prove the power of theater but also come up against its limitations, as drama tends to play to the already-converted and seems to have little effect on those who need conversion. For over twenty years, theater people have lamented the inability of political theater to do more than validate those in the audience who share the playwright's opinions. ACT UP has redefined political theater for the age of mass media. It has shown that theaters are not places to effect social change: theater is a more effective tool for shocking people into awareness of key issues when it is taken out of its conventional home. In *AIDS Demo Graphics*, Douglas Crimp writes:

> For AIDS activist artists, rethinking the identity and role of the artist also entails new considerations of audience. Postmodernist art advanced a political critique of arts institutions—and art itself as an institution—for the ways they constructed social relations through specific modes of address, representations of history, and obfuscations of power.[51]

Crimp is speaking of the visual arts, and his volume is a vivid record of how they have been galvanized into use by and for ACT UP and other AIDS activists. His statement, representative of many by contemporary critics, raises questions about the institutions of theater in a time in which old prejudices and associations need to be exploded.

AIDS theater, then, is played out most effectively in the real world, sometimes with stars like Rock Hudson or Liberace, sometimes with chronically enraged playwrights like Larry Kramer, but most vividly by a cast of thousands, proving, as Hudson inadvertently did, that there are millions of gay men who are not known by the usual, stereotypical signs. They may be forced into being known, or—better—may choose to be known. Like a Cecil B. DeMille spectacular, the power of AIDS as theater is the power of numbers: the cast of thousands in the streets at a gay-pride rally or an ACT UP demonstration is the most powerful sign that the gay community is big and ultimately unbeatable.

Street theater has been a central part of gay life, from the informal and formal costumed processions of Halloween, that celebration of disguise that has become the gay holiday, to the display of sexual and social identity of the gay-pride march. Now gay street theater has been galvanized by AIDS, given a purpose. The flamboyant, celebratory masking has been transformed into potent performances of unmasking aimed at those who are doing nothing, or less than nothing, about AIDS.

AIDS remained as insistent a presence in gay drama as it has in gay life. Later chapters contain discussions of plays that chronicle the changing ways in which HIV, itself changing over the past two decades from something one dies from to something one lives with, has shaped the experiences of gay men. The major change is that AIDS politics has led gay men to refuse the role of victim, as we have refused the other roles the dominant culture has assigned to us.

PART 2

CODES AND CLOSETS

CHAPTER THREE

CLOSET PEDERASTS

"When the audience watches it here, I want them to say to themselves, 'It's homosexual. Nothing is said about it but it's there. It must be there. That's the only explanation for these characters and their story.' So that's what I want. I want to create something without stating it."
JED HARRIS, ON HIS PRODUCTION OF *The Green Bay Tree*

"He was an expert on the adolescent male body. He'd completed an exhaustive study of his subject before I met him. During the course of one magical night he talked to me of his principles—offered me a job if I would accept them. Like a fool I turned him down."
SLOANE, IN JOE ORTON, *Entertaining Mr. Sloane*

This chapter focuses on the presentation of homosexuality in British dramas from the 1930s until 1968, when the section of the Licensing Act of 1737 that mandated the censorship imposed by the Lord Chamberlain's office was revoked. In these plays, one sees how the depiction onstage of gay characters was the result of cautiously showing what could not be shown, and saying what could not be said. By both suggesting and denying the existence of homosexuals, the plays of this period dramatize and maintain the closet. Such "closet dramas" could be written by heterosexuals exploiting the potentially sensational subject matter or, in the case of Harold Pinter, toying with the very restrictions involved in presenting homosexuality at all. Or they could be written by gay playwrights like Noël Coward, dependent on the popularity and rewards of commercial success, or Joe Orton, desiring success like Coward's but wanting as well to place homoerotic desire at the center of his plays.

All the plays discussed in this chapter were also produced in New York (Coward's *Design for Living* was first produced, in 1933, on Broadway) and were, thus, influential in establishing American stereotypes.

ACTORS AND THE CLOSET

In December 1990, British actor and gay-rights activist Ian McKellen became Sir Ian McKellen. While McKellen is hardly the first homosexual to earn a "Sir" before his name, he is the first to proclaim his gayness openly beforehand and to campaign against government attempts to reinstate the closet onstage and offstage. When filmmaker Derek Jarman excoriated McKellen for accepting the knighthood and thereby supporting the heterosexist policies of the government, which McKellen had rightfully attacked, eighteen other British theater people—producer Cameron MacIntosh; playwrights Martin Sherman, Nicholas Wright, and David Lan; and fifteen directors and well-known actors—"came out" and supported McKellen's knighthood as a crucial moment in English gay history. "Never again," their overly optimistic statement read, "will public figures be able to claim that they have to keep secret their homosexuality in fear of damaging their careers."[1] The previous summer, actor Alec McCowen (one of the signers of the letter supporting McKellen) announced that his appearance in a dramatization of Christopher Isherwood's *A Single Man* was his coming out, since the play, about a middle-aged gay man's dealing with the loss of his lover, mirrored McCowen's own recent loss of a lover to AIDS.

While skeptics may note that the statement supporting McKellen was signed only by well-established "personages"—no young actors felt it was safe to sign the statement—optimists can read a number of meanings into these British theatrical comings-out. They are at once a defiance of growing strictures against the public admission of homosexuality in England and an acknowledgment that few Britons care whether theater people are gay. Many simply assume that they are—an equation of homosexuality and artists "in a country in which homosexuality is tolerated as an eccentricity but not accepted as a way of life"[2] that may explain how the British government can both honor a gay activist and enact laws to silence gay activism.

What these British theater people have done in publicly proclaiming their homosexuality is what many American theater people most fear. Here, "outing," announcing that a public figure is homosexual, is a weapon used by activists to attack closeted public figures who, by their silence, support the oppression of their fellow gays.[3] Why is it that American actors have to be dragged out of the closet, while British artists see the importance to the gay community of their visibility as gay people? Why is it that, when outed, gay American actors vehemently deny their sexuality and even, in some recent cases, get married to a woman in an attempt to invalidate the allegation? Why is there less of a price to pay for coming out in Britain than in America? In our society, despite the success of Harvey Fierstein and a few other playwrights, many thespians feel that any tie between the theater and homosexuality must be publicly severed, despite the fact that many of our leading playwrights, composers, lyricists, directors, and designers are and have been homosexual.

While American actors have mastered "playing the closet," many English actors understand the political and theatrical power of coming out. Coming out is a kind of performance, a public proclamation of one's gayness akin to the public demonstration of salvation in an evangelical revival. It is a public joining of private and public life, a public refusal to perform the intricate but limiting roles heterosexist society wants gay men to perform: maintaining silence and denying what others do not want to know or playing the role people want and expect, preparing "a face to meet the faces that you meet," as Eliot's Prufrock so aptly puts it. The performance may be of "playing straight" or playing a stereotype of homosexuality that heterosexist society can grasp. Coming out is a performance that resists a number of other performances.

Much of the public is protected by the performances associated with the closet from knowing what they do not want to know and, therefore, not having to deal with what they do not want to deal with. Eve Kosofsky Sedgwick notes "the degree to which the power of our enemies over us is implicated, not in their command of knowledge, but precisely in their ignorance."[4]

The closet itself is less a place than a performance—or series of performances, maintained by the heterosexist wish for, and sometimes enforcement of, homosexual silence and invisibility. Like any good performer, the closeted individual seeks approval by giving his audience what they want, but in the process he performs his shame at being homosexual.

In this chapter and the next, I will focus on the paradoxes endemic to the dramatic closet. The stage closet resembles one of those garish magician's cabinets that gaudily dressed assistants wheel around the stage: "Now you see him; now you don't." For theatricality—metatheatricality—is essential to the language of the dramatic closet. The phantom homosexual is the character who imaginatively transforms his environment, who turns reality into stage set as a background for his performance. As the homosexual resists conventional categories of sexual identity, the stage homosexual—and the closeted play—are known (only sometimes) by their resistance to the strictures of realistic theater. Dramatizing the closet is also dramatizing the theater of the closet.

One of the most common clichés encountered in discussions of any creation of homosexuals is the "gay sensibility," a universalizing term suggesting that flamboyant, ironic theatricalization, like limp wrists, is a genetic quirk all homosexuals have to one extent or another. This misconception not only denies that homosexuals, like heterosexuals, have more differences than similarities but also minoritizes art as "sissy" because it is more "natural" to homosexuals. I suggest that what has been called the "gay sensibility" is actually a "closet sensibility," an awareness of performance because of the need to perform, and a mockery of the roles one is expected to perform. Closet sensibility seems universal, "natural" to the "unnatural" homosexual, because it is a set of responses to being stereotyped.

Closet drama is tied to two complementary aspects of the closet: the denial of the existence of homosexuality within the audience's social sphere, which is being depicted "realistically" onstage, and the maintenance of stereotypes that assure audiences that the homosexual can easily be recognized and, should he intrude on normal society, marginalized.

THE CLOSET AND THE POLICE

The only truly successful representation of the closet is invisibility and silence—no homosexuality at all; however, like all the other titillating taboo subjects exposed onstage in the twenties and thirties,[5] the horror of homosexuality proved to be an irresistible lure. Realistic drama could afford audiences a glimpse of the forbidden, then banish it from the stage. Historically, homosexuality had moved from the silent and invisible to the unspeakable and unshowable.[6] The theater's challenge was to suggest and indicate without actually acknowledging the existence of the forbidden subject. This is the first visible dramatic closet: the invocation of homosexuality without naming it—or the problematizing of homosexuality without acknowledging its existence. It could be read by those who wanted to see it, particularly homosexuals.

In the United States in the 1930s, depictions of homosexuality were limited, if not eliminated, by legal sanctions against representing homosexuality onstage. These sanctions had been unnecessary until the appearance of such representations. Inspired by a public outrage that had been fueled by the reaction of a moralistic press to Mae West's play *The Drag* (1927) (which never got closer to Broadway than Bayonne, New Jersey) and a sensationalistic melodrama about lesbians, *The Captive* (1927), a translation of a French play by Edouard Bourdet, legislators added the Wales Padlock Act to the New York State Penal Code. The act outlawed plays "depicting or dealing with, the subject of sex degeneracy, or sex perversion." The threatened penalty, if a theater housed a play that "would tend to the corruption of youth or others," was the padlocking of that theater for a year and, potentially, the revoking of its operating license. All persons involved in any way with these productions, or with any "obscene, indecent, immoral, or impure production," were guilty of a misdemeanor.[7] Though it was nominally directed against any stage obscenity, the Wales Padlock Act was supported by the "threat to society" posed by *The Captive*, a play that was hardly an advertisement for the joys of lesbian

behavior. The melodrama was considered dangerous merely because it acknowledged the existence of such behavior.

What seemed most dangerous to the City Fathers was not what happened onstage but the fact that gay characters onstage attracted numbers of
gay people to the audience, thus creating a visible presence and, therefore, a
threat to the enforcement of invisibility. It is clear from newspaper accounts
that the out-of-town productions of *The Drag* and *The Captive* attracted a
large proportion of gay men and women, and the exposure of the public to
displays of "vice and the vicious" on both sides of the footlights probably
contributed to the outcry. Heterosexist Jeremiahs seemed to believe that the
frightening fiction of homosexuals onstage spawned the horrible reality of
numbers of homosexuals in the audience. In declaring *The Captive* obscene,
Justice Jeremiah Mahoney cited police reports that at one performance 60
percent of the audience was female, "and groups of unescorted girls in twos
and threes sat together." One of the dangers of *The Captive*, it seemed, was
the creation of an environment in which women socialized without male companionship or supervision. Mahoney wondered whether obscenity laws should
not protect "the young and immature, the ignorant and sensually inclined,"
for "many people must be protected from their very selves."[8]

The police were eager to do anything they could to stop *The Drag* from
appearing on Broadway. Perhaps the noble protectors of morality could see
the danger of West's piece. According to George Chauncey, West herself had
molded her flamboyant image on Bert Savoy, "one of the first major female
impersonators widely known to be gay."[9] Later a favorite role model for drag
queens, West herself seemed to be a drag queen:

> West's image as been more broadly and frequently associated with *female*
> than with male impersonation [one of her first vaudeville acts had her in
> male drag], implying, paradoxically, that West herself was performing (or
> even really was!) a man impersonating a woman—by popular reasoning, a
> gay male.[10]

It seems logical that, when she turned to playwriting, homosexuality and transvestism would interest her as much as female desire. Clearly, she was determined to test the limits of what could be presented on stage as she did in her
own performances. Nothing could test those limits more than a stage full of
gay men flamboyantly playing gay men (The cast was comprised of drag
performers West "discovered" in Greenwich Village bars, who improvised
many of their lines during the rehearsal period). Critics disagree on whether
The Drag is cynical exploitation or an honest attempt to present gay life of
the period. By the time *The Drag* was in rehearsals, "pansy acts" were staples
of nightclub and burlesque. West may merely have been placing on Broadway
what some nightclub patrons had already seen.

Whatever West's motivation, *The Drag* is an interesting slice of gay history. The narrative, such as it is, centers on a judge's son whose neglect of his wife has become a matter of public notice. The young man, Rolly, is far more interested in men than in his wife, Clair. The first act takes place in the library of Clair's father, a doctor who has studied the most recent literature on homosexuality. The doctor, is, for the time, an enlightened man who sees homosexuality as a medical problem, not a legal one. He tells Rolly's father, the judge, "Still you endeavor by law to force a man born with inverted sexual desires, born to make his way in the world with millions of human beings radically different than he is, to become something which his soul will not permit him to become."[11]

Still, Clair is unhappy and is falling in love with Grayson, the business associate Rolly has take his wife to the opera while he supposedly works but actually parties with his gay friends. The play veers wildly from the enlightened arguments of the doctor to the bitchy camp dialogue of Rolly's gay friends. The centerpiece of the play is a drag ball at Rolly's house, complete with dancing, musical numbers, and a large dose of bitchiness. After the ball, the play veers wildly in another direction. Rolly is shot by a jealous admirer who had come to the doctor for help for his uncontrollable, obsessive, unrequited love (Rolly, typically, is infatuated with a straight man). The doctor convinces Rolly's father, the judge, to be compassionate toward his son and his killer:

> When it's another man's son, you condemn him, it's true, it's true. You've sent many up the river, and you know it, Bob, but when it hits home it's a different story. In this civilized world, we are not civilized enough to know why or for what purpose these poor degenerates are brought into the world. Little did we know that a fine, strong boy like Rolly was one of them.[12]

The judge orders that his son's death be reported as a suicide, thus saving the family's reputation (and the killer).

West's play is hardly great art, but it does express the conflicting views toward homosexuality prevalent in 1927. The most liberal character sees homosexuals as mentally deformed, "degenerate," but at least he pleads for compassion and tolerance. The doctor, the medical model, wins over the draconian judge. The gay characters are flamboyantly, outrageously, in your face queer and hyper-sexual. Not surprisingly, they often sound a lot like Mae West herself. Yet the men represent the dominant contemporary image of the invert as one caught in some sort of gender limbo, neither wholly male or female, but desiring "real men." They are also degenerate, morally weak.

In 1929, West wrote:

> I admit that in my play "Drag" I was a little premature. The public is still too childlike to face like grown-ups the problem of homo-sexuality. How

few are the people who even know what the word means? Because of this universal ignorance I wrote "Drag" with the intention of taking it to all the theaters in the country to teach the people.[13]

Mae West presents herself as a noble sex educator bringing the truth of homosexuality to the entire nation via her cast of Greenwich Village drag queens. If the play was banned in New Jersey and New York City, one can imagine what would happen in the Bible Belt. *The Drag* was much more a piece of exploitation for West, but she does not stand far outside the world she represents. The woman who always presented herself as a sexual outlaw is allowing one group of gay men, also sexual outlaws, to play themselves. For 1928, this is a dangerous play. It would be forty years before anything this openly honest about one segment of gay life appeared on the legitimate stage.

In Great Britain the Lord Chamberlain's office had, since 1737, exercised censorship over all theatrical scripts. This censorship was originally intended to stifle antigovernment satire but later became more concerned with matters of a "decency." Until the Licensing Act was finally revoked in 1968, the Lord Chamberlain was expected to keep homosexual characters and relationships off the British stage. You could evade the Lord Chamberlain's watchful eye only by producing a play in a private club (the Royal Court Theatre had to be turned into a club in order to present John Osborne's *A Patriot for Me*.)[14]

On the American or British stage, then, homosexual characters and relationships could be inferred from the behavior of the actors, though it could not be discussed openly. Such inference could best be shown by a combination of selections from the catalog of gay male stereotypes:

> Effeminacy (mincing, limp wrists, lisping, flamboyant dress)
> Sensitivity (moodiness, a devotion to his mother, a tendency to show emotion in an unmanly way)
> Artistic talent or sensibility
> Misogyny
> Pederasty (as we shall see, this became the stereotypical formula for homosexual relationships, with its connotations of arrested development and pernicious influence)
> Foppishness
> Isolation (the homosexual's fate, if he or she remained alive at the final curtain)

Stereotypes are both necessary and highly problematic. They are necessary because homosexuality does not, like racial or ethnic identity, have any visual signs. Therefore, to represent homosexuality, a catalog of signs was needed, particularly when a character's homosexuality could not be enunciated. As Richard Dyer points out:

A repertoire of signs, making visible the invisible, is the basis of any representation of gay people involving visual recognition, the requirement of recognizability in turn entailing that of typicality. Though not indispensable, typification is a near necessity for the representation of gayness, the product of social, political, practical, and textual determinations.[15]

The purpose of these stereotypes, which assume the validity of certain "universal" signs, is to make homosexuality visible and recognizable. But there is no "truth" to the stereotypes themselves nor to the assumption underlying them: gay people are as different from each other as heterosexuals are.

Further, these problematic stereotypes exist not only to indicate gayness but also to privilege the heterosexual who believes he can identify and marginalize the homosexual. In addition, they help gay people, who can "pass" in a heterosexist society by not enacting the stereotypes. The homosexual character is often trapped in a ritual of purgation—of identifying and eliminating. Visual stereotypes allow the playwright and performers to enact this ritual without ever naming what is considered unspeakable.

As we shall see throughout this chapter and the next, homosexuals were both invoked and marginalized by the very structure of realistic drama. Feminist drama critics maintain that realistic drama necessarily upholds a certain order, one that is as dangerous for gay men as it is for women: "Narrative closure reinstates the preexisting order after instigating its temporary crisis."[16] Jill Dolan reminds us that "if there is an enigma in realism, its structural shape is bent toward unraveling and expunging it."[17] In a structure in which the homosexual is inevitably what Alan Sinfield calls "the outlaw-intruder who threatens the security of the characters and, by inference, the audience,"[18] the purging of the homosexual gives the play closure. Gay playwrights could infuse this formula with irony but could not totally reject it without rejecting the form altogether.

NOW YOU SEE HIM?

Mordaunt Shairp's *The Green Bay Tree*, performed in London and, very successfully, on Broadway with Laurence Olivier in 1933, is a play about a homosexual character and possible homosexual relationship that never mentions or even directly alludes to homosexuality. Shairp managed to succeed where most of his predecessors had failed: he slipped a play about a homosexual relationship past the scrutiny of the Lord Chamberlain and into production and, a few months later onto Broadway without invoking the Padlock Act. Focusing on an elderly homosexual's "tutelage" of an impressionable young man, the play is perforce written in innuendo and depends on stereotypes and judgmental language to make clear the homosexuality that is not written into the script. In discussing *The Green Bay Tree,* Shairp was careful to make his heterosexuality known—in press interviews, he told how he first shared the idea for his play with his wife.[19] This drama about homosexuality was to be seen by the authorities to be clean of any tinge of homosexuality.

The Green Bay Tree, which was to define the formula for the British stage homosexual, established in its Broadway production a recognizable stereotype that dominated American stage and screen for twenty years. It also incorporated homosexuality into the realistic "problem play." In the melodramatic world of *The Green Bay Tree*, the threat of homosexuality lies in the possibility of corruption through pederasty. The worst result of that corruption is, apparently, effeteness verging on effeminacy, a quality that in Noël Coward's *Design for Living* is both chic and sexually ambivalent. In Shairp's play, that sinister effeteness—and hints of pederasty—are the only overt signs of homosexuality in a play that manages to keep its principal subject closeted.

Mr. Dulcimer (no first name, though he is known as "Dulcie," a name precious enough to give him away) is a very wealthy bachelor who lives in elegantly appointed quarters in London. For fifteen years he has been guardian and adoptive father to David Owen, a poor Welsh boy Dulcimer heard sing at an Eisteddfod. Dulcimer fell in love with the purity of the lad's voice and bought the boy from his drunken father for £500. The angelic quality of David's voice, of which the audience hears a recording, signifies the innocence Dulcimer has corrupted, for, since he "bought" the lad, he has shaped him in his own image, teaching him to love his effete life in London and at his country home, Silver Gates (a name suggesting both opulence and imprisonment). Obviously Dulcimer was a good teacher, for David, renamed Julian Dulcimer, is now a handsome twenty-six-year-old ornament, a testament to his training: "My aim was to make him like, and to be unable to do without, what was best for me."[20] For some reason (and this is the most incredible aspect of the play) Julian falls in love with a young veterinarian, Leonora, who took care of his beloved dog, David (clearly his dog has his old name to show that David/Julian is little more than a house pet to Dulcimer). The action of the play centers on the conflict between the effete Mr. Dulcimer and the no-nonsense Leonora over possession of Julian. The role of The Woman here is crucial, as it always is in realistic problem plays focusing on homosexuality. Here the woman is the strong, positive adversary of the evil, homosexual influence. In order to save Julian from Dulcimer, Leonora also must save him from the effete, affluent world into which Julian has been placed and make him a productive member of the middle class.

The "problem" in this melodrama is the sexual corruption of a working-class boy by an older upper-middle-class man. Alan Sinfield notes that it was common for upper-middle-class homosexuals in this period to seek lower-class sexual partners.[21] The romance of cross-class relationships had been central to the literature of gay romance since Edward Carpenter had appropriated Walt Whitman's poetry as a model for loving men around the turn of the century. *The Green Bay Tree* vitiates the myth of the vitalizing sexual force of the working-class man; it also declines to celebrate relationships that cross class lines, relationships that had been an integral component of early gay literature (E. M. Forster's *Maurice* [1913, pub. 1971] is the classic example), and it does so by linking them to pederasty. Shairp connects the age and class differences in his central relationship of Dulcimer and Julian to the corruption of working-class youth, a reworking of the theme of danger lurking for working-class girls, a staple of nineteenth-century melodrama.

The establishment of cross-class pederasty as the model for evil homosexual relations is a crucial aspect of the formula Shairp evolved. Another is the codified presentation of unstated homosexuality. Shairp is meticulous about stage directions, presenting judgments on his characters that the actors are clearly meant to communicate to the audience. Nowhere is this judgmental language clearer than the entrance of Mr. Dulcimer at the opening of the play:

> *He is a man of about forty-five, immaculately turned out, and wearing at present a double-breasted dinner jacket. He speaks exquisitely, in a clear voice, and with now and then a slight drawl. He has a habit of looking at you from under his eyes, and though a complete dilettante, he has an alert, vibrating personality. A man who could fascinate, repel and alarm. Instantly we know that he is the one thing missing in the room, and he seems to know it, too, for he stands a moment inside the doors, almost as if he were 'taking a call' for having created it. (p. 55)*

It does not take a very subtle reading to see the mixed metaphors embedded in Dulcimer's description. His entrance clearly presents him as an actor, a performer in an environment he has made his stage set. An earlier stage description describes Dulcimer's living room as "*artificial,*" but it "*reflects his personality, his sensitiveness, and his delicate appreciation of beauty*" (p. 55). The setting contains not only Dulcimer's tasteful living room but also his hothouse garden; Shairp has mastered the Ibsenesque use of setting as commentary on character. Dulcimer has created a stage on which to perform and, as he is willing to admit, an artificial world in which he can nurture the perfect hothouse flower in Julian.

Dulcimer is the interior decorator as stage designer, but a decorator whose taste is too fine to be shared with the world. The performer and the "complete dilettante," the fop as homosexual, are the stereotypes Shairp uses throughout the play to indicate Dulcimer's homosexuality. An aesthetic sense is connected to *delicateness* and *sensitivity*, words that suggest both effeminacy and its corollary, weakness. Dulcimer is first seen arranging flowers with his butler, Trump, who has obviously been trained to "play" the butler to the hilt. Trump is a fellow performer on Dulcimer's stage, playing a version of Lane, Algernon's butler in Oscar Wilde's *The Importance of Being Earnest* (1895), and that play, with its associations with the "degeneracy" of its creator, ominously echoes throughout Dulcimer's hothouse. Peter Burton points out that Shairp "is setting up Dulcimer as the epitome of effeminacy" and that the opening scene of flower arranging "quickly telegraphs the information to the audience that 'Dulcie' is not a 'real man,' that he must therefore be decadent and, thus is not to be trusted."[22] Indeed, the "effeminate" activity of arranging flowers is the most sinister sign of Dulcimer's effect on Julian. At the end of the London production of the play, Dulcimer's death mask smiles over the set while Julian arranges flowers, a sure sign of his destruction at Dulcimer's hands.[23]

Still, Dulcimer's "performances" raise him out of melodrama and make him a vibrant character. In one extraordinary scene, he stages an elaborate masquerade by inviting Julian and Leonora to dinner and then setting the living room up as a restaurant, complete with menus and with Trump as a haughty *maitre d'*. Julian loves the game, even one-ups Dulcimer by sending Trump for a blank check for the bill, but Leonora sees it as another manifestation of Dulcimer's sinister, unnatural behavior.

Dulcimer's penchant for performance is intended to reflect the aesthete's love of artifice and hatred of the natural—an echo of Oscar Wilde. Like the voice in Eliot's *Wasteland*, Dulcimer hates spring, "that cruel, terrifying time," with its "shattering . . . reassertion of the principle of life" (p. 57). This opposition to nature—and, by implication, to heterosexuality—turns the fop into a demon. The first stage direction presents him as reptilian: *"a man who could fascinate, repel and alarm"* (p. 55). Later, Leonora says, "You fascinate me like a snake fascinates" (p. 82). Earlier, she described Dulcimer as being "rotten to the core" (p. 76). David's father describes Dulcimer as "wicked. He's evil. You don't realize how evil he is" (p. 95). What do we see Dulcimer do that is so evil? He has molded David-become-Julian in his own image and thinks of Julian as his possession, a not-uncommon trait for a father figure in Edwardian drama. The "crime" is not merely the molding but the uncloseted candor with which Dulcimer describes his influence on Julian. Here the mask is off: "I have created comfort and beauty and constant change of scene out of money and a cage for Julian's soul in which he sings to me as sweetly as in that stuffy Welsh schoolroom all those years ago" (p. 93). The "sensitive hothouse flower" (p. 81) is also a bird in a gilded cage. Only a truly diabolical figure would revel in caging souls, though Dulcimer has also provided the money that will guarantee that Julian's cage will be gilded and that he will live in the style to which he has become accustomed for the rest of his life. But there is no place in that scheme for a woman—even one called Leo— and Dulcimer ultimately wins the battle for possession of Julian on economic grounds. He fights for Julian, "because he is to me youth and charm and companionship. I admit the claims of these indefinable things. I must have them" (p. 93).

Dulcimer sees Julian as another possession for his perfect stage set, but there is more in Dulcimer's too-rational explanation of Julian's place in his life: "But I must have a focussing point for all my activities and interests and self-expression. That focussing point is Julian. If you take him away, I'm lost. I admit that. Like you, I have feelings, but with Julian in my life, I'm never troubled by them. He keeps them constant and satisfied" (p. 94).

This is an oblique way of saying that Dulcimer loves Julian and cannot live without him. The coolness of expression is an aspect of Dulcimer's soulless character but also a function of the Lord Chamberlain's censorship. The meaning of the play and the "horror" of Dulcimer's character are meaningful only if we "translate" this line to its most emotionally and physically powerful meaning. What makes Dulcimer so "evil," so dangerous, is that which is never spoken, except in one hint from Leonora: "This man has got hold of Julian body and soul" (p. 94). It is that hold on Julian's body that is so repellent, yet that hold is never seen or discussed beyond that line. Why else would he fight ruthlessly to possess handsome Julian, as we are led to believe he has possessed him since David/Julian was eleven? The luxury is merely the outward trapping of the "diabolical sexual thrall" in which Julian is being held. Contemporary critics saw clearly what was hinted at in *The Green Bay Tree*, and Dulcimer's death by means of his own "exquisitely jeweled revolver" (he is killed by Julian's real father, a drunk-turned-evangelist who is enlisted by Leonora to "save" Julian) is poetic justice.

Julian is not saved, however. Having been "perverted by Dulcimer, Julian at the end *becomes* Dulcimer, arranging flowers sent up from Silver Gates and bantering with Trump:

> TRUMP (*looking up at the mask*): Mr. Dulcimer always said, sir, that a man could never settle down until he'd got women out of his life.
> JULIAN: I expect he was right. He nearly always was. (p. 97)

Except for the butler, who stays on when he discovers that women will not invade the household, Julian is alone at the end of the play, but since he has taken on Dulcimer's identity, one senses that he will soon be taking a trip to Wales to find his own sweet-voiced eleven-year-old. This ending provides an interesting twist on the purging of the outsider essential to the structure of the realistic problem play. Dulcimer, the corrupter, is killed in his own home. Leonora is removed from the scene: she is the outsider in Dulcimer and Julian's world because of her "normal" middle-class values and heterosexual desires. Julian, at the final curtain, is safely ensconced in his hermetic world, removed from "normal" society, sealed in the gilded cage where he belongs. A gay audience could see the denouement not as a sinister picture of corruption but as the survival of the homosexual. Only a portion of the audience will read flower-arranging as a sign of degeneracy.

Yet, while *The Green Bay Tree* presents Dulcimer's elegant surroundings as a gilded cage, the only alternative environment the audience sees is the squalid, Spartan flat of Julian's born-again father and the only alternative

career, veterinary medicine, a ludicrous choice for someone of Julian's up-
bringing and temperament. As in much popular melodrama, an outlandish set
of circumstances and alternatives is presented with utmost earnestness; laughter is precluded.

The issue presented with such earnestness is Julian's corruption at the
hands of a diabolical homosexual, yet all one can do with homosexuality in
The Green Bay Tree is "sense" or "presume," since nothing is overt beyond
what the director and actors perform. Reports of the original London production suggest that there was much overt effeminacy in the playing of Dulcimer
and Julian, but this could be passed off as high camp, which had been an
aspect of British drawing-room comedy for centuries and was not always
overtly tied to homosexuality. However, when in 1933 Jed Harris produced
the play for a Broadway audience, which has always equated camp with effeminacy, he cut out even the hints of homosexuality yet still wanted the
audience to "know" that his characters were homosexual. He told his cast at
rehearsal:

> As you know, in London the entire production was dominated by homosex-
> uality. There was even swishing onstage. I'll have none of that. We've [Har-
> ris and his house playwright, Edward Chodorov] been removing all of those
> references. When the audience watches it here, I want them to say to them-
> selves, 'It's homosexual. Nothing is said about it but it's there. It must be
> there. That's the only explanation for these characters and their story.' So
> that's what I want. I want to create something without stating it.[24]

The few overt references to Julian's "fate," like Leonora's line: "I hope I
shant meet you one day in Piccadilly with a painted face, just because you
must have linen sheets" (p. 92), were cut from the Broadway production. The
audience was left to infer from long glances and meaningful silences:
"They'll know. It's better if they figure it out than if we tell them."[25] Harris
even cut the final tableau of Julian arranging flowers as being too "swish":
"I'll bet half the audience left the theater convinced that they actually saw
Larry [Oliver] arranging the flowers."[26] The onus of reading homosexuality
was on the audience, not the producer, whose show could be padlocked. Yet
the assumed audience ability to read homosexuality into the gestures and in-
nuendoes, to decode the cryptic production, shows that Harris knew his audience had some awareness of homosexuality and some understanding of its
stereotypes.

The Green Bay Tree managed a moderately healthy run without provoking the legal problems of earlier plays about homosexual relationships,
though it hinted at a relationship that was not only homosexual but pederastic
as well. While a number of contemporary reviewers denied that there was
anything sexual in the relationship of Dulcimer and his ward, critic Robert
Garland saw what Jed Harris wanted him to see:

> Reading the reviews printed while I was out of town, I gather that *The Green Bay Tree* has nothing to do with the way of a man with a man. Well, if it has nothing to do with that, it has nothing to do with anything.
>
> If it has nothing to do with that (and "that" is an incident not unknown to the public in general and to patrons of revues in particular), Mr. Shairp's play is the most meaningless play ever written by anybody.[27]

Indeed, if the play is not about "that," it is about destruction by meticulous good taste. But meticulous good taste is code for effeminacy, which equals "homosexual." If Julian has taken Dulcimer's place at the end, then the audience is to infer that Julian has become Dulcimer in all ways. But inference is all the play allows. The meaning of *The Green Bay Tree* is contained in its stereotypical imagery, which audience members could choose to read as they wished. Homosexuality is in the eyes of the beholder and can be "presented" indirectly and nonverbally.

For American audiences, *The Green Bay Tree* established the stereotypical picture of the homosexual as wealthy, effete—and British. He would be played in Hollywood by Charles Laughton or George Sanders. Slightly Americanized in Alfred Hitchcock's films, he would be one of the effete psychopathic killers of *Rope* (1948) and *Strangers on a Train* (1951).

LIFESTYLES OF THE RICH AND FAMOUS

Noël Coward's *Design for Living*, also produced on Broadway in 1933, is another exercise in the masterful manipulation of "reader response." One sees—and hears—what one wants to see and hear. Overtly, the play centers on Gilda, who during the course of the play has relationships with three men: a painter, Otto; a successful playwright, Leo; and an older, staid art dealer, Ernest. Gilda plays musical beds, moving from Otto to Leo to Otto again, then marrying Ernest, and finally giving up her marriage to Ernest to run off with both Otto and Leo. One can see the play as merely a sophisticated sex comedy about free love in the Bohemian set, in which Gilda is the most unconventional character.

However, the "naughtiness" of Gilda's promiscuity is eclipsed by the hints that Otto and Leo were also romantically involved before Gilda came into their lives:

> ERNEST: Otto and Leo knew each other first.
> GILDA: Yes, yes, yes, yes—I know all about that! I came along and spoilt everything.[28]

Now this exchange could be read, as the play has often been read, even by contemporary critics, as an expression of Gilda's awareness that she is the disruptive force in an intense homosocial relationship. The issue, according to this reading, is how to resolve Otto and Leo's friendship with the facts that they both love Gilda and that she loves both of them. However, two more pieces of evidence discourage that reading. The first is Leo's explanation, in the first scene, of the tangled web of affection the play depicts: "The actual facts are so simple. I love you. You love me. You love Otto. I love Otto. Otto loves you. Otto loves me. There now! Start to unravel from there" (p. 21). The other is the famous photograph of Otto, Leo, and Gilda (Noël Coward, Alfred Lunt, and Lynn Fontanne) linked together on the sofa at the end of the play, in a menage that illustrates exactly what Ernest has called a "disgusting three-sided erotic hotch-potch!" (p. 138). The three bodies are all intertwined, and Leo, not Gilda, is in the middle, draped half across Otto's body, half across Gilda's. The truth of the relationships of the central characters is in this design of bodies (see p. 84).

Design for Living was a sophisticated comedy by England and America's most popular playwright, and it starred him and the glittering couple Alfred Lunt and Lynn Fontanne. Did the genre of sophisticated comedy with such stars defuse the danger of the relationship the play depicted? The play itself is a defense of the lifestyles of the rich and famous, asserting, as much celebrity gossip had done for years, that stars live by another code. As Otto tells Gilda:

> We are different. Our lives are diametrically opposed to ordinary social conventions; and it's no use grabbing at those conventions to hold us up when we find we're in deep water. We've jilted them and eliminated them, and we've got to find our own solutions for our own peculiar moral problems. (p. 72)

The weakness of the play is its incessant, didactic harping on the validity, if not superiority, of the trio's own moral code. Ultimately, the butt of the play's jokes is any representative of a morality that denigrates the trio's mutual devotion.

Coward has kept Otto and Leo's sexual relationship hidden in the exposition, and they use terms of endearment that could be read as terms of friendship. The only hint we get of the physical aspect of their relationship is the recounting of a violent argument, in which Leo pushed Otto into a bathtub and doused him with cold water. Their one scene together seems to be a drunken lament over the loss of Gilda, but buried in that scene is another clue:

> LEO (*haltingly*) The—feeling I had for you—something very deep, I imagined it was, but it couldn't have been, could it—now that it has died so easily.
> OTTO: I said all that to you in Paris. Do you remember? I thought it was true then, just as you think it's true now. (p. 89)

Yet within a few lines, Coward covers his tracks by having Leo qualify their relationship: "Do you honestly believe I could ever look at you again, as a real friend?" (p. 89). A gay auditor would understand that "friend" has always been a slippery euphemism in gay parlance and continue to read the scene as a presentation of a homosexual relationship; straight audience members could hear that line as a disclaimer of hints of homosexuality. Here decoding is necessary to read Otto and Leo as either friends or lovers. Coward lays enough hints to allow either reading, though the play makes less sense if Otto and Leo are "just" friends.

The most definitive sign of homosexual behavior in *Design for Living* is Otto and Leo's camp behavior, an echo of the sort of performance that was presented as sinister in *The Green Bay Tree*. In act 3, after Gilda has married Ernest and found a place for herself in New York society (represented by a trio of dreary, witless people), Otto and Leo arrive, dressed to the nines, and proceed to perform a bitchy camp spectacle that, as they planned, drives the guests from Gilda's living room:

> LEO: I always thought Madame Butterfly was over-hasty.
> OTTO: She should have gone out into the world and achieved an austere independence. Just like you, Gilda.
> GILDA: Don't talk nonsense. They both talk the most absurd nonsense; they always have, ever since I've known them. You mustn't pay any attention to them.
> OTTO: Don't undermine our social poise, Gilda, you—who have so much.
> GILDA (*sharply*): Your social poise is nonexistent.
> LEO: We have a veneer, though; it's taken us years to acquire; don't scratch it with your sharp witty nails—*darling!*
> *Everybody jumps at the word "darling."*

Gilda's guests, the New York elite, are discomfited by the way Otto and Leo banter, refer to themselves constantly as a couple, assert that they both lived with Gilda, and, most shocking, use that sophisticated endearment *darling*. In this scene, Otto and Leo are the gay couple horrifying a straight party, but their goal of winning Gilda defuses the danger of forbidden overt homosexuality. The invited guests aren't developed enough to be the targets of satire. They are stand-ins for the audience, composed of similar, wealthy New Yorkers. Their discomfort is the same most members of the audience would feel at such a display of camp behavior. The audience is put in the position of laughing at its own responses.

In his discussion of the play, which is infused with his usual ambivalence toward the homosexuality he exploits and sensationalizes, John Lahr writes: "Coward's comic revenge at the finale [in which Gilda's outraged husband, Ernest, falls on his face as he storms out] is the victory of the disguised gay world over the straight one."[29] However, Coward's focus in

Design for Living is not on homosexuality: Gilda is not a man in disguise. It is precisely on the freedom not to be defined by codes of sexual behavior— not to have to be heterosexual or homosexual. In that the play is most revolutionary. It is the triangle—and the focus on Gilda's anguish and confusion— that hides Otto and Leo's relationship for some, defuses its danger for others. Coward, like Harold Pinter and Joe Orton, removed the danger of homosexual relationships by making his characters bisexual. In doing so, he dramatized the instability of sexual desire. Homosexual desire is there for those who care to see it, neither asserted nor problematized. However, neither is it eroticized nor connected to the possibility of an exclusive homosexual relationship. Like Orton, Coward does not in his plays deny homosexual desire or love, but he does deny exclusive homosexuality as a social identity.

Coward wrote of the audience reaction to *Design for Living:* "People were certainly interested and entertained and occasionally even moved by it, but it seemed, to many of them, 'unpleasant.' "[30] Even glittering star turns and Coward's mots could not hide the hint of homosexuality and the fact that any disapproval of his triangle was either mocked or chastised.

Design for Living had a moderate success in New York, and the Lord Chamberlain eventually allowed it to be produced in London in 1939. A sanitized film version was released in 1933.[31] Still, it was not one of Coward's most successful plays, despite the starry cast, and was not revived until the sexually liberated seventies. In the 1930s, hints of homosexuality among the smart set might be titillating on the larger canvas of a Hemingway or Fitzgerald novel, in which such behavior is a relatively minor detail, but center stage it was too close for comfort for all but the Ottos and Leos in the audience. Coward was never so daring again.

For both Noël Coward and Mordaunt Shairp, homosexuality, whether the stuff of high comedy or moralizing melodrama, was linked to a world of wealth, elegance, and sophistication. The homosexuals were the descendants of the fops of Restoration comedy and, more to the point, of the bachelors in Wilde's *The Importance of Being Earnest*, fashionable in their limited worlds, lacking in erotic charge but containing coded hints of sexual transgression. Coward and Shairp also mastered the art of suggesting without speaking the unspeakable, which for the characters in *The Green Bay Tree* included pederasty and transgression of class. The comic mode of *Design for Living* allowed Coward more latitude than the simplistic melodrama of *The Green Bay Tree*. Coward also was writing his play for both a heterosexual and a homosexual audience, while *The Green Bay Tree*, though it attracted homosexuals delighted to see any version of themselves on the stage, offered them nothing but a negative stereotype.

TRANSITION: THE HOMOSEXUAL AND THE WOMAN

The new generation of British playwrights who appeared in the 1950s were more overt in their presentation of homosexual characters, but this meant, unfortunately, only more fully developed, more articulate versions of the stereotype defined in *The Green Bay Tree*. The homosexual male, seen or unseen, was the effete, feminized male. In dramas of the 1950s, he became identified with female characters and "feminine characteristics."

Among the unseen characters against whom Jimmy Porter rails in John Osborne's watershed play, *Look Back in Anger* (1956), is the homosexual, Webster, who is identified as a friend of Jimmy's wife, Alison. Webster completes a trio of aristocratic men associated with Alison: her father, lost in memories of his powerful position in India during the waning days of Empire; her brother, Nigel, stupid but confident of the power that is his birthright; and her friend Webster, the homosexual. Aristocratic men do not have the "burning virility" associated with Jimmy's rage. The damaging qualities of the aristocracy—moral rectitude, ruthless policing of class boundaries, and, paradoxically, cowardice—are identified with on- and off-stage women. Webster, the homosexual, may be afflicted with a "disease" endemic to his class—a dramatic cliché, as we have seen—but his homosexuality also makes him an outsider and something of a rebel against the morality of his class.

Webster is the only member of Alison's class Jimmy credits with "guts" and "sensitivity."[32] Yet Jimmy has mixed feelings about the group he calls the "Greek chorus boys" (p. 35) and the "Michelangelo brigade" (p. 36)—terms veiled enough to placate the Lord Chamberlain. While he admires their "revolutionary fire" (p. 35), he doesn't like the way they keep reminding people of their difference:

> He (Webster) doesn't like me—they hardly ever do. I dare say he suspects me because I refuse to treat him either as a clown or a tragic hero. He's like a man with a strawberry mark—he keeps thrusting it in your face because he can't believe it doesn't interest or horrify you particularly. As if I give a damn which way he likes his meat served up. I've got my own strawberry mark—only it's in a different place. (p. 36)

The man of "burning virility" is not threatened by homosexuals. He accepts them so long as they don't mention their sexuality, a typical "liberal" point of view. Jimmy is a man of categories as he lives in his attic room with his "mate," Cliff, in the other chair, and his wife or mistress at the ironing board. His heterosexuality makes him terrified of and hostile to the women to whom he is attracted, but Jimmy's sexual pathology is not, as it would traditionally be in the United States, linked with heterosexism.

Osborne's presentation of Webster marks a transitional stage in the dramatization of homosexuality and homosexuals in the English theater. Webster has the old connection with aristocracy but is presented positively. He is the pal of the woman, not the man. Moreover, like Tennessee Williams' homosexuals, he exists only in the closet of exposition. In England, the theatrical closet was still policed.

In Peter Shaffer's *Five Finger Exercise* (1958), we move from the presentation of homosexuality as a moral problem, exemplified in the diabolical and judgmental language of *The Green Bay Tree*, to homosexuality as a psychological problem, the result of a dysfunctional family and the cause of destructive, neurotic behavior.

Five Finger Exercise[33] is the first of a number of Shaffer's plays in which homosexual desire, though unstated, plays a crucial role. Shaffer, who is habitually drawn to simplified Freudian interpretations of human behavior, presents a family that is a textbook Freudian model for the development of a homosexual: a gruff, self-made father in conflict with an overaffectionate mother filled with cultural pretensions that she projects onto her children, particularly her eighteen-year-old son, Clive. When both Clive and his mother become attracted to a young German man who has been hired to tutor the fourteen-year-old daughter, a clash develops that finally destroys the tutor and leads the son to realize fully his membership in a destructive family. Shaffer makes clear that Walter, the tutor, is heterosexual; homosexual desire is never requited in Shaffer's work, thus never more than a source of anguish. Moreover, Clive's crush on Walter leads him to destroy Walter's position in the household and threaten his parent's already fragile marriage. Homosexual desire puts Clive in the position usually given to young girls in problem plays like Lillian Hellman's *The Children's Hour* (1934) and Arthur Miller's *The Crucible* (1953), that of being the purveyor of destructive information. Walter, the heterosexual, is trying to act honorably on a deeply felt desire to be part of a family. Clive, the self-hating neurotic (read homosexual) can only destroy. He and his sexuality are the products of the dysfunctional family, which is presented as basically the fault of the mother, who cuts Walter off when she realizes that he sees her not as a potential sexual partner but as "a second mother." In a quasi-Freudian causality, the woman is to blame for making her son less than a man. Father, however boorish, does know best.

Clive's homosexual desire is expressed in alternating bursts of hostility and cloying dependency. Given that there is no possibility of his desire being requited and, seemingly, no other possible object for it, Clive is the stereotypical miserable, frustrated, malicious homosexual, spiteful of Walter's "normality." His hyperemotionalism is related to his mother's affectations and theatrical behavior. Not surprisingly, the emotional climax of the play is the confrontation of mother and son, who are infatuated with the same young man.

If Clive in *Five Finger Exercise* is the miserable, neurotic, destructive, effeminate, latent homosexual, Geoff in Shelagh Delaney's *A Taste of Honey* (presented in 1958) is the kindly nellie who is the heroine's best friend, another common stereotype. After Jo, the heroine, has been left by her promiscuous mother and made pregnant by a sailor, Geoff moves in to be Jo's companion. He is derided by Jo's mother and her mother's boyfriend. He is a "pansy," a "lily," and a "fruitcake." Yet Jo takes Geoff in. He is, after all, safe: "I always want to have you with me because I know you'll never ask anything from me."[34] Geoff is supposedly homosexual, but he doesn't have any relationships with men, reinforcing the shibboleth that the only acceptable homosexual is celibate. Only his friendship with a woman keeps him alive: "Before I met you I didn't care one way or the other—I didn't care whether I lived or died" (p. 80). Homosexuals may not be sexually attracted to women, but they cannot live without them. Though Geoff has Jo's best interests at heart, he is thrown out when Jo's wayward mother returns. Jo does not get the opportunity to fight for Geoff's presence. Like the traditional outsider, the "problem" in realistic drama, Geoff is expelled from the stage before the final curtain. The close friendship of a woman and a gay man is rejected as a possibility. Yet, at the final curtain, Jo is singing a song Geoff taught her, the artistic legacy of the homosexual.

Neither of these 1958 plays conceives of the possibility of an affirming homosexual friendship, much less a homosexual relationship. One way or the other, the homosexual is isolated by either his "sensitivity" or his effeminacy.

PINTER: PEDERASTY REVISITED

Harold Pinter's *The Collection* (1961) presents interesting variations on established gay stereotypes. A great deal of the obliqueness of *The Collection* stems from the games it plays with television and stage censorship (the drama first appeared on TV) while it extends the stereotypical representation of homosexuals seen in *The Green Bay Tree*. Pinter's play actually gains its force, as Pinter's work often does, from the indirection the subject matter required. *The Collection* is also of particular importance because here, more than in any other Pinter work, homosexuality is tied to the male homosociality and misogyny that are central to Pinter's heterosexuals.

The Collection is set in the fashionable London neighborhoods of Chelsea and Belgravia, where well-behaved, affluent homosexuals were acceptable, even trendy neighbors, and in the women's fashion industry, in which homosexuals occupied key positions. The drama opens in an elegant Belgravia house occupied by Harry, a middle-aged man who owns a fashionable women's clothing business, and Bill, a dress designer. Bill is both much younger than Harry (Bill is in his twenties) and from quite another social world. "I found him in a slum, you know, by accident. Just happened to be in a slum one day and there he was. I realized he had talent straight away. I gave him a roof, gave him a job, and he came up trumps."[35] Harry's remark contains an innuendo Joe Orton would have admired: the, "talent" Harry noticed on first sight probably had little to do with dress design. Harry's history of his slum meeting with Bill (which seems to have taken place some years before, when Bill was a teenager) echoes the pederasty and transgression of class boundaries that formed the dynamic of the relationship between Dulcimer and Julian in *The Green Bay Tree*.

Bill, the slum boy turned dress designer, is the only character in the play definitely out of Pinter's usual social milieu—the working class and the socially displaced—though in being "reformed" he has lost any obvious signs of class. Bill's language, in particular, has lost its identifying characteristics. It is studied and, as a result, lacking in affect: "Every woman is bound to have an outburst of . . . wild sensuality at one time or another. That's the way I look at it, anyway. It's part of their nature. Even though it may be the kind of sensuality of which you yourself have never been the fortunate recipient. What?" (p. 151). Simon Trussler sees the artificiality of Bill's dialogue as a deficiency on Pinter's part: "Mostly, the characters talk not like members of the upper-middle class pretending to be classless, but like upper-middle-class characters imitating people in plays."[36] But Bill is a lower-class character trying to sound posh. Taking the boy out of the slums has made him grammatical and languid, but Bill's new style of language only masks his hostility. The problem for the audience is not that Bill's language isn't convincing—it isn't supposed to be; he's a creature of Harry—but that one cannot imagine Bill going to work. Harry notes that Bill is "supposed to be able to use [his] hands" (p. 124), a stereotypical reference to his origins, but all we ever see is an ornament, one capable, on occasion, of being a flirt.

While the dynamics of Harry and Bill's relationship are left to innuendo, any intimacy they may have shared is clearly on the wane. What is left is the empty familiarity of an old married couple sharpened and threatened by Harry's jealousy and possessiveness. Harry goes off to parties every evening, leaving Bill home alone, because—according to Harry—Bill's "got a slum mind" (p. 155) and isn't fit to socialize with Harry's friends. Since Bill's manners would delight Lady Bracknell, Harry is more likely worried about Bill's slum sexual appetite. There remains a definite authoritarian structure, reinforced by class and age differences. Bill makes breakfast and is expected to fix the broken stair rail. He is also expected to honor Harry's possession of the house and himself. Yet *The Collection* would be more interesting if there were some sign, or at least memory, of an erotic charge in their relationship. It may be that the constraints of censorship supported Pinter in staging a safe, nonerotic homosexual relationship, which was all he could conceive of. The audience is left, as they are in *The Green Bay Tree*, with hints of a sexual relationship: the profession, the neighborhood, the affluence, the circumstances of their meeting, the age and class differences, the domesticity, the jealousy. One reads homosexuality by a process of elimination: why else would these men be living together?

The relationship is more strained by the Pinterian intrusion of James, who seems intent on upsetting Harry and Bill's domestic life as well as his own. James' initial four a.m. phone call, answered by Harry, gives the only clear hint in the play of a sexual relationship between Harry and Bill:

> JAMES: Is that you, Bill?
> HARRY: No, he's in bed. Who's this?
> JAMES: In bed?
> . . . . . .
> HARRY: Do you know it's four o'clock in the morning?
> JAMES: Well, give him a nudge. Tell him I want a word with him. (p. 121)

The call also, like James' subsequent arrival on Harry's doorstep, insinuates a relationship between James and Bill that arouses Harry's possessiveness and jealousy and is the motive force for Harry's antagonism toward Bill, which is expressed in alternate fits of irritability and camp playfulness. It is Harry who raises the possibility that Bill may have been unfaithful on a recent trip:

> HARRY: Did you meet anyone last week?
> . . . .
> BILL: I didn't speak to a soul.
> HARRY: Must have been miserable for you.
> BILL: I was only there one night, wasn't I? (p. 125)

But James plays on Harry's jealousy, as he plays sexually charged games with Bill. In the second television production (1976), directed by Michael Apted, Bill (played by Malcolm MacDowell) picked up what he thought were James' (Alan Bates) sexual clues and flirted very obviously with him, assuming the visits from James would end in bed, or at least with both of them on the living-room floor. James sadistically toys with Bill's assumption, as he toys with Harry's jealousy and his wife's guilt.

Harry's response to James' encroachment on his territory is to get more authoritarian—"Don't touch that paper" (p. 138)—and to go camp, playing theatrical variations on James' appearance at Harry's doorstep. His fantastic descriptions of James are so bizarre as to be frightening, but there is anger under the play:

> HARRY: He didn't dance here last night, did he, or do any gymnastics?
> BILL: No one danced here last night.
> HARRY: Aah. Well, that's why you didn't notice his wooden leg. I couldn't
> help seeing it myself when he came to the front door because he stood on
> the top step stark naked. Didn't seem very cold, though. He had a waterbottle
> under his arm instead of a hat.

BILL: Those church bells have certainly left their mark on you.
HARRY: They haven't helped, but the fact of the matter is, old chap, that
I don't like strangers coming into my house without an invitation. Who is
this man and what does he want? (p. 140)

Bill's response, characteristically, is passive-aggressive evasion, and any information he imparts to Harry (and he must impart some) takes place when
Harry follows Bill upstairs.

James is obsessed with every detail of the recent Leeds hotel-room
fling that Bill and Stella are supposed to have had, an event that may have
happened or that Stella may have made up as an act of passive aggression
against an overly suspicious-husband. We never discover exactly what happened at the Leeds hotel nor, more important, why Stella confessed to it or
fabricated it. What is clear is that the relationship of James and Stella is a
heterosexual mirror of the one between Harry and Bill: an aggressive, possessive man and a partner whose silence and evasions are tools of manipulation and possibly revenge. However, the only character credited with "wild
sensuality," uncontrollable sexual force, is Stella, the woman, who remains
the most enigmatic character.

When James comes to play the wronged husband with Bill, the scene
turns into a combination of flirtation and violence. Pinter practices his own
form of passive aggression by ending scenes like this one before we can see
a character's response. The first scene between Bill and James ends with Bill
still lying on the floor, James still standing over him, and Bill supporting
James' suspicions:

JAMES: You were sitting on the bed next to her.
Silence.
BILL: Not sitting. Lying. (p. 137)

A blackout ends the scene with the focus on Bill's response, which is both
hostile and provocative. Does James want vengeance for Stella's infidelity, or
does he want to enjoy Bill himself? However, the central unanswered question
is: What happens next? How do James and Bill get out of this potentially
sexual pose?

James' acquaintance with Bill gives him a weapon to use against Stella:

He reminds me of a bloke I went to school with. Hawkins. . . . Hawkins was
an opera fan, too. So's whats-his-name. I'm a bit of an opera fan myself.
Always kept it a dead secret. I might go along with your bloke to the opera
one night. He says he can always get free seats. He knows quite a few of
that crowd . . . I mean, you couldn't say he wasn't a man of taste. He's
brimming over with it. . . . After two years of marriage it looks as though,
by accident, you've opened up a whole new world for me. (p. 144)

James, obsessed by his wife's relationship with Bill, avenges his wife by claiming a relationship with Bill, thus appropriating his wife's lover for himself. The allusions to an old school chum, to Bill being an opera queen (a claim for which there is no evidence), to James' having kept his love of opera (a euphemism for homosexuality) a "dead secret," and to Bill's excess of taste—"He's brimming over with it" (p. 144)—are hints of homosexuality, the sort of pre-Wolfenden code by which gay men operated, as well as an elaboration of the stereotype of the affluent, elegant gay man already operative in the delineation of Harry.

In the next scene James is having another tete-à-tete with Bill, which Harry later claims to have orchestrated so that he can talk with Stella. Yet the opening of this scene is more flirtatious than the previous encounter. The undertones of sex lead to Pinterian menace, as Bill picks up the cheese knife and describes it in phallic terms: "Hold the blade. It won't cut you. Not if you handle it properly. Not if you grasp it firmly up to the hilt" (p. 150). While Bill uses the knife as the catalyst for a sexual invitation, James sees the cheese and fruit knives as weapons in a bizarre version of the duel that, in a bygone day, would have reestablished his honor. Still, references to the knives remain phallic:

> BILL: What do you do, swallow them?
> JAMES: Do you?
> *Pause. They stare at each other.* (Suddenly) Go on! Swallow it!
> JAMES *throws knife at* BILL's *face.* BILL *throws up his hand to protect his face and catches knife, by blade. It cuts his hand.* (p. 152)

James' later comment that the knife might have cut Bill's mouth underscores Bill's most potent weapons, words, as he manipulates the narrative of the hotel encounter in Leeds, first denying, then assenting because, "It amused me to do so" (p. 154), and finally claiming that the real truth was that he and Stella spent two hours in the bar talking about what they would do if they went to bed together. "Two hours . . . we never touched . . . we just talked about it" (p. 157).

Bill's story of an encounter far more erotic than a mere hotel-room copulation is his final revenge for James' manipulation and violence and for Harry's vicious vituperation, in which he describes Bill as a slum slug: "He confirms stupid little stories just to amuse himself, while everyone else has to run around in circles to get to the root of the matter and smooth the whole thing out. All he can do is sit and suck his bloody hand and decompose like the filthy, putrid slum slug he is" (p. 155). Bill's final narrative—that he and Stella only talked about what they would do—silences Harry, who has been furiously searching for a denial of the Leeds encounter, and it gives James a story he wants to believe, though Stella holds onto what little power she is allowed by refusing to confirm or deny Bill's story to James.

Bill's encounter with Stella transgresses sexual categories. It is a betrayal of his relationship with Harry and the homosexuality on which that relationship is based. Bill's alleged bisexuality makes him dangerous to all the characters, because it makes him an unstable force. His final story of only talking about sex with Stella may fulfill his own fantasy of having sex with a woman without being in the position of phallic penetrator, a passive-aggressive fantasy that, ironically, empowers him. At the end Bill sits silently sucking the blood from the wound on his hand, an image that is vampiric and narcissistic.

While Bill's passivity becomes connected with his sexual ambiguity, he is in the masculine position of controlling language, of controlling the narrative. Stella, the woman, can only react or deny—yet more passive tactics. Her narrative of her encounter with Bill in Leeds initiates the action but is never heard by the audience and is denied or reshaped by the male characters. Before Bill's final version of the Leeds narrative, James is willing to make peace with Harry and Bill by placing all the blame on Stella: "The fault is really all hers, and mine, for believing her" (p. 156). Bill could have assented to Harry's story, that Stella "made the whole damn thing up," but his final story was his weapon against Harry's possessiveness and cruelty. Harry may be able to keep Bill out of women's beds, but he can't stop him from thinking or talking about such sexual encounters. The homosexual male is still allowed space in the dominant discourse, but the discourse is of heterosexual activity.

Bill, like Harry, knows how to spin a narrative, but while Harry's narratives are fantastic displacements of anger, Bill's are weapons. His power is in his sexual attractiveness to men and to women—"[she] must have found me terribly attractive quite suddenly" (p. 136). Yet Pinter has not presented Bill as an erotic object the way a gay playwright would. The play lacks the erotic charge that would make it powerful and credible.

The Collection is a transitional work that plays with old homosexual stereotypes but also introduces themes and situations that gay playwrights were to eroticize and enliven. Homosexuality is still closeted, still a matter of hints, and must be portrayed through the acting rather than the written script, but it isn't sensationalized. Harry's cautious presentation to Stella of his relationship with Bill is both a dead giveaway and an accurate representation of closeted discourse: "We've been close friends for years" (p. 147). Yet in reality we see not the relaxed familiarity of friendship but the hostility of a sexual relationship on the wane. The interesting, positive move in *The Collection* is to the paralleling and equation of hetero- and homosexual marriages.

The "slum slug," as Harry describes Bill, will become central to Joe Orton's work, but he will be far less passive than Bill Lloyd. Bill has, under Harry's tutelage, become a house pet, as Julian has for Dulcimer. He is like the cat Stella holds and Harry so admires. Orton's slum boys are not so easily domesticated.

JOE ORTON, FARCE, AND THE CLOSET

Joe Orton, clearly influenced in his earlier work by Pinter, infused drama with the homoerotic charge missing from works like *The Collection*. He also kept the sense of ludicrousness found in moments like Harry's description of his meeting with James but moved it out of melodrama and incorporated it into the conventions of farce, which, like the realistic problem play, has a complex relationship with homosexuality.

John Mortimer maintains, "Social conventions are essential to farce,"[37] because farce is about transgression, which requires limits. This is why doors are essential to the setting of farce. In the world of farce, closets, or at least closed doors, abound, and doors never stay fully closed—closets cannot be maintained. The open doors free the libido: sexual ambiguity and confusion of sexual identity seep through the perilously maintained gender order as the behavior of farce characters violates the social order.

In raising questions about the gender order assumed and policed by the closet, farce also raises questions about the stability of hetero and homosexuality, terms that imply their opposites but that also imply a stability of desire counter to the language and vision of farce. In Shakespeare, bisexuality, hinted at, seems to be happily, if cautiously, absorbed by society, but the characters who feel exclusively homosexual desire (the Antonios of *Twelfth Night* and, perhaps, *The Merchant of Venice*) suffer the typical stage homosexual's fate of isolation when the traditional finale of coupling is enacted. Yet Shakespeare's comedies can hover at the brink of polymorphous perversity. In John Caird's brilliant 1989 production for the Royal Shakespeare Company of *A Midsummer Night's Dream*, Demetrius awakes after the love potion has been placed in his eyes and is about to turn his lovesick gaze onto Lysander when Puck turns his head, in the nick of time, toward Helena. In a cartoonlike, high-speed chain of events, Demetrius starts to turn his head back in Lysander's direction, and Puck has to intervene again. Homosexual desire is barely averted. The moment got one of the production's biggest laughs, but it also reminded one of the possibility of homosexual desire lurking very near the surface in many of Shakespeare's comedies. In farce, sexual desire is unstable, settling only with difficulty into the social order some call "natural." Conventional categories are arbitrary expressions of a rage for order.

C. W. E. Bigsby writes: "Farce has always been concerned with the elimination of character, with the creation of an almost hysterical intensity in which character is flung off by the sheer centrifugal force of language and action."[38] In farce, either an individuating characteristic enlarges to engulf the entire character or individuating characteristics disappear altogether. In either case character becomes type. Since typification is the historical condition of the stage homosexual—a reduction to his homosexuality or to mannerisms an audience associates with homosexuality—the gay character can easily become a farce "type." The converse is that, in removing stereotypical mannerisms, the playwright removes any recognizable (to straight audiences), individuating, "comic" characteristics.

To understand the British farce version of the gay type, we need look no further than the English television comedy, "Are You Being Served?," which is a hit on American public-television stations. (It is so successful in the land of Jesse Helms that the North Carolina public-television network ran three episodes back to back in prime time during its 1991 pledge marathon.) This program, which was produced from 1972 to 1984, takes place in an old-fashioned department store in which the sales and managerial staff are a catalog of farce types. One of the salesmen, Mr. Humphries (played to the hilt by John Inman), is a compendium of the mannerisms of the stereotypical farce queen: limp wrist, flounce, high voice (except when he lowers his voice two octaves to answer the phone with the greeting "Men's wear"), flamboyant clothes, constructed face, homosexual innuendo, a tendency to cry, constant phone calls from his mother with whom he lives, of course, and a passion for measuring men's inseams. Since "Are You Being Served?" takes place entirely in the workplace, Mr. Humphries' sexual life is only, though constantly, suggested (talk of being secreted onto a navy warship for the weekend, for instance). When the opportunity for erotic encounter actually appears, in the person of an admiring customer, Mr. Humphries rolls his eyes heavenward and flutters his hands in a combination of panic and disdain. He isn't even "man enough" to respond to homosexual advances. Like the other characters on the program, he is not eroticized at all, therefore no sexual threat. Mr. Humphries is one of many bizarre types in "Are You Being Served?," yet the program caricatures women and the gay man more than it does its collection of dirty old men. Women are bimbos or grotesques, drawn in as broad strokes as is Mr. Humphries.

Farce is more blatant in its presentation of stereotypes than melodrama. Even American television comedy's rare presentation of homosexuals repeats the same stereotypes. Donald in the cable television series "Brothers" or the gay couple who serve as the parents for Tracey Ullman's teen-age character, Francine, on "The Tracey Ullman Show," are prime evidence. The alternative is the "straight" gay who is neither funny nor interesting but there simply to prove that gay men can be as stolid and dull as heterosexuals, like Michael, the gay baseball player on "Brothers."

Peter Shaffer's farce, *Black Comedy* (1965),[39] his next London and New York production after *Five Finger Exercise*, was an extremely popular presentation of the farce gay type. The play focuses on the catastrophic problem a young artist, Brindsley Miller, experiences while preparing to entertain a famous art patron. To impress the millionaire, the young man "borrows" a roomful of antique furniture and ornaments from his neighbor, a prissy, gay antique dealer, Harold. Harold's arrival, in the midst of the power blackout that gives the play its name, and his discovery of the whereabouts of his possessions, is one of the central threads of the farce. Harold, of course, has an unrequited crush on Brindsley and is not very subtly jealous of the young man's girlfriends, though essentially he is a male old maid. Homosexuality in farce involves effeminacy, misogyny, but also chastity, the opposite of male libidinousness. Harold is an upscale Mr. Humphries, another version of the farce queen, this time created by Britain's most successful writer of closet dramas.

Joe Orton, who had his eye on commercial success, aspired to the box-office grosses of *Black Comedy* but also wanted to avoid its stereotypes:

> I hope that now that homosexuality is allowed[40] people aren't going to con-
> tinue doing the conventional portraits there have been in the past. I think
> that the portrait of the queer in Peter Shaffer's *Black Comedy* is very funny,
> but it's an awfully conventional portrait. It's compartmentalization again.
> Audiences love it, of course, because they're safe. But one shouldn't pander
> to audiences.[41]

The safety offered by the farce queen is that of instant, reassuring recognizability. This is what gay people are like. They exist only in beauty parlors, antique stores, and, on occasion, in the men's clothing section of department stores. But, since they have such identifiable characteristics, one is in no danger. Moreover, they aren't in the least erotically provocative. Avoiding the farce queen would be one more tactic in moving the farce—and British drama—toward more danger and greater realism. Orton wrote that he wanted his American production of *Loot* (1965) to be "an amalgam of *Black Comedy* and [Pinter's] *The Homecoming*."[42] Orton wanted farce, but without stereotype or camp. He also wanted the commercial success of Shaffer's comedy combined with the critical praise lavished on Pinter.

The setting and language of Joe Orton's farces (with the exception of *What the Butler Saw* [1969]) is that of the British underclass, of people either on the dole or supported by criminal activity. The language aspires to a respectability that the characters are incapable of attaining. The acting style is to be realistic, not the mannered presentation of farce. Orton told one director of *Loot*, "We must make this absolutely truthful as it would happen in life."[43] Yet the "absolute truth" of Orton's plays is their sexual underpinnings. His farces don't merely play with gender and sexual confusion: that confusion is their only reality and a challenge to any possibility of order. C. W. E. Bigsby writes:

> In Orton's work sexuality is aggression; it is subversion. It is a challenge
> to all authority, including, through its emphasis on incest, the authority of
> the parent, and, beyond that, perhaps of God, who is mocked not only in
> *Loot* and *Funeral Games*, but through a truculent rejection of all values
> except a total freedom of imagination and action.[44]

"Sex is the only way to infuriate them. Much more fucking and they'll be screaming hysterics in next to no time."[45] As this much-quoted diary entry illustrates, Joe Orton saw the graphic depiction of sexual disorder as the primary means to épater la bourgeoisie. The audience and critics of the premiere of *What the Butler Saw* did become "screaming hysterics." Stanley Baxter, who played the libidinous Dr. Prentice, recalled: "They [Orton's vociferous detractors in the gallery] really wanted to jump on the stage and kill us all."[46] While it is not clear how much of the fury could be credited to a misguided production or to the highly publicized circumstances of the playwright's death, Orton got his wish. He would have loved the headline of one review: "DEAD PLAYWRIGHT BOOED BY GALLERY."[47] The reviews echoed the moral outrage American critics were expending on Edward Albee: "Orton's terrible obsession with perversion, which is regarded as having brought his life to an end and choked his very high talent, poisons the atmosphere of the play. And what should have been a piece of gaily irresponsible nonsense becomes impregnated with evil."[48] Harold Hobson's language here verges on the purple as he blames Orton's sexuality (a "terrible obsession with perversion") for his death (blaming the victim once again) and for "poisoning" the play.

Hobson's attack shows how Orton's life, death, and work had become, like Oscar Wilde's, inextricably entwined, another moral parable of the wages of (homosexual) sin. Like Oscar Wilde, Orton became a major "uncloseted" playwright whose life, as a result, was for many more important than his work. John Lahr's exploitation of Orton has only exacerbated this problem. His biography of Orton, *Prick Up Your Ears*, begins with the sensational details of Orton's death, as if that death is the crucial fact in understanding Orton's work (actually it is important only to a biographer of Orton's lover and killer, Kenneth Halliwell). The movie made from Lahr's *Prick Up Your Ears*, a film in which Lahr himself (at his own suggestion, according to Alan Bennett, the screenwriter) became a major character, focuses on Orton the homosexual and sheds virtually no light on Orton the playwright.[49] Bennett was aware of this problem, noting in his introduction how difficult it is to depict on film the act of writing.[50] Yet even the relationship of Orton and Halliwell, on which the film focuses, is presented as a grotesque version of the British stage stereotype of homosexual relationships. Older Nellie Halliwell initiates a working-class boy into homosexual sex and makes the boy his intellectual protégé. Butch Orton transcends his learning both sexually and artistically, becomes a success, and constantly cuckolds Halliwell, who stays home and cooks and cleans. Moreover, the casting of Alfred Molina as Halliwell turns him into a grotesque, which photographs of Halliwell don't support. Molina looks like Orson Welles as the bald, aging, Citizen Kane lumbering through Xanadu in a snit over Susan's defection. The film claims to present the story of Orton and Halliwell as one of the archetypal troubled first marriage of a successful man who no longer needs the spouse who helped him through the early stages of his career: "The idiosyncrasies of the relationship apart, one sees many marriages like this."[51] But one doesn't *see* many relationships as physically grotesque as the marriage of Orton and Halliwell is presented as being, and there is a great difference between the divorce court and murder-cum-suicide.

Who is the audience for *Prick Up Your Ears*? Gay liberationists might see the film as a corrective tale about the dangers of aping heterosexual marriages. They certainly would be disappointed if they expected gay eroticism. Heterosexists, if they went to the film at all, would see evidence for their own prejudices and stereotypes. The casting of Gary Oldman might attract others to a homosexual version of *Sid and Nancy* (the 1986 film version of Sid Vicious' life and death, in which Oldman starred), another sensationalist version of life in the sixties fast lane. The only people who would be disappointed are admirers of Joe Orton's plays. *Prick Up Your Ears* remains on the shelves of video stores when most "gay-oriented" videos disappear, if they have appeared at all, because it is a naughty, titillating picture of gay life for heterosexuals. The Lahr version of Joe Orton popularized in the Frears-Bennett film needs at least an alternative. Orton would have preferred Frears' previous film, *My Beautiful Laundrette* (1985), in which the erotic attraction of working-class youths is candidly and sexily portrayed.

Yet the identification of life with work was not the only thing that turned critics like Harold Hobson against *What the Butler Saw*. Worst of all, for Hobson, Orton's farce dares to be more than "gaily irresponsible" nonsense and thus "becomes impregnated with evil." The "evil" is the sexual violence and polymorphous perversity that the manic action of farce always at least intimates. Like other gay playwrights, Orton was attacked for being superficial, and thus undermining the seriousness of art, and for having too much of the wrong content, and thus not being superficial enough.

Not only did Orton want his audience—and, by extension, his critics—to become "screaming hysterics" but he declared that the outrageous sexual activity depicted in his plays was "the only way to smash the wretched civilization"[52] corrupted by an insane sexual morality and the worship of propriety. When a friend confessed his guilt about his homosexuality, Orton responded: " 'Fucking Judeo-Christian civilization!' I said, in a furious voice, startling a passing pedestrian."[53] Underlying the farce in Orton's work is the anger of a Ben Jonson, turned not against human appetite but against the morality that curbs it: "Reject all the values of society," Orton told his friend, "and enjoy sex."[54] Here in a nutshell is the conflict in Orton's plays. Jonathan Dollimore notes Orton believed, as many in the sixties did, "that sexual transgression and deviance could radically challenge an existing, repressive social order."[55] Society's farcical attempts to curb human appetite were the primary targets of his satire. It is society that is unnatural, not society's notion of unnatural behavior.

The world of Orton's plays is one of unstable sexuality but also one in which the clash of appetite with futile but brutal attempts at social order lead to real violence. People bleed and die in Orton's farces. The police are not the Keystone Cops or the benignly stupid constables of traditional farce. They beat their "suspects" into submission:

> TRUSCOTT *kicks* HAL *violently.* HAL *cries out in terror and pain.*
> TRUSCOTT: Don't lie to me!
> HAL: I'm not lying! It's in church!
> TRUSCOTT (*shouting, knocking HAL to the floor*): Under any other polit-
> ical system I'd have you on the floor in tears!
> HAL (*crying*): You've got me on the floor in tears. (Loot, p. 235)

Yet Truscott is easily bought off and more than willing to send an innocent man to jail. Representatives of authority are as arbitrary and self-serving as the people they police.

Violence is not restricted to officers of the law. Sexual violence is common behavior, the guilty secret that people closet. The closet was not, for Orton, the site of homosexuality but, in the tradition of farce, of any disorderly sexual behavior. In *What the Butler Saw*, the closet becomes the setting for primal familial scenes that would make Sophocles blush, for the family in Orton's plays is the chief example of an arbitrary social order masking a network of desire and violence at odds with the ideals of the society that maintains it. Peter Shaffer's *Five Finger Exercise*, in the simplistic tradition of Freudian melodrama, posits a dysfunctional, destructive family as the cause of homosexual desire. Orton sees the family as a much more complex, volatile combination of repression and desire. The nuclear family that is rejoined at the end of *What the Butler Saw* was literally created in a closet. Its dynamics are an acting-out of the impulses fantasized in Edward *Albee's Who's Afraid of Virginia Woolf?* (1962): a promiscuous wife and intellectual husband spawn children with whom they become sexually embroiled.

In the linen closet at the Station Hotel, one of those monstrous old hostelries attached to a train station, a chambermaid was seduced, which led to the birth of twins. Eighteen years later the same woman finds herself in the same closet with (unbeknownst to her) the son she bore as a result of the previous incident. The encounter is photographed by a hidden camera installed by the young man, who is now attempting to blackmail his "victim," who tells the boy: "When I gave myself to you, the contract didn't include cine-matic rights."[56] When she narrates the closeted assignation to her husband, her role changes from willing partner to innocent victim of an unsuccessful attack: "When I repulsed him he attempted to rape me. I fought him off, but not before he'd stolen my handbag and several articles of clothing" (p. 374). The "victim's" alibi is not totally convincing, particularly given her reputation for nymphomania. Later she tells Dr. Rance, the personification of authoritar-ian, arbitrary social order:

MRS. PRENTICE: The youth wanted to rape me.

RANCE: He didn't succeed?

MRS. PRENTICE: No.

RANCE: (*shaking his head*): The service in these hotels is dreadful. (p. 390)

Mrs. Prentice is much more masterful than Pinter's Bill Lloyd at shifting narratives. Her accounts of the closeted event supplant an "official" version of the story with the "real" narrative of the consensual act, and rape becomes another morally and legally charged term that implodes from misuse during the course of the play. The closet has become not only a place of licentious, incestuous behavior but also the scene of a narrative that hides the sexual appetite and behavior of the woman in question. Even the first closeted event, which led to the birth of her twins, is shrouded in obfuscating language. Two lines after stating that she was raped, Mrs. Prentice says: "I paid for my misdemeanor by conceiving twins" (p. 445), thus acknowledging her complicity in the event. Her husband, who we discover was the alleged rapist, claims that he "debauched" a young lady in the closet, an old-fashioned term that denotes an act short of the violence of rape but that credits him for the young lady's loss of chastity. The event was so exciting that the man wanted to spend his wedding night in the same closet: "If you'd given in to my request, our marriage would never have foundered" (p. 446). The "happy ending" of the play rejoins the parents with their children, who have been more or less willing partners in real and attempted incest, and husband with wife, who from now on will "never make love except in a linen cupboard" (p. 446).

Like the homosexual events in Tennessee Williams' plays, the closeted events in *What the Butler Saw* are not depicted but are enclosed in the play's exposition. The sexual action of the play, like that of much sex farce, is repeated *coitus interruptus*. Nor is the closet a place of homosexual activity, which is only suggested by the compliant young man who, in the style of Orton's young men, will do anything if the price is right. His actions imply a willing homosexual passivity to match his heterosexual aggressiveness: "During my last term at school I was a slave of a corporal in the Welsh Fusiliers" (p. 433). Homosexual activity is shamelessly integrated into the chaotic welter of sexual experience. Even the voice of authority, Dr. Rance, hints that pederasty is not totally unknown to him: "Boys cannot be put in the club [i.e., get pregnant]. That's half their charm" (p. 410). Yet male homosexuality is no more stable than heterosexuality. The outspoken Nick claims: "No position is impossible when you're young and healthy" (p. 370). Like the healthy, bisexual Bobby in Tennessee Williams' *Small Craft Warnings* (1972), Nick has no hang-ups about sex: he is candidly bisexual. Nor does he share his elder's penchant for masking sexual appetite in perversions of morally charged language. In Orton's farces, polymorphous perversity is the way of the world channeled by arbitrary order into fixed categories.

"Unnaturally," Dr. Prentice adheres religiously to his heterosexuality, though his fellow agents of order try to dissuade him:

RANCE: It might have been wiser if you hadn't rejected the young fellow's blandishments.
PRENTICE: Unnatural vice can ruin a man.
RANCE: Ruin follows the accusation not the vice. Had you committed the act you wouldn't now be facing the charge.
PRENTICE: I couldn't commit the act. I'm a heterosexual.
RANCE: I wish you wouldn't use these Chaucerian words. It's most confusing. (p. 411)

Prentice's saw about "unnatural vice" is countered by Rance's gruff pragmatism, which separates acts from moral discourse. Ruin is a matter of words, of being accused, and words can be manipulated until they lose their moral force. "Unnatural" suggests that there is intrinsically "natural" behavior. When Nick (dressed as a girl) asks Dr. Rance, "What is unnatural?," the response, given the current confusion of gender identity, is the opposite of what he intends and suggests that clothing is society's tenuous means of stabilizing gender identity and sexual orientation:

RANCE: Suppose I made an indecent suggestion to you. If you agreed something might occur which, by and large, would be regarded as natural. If, on the other hand, I approached this child—(*he smiles at* GERALDINE [who is dressed as NICK].)—my action could result only in a gross violation of the order of things. (p. 416)

Unconvincing sexual disguise has made it "natural" to proposition the boy. In other words, socially constructed ideas of gender identity define what is "unnatural." No wonder Rance thinks the word "heterosexual" is Chaucerian— archaic and dirty. "Heterosexual" and "homosexual" are arbitrary, like "natural" and "unnatural." When Geraldine, disguised as Nick, declares: "I must be a boy. I like girls," Rance responds, "I can't quite follow the reasoning there" (p. 413) Rance may be authoritarian, but he is properly skeptical about fixed gender definitions and the word "unnatural."

Jonathan Dollimore maintains that the terms "natural" and "unnatural" have, historically, been mechanisms for social control and that Orton clearly perceives the central paradox of the term "unnatural":

The unnatural then becomes a most insidious and paradoxical manifestation of evil: it is at once alien to, and yet mysteriously inherent within, "the human condition." This contradiction surfaces in two especially revealing (and related) anxieties of the post-war period. The first concerns the family, which was presented on the one hand as incontrovertibly natural and on the other as terribly vulnerable to deviant sexual desire, especially from within. The second concerns the homosexual, who was seen on the one hand as a monstrous invert, utterly alien to normal beings, and on the other as capable of corrupting such beings almost on sight.[57]

In *What the Butler Saw*, the closet is not only a site of transgressive sexual behavior but also a manipulation of the normative language of dominant society to hide the sexual appetites and behavior patterns society calls "unnatural." Order is maintained through either linguistic sleight-of-hand or brute force, but even force is a matter of language: "Who are you to decide what reality is?" (p. 440).

The family, the normative center of dominant moral and sexual discourse, is represented by the sexual network of the Prentices: parents who feel nothing toward their children but lust.

> GERALDINE: I lived in a normal family. I had no love for my father.
> RANCE: (*to* DR. PRENTICE): I'd take a bet that she was the victim of an incestuous attack. She clearly associates violence with the sexual act. . . . Did your father have any religious beliefs?
> GERALDINE: I'm sure he did.
> RANCE (*to* DR. PRENTICE): Yet she claims to have lived in a normal family. (p. 382).

The irony of Orton's farce is that Rance's seemingly illogical reading of incest into Geraldine's familial situation is true. Yet Rance's Freudian narratives are confused with the best seller he wants to write (he's a kind of fictional Peter Shaffer). For Rance, Freudian analysis and sensational fiction are identical— arbitrary orders that belie chaotic reality.

In *What the Butler Saw*, homosexual behavior is as "natural" as heterosexual behavior, though heterosexual marriage is a grotesque aberration and exclusive homosexual relationships impossible. Alan Sinfield is right in observing the paradox of Orton, who lived a homosexual life and had a kind of homosexual marriage but who did not present the possibility of exclusive homosexuality in his work. In Orton's plays men have sex with each other, but within the framework of masculine camaraderie, a combination Orton alternately mocked and condoned. He feared above all that his characters would be played onstage with elements of effeminacy. In his notes for an American production of *Loot*, Orton wrote:

> I don't want there to be anything queer or camp or odd about the relationship
> of Hal and Dennis. Americans see homosexuality in terms of fag and drag.
> This isn't my vision of the universal brotherhood. They must be perfectly

ordinary boys who happen to be fucking each other. Nothing could be more natural. I won't have the Great American Queen brought into it.[58]

Nor did he want his female characters played as "one of Tennessee Williams' drag queens."[59] Rance, in *What the Butler Saw*, asserts: "There are two sexes. The unpalatable truth must be faced. Your attempts at a merger can only end in heartbreak" (p. 415). Orton did not like effeminacy or camp caricatures. Men were to be masculine. Orton's untying of homosexuality from the farce queen is as much his own erotic desire for masculine men and dislike of effeminacy as it is a political statement.

In Orton's plays, masculine men are bisexual. In *Loot*, even the law assumes that "perfectly ordinary boys" will have sex with each other: "Two young men who know each other very well, spend their nights in separate beds. Asleep. It sounds very unlikely to me" (p. 233). Though homosexual behavior is assumed to be "natural," Hal and Dennis are sexually omnivorous. As the brutal policeman, Truscott, tells Dennis: "You scatter your seed along the pavements without regard to age or sex" (p. 244). While this bisexuality may seem transgressive, it also denies the possibility of exclusive homosexuality. Orton's boys—Sloane, Hal, Dennis, Nick—are never gay. One wonders whether Orton's insistence on bisexuality wasn't the result of his fear that audiences would tie homosexuality to the effeminacy he despised. Or perhaps, as Alan Sinfield suggests, Orton the dramatist was still, to some extent, in the closet:

> On the other hand, "we're all bisexual really" is the commonest evasion. Hal and Dennis are said to be indifferent to the gender of their partners. . . . That was an unusual and disconcerting thought; it takes the implications of cross-dressing and superficiality quite literally; it could be utopian. But it also keeps a distance from very many actual homosexuals; it was not how Orton lived, or others that he knew.[60]

In the portrayal of Ed, the middle-aged pederast in *Entertaining Mr. Sloane*, Orton wanted to defy the stereotypical assumption that, "the moment you wanted sex with boys, you had to put on earrings and scent."[61] Orton's own self-image—of the leather-clad he-man who liked sex with working-class types in public lavatories—was, like the images of homosexuality he projects in his plays, a counter to the effeminate stereotype, as well as an eroticizing of his own working-class origins. Yet in Ed he also mocks the hypermasculine mythology and athleticism with which Ed not very successfully masks his lust for the teen-age hustler, Sloane:

> ED: Developing your muscles, eh? And character (*Pause*.) . . . Well, well, well. (*Breathless*.) A little bodybuilder, are you? I bet you are . . . (*Slowly*.) . . . do you (*Shy*.) exercise regular?

SLOANE: As clockwork.

ED: Good, good. Stripped?

SLOANE: Fully.

ED: Complete. (*Striding to the window*.) How invigorating.

. . . .

ED: Do you wear leather . . . next to the skin? Leather jeans, say? Without . . . aah . . .

SLOANE: Pants?

ED: (*laughs*): Get away! (*Pause*.) The questions is are you clean living? You may as well know I set great store by morals. Too much of this casual bunking up nowadays. Too many lads being ruined by birds. (p. 87)

Ed's interest in Sloane's "manly" athleticism is, as Sloane well knows, an interest in Sloane's body, as his morality is merely a means of covering his own lack of interest in women and an attempt to encourage that lack of interest in Sloane. By the end of the play, even the word "principles" has become only a euphemism for sex: "He was an expert on the adolescent male body. He's completed an exhaustive study of his subject before I met him. During the course of one magical night he talked to me of his principles—offered me a job if I would accept them" (p. 135).

The linguistic perversions practiced on homosexual desire in Orton's plays are those practiced by most pre-Stonewall drama in masking taboo homosexuality. The difference here is that the language does not succeed in masking the desire. Unlike the farce queen or the closeted pederasts of "serious" drama, Ed in his eroticizing of boys is blatant. And Sloane, who is naked from the waist down when Ed first sees him, is eroticized and fetishized, for Ed's—and the audience's—benefit. In the second act, he is posing on the sofa in the leather pants, the image of Ed's fantasy. Orton's principal contribution to mainstream British drama was the homoerotic charge given homosexual relationships that had been presented, if at all, as sexless. Orton dramatized homosexual desire, not just homosexuality. Like his American counterparts, Williams and Albee, Orton makes the young man the object of the gaze, but he is more blatant; he makes the youth the object of the male character's gaze and thus forces the audience to see him as a gay man might see him. Simon Shepherd notes how in *What the Butler Saw* Nick is framed in the doorway in states of undress and finally appears in a fetishistic costume, underpants and a police helmet, one of many such images of sexy boys.[62] Shepherd also notes that a "straight" production of an Orton play can cancel out its homoeroticism by ignoring the importance of the gaze and the fetishizing of the boys.[63]

Sloane, the object of desire, is young, compliant, bisexual, murderous when threatened. He is a rough-trade fantasy come to life. At the end of the play, he is in sexual thrall to Ed and his grotesque sister, Kath. The menage that ends *Entertaining Mr. Sloane* is another travesty of a family. Kath treats Sloane as both lover and son and, when she becomes pregnant by Sloane, tells him he's going to have a baby brother. Ed plays big brother and lover. When their father is kicked to death by Sloane, brother and sister see this murder only as an opportunity to possess the boy, "not eternally. . . . Just a few years" (p. 148), until he loses his youth and, therefore, his attractiveness.

Orton could not, or did not want to, untie the relationship between homosexual desire and youth. The object of desire is a teen-age criminal. His partners are either his own age or older men who pay for his compliance. Yet the sex lacks affect, as does much of the sex in Orton's diaries:

> The bed had springs which creaked. First time I've experienced that. He sucked my cock. Afterwards I fucked him. It was difficult to get in. He had a very tight arse. A Catholic upbringing, I expect. He wanted to fuck me when I'd finished. It seemed unfair to refuse after I'd fucked him. So I let him. We lay in bed and talked for a while. . . . As I lay on the bed looking upwards, I noticed what an amazing ceiling it was.[64]

In his diaries Orton becomes the performer in his own series of sexual and domestic scenes. It seems clear that he wanted them to be published and that they, like the highly posed, staged photographs of himself as erotic object, were to be a central aspect of his work. Orton was not a performer in the way Wilde was: he did not make public appearances and lecture tours. Nor did he, like Coward, star in his own plays, even though he had trained as an actor. Yet he was in the process of manufacturing an image that, thanks to the devotion and exploitation of John Lahr, has almost overpowered the plays.

The diaries form the picture of Orton as a proto-gay liberationist, if a rather joyless one. The ironic detachment of Orton's descriptions of his sexual activity may represent a literary pose or Orton's lack of emotional investment in his couplings. Yet sex with a fourteen-year-old Moroccan boy is described in much more erotic detail, not just because of the hashish or the sex itself, but because of the defiance and rebellion involved in the act of sodomy and pederasty:

> He went off perfectly satisfied, and not for the first time I reflected that having had a boy of his age in England I'd spend the rest of my time in terror of his parents or the police. At one moment with my cock in his arse, the image was, and as I write still is, overpoweringly erotic, and I reflected that whatever the Sunday papers have said about *Crimes of Passion* was of little or no importance compared to this.[65]

The excitement of pederasty was partly a measure of its illegality, perhaps one reason for its consistent appearance in Orton's plays. Domestic bliss, even with people of the same sex, wouldn't make the audience "screaming hysterics." The family, after all, is in Orton's work a violent, incestuous network. Sodomy and pederasty were the best revenge.

Orton's first produced play, *The Ruffian on the Stair*, despite its too-blatant signs of Pinter's influence, provides a prelude to all that will follow in Orton's work. From its first provocative lines, the play places a homosexual subculture within a supposedly heterosexual setting:

> JOYCE: Have you got an appointment today?
> MIKE: Yes. I'm to be at Kings Cross station at eleven. I'm meeting a man in the toilet.
> JOYCE: You go to such interesting places. (p. 33)

The public toilets, setting for the dark gropings and bizarre, furtive dialogue that fascinated Orton, are presented within respectable dialogue. Throughout the play, it is the ordinary presentation of transgressive characters and situations that give the play its resonance. Mike, it turns out, is a hit man; Joyce is a former prostitute whose fidelity obsesses him: "I'd kill any man who messed with you" (p. 32). Joyce has lived and worked under a series of names: Madelein, sometimes Maddy, and Sarah. While names provide a minimal sense of identity to people who are almost ciphers, they are arbitrary, changeable.

Joyce has read in the paper a record of an "accident involving a tattooed man. He had a heart, a clenched fist and a rose all on one arm. And the name 'Ronny' was on his body in two different places" (p. 32). The signs imprinted on the victim's body—mixed images of sentimentality, eroticism, and violence on the victim's arm and the two appearances of "Ronny" somewhere on the victim's body (Joyce's discretion, or that of the newspaper account, leaves the locations to our imagination)—take primacy over the body itself and its identity. Physical details become the only shreds of identity. When the victim's brother appears on Joyce's doorstep, he asks:

> WILSON: You've heard of him?
> JOYCE: I've heard of his tattoos. (p. 34)

And he then provides more suggestive physical information:

> WILSON: He wore white shorts better than any man I've ever come into contact with. As a matter of fact, strictly off the record, I'm wearing a pair of his white shorts at this moment. They're inconvenient . . . because . . . (*he blurts it out*)—there's no fly. (p. 34)

Later, Wilson tells Mike: "We had separate beds—he was a stickler for convention, but that's as far as it went. We spent every night in each other's company. It was the reason we never got any work done" (p. 49–50). The separate beds, a sop to "convention," are a flimsy cover for the incestuous relationship between the twenty-three-year-old victim, killed by Mike, and Wilson, his seventeen-year-old brother. Mike's moralistic response to Wilson's admission receives a typically Ortonesque rebuttal:

> MIKE: There's no word in the Irish language for what you were doing.
> WILSON: In Lapland they have no word for snow. (p. 50)

Wilson's reply implies that the "unspeakable"—homosexuality, incest—may be all-pervasive. His feelings for his brother certainly were overwhelming: "I used to base my life round him. You don't often get that, do you?" (p. 50). In an understatement, he admits: "I get a bit lost without him, I don't mind admitting" (p. 59).

The young ruffian sets about terrorizing Joyce and ravaging the hallway outside Mike and Joyce's flat. He also plays on Mike's sexual possessiveness of Joyce, calling Joyce by her "trade" name, Maddie, and describing the time his brother had sex with Maddie. Yet Wilson's tactics are not vengeance, but a goad to Mike to kill him.

The play's first director, Peter Gill, told John Lahr that *Ruffian on the Stair* was "the only play where he [Orton] tried to write about genuine homosexual emotions."[66] Wilson's grief is real, however awkwardly stated, and his only purpose is to get the man who killed his brother to kill him as well: "You've got a gun. Kill me with that" (p. 54). Yet Orton's finale is a bizarre combination of farce and melodrama. Wilson tries to stage a moment of passion with Joyce so that Mike, in a fit of jealousy, will kill him. (Since his brother had sex with Joyce, sex seems to Wilson to provide another means of following in his brother's footsteps.) For her part, Joyce is moved to embrace Wilson not by erotic feelings but by pity for the boy. Mike crashes through the door and shoots, but the first shot destroys Joyce's beloved goldfish bowl. From the point when the second shot kills Wilson, the play moves back into Orton's realm of farcical linguistic displacement. "This is what comes of having no regular job" (p. 61), Joyce proclaims before she breaks down, not because of Wilson's death or the realization that Mike *had* killed Wilson's brother, but because her goldfish are dead. Mike's final speech exercises a rhetorical flourish that, instead of justifying his murder of Wilson, reduces it to banality: "I'll fetch the police. This has been a crime of passion. They'll understand. They have wives and goldfish of their own" (p. 61).

The murderer will be let off for his justifiable crime of passion. But the only real passion, other than possession, was that of young Wilson for his brother. The "murder" was really a carefully planned suicide. To confuse matters more, Joyce is not Mike's wife, though he is as possessive of her as a husband, and the equation of wives and goldfish is the clearest sign of the emotional sterility of Mike and Joyce's world.

In one sense *The Ruffian on the Stair* places the possibility of homosexual love above the arid, potentially violent heterosexual relationship, though Wilson's brother was engaged, and so his and Wilson's relationship was thus already coming to an end. Love, however, is an obsessive displacing of identity onto another person, a loss of self. Wilson's only identity is as brother and lover to the dead Frank. Wilson's alienation is one manifestation of a common plight. Mike says of an appointment: "I'm seeing a man who could put me in touch with something" (p. 43), and his jealous attachment to Joyce is based on a fear of loneliness: "I was so lonely before" (p. 57). Left alone in the flat, Joyce talks to herself about the "humiliating admissions" she has made in her life: "You'd think it would draw me closer to somebody. But it doesn't" (p. 40). The only brief moment of connection in the play—Joyce's tender kiss on the cheek of the boy she pities—leads to the grotesque, deadly denouement.

For all their anomie, Joyce and Mike are whore and killer, a literal version of Orton's typical heterosexual couple. And Wilson, the "boy hairdresser," as he was called in an earlier draft (an adaptation of a novel by Orton and Halliwell), is passive, self-pitying, and ineffectual, a far cry from the rough trade Orton eroticizes in his later plays. He can only adore the masculinity and athleticism of his brother, fetishized by those flyless underpants Wilson wears. Wilson's self-inflicted martyrdom is, in Orton's world, more aberrant than the aggressiveness of Sloane or Nick.

The Ruffian on the Stair falls into the traditional structure of realistic drama. Wilson, the homosexual intruder, is shot at the play's climax. Homosexuality is destroyed, yet what is left is a grotesque parody of "normality."

Orton said that Peter Gill's stage production "came over as a sad little play,"[67] which is hardly what he wanted. His notes to Gill make clear that he wanted a combination of "comedy and menace," but they also leave no doubt that Orton saw his characters as unintentionally funny. Their humor, however, could be achieved only through a totally realistic, deadpan performance: "Unless it's real it won't be funny."[68] Orton was as distanced from his own characters as he was from the sad characters he encountered in the toilets. Wilson's love for his brother was as humorous to Orton as the more overtly bizarre conversations of Mike and Joyce.[69]

Ruffian on the Stair is not a farce as *Loot* and *What the Butler Saw* are, yet it treats its most serious moment as farce, and the emphasis on the grotesque—the violent yet funny physical action, the disconnection between language and action—are the seeds that will flower in Orton's later plays. What one does see in this early work is the way in which homosexuality is embodied not in a conventional, sexless stereotype but in obsessive desire rendered with attention to erotic detail. One also sees the mixing of erotic desire with family: pederasty and incest combined in the love of the two brothers. The representative of the force that disapproves of homosexual desire and that killed Wilson's brother-lover is a hired killer, a murderer who is also the voice of conventional morality in the play.

Contemporary gay critics tend to attack Orton for his pre-Stonewall limitations of gay political awareness and social critique. Simon Shepherd notes that "not only was Orton the sort of queer most easily accommodated by straight society, but his adventures celebrate the social and sexual power of the penis."[70] One could add that his plays, like his adventures, are exercises in phallic power. Thus Orton's "contempt for the effeminate, and indeed for women"[71] aligns him with the prejudices behind traditional gay stereotypes even as he was exploding those stereotypes. Alan Sinfield notes that Orton's sexual conservatism was linked to a theatrical conservatism: "His attitudes to homosexuality and theatre tended to assume the milieu of Coward or Rattigan,"[72] which limited him to West End aspirations and left him ignorant of the burgeoning of fringe gay drama. Sinfield's criticism is somewhat naive: Orton aspired to the fame and fortune of his closeted predecessors, and that could be achieved only in the mainstream, commercial theater.

Joe Orton, then, is not the great gay comic writer some heterosexual critics would make him but a transitional figure in gay drama. He rejected the queen stereotype of traditional farce but had no positive vision of homosexuals with which to replace it; he dramatized guiltless homosexual desire but never portrayed homosexual love.

PETER SHAFFER AND THE ENDURANCE OF CLOSET DRAMA

By the time of Orton's death in 1967, censorship had just about ended its long run in Great Britain, and with the advent of gay liberation at the end of the decade, homosexuality could not be treated merely as an open secret. Closet drama was no longer necessary. Yet the genre did not totally fade out of existence. The most popular British "serious drama" of the 1970s (in New York) was Peter Shaffer's *Equus* (1973), a spin on the tradition of British closet drama. In *Equus*, an unhappy middle-aged psychiatrist is assigned a visionary seventeen-year-old boy who has blinded six horses in a stable. Through a series of psychiatric sessions and flashbacks, the analyst discovers that the boy made a religion out of the horses, involving sexual arousal and sadomasochism, and blinded the horses after they witnessed him try (and fail) to have sex with the girl whose father owned the stable.

The girl is very forward in trying to seduce the boy, whose sexual fantasy life has centered on his horse-gods, who are, of course, always masculine (portrayed by tall, athletic men with metallic headpieces in the shapes of horses' heads). The boy's "religion" is romanticized by the doctor as something far more vibrant than his own clinical life and passionless marriage. The doctor sees the boy as a link to the Dionysian ecstasy of ancient Greece, but his job is to cure his patient of this passionate eroticizing of masculinity, which he does, knowing that he has reduced the boy's life to the "Normal":

> I'll give him the good Normal world . . . blinking out nights away in a non-stop drench of cathode-ray over our shrivelling heads! I'll take away his Field of Ha Ha, and give him normal places for his ecstasy. . . . With any luck his private parts will come to feel as plastic to him as the products of the factory to which he will almost certainly be sent. Who knows? He may even come to find sex funny. . . . Trampled and furtive and entirely in control. Hopefully, he'll feel nothing at his fork but Approved Flesh. *I doubt, however, with much passion!*[73]

The psychiatrist's lament over his enforcing of the "Normal" comes after the doctor has covered the boy's naked body. In covering his nakedness, he covers the boy's passionate, aberrant sexuality and his own closeted homosexuality, which has led him to fixate on the boy. The young woman, the cause of the boy's crisis, has been banished from the stage, but "curing" the boy is forcing an adaptation to normal, heterosexual sex. The boy's "religion" is sublimated homosexuality, the result of being raised with a working-class version of the parents in *Five Finger Exercise*—parents who fit the Freudian pattern for homosexual development. The doctor is a repressed homosexual who comes to envy the passion of this seventeen-year-old boy in the way many teachers in the late sixties and early seventies envied and desired their students, whose adolescent freedom they romanticized. It was this fashionable idealization of youth, combined with a denigration of rationality and a celebration of the sixties-style penchant for the spiritual—with the added attraction of an extended nude scene with male and female nudity that led to the success of *Equus*. But under it all is a story of repressed pederasty. *Equus* was a more contemporary reworking of Shaffer's spectacular historical drama, *The Royal Hunt of the Sun* (1964), which had at its center the conflict between a disillusioned middle-aged man and a beautiful semiclad Inca king who thought himself a god;[74] it was a precursor of *Amadeus* (1979), a dramatization of the obsessive love-hate relationship of the established, middle-aged traditionalist, Salieri, and the young, sexually active, eternal adolescent, Mozart. The hope for faith or genius is always a young man who throws a cynical middle-aged man into intellectual and spiritual crisis.

Unlike *Five Finger Exercise* and *Black Comedy*, Shaffer's later plays never present homosexuality directly—or even hint at it; that might have limited their commercial potential. Yet they present a closeted vision of experience and a vision of closeted individuals thrown into crisis by a young man whose very presence challenges their hard-won normality. It could be said that Shaffer keeps rewriting Herman Melville's *Billy Budd*, with the roles of Claggart and Vere combined. The young man becomes a martyr, but he is also the focus of attention. The older man is forced to regard and ultimately to destroy what he doesn't feel he should have. It could also be said that Shaffer keeps manufacturing variations of Shairp's *The Green Bay Tree*, in which the older man doesn't get the boy.

Reflecting on my early experience as a rapt audience member at John Dexter's productions of *The Royal Hunt of the Sun* and *Equus* helped me understand the homoerotics of theater. Dexter's highly theatrical productions foregrounded the homoerotic dimension that was repressed in the script itself. The productions kept one's visual focus on the lithe, often partially clad youth, in *Royal Hunt* on Atahuallpa and even more in *Equus* on the boy, who was clearly presented as the object of the psychiatrist's—and the audience's—gaze. Dexter's productions clarified, for those who wanted to see, what Shaffer's plays were really about. And so a closeted script was uncloseted in production. Both *The Royal Hunt of the Sun and Equus* ended with a vision of an older man standing or kneeling by the prone body of a young man, lamenting what he had lost. Shaffer has a gift for romanticizing, disguising, and mass-marketing homosexual repression that makes a reading of his works a fitting conclusion to a chapter on British closet drama.[75]

CHAPTER FOUR

AMERICAN DREAMS

GRANDMA: And will you look at that face!
YOUNG MAN: Yes, it's quite good, isn't it? Clean-cut, mid-west farm boy type, almost insultingly good-looking in a typically American way. Good profile, straight nose, honest eyes, wonderful smile

GRANDMA: Yup. Boy, you know what you are, don't you?
You're the American Dream, that's what you are.
EDWARD ALBEE, *The American Dream*

"A man knows a queer when he sees one."
BILL REYNOLDS, IN ROBERT ANDERSON, *Tea and Sympathy*

When homosexuality was invoked in pre-Stonewall American drama, it was related to the American concern with "manliness," with a model of masculinity and male bonding that homosexuality endangered. This contrast of homosexuality with masculinity still prevails. It explains the public shock at the illness and death of Rock Hudson in 1985. Before the headlines about Hudson's trip to Paris to be treated for AIDS, most Americans would not believe that tall, lanky Hudson was homosexual (though his sexuality had been known in gay circles for decades). Paula Treichler quotes a *USA Today* article in which a man stated: "I thought AIDS was a gay disease, but if Rock Hudson can get it, anyone can."[1] Hudson was "manly": he couldn't have been gay. The disclosure of Hudson's gayness, a result (as it so often is) of the disclosure of his having AIDS, created a series of narratives, one of which blurred comforting distinctions between masculinity and homosexuality.

Other aspects of the AIDS drama in which Rock Hudson was a central character are pertinent to a discussion of homosexuality in pre-Stonewall American drama. Hudson was adept at "acting straight" on and off the screen. The public fascination with his death arose not merely because he played macho roles or because he was a movie star or because he had AIDS but because he was a closeted movie star.[2] Like many good dramas, Hudson's story was one of discovery, of being "found out." Hudson's "outing" and death proved that the closet is no refuge. Like much gay drama, the moral of Hudson's outing has different meanings for heterosexist and homosexual audiences. To the former, it is a saga of secret guilt and public retribution—the wages of sin are disclosure and death. The closet is no refuge. To many gay men—and women—Hudson's experience demonstrated the futility and, to some extent, the cruelty of the secret life. The closet is no safe haven.

Hudson was an actor, but a central assumption of this book is that closeted individuals are always actors, performing for a reward and approval they don't think they would receive if they were known to be homosexual. Hudson had to choose between being a star and being known as gay, a choice American actors feel they still have to make,[3] as many less public gay men feel they must stay in the closet for fear of rejection of family and friends or heterosexist reprisal. But acting straight also involves internalizing the public's attitudes about homosexuality:

> To accept the closet is to have absorbed society's view of gays, to accept insult so that one avoids harm. Thereby one becomes a simulacrum—a deceptive substitute—of a person: one seems to be a moral agent with ends of one's own and an ability to revise them, but one really is simply a puppet to the values of society.[4]

Like many movie stars, Rock Hudson represented in the late 1950s and early 1960s the masculine American dream. Like most of Hollywood's dreams, Rock Hudson (born Roy Fitzgerald) was as much of a fiction as the characters he played. Roy Fitzgerald's largest acting responsibility was maintaining and protecting the image of Rock Hudson. "Rock," like Tennessee Williams' "Brick," in *Cat on a Hot Tin Roof*, turned out to be an ideal of stolid, unyielding manhood concealing homosexual desire because it is unmanly and, more crucial to stars of the stadium and silver screen, unpopular. While other male stars of the fifties represented a new ideal of male sensitivity, Hudson combined some of their gentleness with old-fashioned stolidity. He couldn't act (real men don't act), but whether holding on to the ranch and Elizabeth Taylor in *Giant* (1956), or assailing Doris Day's virtue in *Pillow Talk* (1959), he was "all man." There is some irony now to viewing *Giant*, in which James Dean, the epitome of the sensitive young man, and Rock Hudson fight over Elizabeth Taylor. Both these embodiments of elements of fifties manhood were homosexual, giving the film a subtext that develops another drama about myths and realities of the American dream of masculinity.

Rock Hudson's drama is a starting point for a discussion of the homosexual texts and subtexts of the plays written in his era, the pre-Stonewall era (Hudson moved in the seventies from the big screen to television). Closets and manhood are the homosexual themes of these plays, yet gay playwrights managed to find space for a critique of the operations of the closet within structures heterosexuals could accept. American gay playwrights deconstructed the image of American masculinity to show its hollowness and cruelty and reconstructed it to include homosexuality. The history of the homosexual in American drama in the fifties and sixties is in large part the story of the reconstruction of the ideal man, the American dream, as object of homosexual desire *and* as homosexual, a task Hollywood had, unknowingly, already undertaken.

The reconstruction includes the homosexual-created character's defiance of the strictures of realistic drama. At the same time, mainstream realistic drama exploited the melodramatic potential of homosexuality while enforcing the norms of heterosexuality and conventional notions of masculinity by raising the possibility of homosexuality but never showing a homosexual character.

WHO'S THE REAL MAN?

Robert Anderson's *Tea and Sympathy* (1953), an enormously successful Broadway play (the Lord Chamberlain banned a London production) and, later, movie, manages, as many mainstream American plays of the fifties did, to raise the specter of homosexuality without presenting any overtly homosexual characters. Anderson's play, like Arthur Miller's *A View from the Bridge* (1955), both raises and dismisses the possibility of homosexuality. In essence, it pushes its characters back into the closet. Yet the Broadway success of *Tea and Sympathy* suggests that hints of homosexuality inspired a prurient interest in a general audience as long as that audience could feel "safe" from any real threat in an era in which homosexuality was linked with anti-American behavior.

Still, *Tea and Sympathy* challenges the normative equation of sexual orientation and gender (heterosexual = masculine; homosexual = feminine). It does so not to validate homosexuality but to challenge the macho mentality that pervaded America during the 1940s. Ironically, in order to subvert the American he-man mystique, Anderson had to color it with hints of homosexuality. The sensitive male is now the heterosexual, the man's man a latent homosexual, and, as in *The Green Bay Tree*, the woman is the instinctive arbiter of sexual orientation. While this new formulation may extend the definition of masculine behavior, it still maintains homosexuality as the negative of masculine. Homosexuality is still taboo, and *Tea and Sympathy* reinforces this sanction by hinting at the possibility of homosexuality while denying its actuality. This double bind is typical of the treatment of homosexuality in pre-Stonewall American drama. Anderson's play, then, is worth a close examination rather than the usual offhand dismissal it receives for political incorrectness; it is as paradigmatic of the treatment of homosexuality in American drama of the 1950s as *The Green Bay Tree* was of pre-Stonewall English drama.

There are two rooms in the single set for *Tea and Sympathy*, which takes place in a New England boarding school (though it must be a school for slow-witted young men, as their median age seems to be eighteen, an age clearly chosen to make their sexual awareness, and the play's famous final scene, less shocking. The larger space is the living room of the apartment shared by Bill Reynolds, the housemaster, and his wife Laura. This is the space in which Laura, a former actress (therefore worldly, sensitive, and likely to have encountered homosexuals) offers the boys "tea and sympathy." Though Bill is the housemaster, Laura dominates this space in which he and other grown men are disruptive forces. Anderson describes the room as "warm and friendly"[5] and Laura as "compassionate and tender" (p. 4), the dominant, positive, "feminine" qualities the play asserts that men too should possess. The fact that the bedroom is invisible is a sign of the sexlessness of Laura and Bill's marriage.

The bedroom the audience sees is Tom's, which represents through its decor ("an Indian print on the bed, India print curtains for the dormer window" [p. 3]) the taste that makes its inhabitant, Tom Lee, "different." At the opening of the play, Tom is sitting on his bed, playing his guitar and singing "The Joys of Love." Tom is defined by his bedroom, and it is his sexuality that will be the focus of the play, as Laura's visit to his bedroom will affirm Tom's heterosexuality and therefore his "manhood" at the end of the play. While Laura is dressed in soft, warm attire, a cashmere sweater and a wool skirt, even though it is June, Tom is dressed as the typical fifties preppie. Though he obviously does not "fit in," his clothing suggests that he is not totally the "off-horse" he is accused of being.

Typical of a McCarthy-era play, *Tea and Sympathy* is about the danger of name-calling. Like its elder sister, Lillian Hellman's *The Children's Hour* (1934), which had been revived as a covert attack on McCarthyism the previous year, 1952, Anderson's play presents not communism but homosexuality as the "big lie," the nastiest possible attack (a ploy used by Senator Joseph McCarthy's team which was, we now know, a classic case of the pot calling the kettle beige). Tom has been seen "skinny-dipping" with a suspect teacher, and Laura's husband, Bill, is leading the campaign to purge the school of the instructor and to purge his house of the "off-horse," Tom, who is so innocent he doesn't understand what he or Mr. Harris could be guilty of. In Bill's eyes,

Tom isn't "all man." He loves music and sings plaintively (shades of Julian Dulcimer); he plays the leading ladies in the school plays. In his first meeting with Laura, he tries on the dress he will wear in a production, appropriately, of Sheridan's *The School for Scandal* (1777), though he clearly takes more interest in Laura's bosom than in transvestism. Tom is called "Grace" by his peers because of his love for Grace Moore in the film *One Night of Love* (1934) (and he isn't gay!). We are told that when Tom's father tried to explain "the facts of life to him," Tom threw up—such revulsion at the thought of sex being presented as healthier than the prurient interest of his peers. When he tries to prove his masculinity by having sex with the town whore, he cannot perform. Yet Tom, the child of a broken marriage, clearly loves the young, beautiful, maternal Laura and plays Marchbanks to her Candida.

When the skinny-dipping scandal breaks, Tom is ostracized by his classmates, and Laura's husband, Bill, becomes obsessed with ridding his school of this pariah. Bill is a real John Wayne type, "large and strong with a tendency to be gruff" (p. 39), but Anderson makes Bill's "manliness" a mask for his latent homosexuality. Bill is a newlywed at forty who apparently showed little interest in women before his sabbatical trip to Europe the year before. Laura's friend Lilly, a sexually outspoken faculty wife, tells Laura of Bill's "safe" past: "Even before he met you, Bill never gave me a second glance. He was all the time organizing teams, planning mountain club outings" (p. 8). Bill's celibacy and professional dedication could be signs that he is the traditional American man's man, but other hints are laid. Bill met Laura abroad on sabbatical, a deceptive time, as Lilly tells Laura: "Teachers on sabbatical leave abroad are like men in uniform during the war. They never look so good again" (p. 9). Yet Bill obviously was a different, frightened person when he met Laura: "I think you're ashamed . . . that you ever let me see you needed help. That night in Italy in some vague way you cried out. . . ." (p. 54). Bill, of course, denies ever feeling anything so weak as fear and now resents Laura's place in his all-male life. Clearly his sexual interest in her has waned now that he is back with his boys: "We don't touch any more. It's a silly way of putting it, but you seem to hold yourself aloof from me. A tension seems to grow between us . . . and then when we do . . . touch . . . it's a violent thing . . . almost a compulsive thing" (p. 112).

Part of being a "man's man" is being able to spot homosexuals, "a man knows a queer when he sees one" (p. 48), but the play supports Laura's claims of even greater powers of perception: "You men think you can decide on who is a man, when only a woman can really know" (p. 173). Like Leonora in *The Green Bay Tree*, Laura has the ability to "spot" homosexuals. In Shairp's play, Leonora's perception was that of any sensible, moral, middle-class person who can recognize evil. Laura's perception is based on a woman's ability to recognize a "real man," a role her husband tries—and fails—to act. In *Tea and Sympathy*, "being a man" is merging masculine and feminine characteristics: "Manliness is also tenderness, gentleness, consideration"

(p. 172), qualities Tom possesses and that Bill and Tom's father are trying to scare out of him. Yet even the perceptive Laura equates homosexuality with her sense of what isn't masculine. Homosexuality, however, is no longer "sinister" or "evil," as it is in Shairp's play: it is merely a weakness.

Laura realizes that Bill married her to advance his chances of being headmaster and to mask his own homosexual feelings: "Did it ever occur to you that you persecute in Tom, that boy up there, you persecute in him the thing you fear in yourself? . . . that was the weakness you cried out for me to save you from, wasn't it?" (pp. 175–176). Bill's response is to order Laura out of his apartment and his life, though it is actually Bill, the latent homosexual, who is dismissed from the audience's view. Laura walks up the stairs to Tom's bedroom, where she offers herself to Tom to allow him to prove his heterosexuality and manhood, uttering the curtain line that is almost as universally known to gay men as Blanche DuBois' final words: "Years from now . . . when you talk about this . . . and you will . . . be kind" (p. 182).[6]

Throughout *Tea and Sympathy*, Tom Lee has been marginalized by the "men," and his isolated bedroom becomes an image of that marginalization— almost a closet—until the end of the play, when Laura enters Tom's room and, in essence, brings it and Tom to the center. The master's parlor, the locus for the values of the "man's world" of the school, now stands empty. The play has moved to the little room on the side.

Manliness has been redefined to include those qualities of sensitivity and tenderness that were part and parcel of the 1950s "new masculinity" embodied by "sensitive" film stars like James Dean, Montgomery Clift, and Tab Hunter. But, to validate masculine sensitivity, homosexuality had to be removed by being displaced to the image of the 1940s macho man. Conversely, the sensitive boy's bedroom may be in perfect taste, but his bed contains a woman. Tom says of himself, "I'm no man. Ellie knows it. Everybody knows it. It seems everybody knew it, except me. And now I know it" (p. 179). Laura responds, "You're more of a man now than he ever was or will be" (p. 181). "Only a woman can really know" who is and isn't a man— who is truly heterosexual and who isn't—and Laura, who understands now that homosexuality was "the weakness" Bill "cried out for me to save [him] from" (p. 176), knows that Tom is "all man."

The language of *Tea and Sympathy*, less indirect than the elliptical hints of *The Green Bay Tree* but equally cautious, combines specific accusations of effeminacy and assertions of masculinity with only the vaguest, most indirect suggestions of homosexuality. It's as if, even in plays that titillate with suspicions of homosexuality, the word itself is still as "unspeakable" as it was for Forster's *Maurice*. Silences—ellipses in the script—are blanks that audience members must fill in for themselves. When her husband tells her of his suspicions about Tom Lee, Laura is uncharacteristically inarticulate: "But, Bill . . . you don't think Tom is . . . (*She stops. Bill looks at her a moment. His answer is in his silence.*) Oh, Bill!" (p. 250). Homosexuality can be presented only as a silence. Mr. Dulcimer's sexual initiation of David Owen (if it did happen) is hinted at but presented as horrific, literally unspeakable. The idea that Mr. Harris and Tom Lee might have at least thought about a sexual relationship is, in *Tea and Sympathy*, unthinkable.

Laura's heterosexual initiation of Tom Lee is presented as a noble, even maternal act (her final gesture is putting his hand on her breast). Bill says to her, "You want to mother a boy, not love a man" (p. 173), and, given Laura's earlier marriage to an eighteen-year-old, her present marriage to an "old boy," and her interest in Tom, his comment seems well targeted, but it is Bill's unacknowledged homosexuality that is seen as the problem, not Laura's interest in offering more than "tea and sympathy" to eighteen-year-olds. Initiating a young man into homosexual sex is unspeakable; Mr. Harris is dismissed on the basis of rumors of that heinous crime. Initiating a young man into heterosexuality is noble.[7]

Typical of 1950s dramas, there is no space for homosexual activity in *Tea and Sympathy*. Mr. Harris, the homosexual teacher who swam naked with Tom but never made sexual overtures to him, is fired. (It is interesting to note that Mr. Harris is the only man in the play described as "good-looking," as if that were a label. Or perhaps it's a liberal gesture to suggest that homosexuals may not be men, but they look good!). Bill, the latent homosexual, is too full of denial mechanisms and too in love with the hearty, all-male world he lives in to act on his "weakness." Bill's preference for the company of adolescent boys is a sign of arrested development that is of a piece with his latent homosexuality. Still, in accordance with the rules of realism, Bill is banished from the scene. And Tom, of course, isn't homosexual. *Tea and Sympathy* proves only that a boy can be a sissy without being a queer, a comforting distinction for some mothers in the audience but not particularly helpful for gay men.

Tea and Sympathy was for its time the classic version of mainstream American treatment of homosexuality. Typical of such plays, accusations of homosexuality taint a male society, and the threat of homosexuality is eliminated by the final curtain. Following the formula established in the thirties by *The Children's Hour* and reinforced by responses to the House Un-American Affairs Committee and McCarthy's witch hunts, homosexuality is the one lie so ugly that it can bring down the accuser (remember Joseph Welch's famous rejoinder to one of McCarthy's accusations of homosexuality, "Have you no shame?"). The rise and fall of McCarthyism spawned political melodramas that enforced the closet by suggesting that homosexuality is the worst allegation anyone can make. Thus, alleging homosexuality labels the accuser as cruel, crass, and insensitive. Moreover, the accuser threatens social stability by violating the silence surrounding homosexuality. However, if the accusation is true, the guilty party must be purged from the scene. Parenthetically, we know now that the real drama of the Army-McCarthy hearings was one of the nastier dramas of closeted homosexuality, with one leading character,

Roy Cohn, a man who, like Rock Hudson, was subsequently, very reluctantly, "outed" by AIDS and who is a prime example of Richard Mohr's dictum: "Outed people will frequently be spiritual basket cases, whom people would not, or at least should not, want as a model for their soul."[8]

In 1960, two successful Broadway plays centered on the use of homosexuality as the "dirty secret" used to blackmail otherwise honorable politicians. While Gore Vidal's *The Best Man* raises and dismisses the issue without ever having a homosexual appear onstage, Loring Mandel's dramatization of Allen Drury's novel, *Advise and Consent*, is a vivid example of the fate of the homosexual in a well-meaning, liberal drama of the period.

Brigham Anderson, an upright young Senator from Utah, chair of the committee to ratify the President's choice for Secretary of State, discovers that the candidate has lied about his membership in a Communist Party cell. Anderson, more upset about the dishonesty than the past affiliation, insists on presenting this information to his committee. To stop him, the Secretary-designate, the President, and their supporters are prepared to uncover a secret in Anderson's life, a brief wartime affair with another man, presented as the result of loneliness and sexual frustration, not "real" homosexuality: "It had been almost three years since a personal thing had happened to me."[9] The play is candid about the sexual atmosphere of wartime, when "every vice you can picture is excused, sex and liquor were patriotic" (p. 66). Yet, despite his wife's support and the rightness of his political position, Brig Anderson shoots himself. While this death is presented as a personal tragedy, it also is a dramatic necessity, according to the regulations of popular drama. The dishonest ex-Communist does not get his cabinet seat, but the man who had a brief wartime homosexual fling does the noble thing and kills himself. He accepts the judgment of his corrupt peers—that he is "morally unfit."

Both *The Best Man and Advise and Consent* present homosexual activity as an unfortunate side-effect of World War II, a far cry from the affirming stories of homosexuality in World War II recounted by Allan Berube,[10] but in the world of these plays, punishment must be meted out for such unspeakable sins. Mainstream popular drama might by 1960 acknowledge homosexual acts and inclinations, but liberalism had clear limits.

WILLIAMS: MASCULINITY AND HOMOPHOBIA

Three of the four most critically acclaimed and commercially successful playwrights of the postwar period were closeted homosexuals whose plays were supported by the critical establishment so long as they maintained the conventions of closet drama. Of the pantheon of Tennessee Williams, William Inge, Edward Albee, and Arthur Miller, only Miller was heterosexual. Thus the central narrative of homosexuality in American drama of the fifties and early sixties was not in popular melodrama written by heterosexuals but in the plays of highly successful homosexual playwrights who chose to operate in the mainstream theater; who saw, as any playwright of their time would, Broadway theater as the only venue that would afford them the possibility of broad exposure and financial remuneration. In the 1950s, Broadway was still a the venue for serious drama, as long as that drama did not offend the sensibilities of its audience. Williams, Albee, and Inge had to negotiate between their experience as homosexual men and the conventions of popular, realistic drama.

The central figure here, Tennessee Williams, paradoxically managed in his most successful work to make homosexuality an insistent presence while keeping it an absence. In an era of enforcement of the closet, Williams managed to dramatize the perils of externally enforced and internalized homophobia. Homosexuality is not silent in his plays, though it is absent onstage. As in American society in the postwar period, homosexuality in William's plays forces the protagonist into a complex relationship with traditional images of masculinity, extending and, to some extent, subverting those images.

The primary issue for Williams' homosexual characters in his plays of the forties and fifties is the devastating one of exposure, of making the private public.[11] When the idea of homosexuality is raised in the plays, it is usually linked to the brutal exposure of a sensitive man who is often a writer. In *A Stretcher Named Desire* (1947), Blanche DuBois tells of "coming suddenly into a room that I thought was empty—which wasn't empty but had two people in it . . . the boy I had married and the older man who had been his friend for years."[12] Typically, this extremely discreet description tells us nothing. What room? What were Blanche's husband and his older friend doing? The unspeakable remains unspoken in *Streetcar*, and the audience is expected to infer a sexual encounter from Blanche's judgmental language: "I saw! I know! You disgust me . . ." (p. 355). Blanche had seen a private moment and reacted by publicly exposing and humiliating her husband: her outburst was not uttered in the mysterious room but on a crowded dance floor. It was Blanche, not Allan, who publicly exposed the unutterable act. What she saw, knew, and was disgusted by was his homosexuality, and her response is the brutal exposure and repudiation homosexuals have long feared. Blanche's speech-act is the exercise of what Richard Dyer calls, "one of the prime mechanisms of gay stereotyping, synechdoche—that is, taking the part for the whole."[13] Blanche cries to Allan, "*You* disgust me," not "your action" or "your sexual betrayal" or "your sexual orientation" but *You*. Allan is reduced to his homosexuality, or, rather, Allan's homosexuality is expanded to be entirely definitive. The all-engulfing homosexual identity engulfs even the artist. "I saw that you are a homosexual—*only* a homosexual. *You* disgust me." Blanche, typical of Williams' characters, cannot exactly name what Allan is, but she can articulate her clear response.

Once made public, the sensitive poet's homosexuality becomes unbearable for him, and he commits suicide, publicly. The audience can accept

Allan's self-destruction as poetic justice: there is no place on stage for homosexual behavior, and Allan's story encapsulates the problem-play resolution for fallen women and homosexuals—disappearance and, frequently, death. Creativity and secret homosexuality are intertwined: expose the homosexual and you destroy the artist. And Blanche's own sensitivity is demonstrated by the fact that she is forever haunted by the memory of her act of extreme cruelty, which is, in a kind of poetic justice, repaid many times over by what she suffers through Stanley Kowalski. As she tells Stanley, "I hurt him the way you would like to hurt me." (p. 282). The action of the play transforms this statement: "You will hurt me the way I hurt him."

Through Allan's invisibility and the inexpressibility of what he has performed with his older friend, Allan is a closeted character in one of the richest and most complex closet dramas. A *Streetcar Named Desire*, though without a living homosexual character or overt gay theme, depicts in a codified fashion a paradigmatic homosexual experience.[14] It is the quintessential closeted gay play, and Blanche DuBois is in many ways the quintessential gay character in American closet drama. Williams himself was quoted as saying, "I am Blanche DuBois."[15] Blanche keeps her sanity by making her world theater, "I don't want realism. I want magic!" (p. 385). She knows about paper moons and cardboard skies and paper lanterns, but she also knows that performance is both her allure and her protection. And William's protection of his homosexual subtext is achieved by hiding it within the actions of a heterosexual female character.

Williams' entire play is a series of complex and sometimes paradoxical transformations. A slum in New Orleans takes on the lurid colors of early Technicolor movies (what an irony that the 1951 movie of *Streetcar* was in dingy black and white, but the film is in many ways a gross act of heterosexualization). Blanche tries to transform Stella and Stanley's tiny flat into a theatrical set, while she changes constantly from spinster schoolteacher to coquette to debutante to Marschalin to whore to helpless maiden. She transforms the paper boy into an Arabian prince and Mitch into her Rosenkavalier (is Blanche aware that Strauss and Hofmansthal's Rosenkavalier, Octavian, is a teenage boy, an idealized version of the objects of Blanche's desire?) The Flamingo Hotel becomes the Tarantula Arms, and her promiscuity there becomes her "intimacies with strangers." She knows that her reality and her defense is in her protean gift. When life is theater, role-playing is not lying. Blanche is sane as long as she knows she is acting. When she tells Mitch that she has "old-fashioned ideals," *"She rolls her eyes, knowing he cannot see her face"* (p. 348), a camp gesture that demonstrates her awareness of her acting.[16] Blanche's theatrical descendants are the transvestite heroines of Charles Ludlam and Charles Busch, playing roles in mock B movies but with camp irony.

Stanley, the heterosexual stud who is Blanche's nemesis, makes no such ironic gestures. His brutality is connected to his lack of awareness of his own role-playing. He does not understand the implications of his urge to get those colored lights going, or the potential self-mockery of his silk pajamas. Seeing himself as a single essence, he wants to reduce Blanche to one consistent identity. But even at the end, now perhaps in saving madness, Blanche has transformed commitment to an asylum into a noble gesture, "I have always depended on the kindness of strangers."

Blanche's famous exit line, "Whoever you are—I have always depended on the kindness of strangers" (p. 418), is also a *double entendre* for the promiscuous Blanche, whose wholesale ravishing of the military has had her declared "off limits." Throughout *A Streetcar Named Desire*, a homosexual code is operative. When Blanche tells Stella that she doesn't know how much longer she can "turn the trick" (p. 332), the language may be surprising coming from a Southern aristocrat and high-school English teacher, but it is not accidental. It is the language of prostitution, and Blanche will have to prostitute herself to marry Mitch, an act of reduction out of economic necessity. But it is also the language of homosexuality. When Mitch confronts Blanche with her past and her supposed lies, he says: "I was fool to believe you was straight," a word Blanche repeats, "Who told you I wasn't 'straight' " (p. 385), suggesting a contrapuntal scenario of the unmasking of a homosexual.[17]

Stanley cannot name exactly what he hates about Blanche, what he must repudiate and destroy, but she knows well the hatred of the "gaudy seed bearer," the heterosexual male who can scream at her before raping her, "What queen do you think you are?" (p. 398). To ignore the homosexual subtext of *Streetcar* is to reduce the play, but to see it as the only text is even more reductive. Yet *Streetcar* is a gay play in its theatricalization, not merely dramatization, of experience; its awareness of the power inherent in understanding the slipperiness of language; its playfulness within scenes of impending entrapment and destruction. It is, in short, about the theatricalization of experience as an act of liberation. Such theatricalization does not destroy the closet but makes the closet bearable. The option is exposure and destruction.

A Streetcar Named Desire presents the "real man," the heterosexual stud, as lure and destroyer: it reverses, in other words, traditional gender roles. In the view from the closet, it is the heterosexual man who is watched (the homosexual is not seen at all). The masculine image is that of the object of desire, not the desiring subject, which could, in Inge's and most of Williams' work, be feminine or effeminate. Looking at the heterosexual male does not render him passive; it excites and empowers him. Stanley's physicality is attractive even to Blanche—though she knows its limits and its dangers—but it is also grotesque and funny. His heaving a bloody package of meat at his wife at the opening curtain is a sign that Williams shares Blanche's view of Stanley. His brutality is not simply a matter of class or ethnicity, a mistake made in a number of productions. It is part and parcel of his gender identity as the "gaudy seed bearer." Stanley's working-class origins are necessary to establish an American version of the British myth of the sexual vitality of the working class: Williams saw D. H. Lawrence as one of his literary models.

Stanley's world is *his* stage, no one else's. Only he is allowed to "get the colored lights going." Yet physically attractive, intensely physical men, studs like Stanley, can be as dangerously attractive to gay men as they are to women. Thus proliferate studs in dramas by homosexual playwrights: Inge's Turk in *Come Back Little Sheba* and Hal in *Picnic*; Williams' Val in *Orpheus Descending* and Chance in *Sweet Bird of Youth*, among others; Albee's Nick in *Who's Afraid of Virginia Woolf?* and Young Man in *The American Dream*. These are all men whose power resides in their sexual attractiveness. They are, in the works of gay playwrights, mocked, feared, sometimes martyred, but always lusted after. Since their attractiveness is so central to their identity, their real power exists only when embodied by an actor who can exude that kind of appeal. Directors will tell you that any number of actresses can play Blanche but finding a convincing Stanley is extremely difficult. The audience must find Stanley sexually attractive, or a crucial part of the play is lost. His body is as important as his words and actions.

Stanley is a unitary essence: as the heterosexual male, he needs only to play variations on his role as dominator and penetrator. Blanche's position is more complex. Theatricality is essential. In his essay, "Homosexual Signs (In Memory of Roland Barthes)," Harold Beaver writes:

> "Human beings," [W. H.] Auden has written, "are, necessarily, actors who cannot become something before they have first pretended to be it; and they can be divided, not into the hypocritical and the sincere, but into the sane who know they are acting and the mad who do not." To be natural, as [Oscar] Wilde observed, is such a very difficult pose to keep up. The result is camp: the whole gay masquerade of men and women who self-consciously act; who flaunt incongruous allusions, parodies, transvestite travesties; who are sanely aware of the gap between their feelings and their roles; who continue to proliferate a protean, and never normative, range of fantasies in social dramas of their own choosing.[18]

I could argue with its implicit essentialism, but Beaver's essay does provide a model for explicating *Streetcar*. Blanche chooses sanity, which means, for the homosexual, choosing camp, a theatricality that is a protective covering and a defensive stance toward the hostile, straight world: "Camp is the desire of the subject never to let itself be defined as object by others but to reach for a protective transcendence, which, however, exposes more that it protects."[19] And indeed, in Williams world such theatricality is not protection but exposure. Only Stanley can be theatrical, but, of course, without the irony, the awareness of acting, that makes theater complex and interesting.

A Streetcar Named Desire suggests that those who "aren't straight" must act in order to survive and that they must imaginatively transform a world in which they are rejected into a bearable place. Allan Grey (and how his gray name contrasts with the lurid colors of Stanley's world) and Blanche cannot exist after they have been exposed. Their world is off the heterosexual stage, if they are allowed any world at all.

In one sense, *A Streetcar Named Desire* is about the place of the homosexual in a world dominated by gaudy seed bearers, but the one visible "gay" character is a heterosexual woman, allowed only the kind of sexual activity homosexuals are allowed in popular drama. Blanche's sad scene with the teenage paperboy figures the pederasty that itself figured the danger and horror of homosexuality in *The Green Bay Tree* and *Tea and Sympathy*. And her rampant promiscuity, which caused her to be declared off limits by the army, is "typical" homosexual behavior, though Blanche remembers it without shame, even with some pride.

Like Blanche DuBois, the artist, Sebastian Venable, in *Suddenly Last Summer* (1958), has an uncontrollable desire for boys and young men. Like Allan Grey, Sebastian is in danger of being publicly exposed by a woman, his cousin and fiancée, and the principal conflict is between her need to tell the truth about Sebastian and his mother's need to keep her beloved son in the closet. But the truth about Sebastian, like the truth about Allan Grey, centers on his death. Sebastian is only memory, manipulated and expressed by the words of the women who knew him.

For the homosexual artist, *Suddenly Last Summer* weaves an interesting set of variations on the theme of exposure. Sebastian Venable has always been a private artist, wishing to be "unknown outside a small coterie."[20] The privacy of Sebastian's art is a corollary to his sense that his art expresses his religious vision; for the rest of his experience, living was enough: "his life was his occupation" (p. 351). Yet that life was to be even more private than his work: "He *dreaded, abhorred!*—false values that come from being publicly known, from fame, from personal—exploitation" (p. 353). But Sebastian's private life became a public matter "*suddenly*" when his cousin, Catherine, saw him killed and eaten by the adolescent boys Sebastian had exploited sexually. To protect Sebastian's privacy, his mother will have Catherine, the witness to his sexual voraciousness and its consequences, lobotomized: "*Cut this hideous story out of her brain*" (p. 423).

The presentation of Sebastian's private homosexuality and public death is accomplished purely by exposition. Sebastian, the artist-homosexual is invisible, dead, literally cannibalized. The only expressions of his vision are what is left of his poems and the garden his mother maintains as she ruthlessly maintains his asexual image, which makes her the only woman in his life:

> The colors of this jungle-garden are violent, especially since it is steaming
> with heat after rain. There are massive tree-flowers that suggest organs of

*a body, torn out, still glistening with undried blood; there are harsh cries
and sibilant hissings and thrashing sounds in the garden as if it were inhabited by beasts, serpents and birds, all of savage nature.* (p. 349)

This setting not only evokes a Melvillian fallen world (*The Encantalas* [1854],
Melville's collection of descriptive accounts of the Galapagos Islands, is mentioned in the play); it represents Sebastian's martyred body and his carnivorous
vision of nature. Moreover, the Venable garden, like Dulcimer's hothouse, is
part of an interior, in this case of another Victorian mansion. It is both savage
and contained, expressive and cut off from public view. Like Dulcimer's hothouse, it is emblematic of its homosexual occupant: "Yes, this was Sebastian's
garden" is the first line of the play (p. 14). As the walled garden is both an
elaborate closet and the physical remnant of Sebastian, the conflicting stories
of his mother and cousin present the public and private selves. The monstrous
Mrs. Venable is quite right to see the public exposure of Sebastian's private
life as destructive of the image of the artist. The death and the sexual appetite
that caused it overshadow Sebastian's poems of summer. *Suddenly Last Summer* questions whether his mother's fierce protection of Sebastian's closet, or
Catherine's truthful narrative, does more violence to Sebastian's memory. The
setting suggests that Sebastian's vision should prevail through his work and
the memory of his death.

There are no artists in *Cat on a Hot Tin Roof* (1955), though the play
is filled with homosexual ghosts. Like *Tea and Sympathy*, the drama focuses
on the fraught relationship of homosexuality to conventional ideas of manhood. Its sexually troubled characters are aging athletes, cases of arrested
development, as the name "Skipper" suggests. Homosexuality is linked to an
inability to grow up into any kind of relationship. However, fortunately, *Cat
on a Hot Tin Roof* is far more complex than that, for it contains Williams'
most interesting attempt at measuring his characters' troubled relationships
against the potential of an abiding love between two men, an attempt that is
mitigated by Williams' inability, or disinclination, to forge a positive language
for the homosexual love the play tries to affirm.

Cat on A Hot Tin Roof takes place in the bedroom once occupied by
Jack Straw and Peter Ochello, a room that expresses both their affluence and
their differentness: *"It is Victorian with a touch of the Far East,"* with a
"quality of tender light on weathered wood," and dominated by the large
double bed the lovers shared for thirty years. For a change, the homosexual's
environment is created to present a positive picture: *"It is gently and poetically
haunted by a relationship that must have involved a tenderness which was
uncommon."*[21] No hothouse or jungle here! The liberation of the Straw-
Ochello relationship is reflected in the walls, *"which dissolve mysteriously
into air"* (p. 15). But the positive image the love of Jack Straw and Peter
Ochello provides is presented only in the stage directions: otherwise, the si-

lence and invisibility surrounding homosexual desire are maintained. The language we hear is no more positive than the heterosexist discourse that pervades Williams' other work.

The plantation the ailing Big Daddy now controls, which is being fought over by his potential heirs, was inherited from Straw and Ochello. In ways both financial and sexual, the legacy of these two lovers lies at the heart of the play, and the love of Straw and Ochello stands as a counter to the compromised heterosexual relationships we see played out. Straw and Ochello do not carry the freight of negative stereotypes other Williams homosexuals carry: they are not frail, like Blanche DuBois' suicidal husband, nor voracious, like Sebastian Venable; nor are they self-hating, like Skipper, the other homosexual ghost in *Cat on a Hot Tin Roof*. They successfully engaged in the masculine enterprise of operating a large plantation, tying them to a world of masculine discourse and power, not the "feminine" world of artistic sensibility. Yet, beyond the stage directions, there is no positive language for Straw and Ochello, who become in the action of the play the targets for Brick's homophobic diatribes.

Straw and Ochello's heir was Big Daddy Pollitt, the cigar-smoking, virile patriarch who admits to loving only two things, his "twenty-eight thousand acres of the richest land this side of the Valley Nile!" (p. 86) and his handsome, ex-athlete son, Brick, who has turned into a drunken recluse since the death of his best friend, Skipper. Brick externally seems to be one of Williams' studs, but, unlike his father, he cannot play the macho role. The central scene in the play is a violent confrontation between patriarch and troubled son in which Big Daddy tries to get at the truth of Brick's relationship with his friend Skipper.

Williams' stage direction tells the reader that Big Daddy *"leaves a lot unspoken"* (p. 115), as he tells Brick of his young years as a hobo and of being taken in and given a job by Jack Straw and Peter Ochello. The implication of the stage direction, and of other hints Big Daddy gives in the scene, is that homosexual behavior is not alien to Big Daddy, who "knocked around in [his] time" (p. 115). Yet Brick is so terrified of being called "queer," that he cannot listen to what his father is trying to tell him:

BIG DADDY: . . . I bummed, I bummed this country till I was—
BRICK: Whose suggestion, who else's suggestion is it?
BIG DADDY: Slept in hobo jungles and railroad Y's and flophouses in all cities before I—
BRICK: Oh, *you* think so, too, you call me your son and a queer. Oh! Maybe that's why you put Maggie and me in this room that was Jack Straw's and Peter Ochello's, in which that pair of old sisters slept in a double bed where both of 'em died!
BIG DADDY: *Now just don't go throwing rocks at*—(pp. 115–116)

The exchange is a brilliant reversal of expectation: the object of suspicion will not listen to expressions of understanding and tolerance, countering them with heterosexist ranting. Brick is obsessed with his terror of being called a "queer" and conscious of the irony of being expected to perform heterosexually in Straw and Ochello's bed. Big Daddy will allow no attacks on Straw and Ochello, but his defense is interrupted by the appearance of Reverend Tooker, "*the living embodiment of the pious, conventional lie*" (p. 116), which allows Brick's homophobic discourse to dominate the scene. In addition to "queer" and "old sisters," Brick speaks of "sodomy," "dirty things," "dirty old men," "ducking [sic][22] sissies," "unnatural thing," and "*fairies.*" Brick's acceptance of the pious, conventional lie is heard in statements that sound like a caricature of the voice of pious respectability: "Big Daddy, you shock me, Big Daddy, you, you—*shock* me! Talkin' so—casually!—about a—thing like that" (p. 119). Yet his stated reason for his shock is not moral, religious, or psychological; it is public opinion: "Don't you know how people *feel* about things like that? How, how *disgusted* they are by things like that?" (p. 119). It is not Brick's heterosexuality, nor moral, legal or religious strictures that make homosexuality such an appalling concept: it is public opinion. Brick lives in mortal fear of exposure.

Brick's homophobia is the core of his sexual and emotional malaise. He is painfully aware that his nonsexual, nominal marriage to Maggie is a far cry from the total relationship the bed signifies, yet Brick occupies a perilous middle state. He does not love his wife, with whom he claims never to have gotten any closer "than two people just get in bed which is not much closer than two cats on a—fence humping" (p. 123), an echo of Big Daddy's loveless sex with Big Mama and an expression of Brick's inability to combine sex with friendship or love; yet he is horrified at the possible perception of a sexual dimension of his friendship with Skipper: "Why can't exceptional friendship, *real, real, deep, deep friendship* between two men be respected as something clean and decent without being thought of as *Fairies*?" (p. 120).

Like the knowing woman in *Tea and Sympathy*, Maggie, Brick's frustrated wife, understands Brick's malaise, that Brick's friendship with Skipper "was one of those beautiful, ideal things they tell you about in Greek legends, it couldn't be anything else, you being you, and that's what made it so awful, because it was love that never could be carried through to anything satisfying or even talked about plainly" (p. 57). Maggie knows that it is Brick's "ass-aching Puritanism" that puts him in such an unhappy position—that he would be better off if he had had the courage to have a complete relationship with Skipper. Maggie told Skipper the truth: "Stop lovin' my husband or tell him he's got to let you admit it to him" (p. 59). Brick blames Maggie for Skipper's death, but Skipper is dead as a result of his own internalized homophobia, and Brick has, as Big Daddy cogently puts it, "dug the grave of [his] friend and kicked him in it!—before you'd face truth with him!" (p. 125).

The bed of Jack Straw and Peter Ochello represents an unstated ideal relationship that seems unattainable for the heterosexual marriages in Williams play. In positing this ideal, the play is subversive for its time, yet the love of Straw and Ochello never seems a possibility for homosexuals either. It is more of a figure of speech than a matter of fact, and a rather paradoxical figure of speech at that, since the only positive words used to describe the relationship are silent hints in the stage directions. The only operative terminology for homosexuals the play allows is Brick's homophobic discourse.

Just at the moment Big Daddy's dialogue with Brick reaches the crucial issue of Brick's relationship with Skipper, Williams offers a lengthy stage direction:

> *The thing they're discussing, timidly and painfully on the side of Big Daddy, fiercely, violently on Brick's side, is the inadmissible thing that Skipper died to disavow between them. The fact that if it existed it had to be disavowed to "keep face" in the world they lived in, may be at the heart of the "mendacity" that Brick drinks to kill his disgust with. It may be the root of his collapse. Or maybe it is only a single manifestation of it, not even the most important. The bird that I hope to catch in the net of this play is not the solution of one man's psychological problem. I'm trying to catch the true quality of experience in a group of people, that cloudy, flickering, evanescent—fiercely charged!—interplay of five human beings in the thundercloud of a common crisis. Some mystery should be left in the revelation of character in a play, just as a great deal of mystery is always left in the revelation of character in life, even in one's own character to himself. This does not absolve the playwright of his duty to observe and probe as clearly and deeply as he legitimately can: but it should steer him away from "pat" conclusions, facile definitions which make a play just a play, not a snare for the truth of human experience.* (pp. 114–115)

Williams begins this statement with a definite interpretation of Brick's panic that places responsibility on the false values of Brick's world, then hedges his bets by qualifying his interpretation, then moves the focus away from Brick to the problems of five people, and finally dismisses definite interpretations altogether in the name of "mystery." The last sentence of William's little treatise thickens the smokescreen: he wants to offer the truth of human experience without facile conclusions or pat definitions. Fair enough, but Williams seems to worry about such things only when homosexuality rears its problematic head.[23] Of course, his printed warning is not shared with his audience, only with his readers, but it allows him to proceed with a scene about homosexuality while denying that is what he is doing. At the end of his statement, he directs that the scene between Big Daddy and Brick be *"palpable in what is left unspoken"* (p. 115). His concern for the unspoken dominates this scene, and what is unspoken here, and in the rest of the play, is the positive force of the love of Jack Straw and Peter Ochello and the unrealized possibility it represents of a positive discourse about homosexual love.

Yet an article Williams wrote in response to critic Walter Kerr's charge that Williams was too evasive, shows that the playwright's understanding of Brick's malaise was much more specific than his vague stage directions indicate:

> Was Brick a homosexual? He probably—no, I would even say certainly— went no further in physical expression than clasping Skipper's hand across the space between their twin-beds in hotel rooms and yet—his sexual nature was not innately "normal." . . . But Brick's sexual adjustment was, and always must remain, a heterosexual one.[24]

Love is not an operative term for the men in *Cat on a Hot Tin Roof*. It is a word used only by Maggie and Big Mama; the men are left to wonder: "Wouldn't it be funny if it were true?" (pp. 80, 173). Not being able to accept the love of women, the men cannot accept the unspoken option of sexual love between men. Nor can Williams convincingly offer that option. Heterosexual marriage, however, is either the hostility of Big Daddy toward the overbearing Big Mama or the grotesque charade of "normality" performed by Gooper and Mae.

The paradox in Williams' presentation of his homosexual characters is that the feared homosexuality, for which there is no positive language, also has the potential for creativity, sensitivity, and, as we see in Jack Straw and Peter Ochello, abiding love. Yet the positive potential is, more often than not, invisible and, at best, only hinted at.

The distance between Williams's work and heterosexist plays like *The Green Bay Tree* or *Tea and Sympathy* is the artistic gap between popular melodrama and deeply felt poetic drama and the political gap between conventional prejudice and radical (for its time) intervention. Sebastian Venable's driven appetite for boys is a far cry from the semicomic Dulcimer's fastidious possession of Julian, just as Brick's crippling sexual fears are miles from Tom Lee's easily solved adolescent predicament. Williams is always interested in the internal and external powers that police homosexual desire. *Cat on a Hot Tin Roof* was, and remains, an enormously popular play. In it, Williams demonstrates an uncanny sense of how far into alien territory his audience can be taken. Yet a successful contemporary production does depict vividly the inner turmoil of a self-hating closeted homosexual, feeling desire his masculine training has taught him is unmanly. The late Ian Charleson's powerful performance in the 1989 National Theatre production was riveting in its intense portrayal of Brick's rage at himself and his terror at being labeled that which he most fears.

While Brick's conflict with Big Daddy provides the apex of *Cat on a Hot Tin Roof*, the central relationship is that of Brick and Maggie, his frustrated wife. Maggie is infatuated with Brick's physical beauty, the focus of much of the first act, which begins with Brick emerging from the shower. Brick is definitely the object of the gaze, and Maggie's unreciprocated desire for Brick is the central aspect of their relationship. Maggie's objective in the play is to get Brick back into bed with her. The denouement suggests that she will succeed but not that their relationship will ever be one of mutual passion: Brick prefers chaste male companionship. Once again, Williams ends with a compromised version of marriage and procreation, as Brick is forced to turn Maggie's lie about her pregnancy into the truth.

Williams, then, was the great dramatist of the closet, a master of the tactic necessary to present homosexuality at all in a particularly repressive period in American society, the era of John Wayne. A product of an earlier time, he was less successful in the later era, when homosexual desire could be presented openly. When Williams decided, after Stonewall, to move his openly gay characters from exposition to the stage, to give them bodies and voices, he projected himself onto those characters in the same way he previously projected himself onto his female characters. The printed text of *Small Craft Warnings* (1972) contains an introductory essay entitled "Too Personal?" in which Williams states: "It is the responsibility of the writer to put his experience as a being into work that refines it and elevates it and that makes of it an essence that a wide audience can somehow manage to feel in themselves: 'That is true.'"[25] In his most successful work, Williams manages just this balancing act. It is interesting to note that Williams was impelled to write this short treatise on the validity and limits of personal writing as a preface to a script containing an openly homosexual character. After the critical attacks he received in the 1960s, he is anticipating charges that such open homosexuality is "too personal." He may also have anticipated attacks from gay men that his homosexual character was anything but a positive representation.

Quentin, the homosexual character in *Small Craft Warnings*, is immediately seen as out of place in the Pacific Coast bar in which the play is set, not because of his sexuality but because of his effete appearance, which announces him as a stereotypical homosexual out of a 1940s movie: "dressed effetely in a yachting jacket, maroon linen slacks, and silk neck-scarf" (p. 240). Williams has returned us to the stereotype of the homosexual as fop. Quentin's face, "which seems to have been burned thin by a fever that is not of the flesh," makes him a brother to Williams' many aging male beauties, but here the wasting is an outward manifestation of the spiritual desiccation that has resulted from Quentin's sexual promiscuity:

> There's a coarseness, a deadening coarseness, in the experience of most homosexuals. The experiences are quick, and hard, and brutal, and the pattern of them is practically unchanging. Their act of love is like the jabbing of a hypodermic needle to which they're addicted but which is more and more empty of real interest and surprise. This lack of variation and surprise

in their . . . "love life" . . . [*He smiles harshly*] . . . spreads into other areas
of . . . sensibility. (p. 260)

The result of this emptying is finally the loss of the "capacity for being surprised," which is the loss of imagination and the possibility of creation. Rather
than being a component of the artistic sensibility threatened by heterosexuals,
homosexuality now destroys the artist. Quentin speaks of himself here in language of textbook heterosexist "objectivity," which is a far cry from the poetic
treatment of promiscuity we find in the language of Blanche DuBois. Desire
is no longer the opposite of death, the spur to the imagination. Williams said
that "Quentin's long speech was the very *heart* of my life,"[26] laying bare the
playwright's own despair as an artist and as a man who no longer found the
kindness of strangers fulfilling.

As Quentin has lost the "surprise" in his sexual life, so has he lost the
ability to create. He is now a screenwriter who does rewrites and adaptations,
a remove even from the limited originality involved in writing a Hollywood
screenplay. Emotionless sex and second-rate hackwork connect in his assignment to "make blue movies bluer" (p. 256).

The spiritual waning that cripples the artist reduced to writing soft-core
pornography links up here with the inevitable cynicism of the aging homosexual who is so self-hating that he can have sex only with boys who are not
homosexual. Quentin is suffering the physical and spiritual ravages of time,
the great nemesis in Williams' world. Yet he also suffers for his awareness
of the brutality of his sex life. The attraction of youth is the attraction of what
has been lost emotionally, and the attraction to young heterosexuals is a yearn-
ing for the possibility of an alternative to the "coarseness" of homosexual
activity.

Part of that coarseness is the need to keep sex on a financial basis, a matter of distancing and control. The worldly wise Leona, another denizen of the
bar, tells Bobby, the boy Quentin has picked up, to take Quentin's payment: "He
wants to pay you, it's part of his sad routine. It's like doing penance . . . penitence" (p. 258). Quentin's expression of the place of homosexuality as one
cause for his sexual and spiritual malaise is reinforced by echoes from other
characters, who present a pathetic image of homosexuality. Leona tells Quentin:
"I know the gay scene and I know the language of it and I know how full it is of
sickness and sadness; it's so full of sadness and sickness, I could almost be glad
that my little brother died before he had time to be infected with all that sadness
and sickness in the heart of a gay boy" (p. 254).

Bill, the heterosexual stud who lives by his cocksmanship with women,
has to prove himself through fag-bashing: "Y' can't insult 'em, there's no way
to bring 'em down except to beat 'em and roll 'em" (p. 241). He at least sees
homosexuals as victims of determinism: "They can't help the way they are.
Who can?" (p. 242). And Monk, the bartender, does not want gay men in his
bar, because eventually they come in droves: "First thing you know you're

operating what they call a gay bar and it sounds like a bird cage, they're standing three deep at the bar and lining up at the men's room" (p. 264).

The only hope for positive homosexual experience is represented by Bobby, the young man who accompanies Quentin into the bar. Like one of Joe Orton's boys, Bobby, Williams' typical fantasy youth, is omnisexual, able temporarily to equate sex with love and enjoy whatever experience comes his way. Bobby has the sense of wonder Quentin has lost, a function of youth, but lacks the sexual specialization he calls Quentin's "hang-up." But Bobby is not homosexual. He is healthily, polymorphously perverse. Like Joe Orton, Williams could romanticize the possibility of such carefree bisexuality but could not present a positive picture of homosexuality.

The wonder-filled youth in *Vieux Carré* (1977) is a young writer, an autobiographical projection of Williams himself, for whom writing and poverty are primary concerns and sex is almost accidental. The drama, like Williams' first success, *The Glass Menagerie* (1944, pub. 1945), is a memory play narrated by the playwright as a young man, here nameless and, alas, faceless. Like much of Williams' later work, *Vieux Carré* is a desperate mining of memory and early fiction ("The Angel In the Alcove" [1943]) for material for a play. The time is the late thirties, when Williams finally had his first homosexual experiences, and the setting is a boarding house in the Vieux Carré in Williams' beloved New Orleans. While the play seems to present Williams' "coming out," that liberation is at best conditional; for *Vieux Carré* is the most vivid evidence for the consistency of Williams' attitude toward homosexuality. In the 1943 story and the 1977 play, homosexual activity is characterized as "perversions of longing" experienced by the young writer and an artist, Nightingale, who is fatally diseased. The narrator, like Tom in *The Glass Menagerie* ruefully remembering events from his young manhood, focuses on speculations regarding his landlady's judgment of his sexual activity with the artist, Nightingale: "I wonder if she'd witnessed the encounter between the painter and me and what her attitude was toward such—perversions? Of longing?"[27] It is interesting that Williams autobiographical artist-narrator seems to internalize the judgmental woman's attitude toward homosexual acts, as it is interesting that he has to imagine a judgmental audience for his sexual initiation.

The "perversions of longing" briefly shared by "the writer" and Nightingale are enacted more spectacularly, though invisibly, by a photographer in the basement with a penchant for "photo sessions" with nude young men. The denizens of the basement are scalded with boiling water poured through a hole in the kitchen floor by the puritanical landlady.

Williams' point of view toward the action of *Vieux Carré* seems as hopelessly muddled as the action itself. At the end, writer and clarinet player head west as the homosexual artist, Nightingale, breathes his last. Has the writer escaped death through his escape with the musician? Williams' last dramatization of the homosexual artist is his most muddled. The move toward affirmation of love between men is tentative.

Donald Spoto quotes Tennessee Williams' most revealing comment about homosexuality in his work:

> You still want to know why I don't write a gay play? I don't find it necessary. I could express what I wanted to express through other means. I would be narrowing my audience a great deal. . . . I wish to have a broad audience because the major thrust of my work is not sexual orientation. I'm not about to limit myself to writing about gay people.[28]

Williams wrote his major work on the assumption, probably correct, that his audience did not want to know that his plays were, in important ways, built on a closeted sensibility. Awareness of the potential for rejection from one's "audience," led to a series of performances of the closet. Sexual desire for men and rejection of homosexuals are major dimensions of Williams' work, and the "other means" by which Williams expressed homosexuality in his plays are fascinating, if sad. Williams was compelled to write about homosexuality, but equally impelled to rely on the language of indirection and heterosexist discourse. Gaining the acceptance of that broad audience meant denying a crucial aspect of himself.

AMERICAN CLOSET GOTHIC

In 1958, Tennessee Williams contributed a short preface to the published text of William Inge's *The Dark at the Top of the Stairs.* Williams' preface is a strange document, obviously hastily written, but focusing on Inge's predilection for the secrets under middle-American life:

> William Inge, the playwright, like William Inge, the gentleman from Kansas via St. Louis, uses his good manners for their proper dramatic purpose, which is to clothe a reality which is far from surface. This nice, well-bred next-door neighbor, with the accent that belongs to no region except the region of good manners, has begun to uncover a world within a world, and it is not the world that his welcome prepared you to meet, it's a secret world that exists behind the screen of neighborly decorum.[29]

This faint praise by William Inge's mentor, friend, one-time lover, and rival[30] could be a description of the exposure and misery of the closet that is the focus of two of William Inge's one-act plays, in which the use of the closet only supports the impossibility of coming out for his spineless secret homosexuals and the inability to imagine a positive image of homosexuality for their creator.

Like Tennessee Williams, Inge was more successful at writing plays in which sexual desire for a man is focal but displaced onto female characters than he was in writing about homosexual characters themselves, as he did in his later, weaker plays, *Natural Affection* (1963) and *Where's Daddy* (1966).

In *Come Back, Little Sheba* (1949) and *Picnic* (1953), the male is the object of the gaze. Turk, the young athlete in *Come Back, Little Sheba* (1950), poses in his track suit for his girlfriend's drawings, and attention is called to the fact that he's not nude: "The women pose naked, but the men don't. If it's all right for a woman, it oughta be for a man."[31] Marie, the coed who sleeps with Turk, rejects him for a more stable, less sexual man, an inversion of the gender roles in the usual drama of the double standard. In *Picnic* (1953), the working-class stud, Hal, who is the focus of attention, appears "bare chested . . . wearing his T-shirt wrapped about his neck."[32] Hal is the prototype of the "straight" drifter-gigolo Williams developed in *Orpheus Descending* (1957) and *Sweet Bird of Youth* (1959), a heterosexualization of the saintly hustler who looms large in Williams' short stories. In Inge's plays, this semi-clad, hypermasculine character is the unsettling force, the outsider who leaves the stage before the play's conclusion.

During the 1950s, the period of his greatest Broadway successes, Inge wrote two one-act plays literally about the "place" of the homosexual; *The Tiny Closet* and *The Boy in the Basement* (both published in 1962). Inge's biographer, Ralph Voss, speculates that the plays, which show a willingness to deal openly and sympathetically with homosexuality not seen in Inge's commercial work, were probably written more as exercises related to Inge's psychoanalysis then as scripts to be produced.[33] The form of the plays, with their heavy, realistic scenic requirements (elaborate for such short plays), also suggests that Inge did not write them for production: they are more short stories written as scripts. Were it not for their subject matter, which would have made production impossible, they could be seen as drafts for television scripts. These two plays seem to be "closet dramas" in more ways than one. Both are dramatizations of shattering invasions of the secret life of lonely homosexual men. They are also symptomatic of Inge's difficulty in tying his homosexuality to received definitions of manhood.

The Tiny Closet takes place in a boarding house in a midwestern city. Its Victorian vintage and decor reflect the values of its inhabitants and its landlady. One of the inhabitants, Mr. Newbold, is, we are told, "always impeccably dressed. . . . He is the sort of man who takes great pride in his grooming."[34] He is also the best behaved of the boarders, a grown-up version of "The Best Little Boy in the World":

> You keep your room spotless, and you're always so correct around the house. My, you're a model guest. You really are. You should open up a class out here at the night school they have for adults and teach 'em how to behave in their rooming houses. The landladies in this town would get together and thank you. (p. 191)

The prissy, well-behaved, aging Mama's boy, Newbold, is obviously, by these signs, homosexual, and his landlady's excessive effusiveness belies suspicion: "If you ask me, it's kinda unnatural for a man to be so tidy" (p. 194). With the introduction of the word unnatural, we're in the realm of heterosexist discourse, which will increasingly be turned against Newbold.

At the beginning of the play, Newbold is very upset at the thought that someone might have looked in his closet: "Mrs. Crosby, a closet is a very small space. That's all I ask in this life. That's all I ask, just that tiny closet to call my own, my very own" (p. 190). Newbold's protection of this private space is enough to whet the landlady's appetite and fire up her moral fervor and unconscious gift for paradox: "I'm a real American, and I say, if anyone's got any secrets he wants to keep hid, let him come out in the open and declare himself" (p. 194). To protect America, the landlady and her friend invade Mr. Newbold's closet. Newbold, expecting such an invasion, has snuck back into the house:

> *He has suspected the two women to do exactly what they're doing. He is very nervous. His heart is pounding. He starts up the stairs and then comes down again. He can't seem to get the courage to confront the women. The starch he showed earlier in the play has dissolved. He is perspiring heavily and twisting his hands in fear and excitement. In a few moments we hear the women on their way downstairs.* MR. NEWBOLD *hurriedly finds a closet to hide in.* (p. 196)

What the ladies find in Mr. Newbold's closet are dozens of beautiful women's hats that Mr. Newbold has painstakingly made for himself. The women bring one of the hats downstairs to admire, but the hats' beauty only underscores hat-making as a subversive activity for a man:

> Why a man who'd make hats and lock them up in a closet, there's no telling what kind of a person he is. He might do any kind of dangerous, crazy thing. . . . I'd rather he was a Communist. At least you know what a Communist is up to. But a man who makes hats? What can you tell about such a creature? (p. 198)

When the women leave, Mr. Newbold emerges from the closet *"shattered"* . . . *"He has become a shy and frightened young girl"* (p. 199). At the end of the play, he puts on a hat and looks at himself in the mirror, but he can no longer find any joy or comfort in posing before the mirror in one of his beautiful hats: *"He drops the hat onto a chair, then himself falls onto the sofa and cries like a helpless child"* (p. 200). Newbold's psychic survival depends on keeping his private self, which is a feminine self, in the closet. Ironically, it is women who cannot find a space for a man who finds joy in

creating and wearing feminine accessories. Inge has presented Newbold's secret self and his collapse through visual images, particularly of the closet in
which Newbold keeps his secret and the downstairs closet in which he hides
after the women have found the hats. Once his closet is invaded, an act that
merely forces him into another closet, there is no longer any space for Newbold, and neither his "performance" as a man nor his fantasies of femininity
offer any comfort. He is, at the end, literally a "hopeless child," asexual and
terrified.

There is no mention of any sexual life for Mr. Newbold. His fantasy
defies gender definitions of appropriate behavior but does not transgress the
boundaries of desire. Yet his wish to dress as a woman is considered subversive and would have been be read as homosexuality. His danger is in his wish
to identify himself privately as a woman. According to the landlady, America
itself is threatened by such blurring of sexual boundaries. It is easy to read
The Tiny Closet biographically, but what is more interesting for our purposes
is how codified Inge's presentation of Newbold's plight is. The closeted man
is a "girl," not even a full grown woman, suggesting femininity but also
presexual innocence. What is feminine is artistic and beautiful but must be
kept literally in the closet. *The Tiny Closet* is an expression of the anxieties
of a homosexual writer who is afraid that even his artistic expression, his
plays, will expose the homosexuality that will destroy his fragile image of
masculinity and bring him, not praise, but rejection. There is here a real ambivalence about the very public position of the playwright, whose work must
be seen and who has, after all, chosen not to operate in a private sphere. Inge
despises the guardians of American morality who "out" Mr. Newbold, but he
can see Newbold only as a pitiable victim who capitulates to prevailing values.

Spencer Scranton, the middle-aged undertaker in *The Boy in the Basement*, is not as asexual as Mr. Newbold. Spencer is an undertaker, living and
working in another Victorian house "of fussy dignity."[35] Spencer still lives
with his invalid father and his powerful, righteous mother. His only personal
space is the basement where he embalms the dead bodies: "One dead body
after another. That's all my life is" (p. 173). His only moments of freedom
are his weekends in Pittsburgh, where he visits gay bars. Unfortunately, on
his last trip, Spencer was arrested and had to have his mother wire two hundred
dollars, ostensibly to repair the car but really to bribe the arresting officer so
that Spencer would not be put in jail and in the local papers. The only bright
spot in Spencer's weekday life in his Victorian prison is the regular visit of
Joker Evans, the eighteen-year-old grocery-delivery boy who sees Spencer as
a "pal," and whom Spencer obviously adores, though he is careful to perform
a kind of hearty he-man role for Joker. But Joker, for all his fond joshing and
heart-to-heart confidences, sees Spencer as a pal because he sees Spencer as
another kid: "I bet in some ways you never grew up, Spence . . . In some ways,
Spence, you're like a kid, too" (p. 173). When Spencer's mother returns home
in a fit of fury and self-pity, having discovered where her money went on the

previous weekend, Spencer musters the courage to leave home. But Spencer's brief escape from home is nothing more than an adolescent spurt of defiance and freedom. The next morning he returns home "defeated" (p. 179) and embraces his mother: *"Undoubtedly, this is the only person* SPENCER *truly loves"* (p. 180). Right after he returns, the body of Joker Evans, drowned while skinny-dipping with some friends, is delivered for preparation for burial. While his mother asks what he wants for breakfast, Spencer, in his basement, faces Joker's naked body, kisses Joker's hand *"warmly"* and prepares to sever the boy's arteries, *"the hardest thing he has ever had to do in his life."*

In *The Boy in the Basement*, Spencer's homosexuality is demonstrated not by effeminacy but by his arrested development and adoration of a domineering mother, the classic Freudian stereotype. Like Newbold, Spencer is not capable of real strength of will. He will continue to live as his mother's son, even denied the secrecy of his trips to the Pittsburgh bars. His infatuation with Joker Evans is adoration of the embodiment of a masculine normality and an adolescent freedom Spencer can appreciate only vicariously: "You were alive. Jesus! And I wanted you to stay that way" (p. 184). Spencer's homosexuality gives him his only real moment of tenderness, his kissing of Joker's hand, and his only moments of freedom from his mother's domination, but it is not connected to any possibility for happiness or fulfillment. Mother is the primary love object, and Spencer's love for Joker is partly longing for the freedom Joker's youth and heterosexuality afforded him.

In these sad little plays, Inge's homosexuals conduct their lives outside, within, or under "normal" human activities—in closets or basements—and their lives are severely crippled by the sexuality that separates them from the rest of society. At their most articulate, they can only idealize what they cannot have. "Normality" is a performance Mr. Newbold and Spencer must continue if they are to have any happiness at all. Mr. Newbold survives by playing "the good boy," and Spencer can engage convincingly in man-to-man banter, though the real self is in a closet or a Pittsburgh gay bar or a basement embalming room. Manhood is just an act covering the fragile ego of a prissy old maid or a pathetic mama's boy. Underneath the performance, there is no possibility of happiness or of an integrated personality for Inge's homosexuals. Yet Inge's realism allows no space for "normal" heterosexuality either. Mr. Newbold lives in a world of women, and Spencer's vision of normality is killed, the usual fate of the homosexual.

The plays exist as explanations of Inge's own unhappy closetedness. They are expressions of despair and misdirected anger. Surprisingly, they posit women as the cause of homosexual self-hatred, which was the result, perhaps of too much Freudian analysis. Yet when Inge tried, later, to write openly gay characters, the results were even more pathetic, as one can see in Inge's version of the pederastic relationship in *Where's Daddy* (1966), a play that brings us almost full circle from *The Green Bay Tree*.

In *Where's Daddy*, Professor "Pinky" Pinkerton, a fat, middle-aged homosexual professor, is—and any irony here is clearly unintentional—the spokesman for "traditional family values." Pinky picked up fifteen-year-old Tom Keen when Tom was an orphaned hustler. The pick-up lasted years, as Pinky became surrogate father as well as lover, paying for Tom's acting lessons and cosmetic improvements. Like Dulcimer in *The Green Bay Tree*, Pinky created something of a monster in Tom, though a heterosexual monster; a self-centered, emotionally limited man who now is going to leave his pregnant wife because a baby might spoil his career chances. Tom's personal limitations are not, like Julian's in *The Green Bay Tree*, the result of being raised by a homosexual: rather they are the effects of his parentless childhood and of the essential vapidity of being an actor.[36] Tom wants to go back to Pinky, which would be a return to immaturity and irresponsibility, but Pinky refuses to take him back, not out of vengeance because of Tom's relationship with a woman, but because Tom should face up to his heterosexual obligations: "You are about to become a father. That means you can no longer be a boy. . . . It's a terrifying step to take, Tom. Some of us never take it, but just grow up into old boys, and go through our lives without dignity or bearing. Take the step, Tom. I beg you. And take your part in this life as a man."[37]

Inge may have finally allowed a homosexual character out of the closet, but only to present the Freudian psychiatrist's view of homosexuality as arrested development. Pinky sees that a homosexual can only grow into an undignified old boy, a living contradiction. The good homosexual believes that "marriage between a man and a woman is a divinely beautiful institution" (p. 62), a sentimentalized, idealized view of heterosexual relationships that denies any possibility of a mature homosexual relationship (the only model for a homosexual relationship is pederasty, with the older man trying to hold onto his lost youth through a boy, preferably a heterosexual boy). Essentially, Pinky's point of view refuses to grant any space to the homosexual. Pinky is a mechanism of abnegation, courting approval of the audience for his awareness of his own inferiority. As a mentor, he must pass onto his ephebe "the truth" about heterosexuality, which inevitably equates with maturity. This is a far cry from the shameless possessiveness of Dulcimer, which looks more and more attractive as one examines the alternatives.

While idealizing heterosexuality, the only language Inge finds for homosexual behavior is that of the outraged mother in *The Boy in the Basement*: "Going to some disgusting saloon, where men meet other men and join together in . . . some form of unnatural vice, in some form . . . of lewd depravity." (p. 177) The moralistic language may seem foolish, even cruel, but it is no more destructive than Pinky's masochistic sentimentalization of heterosexuality. Inge's plays, then, dramatize the closet and are themselves dramatizations of the closet mentality.

The works of William Inge and Tennessee Williams are closet dramas in their evasions, silences, and invisibilites and in heterosexist language with which they surround their homosexual characters. They are also plays about the closet itself and about the terrors of being uncloseted. There isn't much difference between Inge's prissy, effeminate Mr. Scranton, cowering and crying like a child when his closet door is opened, and Williams' macho Brick Pollitt, ranting homophobic epithets to silence the possibility of his father's acceptance of a homosexual bond between Brick and Skipper. Opening the closet door, particularly in the heyday of Williams and Inge, makes one vulnerable to the rejections, insults, and outright violence associated with heterosexism, of which Scranton is a victim and Brick a perpetrator. Not everyone is as tolerant as Big Daddy. Not everyone's closet is the bedroom of a gay couple.

Coming out, in the plays of Williams and Inge, could be linked only to expressions of self-hatred. The playwrights had too successfully internalized the attitudes of their audiences and reviewers. Yet the complex means with which Williams and Inge managed to raise the specter of homosexuality in their earlier, closeted, better work suggests that the restrictions of the dramatic closet were salutary, perhaps necessary, to their writing. It is their rich response to the closet and their mastery of its evasions and projections that made Williams and Inge, in differing degrees, successful writers. For Williams, it was his gift of projecting his personality onto his successful female characters that distinguished his best work: "This mental transvestism is a major key to Williams' art and one of the homosexual artist's principal stratagems for achieving universality."[38] It is also an acceptance of the antipodean relationship of homosexuality and masculinity. "Real men" can be the object of male desire. They can be "trade"—heterosexual men who allow homosexuals to "service" them sexually, usually for a fee. They can also be tortured, repressed homosexuals. But any love between men must be kept offstage. Williams could express his hints of homosexuality more freely than Inge because he was not as trapped in the conventions of realism. His descriptions of settings repeatedly make the point that his plays were not to be visualized realistically. This freed him from the narrative conventions of realistic drama and also gave him the "out" of claiming that his openings of the closet door were part of theatrical, poetic fantasies. In addition to the "mental transvestism" he shared with Williams, Inge had the ability to project a sense of claustrophobia, of compromises characters make for the sake of appearances. When Inge and Williams moved the homosexual subtext from the closet of exposition to the open stage, when they removed the maskings and subterfuges—theatrical tools, after all—which in part made their works interesting, they foundered as playwrights. They couldn't write overtly gay plays that were in any way affirming.

OUTING, THE CRITICS, AND EDWARD ALBEE

The closet was an agreement between playwright and audience and between playwright and critical establishment. Academic critics did not touch upon areas that were to be kept silent or disguised. Even gay critics managed to write about Williams and Inge without violating their artistic disguises: the closets that were created and maintained by academia and the heterosexism that was rife in literary, and particularly dramatic studies, could fill another volume.

For decades, the works of Tennessee Williams, with their not-very-subtle homosexual codes, were celebrated by New York reviewers. In the wane of the brief heyday of American drama, Williams and Inge represented substantial playwrights who could merge art and commerce, a necessity for reviewers, as well as for producers and theater owners. The considerable success of the sanitized film versions of their plays (usually the sanitizing entailed ludicrous attempts to remove all hints of homosexuality from the original Broadway hits) made both playwrights as close to household words as playwrights can become in the United States. The theater needed these playwrights as much as they needed the theater.

By 1963, Williams and Inge had lost some of their control over their material. The closet door was, perhaps unintentionally, opened by the wane in the playwrights' work. The homosexual subtext became less carefully hidden. In Inge's case, his focus on pathological Oedipal relationships and sensitive young men instead of on the macho men and repressed women of his fifties plays raised red flags for critics. Mama's boys meant homosexuals. The cartoonlike middle-aged women and saintly hustlers who began to dominate Williams' plays made homosexual decoding inevitable. And his heroines had aged, making them seem more autobiographical.

One can see from the critical response to the later plays of Williams and Inge, and particularly to the Broadway plays of Edward Albee, that a number of critics saw themselves as guardians of the dramatic closet. By 1963 it was time to warn audiences of the pernicious influences of closeted homosexual drama. In 1963, Howard Taubman, then the *New York Times* reviewer, wrote a "Primer," as a "public service": "Helpful hints on how to scan the intimations and symbols of homosexuality in our theater." Taubman cites Inge's unfortunate melodrama of a son's murderous Oedipal fixation, *Natural Affection* (1963), as a palpable example of a play with "homosexual content," as if any play with a pathologically Oedipal young man who is violent toward women is inevitably homosexual in content, a stereotypical view, to say the least. *Natural Affection* does have one character who feels homosexual desire for another man. But the play is an easy target—a bad play whatever its sexual dynamics. Taubman is more interested in pointing out the hallmarks of insidious, *disguised* homosexual dramas. His telltale signs of homosexuality are worth noting:

Look out for the male character who is young, handsome, remote and lofty
in a neutral way. . . .

Be on guard for the male character whose proclivities are like a stallion's.

Beware the husband who hasn't touched his wife for years.

Beware the woman who hasn't been touched by her husband for years.

Look out for the baneful female who is a libel on womanhood.

Look out for the hideous wife who makes a horror of the marriage relationship.

Be suspicious of the compulsive slut . . . who represents a total disenchant-
ment with the possibility of a fulfilled relationship between man and
woman.

Be alert to scabrous innuendo about the normal male-female sexual relationship.[39]

Taubman concludes by lamenting, "if only we could recover our lost innocence and could believe that people on the stage are what they are supposed
to be!" (p. 1). What does it mean to demand that fictional dramatic characters
be "what they are supposed to be," unless they are supposed to be heterosexual
and to support a myth of universal heterosexual happiness and harmony—the
myth of "normality?"

Taubman's warning signs could make his reader suspicious of an enormous amount of "heterosexual" drama, particularly of plays by the *Times'*
favorite, Eugene O'Neill, as well as most of Tennessee Williams' work (Taubman's warnings describe *A Streetcar Named Desire* and *Cat on a Hot Tin
Roof*, among other plays).[40] However, there was one play on Broadway at the
time of Taubman's diatribe that is clearly his target: Edward Albee's *Who's
Afraid of Virginia Woolf?* (1962), which had been running since the previous
October. The "aloof, lofty" Nick claims that he will "plow a few pertinent
faculty wives," though he plans to mount faculty wife Martha not like a stallion but "like a goddamn dog."[41] And Martha could be interpreted as "making
a horror of the marriage relationship"; she also claims to be a compulsive slut.
Moreover, *Who's Afraid of Virginia Woolf?* could be said to be filled with
"scabrous innuendo about the normal male-female sexual relationship," though
the scabrous commentary on marriage goes far beyond innuendo.

In the sort of move reserved for homosexuality in the dramas of the
closet we have discussed, Taubman defines *Who's Afraid of Virginia Woolf?*
as a closet drama, yet, by not mentioning which play he is talking about,
keeps the play in the closet. He will mention the unsuccessful *Natural Affection* by name but keeps the hit play shrouded in innuendo. Is he afraid of
accusing the large audiences for Albee's play of guilt by association?

In covertly singling out Albee's excoriating attack on the state of American domestic bliss, Taubman attempts to invalidate the play's satire by re-
ducing it to a homosexual code and, at the same time, maintaining the myth
of "normal male-female sexual relationships" the play explodes. Perhaps the

play hit a nerve in Mr. Taubman that forced him to protect his readers from its pernicious, corrupting influence. Readers needn't worry: Albee's play is *really* about inevitably miserable homosexual relationships, not inevitably happy heterosexual marriages. The belief that homosexuals know nothing about heterosexual marriage, therefore cannot write "truthfully" about it, is one of the most inane weapons in the heterosexist critic's arsenal. Where, after all, do homosexuals come from? They are raised and learn about marriage through spending their childhood and adolescence in heterosexual households. That seventeen or so years of experience should provide some grist for later fiction.

Taubman's covert caveats became interpretive clichés about Albee's play, even inspiring Ingmar Bergman to create a Swedish production in which George and Martha were played by men. Albee was not going to "get away with" the adaptations and transformations allowed Williams and Inge. He had dared to attack too many sacred cows and shibboleths of the American middle class. Yet, despite an overwrought film adaptation and the critical attempt to marginalize the play, *Who's Afraid of Virginia Woolf?* has become a "standard," revived often by professional and amateur theaters across the country.

While Albee's off-Broadway plays, *Zoo Story* (1959), *The Death of Bessie Smith* (1960), and *The American Dream* (1961) had made the playwright critically fashionable, the closeted homosexuality in his Broadway productions inspired the ire of the critics. There was, it seemed, one set of standards for Broadway, another for adventurous off Broadway.

Brickbats were hurled at Albee by respected members of the artistic left. Richard Schechner, soon to be guru of the New York University School of Drama and of sixties avant-garde theater, proclaimed in his journal, *Tulane Drama Review* (later to become TDR), the house organ of the theatrical left: "I'm tired of morbidity and sexual perversity which are there only to titillate an impotent and homosexual theater and audience. I'm tired of Albee."[42] The context was a jeremiad against *Who's Afraid of Virginia Woolf?*—to Schechner a dangerous example of dramatic "decadence," "which is likely to have an infective and corrosive influence on our theater."[43] Schechner's choice of metaphors of disease and destructive chemical reaction was typical of the tactics of those who warned against the threat of homosexuality. One can see more vividly in his diatribe than in Taubman's cautious warning the sense of danger and infection the supposed homosexual subtext in Albee's plays inspired. In an extension of the old superstition that pernicious influence can make an unsuspecting soul homosexual—homosexuality as vampirism—it was believed that Albee could taint and corrupt the American theater itself as well as individual audience members.

Albee's next original play, produced in 1965, was *Tiny Alice* (the adaptation of Carson McCuller's *Ballad of the Sad Cafe* intervened). It lit a fire under novelist Philip Roth, the bard of masturbation and Jewish sexual neurosis: "The disaster of the play, however—its tendentiousness, its pretentiousness, its galling sophistication, its gratuitous and easy symbolizing, its ghastly pansy rhetoric and repartee—all of this can be traced to its own unwillingness to put its real subject at the center of the action."[44] *Tiny Alice* is really a "homosexual daydream" (of course Roth is an expert on those) in which a celibate man in skirts is seduced by a strong woman, betrayed by a male lover, and killed by a representative of the law.

Like Schechner, Roth cites Jean Genet as a model for homosexual playwrights. Most of Genet's plays received off-Broadway productions during the fifties and sixties with some degree of success. But, while Genet was openly homosexual in his memoirs and fiction, his plays, except *Deathwatch*, were no more overtly homosexual than Albee's *Tiny Alice*, which bears some marks of Genet's influence. Genet explored the metaphoric potential of some aspects of the gay experience—drag and camp—but totally outside the conventions of naturalistic theater. The celebration of Genet was partly a result of his status as a chic European playwright outside the loop of commercial theater. It was absurd to think that Genet's linkage of homosexuality with criminality and marginal social status could provide a model of appropriate uncloseted behavior for an American homosexual. Nor could his plays offer a model for a commercial American playwright. The subtext of the invocations of Genet by Albee's detractors is that gay theater belongs off Broadway and that gay men belong outside the mainstream.

Roth calls for an uncloseted homosexual drama: "How long before a play is produced on Broadway in which the homosexual hero is presented as a homosexual, and not disguised as an *angst*-ridden priest, or an angry Negro, or an aging actress; or worst of all, Everyman?"[45] Perhaps the answer is that openly gay drama would be possible when critics stop using words like "pansy." Roth praises Genet but denies Albee the right to the kind of displacements that dominate Genet's drama. He doesn't want magic, he wants realism as pedestrian as his own. It should not be surprising that the chronicler of neurotic heterosexual males should be disturbed by homosexuals invading his turf.

A year after Roth's diatribe, Stanley Kauffman, the new *Times* drama critic, raised the subject of "disguised" homosexual drama again, this time following Roth's example of virulent heterosexism tinging a plea for an openly homosexual theater. On January 23, 1966, eleven days after Albee's adaptation of James Purdy's novel, *Malcolm*, opened to critical brickbats, Stanley Kauffmann's column, "Homosexual Drama and Its Disguises," appeared on the front page of the Sunday *Times*' "Arts and Leisure" section. Kauffman's article was inspired not by Albee's failed work alone but also by the imminent arrival on Broadway of plays by Williams (*Slapstick Tragedies*) and Inge (*Where's Daddy*). None of these plays, as it turned out, would need Kauffmann's help in failing, but it is interesting that this sort of attack would appear in advance of Williams' and Inge's openings.

Kauffmann began by noting that "all of us admirably 'normal' people wish [the subject of homosexuality] would disappear," but since "three of the most successful American playwrights of the past twenty years are (reputed) homosexuals and because their plays often treat of women and marriage,"[46] the subject must be raised. That "reputed" in parentheses looks like a lawyer's addition, but it reflected the *Times'* inability to admit that anyone really was or could be homosexual, a myth the playwrights in question publicly supported.

What bothered Kauffmann was the *"disguised* homosexual influence." He could understand how playwrights, because of the "defiant and/or protective histrionism they must employ in their daily lives" were drawn (passive construction, of course) to the theater. Here superstition and universalizing have already pigeonholed the homosexual and, at the same time, created a paranoid fantasy. Either there are very few homosexuals, since he could allude to only three playwrights, or there are millions being "drawn to" the theater, armed and ready to undermine "normal" life. While Kauffmann could blame society for forcing homosexuals to dissemble, to write plays "streaked with vindictiveness toward the society that constricts and, theatrically, discriminates against them," and while he could forgive "their distortion of marriage and femininity," since "the marital quarrels are usually homosexual quarrels with one of the pair in costume and . . . the incontrovertibly female figures are drawn less in truth than in envy or fear," he drew the line at camp, though he kept the term in the closet along with the playwrights' names. The real crime of homosexual playwrights is that they "exalt style, manner, surface. They decry artistic concern with the traditional matters of theme and subject because they are prevented from using fully the themes of their own experience." While this wildly inaccurate generalization dismisses or reduces the "matters of theme or subject" in Williams', Inge's, and Albee's major work because they were homosexual and leaves them only surface, Kauffmann, with no sense of the irony involved, then joined the chorus of praise for Jean Genet as "one of the few contemporary dramatists whose works are candidates for greatness," because Genet "is a homosexual who has never had to disguise his nature."

I describe Kauffmann's column in detail because it is a prime example of the heterosexist attacks that plagued homosexual playwrights in the decade before Stonewall, an echo as well of some of the posthumous attacks Joe Orton's work received. Moreover, Kauffmann was considered by some an "intellectual" critic of the *New York Review of Books* variety, one who represented a more thoughtful, reflective brand of analysis than newspapers usually offered. But liberal, "intellectual" critics were the most avid exponents of heterosexism. It was, after all, in the *New York Review of Books* that Roth's attack appeared. Kauffmann's column is a classic example of the mixed signals that entrapped American playwrights: a few liberal posturings about society's responsibility for the closet, as if Kauffmann himself weren't maintaining the closet, followed by gross oversimplifications that dismiss the work of the dramatists in question, followed by praise of Genet.

Two weeks later, in response to a spate of angry letters that pointed out the gross oversimplifications in his column, Kauffmann wrote a sequel that softened the heterosexism and raised the volume on the liberal white noise: "I mean simply (to repeat) that homosexual dramatists need the same liberty that heterosexuals now have."[47] Kauffmann's response when homosexual dramatists took the liberty he offered them can be seen in his review, in the *Saturday Review*, of Martin Sherman's *Bent* (1979), in which he consistently, almost defiantly, referred to the characters as "queers."[48] For Kauffmann, Harvey Fierstein's *Torch Song Trilogy* (1981), which places gay experiences squarely within the patterns of heterosexual marriage and child-rearing "is not the first valuable, nonvindictive work, but it takes first place in the field so far" after years of "artistic trash and social vengeance."[49]

Clearly these critics were most offended in the sixties by Edward Albee's work and took it upon themselves to unmask Albee's "vindictiveness," dismiss his considerable strengths as a playwright, and reduce his plays to homosexual codes. Yet postliberation gay critics, with their own, very different agenda have been eager to ride the same hobby horse. In his pioneering study of homosexuality in American literature, Georges-Michel Sarotte goes further than Albee's detractors:

> *Who's Afraid of Virginia Woolf?* . . . is a homosexual play from every point of view, in all its situations and in all its symbols. It is a heterosexual play only in outward appearance, since in 1962 it had to reach the mass public, and also because Albee *does not want* to write a homosexual work. However, as is the case with all homosexual writers, his obsessions emerge, despite all he can do, to color and contravene his best intentions.[50]

Sarotte makes Albee a homosexual in spite of himself. His supposedly affirming thesis is that homosexual writers cannot closet themselves: the "truth" of their vision and experience will out. This universalizing removes from the writer any will and any control over his work. It is a kind of extreme Freudianism in which the subconscious of the author will dominate all his writing. It also reduces Albee's play (and many other works Sarotte discusses) to only one subject and reduces Albee to his homosexuality. If *Who's Afraid of Virginia Woolf?* is only a lengthy feud of two homosexual couples, a better written Mart Crowley's *Boys in the Band* (1968), it is nothing more than the testament to homosexual self-hatred its detractors see. But Sarotte had already one-upped heterosexist critics by titling his chapter on William Inge "Homosexual Spite."

Canadian playwright and drag artist Sky Gilbert echoes Howard Taubman's critique from a militant gay point of view. Like Taubman, he catalogs identifying characteristics of closet drama, "all of which are present in *Who's*

Afraid of Virginia Woolf?," which Gilbert calls "Albee's great closet gay play":[51]

> 1. A quiet, intellectual, slightly effeminate, autobiographical male hero with little or no personality and a mysterious past. . . . The leading character in these cases is, in actuality, a gay man, but because the writer has refused to reveal this, the character remains mysterious, not very fleshed out, but with certain, obvious, stereotypical gay characteristics. 2. Misogyny. The female characters are in effect men in drag, but because the writer is not honest about this, the presentation of women is sexist and misogynistic. 3. Unrealistic and not very closely observed heterosexual relationships that resemble gay ones. Sure, heterosexuals act like this, but this is not a closely observed heterosexual relationship; it is a closely observed gay relationship masquerading as a straight one. So the observations are less piquant, less truthful, more off-putting and confusing.[52]

According to Gilbert, the closeted Albee does justice neither to the heterosexual relationships he claims to be depicting nor to the homosexual relationships he cannot help but depict. What he is hiding is an antigay play, not just a portrait of a gay relationship: "Not only is the play about gay men, it is a critique of their lifestyles and presents many of Albee's antigay feelings, but buried deep inside the closet."[53]

Albee has been attacked from all sides: by Kauffmann for being closeted and, therefore, distorting the truth of heterosexual relationships and by Gilbert for being closeted and, therefore, distorting the truth about heterosexual relationships, women, and homosexual relationships. Yet Albee's plays seem less about sexuality, either homo- or hetero-, than do the more naturalistic plays of Williams and Inge, in which sexual desire is the overt focus. As Foster Hirsch observes: "Typically, sexual drives in Albee become transfigured into mock-religious acts of sacrifice, penitence, immolation; sex is incorporated into a lofty, symbolic framework. . . . Albee's characters customarily use sex either as a deadly weapon in ferocious marital battles, or else abstain from it altogether."[54] Sex in Albee involves recollection of adolescent freedom; for his adults, it is a diminished thing or a weapon. It is linked not to fertility but to sterility: George and Martha's childlessness, Honey's abortions, Tobias' "spilling his seed" in *A Delicate Balance* (1966). It is not the motivating desire, the agent of chaos, the underlying "truth" that it is in Williams and Inge. To some extent, Albee's plays are interesting because they question the very assumptions of naturalism—rationality, the belief in a "truth" one can grasp, the primacy of sexuality. Critics tied this skepticism, this nihilism, to Albee's sexuality in ways that denied him anything but his homosexuality and looked for homosexual codes where they were perhaps present but not central. They refused to acknowledge the potential validity of Albee's insistence that loneliness and emptiness are universal conditions. That's all right for heterosexual Eugene O'Neill to say, but from a homosexual it is an impertinence.

However, Albee's peek-a-boo alternation of overt references to homosexuality and subsequent denial of homosexuality only tantalized his heterosexist detractors (in the fifties and early sixties gay audiences for the most part were happy with any hint they could get). It didn't take a philosopher to discover that Albee was not so much a philosophical nihilist as no philosopher at all: this is no crime. Playwrights are seldom philosophers and philosophers are even more rarely playwrights. Albee's detractors had a point. Ultimately, what Albee shared with Williams and Inge was that the very elements that make his better plays so theatrically vibrant are those that make them the closeted gay dramas both gay and straight critics agree they are.[55] These are not the only aspects of the plays but account for their power more than the rehashes of truisms about the alienation of modern man.

In *Zoo Story* (1959), which some critics have read as a bizarre homosexual encounter, the "intruder," Jerry, admits that at age fifteen, during an eleven-day affair:

> I was a h-o-m-o-s-e-x-u-a-l. I mean I was queer . . . queer, queer, queer . . . with bells ringing, banners snapping in the wind. . . . I think I was very much in love . . . maybe just with sex. But that was jazz of a very special hotel, wasn't it? And now; do I love the little ladies; really, I love them. For about an hour.[56]

Jerry's adolescent romance was the closest thing to love he has ever felt, but he still claims heterosexuality, though he is incapable of more than a one-night stand with the "little ladies." Heterosexuality seems an accommodation in a world that demands the compromise of unhappy heterosexuality, though it is a world in which "GOD IS A COLORED QUEEN WHO WEARS A KIMONO AND PLUCKS HIS EYEBROWS" (p. 18). Jerry wants Peter to acknowledge and understand his world of marginal people, yet he denies the homosexuality that marginalizes him. The mock sexual and religious crucifixion that ends the play, with its sexual pun, "I came unto you (*He laughs, so faintly*) and you have comforted me" (p. 26), is nominally an example of the combination of love and cruelty that Jerry claims is "the teaching emotion" (p. 19). If *Zoo Story* has a homosexual subtext, it is one of thwarted love through the self-hatred of denied, closeted homosexuality, but the negativism is directed at the homosexual. Homosexual love is an adolescent idyll; adult reality is heterosexual promiscuity combined with misogyny and fear of commitment, or unhappy, castrating marriage and routine. "What is gained," Jerry says in his story of the dog, "is loss," but is that loss as inevitable as Albee thinks? Only if heterosexuality is inevitable.

In William Inge's plays, the beautiful young man was the image and agent of liberation. In Williams' plays, the beautiful young man was the martyr to sexual desire. Both playwrights idealized and sentimentalized male beauty. The dream of their hunks is Hollywood, that apex of narcissism and factory for American dreams, but they are too nice and too innocent to succeed in such a predatory environment. The unfeeling, narcissistic hunk who is the American dream in Albee's 1961 play of the same name is a Freudian nightmare, a result of the classic pattern of domineering, castrating mother and ineffectual father. He is a loveless sexual receptacle, the receiver of the gaze and nothing more. He is the opposite of his twin brother, who was dismembered for not focusing all his attention on his monstrous parents. Albee's title, *The American Dream*, presents this spiritually sterile hunk as an image of cultural aspiration, but the story of the unfortunate twins is really a parable of the Freudian formula for the making of the homosexual.

Who's *Afraid of Virginia Woolf?* (1962) is a more realistically rendered elaboration of the one-act plays. George and Martha, named to suggest that they are American icons, are fuller versions of the domineering Mommy and castrated Daddy of *The American Dream*, and their treatment of their imaginary son is relegated inevitably to exposition. He is like the castrated, mutilated son of Mommy and Daddy, the twin brother of the American dream, who emerges, fully clothed in the later play as Nick, the cool, smug biologist on the make. In *Who's Afraid*, the ineffectual husband finally triumphs over his monstrous wife by robbing her of her fantasy of motherhood—of womanhood. Nick is ultimately put in the position of Peter in *Zoo Story*, of learning the truths of marginal lives, of the underside of the "normality" he seems to represent; he is forced to see that the truth is that love and violence are intertwined for self-hating people. Martha is a descendant of Ibsen's *Hedda Gabler* (1890), a Daddy's girl trapped in a marriage to a mediocre scholar, and her battles with George echo Strindberg. Albee acknowledges his debt to the Scandinavian naturalists but cannot commit himself fully to their belief in logic and causality. At the heart of the exposition—the imaginary child who is the guilty family secret—is nothing more than a fantasy. Naturalism is both used and undermined—a reflection of the gay writer's usual ambivalence toward the dominant mode of modern theatrical structure, which functions both to explain and to dispense with the outsider, the problem.

In *Who's Afraid*, the outsider who must be humiliated and purged is the handsome, brilliant, but vacuous Nick. What threat does Nick really pose? He is relatively humorless, he is uncomfortable being thrust into the fighting and game-playing of George and Martha, he doesn't love his wife (for whom the playwright reserves the brunt of his contempt), he is ambitious and vain, and he doesn't play the games very well. In other words, he has the makings of a theatrically dull character but doesn't deserve to be punished. Like Williams' Stanley Kowalski, Nick is a version of "masculine," heterosexual, "normality," but Albee disarms Nick. The potent danger is not from conventional virility, but from George's theatrical authority, spearing Martha not with his penis but with snapdragons.

Unlike Williams and Inge, Albee is not good at writing women. Honey is a hateful caricature, a horrid case of arrested development. Martha, like Albee's other theatrically lively women, is, as Sky Gilbert suggests, a drag queen: loud, self-mocking, highly performative (the next Martha, Claire in *A Delicate Balance*, even trots out an accordian at a climactic moment). Martha is a cartoon of a woman, if a woman at all. William's transvestite displacement was successful because he wrote women's voices more convincingly than he wrote men's. Albee did not have the ear, or the sympathies, for such ventriloquism.

What is offered Martha instead of the phallus she desires, at times claims, for herself, or which she at least wants from a man, is a pop gun—a trick, a theatrical device, but it gets her sexually excited:

> (GEORGE *takes from behind his back a short-barreled shotgun, and calmly aims it at the back of* MARTHA'S *head. . . .* MARTHA *turns her head to face* GEORGE. GEORGE *pulls the trigger.*)
> GEORGE: POW!!!
> (*Pop! From the barrel of the gun blossoms a large red and yellow Chinese parasol* HONEY *screams again. . . .*) You're dead! Pow! You're dead!
> . . . .
> (HONEY *is beside herself.* MARTHA *laughs too . . . almost breaks down, her great laugh booming.* GEORGE *joins in the general laughter and confusion. It dies, eventually.*)
> . . . .
> MARTHA (*joyously*): Where'd you get that, you bastard?
> . . . .
> GEORGE (*leaning over* MARTHA): You liked that, did you?
> MARTHA: Yeah . . . that was pretty good. (*Softer*) C'mon . . . give me a kiss.
> GEORGE (*Indicating* NICK *and* HONEY): Later, sweetie.
> (*But* MARTHA *will not be dissuaded. They kiss,* GEORGE *standing; leaning over* MARTHA'S *chair. She takes his hand, places it on her stage-side breast. He breaks away.*) (pp. 94–95)

George's theatrical performance of a potency he does not in actuality possess excites Martha to initiate sexual activity, which George rebuffs: "What are we going to have . . . blue games for the guests?" (p. 95). As George has performed a cartoon of the phallus, Martha performs an exaggerated sexual overture in which she is the aggressor, her husband the passive receiver of the "pass" that he must rebuff. While much has been made of the many instances of conventional sex-role reversal in the play, the central dimension of the moment is the presence of the audience. The gun play and the sexual overture are performed, as George's rebuff is performed, for the audience onstage, Nick and Honey. The death of George and Martha's imaginary son is the denouement of a series of scenes they have acted out for each other for years. Near the beginning of the play, before Nick and Honey enter, George warns Martha not to "start on the bit . . . the bit about the kid" (p. 77). The theatrical definition of "bit" is an entertainment routine, an "act," which is exactly what their son is. The insupportable rule is that their act is not to be played in front of an audience, which makes it no act at all. Bits need an audience, and their chosen audience, the young couple, is a parody of heterosexual "normality," and as such a parody of many in the real audience in the Billy Rose Theater. The bit about the son is also a parody of heterosexual "normality," of the family George and Martha cannot have and that they would destroy, as they destroy him in their bits.

The "What a dump" exchanges at the beginning of the play are also performance, by inference acknowledging an audience—why else would George and Martha do "bits" so blatantly? The theatrical "Screw you" at the opening of the door to reveal Nick and Honey switches the focus from real to surrogate audience, as the young people are both audience and target of George's satire. The only private "overheard moments" are at the play's coda, when the audience is to believe George and Martha are alone because they have, for the first time, stopped performing.

The emphasis in *Who's Afraid of Virginia Woolf?* is on performance as superior to real experience. After Nick's exposure and humiliation in "Get the Guests," Nick threatens to join the performance: "I'll play in your language . . . I'll be what you say I am" (p. 136). Nick's very statement, confusing "play" and "be," shows his inferiority to George and Martha. Nick doesn't know how to perform and ultimately becomes the butt of jokes in George and Martha's "bits." Even in the midst of their war, George and Martha join in a musical mockery of Nick:

> NICK: I'm nobody's houseboy.
> GEORGE *and* MARTHA: . . . Now! (*Sing*) I'm nobody's houseboy now. . . .
> (*Both laugh.*)
> NICK: Vicious. (p. 156)

Onstage, theatricality triumphs, and George and Martha's home is a theater in which the rules of theater prevail. Experience and fantasy, truth and illusion, are turned into art, and the hilarious, fun surface only partially masks Albee's hatred of the Nicks of the world, disgust at the Honeys, and ambivalence toward the Marthas. The play is, in its best moments, as its straight and gay detractors claim, an exercise in camp. Whatever social or philosophical message Albee claimed for the satire in the play, it is greatly an exercise in gay metatheatricality and an exorcism of the claims of heterosexuality. When the bitchiness and game-playing end, the play's *raison d'être* is eliminated and one is left with an empty, joyless conclusion.

This is not to say that *Who's Afraid of Virginia Woolf?* isn't a brilliant play, but its brilliance is on the surface. Dig too deep and, like Julian in Albee's *Tiny Alice*, you'll find yourself wedded to nothing at all, though Albee insisted on making claims for that nothing as though it were a form of depth. As he couldn't claim his homosexuality, he couldn't claim that surface in his plays is almost everything. The joy is in the bitchy language, in camp feminine diminutives like "snoozette" (what straight man would conceive of such a playful diminutive?), and in the travesty of femininity and sexual appetite Martha enacts.

Albee, like Williams and Inge, couldn't write homosexual scenes. He couldn't believe in their acceptability (Albee saw himself, as Williams and Inge did, as a "Broadway writer"). In a way, it's a good thing for gay men that he didn't; for a gay *Who's Afraid of Virginia Woolf?* would also be antigay, as would a gay *Streetcar Named Desire* or a gay *Picnic*. Albee's gift, to a lesser extent than Williams', was the ability to stage a version of heterosexuality from the "other side" that was theatrically vibrant, more so than many pictures of heterosexual life created from within. Perhaps the complex relationship Albee, Williams, and Inge had toward heterosexuality, as well as toward their own "marginal" sexual status, gave them the tools to theatricalize the other for whom they were The Other. No heterosexual playwright has done it so well since. Still, I must agree with Alan Sinfield that "decoding the work of closeted homosexual artists ought to produce a recognition of oppression rather than a cause for celebration."[57] In the works of Albee, Williams, and Inge, successful drama is produced from, and itself dramatizes, the considerable self-loathing reinforced by the closet.

FRANK RICH AND THE NEW CLOSET DRAMA

In the eighties, Terrence McNally became the house playwright of the Manhattan Theatre Club, which moved from modest surroundings to a theater in the New York City Center and a four-million-plus annual budget. While his openly gay *The Lisbon Traviata* (1985/1989, discussed in Chapter 6) was successful enough to merit a move to one of the larger off-Broadway houses, McNally's big hits have been *Frankie and Johnny in the Clair de Lune* (1987), which had a long off-Broadway run and a West End run in London and has been turned into a film with Al Pacino and Michelle Pfeiffer, and *Lips Together, Teeth Apart* (1991), which earned a rave review from Frank Rich and sellout business.

Frankie and Johnny in the Claire de Lune, like Lanford Wilson's highly successful *Talley's Folly* (1980), is a romantic play about a couple of socially inept people in which a man must break down a woman's resistance to a relationship. In Wilson's play, the issue is the viability of a nonprocreative marriage (the woman cannot have children; the man doesn't want to bring children into a world he sees as evil). The Talley trilogy, which culminates in *Fifth of July* (1978), with its central gay couple, ultimately affirms nonprocreative gay and straight relationships, a challenge to the "traditional family." The middle American nineteenth-century farmhouse is inherited by a gay couple. The biological future is the formal garden one of the lovers is developing.

In McNally's *Frankie and Johnny,* the names suggest a gender ambiguity—the names could be masculine or feminine, the couple could be gay or straight. In the preface to the published version, McNally claims that it is his most autobiographical play, a response to the loss of dear gay friends to AIDS.[58] Yet one sees and hears a man and a woman. As a matter of fact, one sees and hears one of the best romantic dramas in years. But there is very little gay in *Frankie and Johnny in the Clair de Lune*. There is one cautious reference to caution in the age of AIDS, yet a few minutes later Johnny (the man) is sucking blood from Frankie's cut finger, a blatant act of unsafe intimacy. Frank Rich called this play "the most serious play yet about intimacy in the Age of AIDS."[59]

McNally's most recent play, *Lips Together, Teeth Apart,* presents two heterosexual couples in a Fire Island house inherited by one of the wives from her brother, who recently died of AIDS-related infections. In *Lips Together, Teeth Apart,* Nathan Lane and Anthony Heald, who played the gay central characters in *The Lisbon Traviata,* are the troubled heterosexual husbands. Gay men are background noise—on Fire Island! They make love in the bushes while the onstage heterosexuals rail—and avoid the pool because they might catch AIDS from it!

Frank Rich, in a rave review, proclaimed, "The play's great generosity can be found in its insistence on letting the audience see each camp through the eyes of the other without distorting either point of view, and, as it happens, without bringing a gay character onstage."[60] *See* is the operative verb in Rich's sentence, yet precisely what the audience does not do is "see" gay men. If anything, McNally is overly generous toward the heterosexuals in his affluent Manhattan Theatre Club audience—and toward Mr. Rich—they are spared the awkwardness of "seeing" gay characters. McNally, who more blatantly than his colleagues, put gay men on the Broadway stage in *Bad Habits* and *The Ritz,* now receives praise for pushing homosexuality at least into the wings. Otis Stuart rightly laments that "*Frankie and Johnny in the Clair de Lune* and *Lips Together, Teeth Apart,* which contain not a single gay character, can be seen as the return to the era of the invisible homosexual."[61]

In a recent interview, McNally noted: "Unless you write a play for a specific audience now, you don't know who's sitting out there, whereas in the '60s I knew who came to my plays. We were all against what we saw as the establishment. Now we've become the establishment."[62] McNally does write for a specific audience—the well-heeled, New York "liberal" audiences who support the Manhattan Theatre Club. He has made clear that for him, the New York theater is "the only place to be if you want to work with the best directors, actors, and designers in the American theater."[63] But one also works with the New York audience and must please Frank Rich, the latest *Times* drama critic who, like his predecessors, has a clear sense of the place of gay men on the New York stage. McNally is praised for his "straight" plays and given more qualified eccomiums for his gay plays.

In 1990, playwright Craig Lucas wrote an article for *American Theatre,* "A Gay Life in the Theatre,"[64] and the film about the effect of AIDS on a group of affluent gay men, *Longtime Companion.* He also managed to create a critical and commercial success with *Prelude to a Kiss,* which premiered at the Circle Repertory Company, the old stomping ground of Lanford Wilson, and moved for a long run into the same Broadway theater that housed *Torch Song Trilogy.* Film stars Alec Baldwin, Timothy Hutton, and Steve Guttenberg were willing to play Peter, the heterosexual leading character in Lucas's play while, ironically, lesser-known stage actors played the gay men in Lucas' film. The larger irony is that Lucas could write a successful film about gay men, but his big dramatic success was a heterosexual love story, if one with a twist only a gay playwright could execute sensitively. The "prelude" to a kiss is a whirlwind courtship of Peter and Rita, two yuppies in love. On their wedding day, Rita is kissed by an old man and she and the old man exchange bodies. Peter finds himself with the body of his wife, but with a stranger occupying that body. As his mother-in-law points out, this is not an uncommon experience for a newlywed. He is reunited with the person he loves, now in the body of a cancer-ridden old man. *Prelude to a Kiss* is a sweet, deftly written play with some gentle reflections on mortality and the difference between youthful spirit and aging, decaying flesh. However, in the manner of contemporary commercial theater, it is totally unthreatening, totally accommodating to its audience in ways Lucas did not think would be necessary in a screenplay.

In one moment just before the wedding, Peter's best friend and best man kisses him on the cheek and mouths "I love you" to the groom.[65] The friend claims never to have *sex.* Is this the typical gay man in the age of AIDS, safely virginal out of fear of disease and playing the closeted, stalwart sidekick to his beloved straight friend? Peter spends his honeymoon having sex with an old man in the body of his wife. What if it had been a gay young man in his wife's body? That might have been too threatening. Frank Rich's proclamation, "I loved this play!" is emblazoned on the front of the dust jacket.[66]

The off-Broadway success of the 1990–1991 season was David Stevens' *The Sum of Us,* an Australian play about the relationship of a butch gay working-class man and his father. Though it is hinted at the end that the son may have found a lover, throughout his only close relationship is with his adoring father, whose voice is privileged through his lengthy monologues. *The Sum of Us* focuses on a father's tolerance of his son's not very active homosexuality and the son's primary relationship with his father. While the only loving, sexual relationship celebrated in the play is that of the father's mother with her lesbian lover, the audience never sees a loving, sexual gay (or straight) relationship.

This is the commercial theater in the nineties—an "outside" comedy-drama of a "good" gay son is a hit and openly gay playwrights now proudly write the sort of play closeted gay playwrights previously wrote. The offstage openness of the playwrights combined with their sensitivity to their audiences wins the praise of Frank Rich and success in commercial theater in which the most powerful, successful producer is an openly gay manufacturer of hetero-sexist lowbrow musical fantasies.

The return of the closet in the early nineties may be the clearest indi-cation of what Williams' *A Streetcar Named Desire* metaphorically asserts and his more realistic plays bear out—that in traditional, realistic drama, there is no meaningful place for gay experiences or explorations and expressions of what has been inadequately called the "gay sensibility."[67] In the discussions of the contemporary gay drama in part III, we will see that it is in pushing beyond the limits of realism and the expectations and sensibilities of the au-dience for mainstream theater that gay drama most vividly stages gayness.

PART 3

STAGING "A CULTURE THAT ISN'T JUST SEXUAL"

CHAPTER FIVE

DRAMATIZING GAY
MALE HISTORY

"The only way we'll have real pride is when we demand recognition of a
culture that isn't just sexual. It's all there—all through history we've been
there; but we have to claim it, and identify who was in it, and articulate
what's in our minds and hearts and all our creative contributions to
this earth."

NED WEEKS, IN LARRY KRAMER, *The Normal Heart*

On the 1991 season finale of CBS' *Northern Exposure*, two good-looking,
well-dressed men arrive at an Alaska wilderness town. One is bearded and in
his early forties, the other fair, a bit younger; their looks, clothing, and comfort
with each other make them instantly recognizable to gay men as a gay couple.
They want to buy an old house, restore it, and turn it into a bed-and-breakfast.
Maurice, the burly ex-astronaut who owns the building and most of the town,
smelling money, invites the two men to dinner to help solidify the deal. The
couple sees Maurice's well-equipped kitchen, antiques, and large collection
of original-cast albums and assumes he, too, is gay. Having found, they presume, a kindred spirit, they feel totally at home, so much so that they hold
hands at Maurice's dinner table. The next day, Maurice, thrown by the mis-
perceptions of the previous evening into a major image crisis, gives away his
Cuisinart and Broadway albums (if he had any knowledge of gay literature,
he would also change his name). When he asks the hip DJ at the local radio
station what he would assume about men who loved cooking and show tunes,
the immediate answer is, "I'd think they were homosexual."

To protect the town from an invasion of "Nancy boys," Maurice tells
the couple he won't sell them the house. Their assumption is that Maurice is

a closeted gay who is out to get a higher price. They offer him the house's outrageous list price, throwing Maurice into a conflict between heterosexist principles and greed. Greed wins.

In the final scene, Maurice is buying the two men a drink in the community's bar (Maurice's fears have been assuaged by the knowledgeable DJ's telling him that there were bloodthirsty, militaristic homosexuals in the Ottoman Empire and that excessive fear of homosexuality is frequently a sign of homosexuality). When a couple begins slow-dancing to the jukebox, other couples join in, including the gay couple, who slow-dance with their arms around each other. The camera pans from them, past other dancing couples, including two Native American women, and then moves behind Maurice and the DJ, who stand watching, the DJ with his arm around Maurice's shoulders in a friendly gesture that could have been—but wasn't—misread as a sign of homosexuality. In this situation, Maurice is the outsider, the viewer of an integrated society, but he is accepting the affectionate touch of a male friend.

The gay couple has been integrated into this town of eccentrics without any compromise. They had to buy their way in at an inflated price, but they didn't back down when faced with Maurice's homophobia. More important, they weren't scared to dance; nor did their dancing cause any consternation. This episode of *Northern Exposure* presented a sweet, idealized picture of assimilation. The show did not completely ignore stereotypes—it wouldn't exist without them—but it did mock dependence on stereotypes, and the joke was in the reading and misreading of signs. It offered the healthiest dramatic image of gay men television has yet presented: two men who wouldn't think of being marginalized establishing their place on a dance floor and slowly dancing, arms around each other, like everyone else. Homosexuality was never problematized, nor were homosexuals; it was Maurice who had the problem.

Post-Stonewall gay drama is basically about finding a place on the dance floor, a place in society where a gay man can safely not act straight. It is about the experience of being gay as seen from inside. The situations are often the same as those shown in "outside" drama about gays, but the point of view is now that of a gay character. If gay men choose to assimilate, as television and much drama assumes they will, the central question remains: What does it mean to be gay? This is a question that has until recently been answered for lesbians and gay men by the dominant culture. What is gay identity apart from sexual-object choice? Canadian dramatist Robert Wallace has written that "the essential strangeness of being gay in a heterosexual society is the common denominator that united the millions of lesbians and gay men openly involved in the construction of "sexual community."[1] Don Shewey adds that this "essential strangeness of being gay is being something other than what one was brought up to be."[2] "It is," Philip Brett notes, "the special characteristic of the homosexual stigma (unlike that of being black or Jewish) that it is almost always reinforced at home and thus the more readily 'internalised.' "[3] This strangeness is reinforced by homophobia, or heterosexism, the resultant rejection, and the potential for violent attack from hostile outsiders.

In part the two gay men on *Northern Exposure* were accepted because they were a couple joining other couples. One of the major questions in the years since Stonewall has been that of relational values: what are the most appropriate gay relationships and what does love mean in a gay context? These issues of alienation, internalized heterosexism, and the possibility of loving relationships are so interrelated that they inevitably become intertwined in gay drama.

A gay couple can fit more comfortably into the world of *Northern Exposure* than into that of the typical "serious" television drama because *Northern Exposure* is not dependent on the conventions of realistic drama, as were telefilms like *An Early Frost* and *Our Sons*. The show is an interesting generic mix—comedy, farce, parody, melodrama, fantasy—that defies linear narrative. The moon over Cicely, Alaska, is full, and characters aren't expected to behave in accordance with realism's laws of rational causality. Homosexuality needn't be problematized, nor do issues have to be resolved in a conventional, realistic manner. In other words, to paraphrase Blanche DuBois, magic takes precedence over realism. This is the thrust of contemporary gay drama; and what unites many gay plays is the dialogue with, defiance of, or elimination of the conventions of realistic drama that would otherwise entrap gay characters. Moreover, the plays are unabashedly metatheatrical, revelling in their own theatricality, underlining the essential fact that acting has been, to some extent, an essential part of the gay man's life.

I divide post-Stonewall gay drama into two categories. This chapter will be devoted to the development of an affirming gay history, the next to depictions of contemporary gay life that focus on what it means to act gay.

THE HISTORICAL IMPULSE

Eve Kosofsky Sedgwick has defined a potential alternative canon of lesbian and gay male literature as "a literature of oppression and resistance and survival and heroic making."[4] Oppression and resistance and survival and heroic making are the stuff of gay history, and much of gay drama is an expression of what might be called the "historical impulse" in gay literature—the impulse to depict and define the collective past of gay men to affirm a sense of identity and solidarity and to educate the dominant culture about the brutal effects of its heterosexism.

The historical impulse is expressed in Christopher Marlowe's *Edward II* (1594), which not only focuses on the homosexual desire of its central character but also celebrates and affirms Edward's love for Piers Gaveston by linking it with a catalog of celebrated male lovers of classical history and myth:

The mightiest kings have had their minions,
Great Alexander loved Hephaestion,
The conquering Hercules for Hylas wept,
And for Patrochlus stern Achilles drooped:
And not kings only, but the wisest men:
The Roman Tully loved Octavius,
Grave Socrates, wild Alcibiades.[5]

Such list-making was the central historical act in the early days of gay liberation, when identity and pride came from a symbolic joining with celebrated
homosexuals of the past and present. Larry Kramer has Ned Weeks, in *The
Normal Heart* (1985), incant such a list of past homosexuals:

> I belong to a culture that includes Proust, Henry James, Tchaikovsky, Cole
> Porter, Plato, Socrates, Aristotle, Alexander the Great, Michelangelo, Leo-
> nardo da Vinci, Christopher Marlowe, Walt Whitman, Herman Melville,
> Tennessee Williams, Byron, E. M. Forster, Lorca, Auden, Francis Bacon,
> James Baldwin, Harry Stack Sullivan, John Maynard Keynes, Dag Ham-
> marskjold.[6]

Kramer's list manifests the problems inherent in such compilations. What
meaning is there in invoking such names? And, once we have the names in
place, what do we do with them? After all, many of the people on Kramer's list,
including Christopher Marlowe, could not conceive of homosexuality as we understand it,[7] and others who could were not known for proudly asserting their
gayness. Yet this cataloging both represents an urge to make historical connections and, to use Kramer's Ned Weeks' words, calls for "the recognition of a
culture that isn't just sexual."[8] Kramer's Ned Weeks recited his list as a rebuttal
to the charge that his pleas for gay men in the AIDS epidemic to stop their promiscuous behavior were destroying the foundation of the gay community,
which was sexual liberation. His list is an assertion that there is more to the gay
experience than sex, which forms but one element in a long history of artists,
leaders, and heroes. The assertion can be made more effectively as a counter to
heterosexist reductions of gay people to their "abnormal," "deviant" behavior.

The *historical impulse* in gay theater—the urge to dramatize the history
of "oppression and resistance and heroic making"—is linked in complex and
interesting ways with three other central impulses in gay drama:

> The *anarchic impulse* to celebrate, sometimes even in its nonlinear structure,
> creative anarchy as a positive counter to oppressive order.
> The *romantic impulse* to posit loving relationships as the norm for gay
> men—to posit the right to love, not merely the right to sex, as the stake
> in the battle against oppression.

The *canonical impulse* to celebrate gay creativity by dramatizing the experience of gay artists, thus reinforcing awareness of the kind of pantheon of creative figures that Kramer's Ned Weeks hailed. Those names establish that much of Western culture is gay culture, and they claim a space in this culture for an openly gay identity.

I shall devote this chapter to a consideration of four types of history play. First I shall evoke a canonical model, Marlowe's *Edward II*, which can be seen to point the way toward contemporary gay history plays by evoking a homosexual martyr and defining a conflict between the "official" world and what one might call "the right to love." The second section focuses on three plays that dramatize the complex relationship of homosexuality to privileged all-male societies. In these mainstream plays, the homosexual, seen from outside, cannot be fully integrated into the society in which he places himself. His marginalization is symptomatic of a complex social malaise. I will then discuss three contemporary history plays that focus on three pivotal events in modern gay history: The Oscar Wilde trials, the Nazi persecution of homosexuals, and the Stonewall riot (the Boston Tea Party of gay history). All three of these "inside" plays—Noel Greig and Drew Griffiths' *As Time Goes By* (1977), Martin Sherman's *Bent* (1979), and Doric Wilson's *Street Theater* (1982)—mix a politicized view of history with a project for love between men. Finally, I shall look at some dramatic representations of gay artists that serve as examples of how the canonical impulse merges with the romantic and anarchic impulses.

THE CANONICAL MODEL

Two post-Stonewall productions of Christopher Marlowe's *Edward II* (1594) have become particularly famous. In 1969, Ian McKellen played Edward in repertory with a play that shows its influence, William Shakespeare's *Richard II* (1595). The production inspired outrage, particularly for the kissing scene between Edward and Gaveston. Tabloid newspapers referred to the moment as the "shock kiss"; and a photograph of the kiss was included in a book called *The Erotic Arts*. McKellen's *Edward II* was videotaped and shown in America as well as in Great Britain. In 1990 Gerard Murphy directed a production for the Royal Shakespeare Company at Stratford-upon-Avon that moved to the RSC's London home in 1991. These productions are not only revivals of a masterpiece but recognitions by gay artists of the centrality of Marlowe and *Edward II* in the gay canon. This centrality has been reinforced by the 1991 film version by the gay British director Derek Jarman.

Marlowe himself has become a gay hero, romanticized by some artists:

When Edward gets fatally screwed for letting the world go screw itself, you sense Marlowe's unflinching confrontation of his own emotional self-indulgence. Edward chooses to reject his responsibility as a King to his Country, as Marlowe rejected his responsibility as a writer to his talent; and you can't blame either.[9]

He has been seen by gay scholars and critics as a poststructuralist gay hero: "Like the heroes he created, Marlowe lived and died in the impossible project—as author, government spy, and homosexual—of the marginalized, negativized existence permitted him."[10]

Edward II fulfills one of the prime functions of a gay history play; it establishes a pantheon of historical and literary figures who form "a culture that isn't just sexual." The text is based on chronicles of English history, and the text also creates its own chronicles of gay history. *Edward II* places a character motivated primarily by homosexual desire in a world in which this motivation alienates him both politically and domestically.

The "official" view might be that Edward's blatantly sexual love for Gaveston and Spenser can be seen only as fatal political error. In this interpretation, the sex of Edward's love objects is not the issue but rather their class and the power Edward grants them. Edward abuses kingly privilege to defy aristocratic privilege. "Traitor" and "treason" are important words in *Edward II* and the "lovesick" king invites civil war and ignores strife in France. To Edward, everyone who stands in the way of his will is a traitor to his kingship, but ultimately Edward himself, along with Gaveston and Young Spenser, is punished as a traitor to the realm.

If, however, we see *Edward II* as a play about gay history instead of English history, varied alternative readings emerge. Director Gerard Murphy sees homophobia as a crucial element. Murphy thinks that when Edward takes Spenser as his lover

> he has learned a lot about the complexity of the reasons why people hated Gaveston and actually endangers Spenser's life by saying, "You are now my official boyfriend." The turning point is when a messenger comes from the barons and says, "Right, we've got rid of Gaveston and if you want this to end happily you'd better get rid of Spenser." The underbelly of anti-gay feeling now becomes ulcerous. And Edward's murder, with the poker thrust into his anus, is not accidental.[11]

More historically oriented critics, like Alan Bray and Jonathan Goldberg, see *Edward II* as a case history of the complex Elizabethan attitude toward sodomy, a term that still has resonance and legal power for many gay people. Not only are a number of state sodomy laws still on the books, but in 1982, in the *Bowers v. Hardwick* ruling, the United States Supreme Court declared that Georgia's sodomy laws take precedence over an individual's right to privacy.[12]

No gay critic can ignore the play's lavishly expressed homoeroticism, a subject that heterosexist critics either ignore or decry. Purvis E. Boyette writes that *Edward II* is "about the erotic consciousness and its play through all the tensions of the drama. . . . The homoeroticism of the play expresses a plausible consciousness no dramatist had explored before Marlowe, and for him traditional judgment becomes irrelevant, a fiction he chooses to ignore."[13]

The play begins with a speech by Gaveston, who represents the magnet to which Edward is drawn. In Marlowe's play, Gaveston may be a commoner, a Frenchman, a sycophant, and a ruthless opportunist, but he is also the representative of a free play of imagination and erotic charge presented in language far more attractive than that of the edicts of his dour adversaries, the barons. Gaveston's opening speeches evoke the worlds of beauty, art, and music, but particularly the world of theater:

> Music and poetry is his delight,
> Therefore I'll have Italian masques by night,
> Sweet speeches, comedies, and pleasing shows. (I,i,53–55).

But the theater is one of sexual ambiguity and homoerotic desire:

> And in the day when he shall walk abroad,
> Like sylvan nymphs my pages shall be clad
> My men like satyrs grazing on the lawns
> Shall with their goat feet dance an antic hay;
> Sometime a lovely boy in Dian's shape,
> With hair that gilds the water as it glides,
> Crownets of pearl about his naked arms,
> And in his sportful hands an olive tree
> To hide those parts which men delight to see. (I,i,56–64)

The "my" paints Gaveston as creator, producer, and director of an erotic spectacle in which, as in the Elizabethan theater, boys play women, but in which those boys are also erotic objects in themselves. Stephen Orgel summarizes the Elizabethan attacks on boy actors playing women: "Male spectators, it is argued, will be seduced by the impersonation, and, losing their reason, will become effeminate, which in this case means they will lust not after the woman in the drama, which would be bad enough, but after the boy beneath the woman's costume, thereby playing the woman's role themselves."[14] This, in essence, is what Gaveston intends his spectacle to do to Edward, to allow him to "draw the pliant" (that is, effeminate) king. Alan Bray rightly asks whose parts are those "men delight to see," Dian's or those of the boy actor playing her?[15]

Gaveston's speech establishes a central aspect of his relationship with, and attraction for, Edward. Gaveston is the spirit of theater which is attractive and dangerous. Bruce R. Smith warns: "The lovers' fascination with dressing up, with role-playing, with acting things out threatens to drain the world of substance and set up instead the infinite regressions of Ovid's *Metamorphoses*."[16]

Gaveston's motives are more Machiavellian than they are loving, but of all the characters, only Edward isn't a scheming pragmatist. Still, Gaveston's ornate language and richly erotic vision link him and Edward not only to art and pleasure but to a rich mythological past. This opulent vision could not be further from the matter-of-fact threats of Young Mortimer, the baron who is most militant in his demand that Edward renounce his beloved:

> Come uncle, let us leave the brain-sick king,
> And henceforth parley with our naked swords. (I,i,124–125)

Mortimer's language represents the norm of violently imposed order and brutality, which sees Gaveston in the typically gay role of agent of anarchy: "If you love us, my lord, hate Gaveston" (I,i,79). Simon Shepherd sees Mortimer's hatred of Edward's love for his minions as predicated on the Elizabethan concept of manliness that Edward transgresses not by loving a man but by his uneconomical emotional expenditure: "The ideology of manliness, or masculinity, inscribes the individual within interpersonal competition and denigrates emotion without actions."[17] As Edward is in thrall to Gaveston's eloquence, he will become captive to Mortimer's manly action. Both are dangerous; Gaveston's opulent, eloquent shows of love have a sinister dimension that supports the barons' mistrust:

> It shall suffice me to enjoy your love,
> Which whiles I have I think myself as great
> As Caesar riding in the Roman street
> With captive kings at his triumphal car. (I, i,170–173)

Gaveston sees himself as Caesar; Edward is a "captive king." Edward sees Gaveston's performance as one of love—"he loves me more than all the world"—the play presents it much more skeptically.

It is not Gaveston but Young Spenser, his successor in Edward's affections, who is allowed to grow from pragmatist, interested only in his own advancement, to loyal lover. In Gerard Murphy's production, Gaveston was never more than a preening love object: there was no sign that he reciprocated Edward's love. Young Spenser is more complex. He is first seen in bed with his lover Baldock, a sign that homoerotic desire is more than show for this pretty young man, but his conversation is of favor and patronage:

But he that hath the favor of a king
May with one word advance us while we live. (II, i,8–9)

Spenser has read his Machiavelli, and he wants advancement for himself and his scholarly lover, but his youthful exuberance is no match for the mature resolve of the barons, who see Edward transferring his affections to a mere boy. Spenser, however, moves from teen-age Machiavellian pragmatist to the voicer of a glorious lament for his martyr king:

Oh is he gone? is noble Edward gone?
Parted from hence, never to see us more?
Rent, sphere of heaven, and fire, forsake thy orb,
Earth melt to air, gone is my sovereign,
Gone, gone alas, never to make return. (IV, vi,99–103)

In a world of deceit, Spenser's eloquent lament is a brief moment of honest love. It contrasts with the false tears of Lightborn, the hired assassin, who seduces Edward for the last time. In Murphy's production, Lightborn's execution of Edward was indeed a seduction, the most graphic sexual moment in the play. Lightborn boasts as he prepares to meet the king:

ne'er was there any
So finely handled as this king shall be. (V,v,37–38)

Like Gaveston, Lightborn will "draw the pliant king which way I please," a deadly seduction that is a brutal perversion of the act it punishes.[18] Claude Summers observes:

The "anal crucifixion" combines elements of sexual desire and violent "policy" into a horrible triumph of the will. In so doing, it forcefully juxtaposes the world of erotic freedom and sexual fulfillment represented by Edward's love for Gaveston and the symbolic world of power politics symbolized by the union of Mortimer and Isabella, whose love "hatcheth death and hate."[19]

To embrace his "minions" publicly is to inspire classical heterosexist imagery. In defending the king's youthful love for his minion, Old Mortimer presents homosexual desire not only as a quality that connects Edward to great figures from the past but also, paradoxically, as something he will outgrow: "For riper years will wean him from such toys" (I,iv,400). Young Mortimer evokes the virulent imagery of disease: Gaveston will be killed, "purging" the realm "of such a plague" (I,iv,270).

In the first English drama about a character who is what modern parlance would term a homosexual, that character is imprisoned in sewage, forced to shave in fouled water, and fatally sodomized with a hot poker. In the grand, grisly catalog of deaths in Elizabethan and Jacobean drama, Edward's execution is one of the most gruesome and humiliating, and Marlowe lingers on those final humiliations, not as justice for the petulant humiliations Edward caused others nor as punishment for insults of his beloved but to present his audience with a pathetic, if not tragic martyrdom:

> This dungeon where they keep me is the sink
> Wherein the filth of all the castle falls.
>
> . . .
>
> And there in mire and puddle have I stood
> This ten days space, and lest that I should sleep,
> One plays continually on a drum;
> They give me bread and water being a king;
> So that for want of sleep and sustenance,
> My mind's distempered and my body's numbed,
> And whether I have limbs or no I know not. (V,V,55–56, 58–64)[20]

Edward's final scream of pain at the combination of rape and death blow is loud enough to "raise the town" (V,v,113).

Like later gay heroes, Edward is shown as a martyr to his own desire, which is presented as being more positive than any other human feeling in the play, except, perhaps, Young Spenser's imprudent devotion. Marlowe's graphic dramatization of Edward's suffering and death begins a pantheon of martyrs to homosexual love as it evokes a glorious history of heroic lovers. Edward is also an agent of disorder in a world where order is brutal, repressive, and unloving. When order is the enemy, anarchy is a just cause.

Admittedly, this is neither an old—nor a new—historical reading of *Edward II* but one that places the play in a canon of gay history plays that set erotic desire and imagination against official repression. What is at stake is not only homoerotic desire but the possibility of the theater of male love envisioned and voiced by Gaveston as a splendid alternative to the dour world of order and power. Edward, like many characters in gay history plays, is both martyr and traitor, but he is incapable of the imaginative liberation Gaveston represents or of the love and loyalty of Young Spenser.

TRAITORS

Edward II dramatizes the adversarial position of a man who chooses to live through his homosexual desire, which places him in opposition to the representatives of a repressive male authority. Edward's execution is the painful, humiliating punishment of a sodomite, an agent of disorder. Edward is the first gay martyr in drama, branded traitor and destroyed by the dominant society.

Hugh Whitemore's *Breaking the Code* (1986) dramatizes the life of Alan Turing, a British mathematician and pioneering genius in computers. Turing became a hero in World War II by breaking German military codes, in particular one code—created by a machine called Enigma—that the Nazi command used to communicate with its U-boats. Turing's service to his country did not prevent his being imprisoned, shot up with female hormones, and treated as a traitor when his homosexuality was discovered. In the play, when it becomes clear to the uncompromisingly honest Turing that he is an object of constant suspicion and scrutiny, he remarks to his superior:

> Day after day I came up with new ideas, new solutions—the Germans always seemed to be one step ahead of us. But I persevered, and—after years of exhaustive effort—the U-boat Enigma was finally broken. It took much more than mathematics and electronic ingenuity to do that. It needed determination, tenacity—moral fibre, if you like. That's what made it so deeply satisfying. You trusted me then. Why not now?[21]

Turing's sexual orientation made him a security risk, a potential traitor, able to enjoy intimacy and companionship only with young, working-class toughs. His mistreatment at the hands of the government he so ably served (and his subsequent suicide) make Turing another gay martyr, one who is included in Larry Kramer's gay pantheon.[22] Treason, like disease, both physical and mental, has been a controlling metaphor for gay men, but it can also contain the germ of an empowering metaphor. Freedom, and a sense of private revenge, can come from consciously playing out the role one is assigned, but such duplicity traps one in a constant performance. Treason is another closet in which the gay man has the illusion of control.

Both John Osborne's *A Patriot for Me* (1965), and Julian Mitchell's *Another Country* (1981), depict historical figures who chose to become traitors to the privileged societies that nurtured and empowered them but that, ultimately, marginalized them. The two plays focus on masculine societies—the military and the English boarding school—that both enforce and celebrate discipline; however, in these societies tension exists between the forces of order and those of anarchy. The ultimate threat to the discipline that tenuously holds the society together is the openly homosexual character, who is, or is perceived as being, the traitor whose behavior will undermine that society. As the person who threatens to bring into the open his society's hidden secret, he must be contained or destroyed. Yet the central characters of these plays have been raised and trained to want, above all else, positions of power in their societies. If treason is the only way to have power, then these men will embrace the role of traitor. Both *A Patriot for Me* and *Another Country* are as much critiques of the values of aristocratic male societies as they are depictions of the role of homosexuality in those societies. Ironically, as in

Edward II, the homosexual traitor has more integrity than the supposedly principled men around him.

Osborne and Mitchell draw obvious parallels between their dramatic situations and the British spy and sex scandals of the fifties and sixties. Homosexuality and treason are seen in Osborne's play from the vantage point of 1960s Britain (two of Britain's most infamous spies, Guy Burgess and Anthony Blount, were homosexuals), and the parallels between Mitchell's Guy Bennett and British spy Guy Burgess are obvious.[23] For both writers, from different vantage points, the issue is the link between homosexual and traitor in a society that protects as well as punishes homosexuality.

A Patriot for Me and *Another Country* are separated by the degree of their authors' identification with the homosexual subject matter. Osborne's play was so daring in 1965 that, to avoid the wholesale cuts demanded by the Lord Chamberlain's office, the Royal Court had to be turned into a private club for the run of the play.[24] Yet, however important it was in opening up space for homosexual subject matter in the censored British theater, *A Patriot for Me* presents its homosexual hero from the point of view of a well-meaning but not totally convinced liberal. Its treatment of homosexuality is typical of that of mainstream drama. Mitchell's play, though a commercial success in the West End, is more like gay drama in that it presents its society through the eyes of its homosexual hero.

A Patriot for Me chronicles twenty-three years in the life of Alfred Redl, ostensibly one of the most promising, fast-rising *Wunderkinder* in the pre-World War I Austro-Hungarian army. Redl, though not an aristocrat, the usual prerequisite for speedy ascent in military circles, moves quickly to the top of Army Intelligence. Ironically, Redl's private life as a spy makes him prey to manipulation by Russian spies. Redl never resists being a traitor: as the title suggests, his real loyalty is not to his country, but to his own impulses.[25]

Osborne's play begins and ends with the linking of violent death, heterosexism, and anti-Semitism. In the first scene, Redl, a young lieutenant in the Galician infantry, is in a predawn conversation with an extremely handsome fellow officer, August Siczynski. Redl has agreed to be the young man's second in a duel with the aristocratic von Kupfer, who has offered Siczynski the double insult of calling him "Fraulein Rothschild," thus labeling him both Jew and homosexual. It is for the latter insult that Siczynski has challenged von Kupfer.

The setting for this predawn dialogue between Redl and Siczynski is an army gymnasium, the cathedral for the masculine society in which these officers live. Climbing bars, a thick rope, and a vaulting horse define the scene. Yet within this space, Redl and his comrade display, however cautiously, their attraction to one another. These are men with something to hide, yet they are open, almost intimate, with each other, defining, again paradoxically, both their need for such intimacy and their awareness of its impossibility:

SICZYNSKI: What, what does one, do you suppose, well, look for in any-
one, anyone else, I mean?
REDL: For?
SICZYNSKI: Elsewhere.
REDL: I haven't tried. Or thought about it. At least . . .
SICZYNSKI: I mean: That isn't clearly, really, clearly, already in oneself?
REDL: Nothing, I expect.[26]

After this halting verbal exchange, the scene ends with two crucial, contrasting
physical images: the brutal duel between von Kupfer and Siczynski and the
final tableau of Redl cradling the dead Siczynski's body in his arms. By winning the duel, von Kupfer has done his aristocratic duty of purging his world
of Jew and homosexual. Redl, unacknowledged Jew and homosexual, in cradling Siczynski is embracing not only a body, one for which he had an unacknowledged attraction, but also a victim of the forces that will always keep
him an outsider. Moreover, his embrace demonstrates the uncontrollable force
of impulse that will always be at war with his fierce sense of discipline. Redl
will always embody both order and anarchy.

In a real sense, Redl never leaves the gymnasium in which the play
opens. His world is defined by physicality, discipline, and violence. It is a
place with virtually no space for women, yet it denies honest expressions of
love between men. Redl is an almost schizoid figure in this gymnasiumland.
He is constantly described as the most disciplined of men, working all hours
and achieving through ability and effort the rank and power that are usually
the privilege of the aristocratic birth he was denied. His discipline is also a
weapon in his battle against his own sexual impulses: "Tried everything, apparently. Resolution, vows, religion, medical advice, self-exhaustion. Used to
flog a dozen horses into the ground a day. And then gardening, if you please,
fencing, and all those studies they do, you do, of course—" (p. 82–83). Redl's
success, then, is the result not only of ambition and excellence but also of
repression of a strong sexual force; but it is homosexuality itself, in both its
repression and its expression, that is most linked with violence as Redl moves,
in the ten scenes of the first act, from repressed to practicing homosexual.
That violence is chronicled in the two scenes that end the act. In the first,
Redl attacks a young homosexual at a cafe who says to him, "I know what
you're looking for," another version of the accusation Siczynski took as a
challenge to his honor. Redl grabs the young man by the throat "*with ferocious
power.*" Yet in the next scene, Redl, after his first sexual experience, cries,
"Why did I wait—so long?" But shortly thereafter, Redl is brutally beaten by
four friends of his young sexual partner, who steals Redl's money and jewelry
and who leaves with the advice, "Don't be too upset, love. You'll get used
to it" (p. 67–69). Allowing the erotic dimension of one's feelings for men to
emerge is moving from a world of brutal repression and power to one of
brutal victimization.

Acting on erotic attraction also makes a person vulnerable to those who know information is power. As Redl spies, he is spied upon by the Russians and is blackmailed into being a double agent, a role he accepts because to do otherwise and be exposed as a homosexual would be to lose the only world in which he feels comfortable, not simply because of its known systems of reward and privilege but also because of the security of its all-male society. When he is ultimately, inevitably, exposed, he commits suicide, not as an acceptance of the strictures against his sexual behavior but for the same reasons he became a double agent: he could not live outside a military society.

Unlike Osborne's earlier central characters, Redl is an almost totally physical person, whose sexual appetite and violent nature lie close to the surface. Physicality is everything to Redl, and his love for young men is in part a connection to his lost physical youth. This also means that Redl's treason is unreflective. It is not a reasoned response to his place in society.

The principal question is what Redl's sexuality has to do with his being a spy, a master of "the treachery that leads to wars. The game" (p. 96). Osborne's answer is that the greatest outsider is the greatest traitor. It is not just that Redl is homosexual—so are many of his comrades. Nor that he hides his Jewish blood—so do many others. But, in addition, Redl has had to master a class system that did not privilege him and will not protect the outsider who made it by will and talent, not by birth. Yet the goal of Redl's life is the creation of a space for the expression of his homosexual desire, which he achieves but with greater and greater indiscretion. Redl has no loyalty to country or class, but he is loyal to his own impulses and to his world—the military, in which those impulses are both repressed and condoned in ways familiar to him.

Redl the outsider is constantly at war. His conflicts with the aristocracy are seen in the vicissitudes of Redl's friendship with von Kupfer, who killed Siczynski but who becomes Redl's aide and protector, lives in Redl's quarters, and wants to be Redl's friend and lover. Redl frames him as a spy (he knows too much). Redl's sexual battles are revealed in the partners he chooses, who are either whores or opportunists. Ultimately it is an old friend who exposes his spying and gives him the pistol.

The old baron, who hosts a spectacular drag ball, a travesty of Viennese aristocratic life, says: "This is the celebration of the individual against the rest, the us's and the them's, the free and the constricted." (p. 77). Osborne takes great pains to make this drag ball, which opens the second act, as realistic as possible (by means of a two-page footnote), and he understands that the contrast between this festivity and the stodgy, aristocratic ball of act 1 defines the attractiveness of the ironic and richly theatrical gay subculture. In the same way, the contrast between Gaveston's language and Mortimer's defines the seductive attractiveness of homoeroticism in *Edward II*. It is only within this splendid, make-believe world that, we are told, Redl can "be himself for once"

(p. 83), but Redl finds no more than temporary and partial freedom at this gathering. He remains in uniform, becomes his old, repressed self when confronted by von Kupfer, and leaves after violently attacking an effeminate young man with whom he had joked earlier. The ball makes clear, as Arnold P. Hinchcliffe puts it, that "neither style—Hofburg nor drag—suits him."[27]

A Patriot for Me shows Redl's suicide, like the earlier duel, as a secretly sanctioned means for society to dispense with its uncontrollable elements. In taking his own life, Redl allows his world to rewrite his history in order to control its image. His homosexuality is erased while his Jewish blood, heretofore secret, is published. The homosexuality that seems an inevitable corollary of the hypermasculinity of Redl's world remains the privileged secret of that world.

Yet, with characteristic confusion, Osborne does not see Redl's death as a martyrdom for his sexuality but as the inevitable self-destruction of another Osborne outsider. In *A Patriot for Me*, as in his previous plays, *Look Back In Anger* (1956, pub. 1957) and *Inadmissable Evidence* (1964), Osborne gives mixed signals in his depiction of the homosexual. Homosexuality is Redl's badge of status as outsider-victim, yet it is also a measure of the decadence of his society. Nor can the playwright resist throwing an anachronistic attack on gay liberation into the play: "God, I'm weary of your self-righteousness and all your superior railing and your glib cant about friendship and the army and the way you roll out your little parade: Michelangelo and Socrates, and Alexander and Leonardo. God, you're like a guild of housewives pointing out Catherine the Great" (p. 101–102). Since no one in the play has uttered the "cant" the Countess attacks, the speech seems wildly out of place, unless Osborne is offering a rejoinder to anyone who thinks he is promoting a positive view of homosexuality.

No such mixed signals exist in Julian Mitchell's *Another Country* (1981), which is also about how the brutality and hypocrisy of a closed, privileged, masculine society, when turned against a homosexual member of that society, creates a traitor. The society in question is the English public school, the training ground for the power elite. Militarism, fake piety, and anti-intellectualism are the hallmarks of this corrupt training ground. The time is the mid-1930s: the Depression is on and Europe is moving toward a world war, but Gascoigne School operates as it always has, oblivious to the movements of history.

We discover volumes about the mores of the young men at Gascoigne School through the suicide of one of them, Martineau, who hangs himself from the chapel bell tower. Martineau was caught with his pants down, literally, in the school darkroom. Reactions to his death are the litmus paper by which we judge the values of the students at Gascoigne's. For most of the select group of young men who run the house, the Prefects, Martineau would have been alive if a teacher hadn't interfered in something that wasn't his business: "If you ask me, it all comes of having masters who aren't old boys . . . An old boy would have had more sense than to go prowling around Phot. Soc. Dark Room in the evenings."[28] The students have their own code of morality and discipline, and in their eyes, the real crime is "letting themselves be caught" (p. 24). The punishment is flogging with a cane, which is both the infliction of physical pain and a public humiliation. It is punishment and containment of the school's guilty secret, which is rampant homosexual activity.

Another Country is about the subtle and the violent marginalization of outsiders—the believer, the Communist, and the homosexual—who threaten the system of appearances the school upholds. The students are united in scheming to keep the absolutist, Fowler, from attaining authority because he believes in the principles underlying the school's code of discipline. He believes in right and wrong, rather than in the appearance of right and wrong. His view of Martineau's transgression has the simplicity of the extreme conservative, "Immorality is immorality" (p. 24), but his belief in his code blinds him to the fact that his peers use the code to hide their own sexual activity. If there is an investigation into sexual activity at Gascoigne's, it will affect the students' future in the world of power to which they aspire.

Tommy Judd, the Communist, believes that the system represented at Gascoigne's must be overthrown by world revolution. Like Fowler, he has strong principles, but Tommy sees no way for the present system to be honorable. Both Fowler and Tommy Judd can be, and are, defused without violence because their idealism validates the system in which they are placed. As long as they don't have enough power to upset the old order, there is a place for the absolutist and the intellectual revolutionary. But Guy Bennett, the homosexual, is dangerous and must be dealt with violently.

Guy is the only character who understands what Martineau's death means: "Martineau wasn't a hypocrite. That's why he did it [committed suicide]. This ghastly school persuaded him its footling, meaningless rules actually stood for something real. Moral principles! Rules of life!" (p. 34). Guy understands that the system is a game, yet he aspires to be one of the winners. He wants his place high in the Foreign Service. Yet he is aware that, unlike so many men for whom homosexual activity is merely the only sexual release in an all-male society, he, like Martineau, is compelled to *love* another man. This, for him, explains the discovery of Martineau with Robbins in the darkroom:

> For Robbins it was just a game. Assignation—excitement—hands fumbling with buttons in the dark—all perfectly normal! School practice! But then poor Martineau—he went and told him [he loved him]. And Robbins was revolted—disgusted. He shoved him away. *That's* not what he'd come for! And Martineau knocked something over and Knickers came in to see what was happening and—(p. 96)

It was not just another instance of sex, but Robbins' violent response to Martineau's confession of love, ironically, that got them caught. Gay history dramas typically posit love, not sex, as the forbidden, dangerous impulse.[29] Martineau, through suicide, saved himself from a life of humiliation and verbal violence: "Think of that for a lifetime. Think of the names. Pansy. Nancy. Fairy. Fruit. Brown nose" (p. 96). The violence of heterosexist language is, for Guy, more bitter, more enduring, than the violence of caning.

Guy Bennett is in love, as Martineau was, with a boy from another house, and it is the mixture of real love with homosexual activity that brands him as an outcast. More practically, engaging in sexual activity with a boy from another house is seen as the worst of crimes because it increases the possibility of scandal, and containment of scandal is the primary objective of this society.[30] Guy is able to stave off a caning by playing on his peers' worst fear: "I just thought you'd like to know—if one stroke of Fowler's cane lands on my arse, I shall go straight to Farcical [the Master] and tell him the names of everyone I've done it with over the last three years" (p. 86). When Fowler discovers a love letter, Guy must be punished to maintain appearances; he receives the requisite brutal caning and loses his chance for a position of authority in the house. He is punished and contained. Guy's response is to vow to become a traitor. When his friend Tommy Judd tells him, "Either you accept the system, or you try to change it," Guy responds: "Why not both? Pretend to do one while you really do the other. Fool the swine! Play along with them! Let them think what they like—let them despise you! But all the time—" (p. 99). The homosexual will become a double agent, accommodating to society while subverting it. For Guy, treason is revenge against a society that despises him, a form of passive aggression. Martineau committed suicide not because he was discovered but because he knew he was really homosexual and would, as Bennett puts it, "face a lifetime of *that*," "that" being hatred and punishment. Guy Bennett admits to his idealistic, Communist friend that he prefers love to justice. *Another Country* laments the necessity to make a choice between the two.

WAR

David Rabe's *Streamers* (1976), is the American counterpart to Osborne's and Mitchell's plays about the homosexual in an all-male society. Like *A Patriot for Me*, it is not written from the point of view of the homosexual character but uses the homosexual as a type, an outsider who is allowed provisional space in his environment. *Streamers* powerfully dramatizes the problems of acting gay in a heterosexist community. It is 1967, early in the Vietnam War, a year of racial unrest in Newark and other American ghettos. The Stonewall riots are still two years away. Set in an army barracks that is a way station between American society and the chaos of Vietnam, *Streamers* connects homosexuality to a network of related issues—racism, male bonding, role-playing in a male-dominated society, and the forces causing the Vietnam War. Homosexuality is not a secret to be maintained and contained as it is in the Austro-Hungarian army or the British public school. Attempts to deny the homosexual a place in this fortress of American middle-class values ultimately fail.

The barracks Rabe shows us is a peculiar one containing only four young men whose position in the army (and in American society) has allowed them special status. One is a college-educated "All American Boy" from Wisconsin, another an assimilated black, a third a wealthy urban homosexual who, of course, can't be fully labeled until he stops "playing straight" (the fourth disappears from the scene early in the play). The false appearance of uniformity in the army allows these men to live together as if their differences don't exist. Billy, a college graduate from Wisconsin, falsely claims to be a school drop-out and affects a kind of "street talk" to erase his differences with Roger, who has learned to play the kind of assimilated black who does not endanger whites. Richie, the homosexual, has declared his place among heterosexuals by taping a female pin-up to the inside of his locker door. "Acting" is the operative term for the behavior of all these young men, and acting means finding a common language that denies any differences.

All the young men in the barracks are suffering from some form of pre-Vietnam anxiety that will foreground their real identity and propel the action toward violence. As the play begins, one of them, Martin, has slashed his wrists, an act that will lead to his discharge from the army. The remaining men manifest their anxiety in less overtly self-destructive ways. Roger has been to the camp psychiatrist because of tension headaches, Billy feels "sick-like,"[31] and Richie has moved from hiding his homosexuality under a common language and a *Playboy* pin-up to aggressively performing his difference: "ever since we been in this room, he's been different somehow" (p. 16).

Though Billy's first action in the play, symbolically, is to bring Richie a piece of American pie, Richie's performance of his homosexuality moves him outside the male bond that has been formed between Billy and Roger, a bond Richie sees as phony. When Billy slips and uses a four-syllable word, Richie shows that he is "on to" Billy's affectations: " 'Obliterate,' did you say? Oh, Billy, you better say "shit," "ain't" and "motherfucker" real quick now or we'll all know just how far beyond the fourth grade you went" (p. 14). The gay man, used to playing a role himself, is particularly sensitive to others' role-playing.

What Billy and Roger share, beyond fear of their impending duty in Vietnam and a series of common rituals to overcome that fear (push-ups, cleaning the barracks), is heterosexism. Richie's behavior inspires in Billy and Roger a number of manifestations of their prejudice and hostility. Roger vehemently denies Richie's homosexuality in the face of Richie's protestations:

ROGER: You ain't sayin' you really done that stuff, though, Rich.

RICHIE: What?

ROGER: That fag stuff.

RICHIE: (*He continues looking at Roger and then he looks away.*) Yes.

ROGER: Do you even know what you're sayin', Richie? Do you even know what it means to be a fag?

RICHIE: Roger, of course I know what it is. I just told you I've done it. I thought you Black people were supposed to understand all about suffering and human strangeness. I thought you had depth and vision from all your suffering. Has someone been misleading me? I just told you I did it. I know all about it. Everything. All the various positions.

ROGER: Yeh, so maybe you think you've tried it, but that don't make you it. (p. 28–29)

Roger's denial finally dismisses any protestation from Richie: "Ohhh, ohhh, you ain't no screamin' goddamn faggot, Richie, no matter what you say" (p. 29), before proceeding to vivid descriptions of fag-bashing in his neighborhood.

Richie's adolescent boastfulness about his homosexuality ("I know all about it. Everything. All the various positions") is a means of asserting himself in an alienating environment. Billy finds it necessary to respond with moral outrage. His attitude toward homosexuality is manifested in a long story he tells Roger, within Richie's earshot, about how he and his friends used to take advantage of homosexual men:

> So we'd let these cats pick us up, most of 'em old guys, and they were hurtin' and happy as hell to have us, and we'd get a lot of free booze, maybe a meal, and we'd turn 'em on. Then pretty soon they'd ask us did we want to go over to their place. Sure, we'd say, and order one more drink, and then when we'd hit the street, we'd tell 'em to kiss off. We'd call 'em fag and queer and jazz like that and tell 'em to kiss off. (p. 48)

One of Billy's gang began going home with the men who picked him up and eventually admitted that he was a homosexual. For Billy, his friend Frankie's homosexuality was an addiction Frankie could have avoided by not succumbing in the first place: "He had got his ass hooked. He had never thought he would and then one day he woke up and he was on it. He just hadn't been told, that's the way I figure it" (p. 49). Billy's story, the moral of which is "Just say no," is meant to be a cautionary one for Richie, as if he is making sure that Richie, unlike poor Frankie, is told what he needs to be told to avoid being a "fag." As Billy misunderstands homosexuality and Richie, Richie, who has a crush on Billy, misreads Billy's story: "Well, was it . . . about you? (*Pause*) I mean, was it ABOUT you? Were you Frankie?" (p. 71). Billy rightly responds: "You didn't hear me at all!" (p. 71).

Out of a desperate need to assert his confused sense of himself, and out of a genuine attraction for Billy, Richie unconsciously performs what amounts to a parody of Roger and Billy's stereotypical "faggot." The underwear-clad Richie jumps on to Billy's bunk and lies next to him:

RICHIE: And what time will you pick me up?
BILLY: (*He pushes at* RICHIE, *knocking him off the bed and onto the floor.*)
Well, you just fall down and wait, all right?
RICHIE: Can I help it if I love you? (p. 14–15)

Richie is not only *being* gay, he is *acting* gay with a vengeance, and in doing so acting what disturbs Billy most about "queers"—their unwillingness to believe he isn't one of them: "So you tell 'em you're straight and they just nod and smile. You ain't real to 'em. They can't see nothin' but themselves and these goddamn games they're always playing' " (p. 17). Billy assumes a reality, which is, of course, straight, and sees gay behavior as narcissistic game-playing, and the presumption that he might be gay as "lookin' out and seein' yourself" (p. 27). Billy's responses to Richie mount from nasty attacks, "you go up and down like a Yo-Yo and you go blowin' all the trees like the wind" (p. 25), to threats of rejection that he presents as "straight talk," "If you don't cut the cute shit with me, I'm gonna turn you off. Completely" (p. 27). Like Brick in *Cat on a Hot Tin Roof*, Billy has the power to "hang up" on Richie—to deny him any recognition at all.

But Richie's character is built from traditional stereotypes. Even his powdering ritual after showering smacks of effeminacy, as does his half-mocking claim that he's "so pretty." Richie is also the most affluent of the men, as if homosexuality were, as it seemed to be in *The Green Bay Tree*, linked to the corruption of wealth: "But I've just done what I wanted all of my life" (p. 28). Julian Dulcimer joins the army! It is not clear why Richie, who reads film critic Pauline Kael in his free time, has enlisted in the army (all three occupants of the barracks have enlisted), though Roger may be right in assuming that Richie joined the army to "get away from" his homosexual past: "And now you're gettin' a chance to run with the boys a little, you'll get yourself straightened around" (p. 35)—if the boys will teach Richie how to act straight and if Richie can keep up the act!

Into this tense situation comes Carlyle, a frightened ghetto black. As Richie's effeminacy, sexual aggressiveness, and air of superiority are homosexual stereotypes that force a response from straight men, so Carlyle's volatility and hostile language evoke the stereotypical black man white men fear most. Carlyle comes into the barracks to meet another black man, but whites like Richie and Billy are alien and frightening to him. Carlyle catches Roger staring at Billy's pinup (Roger is trying to figure out whether Richie is what he claims to be), and Roger, to counter Carlyle's accusations of his being attracted to white women, proclaims, "This here the locker of a faggot" (p. 18), leading Carlyle to misread the dynamic among Richie, Billy, and Roger as a kind of sexual ménage he might be able to join: "You and Roger are hittin' on Richie, right? . . . I'd like to get some of him myself if he a good punk" (p. 68). Billy's response, interestingly enough, is not to protest his own "straightness," but to defend Richie's: "He's not queer, if that's what you're sayin.' A little effeminate, but that's all, no more, if that's what you're sayin" (p. 68). Billy's denial is a means of protecting the central myth of an all-male society: it contains no homosexuals.

Later in the evening, after a lot of drinking, Richie and Carlyle ask Roger and Billy to leave the barracks so that they can have sex. Richie wants to make Billy jealous; Carlyle just "wants his nut" and wants to feel part of this group. Roger reads Richie's motivation in purely racial terms: "Richie one a those people want to get fucked by niggers, man. It what he know was gonna happen all his life—can be his dream come true . . . Want to make it real in the world how a nigger is an animal" (p. 84), but he won't endanger himself by taking a stand on what is happening in his barracks. He tells Billy: "Get up in the rack, turn your back and look at the wall" (p. 82). Billy, however, is impelled to impose his white, heterosexist values and sense of territory: "It ain't gonna be done in my house. I don't have much in this goddamn army, but *here* is mine" (p. 84). Richie misreads Billy's stand as an expression of his latent homosexuality ("Jealous, Billy?"), but Carlyle, in fury and frustration, cuts Billy's hand, and Billy, in retaliation, turns on Carlyle with a straight razor—demonstrating that he too can be irrational, violent. Instead of attacking with a the razor, Billy flings it aside and attacks with words that assert his superiority: "I put you down, I put you down—you gay little piece of shit cake—SHIT CAKE, AND YOU—you are your own goddamn fault, SAMBO! SAMBO!" (p. 88). Carlyle responds by stabbing Billy fatally, thus silencing the voice of white, heterosexist middle America.

After Billy's body has been carried out, Carlyle arrested for Billy's death, and a drunken sergeant killed while trying to attack Carlyle, Roger, the assimilated black, and Richie deny any responsibility for what happened. The violence has not taught the survivors anything: Roger still denies that Richie told him he was homosexual, and Richie still insists that Billy returned his feelings:

> RICHIE: I've been telling you. I did.
> ROGER: Jive, man, jive!
> RICHIE: No!
> ROGER: You did bullshit all over us! ALL OVER US!
> RICHIE: I just wanted to hold his hand, Billy's hand, to talk to him, go to the movies hand in hand like he would with a girl or I would with someone back home.
> ROGER: But he didn't wanna; *he* didn't wanna.
> RICHIE: He did.

ROGER: No, man.
RICHIE: He did, he did. It's not my fault. (p. 102–103)

Roger claims to understand Richie, but at the end he can only call Richie "a queer." The only compassion comes from a drunken sergeant who has been told he's dying of leukemia: "There's a lotta worse things in this world than bein' a queer. I seen a lot of 'em, too" (p. 107).

Rabe uses Richie to dramatize sex as the great destroyer of the male bond. Whites and blacks can get along as long as a common language can be found, but homosexuality is taboo. The history of oppression of blacks has not made them sympathetic toward homosexuals.

At the end of the play, Richie lies on his bunk weeping, though he does not understand why he is unhappy: "I don't know what's hurtin' in me" (p. 107). Richie is unable to put a name on his pain—is it pain at being homosexual? at being rejected? at seeing a love object die? at awareness at some level of his complicity in that death? or is it confusion in the face of the meaningless violence he has seen?

In the hermetic, all-male world of *Streamers*, the homosexual, the object of irrational fear and hatred, becomes a symbol of the chaotic, hostile forces men unleash on one another. In Rabe's world, the homosexual is neither innocent victim nor traitor, but, like everyone else, he is sealed in a world of misunderstanding. The homosexual, not the representative of white, heterosexist values, survives, but it is 1967, and he has not yet found his own society or waged his own war.

RESISTANCE

Noel Greig and Drew Griffiths' *As Time Goes By* (1977), Martin Sherman's *Bent* (1979), and Doric Wilson's *Street Theater* (1982) move their gay characters from acquiescence of their status as outsiders or criminals to militant assertion of their gay identity, the beginning of gay liberation. The characters for the most part are fictional, but the settings and situations are evocations of crucial moments in gay history. In *As Time Goes By*, Victorian Englishmen flee to France to escape imprisonment in the wake of the Oscar Wilde scandal, and young Germans in 1934 try to flee Nazi Germany to avoid imprisonment and death. Among the English characters, Edward Carpenter provides a counterpoint of idealism and courage in the 1890s, and Magnus Hirschfield provides a model for self-acceptance for German homosexuals, but the fictional characters are not ready to live the example of their real prototypes. *Bent* focuses again on gay men in Nazi Germany, which has become a real historical site and a metaphor for oppression of gays, as the pink triangle worn by gay prisoners in concentration camps has become a symbol of gay identity and resistance. The Stonewall riot, which provides the finale for *As Time Goes*

By, is the subject of Doric Wilson's *Street Theater*, a satire of closeted gays and a celebration of a central moment in modern gay history. Within these historical moments, the most positive act is the rejection of oppression from without and within and, in Richard Hall's words, "choosing sides": "Gay theater will bear witness to some sense of community, to a shared experience of choosing sides, that is a central fact of gay life. Events onstage will be joined somehow to our choices offstage. 'Us' under the spotlight will be different from 'them.' "[32] In all three plays, we watch characters move from seeing themselves as "them," the outsiders and criminals that society sees, to asserting an "us," a positive identity.

In a homosexual brothel in London in 1896, the brothel keeper begins his presentation of his stable of young men to an audience of noblemen by quoting Gaveston's speech from the first scene of *Edward II*. The young men, clad in Greek costumes, quote poetry by Edward Carpenter. Thus begins Noel Greig and Drew Griffiths' history play, *As Time Goes By*, an example of historical gay drama fulfilling its traditional function of education and assertion of a gay culture. The play creates a catalog of literary and historical personages and events, as the action moves from Victorian England to Nazi Germany to Stonewall, through Oscar Wilde and Edward Carpenter, through Magnus Hirschfield and Cole Porter and Ernst Rohm, to a number of 1969 gay types, in order to show that the history of gay liberation did not begin on Christopher Street in 1969. The play also, through its choice of events, defines what are seen as three key symbolic events in the one hundred years of pre-AIDS gay history: Oscar Wilde's trial, the Nazi purge, and Stonewall. Within this framework Greig and Griffiths' reading of history shows that love relationships are only possible for those willing to be "out" and opposed to capitalism, which bases all relationships on money and ownership.

Each of the major episodes of *As Time Goes By* takes place in a setting that is both a gay meeting ground and a symbol of economic exploitation—an 1896 London brothel in which poor boys are kept to amuse wealthy noblemen, a gay nightclub in Berlin in 1929, a Mafia-owned gay bar in New York—and each episode contrasts those who accept the status quo with the revolutionaries of the time.

As the wealthy Londoners are endangered by a police raid on their favorite brothel, Edward Carpenter and his working-class lover have found their "Uranian [the favored term of many nineteenth-century writers, for homosexuality] Utopia." The wealth of the Londoners allows them to support the system that oppresses them and, in the process, to oppress the boys they buy for sex. Greig and Griffiths scathingly satirize the point of view of the wealthy closet queens as they sail to France to avoid imprisonment:

> TREVELYAN: I agree with Oscar Wilde and his socialist friends, but I'll certainly not fight alongside them for my sexual rights, because I can afford to pay for them.

REGINALD: Yes, at two sovereigns a time.

TREVELYAN: And worth every farthing. Lovely boys. Now who can say we corrupted them.

REGINALD: For goodness sake, we bought them.

TREVELYAN: They were poor, they needed to earn a living. Some of them probably did it just for the cash, but I'm certain that if they'd means of their own they wouldn't be out courtin' the girls. No, they'd be throwing their legs up in the air just the same, but for other young boys. They'd all be running off to set up house together. How dull for us. We'd only have each other.[33]

In the second part, Greig and Griffiths present Berlin from 1929 to 1934 as an object lesson in the price of remaining apolitical by contrasting the courage of Magnus Hirschfield with the blindness of the typical bar queen. The central event is the destruction of Hirschfield's Institute of Sexual Science and the collapse of Hirschfield's gay movement, not because of the Nazis but because of the indifference of gays: "No, what we've got to do is stick together and make a cozy little nest for ourselves, and let the rest of the world go by" (p. 50). The gay men of Berlin have no allies on the left or the right. As a friend tells Hirschfield: "The left supported you for the same reasons the Nazis are attacking your work. Power" (p. 47). At the end of the Berlin sequence, it is 1934 and everyone is fleeing for his life.

For Greig and Griffiths, Stonewall is a new chapter of continuing saga, a chapter of unity and courage. The sequence is made up of monologues, signifying a fragmented community, until the denizens of the bar—a disaffected student, a drag queen mourning the death of Judy Garland, and a businessman who has lost his black lover to separatist politics—join to fight the police. Finally gay men refuse to flee and stay to fight those who would deny them a place.

The Stonewall scene acknowledges the importance of the rebellion to gay liberation in England and Europe. In Philip Osment's poignant panorama of English gay life in the eighties, *This Island's Mine*, a character remembers:

Then came the rumours from New York
Of riots in Greenwich Village,
And a new sort of Pride was born
Which quickly spread to Europe.[34]

The birth of that pride comes, in *As Time Goes By*, with a simple, definite "No!" shouted to a policeman.

The spirit of Marlowe's Gaveston lives: *As Time Goes By* celebrates the opulence and playfulness of gay culture through musical numbers and parodies. From the Greek extravaganza at the brothel to the Berlin nightclub show to the drag queen's lament for Judy Garland, the play displays the the-atricality of gay life. In a typical gay cultural gesture, the play ends by ap-propriating the song "As Time Goes By" as a gay hymn: "A kiss is just a kiss/ A sigh is just a sigh,/ The fundamental things apply,/ As Time Goes By" (p. 70).

As Time Goes By was written by and for the gay community, providing a celebration of "oppression, resistance, survival, and heroic making." It coun-sels courage as a way of life for the gay man—for only in declaring himself and fighting his oppressors will he be free—and urges solidarity for a com-munity united to affirm and protect itself. The play's heroes, from the cele-brated Edward Carpenter and Magnus Hirschfield to the ordinary denizens of Christopher Street, provide examples of courage.

Martin Sherman's *Bent* (1979) uses the Nazi period to frame a more specific agenda. Through presenting a harrowing picture of oppression from without and within, *Bent,* as a mainstream gay play, also calls for assimilation through assertion of conventional values. Max, the leading character, pro-gresses from absorption in a negative version of the "gay lifestyle"—prom-iscuity, drugs, and the inability to embrace a love relationship fully—to an education in love for another man. The Holocaust provides a background of brutal oppression, but the real issue of the play is self-oppression, as mani-fested in behavior that would be considered typical for urban gay men in 1979. The opening of *Bent* is purposely ambiguous about its time period. We are warned to see homophobia, or heterosexism, as a constant possibility, but we are also encouraged to see Max's education in love as a gay *Pilgrim's Pro-gress.*

At the beginning of *Bent,* Max is a rather unsettled thirty-four-year-old who shares a sparsely furnished apartment with his lover, Rudy, a dancer in a drag show. Max and Rudy's relationship is fashionably "open," though Rudy does not share Max's penchant for bringing home lovers for him and Max to share, nor for his flirtation with sadomasochism: "I know pain is very chic just now, but I don't like it, 'cause pain hurts."[35] References to cocaine, mén-ages à trois, and fashionable S&M activities underscore the parallels between 1934 Berlin and pre-AIDS urban gay life. However, a knock at the door brings Nazi soldiers, who kill the young SA officer Max had brought home the night before. Max and Rudy are forced to run for their lives. It is the morning after the Night of the Long Knives, and its aftermath will reinforce the lesson in self-oppression Max learned years before when his father fired a young worker Max loved: "Queers aren't meant to love" (p. 132).

After the Nazi invasion of the stage at the end of the first scene, the remaining short scenes of act 1 trace the two years from Max's flight to his arrival in Dachau and show Max's growing denial of his own sexuality, as a strategy for staying alive. In one scene, Greta, the opportunistic drag queen who employed Max and Rudy, denies his gayness, too: "Everyone knows I'm not queer. I got a wife and kids" (p. 93). Denial is survival.

In another scene, Uncle Freddie, a middle-aged closet queen who has maintained the proper image while secretly being a "fluff," comes to tell Max that his family will help him escape from Germany but will do nothing for Rudy, with whom Max has spent more than a year in hiding (living in tent colonies and in the forest), while Max tried to "swing a deal" to get them out of Germany. Max knows that to win the cooperation of his family, he will have to play by their rules: "Remember that marriage Father wanted to arrange. . . . Make the arrangements again. I'll marry her. Our button factories can sleep with her button factories. . . . If I want a boy, I'll rent him. Like you. I'll be a discreet, quiet . . . fluff. It's what Father always wanted" (p. 97). Neither Max nor Uncle Freddie is aware that "decent, quiet fluffs" are also an endangered species.

Although he gives up his family's offer of escape because he is committed to protecting Rudy, who is neither strong nor particularly bright, Max cannot admit to loving him: "What's love? Bullshit. I'm grown up now. I just feel responsible" (p. 97). Later, in a brief moment of happiness, Max and Rudy hold hands by the campfire in their forest hideout: a searchlight is turned on and they are immediately arrested. Max's edict, "Queers aren't meant to love," is again reinforced on the train to Dachau, when Max, in order to survive, must not only deny his relationship to Rudy—"If you want to stay alive, he cannot exist" (p. 105)—but also deal the deathblow to his lover.

Max must further betray his dignity and self-respect to prove he isn't "bent" by performing an act of necrophilia with an adolescent Jewish girl. Thus Max earns a yellow star—the badge of the Jew—rather than a pink triangle—the badge for the bottom of the Dachau pecking order in 1936— but in the process loses what remains of his self-respect: "You mustn't touch me. I'm a rotten person" (p. 112). By the end of the first act, Max is a picture of shame and self-hatred.

The short scenes that compose the second act are devoted to Max's reeducation by Horst, a young political activist who is a well-drawn version of a conventional character in gay drama and film: the proud gay who is the teacher, foil, and lover of the ambivalent hero (Saul in *As Is*, Felix in *The Normal Heart*, Peter in *An Early Frost* are other examples). During act 2, as Max and Horst perform the maddening task of moving rocks from one pile to another and back again, Horst teaches Max that to do more than survive, "You should be proud of *something*" (p. 118). The basis of that pride is the love Max has long forbidden himself. Because Max and Horst are not allowed to touch each other, or even look at each other, their relationship must progress solely through language, thus presenting an ironic reversal: usually it is not sex gay men are denied by a heterosexist society but the right to speak openly of their desire, the right to express their love.

For Max, speaking of sex is one thing, but love is alien territory. When Horst proclaims his love, Max can respond only with self-hatred: "Hate me. That's better. Hate me. Don't love me" (p. 132). Horst counters by asserting the telling difference between him and Max: "I love myself. Poor you, you don't love anybody" (p. 133). Horst also echoes Rudy in his rejection of Max's need to inflict pain as part of sex: "You don't make love to hurt" (p. 137), and he forces Max to enter the alien territory of real emotional intimacy signified by a loving, nonsexual embrace, even though this embrace must be in word, not in deed. Tenderness replaces rough sex and love replaces self-hatred, but in this world of oppression, Max's first real physical embrace of Horst comes after Horst has been fatally shot: "I love you. What's wrong with that? What's wrong with that?" (p. 147).

Horst dies running toward the soldier who is harassing him. His death is an act of defiance and resistance. Max puts on Horst's jacket, thus exchanging yellow star for pink triangle, and walks into the electrically charged fence. His suicide, too, is an act of resistance. He dies a proud, gay man. His identity has been forged and is proudly asserted. Dachau allows no riot against authority, but a man can assert his identity and choose his death. Shortly before he dies, Horst affirms a central lesson of gay history: "Well . . . what the hell. There are queer Nazis. And queer saints. And queer mediocrities. Just people. I really believe that. That's why I signed Hirschfield's petition. That's why I ended up here. That's why I'm wearing this triangle. That's why you should be wearing it" (p. 141).

For all its grim subject matter, *Bent*, like *As Time Goes By*, celebrates theatricality, from the song of the Berlin drag queen to the celebrated verbal sex scenes, to the unabashedly melodramatic ending. Moreover, it never loses its sense of the ironic humor that enables its characters to endure.

As both *As Time Goes By* and *Bent* use Nazi Germany as a metaphor for gay oppression, both *As Time Goes By* and Doric Wilson's *Street Theater* (1982) present the Stonewall riot as the beginning of gay liberation and a true gay community. *Street Theater* is also an exemplar of inside gay drama, written by a gay playwright for gay audiences and performed, for part of its New York run, at The Mineshaft, a Greenwich Village sex-on-premises leather bar. During its run at The Mineshaft, *Street Theater* was being performed not in some theater removed from the life of its audience but literally within the gay male community, a kind of indoor street theater. Jack, the leatherman who is one of the play's principal characters, could have been one of The Mineshaft's regular customers. The bar itself, with its leather costumes, S&M trappings, and the performance of sex as theater, showcased those theatrical aspects of gay life that the play celebrates.

Wilson's play seems to stem from a comment by playwright William M. Hoffman, "The Stonewall Riots of 1969 might be viewed as gay street theater,"[36] for *Street Theater* is a memorial to Stonewall and also a celebration of the theater of gay life, presenting a catalog of pre-Stonewall gay types: the catty drag queen, the leatherman, the kid from the Midwest, the diesel dyke, student radicals, and young and old closet queens—including Michael and Donald from Mart Crowley's play, *The Boys in the Band* (1968), which was still presenting a picture of gay self-hatred when the Stonewall riot took place. It also presents caricatures of gays' adversaries: the undercover police who relish the assignment of entrapping gays and the mafia-connected gay bar owner.

Street Theater begins with the voice of Murfino, the "cigar in the mouth slob" who runs the Stonewall Inn for his "partners in New Jersey."[37] Murfino sees himself as the narrating stage manager of Thornton Wilder's *Our Town* (1938), which he acknowledges was written by someone "of your lavender leaning" (p. 8), but the allusions to *Our Town* only distance Wilson's play from that idealized picture of small-town life written by a closeted homosexual. Nor will the stage of this uncloseted extravaganza remain bare, as it does in *Our Town*. A diesel dyke and leatherman bring on scenery that colorfully depicts the Christopher Street of June 1969, and Murfino's voice is eventually drowned out by the voices of gay people.

The principal action of the play is the creation and mobilization of a gay community, which at the beginning seems a ludicrous fantasy: "You couldn't find two faggots who agree on the recipe for cheese fondue" (p. 28). In the first act, Wilson presents, in a series of comic confrontations and unsuccessful assignations, caricatures of the self-hatred that divides the community, most fully personified in Sidney, a middle-aged closet queen who revels in the masochism of unfulfilling relationships: "My dear man, you underestimate my capacity for self-destruction. When the wrong man comes along, I'll know him" (p. 45). Sidney is an older version of Michael and Donald, who, like their namesakes in *The Boys in the Band*, are victims of psychoanalysis: "You have no idea how good I feel about how bad I feel" (p. 22).

The climax of the second act is the Stonewall riot. At the end of the play, Sidney gives up the closet and joins the gays who are rebelling against police harassment. Only Michael and Donald remain on the side of their oppressors:

> DONALD: You faggots are revolting!!
> (SIDNEY, *horrified at* DONALD, *makes his decision, tosses his sunglasses in the gutter, joins* CEIL *and the others.*)
> SIDNEY (*to* DONALD *and* MICHAEL): You bet your sweet ass we are!
> (p. 77)

Sidney joins his fellow gays in "a grouping worthy of a statue in Sheridan Square" as the play ends. The police are silenced: the united gay men and women are the dominant voice, chanting "The street belongs to us."

The revolt dramatized in *Street Theatre* is not so much against outside forces as it is against the internalization of those forces. Internalized heterosexism maintains the closet and prevents community. The gay community that coalesces to resist exploitation and police harassment is a motley assortment of gay types. The Stonewall of *As Time Goes By* is linked to the struggles of blacks and women, part of a pattern of issues of identity and civil rights raised by the protests of the sixties. *Street Theater* focuses on the theater of gay life and the forging of its existence as a political reality.

As the plays about traitors focused on creating and maintaining masks, these plays focus on moments of unmasking. *As Time Goes By* moves from theater to the real life of gay oppression. *Bent* moves to a moment of honesty in which Max removes his disguise, the yellow star, and proudly dons the jacket with the pink triangle. At the end of *Street Theater*, Sidney doffs his dark glasses and joins the gay community. These unmaskings provide a positive counter to the dramas of duplicity that chronicle a sad chapter of gay history.

HEROIC MAKING

Larry Kramer's list of culture heroes was basically one of artists and intellectuals. His "culture that isn't just sexual" is, with a couple of exceptions, a list of makers of high culture: philosophers, artists, writers, musicians. In gay drama, one alternative to the dramatization of criminals as rebellious gay martyrs is the depiction of gay artists as heroes. These biographical dramas establish and reinforce a gay canon. They educate gay audiences about men whose lives make them part of gay history while making sure the mainstream audience understands the centrality of homosexuality to the experience and work of these artists. The plays are also reminders of the major role gay artists have had in high culture and assertions of a continued investment in that culture, which drama itself represents. The common bond between gay and heterosexual members of the audience is an appreciation of the creative work of these men, for the plays assume a knowledge of the creative output of their subjects.

Since one function of these plays is to establish the link between homosexual desire and the work of these creative men, they are also love stories, chronicling the problems for creative gay men in establishing relationships in a world hostile to homosexual love. These biographical dramas, like the depictions of gay life discussed in the next chapter, place gay love relationships within a pattern familiar to all members of a mainstream audience, defy heterosexist assumptions that gay love is impossible, and sanction the display of such love.

Christopher Hampton's *Total Eclipse*, produced at the Royal Court in 1968, a daring work for its time, candidly depicts the turbulent, sporadic affair of the nineteenth-century French poets Arthur Rimbaud and Paul Verlaine. Rimbaud was a sixties hero (Jim Morrison declared that Rimbaud was a major influence on his work), and in choosing him as a subject, Hampton was focusing on a contemporary ideal of the antisocial artistic rebel. In terms of gay

drama, *Total Eclipse* combines the dramatization of the homosexual as criminal and outsider with an exploration of the relationship between art and love.

The play begins with Verlaine's voice remembering Rimbaud's fascination with the underclass and his combination of beauty and power, which
would lure Verlaine from his bourgeois womb: "He moved with the grace of
a little girl at catechism. He pretended to know about everything, business,
art, medicine. I followed him, I had to!"[38] After Rimbaud's death, Verlaine
claims that "Rimbaud is trapped and living inside me" (p. 71), that Verlaine
speaks with Rimbaud's voice. By beginning and ending with Verlaine's voice,
the play underscores its focus on Verlaine's appropriation of Rimbaud. The
final sentence of his first speech, "I followed him, I had to!" defines the
compulsive nature of Verlaine's attraction to the teenage genius' beauty, his
imagination, and his stronger will.

At the beginning of the play, Rimbaud enters the living room of Verlaine's in-laws, where Verlaine and his pregnant wife have resided since he
gave up his civil-service position. Rimbaud is filthy, but he is also "extremely
good looking: thin lips, cold, grey eyes" (p. 11). When Verlaine enters, he is
"transfixed by Rimbaud's appearance" (p. 11) and overwhelmed by Rimbaud's
articulation of his loathing for bourgeois cant and mediocre poetry. Verlaine
is first seen as opposite to this personification of the starving, rebellious artist:
he is "well dressed and looks like a civil servant with private means" (p. 11).
He seems a balding, self-indulgent sentimentalist who doesn't have the courage to be a rebel. When Verlaine's wife agrees with her father's edict that
Rimbaud leave the house (among other things, Rimbaud has been stealing
objects d'art), Verlaine, drunk and enraged, throws her down and punches her
in the face.

Although Verlaine cannot muster the courage to sever all ties with his
wife, he becomes Rimbaud's companion and lover, half of an Odd Couple of
nineteenth-century sentimentalist and modern, pessimistic realist. Verlaine all
too easily relies on vague words like love, while Rimbaud realizes that "Com-
placency exists. But not love. It has to be reinvented" (p. 23). Love cannot be
what "binds families and married couples together out of stupidity or selfish-
ness or fear" (p. 23). Love must be "reinvented" out of physical desire and
human need: Rimbaud sounds here like a 1968 sexual liberationist.

The action of the play revolves around the faltering attempts of the
two men to forge a love relationship without the language or the models and,
in Verlaine's case, without the strength of character to support such an endeavor. Rimbaud is constantly frustrated in his attempts to strengthen Verlaine:
to make him leave his wife and her world, which is antithetical to the making
of poetry, to force him to be more precise in his use of words, and to help
him understand that poetry begins in pain. He tells Verlaine of being raped
by four drunken soldiers: "It clarified things in my mind which had been
vague. It gave my imagination textures. And I understood that what I needed,
to be the first poet of this century, the first poet since Racine or since the

Greeks, was to experience everything in my body" (p. 23). Verlaine must realize that the body is not merely the source of indulgence, sentiment, or nostalgia, and it is for this purpose that Rimbaud stabs his lover's hands with a knife: "The only unbearable thing is that nothing is unbearable" (p. 35).

While the audience at *Total Eclipse* sees no love scenes between the two men (though we are told of their anal intercourse), we do see a series of scenes chronicling a troubled homosexual relationship without a community to offer them support or a choice of more appropriate lovers. Verlaine vacillates between "respectability" and marriage on the one hand and debauchery with Rimbaud on the other. He is afraid, above all, to be alone, because "I don't exist without someone else" (p. 53). Rimbaud, who is incapable of supporting himself or of living his own philosophy, stays with Verlaine but rationalizes his dependency and inertia as free will: "You're here, living like this, because you have to be. It's your life. Drink and sex and a kind of complacent melancholy and enough money to soak yourself oblivious every night. That's your limit. But I'm here because I choose to be" (p. 49). When Rimbaud finally musters the courage to leave an unsatisfactory relationship, Verlaine shoots him in the hand:

> RIMBAUD *begins to laugh hysterically.*
> VERLAINE: Oh God, what have I done?
> RIMBAUD: You missed. (p. 55)

Verlaine turns the shooting into a melodramatic scene with the appropriate cliché; Rimbaud sees the shooting as another ludicrous failure. Rimbaud presses charges out of his anger that Verlaine will not let him leave freely but insists on possessing him. The resultant trial focuses more on sodomy than on the shooting, and Verlaine is sentenced to two years in prison.

The final meeting between the two poets also ends in violence. After imprisonment, divorce from his wife, and a not-very-convincing religious conversion, Verlaine wants to reestablish his relationship with Rimbaud, who has stopped writing and wants to make a final break out of their problematic relationship: "I no longer have any sympathy for you" (p. 61). Rimbaud's only means of escape from Verlaine's clinging, desperate embrace is a series of swift punches.

The final scene takes place fifteen years later. Rimbaud has died of cancer. His family is trying to destroy the poems that would sully his, and their, reputation and to ban the anonymous preface containing biographical details not consonant with their image of Rimbaud as a Christian convert. Verlaine, a fat, pathetic, middle-aged drunk, lives only for his sentimentalized memory of the past with Rimbaud: "We were always happy. Always, I remember. . . . He's not dead, he's trapped and living inside me" (p. 71). But it is Verlaine who is trapped within his distorted memories of Rimbaud that no longer have any relationship to truth: "We were always happy. Always. I remember" (p. 71). Verlaine is neither with wife nor male lover: he now is in the company of a "semiretired prostitute."

Total Eclipse is not only a chronicle of the unhappy relationship of two artists. It is also the depiction of a relationship for which the participants' culture or psyches did not equip them. Verlaine, however talented, could not escape his own weakness and dependence. Rimbaud could not find a place for his sexuality or poetry. This picture of what contemporary pop psychology calls codependency is also an attack on past and present complacent, middle-class culture.

In *Total Eclipse*, Christopher Hampton employs the episodic structure and objective realism Osborne used in *A Patriot for Me* to depict the relationship of Verlaine and Rimbaud. The recurring images that give the play its power are of violence to the body, from the punching, stabbing, and shooting to Rimbaud's sister's lengthy description of the amputation of his cancerous leg. The living-through-the-body Rimbaud envisioned has more to do with pain than pleasure. The play does not show Verlaine and Rimbaud in their roles as poets beyond presenting a few artistic arguments and Rimbaud's physical attack on a mediocre poet, nor does it attempt an explanation of the relationship between their turbulent romance and their poetry. As a matter of fact, one is hard put to imagine Hampton's Verlaine writing poetry at all, much less poetry of the quality of his real counterpart. The mysteries of Rimbaud's life after his break with Verlaine are left unexplained. Yet, like *A Patriot for Me, Total Eclipse* is presented as a case study that does not veer from selected facts.

Noel Greig's *The Dear Love of Comrades* (1979) is a more positive picture of the forging of a gay life away from the norms of conventional society. Edward Carpenter, its protagonist, is a figure in the pantheon of gay history; a poet, socialist, and early writer on homosexuality. Carpenter tried to practice what he preached, attempting to found a Utopian gay community in the midst of Victorian England. Here the relationship between life and work is central: Greig's play focuses on the relationships of his central character, as he moves to the full experience of the homosexual love he writes about. The play shows the troubled relationships between Carpenter and each of the three working-class Georges who were his lovers (Adams, Hukin, and Merril) in the early nineties and presents their problems in living by Carpenter's ideals of nonpossessiveness. Adams and Hukin are married; though their wives are never seen, they offer a protective cover for their relationships with Carpenter. Adams, the most problematic of the lovers, cannot be cured of his capitalism: he wants Carpenter's farm to be profitable. Nor can he avoid feelings of possessiveness that the play attributes to his capitalistic principles of ownership. George Hukin is too much Carpenter's disciple, too much a believer in his philosophy, to be his satellite. He loves Carpenter but also loves his wife and George Merril. At the end, he demands that Carpenter practice what he preaches, first by not being jealous of Hukin's sexual relationship with Mer-

ril—Carpenter has difficulty ridding himself of feelings of jealousy and possession—and then by accepting and affirming his own sexual orientation.
Hukin tells Carpenter: "Write till there's not a scrap of paper and the ink's
run dry. One day it might all come true, but there's people living now who'll
thank you much more for doing the *one thing* that you're not supposed to do.
Which is to be homosexual. Not think and write and talk about it, but be it."[39]
Hukin leaves Carpenter with the challenge he most fears, of living the life he
has theorized with the earthy George Merril.

The *Dear Love of Comrades* is narrated by a character who represents
the English author E. M. Forster, who in the 1940s gave a radio talk on Carpenter. Forster's hatred of his own homosexuality makes him Carpenter's opposite: "He [Carpenter] was also a homosexual, although I did not announce
this fact over the airwaves. How could I admire in someone else a quality that
I loathed in myself?" (p. 74). The prologue of the play begins with Carpenter
and the three Georges singing a setting of Walt Whitman's "I Sing the Body
Electric," the antithesis of Forster's description of his reaction to being
"pinched on the bottom" by George Merril: "The electric shock that entered
my spine did not reach my brain. I drew a veil between myself and the world"
(p. 75). The juxtaposition of Forster's voice and Whitman's poem provides an
ironic frame for the action of the play, but it is Whitman's words, and the
voices of Carpenter and the three Georges that are, literally, the last word.
Carpenter taught his working-class friends principles, but they taught the
middle-class writer from Brighton to revel in a physical world, to "sing the
body electric." Greig's play reinforces the traditional notion of working-class
physicality vitalizing the middle and upper classes. It celebrates the class and
age differences that were presented as evil in *The Green Bay Tree*.[40]

The Dear Love of Comrades is written in the nonlinear, non realistic
style of many Gay Sweatshop plays, presenting a collage of scenes and songs
whose roots are in Brecht. But where Brecht uses irony, Gay Sweatshop productions offer a more expansive, optimistic humanism, more Carpenter than
Marx. On the one hand, Greig's play is a carefully researched documentary
by a student of Carpenter's work; on the other, it is a finely shaped theater
piece whose meaning comes from juxtaposition and repetition, not linear narrative. *The Dear Love of Comrades* celebrates a chapter of gay history before
Stonewall that offers an alternative to the martyrdoms depicted in many historical dramas. The play gives historical perspective to the principles of gay
liberation and reveals the links between that liberation and socialism. Like
Hampton's play, it challenges by stressing the great difference between concept and actuality, between idea and life.

When Noel Greig read about Carpenter's life, he found not only subject
matter but inspiration:

> Here was proof that a movement in which I held faith—the impulse towards
> a radical shift in the structures of society—held within its early stages an

open advocation of something even closer to me—my own sexuality. Some
sense of isolation dissolved—the feeling of having no personal part in the
movements of history. In the early 1970's that starting point for many of us
in the Gay Liberation Movement was the phrase "the personal is political."
For myself Edward Carpenter gave this a historical dimension.[41]

Greig's play is not only an expression of his commitment but also a clarification of the values the Gay Sweatshop represented and of the style it developed.

   Total Eclipse and *The Dear Love of Comrades* are set in the late nineteenth century, when homosexuality was just beginning to be an operative
concept: the term "homosexuality" was coined in 1869; the action of *Total
Eclipse* begins in 1871. Verlaine and Rimbaud, through their attraction to one
another, were launched into uncharted territory. Edward Carpenter, at the end
of *The Dear Love of Comrades*, which takes place in 1896, overcomes his
fears and commits to living out the homosexuality he theorized in his writings.
Unlike Edward Carpenter, who wrote about homosexual love, or Paul Verlaine, who made his relationship with Arthur Rimbaud a matter of public
record, the English composer Benjamin Britten was reluctant to discuss his
homosexuality. Only after Britten's death did his artistic collaborator and lover
of almost forty years, tenor Peter Pears, openly discuss their relationship. Paul
Godfrey's play, *Once in a While the Odd Thing Happens* (1990), places center
stage the aspects of Britten's life that remained, while he was alive, an open
secret.

   The Britten-Pears relationship was something of a paradox. On one
hand, it was one of the best known artistic and personal collaborations in
musical history and in gay history; however, Britten could not see his homosexuality in positive terms. Unlike his sometime friend and collaborator,
the poet W. H. Auden, Britten remained a closeted man and artist, yet he
wrote a series of eloquent theater works about men who cannot find a positive
outlook for their sexuality: Claggart and Vere in *Billy Budd*, Aschenbach in
Death in Venice, Quint in *The Turn of the Screw*, and Peter Grimes. Musi-
cologist Philip Brett has commented that Britten, in his work, expressed "his
own shame and loneliness . . . so powerfully that he encapsulates the social
experience of gay people since homosexuality was defined in 1869."[42] As
such, Britten's operas are themselves central to twentieth-century gay theater.

   However unable Britten was to find positive terms for his homosexuality, the texts he chose to set to music create a gay canon: Rimbaud's "Les
Illuminations," Michelangelo's sonnets, W. H. Auden's poems, Henry James'
The Turn of the Screw and "Owen Wingrave," Melville's *Billy Budd* (with a
libretto by E. M. Forster), and Thomas Mann's *Death in Venice*. Even Britten's adaptation of George Crabbe's poem, "The Borough," into the opera
Peter Grimes can be given a gay reading: an emotionally thwarted man is

violent toward the boys to whom he is attracted, and his expulsion represents the exile of the "different" man from his community.

Building on the writings of Britten experts like Philip Brett and Clifford Hindley,[43] who have focused on the gay elements in the composer's work, Paul Godfrey, in *Once in a While the Odd Thing Happens*, gives the reticent Britten a voice and a language in which to express his love for Peter Pears and to describe the relationship between that love and his music, much of which was written for Pears to perform. Godfrey's preface to the published text of his play insists on its authenticity, developed out of interviews with people who were closest to Britten, including Pears and Britten's sister, Beth. Godfrey's claims for his play are complex and contradictory: "The play is fiction, but I have portrayed the characters as I believe they were and shown events as I understand them. The purpose was not to do a biographical drama but to use these specific figures to create a play with the widest resonance."[44] Though he lists his sources, Godfrey claims artistic license in his treatment of the facts, impressions, and memories of conversations that he amassed in his research. Godfrey did not want to be tied to the details of time and place that often limit biographical drama. He opts for the representational freedom of Gay Sweatshop playwrights rather than the literal detail of *Total Eclipse*. Most playwrights, I assume, aim for the "widest resonance," but in this case the aim is to create a play that aspires, in its use of free verse, to the emotive and suggestive power of Britten's music, which W. H. Auden describes in the play as "mercurial, but eloquent, yet uncomfortable" (p. 72).

Philip Brett has written that the gay man, "and in particular the artist, needs to come to terms with himself as well as society, and settle the linked questions of 'roots' and sexuality."[45] These related issues are the focus of Godfrey's play, which is structured on events in Britten's life in the decade leading to the premiere of his first grand opera, *Peter Grimes* (1945): the unhappy move to America, influenced by Auden; the development of the relationship with Pears and the break with Auden; the return to England and commitment to Aldeburgh, a village on the North Sea, as the locus for his life and work; and the dedication to the seemingly quixotic goal of creating English grand opera. Godfrey's Britten makes meaningful connections—between his sense of place and his art ("I should have known I could never live anywhere else" [p. 57]) and between his passion for Pears and his music. The unique quality of the Britten-Pears relationship is its complete merger of art and love. Britten puts Pears' voice "at the centre of everything" (p. 63), while Pears himself is "the source of my joy" (p. 64).

The play tracks the events of this ten-year period in a free-flowing succession of short episodes. Time and place are conveyed only by the language, not by realistic scenery or devices. The play's detachment from the realistic apparatus of scene-setting used by plays like *A Patriot for Me* and *Total Eclipse* mirrors Britten's own separation from the key events of the period, the Depression and World War II, to which he was a conscientious objector. Britten's commitment to his art separated him from history: during the war he devoted himself to writing *Peter Grimes*: "Little else matters but getting this done" (p. 62).

Godfrey's Britten is as steadfast in defending his personal life and work as he is to his principles as a conscientious objector. When a chorus member tells him he should cancel "your precious opera with your 'friend' in the starring role" so that opera lovers can celebrate the end of the war with a familiar work, Britten stands firm:

> BRITTEN: You do it!
> CHORUS: Careful, you may regret this one day.
> When we come to round up people like you.
> BRITTEN: I am not ashamed!
> *Exit* CHORUS
> (I am ashamed?
> No.)
> Here
> I am. (p. 80)

The chorister tries to make Britten the outsider, as the villagers of Aldeburgh do to Peter Grimes. Britten's simple "I am" is an eloquent expression of self-acceptance, tied to his love for Pears and pride in his work. The greatness of Britten's operas are linked to his love for Pears, "I wrote it for you, you know that" (p. 84), as they vividly portray men bereft of the kind of love Britten and Pears experienced.

Godfrey has written Benjamin Britten as a gay artist-hero. To do so, he omits the negative image of homosexuality Britten internalized and expressed in his work. Godfrey's Britten is proud and loving, if also, like his protagonists, willful and obsessed. This is a revisionist Britten, one contemporary gay men can unreservedly celebrate.

The production of *Once in a While the Odd Thing Happens* was itself a page of gay history. In the era of Clause 28, which above all bans government money for positive depictions of homosexuality as an alternative to family life, the government-funded National Theatre commissioned and presented a play that did just that. It is Britten's married sister, the representative of conventional family life in the play, who says of Britten's relationship with Pears, "I think such happiness is too rare to dismiss it" (p. 76). The word "odd" in Godfrey's title, which is the first line of a chorus from Britten and Auden's American folk musical, *Paul Bunyan* (1941), defines the relationship: considered "queer" by some, it is all too "uncommon."

Benjamin Britten's love for Peter Pears and his collaboration with Pears are inextricably connected to the experience of Britten's work, particularly on disc, where Pears' definitive interpretations have been recorded for posterity.

History and literature have preserved the details of Edward Carpenter's life with George Merril and Paul Verlaine's sad, turbulent relationship with Arthur Rimbaud. The movement from the doomed relationship of Edward II and his "minions"; through the unhappy outsiders of *A Patriot for Me, Another Country, and Streamers*; to the violence and self-destruction of the poets in *Total Eclipse*; to the proud, angry self-assertion of the participants in the Stonewall rebellion and the loving relationships of Edward Carpenter and George Merril, Benjamin Britten and Peter Pears, offers a positive, even optimistic vision of gay history, affirming the centrality of the right to be gay and to love.

CHAPTER SIX

FASHIONING A GAY SELF

It's about growing up,
Getting older,
Living on a lover's shoulder,
Learning love is not a crime.
MARVIN, IN WILLIAM FINN, *Falsettoland*

In John Guare's *Six Degrees of Separation* (1990), the young black gay man whose acting of the role of Sidney Poitier's son has given him entree into an affluent, white home, tells his hostess:

> The imagination has moved out of the realm of being our link, our most personal link, with our inner lives and the world outside that world—this world we share. . . . Why has imagination become a synonym for style? I believe imagination is the passport we create to take us into the real world.[1]

Paul's comment can be seen as a gloss on the dramatic depictions of the stasis and progress of gay men I shall discuss in this chapter. These depictions present imagination first as a means of separation and isolation, then as a tool for forging a gay identity, and finally as a bridge to other people.

In the closet dramas discussed in part 2, the fate of the homosexual was isolation. Corrupted Julian controls the action at the end of Mordaunt Shairp's *The Green Bay Tree* (1933). Unlike his corrupter, Mr. Dulcimer, he is allowed to survive, but he is cut off from realism's version of the "real" world—of productive activity, marriage, and children. At the end of the play,

Julian is arranging flowers, turning nature into art just as he, the homosexual as aesthete, is a work of art, created in the image of Mr. Dulcimer. In Tennessee Williams' plays, the gay artist who tries to join his vision to the real world is destroyed. In *Suddenly Last Summer* (1958), the poet Sebastian Venable is eaten alive by the boys he has had sex with. Allan Grey, another poet, is exposed by his wife; rejected and humiliated, he shoots himself. If we read Blanche DuBois as a crypto-gay character, we see a person who tries to redeem a threatening heterosexual world by turning it into theater. In the end, Blanche is not allowed to find a space in which to create a livable, tolerable world. Inge's Spencer Scranton, in *The Tiny Closet* (pub. 1962), can only hide in another closet when his locked closet is opened, revealing the women's hats that are the products of his imagination, his sexuality, and his gender identity. Like the closet, the parallel world of the imagination and of imaginative creation is not necessarily a safe haven.

"Realist" Stanley Kowalski shouts at Blanche in Williams' A *Streetcar Named Desire* (1947), "There isn't a goddam thing but imagination,"[2] as though imagination were the opposite of a stable truth. Gay drama centers on the conflict established in Blanche DuBois' cry, "I don't want realism. I want magic!" In Williams' play, the realism that crushes Blanche's performances is a fabric of lies and denials far more damaging than Blanche's theatrical illusions. Imagination can liberate, but imagination can also create and reinforce an isolated, hermetic world for the gay character. Many of the plays discussed in this chapter enact a pathology of the imagination, while others show the liberating possibilities of a gay man's imagination. I also postulate that a reassertion of imaginative, nonrealistic theater can liberate gay drama from the prosaic, conventional norms and strictures reinforced by realism.

In the plays discussed in this chapter, two related metaphors link the gay character's experience to the world of imagination: performance and writing.

Performance can entail the exaggerated acting of roles created and defined outside oneself, expressions of one's internalized heterosexism. Such negative exhibitions usually connect assumptions about oneself to a supposed fixed reality of gender identity that postulates that homosexuals aren't men. Exclusion from conventional representations of manhood or outright opposition to them can result in various exhibitions of identification with women: imitations of women—which means drag; identification with larger-than-life depictions of victimized women from opera, ballet, and camp movies (the Judy Garland cult being the most famous example in this area); or performing a stereotype of effeminacy. The problem for the gay character is to liberate himself from the stereotype of effeminacy without merely aping the behavior of heterosexual men. The ideal performance would be unmoored from conventional notions of masculinity and femininity—an imaginative self-creation possible onstage only outside the framework of realistic drama.

Another mode of performance is the play of anarchic wit, the virtuosic manipulation of language as a means of dismantling censorious judgments. As the exercise of wit has been for gay men a successful defensive measure— at times even a liberating tactic—wit, too, has been a liberating tactic in gay drama since the epigrams of Oscar Wilde's crypto-gay characters deflated the shibboleth of Victorian propriety. Doric Wilson's *Street Theater* of 1982 (discussed in chapter 5) recreates gay history through parody and satire; even the climactic moment is built on a pun, "You faggots are revolting," an expression of internalized heterosexism here converted into a call to arms.

Christopher Durang has based his most hilarious yet disturbing plays on parodies of the language of oppression. *Sister Mary Ignatius Explains It All For You* (1979) has a particularly virulent representative of the Catholic church unwittingly demonstrate how the theology and doctrine of her religion oppresses women and gay men, who "do that thing that makes Jesus puke."[3] For Sister Mary Ignatius, words aren't enough to purge the world of such sin, so she, carrying out her own inquisition, shoots the young man who has proudly proclaimed his gayness: "I've sent him to heaven!" (p. 206). In *Beyond Therapy* (1981), a female psychiatrist has an honest, if manic, reaction to a character's admission of gayness:

> COCKSUCKER! Oh, I'm sorry. It was just this terrible urge I had. I'm terribly sorry. (Gleefully.) COCKSUCKER! (*Screams with laughter, clutches Snoopy, rocks back and forth.*) COCKSUCKER! Whoops! Sorry. Oh, God, it's my blood sugar. Help, I need a cookie.[4]

Wit enables Durang's characters to parody and dismantle destructive languages, but the effect is limited. It seldom helps them shape a positive vision of gay experience. Similarly, the wit of many characters in gay drama helps them dismantle oppressive language, but it is not the only imaginative tool necessary in constructing a positive self. Wit is often only an expression of futility.

Writing links the gay character to the world of art and to the written world of the play he inhabits. The protagonists of many gay dramas are failed writers, masters of language too often turned against themselves instead of being shaped into art. Only after mastering the articulation of a positive self-image, which requires revising a language that has, for gay men, been oppressive, is a character finally able to write.

The metaphoric actions of performance and writing are joined in the creation of the gay self, a work of art, the product of a critique, revision, and, to some extent, rejection of the self-image and the language that have been taught by an education in a heterosexist society. Only when the gay character has embarked on such a self-creation can he forge relationships that meaningfully and honestly connect him to other people—lovers, friends, family. Like the self, relationships and the languages of relationships must be forged anew out of words that have limited or negative meanings for gay men. A major example of this is the discourse of marriage and family.

ISOLATION

The most significant nurturing place for "inside" gay drama was the Caffe Cino in Greenwich Village, which for almost a decade presented a series of new dramas, many of them gay-oriented. The cafe, owned by a gay man, Joe Cino, was from 1958 until Cino's death in 1967 a workshop for a group of young gay playwrights, including Lanford Wilson, Robert Patrick, Doric Wilson, and William M. Hoffman.

Lanford Wilson's one-act play *The Madness of Lady Bright* (1964) was one of the first big hits of this fringe theater (164 performances) and proved that gay drama—and off-off Broadway itself—could be commercially viable. In this prototypical inside gay drama, a gay character imaginatively transforms his environment.

The setting for *The Madness of Lady Bright* is on *"the stage within a stage."* The audience is not to forget that Wilson's play is just that—something enacted. The stage as frame also underscores the performative nature of Leslie Bright's life. Leslie fashions the space in which he lives as a reflection of himself, but doing so is an act of exclusion as well, of controlling the encroachment of reality. The walls of Leslie's one-room apartment are covered with signatures of the men Leslie has had in his bed. The names are a memorial to Leslie's sex life. The walls on which the names are inscribed are Leslie's memory: *The Madness of Lady Bright* really takes place inside its central character's mind.

The young man and woman who share the stage with Leslie portray the voices in Leslie's head, of his mother, of his past lovers, of imaginary companions, and the internalized voices of "normal" society. Having no real audience left, Leslie Bright imagines one, as he imagines his fellow performers. Leslie's head is also filled with music—Mozart, Judy Garland, *Giselle*, rock 'n' roll, and striptease accompaniments—heard sometimes separately, sometimes cacophonously. Leslie has not created the art that defines him; he has imported it from a space he does not wish to inhabit.

Images of performance and writing begin the play. The boy and girl are an imaginary audience for Leslie's monologue, but Leslie also has an urge to write down—to record—his utterances. He becomes inarticulate, however, the moment he tries to write:

> You are a pile of paper addresses and memories, paper phone numbers and memories, and you mean nothing to me. (*Trying to catch the line just said*)
> You—I am surrounded—I am left with (*Rather desperately trying to catch*

the right phrasing of the line to write it down) a—with paper memories and
addresses. (*Finding a piece of paper at the desk. With a pencil, bent over
the desk*) I am—how?[5]

The play moves from this futility, which reflects Leslie Bright's loss of the
ability to order his experience, to the imaginative enactment of real and imaginary scenes from the past, particularly reminiscences of Adam, the first signer
of Leslie's wall and the man Leslie claims to have loved. Leslie's fixation on
the one man memorialized on his wall with whom he didn't have sex is a
prime manifestation of his self-hatred and masochism. Like many gay protagonists, he romanticizes the roles of victim and outcast, thus making his isolation both bearable and inevitable.

For Leslie, his drag is not only a performance of femininity related to
his sense of failed masculinity—"But, whatever your dreams, there is no possibility whatever of your ever becoming, say, a lumberjack" (p. 181)—but it
is also a veneer of eternal youth covering his aging body. As he puts on
lipstick, he proclaims, "I will never be old" (p. 196). Leslie may be "built like
a disaster," but his assumed femininity is the basis for his fantasies of beauty,
love, and freedom. Leslie imagines himself as the ballet heroine, Giselle.
Giselle is one of the Wilis, specters of young women who have died of unrequited love; they reappear every night to lure the men who abandoned them
to dance to their deaths. Giselle, however, tries to save her faithless husband's
life. Leslie identifies with Giselle, who, with the masochism of a male-created
nineteenth-century heroine, continues to sacrifice for the man she loves. At
the end of the play, Leslie tries to dance *Giselle* but collapses. Unlike Giselle,
he is tied to a failing body. Throughout Leslie's dancing, the young man and
woman dance together, an imagined couple and a complement to the visual
image of Leslie's isolation.

With only memory and imagination, bereft of new experiences to feed
on, Leslie is going mad, his mind deteriorating in counterpoint to the aging
of his middle-aged body: "I grow brittle and I break. I'm losing my mind,
you know. Everyone knows when they lose their mind. But I'm so lonely"
(p. 196). At the end, Leslie can only repeat "take me home," which becomes
a pathetic cry for help, a plea for death.

With a nod in the direction of Samuel Beckett monologues like *Krapp's
Last Tape* (1958), Wilson has fashioned a vivid theatrical portrait of a man
disconnected from the outside world (no one answers the phone when Leslie
calls except Dial-a-Prayer). Leslie's imagination, now out of control, frightens
him. He hears the voices of people who have briefly loved him and the in-
escapable voices that molded his self-hatred. Leslie Bright is not loved. He
doesn't even have the solace of the performer's substitution for love—adu-
lation. *The Madness of Lady Bright* is a depiction of the imagination and·
theatricality that have made life bearable for this lonely man, yet isolated him.

Wilson's comrade at the Caffe Cino, Robert Patrick, has written, "I met here [in Greenwich Village], the kind of brave and brazen gay men I longed for, but half the time they were so crippled by identity crises and simple self-hatred that they couldn't maintain an affectionate erection, much less a relationship."[6] In Patrick's *The Haunted Host* (1964), this dilemma is not the core of classic American realistic melodrama, but of comedy. The setting is realistic, a Greenwich Village apartment "set just above the main homosexual cruising crossroads,"[7] but the action mixes fantasy and reality. Again, writing and performance dominate the action. Jay, the protagonist, is a playwright whose life and work are now crippled by the ghost of his lover, who committed suicide after Jay left him. The lover, Ed, was a handsome young would-be writer who was also Jay's protégé. Jay's way of showing his love for Ed was to pour his own self and creativity into him. This act of "ghost-writing" figured the ways in which Jay gave over his whole identity to his lover, more a sign of self-hatred than of love. When he didn't feel that Ed was returning all he had invested in the relationship, Jay ended it: "What was I supposed to do, go on producing indefinitely for you to keep on confiscating?" (p. 120).

When the play opens, Jay's home is in disarray and is still dominated by Ed, whose picture hangs on the wall and whose manuscripts cover Jay's desk. The chaotic room is an image of his mind, stricken with grief and guilt. Jay has become a recluse, conversing only with Ed's ghost. Into the hermetic world of this drugged-out, manic, and self-hating failed writer comes Frank, who is the spitting image of Ed, looking for a place to spend the night, advice on his playwriting, and, though he claims to be heterosexual, perhaps an exotic homosexual adventure. Jay tries desperately to avoid responding to his unwelcome guest, the embodiment of his ex-lover, sure that he is living through some awful punishment.

Jay's defense against this intruder is to perform, to camp, and to cut off any chance for communication by carrying on a frenetic monologue. When Frank asks for advice on his writing, Jay mounts a filibuster, boring Frank to sleep by reading his own plays, a not-too-subtle means to avoid helping Frank write. When Frank tries to defend himself, Jay drugs him into unconsciousness. Above all, Jay fights the bids for artistic advice and the sexual ploys that are temptations to relive the past: "You want me to do it all over again! Jay, the mad scientist! You want me to praise you and pour myself into you and write your plays for you. You want me to take my brain out and put it into your body and make a corpse out of you and a ghost out of myself" (p. 132). Jay makes Frank, and himself, realize the sickness of his past relationship with Ed and why he cannot let history repeat itself: "The minute you try to live someone else's life for him, or let him live yours—it's suicide" (p. 135). In trying to avoid repeating a mutually destructive relationship, Jay avoids all affection, all contact, and has sealed himself in his apartment. Before Frank leaves, he says the one thing he thinks can "break" Jay: "I love you." The ideal of being loved may be frightening to Jay, but Frank is the wrong person to offer it.

Frank, eager at first to assert his heterosexuality, tries to cast Jay as the "other," but Jay's wit enables him to turn Frank's heterosexist judgments around and direct them back to their source:

> FRANK: Tell me, did you ever see a psychiatrist?
> JAY: You mean one of those people who tell you society is sick then offer to help you adjust to it? (p. 97)
>   . . . .
> JAY: Tell me, Frank, how long have you been heterosexual? (p. 99)

Frank can only dismiss Jay's turning of the tables as sick, a standard heterosexist ploy.

Frank has all the makings of a realistic playwright. He wants to write "Honestly! Truthfully! Fearlessly!" (p. 115), based on his own experience— as if he has had any. He brings to his work what Jay would call the "cookie cutters" of conventional interpretation ("I took psychiatry") and generalizations from a white, heterosexual point of view ("trying to get you people to be serious is murder"). Jay has his own revelations, based on a point of view and experiences Frank cannot comprehend.

When Frank leaves, Ed's ghost leaves as well. Jay is ready to move out of the past. He throws into the wastebasket Ed's manuscripts, the remnants of an unhealthy relationship that wasn't a collaboration. Jay reaches a crucial turning point. He has gained enough understanding of the past and enough pride in himself to exorcise his ghost. Frank accused him of being tough, but toughness was essential for the survival of gay men in the 1960s—and beyond. When Frank asked Jay whether he was a homosexual, Jay responded, "I am THE homosexual," a glib remark but one showing the beginnings of the sense of pride that will allow Jay to write his own script instead of pouring himself into someone else's. Jay's witty, manic performance has both dismantled Frank's judgments and liberated Jay from constantly reliving his past series of self-destructive infatuations. At the final curtain, Jay, too, leaves the apartment. His exit from the scene suggests a re-integration into the gay society that teems right outside his apartment.

At the end of Mart Crowley's *The Boys in the Band* (1968), Michael leaves his apartment to go to midnight mass, hardly a place to give a gay man much positive reinforcement. Michael is a failed writer whose self-hatred keeps him from creative activity. Unlike Lanford Wilson and Robert Patrick, Crowley does not make anything of the metaphoric potential of his protagonist's profession or of the connection between his self-hatred and his inability to write. Michael's profession as writer is merely linked to a general sense of his articulateness. His only narratives are self-oppressing or misconstructions of others' lives. Language for him is always a weapon. Michael's home is the locus for the gathering of a group that represents middle-class urban gay society. In the course of the play, Michael assembles the group and dismantles it, reinforcing his own isolation.

I mentioned in the previous chapter how Michael and his friend Donald are parodied in Doric Wilson's *Street Theater* (1982). They are the most eloquent spokesmen for the men in power, "People like us don't have rights," Wilson's Michael says to his fellow gays, "we haven't earned them."[8] They are the only gay characters who attack the participants in the Stonewall riots from the sidelines: "You faggots are revolting!" Wilson realized *The Boys in the Band* was itself an important event in gay history and gay drama and that Michael and Donald are not merely malicious fictions but frequently encountered types of self-hating, closeted gay man who have internalized the language of their oppressors. After all, the self-hatred that Michael and his friends act out was present in *The Madness of Lady Bright* and Patrick's own play, *The Haunted Host*. Yet *The Boys in the Band* has become for its detractors, particularly those who did not experience gay life before Stonewall, a paradigm of politically incorrect gay drama. For some, this antipathy to the play is based on its lack of a sense of the sadder elements of gay history. For others, the problem with *The Boys in the Band* is one of audience. Kaier Curtin notes that during the first weeks of its run, *The Boys in the Band* played to predominantly gay audiences but that eventually it attracted a large number of heterosexuals.[9] It is one thing to show a gay audience the dark side of its life; it is quite another to profit by parading this before a mainstream audience.

Many of the actors did all they could to distance themselves from their characters, thereby reinforcing stigmas against gay people. A *New York Times* feature article on one of the actors was entitled, "You Don't Have to Be One to Play One." As his wife pours his beer, actor Cliff Gorman tells the reporter, "I already knew how to lisp because I'd been telling gay jokes since I was a kid."[10] Gorman also pointed out that gay actors were asked to read for the part of Emory, whom the same *Times* article described as "The Definitive Screaming Queen" and refused. Acting gay was professionally risky: the reticence of the actors reflects the fact that being gay in 1968 was not something one advertised. This public distancing of actor and character helped maintain the distance between the play and its audience.

At the same time, as playwright William M. Hoffman has noted, "Whatever one thinks of it, *The Boys in the Band*, more than any other single play, publicized homosexuals as a minority group."[11] The very existence of such a performance was in some sense empowering. The production ran for years, and the original cast made a film version in 1970, which is still available on videotape. Heterosexuals may find the video a reassuring, if inaccurate, picture of the unhappy lives of "those people"; gay men can see it as a quaint period piece or a slice of pre-Stonewall gay life. Film critic Vito Russo believed that the film "summed up a generation of gay men who were taught to blame all their troubles on their homosexuality."[12]

The Boys in the Band follows the structural pattern of *The Haunted Host*, but in doing so inverts the traditional place of gay men in commercial drama: an outsider disrupts a hermetic, "realistic" society and leaves the stage at the climax of the action, but in Crowley's play this outsider is not expelled as the homosexual was in traditional drama. He leaves voluntarily, rejecting the world presented on the stage. The play's point of view is both that of the self-hating gay man and that of the outsider, who represents the audience on the other side of the fourth wall. What the outsider and the audience see and hear is purported to be a slice of life, the "off-stage" activities of closeted gay characters when they're not "playing straight." For the first time, mainstream audiences see gay men talk openly about their sexual predilections, dance together, kiss, and retire upstairs for sex. Characters acknowledge a common gay culture with their references to the plays of Tennessee Williams and Edward Albee and their homages to camp movie queens like Maria Montez. The silences and indirections of closet drama no longer prevail, but the play is still trapped within the normative sphere of realistic drama. The actions of the characters become performances, watched and judged by the "normal" outsider who offers society's judgments, which the characters too readily accept. Just as the fallen woman of nineteenth-century drama accepted and articulated the judgment of the patriarchs who decided her place in society, the boys in the band know that they are gay, alone, and unhappy—that they would be happier if they were straight. They can articulate these judgments with the solipsism and eloquence developed through years of psychotherapy, whose theories and strategies are presented without skepticism.

In the first scene between Michael and Donald, best friends who "tricked" together years ago when they were in college, Donald, degreed but doing menial work because he is too anxious and self-hating to pursue a career, defines himself as sick, "I'm not that well yet."[13] His sexual orientation is one expression of his "sickness." Michael, a compulsive shopper and reformed alcoholic (until the end of act 1), defines himself as "spoiled rotten, stupid, empty, boring, selfish, self-centered" because his overprotective, domineering mother "refused to let me grow up" (p. 23). The classic Freudian stereotype of arrested development is linked to psychoanalytic interpretation—"Christ, how sick analysts must get of hearing how mommy and daddy made their darlin' into a fairy" (p. 19)—without attacking or even questioning the role of the psychiatrist in maintaining that interpretation. Michael's sporadic dependence on the Catholic Church only intensifies his masochism. A heterosexist audience could see Michael and Donald as pathological and unproductive—intelligent men who have failed to fill a useful role in society. Thus they can be judged both sick and unmanly.

After fifteen minutes or so of masochistic self-analysis, Michael's party guests begin to arrive and, when assembled, are presented as a microcosm of the gay community: Emory, a mincing Nellie queen and interior decorator; Bernard, a black librarian who masochistically endures racial slurs; a bickering couple comprising Larry, a wayward, promiscuous artist, and "athletic-looking" Hank, a schoolteacher who has recently left his wife to move in with Larry; and a vapid, stupid, but beautiful hustler with a heart of gold: "I try to show a little affection—it keeps me from feeling like such a whore" (p. 174). The hustler is a birthday present for the guest of honor, Harold, a former ice-skater and self-described "thirty-two-year-old, ugly, pock-marked Jew fairy" who veils his own self-loathing under a cloud of marijuana smoke. Clearly the only things that connect the members of this bickering group are their gayness, their self-hatred, and their middle-class credentials. The only thing they share with their presumed audience is their position in the middle class. The vituperation and game-playing that ensue at Harold's birthday party owe a considerable debt to Edward Albee's *Who's Afraid of Virginia Woolf?* (1962)

The surprise arrival of the supposedly heterosexual Alan, Michael's former college chum, the only representative of the straight world, is the catalyst for cruelty from cruelty-prone Michael. When confronted with a roomful of homosexuals, Alan, "who is so pulled-together he wouldn't show any emotion if he were in a plane crash" (p. 29), lashes out at effeminate Emory with a catalog of homophobic epithets worthy of *Cat on a Hot Tin Roof's* Brick Pollitt:

> ALAN: (*Lashes out*) Faggot, fairy, pansy . . . (*Lunges at* EMORY) . . . queer, cocksucker! I'll kill you, you goddamn little mincing swish! You goddamn freak! FREAK! FREAK!
> (ALAN *beats* EMORY *to the floor before anyone recovers from surprise and reacts*)

By the end of the play, Alan has vomited, vehemently denied Michael's accusations that he had a homosexual affair in college, and vowed to return to the wife he has recently left, thanking Michael for shocking him back into his marriage. The play hints—merely hints—that Alan's leaving his wife and his behavior at Michael's party are signs of homosexual panic. Alan's continued presence at the party is at least a sign that he is as much as masochist as the others: "He was dying for somebody to let him have it and he got what he wanted" (p. 180). However, the shock of this nasty party has scared Alan back into a heterosexual commitment. Even if Alan has acknowledged homosexual impulses, the play does not question his return to a heterosexual life; it has to be happier than what he has seen at Michael's party and, after all, Alan has children.

Alan's presence brings to the fore all of Michael's guilt and self-loathing. He attacks his friends viciously and tries to destroy their illusions and frail self-respect, but he succeeds only in displaying his own misery. Harold, the birthday boy, who has repeatedly, accurately labeled Michael's behavior as "hateful," silences Michael's cruelty by making him face the truth about himself: "You are a sad and pathetic man. You're a homosexual and don't want to be. But there is nothing you can do to change it" (p. 173). After the guests have left, a guilt-stricken Michael goes off to midnight mass, leaving his friend Donald alone in the apartment reading a book. Donald will finish the bottle of brandy and drive back to Long Island. Though these two neurotics are best friends, neither could possibly have a relationship. They, like most of the characters in the play, are doomed to be alone until "we learn not to hate ourselves so much" (p. 178).

While positing unhappy isolation for most of its characters, *The Boys in the Band* also defined a subgenre of gay dramas about redefining the rules of gay men's relationships. The one couple in the play, Larry and Hank, are fighting over Hank's equation of relationship with monogamy. Hank and Larry have been lovers for two years. For Larry, it is an attempt at a long-term relationship after a history of sexual promiscuity. It is Hank's first gay relationship; he left his wife and children to be with Larry. Hank wants the same rules to prevail in his relationship with Larry that prevail in a heterosexual marriage; "till death do us part" and total sexual fidelity." The tension caused by this disagreement over the rules of their relationship causes cycles of bickering. The more Hank suspects Larry of infidelity, the more Larry asserts his right to have other lovers. Larry also would like Hank to be unfaithful, so that he would be free to follow his impulses. Larry doesn't believe the fidelity Hank wants is even possible: "The ones who swear their undying fidelity are lying. Most of them anyway—ninety percent of them. They cheat on each other constantly and lie through their teeth. I'm sorry, I can't be like that and it drives Hank up the wall" (p. 157). The couple's conflict is resolved by an agreement to try Larry's rules: "Respect—for each other's freedom. With no need to lie or pretend" (p. 160). The contract Hank and Larry establish is their solution to the conflict the gay liberationist sees between male need for sexual variety and the affectional need for a stable, loving relationship. Larry teaches Hank that love is not a matter of sexual possession or even sexual fidelity. Larry and Hank resolve their dispute, at least temporarily, and go upstairs to make love, the one happy ending in the play. In this resolution, Crowley asserts both the possibility of a relationship and the fact that the rules cannot be the same as they are for heterosexuals. Marriage is redefined but upheld, and Larry and Hank leave the neurotic game-playing. Crowley makes his positive judgments indirectly; Larry and Hank are the most "masculine" of the guests and the ones with active professions.

As for Michael, Donald, Emory, Bernard, and Harold, *The Boys in the Band* allows its heterosexual audiences a liberal compound of pity, tolerance, and superiority. Homosexual audiences saw that the characters' "problem" was not their sexual orientation but their "internalized homophobia," their acceptance of the judgments of family, medicine, law, and religion.

Doric Wilson's *Street Theater* (1982) shows that the Michael and Donald of Crowley's play, and their "real life" counterparts, were not immediately converted by the events of June 27, 1969. Larry Kramer's *Just Say No* (1988) depicts the Michaels and Donalds a generation later but turns the closeted, self-hating, but ever-so-well dressed gay men into the best friends and supporters of a certain ex-actress who is the First Lady of the United States and into enemies of the gay community. Kramer's version of Michael and Donald dread exposure because they would no longer be invited to the best parties. Larry Kramer and Doric Wilson see Michael and Donald as real devils that gay life and gay drama must exorcise.

The Boys in the Band was a bellwether for gay drama in a number of ways. It not only proved that uncloseted gay drama could be "commercial" (it ran over a thousand performances) but it also offered a formula for appropriating the conventions of realistic drama while demonstrating their limitations. The conventions can provide an effective means of presenting "problems" or affirming relationships, but they cannot depict what it means to act gay. In moving gay drama "uptown," Crowley's play moved it into the language of American realism, in which aberrant behavior has to be explained and cured. There is a plodding literal-mindedness about the play, the result of a drive to make sure the audience has a reason for everything and everyone, but such full explanations are characteristic of commercial plays. You can't blame Crowley for succeeding in the popular arena (he moved on to produce the successful television series "Hart to Hart," which began in 1979). The challenge for post—*Boys in the Band* and post-Stonewall gay dramatists is to find forms more suited to the creation of a positive gay self.

In the worlds of *The Madness of Lady Bright, The Haunted Host,* and *The Boys in the Band*, the gay world is a dangerously closed society. Domestic space becomes a refuge from a hostile, terrifying world. "Out there" are hostile heterosexuals; inside, gay men face their own private demons (created by the people out there). Isolated within the domestic space, the creative gay man is at a dead end. This isolation did not stop with Stonewall. Robert Patrick wrote in 1988, "*The Boys in the Band* was no fantasy. It still isn't, for that matter."[14] The AIDS epidemic becomes for some characters another reason to withdraw.

Terrence McNally's *The Lisbon Traviata* (1985/1989) weaves a disturbing set of variations on the themes of fantasy, performance, and isolation within a gay world at the height of what one character calls, "our very own bubonic plague."[15] Mendy and Stephen, its central characters, are holdovers from an earlier time, self-hating gay men who use elements of gay culture to encase themselves in a bearable world. Mendy and Stephen's escape and solace comes from that cornerstone of gay culture—opera. McNally, himself a regular on the "Opera Quiz" feature of the live Texaco Metropolitan Opera radio broadcasts, uses his two protagonists to analyze the gay man's fascination for opera and to draw its dangers vividly.

Jokes abound in the gay community about macho types in leather bars arguing over the merits of rival divas and describing the lobby of the Metropolitan Opera at intermission as the Easter Parade for gay men. To more than one generation of homosexual men opera offered not only a liberation but the chance to participate in a sport; the merits of various singers could be argued as another group of men might argue baseball statistics. Part of the imaginative experience of opera is the audience's substituting of an imaginary body for the body of the overweight, unglamorous diva. Opera, above all, purports to transcend bodies. Substituting one sex for another—imagining oneself as the larger-than-life character or as the performer—is the next logical step. Opera cries out for such rereading. The opera queen's identification is usually less with the role than with the performer: he projects himself onto the diva who can, through voice and force of will and personality, make an audience believe she is a grand, beautiful, tragic victim. One of New York City's great institutions is La Gran Scena Opera Company di New York, in which the all-male cast present scenes from the great operas filtered through a gay sensibility. The men are capable of singing all the great soprano roles and acting with all the magnificent excess of the great divas. The more one knows about opera, the more one can appreciate the detail of their parody of specific artists, but anyone who knows even the bare bones of the story can appreciate diva Vera Galupe-Borzkh (Ira Siff) singing Violetta's poignant "Addio del passato" from the third act of Verdi's *La Traviata* while caressing her lover's briefs. The male characters are fools, unworthy of sharing the stage with the grandly suffering diva who is an unlikely combination of vulnerability and toughness, of faith and cynicism. What Mme. Vera Galupe-Borzkh and her colleagues perform is the self-absorption of the diva—the total performer.

Generations of opera queens have idolized Maria Callas, the temperamental Greek-American soprano whose vocal limitations were overcome by force of will, intelligence, and fierce temperament; whose career languished early when vocal problems became insurmountable; and who died, alone, in Paris, having never recovered from the loss of her two great loves, her singing and her Greek tycoon, Aristotle Onassis. Her story is itself operatic—grand, sentimental, a bit unbelievable, built on the suffering and loneliness of an extraordinary woman.

In *The Lisbon Traviata*, Stephen, a failed writer, and his friend, Mendy, live for opera, particularly for the memory of Maria Callas, around whom they have erected a mythology that has little connection to her or to their own reality. The "Lisbon Traviata" of the title is a pirated recording of Callas singing the part of Violetta in a Lisbon performance that Mendy has not yet heard and that fills the air at the end of the play. Mendy has given up wife and family to live hermetically sealed in a nineteenth-century setting, drapes shut, doors locked, listening to opera, as though doing so were his profession. Even his gay society centers on opera and Callas. His annual party is on Callas' birthday, and his friendship with Stephen is based on their mutual adoration of the Brooklyn-born diva.

The first act, set in Mendy's ornate, campy world, is comedy, dominated by an opera queen enacting his passion: "She's given me so much:

pleasure, ecstasy, a certain solace, I suppose; memories that don't stop. This doesn't seem to be such a terrible existence with people like her to illuminate it" (p. 34). Mendy speaks of Callas in terms like "truth" and "intensity." Her singing provides feelings Mendy cannot get from his own life—from his estranged wife, his son, his friends. Yet he wonders why he can't find a lover. Beyond the closed drapes of Mendy's shrine to Callas is a troubled real world of men dying of a real disease, AIDS, but Mendy and Stephen are oblivious to real suffering. All emotions have been focused on their fantasy of Maria Callas. Mendy can think only of obtaining a recording of the Lisbon *Traviata*. At the end of the first act, the audience hears, with Mendy and Stephen, director Franco Zeffirelli's voice on a videotape of a documentary about the soprano: "There has been perhaps one faithful companion to Maria throughout her life, her loneliness. The price sometimes one has to pay for the glory and the success" (p. 49). Mendy and Stephen's loneliness is not connected to such glory, but to their own self-absorption. Where Mendy sees opera as a substitute for an emotional life he cannot have—"Opera doesn't reject me. The real world does" (p. 24)—Stephen, a writer and editor whose professional and personal life are on the rocks, sees his own emotional life as opera. The second act, which veers toward operatic pathos, depicts the end of Stephen's relationship with Mike, a doctor enmeshed in the real world of dying patients and dying friends—and in a new relationship. Mike tells Stephen: "You live in TOSCA. You live in TURANDOT. You live in some opera no one's ever heard of. It's hard loving someone like that" (p. 86). Stephen refers to Mike, his estranged lover, as "my life's salvation" (p. 87), but cannot even give Mike his full attention; he is impelled to focus on whatever opera is blaring from the stereo. Mike leaves because, "I just want to be away from you" (p. 85).

At the end, after Mike has left, Stephen loses himself in Callas' Violetta, the operatic version of *La Dame aux Camélias*, singing "Sempre libera"—"Always free"—an ironic commentary on Stephen's entrapment in his own fantasy world: *"He throws his head back with her as she reaches for a climactic high note but no sound comes out. . . . Callas is all we can hear"* (p. 88). Stephen's only union is with Callas: he will listen to her while avoiding his lover's attempts at connection.

On one level, *The Lisbon Traviata* is a satire on opera queens filled with diva jokes that only opera queens would understand. One can laugh at Mendy, who is a parody of a familiar type, but Stephen is neither funny nor sympathetic. His cruelty toward his fellow gays who have died of AIDS—"Wouldn't you rather be at a nice restaurant than sitting here moping over someone who probably, if the truth could be faced up to, even just a little bit, got what was coming to him" (p. 80)—is the expression of someone totally severed from reality and compassion. His desperate, futile attempts to humiliate Mike's new lover and to keep Mike from leaving are pathetic.

The second act is filled with messy verbal and physical violence, a contrast to the bloodless, noble deaths of opera. Mike punches Stephen for blaring opera on the stereo as a means of driving out Mike's new lover. Stephen threatens to stab Mike with a pair of scissors. Unconsciously, Stephen and Mike speak the lines from the final scene of Georges Bizet's *Carmen*, but without the music and within a Manhattan apartment, such operatic moments are banal.[16] Mike leaves the apartment for the real world of professional commitment, family (he is going to stay with his brother), and the potential of a relationship with a productive human being. Stephen, who no longer writes or even cares about his editing job, is alone and silent, bonded only to Maria Callas. Even his friend Mendy has beome only a voice on the phone.

FATHERS AND SONS

The protagonists of *The Madness of Lady Bright*, *The Haunted Host*, *The Boys in the Band*, and *The Lisbon Traviata* turn their domestic spaces into stages on which their own neuroses and fantasies are played out. Ultimately, these performances create or maintain isolation. Imagination is used by these gay characters to project themselves onto other people or to absorb others into themselves but not to create. In another group of plays, the protagonist liberates his imagination by forging links with a redefined family, albeit a nontraditional one.

In Albert Innaurato's *Coming of Age in Soho* (1984), a writer's reunion with his fourteen-year-old son leads to a reintegration for him of experience and art. At the beginning of the play, Bartholomew Dante, known to his friends as Beatrice, unsuccessfully isolates himself in order to try to find himself. This search first involves divesting himself of compromises with the outside world, "I want to stop working to define myself by every standard but mine."[17] His ultimate goal, though, is artistic expression. Beatrice is a writer whose books thus far reflect his own immaturity; he is best known for a children's book entitled *Little Boy Bound*. The link between work and creator is made abundantly clear in the first moments of the play, when a young man, tied to a chair, emerges from Beatrice's bedroom. In addition the book's title presents an image of its author's immaturity. Beatrice is also the creator of a video game, "Death in Venice," involving a chase between an old man, a young boy, and cholera. The game is a reflection of his life in the age of AIDS.

Beatrice has left his wife to start life over in a Soho apartment, but she, the ambitious daughter of a Mafia don, wants him back; she needs a husband to legitimize her campaign for political office. Beatrice is through with acting heterosexual: "If I wasn't acting a hundred percent, I was acting forty or fifty percent" (p. 30), but he also wants to avoid the stylized performance associated with acting gay: "I've forgotten how to respond naturally. I seem to camp automatically now, to expect insincerity, and admire finely wrought falsehood, and I shrug off everything" (p. 36). Beatrice's choice of nickname reflects the idea that finding oneself is in part a matter of working out one's sexual identification. He is not, as the name would suggest, a drag queen, but "conventionally masculine in manner" (p. 3). He is, as a matter of fact, both Bartholomew and Beatrice, both masculine and feminine, both public ('Bartholomew' is his pen name) and private.

Beatrice wants to "raise" himself, but his home is invaded by two teenage boys: Dy, a runaway preppie, and Puer, Beatrice's son by a brief marriage to a German radical. Dy has run away "to be free" (p. 9); Puer, to "feel less singular and alone" (p. 24). Beatrice falls in love with Dy but is disturbed by his lack of feeling toward his son's efforts to win his love. Beatrice tells Dy that "One of the problems of life" is "sorting out love and friendship and sex" (p. 28), which he manages to do as he works through his attachments to these two boys. Dy finally agrees to go back home, and Beatrice decides to let his son stay with him. At the end, Beatrice and Puer put the contents of Dy's journal of living with Beatrice, "Coming of Age in Soho," into the computer as a starting point for Beatrice's own writing: "Maybe there's something in there about me, or about us, or maybe about the three of us I can expand" (p. 77). As Puer types into the computer, Beatrice begins his writing: "It was the worst of times, but Bartholomew Dante began to come of age and this is his story" (p. 78).

At the end Beatrice is again Bartholomew, the author of *Little Boy Bound* is writing about coming of age, and the man who liked to tie boys up has freed himself and embraced his son. Coming of age is realizing one is both boy and man, both masculine and feminine. This drama of the maturation of man and artist is presented with an almost operatic mixture of realism and outlandish theater, from the invasions of Mafia goons who try to force Beatrice back to his wife to Puer's outlandish attempts at looking like the all-American boy. Character's names (Odysseus, Trajan, Puer) free them from the confines of realistic drama. The echo of Charles Dickens ("It was the best of times, it was the worst of times" is the first line of his 1859 novel, *A Tale of Two Cities*) in Beatrice/Bartholomew's last line is appropriate; Innaurato's play is Dickensian in its reliance on coincidence, its veering from comedy to pathos, its narrative freedom, and its generosity of spirit.

Harvey Fierstein's *Torch Song Trilogy* (1981) also moves its central character to an embrace of fatherhood. At the end of the trilogy a gay family has been forged, and Arnold's acceptance of love is linked to the acceptance by his ambivalent lover, Ed, of his own homosexuality. Arnold's troubled relationship with Ed is the through line that connects the three plays.

Each of the three plays in *Torch Song Trilogy* is written to be performed in a different style, moving from musical theater to domestic realism. The first play, *International Stud* (1978), alternates scenes and torch songs sung by "Lady Blues." The songs create the world Arnold inhabits. Instead of identifying with divas, like the protagonists of *The Lisbon Traviata*, Arnold identifies with the tough female voice of the torch singer, suffering and surviving unworthy men. Arnold is "the last of a dying breed,"[18] an old-style drag queen who makes his money singing torch songs in gay bars. When Arnold starts talking about what he wants in a man, "the international stud," he begins to sound like a torch-song lyric:

> A guy who knows what he wants and aint a'scared to go out and get it. A guy who satisfies his every need and don't mind if you get what you want in the bargain. Matter of fact, he aims to please. He'd be happy to be whatever you wanted him to be, 'cause you're happy bein' what he wants you to be. (p. 16)

Arnold does not yet see that what he wants in another man is what he must become. He does know that he needs this "stud" not for his on-stage female role but for his off-stage male one, "the part that's not so well protected" (p. 16).

Arnold's first monologue is addressed directly to the audience as he prepares to perform. In it he confesses the failing that makes a connection with the international stud—or becoming the international stud—impossible, the lack of self-love that prevents accepting love. We see Arnold's meeting with Ed Reiss as Ed's monologue. In essence, it is Ed's performance, the "line" he delivers to prospective "tricks" in gay bars; self-assured, clear in what he wants, though not without its red flags: "I'd ask you back to my place but I have this straight roommate. He's got a hangup about gays. . . . I date women too" (p. 18). This line signals Ed's inability to accept his homosexuality: "I've got to be proud of who I am" (p. 30). Ed has run away from Arnold precisely because he does love him and is terrified. He says sex with Arnold was "out of control" and refers to "losing" himself, both expressions of passion Ed finds terrifying, particularly when it means giving up ties to conventionality.

The simple platforms that make up the setting are stage "islands," allowing theatrical distance between Arnold and Ed to mirror their irreconcilable differences. A tape of their dialogue on their first night together is heard between choruses of one of Lady Blues' songs, as if the dialogue itself were the raw material for a torch song. Only in the final scene, in which Arnold takes control of the relationship by rejecting Ed's manipulative advances, are both actors visible in the same playing area. Ed, at that point in the throes of panic and indecision, wants Arnold to take charge and force him to give up Laurel, but Arnold has come to separate torch song from reality: "Maybe he's treating me just the way I want him to. Maybe I use him to give me that tragic torchsinger status I so admire in others. If that's true . . . then he's my International Stud. I love him. . . . But do I love him enough? What's enough? This is enough" (p. 43). Masochism should be left to performance, to torch songs. Arnold will not suffer through Ed's vacillations.

The monologues isolate their speakers, whose fears of commitment prevent honest dialogue. Yet, unlike Wilson's Lady Bright, Arnold has a real audience. The fourth wall of realistic theater has been razed and *The International Stud* begins and ends with direct address to the audience. The music, the torch songs, are not figments of Arnold's imagination but part of a meta-theatrical performance. Fierstein has successfully mixed genres: drag act, cabaret, comic monologue, and dramatic scene.

Fugue in a Nursery (1979), the trilogy's second play, takes place at Ed's upstate New York farmhouse. Laurel, with whom Ed now lives, has invited Arnold up for the weekend in order to size up the competition (Laurel knows Ed is not over his feelings for Arnold). Alan, Arnold's lover, insists he and Arnold go; he knows Arnold has not recovered from Ed. *Fugue in a Nursery* is not presented within the conventions of realism. The setting is a gigantic bed, in which all the action takes place, underscoring the dominant role in sex of game-playing. The bed is a stage on which the four characters do a lot of acting. The scenes are accompanied by and interspersed with an instrumental quartet, each instrument representing one of the characters. The linear action is clearly defined, but the nonrealistic style of performance focuses on the interrelationships of characters and scenes.

Arnold's antagonist is Laurel, who rightly sees Arnold as a rival and wages a battle she only partially and temporarily wins. All of Laurel's relationships have been with gay or bisexual men, and she is not about to suffer another rejection. Arnold, on the other hand, has no intention of actually returning to Ed, no matter how strong his feelings are.

Alan, Arnold's new beau, is a beautiful, eighteen-year-old hustler who sees Arnold as both lover and parent. Alan has every reason to be insecure about Arnold, who never will say he loves Alan because he doesn't, or at least, because he won't admit he does:

> ARNOLD: So, maybe I don't love him, but I need that gorgeous imbecile, and I like to think that he needs me.
>
> . . . .
>
> ED: Don't you think he deserves to be loved?
> ARNOLD: Of course he does. Who doesn't. But who is? (p. 75)

Ed and Alan have, literally, a roll in the hay, an act that has less to do with their attraction to each other than with their feelings for Arnold. The aftermath is that Ed and Laurel get married, and Alan and Arnold make a formal commitment to their relationship. Both are compromised relationships. Ed's marriage is the result of Laurel's manipulation and his cowardice. Arnold still will not admit he loves Alan. The play ends with Arnold as writer and performer, singing his new torch song, which is both a rejection of Ed and a recognition of what his relationship with Alan will be:

> I can't live on love alone.
> Want somebody all my own. (p. 101)

The fact that the song is directed to Ed, not Alan, is a sign that he has not been forgotten:

> Keep my number by the phone
> Call me if you should atone. (p. 101)

Again, Arnold ends the play alone onstage, where he is in control of the action. Offstage, events and characters are messier and not so easy to manipulate.

The final play, *Widows and Children First* (1979), takes place five years later. Arnold is still grieving over the loss of Alan, killed by gay-bashers. Arnold's memories of Alan are of a more loving and reciprocal relationship than was evident in *Fugue in a Nursery*. This may be in part because, as Arnold admits, ". . . it's easier to love someone who's dead; they make so few mistakes" (p. 172).[19] It is also because a real love developed between Arnold and Alan during the five years they were together. Arnold is in the process of fulfilling his and Alan's ambition of adopting a gay son, and fifteen-year-old David is living with Arnold on a trial basis. So is Ed, who has left Laurel and "temporarily" moved into Arnold's living room. While the play moves toward the formation of a new nuclear family consisting of Arnold, Ed, and David, its focus is on Arnold's tempestuous break with his mother.

Widows and Children First is, as the title suggests, about "widows" and their children. One widow is Arnold's mother, and the play concerns in part her inability to establish a peaceful relationship with her gay son; the other is Arnold himself, "widowed" by Alan and trying to raise David, Arnold's street-wise foster son. The basic issues of the play are two related, politically charged issues for gay men: a young gay's right to a nurturing, gay-positive home and a gay man's right to be a surrogate parent to young gays.

The action has moved to a realistic setting, Arnold's apartment, thus moving into the most familiar territory of American drama, domestic realism, though, as is typical in gay drama, a member of the "normal" middle-class family is the outsider who is later to be removed from the scene. *Widows and Children First* depicts the conflict between parent and gay son that has since become the formula for television dramas about gay men, but Fierstein makes Arnold's mother a classic nightmare of a Jewish mama, powerful but unintentionally funny, in the grand tradition begun by Clifford Odets in *Awake and Sing* in 1935. Arnold's mother cannot see her son as a fit father for David nor her son's feelings of love and grief for Alan as equal to hers for her husband:

> ARNOLD: How dare I say I loved him? You had it easy, Ma. You lost your
> husband in a nice clean hospital. I lost mine out there. They killed him there
> on the street. . . . Children. Children taught by people like you. 'Cause every-

body knows that queers don't matter! Queers don't love! And those that do
deserve what they get! (p. 145–46)

While he is still wounded by his mother's disapproval, she is angry that Arnold
never really confided in her, even after she flew up to New York to attend Alan's
funeral: "Maybe I could've comforted you" (p. 172). Arnold and his mother do
share strength, temperament, stubbornness, and their status as widows.

As Arnold lays down the law to his mother, his new son sets terms for
Arnold's relationship with him. Though Arnold has given this former battered
child the only loving home he has ever known, David doesn't want to be an
excuse for Arnold's isolation: "I'm tellin' you now: I'll walk if you try to use
me as an excuse for sitting home alone, or to pick a fight with your mother
or with Ed. Hey, you do what you gotta do. I aint judgin.' Just don't blame
anybody but yourself" (p. 158). As David wants Arnold to understand that he
has to take full responsibility for his life, Ed, now separated from Laurel and
sleeping in Arnold's living room, wants Arnold to trust his love: "Arnold, the
time I've spent here with you and David . . . it's been the closest thing to
whatever it is I want" (p. 164). At the end, Arnold and Ed begin negotiating
the sort of relationship they want, though they have no clear models: "Christ,
I mean, I don't even know what this is supposed to be. I can't exactly buy a
book or study some *Reader's Digest* article that's gonna tell me. All I know
is whatever this is, it's not a grade B imitation of a heterosexual marriage"
(p. 166).

Nothing is completely resolved at the end. Arnold is once again alone
onstage, listening to a song on the radio that David has dedicated to him.
Arnold, who needs "nothing from anyone except love and respect" (p. 152),
will cautiously build a strong relationship with Ed. The ending intimates that
a loving gay family is being forged, without the support of biological ties or
received rituals.

Torch Song Trilogy advocates the right of gay men to have what the
other 90 percent of society takes as its birthright—a loving home. Arnold,
like Beatrice Dante in Innaurato's *Coming of Age in Soho*, has moved from
loving a teenage boy to being a father to one. Yet the domestic realism of
Widows and Children First reinforces a misconception that there is no difference between Arnold's family and a heterosexual family, that the gayness of
Arnold, Ed, and David makes no appreciable difference. Could not Fierstein
have used a dramatic idiom that suggested this home was going to be enliv-
ened by its occupants' gayness, or at least by the imagination that shaped the
first two plays? In *Widows and Children First*, the only music comes from
the on-stage radio. While this might be a sign that Arnold has distanced himself from the role of torch singer in his own life, we miss the music. Moving
Arnold from the world of experimental theater to that of Neil Simon may be
comforting for a Broadway audience, but it is a reduction.

GROWING UP TO MUSIC

The very title *Torch Song Trilogy* connects the action to music: two of its three plays are musical theater. The actions of all but one of the plays I have discussed in this chapter are set against or within forms of musical theater. In various ways, music has been a figure for both entrapment and liberation. In Wilson's *The Madness of Lady Bright*, the sound of Mozart wafting from another apartment is the cue for one of Leslie's theatrical transformations, as he turns his apartment into the lobby of a concert hall and imagines himself engaged in an intermission conversation. Yet Leslie is also aware that the music he hears is probably the accompaniment for a real tête à tête. Ultimately the music spinning out of Leslie's control is the most vivid metaphor of his madness. In McNally's *The Lisbon Traviata*, music is also a sign of the central characters' pathologies. The strains of Gustav Mahler's "Das Lied von der Erde" in Innaurato's *Coming of Age in Soho* represent first Beatrice's wish for solitude and later his loss of Dy. At a climactic moment, the strains of verismo opera accompany the threats of Beatrice's wife and her Mafia friends. In these plays, music is part of a culture with which gay men identify themselves. In Crowley's *The Boys in the Band*, dancing is one of the most important visible signs of homosexual behavior that is forbidden by "normal" society. Twice Alan's entrances interrupt dancing, a sign of the conflict between straight and gay society. Michael's only moment of happiness in the play is in the opening scene when he dances alone to bossa nova music being played on the radio.

If music and musical theater have been to gay playwrights such important aspects of the gay experience, offering positive and negative role models; if, as stated by the DJ in "Northern Exposure," a love of show tunes is a sign of homosexuality; musical theater should be a powerful medium for depicting the contemporary gay experience. I described in the previous chapter how London's Gay Sweatshop, following Brecht's example, used songs in their recreations of gay history, as part of a theatrical form that defied the constraints of realism. In America, William Finn's three musicals about the coming of age of Marvin—*In Trousers* (1979), *March of the Falsettos* (1981), and *Falsettoland* (1990)—are a compendium of the actions and themes of gay drama during the past three decades, but freed from the constraints of conventional drama. Of all the works discussed in this chapter, Finn's trilogy of musicals about Marvin present the richest, most complete picture of the emotional development of a gay man through his love for another man.

Finn's three musicals are not conventional Broadway musical extravaganzas. They are small in scale, with small casts and bands and simple, nonrepresentational scenery. Solos are rare in Finn's musical structure and are used like Shakespearean soliloquies to allow a character to explain himself. Most of the music is made up of elaborate ensembles that define relationships and conflicts. The artifice of song allows the thoughts of the characters to be voiced as "naturally" as their words. Like many contemporary composers of musicals, Finn through-composes (there is no dialogue), thus creating intimate operas written for Broadway voices. Finn, like Stephen Sondheim, uses music to set complex, sophisticated, witty lyrics at least as literate and precise as any script discussed in this chapter.

The three Marvin musicals are connected by Marvin's relationships with his nuclear family—his wife and son—and with his lover, Whizzer. They move from Marvin's first sexual encounter with Whizzer in 1979 to Whizzer's death from AIDS three years later. Each of the musicals tells the story of a key moment in this history.

In Trousers (1979) chronicles Marvin's move out of the conventional heterosexual world; he leaves his wife and son and moves in with Whizzer. The only characters other than Marvin are his high school teacher, Miss Goldberg, his high-school sweetheart, and his wife, Trina. The emphasis is on figures from Marvin's adolescence because Marvin remains a spoiled, petulant adolescent, prone to fits when he doesn't get his way. The central moment is Marvin's starring role in a school play about Christopher Columbus. After meeting Whizzer, Marvin presents a new play about the discovery of the new world, in which Columbus has a shipboard romance with Amerigo Vespucci and names the new world after him. "The thing about explorers," Marvin says, "they discover things that are already there."[20] Marvin's new world is his homosexuality, but at first this is just another appetite to be satisfied. Sex with Whizzer is described joyously and graphically in "Whizzer Going Down," a contrast to the chaste avoidance of sex in most gay plays. However, Marvin's nonsexual expectations of his relationship with Whizzer are immature and unrealistic:

> Whizzer will act very parental,
> Completely gentle,
> Absolutely swell. (p. 71)

Whizzer's invisibility in *In Trousers* is a sign that he is now little more than a virtuosic sexual performer and the object of unrealistic expectations.

At the opening of *March of the Falsettos* (1981), Marvin wants to keep his entire universe intact:

> I want a tight knit family.
> I want a group that harmonizes.
> I want my wife and kid and friend
> To pretend
> Time will mend
> Our pain. (p. 98)

Wife and kid and friend have other ideas. Trina marries Marvin's psychiatrist, adolescent son Jason worries that he will grow up like his father (he already acts as petulant), and Whizzer, disgusted with Marvin's "family charades," packs his bags.

Marvin has poisoned his relationship with Whizzer with the assertions of conventional masculinity. In place of the ecstatic descriptions of sex in *In Trousers*, Marvin and Whizzer now fight. Like their chess games, Marvin sees his relationship with Whizzer as a series of contests he must win. Worse, he sees it as a conventional, patriarchal marriage:

> Whizzer's supposed to make the dinner—
> Make the dinner, look to screw.
> That's what pretty boys should do. (p. 129)

At the end, Marvin and his son, Jason, are alone onstage together. Marvin gives Jason a fatherly assurance, "You'll be, kid, a man, kid, whatever the song" (p. 175), but the principal question raised in *March of the Falsettos* is what does it mean to be a man. Manhood—conventional masculinity—is a set of baggage that the men of *March of the Falsettos*, gay and straight, must rethink. The title song, sung in falsetto by Marvin, Whizzer, Jason, and Mendel (Trina's new husband) is a challenge to sing without the voice—the vanity, competitiveness, and hierarchical demands—of conventional masculinity.

> Who is man enough to
> March of the Falsettos? (p. 153)

It is the masculine voice that keeps these men from giving and accepting love from anyone, that leads them to be frightened of love.

Falsettoland (1990) is, as its opening song states:

> About growing up,
> Getting older,
> Living on a lover's shoulder,
> Learning love is not a crime. (p. 185)

To the five characters of *March of the Falsettos*, Finn has added a lesbian couple: a doctor, Charlotte, and a caterer, Cordelia. Doctor and caterer become crucial characters in the two related actions of *Falsettoland*, Whizzer's illness and Jason's bar mitzvah.

Marvin and Whizzer are reunited when both go to see Jason play baseball (Jason likes Whizzer the best of the men in his life). Another song of their sex life shows how far Marvin has "been revised" since "Whizzer Going Down"

> It's been hot,
> Also it's been swell.

More than not,
It's been more than words can tell.

. . .

We take it day by day.
What more can I say? (p. 216–217)

Love has made Marvin less articulate, less forceful. He trusts language less. The prevalence of AIDS among her patients has made Charlotte even more conscious of the limitations of language: "Something so bad that words have lost their meaning" (p. 219).

When Whizzer is hospitalized with an HIV-related illness, Marvin's ex-wife and son realize that Whizzer has become part of their family:

Trying not to care about this man Marvin loves.
But that's my life.
He shared my life. (p. 224)

Trina articulates what all the characters have to accept: "Life is never what you planned" (p. 224).

At Jason's behest, his bar mitzvah is held in Whizzer's hospital room. There at this family gathering, Jason is hailed as:

Son of Abraham, Isaac and Jacob
Son of Marvin, son of Trina, son of Whizzer, son of Mendel.
And godchild to the lesbians from next door. (p. 244)

Whizzer dies without a death scene, that celebration of victimization that typically culminates nineteenth-century opera. Whizzer is too tough to indulge in such melodramatics:

Give me the balls to orchestrate
A graceful leave.
That's my reprieve. (p. 239)

At the end, Marvin sings a song to, and with, his memory of Whizzer, affirming not only their love but the man he has become because of that love:

Who would I be
If I had not loved you?
How would I know what love is? (p. 245)

Marvin has matured enough to celebrate what he had instead of regressing to his earlier petulance and self-pity. Loving has come of age.

In the final chorus, characters sing that Falsettoland "is where we take a stand" (p. 248), and Finn's stand is uncompromising. He has celebrated the sexual component of Marvin and Whizzer's relationship, as well as their growth from sparring partners to friends. He has placed Marvin and Whizzer's relationship within a network of marriages and, in the process, created a new sense of family. Everyone, not just the gay protagonist, has come of age, a bittersweet process that means:

> Holding to the ground as the ground keeps shifting.
> Trying to stay sane as the rules keep changing. (p. 224)

Unlike the other protagonists discussed in this chapter, Marvin is not an artist—we don't know what his profession is—but he is presented within a self-reflexive work of art that, as musical theater tends to do, celebrates the acts of creation and performance as it celebrates the ways in which Marvin and the members of his family bravely forge their lives and the links between them. Marvin and his family are highly conscious of language. Created within a world of verbal and visual metaphor, the characters seem always aware of the power of metaphor and of their own experience as metaphor, a gift denied most inhabitants of the real or realistic worlds and harking back to the world inhabited by characters in Elizabethan drama.

Both of my chapters on openly gay drama have ended with works that defy the conventions of post-Ibsen representational theater and the compromises of the realistic, domestic problem play. Other forms are more suited to convey the gay experience as something richer than a social problem to be solved or a domestic intrusion to be expelled. Gay playwrights present their protagonists as artists, particularly as writers and performers, and it is in the world of admitted artifice—poetry, music, theater—that the richness and challenge of acting gay can be most fully depicted. Realism defines and reinforces limits. Works like Finn's Marvin trilogy and Paul Godfrey's *Once in a While the Odd Thing Happens* (1990) allow characters and audience to transcend every given except the free play of imagination possible in the theater. In this freedom, the protagonist can grow into gayness and learn to love.

A culture built on the necessity of acting—in which freedom from the constraints of conventional gender roles can mean the possibility of life of the imagination, in which alternative readings of musical theater offer a supportive mythology in an opulent parallel world, and in which a play of language defuses oppressive judgment—is best re-created by a theater freed from the literal-mindedness of most mainstream realistic drama. Marlowe's Gaveston said of Edward, "Music and poetry is his delight," then described an opulent theater that blurred gender and celebrated homoerotic desire. In the meta-theatrical world of *Falsettoland* and other gay theatrical works by Martin Sherman, Neil Bartlett, Paul Godfrey, Doric Wilson, Philip Osment, Noel Greig, and Drew Griffiths, we see vividly the positive meanings of acting gay. Freed from the restraints of the structure, conventions, and assumptions of realistic drama, their works show us characters with complex protean identities. Theater in these works is not a slick metaphor for illusion. Theater is the mirror of the role-playing and stereotyping gay men experience every day. More important, it reflects the complex and multifaceted identities of people who have created their affirming personae. Gay theater cannot solve the problems of heterosexism or AIDS, but it can offer a liberating vision of what it means to be gay.

CHAPTER SEVEN

CELEBRATING OUR GAZE

SALLY: I don't think I have anything against gay men. I just
don't want to be the only non-gay people here.
CHLOE: You don't want to be a token anything. I hear you.
Who wants to feel everyone's staring at them?
—TERRENCE MCNALLY, *Lips Together, Teeth Apart*

We won't die secret deaths any more. The world only spins forward. We
will be citizens. The time has come.
—TONY KUSHNER, *Angels in America: Perestroika*

In the 1990s, gay drama focuses on how gay people see the society which
denies them an equal space rather than on how that society sees and polices
them. The gay vision is both aesthetic and moral. While continuing to find
joy in the play and transformation central to theater, more than ever, in the
face of AIDS, lesbians and gay men fight to save a gay culture. In doing so
we realize the importance of difference as we question the ideal of assimilation. On the stage as well as in the streets, lesbians and gay men affirm the
value of queerness, of radical difference, as something not to be surrendered
in the move to assimilation.

   The film sensation in 1992 was an Irish romantic thriller in which the
supposedly shocking moment is a close-up of a penis on a body which the
central character, Fergus, and those in the audience who did not know how
to spot a drag queen, wanted to believe was female. Neil Jordan's *The Crying
Game* ultimately asks the question whether the gender or sexual orientation
of a loved one is relevant.[1] The American distributors of *The Crying Game*

begged critics and audience members not to give away the film's big surprise—that the "heroine," Dil, is a male—partly because they believed that
the surprise is essential to the film but more, I think, because they were un-
derstandably reluctant to be up front about the fact that *The Crying Game* is
a male-male love story in which the penis is not hidden. By placing the penis
at the center of the film, *The Crying Game* displays the terror at the heart of
male bonding narratives—that the woman who keeps the bonding from appearing homosexual, who ratifies the heterosexuality of the male homosocial
order, might not be a woman at all. From the point at which the central
character and the audience are confronted with that which films are most
reluctant to show, the male penis, we are aware that he and they see what he
has always wanted.

There were outraged letters and phone calls from members of the audience when National Public Radio's Saturday morning show gave away the
film's secret by announcing that Jaye Davidson, who plays the transvestite,
Dil, had been nominated for an Academy Award as Best Supporting *Actor*.[2]
Would audience members be so affronted simply because a plot twist was
disclosed, or was there fear of taking the secret of *The Crying Game* out of
the closet? Did audience members feel some need to keep the film's homosexuality closeted so as to disassociate themselves from any complicity with
the meaning of Dil's penis? For in *The Crying Game* the male penis once
again figures homosexuality which explodes conventional gender definitions.

The central character does not reject Dil when he discovers that she is
male. Instead, he tries to remove her drag and put her into ill-fitting clothes
of the man both of them loved. The film bears out the basis of much gender
theory, most cogently voiced by the New York drag star, RuPaul: "I always
say you're born naked and the rest is drag."[3]

Sadly, Neil Jordan's brilliant, provocative film is richer than any depiction of gay men now seen on the London stage. Its enormous success in
The United States is a reflection of the passionate debate about sexual identity
and orientation now being waged. *The Crying Game* is a challenge to audiences, particularly male audiences, to face their fears and hatreds. While *The
Crying Game* is a film Hollywood would not have had the courage to make,
the critical establishment and the American film industry realize the film's
importance and its centrality to the strident dialogue now taking place.

If the American success of *The Crying Game* reflects the nation's pre-
occupation with things sexual, particularly homosexual, the lively renaissance
in American drama right now is almost totally the result of the enormous
amount of gay drama that is being written and produced across the country.
It is difficult to believe that only three decades have passed since the virulent
critical attacks on homosexual playwrights I chronicled in chapter 4 and that
uncloseted gay drama is a historical inevitability and the lifeblood of the
contemporary American theater. Conversely, drama remains, in American gay
culture, a primary medium of communication and transmission of ideas.

STRAIGHT AND NARROW

I devote the great majority of this chapter to American gay drama because British drama, gay and straight, seems to be in a worse slump than the British economy. The parlous state of gay drama only reminds us that, despite the efforts of radical theater groups in the seventies and eighties, a tradition of affirming gay drama never developed in Great Britain. The gay presence on the British stage is greatly the result of American imports. It was wonderful to see that Tony Kushner's *Angels in America* was such a hit at the Royal National Theatre, but sad that England did not have its own counterpart to Kushner's gay fantasia on America. It was moving to see the successful fringe production of Bill Russell and Jane Hood's *Elegies for Angels, Punks, and Raging Queens*, but it is a British production of an eloquent American tribute to Persons With AIDS in New York City, not London or Glasgow. And the brilliant 1993 revival of J. R. Ackerley's 1925 play, *The Prisoners of War*, only shows that much British gay drama is artistically inferior to and no more gay affirming than what Ackerly wrote almost seventy years ago.

Case in point: Jimmie Chinn's *Straight and Narrow*, which had a successful run on the West End, played to the prejudices of a heterosexual audience. Bob, a young building contractor, although he has been sharing his home with his male lover of many years, cannot bring himself to come out to his mother. Bob's lover, Jim, is in the throes of agony and self-abnegation because he has not fathered a child. Chinn does not see the gay political ramifications of his topic—that perhaps Bob and Jim are trying too hard to be just like heterosexuals and should stop judging themselves against the norms of heterosexual marriage, particularly against the dysfunctional heterosexuals surrounding them. Chinn allows his characters to voice their awareness that, no matter how hard they try to be just like the straights in the audience, they are "naturally" inferior because they do not procreate. Ultimately the play calls for pity. *Straight and Narrow* was written by a television writer and featured television sitcom stars. The advertising campaigns and low prices were "aimed at heterosexual and non-theatergoing audiences."[4] Like television dramas about gay men, *Straight and Narrow* tried so hard to make its homosexuals "normal" that they became, except for their displays of guilt, bland, characterless, above all sexless. There was nothing in the play to frighten heterosexuals, but neither was there much for gay men to identify with. That this television-fare drivel played just across the Thames from *Angels in America* showed how far English theater has to go.

At the Royal Court Upstairs, Chay Yew's *Porcelain*[5] presented a more melodramatic picture of gay anguish. A beautiful, intelligent Asian man can find sexual fulfillment only in public toilets. There he meets and falls in love with a brutal closet queen whom he ultimately murders. One wanted to scream at the central character, "Get a life!" Instead of exploring the social causes of

the central character's self-hatred or depicting his conquering of his masochism, the play presents another object of pity. This was the gay not-so-sub-
text of David Henry Hwang's *M. Butterfly*, but without the possibility of love.[6]
Ironically, Daniel York's performance as the self-hating young Asian was so
charismatic that it made his misery all the more unbelievable.

British drama seems to find a space for homosexual love only in depictions of historical relationships. John Byrne's rather messy dramatization
of the even messier love and career of the Scottish artists, *Colqu'houn and
MacBryde*, like its predecessors, Christopher Hampton's *Total Eclipse*, and
Paul Godfrey's *Once in a While the Odd Thing Happens*, explores the way a
personal relationship impinges upon the creative life of two artists.[7] But the
gay man as a political creature in contemporary Britain, or as a person who
has managed to create his own positive domestic and social space, does not
seem to be viable material for contemporary dramatists.

While England, much more than the United States, is considered a
theater culture, gay playwrights have not carved their space within that culture.
Or have they relinquished it? The Gay Sweatshop seems to be dead, and no
politicized gay theater has replaced it. In the 1990s the West End can display
a piece of hateful anti-gay (and misogynist and anti-Semitic) rant like John
Osborne's recent debacle, *Deja Vu*, but not a nineties equivalent of Joe Orton.
Sadly, the question of where are the gay British playwrights is superseded by
the question of where is the younger generation of British playwrights. The
new plays being produced by the mainstream theaters are by the playwrights
who came of age in the sixties: Tom Stoppard, Peter Shaffer, and David
Storey. Britain desperately needs the kind of theatrical renaissance young gay
dramatists are giving the United States.

In this environment, it is not surprising that one of the most noteworthy
events in recent British gay theater was the 1993 fringe revival of J. R. Ackerley's *The Prisoners of War*. Set in Switzerland in 1918, the drama presents
a group of British and Canadian prisoners who have been interned in neutral
Switzerland because of the severity of their war injuries. Quartered in a mountain inn with all the comforts of tourists, their lives are far from Spartan. Still,
they feel removed both from their native lands and from the war raging in
neighboring countries. The action focuses on the unrequited love a twenty-
four-year-old captain, James Conrad, feels for a nineteen-year-old lieutenant,
aptly named Grayle. Conrad seems both to know that he is infatuated with
another man, and that he doesn't have any words for it. History has taught
him that there was an ideal of loving male friendship represented by what one
character euphemistically calls "The Theban Band": "Each man used to take
his intimate friend to war with him, didn't he? And they'd protect each other.
It gave a man something real to fight for."[8] Conrad knows that such loving
comradeship is what he needs: "There's no one who shares me, frees me,
takes me out of myself" (105). For Conrad, Grayle "fills gaps," but clearly
the selfish, callow young man doesn't fill them very effectively.[9]

What was realized brilliantly in Ashley Russell's complex, sympathetic depiction of Conrad was the extent to which Ackerley has imbued Conrad with self-knowledge and pride in his capacity for love. Though suffering from combat fatigue and verging on, finally succumbing to, a nervous breakdown, Conrad is not ashamed of his homosexual feelings, even if he doesn't have positive words for them: "I know all my weaknesses and I cherish them. I value them more than my strength" (126). When a female camp follower who is interested in Grayle says to Conrad, "I have heard you do not like much the fair sex," Conrad replies with no irony, "The fair sex? Which one is that?" (119).

Conrad does not crack because he is a homosexual: he cracks because he, an ambitious man of action, cannot stand the hothouse world of his internment and because of the intense pain his head injuries cause him.[10] Conrad is trapped, too, in an all-male society that does not acknowledge its homoerotic subtext. He lavishes his affection on Grayle because the hothouse offers few other objects for his affection: Grayle, as he says, "fills gaps" (107). The sympathy of the playwright and the sensitive characters is with Conrad, whose main weakness is the lack of a protective sense of irony, which has been a principal weapon in the gay man's arsenal.

At one point, Conrad says to another lieutenant, Tetford, who is clearly in love with a rather bumptious Canadian, "We're both in the same boat," to which Tetford replies, "Are we? I wonder?" (110). At first hearing, this line seems to be Tetford distancing himself from Conrad's homosexual longing for Grayle, but in this revival it is clear that the difference between Conrad and Tetford is that Tetford is willing to settle for what comradeship he can have with a man with whom he has little in common and who may not be able to return his love fully. Conrad is all too aware of what Grayle does not offer or return. Tetford and his comrade will go off to Canada together after the war. They may never have sex, but they will be inseparable "buddies." Conrad wants more, but knows he may never find it.

At the end of *The Prisoners of War*, Grayle is very reluctantly serving his shift, keeping watch over the mad Conrad, who comes over to Grayle and, almost like a blind person, runs his hands over Grayle's face, then returns alone to the veranda. Stunned, terrified Grayle cannot even imagine what Conrad felt for him, or what he is incapable of feeling himself. Though Ackerley's play never becomes more explicit than the lines I have quoted, the revival managed to illuminate the homoeroticism underlying all the homosocial alliances in the script.[11]

The Prisoners of War was an extraordinary achievement by a writer in his mid-twenties who, unfortunately, never wrote another play. The times were not right for the kind of gay-positive play Ackerley envisioned, so he moved to the less censored genres of autobiography and fiction.[12] The 1993 revival of *The Prisoners of War* reminds us what theater lost. It also reminds us how little has changed in mainstream British gay drama over the past seventy years.

Such pessimism is somewhat abated by a superb new play by another twenty-five year old. In *Beautiful Thing* (1993), Jonathan Harvey has written a play that is a breakthrough for British gay drama in the nineties.

Harvey's *Beautiful Thing* is a textbook example of how gay drama liberates and transforms the oppressive givens of realistic drama. The problems of the urban poor, the stuff of soap opera in England,[13] are the wellspring of the action, but Harvey turns a tenement into a setting for romance as he turns inarticulacy and urban slang into poetry. Set in a grim concrete council estate in South London, *Beautiful Thing* chronicles the blossoming first love of two sixteen-year-old boys from broken homes. Jamie lives with his mother, a brash bartender, and a succession of her young boyfriends. Frightened of sports, resigned to not fitting in with his peers, Jamie is a timid, bookish dreamer. Next door, Ste is beaten regularly by his brutal, alcoholic father and his older brother. Ste plans for a future working in a gym. He loves sports, particularly swimming, because "You're on your own when you're swimming. You can't think about nothing else."[14] Harvey tenderly and humorously depicts the tentative courtship and coming out of these two boys from their first sexual overtures to their first reading of a gay magazine to their first attempt at camp behavior when they see themselves as Cagney and Lacey:

> JAMIE: Give us a kiss.
> STE: No!
> JAMIE: Let's go to the stairs, no one can see there.
> STE: There's no such thing as just a kiss. I'll knock you up in the morning, yeah?
> JAMIE: *(Christine Cagney)* Knock away Marybeth, knock away!
> STE: See you Christine. (87)

Like many young gay couples, Jamie and Ste's romance begins with sex, then a struggle with accepting their gayness, then an affirmation of their love. Actually, their gayness and their love frees them from the traps and despair of urban poverty.

While Ste is terrified that his father will discover and literally kill him, the boys gain the protection of Jamie's mother, Sandra. Abandoned by her own unmarried mother, Sandra is on one hand fiercely protective of Jamie to the point of robbing to feed him when he was an infant, but in many ways she has never grown up herself, and the violent fights she has with Jamie resemble sibling battles more than mother-son arguments. Jamie resents that Sandra doesn't act more like a mother. At the end of one violent argument which turns into a physical battle, Sandra tells her son: "You're all right. You're not weird, you're just fifteen. Okay, so you got me for a mother, but who said life was easy?" (48).

Sandra has often taken in Ste after his beatings and let him sleep "top to tail" in Jamie's bed. Unbeknownst to Sandra, "top to tail" eventually turns into what she calls "seventy minus one." When Jamie tells Sandra that Ste isn't coming round as much because "he's in love" (Ste actually is experiencing a mild case of homosexual panic), Sandra naïvely gives the confused boy five pounds to buy his new girlfriend a present and Ste uses the money to buy Jamie a knit hat. Sandra's ignorance of the budding romance under her roof doesn't last long. She discovers that Jamie has been beaten up for being a queer and that he and Ste have gone to a gay pub. When she confronts Jamie, mother and son manage to have the most constructive conversation they have had in the entire play:

> SANDRA: Do you talk to him?
> JAMIE: Me and him's the same.
> SANDRA: He's sixteen years of age Jamie. What pearls of wisdom can he throw your way? He's never even had a holiday.
> JAMIE: It's difficult, init.
> SANDRA: Am I that much of a monster?
> JAMIE: No!
> SANDRA: Don't get me wrong. I like the lad. Always have. All I'm saying is he's young.
> JAMIE: He's good to me.
> SANDRA: Is he?
> JAMIE: Yeah. (75)

For Sandra, this conversation shows her that Jamie has found what she hasn't—a man worthy of love. She realizes that it's time for her to grow up and dump the garbage out of her life. She gets a job as a pub manager and throws out the latest unsatisfactory young boyfriend.

Throughout *Beautiful Thing*, the music of Mama Cass provides a counterpoint to the dreary life on the council estate. Leah, another neighbor, is an unhappy fatherless sixteen year old who lives in a fantasy world built around Mama Cass, the homely fat girl who sang like an angel. The play opens with her singing "It's Getting Better" and closes with Jamie and Ste dancing cheek-to-cheek to "Dream a Little Dream of Me." As Jamie and Ste discover who they are and Sandra determines to change her life, Leah realizes that she can't "wrap [her]self up in a dead fat American git" and will instead "Find meself a nice dyke" (89). Leah slow dances with Sandra, leading the audience to imagine that their liberation from being "slags" will come from other women. As the two couples dance, music wins over words. The dance sums up Harvey's sense of the liberation gay love can offer from a bleak world.

Beautiful Thing is unabashedly optimistic and romantic, a charming unlikely mix of comedy, sentiment, and urban realism that elicited joyful cheers from staid British audiences. By making his lovers sixteen year old virgins, Harvey is able to write a gay drama that eludes the specter of AIDS.

Yet the age of the lovers scores an important political point in a country in which the age of consent for homosexual sex is twenty-one. The sweet love we have watched blossom is literally illegal in England. On the cover of the playbill and published script of *Beautiful Thing* is a Cecil Beaton photograph of the young Truman Capote, arms raised, leaping like a dancer. Capote is joyfully aloft, defying gravity. It is this sense of liberation that Harvey offers his characters and audience. *Beautiful Thing* is selling out at the tiny but prestigious Bush Theatre on the fringe. It's the kind of working-class romantic fantasy J. R. Ackerly dreamed of in 1925. Now, perhaps, its success might just liberate young gay playwrights and, eventually, make mainstream British drama gayer and livelier.

THE GAY LOOK

In the United States gay is everywhere. The 1992 Republican National Convention was an orgy of gaybashing reflecting the fact that the paranoid wing of the party has found its replacement for the evil empires of communism in homosexuality and the televangelists have found homophobia to be an effective cash cow. At the same time, the hate mongering reflected the fact that the closet door is frighteningly ajar and even flocks of the righteous can't seem to close it. While the 1992 election gave the country a president willing to acknowledge the existence of gays and lesbians and speak to their concerns, Colorado, in a state referendum did away with banning discrimination against gay people. And, in early 1993, Clinton's statements of intention to open the closet door policed so long by the military led to cries of outrage and terror from those who can be counted upon to make such noises and acts of brutality encouraged by the strident voices of homophobia and heterosexism, but it also led to such massive media coverage that homosexuality in America can never truly be closeted again.

Despite the hatemongering and the simplifications, distortions, and condescensions of straight and closeted television pundits, America's image of gay men and gay men's self images have changed radically. Consider, for instance, the full page ad on page 3 of the February 1, 1993 issue of the *New Yorker*. The ad is for GAP menswear. The striking Annie Leibovitz photograph is a head and shoulders shot of Andrew Sullivan, the openly gay editor of *The New Republic*. While Mr. Sullivan is ostensibly modelling a GAP t-shirt, the picture—unlike those of most GAP ads—focusses not on the body, but on Sullivan's face, particularly his intense eyes. This is a picture of intellectual energy and piercing wit, qualities many gay men have valued and achieved, but also contained within a defiant, macho pose, complete with two day growth of beard. This is the gay man for the nineties—smart, powerful, attractive, but with the focus on what is above the neck. Sullivan's slightly defiant look says, "I'm here. I'm queer. Get used to it." That openly gay Andrew Sullivan, editor of a non-gay news magazine, is a model for a GAP ad is a great sign of the times. Sullivan's intense, defiant pose is the 1990s gay look. The visible presence of ACT-UP, Queer Nation, and a myriad of other gay support and pressure groups show that lesbians and gay men are coming out and fighting back. The sissy image is gone and pity or tolerance are not enough. Sullivan's GAP photo is a commercial corollary to the photos and televised images of a brave individual, Keith Meinhold, refusing to acquiesce in the military's attempts to remove him from service, or the hundreds of thousands of lesbians and gay men marching in Washington to remind the government and the rest of the country that they won't be closeted or forgotten.[15]

This new image is reflected and depicted in American gay drama in this decade. There are no more coded gay figures, no more calls for pity for moody, troubled young men, no more gay Camilles pleading for tolerance, and no more uncritical presentation of stereotypes.

As the battle lines are drawn on the issue of just how far Americans will go to embrace or bash gays, gay drama seems to be everywhere. William Finn's *March of the Falsettos and Falsettoland*, discussed in the last chapter, have been running on Broadway as *Falsettos*, albeit in a production that dilutes the work's impact.[16] Tony Kushner's two-part "gay fantasia," *Angels in America*, was eagerly sought by all the New York theater owners. Before it arrived on Broadway, previous productions in London and Los Angeles had earned rave notices from *Times* critic, Frank Rich. A musical, *The Harvey Milk Show*, was so successful in its run at Atlanta's Actor's Express that it had to be brought back for another season, and the ambitious little theater had to double its seating capacity. Larry Kramer's strongest play yet, *The Destiny of Me*, replaced Terrence McNally's long-run hit, *Lips Together, Teeth Apart*, at the Lucille Lortel Theater in Greenwich Village, while, a few blocks uptown, David Drake performed his one-man panorama of gay life, *The Night Larry Kramer Kissed Me*. The comic hit of the season was Paul Rudnick's *Jeffrey*, a witty exploration of being gay in the age of AIDS. And 1993 was the year in which a musical version of Manuel Puig's *Kiss of the Spider Woman*, whose "climax" is sex between two men in a South American prison, won awards in London and on Broadway.[17] Gay theaters exist even in small cities like Durham, North Carolina, where Mac Wellman's *7 Blowjobs*, a wickedly funny satire on a certain hateful southern senator's reaction to photographs very like Robert Mapplethorpe's, was one of many gay-positive plays to pack the adventurous Manbites Dog Theater.

What these theaters and plays represent is one side of the most important contemporary battle being waged about homosexuality, the final destruction of the closet as the appropriate, carefully policed space for gay men.[18] These plays are theatrical acts of coming out; for the characters, for the playwrights, for the productions themselves. They privilege openness over closetedness, liberation over acquiescence to control. Like the photo of Andrew

Sullivan used to sell GAP clothing, they place gay men in an empowered and empowering position within a capitalist system.

SAVE THE CHILDREN

In Dan Pruitt and Patrick Hutchison's musical, *The Harvey Milk Show*, Harvey, furious at Anita Bryant's homophobic "Save the Children" campaign, sings of the gay children who need saving:

> What of the kid from West Virginia
> Who now turns away from suicide?
> And what of the kid from eastern Texas
> Who tries to find his place—
> The grace he's been denied . . . [19]

The kid from east Texas is Harvey's lover, Jamey, a young man who was thrown out of his home when he came out to his father. Self-hating and self-destructive, Jamey ran away to San Francisco where he became a hustler. Harvey Milk takes Jamey home to heal his wounds after a fag bashing, and Jamey finds in Harvey the loving father, hero, and lover he has been looking for.

The Harvey Milk Show celebrates one of the hero-martyrs of gay history and through his story shows heterosexuals some of the battles gay men fought and continue to fight. More important, through Jamey's story the musical challenges gay audiences to look beyond heroes to their own responsibility for their futures. The relationship of Harvey and Jamey is not just the fictional spine of a romantic musical. It is a challenge to activism, to healing the wounds left by one's biological family and embracing one's gay family.

When Harvey challenges Jamey to believe in the possibility of fighting for social change, Jamey answers:

> What I believe in, Harvey, is you. I believe that you believe it, and that's
> enough for me. It comes to the same thing.
> HARVEY: No, baby, it's not even close.

Jamey sees Harvey as a lovable dreamer, a Don Quixote. Older and wiser Harvey knows that meaningful action comes out of self reliance and the realism born of disillusionment:

> Life has its mean little job to do.
> Young man, you've got to believe in you.

Only Harvey's death and the grotesquely light sentence granted to his murderer, Dan White, makes Jamey see that Harvey's fight was serious and necessary, that the rage inside him, from the rejection of his father and the brutality and hatred of homophobes is justified and the beginning of action. He sends his sister away when he realizes that his biological family is no longer the site of real kinship:

> The world has always drawn a line between us—those of us like me and those of you like you. And we've never been allowed to cross that line— not really. Now you can't cross over either. Not unless you know what it feels like to be despised for this—the things here—to be despised for your very heart.

The epilogue takes place four years later, on the day Dan White is to be released from prison. Jamey, disillusioned and drunk, is visited by Harvey's spirit, who reminds him and the audience that there's "So very, very much left undone."

The Harvey Milk Show turns its title character into a Christ figure who works miracles on earth, is executed, and reappears to strengthen on his disciple's resolve. The two most rousing numbers in the show echo Protestant hymns; one is even entitled "Anthem." Yet it is this old-time religious quality that made this musical of a sixties San Francisco politician written by a small town boy from South Carolina a long-running hit in the gayest city in the south. This Harvey is not a character Randy Shilts—or Harvey Milk, for that matter—might recognize. The show raises him and the beginnings of gay politics to mythic status. By presenting Harvey through Jamey's eyes, the show challenges the audience to see that love or a sentimental look at the past isn't enough, that disillusionment should lead one to keep fighting: "Look inside—learn to use the scars/Look to each defeat to teach you to fight." Above all, the show asserts that pity or self pity are not constructive responses to the battles gay people are still waging decades after Harvey's death.

There are aspects of *The Harvey Milk Show* its namesake might disagree with. The sixties sexual liberation Harvey and so many others came to San Francisco to enjoy are replaced by the "marriage" of Harvey and Jamey. The show joins many other works of gay theater in proclaiming the right to a loving relationship as that which is worth fighting for.

The musical is gay theater at its best. From Anita Bryant's anti-gay sermons presented as a Carmen Miranda-like drag act—

> And don't let some big banana
> Who's a plant from New Havana
> Tell you children should be learning from a fruit!

to the camp and glitter of Harvey's political and musical back-up group, The Milk Duds, to the blatantly physical romance of Harvey and Jamey.[20]

The Harvey Milk Show celebrates gayness and shows straights in the audience that caution and defensiveness are signs of shame that don't belong in gay theater while it centers on the conflict between middle-aged Harvey's tenacity and young Jamey's skepticism. Ultimately, even in death, the middle-aged activist has the last word. The final duet ends with his challenge to do what is left undone. The central relationship in Larry Kramer's new play, *The Destiny of Me* is between middle-aged Ned Weeks—despairing of the value of his past activism and now HIV-positive, begging for time from the very medical institution and superstar he has previously excoriated—and his former self, young Alexander Weeks who will lose his dreams and ideals and become Ned. *The Destiny of Me* ends, as it begins, with middle-aged Ned and his younger self singing a show tune, "Make Believe" from *Showboat*. The song, at the end, becomes one of self-acceptance, of reconciliation of youthful hopes and mature defeats and disillusionment.[21] It is high praise to assert that *The Destiny of Me* deserves comparison with the works of such canonical American dramatists as Clifford Odets, Eugene O'Neill, and Arthur Miller. Kramer's powerful, evocative, disturbing play is a capstone to the tradition of naturalistic American family tragedy. Yet, for a student of gay drama, it is Kramer's alliance to this dramatic tradition that causes the play's infuriating flaws. Like the work of Miller and O'Neill, an air of determinism, of grim defeat, of hopelessness, pervades the work. Kramer succumbs to a heterosexist Freudian scenario even as he attacks it. For a gay writer and activist this is particularly perilous.

The Destiny of Me begins with Ned Weeks, Kramer's alter-ego, entering a hospital room at the National Institute of Health. Outside the hospital, members of the AIDS activist group Weeks/Kramer founded are demonstrating in increasing numbers and with increasing violence. Ned feels isolated, separated from the activists and has given up on activism: "We've lost" (1,3). He has come to try an experimental treatment which might stymie the HIV that is weakening his immune system. The treatment will be given by the very man Ned has attacked for his bureaucratic compromises, Dr. Anthony Della Vida, head of the AIDS division and a thinly veiled version of Kramer's nemesis at the National Institutes of Health. Ned will be treated by Tony and his wife, thus putting his medical fate in the hands of a heterosexual couple.[22] Ned is, as he admits, "here begging" for a few more years of his life. Throughout the play, Ned is the dependent but hostile child, attacking Tony and his wife as he risks the experimental treatment that might help him or hurt him.

The play alternates present scenes with memories of Ned's relations with his family over the period from his adolescence in the 1940s until his mother's recent death. However much Ned and his creator blame psychoanalysis for his unhappiness, the presentation of Ned's development is dominated by a monstrous version of Freud's Oedipus complex. Ned and his younger self, Alexander, experience his father's extreme hostility to his "sissy" son, his mother's manipulativeness, and the revered older brother's judgment of his homosexuality. Somehow Ned's father, the epitome of masculine emotional constipation, manages to walk in on Alexander's most intimate adolescent moments; as he spreads depilatory cream around his privates to avoid the embarrassment of being the first in his class to have pubic hair and as he puts on drag to appear in a boy scout play (!). In one scene the father strips his son and tries to grab his penis in front of the boy's mother. The father's responses to his "sissy" son range from physical brutality to pronouncements out of the worst Oedipal nightmare: "I should have shot my load in the toilet." On his deathbed, the father and son reconcile through the father's narrative of his loveless father, a mohel, a remover of foreskins, whose life was ruined when he once cut off a bit too much. The literal and symbolic castration of the fathers is passed on to the sons and grandsons.

Alexander's adolescent scenes with his mother center on physically intimate moments like helping her with her clothing while asking her what the function of the penis is. Her answer precludes both pleasure and homosexuality:

> ALEXANDER: Hi, Mom. Dad says to ask you what's a penis.
> RENA: I told you.
> ALEXANDER: Tell me again.
> RENA: When you grow up, you'll insert it into the woman's sexual organ, which is called the vagina. The penis goes into the vagina and deposits semen into my uterus and if it's the right time of the month pregnancy occurs resulting, nine months later, in a child. (23)

Her limiting answer furthers the horrific Freudian Oedipal scenario Kramer has constructed. Rena is assigned the father's job of explaining the function of the penis, and in the process her explanation moves from the objective scientific use of articles to personal pronouns that reinforce the Oedipal scenario ("*my* uterus"). While Rena confides to Alexander that she loved another man more than her husband, she does not defend him against his father's castrating rages. While describing graphically her miscarriage, she fails to mention that it actually was an abortion. And, though Rena proclaims that she wants her son "to become a leader in the fight against discrimination and prejudice" (36), she never accepts his homosexuality.

Ned/Alexander's salvation from an unhappy home is his beloved big brother, Ben, for whom Ned's feelings verge on the incestuous. However, Ben is also a source of Ned/Alexander's maladjustment. When Alexander confides to Ben that he is homosexual, Ben convinces him to go into psychoanalysis to cure something that will "do nothing but make you unhappy" (83). Eventually, Alexander, in a speech more revealing than Kramer knows, confronts Ben with a series of crucial questions:

> Why do I obey you? You don't put a gun to my head. Why don't I say: get out of my life, I'll make my own rules? I could be loved! But you do put a gun to my head. You won't love me unless I change. Well, it's too powerful a force to change! It's got to be a part of me! It doesn't want to die. And fights tenaciously to stay alive against all odds. And no matter what anyone does to try and kill it. (91)

This central speech voices two of the most problematic questions Kramer's play raises. First, why is Ned so passive? Why indeed does he let his brother tell him what to do? Why does Ned continue through a series of therapists when he knows they do him more harm than good? Why does he remain loyal to parents who have, to say the least, not supported him? Why does Ned so passively put himself in the hands of Anthony Della Vida and his wife when he is HIV positive, but not suffering from one of the classic infections that define AIDS? Why doesn't he follow the example of the protesters outside his window instead of worrying about failing to lead them? Second, is Kramer aware that Alexander's description of his homosexuality, the "it" that doesn't want to die, intimates an equation between homosexuality and the tenacious HIV? Earlier, Ned has said of his alter-ego, "You're like the very virus itself and I can't get rid of you." But Alexander is the burgeoning queer Ned's passivity has turned into an angry, lonely, despairing, middle-aged homosexual victim.

As I watched *The Destiny of Me*, I was reminded of David Bergman's analysis of Kramer's attraction to the rhetoric of heterosexual family:

> I can detect [in Kramer's essays] at least three major strains: the grating soprano of the enraged child, the wounded contralto of the guilt-inducing mother, and the rasping bass of the humiliating father. Because I hear these voices coming not only from Kramer's page, but also from my own head, I respond to them with unusual intensity. Kramer's ability to address the subconscious of gay readers [and audiences] accounts, I think, in large measure for his nagging power and the anger he arouses.[23]

Like a family member, Kramer can ingratiate and infuriate gay men, and can touch in us frightening chords. What one sees in the family scenes in *The Destiny of Me* is such an extreme case scenario that one responds as to a bad dream.

Wayne Koestenbaum has written: "Home has grim meanings for the gay kid on the verge of claiming an ambiguous identity. Home is the boot camp for gender; at home we are supposed to learn how to be straight. Queer identities arise against normative strictures of home, whether or not we faithfully replicate the canons of domesticity."[24] The Weeks family is certainly a boot camp, but they did not make Ned/Alexander Weeks homosexual any more than they made his brother heterosexual. Yet Kramer's Freudian patterns suggest a causality. Alexander Weeks, like many gay kids, realizes very young that he is "different" but receives no support for that difference. However, Kramer, typically, takes that sense of difference to an extreme register:

> ALEXANDER: Oh, Ned. Nobody I know is interested in what I am interested in. And I'm not interested in what they are interested in.
> NED: And you're never going to be able to accept or understand this. (20)

This sense of isolation distances Ned not only from those who have hurt him, but also from the gay community, toward which he claims he wants to be "a Moses," rather than a brother. Does Kramer really aspire to being a Moses, an instrument of God's wrath and God's law? And are gay men like the heathens worshipping the golden calf, to be destroyed for not listening? What does that make AIDS? The image of Ned Weeks isolated in an eleventh floor hospital room, removed from everything but his adversaries and his traumatic memories, contains the real "destiny of me."

At the end, in a coup de theatre, Ned, after finding out that the failed experimental treatment has lowered his T-cell count, breaks bags of blood all over the stage, a solitary imitation of the communal action the protesters staged earlier. As Ned splatters his infected blood all over the stage, he laments:

> "My straight friends ask me over and over again: Why is it so hard for you to find love? Ah, that is the question, answered, I hope, for you tonight. Why do I never stop believing this fucking plague can be cured?" (122)

The speech exemplifies the way in which Kramer's play links AIDS with the monstrous family narrative Kramer has dramatized. Is the plague AIDS or Kramer's isolation and unhappiness? Why is it only Kramer's straight friends who ask him why it is hard for him to find love? Why, as the question intimates, is it more important to answer his straight friends than his gay comrades? Hasn't the play's action demonstrated the danger, if not foolishness, of being answerable to straight people? It is to Kramer's credit that his play does not, as claimed, offer answers to the questions he poses. However, Ned's final speech suggests that Kramer thinks it has.

The Destiny of Me may explain some things about Ned Weeks, for those who believe in ironclad, deterministic narratives, but it leaves him in limbo. What good does his final tantrum do? One can only hope that in embracing Alexander, he affirms some of the playfulness and camp humor of his former self. Regaining some of the strength and irony of the queer Ned left behind would help link him to his gay brothers outside; not as Moses, but as, in the spirit of the play's epigraph from Walt Whitman, loving comrade.

"EVEN BRECHT WROTE MUSICALS"

The Harvey Milk Show presents a hero martyr. Larry Kramer's plays offer grand-opera pathos: a deathbed wedding (*The Normal Heart*) and a mad scene complete with blood bags spraying the walls (*The Destiny of Me*). The innocent young queen in *The Destiny of Me* turns into an isolated, failed Jeremiah. These plays are typical of much classic gay drama which ennobles gay men's experience by connecting it to pathetic myths of victimization. AIDS, which has inspired playwrights to create dozen of sons of Camille, has only exacerbated an existing tendency. The beauty of Paul Rudnick's *Jeffrey* (1992) is its refusal to authorize pathos. *Jeffrey* is a healthy, irreverent satire on gay life in New York City in the age of AIDS. More important, it is a challenge to live joyfully in perilous times. Paul Rudnick has written: "AIDS is not the end of gay life or gay laughter."[25] His central character, Jeffrey Calloway, finally realizes this.

Jeffrey is a thirtysomething "innocent" who "believes that life should be wonderful."[26] A would-be actor who supports himself as a waitperson, Jeffrey has, above all, lived for sex, which is for him spiritual as well as physical: "It's just one of the truly great ideas. I mean, the fact that our bodies have this built-in capacity for joy—it just makes me love God. Yes!" (7)

But sex ceases to be fun when it becomes connected to terror of broken condoms and virulent body fluids: "Sex is too sacred to be treated this way" (7). So Jeffrey will renounce sex and plunge into anxiety. Through a series of vignettes, Rudnick traces Jeffrey's attempts to find a cure and substitute for his love of sex. In the process Jeffrey travels through many of the institutions of contemporary gay New York: the gym, AIDS fund raisers, hospitals, memorial services, self-help groups, masturbation clubs, gay bashing, new age evangelism, and even St. Patrick's Cathedral. No place can protect him from the two realities of his life as a gay man in the nineties: his unquenchable desire for sex and romance and the terror of AIDS.

In his first unsuccessful attempt to rechannel his libido, at a gym filled with humpy men, Jeffrey meets and is instantly attracted to charming, handsome Steve, "a master at outrageous, successful flirtation" (8), who henceforward zeroes in on Jeffrey wherever Jeffrey goes. True to his new devotion to celibacy Jeffrey tries to avoid Steve's determined advances. He tries even harder when he discovers that Steve is HIV-positive, embodying the very danger Jeffrey wants to avoid. In *Jeffrey*, HIV is not a cue for melodrama, but rather a challenge to get on with life as happily as possible. Steve tells Jeffrey: "Don't admire me! Fuck me!" (60), but Jeffrey wants sex not only to be joyful, but also totally carefree. He cannot face the idea of beginning a relationship with someone whom he might have to watch get sick and die, tragedies people had to experience long before AIDS.

Rudnick's play provides a healthy counter to other AIDS plays in its insistence that AIDS isn't Jeffrey's primary problem: it is his inability to accept and live happily in a compromised world. When Jeffrey goes to pray in St. Patrick's, he is accosted by a randy, musical comedy loving priest who leads him into the bowels of the church for sex, but instead delivers a homily which, though no doubt unacceptable to Cardinal O'Connor and the pope, is the antidote to Jeffrey's despair: "Of course life sucks, it always will—so why not make the most of it. How dare you not lunge for any shred of happiness" (69), but that happiness can come only with the rejection of deterministic myths, including that of God the puppeteer. God is, for the priest, the balloon children hit aloft to keep it from touching the ground: "The very best in all of us" (69). Toward the end of the play Jeffrey is at the memorial service for his friend Darius, who was a dancer in *Cats*. Darius' ghost, decked out in a shiny cat costume, appears to Jeffrey and delivers the mandate: "Hate AIDS, Jeffrey. Not life" (84). Finally Jeffrey takes the advice of the priest and Darius and gambles on love with Steve. The play ends, romantically, on top of the Empire State Building with Gershwin's "Embraceable You" in the air and Jeffrey and Steve keeping a red balloon aloft.

In *Jeffrey*, Paul Rudnick has written, out of the grief and fears of contemporary gay men, one of the best American comedies in years, filled with memorable one-liners George S. Kaufman would have envied. His satire is deft, but always affirming. Most important, however, Rudnick affirms the spirit and substance of all great comedy—love and community in a compromised, fallen world.

TURNING THE TABLES

In some of the most celebrated works of contemporary American drama, gay playwrights offer corollaries to the critiques of the "gender trouble" (as Judith Butler calls it) of American society which is the subject of much feminist and gay theory.[27] At a time when "performance" is a buzzword in critical theory, contemporary gay drama shows how theorists' sense of performance can be realized.[28]

In focussing on the performative aspects of gayness, homophobia, and gender, some contemporary gay plays reverse and explode the outside/inside categories of gay drama on which I have structured much of this book. "Mainstream" gay drama, written for a predominantly heterosexual audience in the commercial theater, and "inside" gay drama, written by gay playwrights for a predominantly gay audience, operate under different sets of assumptions and with different sets of signs. My terminology mirrors the inside/outside distinction delineated by theorists like Diana Fuss:

> To the extent that the denotation of any term is always dependent on what
> is exterior to it (heterosexuality, for example, typically defines itself in crit-

ical opposition to that which it is not: homosexuality), the inside/outside polarity is an indispensable model for helping us to understand the complicated workings of semiosis. Inside/outside functions as the very figure for signification and the mechanisms of meaning production. It has everything to do with the structures of alienation, splitting, and identification which together produce a self and an other, a subject and an object, an unconscious and a conscious, an interiority and an exteriorty.[29]

My formulation has underscored the ways gay men have been dramatized as "other" in modern drama, outside the frame of reference of the mainstream audience, only to be incorporated within the familiar heterosexist structures of that audience and its spokesmen, the newspaper reviewers. Gay playwrights who want to support themselves in the theater have to find a way to speak to a larger audience than that for "inside" gay dramas, to present gay experience in a wider context. Such playwrights must perforce be assimilationists, finding a place for gay experience within the mainstream. Contemporary dramatists assert further that the heterosexuals in the audience must also be assimilationists, which entails that they see, understand, and learn from a gay point of view.

Paula Vogel's *The Baltimore Waltz*, Terrence McNally's *Lips Together, Teeth Apart,* and Tony Kushner's *Angels in America* critique the homophobia and heterosexism still dominant in American society and the social, spiritual, and institutional malaises that support and are expressed by such homophobia. Rather than focusing on homosexuality as "the problem," the plays turn the tables in suggestive ways, presenting "the problem" as that of the predominantly heterosexual society represented by the audience.[30] Rather than simply satirizing or attacking the audience, these plays toy with the very idea of audience. By doing so, they play with the idea of "who's watching," a primary question for theater and for homosexuals.

Equally important, this new wave of gay drama resists remorse and victimization, which have been the central points of mediation for gay characters and heterosexuals in the audience. Thomas E. Yingling wrote, "Until quite recently, the homosexual has been almost literally unable to speak of itself coherently except in a vocabulary of remorse,"[31] which was anything but enabling.

A classic expression of this "vocabulary of remorse" is the longest monologue in *A Chorus Line*, which opened on Broadway in 1975 and ran into the late 1980s; Paul's shame-filled confession of his homosexuality and description of the night his parents came to see him in a drag revue. Paul's shame and self-pity should have been obsolete by the mid-seventies, particularly in a gay-written show; yet then, and even now, Paul's confession usually receives an ovation, even though Paul is the only principal character whose experience is not crystallized in a song (only heterosexuality is musical?). Paul's pitiable state continues as an old knee injury forces him to collapse in pain at the audition and be taken to the hospital. Paul is not only gay, but also a former drag performer; not only pitiable, but also physically weak.

While it would be nice to think of Paul as a dated piece of seventies theatrical condescension, he is still for many people the acceptable homosexual.[32] Unlike the other characters whose life stories are narrated in front of the other auditioners, Paul's is told on a bare stage, underscoring his isolation (the only other gay character was dismissed at the first cut). Paul is first isolated, then dismissed from the scene like the gay scapegoat of traditional problem plays. *A Chorus Line* perpetuates the ridiculous fiction that the choruses of Broadway musicals, and society itself, are totally heterosexual. More dangerous, the musical offers an uncritical presentation of the American notion that personality and private life, not talent or mastery of one's craft, get one a place on America's figurative chorus line.

Paul is under the judgmental gaze of the director who from his position in the audience manipulates the action, and the audience who share the director's point of view toward the characters. The director forces Paul to confess and abject himself to earn a place on the chorus line. What if the director were gay and forced the heterosexual men in the cast to isolate themselves from the tribe and share their sexual insecurities and their guilt and shame? The audience would be put in the challenging position of seeing dramatized experience through gay eyes.

It is this traditional audience/actor relationship that *The Baltimore Waltz, Lips Together, Teeth Apart,* and *Angels in America* try to reverse and revise in order to examine what separates and what connects gays and straights in American society. AIDS plays an important role in this revision of gay drama, for the disease has brought to a crisis point the fear and hatred of gay men that has been institutionalized and, in various ways, protected by societal norms and laws. David Wojnarowicz's angry proclamation—"WHEN I WAS TOLD THAT I'D CONTRACTED THE VIRUS IT DIDN'T TAKE ME LONG TO REALIZE THAT I'D CONTRACTED A DISEASED SOCIETY AS WELL[33]—could be the adage for contemporary gay drama.

BREAKING THE CODE

In Paula Vogel's *The Baltimore Waltz*, a woman is baffled by the fact that her brother and a series of mysterious men make contact by flashing stuffed rabbits. She witnesses one furtive encounter in which her brother and a suspicious man in a trenchcoat fondle the obviously phallic ears of each other's stuffed bunnies. After one performance, in Baltimore of all places, an intelligent sophisticated woman asked me what the bunnies meant. I wondered whether she thought I was likely to understand better than she because I write on drama or because I am a gay man. Regardless, my friend knew that a code was operative and that she was not privy to it. Indeed, few plays operate so successfully both to use and to deconstruct the codes by which much of gay performance has been mediated for its audiences.

In her script, Paula Vogel explains that *The Baltimore Waltz* is meant to be a memorial to her gay brother who died of AIDS-related infections at the Johns Hopkins Hospital in Baltimore. On the title page is included the dedication: "To Carl, because I cannot sew."[34] As the panels of the AIDS Memorial Quilt are ornate, often playful visual tributes to those who have died of AIDS-related infections, so Vogel's play is a less silent testament. The script also contains a letter from Carl Vogel to his sister detailing his instructions for his memorial service: "Well I want a good show, even though my role has been reduced involuntarily from player to prop" (vii). The "good show" becomes the play, Vogel's dramatization of "a journey with Carl to a Europe that exists only in the imagination" (vii), which reflects and honors her brother's camp sensibility. While her brother was openly gay, *The Baltimore Waltz* is playfully, ironically, self-consciously (is there any other way?) closeted.

The play is full of reversals. The mysterious, lethal virus is in the system not of the gay man, but his sister, Anna, who is diagnosed with Acquired Toilet Disease, a lethal virus whose mode of transmission is toilet seats which have been used by small schoolchildren (the younger, the more virulent), and whose target population is unmarried female schoolteachers. The whimsy of this virus underscores the silliness of blaming the victim for having the HIV in his system. If any population can be blamed for being the carriers, it is that which is usually considered to be the most innocent. Anna's response to the news of her medical condition is that which is considered most "taboo" in men infected with HIV—she wants to "fuck [her] brains out"—and spends the European trip shared with her brother in a series of anonymous sexual encounters while searching for the cure for her deadly disease.

Meanwhile Carl, her brother, searches for Harry Lime (the villain played by Orson Welles in the classic Graham Greene/Carroll Reed film, *The Third Man,* who makes his living in postwar Vienna selling lethal, watered-down penicillin) who has the drug which can cure ATD. Carl's entree into a world of sinister male strangers is his stuffed bunny and the encounters are coded homosexual encounters. In the great tradition of coded mainstream gay drama, heterosexual encounters are overt; homosexual encounters are coded, covert, chaste.

All this "play" may seem to trivialize or even mock the seriousness of AIDS discourse. It succeeds in putting the audience off guard, signalling a "safe," inoffensive approach to a perilous subject, while at the same time showing the ludicrousness of most AIDS homophobia. Yet Vogel's play is not that simple or that shallow. The crucial scene is a slide show that Carl narrates of their travels in Germany. As Carl presents a narrative of German locations, the audience sees slides taken in and around the Johns Hopkins Hospital, where the "real" Carl died. The stark reality of these slides of an inner city hospital and Anna's memories of a very real Baltimore, intervene while Carl's narrative attempts to maintain the fantasy of the European trip. Finally, as Carl describes his trip to the Neuschwanstein, the slides change to a castle in Disneyland where Mickey Mouse and Donald Duck wave to tourists. Carl lashes out at what he sees as Anna's mockery of their trip:

> CARL: I went to Europe. I walked through Bavaria and the Black Forest. I combed through Neuschwanstein! I did these things, and I will remember the beauty of it all my life! I don't appreciate your mockery.
> ANNA: It's just a little—
> CARL: You went through Germany on your back; all you remember are hotel ceilings. You can show them your Germany.
> *Carl rushes off, angry.*
> ANNA: [*to audience*]: Sometimes my brother gets upset for no apparent reason. Some wires cross in his brain and he—I'm sorry. Lights, please. (52).

Through the slides, the audience is confronted with the reality of Carl's experience (all the more vivid in a performance in Baltimore) which can no longer be displaced or denied. The intrusion of Disneyland, where the world becomes a meaningless performance, is a metaphor for the way American popular culture gives everything a ludicrous language of denial. Carl's adherence to *his* reality is a kind of mad scene in which the audience is brought into the harsh reality of AIDS where denial, illusion, and play become impossible. Yet, visually, the play has never allowed the audience to ignore its central reality: the action takes place in front of a white hospital curtain and Carl throughout wears pajamas, reminding us that, despite the fantasy action of the play, it is he, not Anna, who is the invalid.

The slide show is a performance which acknowledges and speaks directly to the audience who understand the discrepancy between word and picture and the "play" that is the core of the scene, as they see vividly through the scene that such play cannot deny the reality of AIDS any more than the silence, scorn, or indifference of public figures can deny its reality. Even the supposedly idyllic German trip of the narrative contains dangers like Dachau, a memorial to hatred and social pathology, as well as the stark reality of illness and death.

Throughout the play, the characters/actors perform delightful, if futile transformations that also acknowledge and transform their audience. In the first scene, in which we see Carl in his job as children's librarian at the San Francisco Public Library, Carl transforms the audience into children whom he tries to politicize by having them make and wear pink triangles. Play time, the cutting of colored paper, has become serious. Those bits of paper have become a text—a memorial and a political challenge. Carl's superiors know that these are not just paper triangles—that play can become serious and must be policed—and members of the audience must decide whether they identify with the children or the policing supervisor who has Carl fired for his open homosexuality.

At the beginning of the play, Anna admits that "I've never been abroad. It's not that I don't want to—but the language terrifies me" (1). Anna's trip is to an imaginary Europe, where she doesn't know the languages, to the medical world where she cannot penetrate the inscrutable jargon, and to the imagination, where the language is liberating, but frightening. Only death leaves her totally speechless. Carl's death is presented as the grotesque, mute waltz of Anna and his recalcitrant corpse.

Language is one of the sign systems the play explores. More important, *The Baltimore Waltz* is an exercise in the transformation of signs often identified with homosexuals. Thomas E. Yingling wrote:

> The gay absorption into signs, meanings, interpretation, and art is related to the fact that for the homosexual, the "problem" of homosexuality is in fact the problem of signs. The problem of signs for the homosexual is inescapable. One is taught young, for instance, that homosexuality is a semiotic, that there are *signs* of it, and that one ought not to produce those signs.[35]

Signs abound in Vogel's play, beginning with the cutting of the pink triangles. Here a sign is properly interpreted by the library staff, who react as the sign signifies—as Nazis. The pink triangle, after all, is historically more a sign of oppression than of liberation. More precisely, it is a sign of how the gay movement, like many oppressed subcultures, is built on signs that signify both a history of oppression and the potential for liberation. Once the play moves further into fantasy, signs are created and transformed. The stuffed rabbit, like all such children's objects, is a source of comfort—something to hold—and an image of sexual activity ("fucking like a bunny"). At the end, after Carl's death, the rabbit becomes a sign for Carl and his liberating imagination. AIDS—a sign for much more than an immune system breakdown—is converted into another disease and sign system.

Vogel dramatizes the playful manipulation of signs which has been, for the gay person, empowering. Anna and Carl take control of their own signs. The audience feels loss at the end, not only because Carl dies, but because with his death the play moves into the literal world of heterosexist AIDS melodrama in which a doctor is only a doctor and a stuffed bunny only a remnant of someone who has died. The tragedy of AIDS is that it seems to rob the world of gayness, of the play with signs, of the free sexuality. Without that play, experience, even relationships, become frightening: "I feel it's simply not safe for me right now to see anyone" (81).

Anna takes on not only Carl's disease but also his gayness, his liberating, empowering play with signs. Such play cannot combat disease or mortality, but it can cut through the oppressive language of heterosexist representations of gay people. The codes exist in *The Baltimore Waltz* not as a means of hiding the homosexual content of the play or of enacting a compromise with the audience—contemporary gay playwrights refuse to compromise. They are there to force the audience to experience a different means of seeing and dealing with experience.

"I HOPE YOU BOYS DON'T MIND A LITTLE SHOW"

Terrence McNally's *Lips Together, Teeth Apart* turns the tables by making four heterosexuals the object of the homosexual gaze and locates those heterosexuals literally in the middle of a gay subculture with which they refuse to assimilate. The play avoids the usual problematizing of gay characters by privileging a gay point of view toward heterosexual behavior.

McNally's play is structured on the clash between the often ludicrous performance the characters to give to hide their anger and anxiety and the voicings of the character's most self-defining thoughts which are unexpressed to the other characters because: "No one wants to listen to who we really are. No one really."[36] McNally has repeated here the technique of "inner monologue" Eugene O'Neill used in *Strange Interlude*. In O'Neill's play, the monologues are tied to a quasi-Freudian pattern which rigidly fixes characters in behavior patterns that are ultimately out of their control. In *Lips Together, Teeth Apart*, the inner monologues reveal the extent to which the characters are unformed, unmoored. They are not, as O'Neill's characters are, overdefined; rather their unhappiness stems from their feeling underdefined. Yet, like O'Neill's characters they feel fixed, unchangeable, while hating what they are.

Lips Together, Teeth Apart focuses on seeing and being seen, particularly seeing and being seen by gay men. Seeing and being seen become linked to the play's two principal themes; performance, particularly performance of gender, and mortality, particularly the heterosexual's death wish set against the gay men's celebration in the face of death. The time is a symbolic July 4th, the holiday on which America celebrates itself; the place is Fire Island, one of the few places in America where heterosexuals are in the minority. Two heterosexual couples are spending the weekend in a house left to one of the wives by her brother who recently died of AIDS. Self-consciously isolated, the characters watch the alien activities around them, rituals of death and sexually charged revelry. To the two couples, everything seems alien and frightening, even the swimming pool, which they fear might be "polluted" by the equated HIV and homosexuality: "One drop of water in your mouth or on an open sore and we'll be infected with my brother and his black lover and God knows who else was in here" (80).

The legatee, Sally, spends much of the weekend apart, painting. Sally is isolated by her grief at her brother's death, her anger at his homosexuality, and her guilt at the strength of that anger. She cannot bring herself to accept the revelry of the gay men around her: "Seeing them touching sort of sickens me. I can't help it. I'm glad I never saw my brother dancing with another man and now I never will" (90). Early in the play, she sees a man take off all his clothes, wave in her direction, then swim out to sea in what is a suicidal journey. Later she sees the drowned body of the swimmer and obsesses on her complicity in the man's death and her identification with his wish to die:

> My eyes didn't say "Stay, life is worth living." They said "Go. God speed. God bless." My wave didn't say "Hurry back, young man, happiness waits you ashore." It said "Goodbye. I know where you're going. I've wanted to go there too." (75)

Sally is riddled with guilt about her lack of acceptance of her gay brother, about helping him to die, and about her inheriting his house which rightfully should have gone to his Black lover. The willful journey of this young man into the sea and to death becomes her obsession during the play as she watches it from the safety of her deck: "I saw what happens when we're not loved and protected and we feel so alone" (74). She remembers the moment at her father's funeral when she stood silently while her mother told her brother that "he couldn't really understand her loss, or what she was feeling, that the love between a man and a woman was different" (21). Her brother David's response was that he felt "rejected and diminished" by both his hostile mother and his silent sister. And Sally, unable to bring a pregnancy to term, feels herself alienated from her fertile companions, out of the loop of real heterosexual "normality." Her legacy from her brother is her own sense of apartness, her own vision of alienation: "I wouldn't want me for a mother either. Too frightened, too sad, too late" (15).

The only things that Sally's husband, Sam, seems to have in common with her are self-hatred and homophobia. As Sally is sure that her inability to carry her pregnancies to term is a sign of her potential failure as a mother, Sam is terrified of fatherhood because he is sure he has nothing children could love. "You don't love empty" (143). Sam's sense of inadequacy has been intensified by the knowledge of his wife's affair with his brother-in-law and by the surrounding gay presence: "I don't know about pools and AIDS and homosexuals. I don't want to. It frightens me, all right? All of this" (82). Toward the end of the play, Sam watches two men make love in the bushes next to the house. He wonders first if this is what "we look like when we make love. I see huffing and puffing and biting and licking and kissing and hugging and grunting and groaning, but I don't hear anyone say 'I love you' " (85). Yet this act, which the homophobic Sam has described in bestial terms, becomes romantic:

> They lie in each other's arms on the sand, in the poison ivy, under a full
> July moon, the sound of the Atlantic Ocean and Ella Fitzgerald wondering
> "How High the Moon." And now I hear it. I hear I love you. (86)

At that moment, like a Hollywood climax, fireworks fill the sky, ratifying the
beauty of the passion Sam has voyeuristically seen and heard. The love Sam
has witnessed is the normality from which the heterosexuals are separated.
The blissful sexual act is the counter to the isolation and alienation the two
couples feel. Their sense of emptiness, of self-hatred, of separation can be
countered by the dancing and coupling that surrounds them. Their gay neighbors revel in the face of hatred, loneliness, and death.

Sam's brash sister, Chloe, sees the physical attractiveness of her gay
neighbors: "You compare that [Chloe's husband, John] or your brother or your
neighbors next door with the hi-fi to our two and you have to ask yourself
something: don't straight men think we have eyes?" (32)[37] Sally sees their
naked romantic confrontation with mortality and the isolation she supported.
Sam eventually sees their nakedness, their sexuality and their love. But in
seeing, Sally, Sam, Sam's sister, Chloe, and her husband, John, are like audience members, responding from a safe, irresponsible distance. They are
viewers of another, separate society:

> SALLY: He had a beautiful body.
> SAM: I'm sure he did. Most of them do. It's one of their requirements. (11)

More crucial to the play, Sally, Sam, Chloe, and John are painfully aware that
they are also performers for whom the neighboring gay men, whose balconies
overlook the poolside deck on which the play takes place, become an audience. In self-consciously performing, the characters become stereotypes of
neurotic, unhappy heterosexuals.

Chloe is an obsessive housewife, constantly cooking and waiting on
people in a flurry of unreflective activity. When she is not cooking or serving,
she is rehearsing for her next musical at the local community theater. She is
a constant performer on- and off-stage, and the larger-than-life characters she
performs in the musicals—the sort of characters supposedly adored by gay
men—are corollaries to her exaggerated, performed domesticity. Chloe is
aware that her performance covers, not too successfully, a total lack of self-
worth: "Honey, just about everyone is superior to me" (48), and an awareness
that her constant performance keeps reality at bay: "I talk too much because
it's too horrible to think about what's really going on" (48).

The four heterosexuals perform, but are terrified of being seen. When
Sally comments that she doesn't like being the only non-gay in a gay society,
another turning of the conventional tables, Chloe responds: "You don't want
to be a token anything. I hear you. Who wants to feel everyone's staring at
them?" (46). Sam worries that the gay men will think he is "one of them":

SAM: That guy in the red bikini is looking down here.
JOHN: Ignore him.
SAM: I'm trying to. He waved at me.
JOHN: So wave back.
SAM: You wave back. Imagine if they thought we were queer. I'm gonna sit with my legs apart and smoke a cigar all weekend." (13–14)

The guy in the red bikini was not only looking; he was also trying to establish a friendly relationship with his neighbors, which they rejected. Sam is more concerned with proving he is heterosexual which, of course, can only be done by performing what he envisions as the opposite of homosexuality, a stereotype of heterosexuality. However, unlike the gay man, who is always aware that gender is a series of performances, Sam sees no irony, no absurdity, no mockery in his pose of heterosexuality. For the gay man, as Richard Dyer has aptly claimed, "Performance is an everyday issue, whether in terms of passing as straight, signalling gayness in coming out, worrying which of these turns to do, unsure what any of that has to do with what one is."[38] However, for the heterosexual, as Judith Butler has defined him, heterosexuality is

> an incessant and *panicked* imitation of its own naturalized idealization. That heterosexuality is always in the act of elaborating itself is evidence that it is perpetually at risk, that it "knows" its own possibility of becoming undone: hence, its compulsion to repeat which is at once a foreclosure of that which threatens its coherence. That it can never eradicate the risk attests to its profound dependency upon the homosexuality that it seeks fully to eradicate and never can or that it seeks to make second, but is always already there as a prior possibility.[39]

To associate with a gay man would be to be identified as gay. To avoid that identification, Sam performs "straightness," which is really only anti-gayness. Sam fears more than being misidentified. In a telling double entendre, he expresses his sense of inferiority: "The first thing we're going to do if we keep this place is build a deck higher than theirs. I don't want people looking down on me" (14)

When Sam and John's tension (John has had an affair with Sally) erupts into a ridiculous fight, Chloe's concern is whether the gay "audience" is watching and how to explain the fight to them: "They were rehearsing *West Side Story!*" (53).

Chloe's passive-aggressive husband, John, is troubled not only by the intensified homophobia he experiences in gayland, but also by the fears engendered by his newly diagnosed cancer and the attendant awareness of his mortality. Heterosexuals are not immune to diminished life spans: "Not everyone is dying of AIDS, Sally. There are other malevolent forces at work on God's miraculous planet" (83). Yet John's fears do not give him a sympathy for, or an imaginative link to, the gay men around him who are dealing with a plague. His bigotry is his only source of power: "Fucking nigger, dumb cunt, idiot faggot. I kill a hundred of them a day in my impotent fashion" (55).

Ironically, what the two heterosexual couples perform are traditional homosexual stereotypes: artistic temperament, shame, lack of self-worth, disease, camp, and petty bickering. Terrence McNally has turned the tables on straights, but not as an act of what sixties homophobic critics would call "homosexual spite" or as closet drama inversion or projection. McNally, from his viewpoint as a gay man, is showing how traits commonly considered homosexual are really American.

Above all, these husbands and wives, brother and sisters don't know how to talk with each other. When they do move from inner monologue to painful confession of their fears and inadequacies there is the possibility of moving toward intimacy and liberation. Yet the self-loathing is still there. John confesses: "With or without cancer I'm still the same person, so there's no reason to change your opinion of me. I mean, riddled with the stuff I'm still going to be the same rotten son of a bitch. I wish I could change. I really, really, really do. Profoundly. I can't. I just can't" (97).

The isolation from the surrounding community, too, remains. The couples refuse the invitation to join the gay Fourth of July party next door, but when the fireworks appear in the sky over the beach, the gay neighbors throw down American flags for the heterosexuals to wave. Whether the two couples accept it or not, America belongs to gays and straights and for a moment of flag waving during the fireworks, there is an unacknowledged community.

Sally understands that "these are difficult times to be anything in," but McNally sees that gay men have something to teach their straight neighbors onstage and in the audience. At the end of the play, *"audience and actors are in the same bright light"* signifying the kinship between performance and audience and the community the play offers as an antidote to the isolation and alienation the audience has seen. Community comes when there is no separation of performer and audience, self and other, gay and straight.

Like Lanford Wilson's *Fifth of July,* McNally's *Lip's Together, Teeth Apart* uses the idea of our national holiday, a day of celebration of America's two primary but conflicting national aspirations, independence and community, to show what is missing in the American notion of domestic and national family. The play limits itself to the upper middle class, the socioeconomic plateau of the majority of its audience. It does not offer a revolutionary vision, but it does offer a potentially healing gay vision of America.

LOVE AND JUSTICE: THE CULMINATION

Gayness and America are also the foci of Tony Kushner's ambitious two-part, seven hour *Angels in America*, which has become the most talked about, written about, and awarded, play of the past decade or more. Like *Lips Together, Teeth Apart*, Kushner's extravaganza challenges the heterosexuals in its audience to see with gay eyes, while challenging gay men to be the revolutionaries our social position enables us to be. *Angels in America* is uncompromising and proud in its gaze.

Seeing, being seen, and performing are central to Kushner's play, and what is seen in the first part of the play is what some of the characters, and many in the audience, do not want to acknowledge—homosexual acts. Joe Pitt, the young Mormon lawyer, discovers his gayness through going to Central Park at night and watching the furtive, anonymous sex of gay men. In the central scene of Part I, the audience experiences what Joe has experienced: they are forced to see such a late night Central Park sexual encounter presented simultaneously with and in counterpoint to a scene between Joe and the monstrous closet queen, Roy Cohn. Male-male sex, which Joe fears, watches, and wants is uncloseted as Joe talks of the difficulty of "passing," of performing what one is not. Joe's tentative expression of his homosexual desire moves him from audience to participant. Yet hiding one's sexual orientation, as Roy Cohn has done, and as Joe has tried to do, is achieved by performing the heterosexual moves and gestures expected of men.

In many ways, *Angels in America* is a momentous play, a turning point for gay drama and American drama. This uncompromising, unabashed "gay fantasia on national themes" is as grand and ambitious as the largest of O'Neill's works, but redeemed from O'Neill's ponderousness by its sense of transformation and play. Kushner allows the best elements of gay performance to liberate traditional American drama's penchant for the rigid formulas of naturalism. More than anyone before him, Kushner has linked in a positive way the traditions and conventions of classic American drama with those of gay theater. David Savran has written of Tennessee Williams's works' "ability as a text of bliss and desubjectivication to lead the reader or spectator simultaneously to recognize the oppressiveness of the present historical moment and to think the unthinkable alternative."[40] Kushner makes the gay alternative not only thinkable, but also necessary and inevitable.

Angels in America is structured like a Shakespearean romance. A seemingly stable world atomizes to be reconstructed and redeemed. Relationships are quickly brought to a crisis point. Destiny or coincidence causes unlikely collisions. Characters thought dead miraculously reappear. The real and the dream merge. Seemingly disparate actions are analogous. Comedy and tragedy alternate and, at times, coalesce. Kushner takes the multiple plot lines of Shakespeare a step further by using a "split screen" method and playing analogous scenes simultaneously.

As in Shakespeare's romances, an overriding question in *Angels in America* centers on what the relationship is between the concrete, historical world and the source of the play's miraculous and metaphysical interventions. In *Angels in America* there are angels, but God left heaven on the day of the 1906 San Francisco earthquake. Having tired of the eternal sexual bliss of paradise and its ever adoring angels, he followed the example of his creation, man:

> His lust gave way to wanderlust
> In mortifying imitation of you, his least creation.[41]

The angels want an end to human movement, migration, change, typical of the battles waged throughout *Angels in America* between order/stasis and chaos/change. The rabbi whose burial sermon begins *Part I: The Millennium Approaches* laments the change and assimilation that was the result of the Jews' westward migration to America: "and how we fought, for the family, for the Jewish home, so that you would not grow up *here*, in this strange place, in the melting pot where nothing melted."[42] The rabbi's lament is echoed at the beginning of *Part II: Perestroika*, when the world's oldest living Bolshevik mourns the new chaos, the "mad, swirling planetary disorganization" not founded on theory which allows one to see creation as a "mountainous, granite order" (P1). But the world is not orderly; it is chaos, movement. Kushner and his characters can both lament and celebrate this chaos, endowing the play with a mixture of elegy and celebration that makes it a post-modern *Winter's Tale*.

Angels in America focusses on four homosexual men who represent, in various ways, not only positive and negative possibilities for homosexuals, particularly the perils of the closet, but the moral and spiritual plight of America. The symbolic center is Roy Cohn, the powerful, ruthless, closeted conservative who died of AIDS in 1986.[43] For Cohn, one is defined by one's power, not one's sexuality, and power and gay identity are irreconcilable opposites. He, after all, helped create an inquisition against homosexuals. When Cohn is diagnosed with AIDS, he tells his doctor:

> Homosexuals are not men who sleep with other men. Homosexuals are men who in fifteen years of trying cannot get a pissante anti-discrimination bill through City Council. Homosexuals are men who know nobody and who nobody knows. Who have zero clout. Does this sound like me?
> . . . Because what I am is defined entirely by who I am. Roy Cohn is not a homosexual. Roy Cohn is a heterosexual man who fucks around with guys.
> . . . AIDS is what homosexuals have. I have liver cancer. (M31–32)

For Roy Cohn, the universe is all chaos and terror: "I see the universe, Joe, as a kind of sandstorm in outerspace with winds of mega-hurricane velocity but instead of grains of sand it's shards and splinters of glass." (M4), but Cohn affirms this maelstrom: "You have to love the madness of the world to live in it. All else is vanity" (P70).

Within this chaotic, dangerous universe, the law becomes not an agent of order, but an expression of the chaos. Cohn believes that one either makes laws or is their subject, and he chooses to be a maker; for power is not being subject to laws. Roy Cohn, the self-proclaimed "heart of modern conservatism," is a lawyer who admits: "I know no rules" (M48). He is a moral monster, "the polestar of human evil," but his energy, both godlike and demonic, makes him an image of America itself. As his nurse, the Black drag queen Belize says: "I could show you America. Terminally ill, crazy and mean" (P95). Like order and chaos, the mixture of individualism, vitality, and malice that is Roy Cohn is a basic, American contradiction that must be understood, if not embraced.

Cohn's protege, another closet case, is a young Mormon lawyer, Joseph Porter Pitt. Joe believes in the new order of the Reagan revolution (it is 1985) and the Jehovah-like fury and arbitrary power of Roy Cohn. When asked to justify the homophobic court decisions he has drafted, Joe can say: "It's law, not justice, it's power, not the merits of its exercise" (P117). Like Cohn, Joe has learned to detach moral principles from inherently moral concepts. Like Cohn, Joe cannot fit his homosexuality positively into that order. Since homosexuals do not exist in the Mormon faith, or in the Reagan revolution, Joe has tried his best to deny his sexuality and live with a loveless marriage, performing the "cheerful and strong" persona demanded of Mormons. When his wife asks him if he is a homosexual, Joe responds: "Does it make any difference? That I may be one thing deep within, no matter what, no matter how wrong or ugly that thing is, so long as I have fought, with everything I have, to kill it" (M27).

While the shameless Cohn can live his contradiction happily, Joe hates his contradiction and sees himself only as "a shell" (M27). Joe can no longer hide his homosexuality and his anguish and suffers from the emptiness and self-hatred the play presents as part of being American, of being Reagan's children, the offspring of a family that isn't a family at all: "I think we all know what that's like [to be Reagan's child]. Nowadays. No connections. No responsibilities. All of us . . . falling through the cracks that separate what we owe to our selves and . . . what we owe to love" (M52-53). Joe leaves his unhappy, valium-addicted wife, Harper, and joins in a turbulent liaison with another self-hater, the literal and figurative "word processor," Louis Ironson:

> LOUIS: Strange bedfellows. I don't know. I never made it with one of the damned before. I would really rather not have to spend tonight alone.
> JOE: I'm a pretty terrible person, Louis. . . . I don't think I deserve being loved.
> LOUIS: There? See? We already have a lot in common. (M89)

Louis has left his lover, Prior Walter, because he cannot deal with his lover's AIDS-related illnesses and impending death. He has failed "the hard law of love," and put his own needs and fears before those of his partner. Linked in their attraction and their self-hatred, Joe and Louis feel that they are doomed. Both have betrayed their commitments to lovers. They cannot go back, neither can they forgive themselves.

Kushner's Cohn says, "Either make the law or be subject to it" (M83), but law in Kushner's play is a gigantic, over-arching concept, embracing the personal and the political. In the premiere production of both parts of the play at the Mark Taper Forum in Los Angeles, the action was played in front of John Conklin's setting of a decayed, cracking replica of the Hall of Justice in Lower Manhattan. Cohn's devotion to law and power denies him any personal relationship beyond that of sexual liaison or surrogate father. Love gives one no clout. But Louis, Joe, and their partners and friends want love as well as law. Louis' friend Belize, a Black drag queen, says: "I don't understand what love is. Justice is simple. Democracy is simple. Those things are very un-ambivalent. But love is very hard. And it goes bad for you if you violate the hard law of love" (77).

The problem is in discovering what that "hard law of love" is. Certainly it involves more self-acceptance, more self love than guilty, self-hating Joe or Louis can muster; more of a sense of community than Roy Cohn can conceive of. When Harper, toward the end of Part I, has her hallucination of Antarctica, a place which should be a total escape from other people, what Mr. Lies calls "a deep freeze for feelings," ultimately Harper cannot conceive of this desolate waste without a child in her womb and an Eskimo companion. It is not separation she wants, but love. And the Angel appears not to the most powerful, but to the most loving and self-accepting, Prior, of whom Harper, in an amazing mutual dream scene, says "Deep inside you, there's a part of you, the most inner part, entirely free of disease" (M22). Prior and Belize, the two gay men who refuse to be closeted, are the only characters in the play of whom that could be said.

John Lahr has compared the state of the characters in *Angels in America* with Alexis de Tocqueville's prophetic vision of Americans in his commentary of the early nineteenth century, *Democracy in America*, a work Louis mentions in Kushner's play. De Tocqueville wrote:

> Thus not only does democracy make every man forget his ancestors, but it hides his descendants and separates his contemporaries from him. It throws him back upon himself alone and threatens in the end to confine him entirely within the solitude of his own heart.[44]

It is this dark side of democracy—the isolation and solitude—which has haunted American literature from Hawthorne and Melville through Emily Dickinson and Ernest Hemingway and William Faulkner to contemporary writers. It is what we see in the noncommunication of the married couples and siblings in *Lips Together, Teeth Apart*. It is poignant in the failures of Louis and fears of Harper in *Angels in America*. It is terrifying in the colossal amorality and isolation of lawyer Roy Cohn, who is a postmodern Ahab.

Part One of *Angels in America* is a picture of dissolution of the social fabric. Old ethnic communities are gone. So are old power structures, old faiths and illusions, and relationships not based on honesty or love. Characters move from the familiar to the unknown. The watchword is not community or relationship, but isolation. All the characters, isolated at the end, began as outsiders through a combination of religion, race, sexual orientation, agoraphobia, disease, or disillusionment. Yet the characters are also joined in uncanny ways. Prior, having donned drag to console himself after receiving his diagnosis of Kaposi's sarcoma, dreams a meeting with Joe Pitt's valium-addicted wife, Harper, who simultaneously hallucinates a conversation with Prior:

> HARPER: What are you doing in my hallucination?
> PRIOR: I'm not in your hallucination. You're in my dream. (M20).

In this mystical merging of fantasies, Prior tells Harper that Joe is homosexual. How does he know? "Threshold of revelation" (M22). When Roy Cohn collapses, the ghost of Ethel Rosenberg, whose execution Cohn arranged, appears to dial 911 for an ambulance. Ethel tells Roy, "History is about to crack wide open" (M86).

The dissolution of relationships and the various unmoorings seem to be the prelude to a revolution, the creation of a new order, heralded by the climactic, spectacular, "very Steven Spielberg" appearance of an angel to the ailing Prior Walter.

The assumption is that this divine intervention will change things, or at least issue a redemptive call for action. However, when *Perestroika* opens, Prior learns that the angel, instead, calls for stasis, death:

> In your blood we have written STASIS!
> In you we make an ENDING! (P14)

Prior, however, wants "more life" and will, like Jacob, wrestle with the angel to get it. When Prior ascends the ladder to heaven to argue for his life, he finds that heaven is more tedious and more specific than Shaw foresaw in *Man and Superman*. God has disappeared, and heaven is a simulacrum of San Francisco after the 1906 earthquake, ruled by squabbling, leaderless angels. Prior tells the angels: "We're not rocks, we can't just stop, progress, migration, motion is *animate*" (P146). As for God, Prior, who sees God's desertion as analogous to Louis', declares, "Sue the bastard for walking out" (P146). God will have Roy Cohn as his defense attorney: "You're guilty as hell, no question, you have nothing to plead, but not to worry, darling. I will make something up" (P161).

Perestroika continues and develops a series of alliances and misalliances begun in *The Millennium Approaches*. The brief romance of Louis and Joe ends in a fight which gives Louis, at least, the punishment he wanted for abandoning Prior. Joe's mother, Hannah, becomes Prior's caregiver. Belize, the Black drag queen, becomes Roy Cohn's private nurse and guardian of his stash of AZT. But this conventional series of collisions and separations is punctuated by more mysterious interventions, more links between historical and spiritual.

These mysterious and metaphysical interventions are rooted in the two religions that shape the characters: Judaism, an "ancient, ancient" religion imported from the old world which is the religion of Roy Cohn and Louis Ironson; and Mormonism, the indigenous American religion, founded upon an angelic vision. Both historically see themselves as separate communities, apart from the mainstream. The play is saturated with elements of both religions. It opens with the speech of a Rabbi at a Jewish funeral. When Louis asks that Rabbi for advice and forgiveness, the Rabbi tells him to find a priest: "Catholics believe in forgiveness. Jews believe in guilt" (M15), and Louis anguishes unconsolably over his desertion of Prior: "Some things. Are unforgivable, Mr. Pitt. Nobody does what I did" (P19), seeing Joe not as salvation, but as "punishment" (P54). Louis sees Joe's beating as "Expiation. For my sins" (P133). Through the intervention of Ethel Rosenberg's ghost, Louis, who does not know Hebrew, chants Kaddish over Roy Cohn's corpse, though both end the Hebrew prayer with the English refrain, "You sonofabitch!"

Mormonism and Judaism are linked by the recurring image of Jacob's wrestling with the angel. Joe tells Harper how, as a boy, he was fascinated by a picture of Jacob and the angel:

> Jacob is young and very strong. The angel is . . . a beautiful man with golden
> hair and wings, of course. I still dream about it. Many nights. I'm . . . it's
> me. In that struggle. Fierce and unfair. The angel is not human, and it holds
> nothing back, so how could anyone human win, what kind of a fight is that?
> It's not just. Losing means your soul thrown down in the dust, your heart
> torn out from God's. But you can't not lose. (M35)

For Joe, the angel represents the overpowering temptation of his homosexuality, a battle he must fight, but can't win. Prior's actual encounter with the angel is a fight for his life. After Prior wrestles with the angel and wins, Prior visits heaven where Louis' aunt and the old Rabbi send a message to Louis: "he should *fight* with the almighty. It's the Jewish way" (P152), an injunction impossible in a world deserted by God.

Where Judaism is a religion of guilt and atonement, Mormonism is supposed to be the faith of the "cheerful and strong." Kushner has said of Mormonism:

> The theology is an American reworking of a western tradition that is uniquely American: the notion of an uninhabited world in which it is possible to reinvent. It's part of the political project of westward expansion and genocide against native American populations, because it gives a moral ranking to colour of skin: the darker you are, the farther away you are from goodness. . . . They're very interesting people, the ones I have met and known personally, I've always liked them a lot. They're very decent, hardworking, serious, intelligent people. But they're very reactionary.[45]

The brief relationship of Louis and Joe is in part a collision of Judaism and Mormonism. Neither faith can support the moral lapse the men enact in leaving their partners. Nor can either faith support homosexuality. When Joe comes out to his mother via a four A.M. phone call to Salt Lake City, she pretends not to hear: "We'll just forget this phone call" (M56). Yet the call leads Joe's mother, Hannah, to sell her house in Salt Lake City and search for her son in New York City. Hannah is tired of the Latter Day Saints: "Abundant energy; not much intelligence. That's a combination that can wear a body out. No harm looking someplace else" (M62).

In *Perestroika*, Harper takes up an unofficial residency at the Mormon Visitor's Center on Manhattan's West Side and Hannah takes a job as volunteer to watch over her. Mormonism there has been reduced to a diorama presenting its history as a quaint piece of frontier nostalgia created by dummies and taped voices. Harper finds the tacky nostalgia comforting: "this isn't a place for real feelings, this is just storytime here" (P47), but there is trouble even in storytime. In the diorama, only men have voices. Women are mute props. In reality, the positive voice of Mormonism is that of a woman, Hannah Pitt, who gives Prior the advice that empowers him: "An angel is a belief. A Theory with wings and arms, that can carry you, that can lift you up. If it lets you down, you have to send it on its way, seek for something new." (P111)

Secular religions keep overwhelming the metaphysical. Roy Cohn advises Belize: "Hire a lawyer, sue somebody, it's good for the soul. Lawyers are . . . the high priests of America. We alone know the words that made America. Out of thin air. We alone know how to use The Words." (P81–82)

When Harper and Prior watch the show at the Mormon Visitor's Center, they envision the Mormon frontier patriarch turning into Joe Pitt, and Louis enters the scene to argue the political implications of Mormonism with him. Once again, Harper and Prior have broken through the "threshold of revelation" to a truth about the connection between them:

> PRIOR: I JUST SAW MY LOVER, MY . . . ex-lover, with a . . . with your husband, with that . . . window display Ken-Doll, in that . . . *thing* . . . (P47).

In seeing the relationship between Louis and Joe, Prior also sees the truth of that relationship, the squabbles that reveal the political and religious gulf separating these men who have in common only their desertion of their loved ones. Louis and Joe's Shavian arguments offer an even-handed presentation of the contradictions and failings of two central American secular religions, conservatism and liberalism. While Louis cogently defines the basic, unbreachable conflict in the Republican party between the "half religious zealots wanting to control every breath every citizen takes and half ego-anarchist libertarian cowboys shrilling for no government" (58), Joe can assert what is positive in American conservatism and what is the source of Louis' personal and political impotence: "we haven't lost sight of what really counts, freedom, not dependency, responsibility, individual responsibility, what's most good and most human in us, not a celebration of weakness and collapse. With you it's just guilt, guilt, guilt and anyone can feel guilty" (58). Joe fails to see the lack of compassion that destroys the credibility of his political faith. For Louis, politics is his religion. He believes until the end that "only in politics does the miraculous occur" (P163), but he does not see the need for affiliation or action.

Tony Kushner has said that "the question I am trying to ask is how broad is a community's embrace. How wide does it reach? Communities all over the world now are in tremendous crisis over the issue of how you let go of the past without forgetting the crimes that were committed."[46] While Louis is right in asserting that: "Power is the object, not being tolerated. Fuck assimilation" (M68), the principal issue in *Angels in America* is not what stance heterosexuals should take toward gay people (the answer to that is obvious), or even the more complex question of what stance gay people should take toward heterosexual adversaries, but what, in defining our community, do gay people do with homosexual adversaries like Roy Cohn or Joseph Porter Pitt?

The answer comes from the key words in *Perestroika*; "blessing" and "forgiveness." The dying Roy Cohn blesses his protege, Joe. Prior demands a blessing from the angel. The larger question is who can forgive and who can accept forgiveness. Ethel Rosenberg tells Roy Cohn: "I came to forgive, but all I can do is take pleasure in your misery" (P122). Belize, who is the moral center of *Perestroika*, enacting what others theorize, says before Roy Cohn's corpse: "He was a terrible person. He died a hard death. So maybe . . . A queen can forgive her vanquished foe. Noblesse oblige, forgiveness. Love and justice meet there, I think. It isn't easy. It doesn't count if it's easy. It's the hardest thing." (P135)

Belize's speech joins the two opposing forces, love and justice. It is the cement of a new gay community. Belize can forgive Cohn. Prior can forgive Louis, though he knows the limits of Louis's love. Harper can offer Joe the benefit of her experience—"Sometimes, maybe lost is best. Get lost. Joe. Go exploring" (P158)—and two valiums to help him on his way. Only

God, who abandoned all his creation, cannot be forgiven: "He walked out on us. He ought to pay" (P149).

As Harper soars to the real San Francisco, which Prior has described to her as "unspeakably beautiful," the end of the American frontier, she realizes: "Nothing's lost forever. In this world, there is a kind of painful progress. Longing for what we've left behind, and dreaming ahead. At least I think that's so." (P160). Her abandonment and isolation have given her a new faith born of experience and her visions, but her final, personal rejoinder also makes clear that revelation is personal, hard-earned, not communal or institutional. Her belief in progress is echoed by Prior in the final scene, whose proclamation, "The world only spins forward" (P165), combines the swirling, chaotic vision of Roy Cohn with an expression of the traditional American faith in a beneficent progress.

The final scene takes place in 1990, four years after the main action of the play. Prior has survived AIDS longer than he lived with Louis. Louis and Belize are still arguing politics. Hannah Pitt is still Prior's companion and caregiver, bolstering his faith in his survival. The foursome sit under the stone angel which stands on the Bethesda Fountain at the southeast corner of Central Park, Prior's favorite place and favorite angel: "I like angels best when they're statuary. They commemorate death but they suggest a world without dying" (P163). Prior, the prophet, steps forward and addresses the audience: "You are fabulous, each and every one. And I bless you. *More life.* And bless us all" (P165). This benediction is an act of forgiveness which breaks down the most obvious wall, that between stage and audience. Terrence McNally also does this at the end of *Lips Together, Teeth Apart* in a gesture of reconciliation and unity. The antidote for the isolation, unhappiness, and self-hatred of the characters in both these plays is the move to community, but the forging of that community is a challenge to the audience as well as the characters and actors.

The appearance of *Angels in America* on Broadway marks a turning point in the history of gay drama, the history of American drama, and of American literary culture. Tony Kushner's gigantic play, longer and more sweeping than Eugene O'Neill's most mammoth work, removes from the closet once and for all the enlivening relationship of gay culture and American theater and the centrality of the homosexual gaze in American literature from at least as far back as the works of Melville and Whitman that homosexual critic F. O. Matthiessen first canonized as expressions of an "American Renaissance." It is a turning point for the inevitable, eternal, if turbulent relationship of gayness and theater, the climax to this chapter of its history.

PART 4

AT THE MILLENNIUM:
FROM INSULARITY TO ENGAGEMENT

CHAPTER EIGHT

LOVING COMMUNITIES?

> All in all, there was a lot of love in Gregory and Bobby's house that first
> night of the first holiday weekend of the summer.
> —*Love! Valour! Compassion!*

After the enormous artistic and critical success of Tony Kushner's *Angels in
America,* which had its first and best production in London, the two most
successful gay plays with critics and audiences have been Terrence McNally's
Love! Valour! Compassion! in the United States and Kevin Elyot's *My Night
With Reg* in London. Since its New York run, McNally's play has been produced successfully by many smaller theaters around the country. Both plays
have been turned into films. While *My Night With Reg* had a short Off-
Broadway run, neither play has transferred well across the Atlantic. To some
extent they represent different cultural views of drama and of being gay. The
optimism and sentiment of McNally's three hour play, built on an alternation
of dialogue and direct address to the audience, is miles from the post-Pinter
bleakness and mordant wit of Elyot's more realistic ninety minute one act
play, imbued with skepticism about meaningful communication, community,
and love. Another cultural difference in these plays and their reception is
summed up in British journalist James Collard's statement: "in America 'gay'
is something you are while here in Britain, while we have co-opted a lot of
American gay culture, including the notion of gay identity, we also draw on
an older, European idea of 'gay' as something you do."[1] American gay plays
tend to focus on identity and politics while British plays present sexual practice as the primary bond joining gay men.

    My Night With Reg and *Love! Valour! Compassion!* represent the high points thus far in the careers of these veteran writers. Terrence McNally has written, "I think I wanted to write about what it's like to be a gay man at this particular moment in our history."[2] In doing so in *Love! Valour! Compassion!*, McNally has written a play that is in conversation with the major works of gay drama of the last three decades, from *The Boys In the Band*, to McNally's earlier work, to *Angels in America.* Elyot's play also echoes Crowley's work. Like *The Boys in the Band* and *Love! Valour! Compassion!*, *My Night with Reg* depicts the social interactions of a group of gay men to show how far we have, or have not, come in the quarter century since Crowley's play. Written before protease inhibitors redefined infection for middle-class gay men, AIDS hovers over these plays as the defining element of gay experience.

GAY DRAMA VS. QUEER DRAMA: MCNALLY AND KUSHNER

It was sheer coincidence that the Broadway run of Terrence McNally's *Love! Valour! Compassion!* occupied the same theater that housed Tony Kushner's *Angels in America.* For those with no interest in theater history, this factoid is irrelevant. It was inevitable, however, that these two plays would be compared; for these two highly successful plays represent differing points of view within that fictional entity called "the gay community." Kushner's *Angels in America* (1992) is the most discussed play of the nineties. It has been seen as a political critique and an exhortation (Prior's final speech has even been published separately as if it were the Sermon on the Mount), as well as a groundbreaking work of theater combining high art and low. With a style that seems to be equally influenced by Shakespeare and soap opera, *Angels in America* has been excoriated by the religious right and celebrated by liberals of all sexualities. Terrence McNally's *Love! Valour! Compassion!* (1994) was celebrated by mainstream critics and attacked by the gay left for its parochialism.

Kushner's seven hour extravaganza ended with an odd counter-cultural quartet onstage: a former drag queen living with AIDS; an African American ex-drag queen, now nurse; a feckless gay Jewish man who talks politically correct talk but who seems incapable of responsible action; and a Mormon matron who, having lost her son and daughter-in-law (who have disappeared), takes care of the person with AIDS. Even more interesting is who is not on stage—the only character in the seven hour play who goes through a real dramatic conflict and crisis, the conservative Mormon lawyer, Joe Pitt, who is thrown into a tailspin by his coming out.[3] Joe represents a lot of gay men who have been brought up with a set of religious and social beliefs that he finds difficult to reconcile with his newly acknowledged homosexuality (or is it bisexuality?). Kushner drops Joe off the face of the earth shortly before the end of *Perestroika,* as if he is unredeemable or simply not very interesting.

Blond, blue-eyed Joe Pitt, described disdainfully by one character as "the Ken doll," is like Edward Albee's Nick in *Who's Afraid of Virginia Woolf,* a gay playwright's representative of what is wrong with society and conventional American masculinity, dismissed before the final curtain. Joe's wife, Harper, tells him to "Get lost," and we are to believe he does. Perhaps, in Kushner's world view, if or when Joe loses the baggage of his conservatism, his wish for social order, he can be redeemed and join the elect at Bethesda Fountain where the play ends. Joe's capacity for love, his complexity, his wish, however misdirected, for a redeemed and redemptive society, count for nothing in Kushner's scheme.

Yet in every production of *Angels in America* I have seen, Joe is the character I care about, anguish over. He is the character who cares about combining his homosexuality with the important elements of human experience, straight or gay, that are left out of Kushner's vision of America: loving, committed relationships; meaningful work; and a constructive politics. Of course, Joe's politics are dreadful, his distinction between law and justice is an appalling, if somewhat accurate reflection of our legal and political system, and his search for a benevolent patriarch in Roy Cohn woefully misguided, but he at least wants to be politically and personally effective. Is it reprehensible to be gay and not be counter-cultural? Is it morally wrong to be gay and conservative?[4] Joe is not a monster like the play's arch enemy, the homophobic, antisemitic gay Jew, Roy Cohn. Joe is capable of love, he is educable, and he is on the verge of coming out. Indeed it could be said that rather than help Joe Pitt out of the closet, the other characters—Louis, Roy Cohn, and Prior—do all they can to drive him back in. Joe's erstwhile lover, the ineffectual leftie, Louis, doesn't engage Joe in political argument; he hectors him and goads him into enacting the physical punishment Louis wants for his fecklessness.

Kushner privileges Louis's ex, Prior Walter, the former drag queen living with AIDS, but what does Prior represent except a particularly endearing representative of the fashionable but dangerous Cult of the Victim? His best scenes in the play are the comic ones in *Perestroika* where he plays a kind of queer Lucy to Belize's Ethel. Only AIDS gives Prior the right to the moral superiority Kushner claims for him. What makes Belize worthy of a place at the end of the play beyond his race?

The basic difference between *Angels in America* and *Love! Valour! Compassion!* is that the former purports to be a queer play while the latter is definitely a gay play. To understand the distinction, one must understand the different political ramifications of the words "queer" and "gay." While "gay" signifies a male who openly declares his desire for someone of his own sex, "queer" has more complex, more politically charged connotations: a reveling in difference, a belief in performativity over stable essence, a celebration of marginality. In its most radical, Queer Nation definition, according to Alexander

Doty, "queer" "means to be politically radical and 'in-your-face': to paradoxically demand recognition by straight culture while rejecting this culture. Part of what is being rejected here are attempts to contain people through labeling, so 'queer' is touted as an inclusive, but not exclusive category, unlike 'straight,' 'gay,' 'lesbian,' 'bisexual.' "[5] For Eve Kosofsky Sedgwick, "queer" is a word that includes all individuals who demonstrate by their claims and actions that definitions of sexual identity are fluid, unstable:

> That's one of the things that "queer" can refer to: The open mesh of possibilities, gaps, overlaps, dissonances and resonances, lapses and excesses of meaning when the constituent elements of anyone's gender, of anyone's sexuality aren't made (or *can't be made*) to signify monolithically.[6]

For its advocates, "queer" shows both the failure and the power of hegemonic discourse. It covers what there are no nice words for, because it is an umbrella for proscribed sexual acts, roles, and orientations. More important, for Sedgwick "queer" is a choice of performance rather than a definition based on empirical analysis of experience:

> But "gay" and "lesbian" still present themselves (however delusively) as objective, empirical categories governed by empirical rules of evidence (however contested). "Queer" seems to hinge much more radically and explicitly on a person's undertaking particular, performative acts of experimental self-perception and filiation. A hypothesis worth making explicit: that there are important senses in which "queer" can signify only *when attached to the first person.*[7]

"He's a queer" is an insult, like "he's a faggot," for it places the object inside negative discourse, hate speech. "I'm a queer," says "I am not like you and I do not accept the systems on which you might base a negative judgment of me." Queer, then, is a matter of philosophical assumption, politics and style. One can be gay without being queer. In fact, to be queer is to deny the assimilationist goals of much of gay politics (one might add that it denies the philosophical underpinnings of political action). Queerness will lead to its own revolution in which individual perception and desire is the only valid law. As one critic of queer theory puts it:

> Queers do not want a place at the table. They want universal acknowledgment that the table has three legs. And yet, in queer writing, "queerness" always comes down to being gay. Worse, it often seems that calling oneself queer is a tactic for not acknowledging that one is merely gay, for not shouldering the burdens of coming out or the responsibilities that come with accepting the inevitable reality of a sexual identity and getting on with the rest of life.[8]

This sort of queerness informs *Angels in America.* We are to identify with Louis Ironson because of his marginality. "He could have been a contender," to paraphrase *On the Waterfront,* but instead of being a lawyer, he is a word processor; instead of being a devoted lover to his ailing partner, he runs from him when AIDS strikes, but revels in the guilt that betrayal provokes. Louis is brilliant, well-read, even theoretically sophisticated—he sounds like my graduate students—but, unlike them, he would drop out along the way and fester over his failure. However, we are not to lament over Louis's wasted potential. There he is at the end, still loved by the man he betrayed, along with the queer, as opposed to gay, Prior and Belize, and the potential lesbian Mormon matriarch, Hannah Pitt. In Kushner's vision, queerness is valorized, but it is also ineffectual. To paraphrase Mr. Faulkner, queers endure, but they do not prevail. They are wise enough to know that "The world spins only forward"—that motion is inexorable but not linear and that any form of conservatism that tries to stop the motion is doomed to fail—sometime. But for all the talk about politics, *Angels in America* does not call for political action. You are okay as long as you don't think like a conservative, but in Kushner's America, profession, middle-class aspiration, and conservatism are equated. At the end we are all blessed, liberal and conservative, homosexual and homophobe. No threat there. *Perestroika* is not a call for political action; it is a celebration of forgiveness. Everyone is forgiven—except Joe Pitt. *Angels in America* manages to be queer without offending the sensibilities of those well-heeled enough to pay the $130 it took to see the entire play on Broadway. It is a brilliantly written play, better in small-scale productions where one can better follow its arguments and enjoy its language and the great opportunities it gives actors. However, like other classics of American social drama—*Death of a Salesman, Awake and Sing*—it lets its audience off the hook. Like much of gay drama, it does not question the assumed righteousness of out gay men of liberal to left political persuasion.

"Gay," like "queer," has taken on specific political connotations. Even if Kushner allowed Joe Pitt a reformation, he would have at best become an upper middle-class *gay* man—a successful lawyer cautiously out in his everyday life, living in a domestic partnership with a socially compatible lover, perhaps belonging to a church with a lesbian and gay group (what is now known as a "welcoming congregation"). He might read Bruce Bawer's *A Place at the Table* and agree with Andrew Sullivan's writings.[9] He would belong to a gym and some gay biking group and, perhaps, be a Log Cabin Republican. He might subscribe to *The Advocate.* And he could afford to go to Broadway to see *Angels in America* and *Love! Valour! Compassion!* Joe Pitt would be gay, not queer. He would acknowledge his sexual orientation, believe that it should be socially acceptable as long as it fit within certain parameters, but would want to assimilate into American society. Indeed assimilation would be at the heart of his politics. But Louis Ironson, who seems to be Kushner's mouthpiece, cries "Fuck assimilation!"

I do not present this picture to denigrate it. My sympathies are more with this hypothetical Joe Pitt than they are with Louis Ironson. Yet Joe Pitt raises some of the most contentious questions for gay men: whether a mainstream politics can or should gel with gayness. This issue is an offshoot of the larger debate over the extent to which gay men should uncritically accept their patriarchal privileges as men. As Leo Bersani so cogently points out, "Gay men are an oppressed group not only sexually drawn to the power-holding sex, but belonging to it themselves."[10] Gay Joe Pitt, still unquestioning the fact that his power and conformity have placed him in a morally untenable position, does not, according to his creator, deserve to sit with the independent woman, the person with AIDS, the African American queen, and the left-wing intellectual.

Gay (as opposed to queer) drama tends to be about the gay bourgeoisie and tends, as mainstream drama does, to accept middle-class ideals and aspirations even as it critiques them. Everyone is allowed a place in the finale of *Love! Valour! Compassion!:* lawyer and accountant as well as costume designer and choreographer. While the end of *Angels in America* essentially celebrates the individual, the end of McNally's play celebrates the group, but it is a very privileged, insular group. I would suggest, however, that the end of *Angels in America* is more comfortable to a homophobic middle-class audience member than the end of *Love! Valour! Compassion!.* The reaching out for blessing from a marginal, relatively unthreatening position is easier to accept than the idealized community of relatively happy, prosperous *naked* men we see in the latter play.

Neither play is radical, but they differ in the extent to which they valorize marginality and accept some basic aspects of upper middle-class American culture. Gay drama is less interested in social critique or change than in staking a claim for gay people within a more compassionate, open society. Leo Bersani sees the negative aspect of this sort of gayness:

> We want to be recognized, but not as homosexuals (the essentialist identity).
> It is doubtful that we will be mistaken for other oppressed groups by the
> dominant culture (which is, for obvious reasons, concerned with questions
> of identity): we may, however, easily be mistaken for the dominant culture.[11]

Or, for assimilationist gays, we may too easily believe that we occupy a safe place in the dominant culture, forgetting that a lot of people do not want us there, particularly not wanting us to live as comfortably as they do, for that would make a bold statement that homosexuality is an attractive option and that compulsory heterosexuality is not necessary nor necessarily right. However, gay drama often forgets that there are many more people less privileged than we and that urban, highly-educated, upper middle-class gay men are not representative of the majority of gay men in America. As novelist John Weir, who has become a rabid critic of gay culture, puts it: "The true division in the gay community is between the entrenched, privileged, politically active urban and suburban trend-setters and policy makers, and the mass of people with homosexual urges who feel represented more by *Reader's Digest* and *Soldier of Fortune* magazine than by *The Advocate*, or *Genre* or *10 Percent* or *Frontiers* or *Deneuve* or *On Our Backs* or *Out*. If indeed they have even heard of them."[12]

STATE OF THE UNION

I'm butch. One of the lucky ones. I can catch a ball. I genuinely like both my parents. I hate opera. I don't know why I bother being gay.
—*Love! Valour! Compassion!,* p. 100.

This characteristic bit of humorous self-deprecation is spoken by Arthur, a gay accountant who has been in a relationship with Perry, a lawyer, for four-teen years. Arthur and Perry represent an upper middle-class gay marriage. Two solid professions, a nice home filled with all the necessary and unnec-essary appliances and electronics coveted by members of the American bour-geoisie, and a state-of-the-art car for their weekend trips. Arthur and Perry do good works. They contribute to charities, work for AIDS groups, and do pro bono work for arts organizations. They're good, solid citizens. Arthur and Perry would never be invited to join the gathering at Bethesda Fountain at the end of *Angels in America*. Not only do they represent the white bourgeoisie Kushner mistrusts, they are also politically and socially conservative. When one of their party starts talking about a newspaper photograph of a starving Somali child, Perry rejoins:

> I think the point is that we're all sitting around here talking about something, pretending to care . . . when the truth is there's nothing we can do about it. It would hurt too much to really care. You wouldn't have a stomachache, you'd be dead from the dry heaves from throwing your guts up for the rest of your life. That kid is a picture in a newspaper who makes us feel bad for having it so good. But feed him, brush him off and in ten years he's just another nigger to scare the shit out of us. Apologies tendered, but that's how I see it. (p. 52)

Though his lover and friends are appalled at the callousness and political incorrectness of Perry's statement, they share his fear of a world in which everything seems threatening and nothing works properly. Later, when they are alone, Perry tells Arthur: "I hated what I said at the table. . . . I just get so frightened sometimes, so angry." Arthur reassures him that "we all do" (pp. 60–61). When Bobby arrives, he tells his lover, Gregory, how things are at their city home: "The city is awful. You can't breathe. They still haven't fixed the dryer" (p. 37). Perry's fear and anger is one way of responding to chaos. Buzz, the ultimate Musical Comedy Queen, has another:

> You may wonder why I fill my head with such trivial-seeming information
> [data about arcane musicals]. First of all, it isn't trivial to me, and second,
> I can contain the world of the Broadway musical. Get my hands around it,
> so to speak. Be the master of one little universe. (p. 25).

A sense of order, of control is crucial to these gay men of the 1990s. They suffer from the usual fears of our age plus those particular fears of gay men, painfully aware of their place in American society: "They hate us. They fucking hate us. They've always hated us. It never ends, the fucking hatred" (p. 107). And they are either living with AIDS or with the fear and survivor guilt AIDS inspires. HIV-negative Arthur tells his lover: "I will always feel like a bystander at the genocide of who we are" (p. 122)

Most of the men in *Love! Valour! Compassion!* are all prosperous, relatively apolitical, artists or supporters of the arts. The artists depicted in *Love! Valour! Compassion!* don't create "queer" work. There are no Tim Millers invited to this country house. Indeed the play's straight audience senses a commonality with the characters because of the bourgeois status they share. We are told that the lawyer and accountant like to play rough in bed, but they do not wear leather and nipple rings. They don't display their difference. The two queens, Buzz and James Jeckyll, do not share the others' privileged economic status. In one of the few statements in the play that suggest that there is a world other than that of the more affluent characters, Buzz says:

> I can't afford to be fair. Fair's a luxury. Fair is for healthy people with
> healthy lovers in nice apartments with lots of health insurance, which, of
> course, they don't need, but God forbid someone like me or James should
> have it. (pp. 131–32)

As usual in popular representations of gay men, it is the more flamboyant, effeminate queens who stand outside the bourgeois world of profession and affluence.

McNally's characters could be, and have been, seen as stereotypes, the nineties version of the eight men who gather in Mart Crowley's *The Boys in the Band*. Indeed, McNally seems to be consciously placing his characters within a framework of canonical gay drama. We are told in Act II that "We would have a fabulous 5th of July," an allusion to Lanford Wilson's 1978 play, *5th of July*, about a gay couple in middle America. (see pp. 18-19) Even the casting—Stephen Bogardus (*Falsettos*), Nathan Lane (*The Lisbon Traviata*), and Stephen Spinella (*Angels in America*)—reinforces the referentiality. The play, like Kevin Elyot's *My Night with Reg,* is, among other things, a kind of State of the Union for one group of gay men, showing us how much has changed since Crowley wrote his play. What remains the same is a sense of insularity, of separateness from heterosexuals that is not typical of the experience of gay men outside the gay ghettoes. Most gay men no longer live in such a separate society, but have heterosexual friends and stronger connections with their own families. Most also do not socialize in such an exclusively male milieu.

Like *5th of July, Love! Valour! Compassion!* takes place in and around a beautiful old country house. Here a group of old friends spend their summer holiday weekends. What the six middle-aged men share is a sense of their own mortality. For McNally, there are both physical and spiritual malevolent forces. There is the mortality we all must deal with—aging and the loss of feeling desirable without the attendant loss of desire and the horrid diseases particularly ravaging gay men. How does one cope gracefully with these? Also, for those like John, there is the curse of feeling unloving and unlovable, of being evil. The embittered John in *Lips Together, Teeth Apart* has his counterpart in another John Jekyll, the evil twin in *Love! Valour! Compassion!* Both Johns suggest that mean-spiritedness may also be an incurable disease that lodges in certain people and is as virulent as cancer and the HIV virus. John Jeckyll tells his good twin, James:

> I resent you. I resent everything about you. You had Mum and Dad's un-
> conditional love and now you have the world's. How can I not envy that?
> I wish I could say it's because you're so much better looking than me. No,
> the real pain is that it's something so much harder to bear. You got the good
> soul. I got the bad one. Think about leaving me yours. (p. 124)

Unlike Kushner's evil genius, Roy Cohn, who exults to the last in his splenetic displays of malevolence, a Richard III for the 1990s, McNally's bad souls are pained by their own isolation. Yet John Jeckyll is not nasty because he is homosexual. This is not a repeat of the "Oh, God, why am I such a miserable nasty fairy?" refrain of *The Boys in the Band.* McNally's alternation of plays about homosexuals and heterosexuals shows that poverty of the spirit and lack of compassion are human traits that in heterosexuals are most dramatically seen in their hatred or fear of homosexuals.

While McNally seems to be suggesting that *Love! Valour! Compassion!* can be seen as a new look at the sort of group Mart Crowley presented in *The Boys in the Band,* one can see by reading the work in the context of McNally's other works, that homosexuality does not define personality here. Yet, as in Crowley's play, there is an attempt in *Love! Valour! Compassion!* to present as much of a cross-section of New York gay society as would credibly be invited to Gregory's house. Arthur and Perry can be seen as the nineties version of Crowley's "straight acting" couple, Larry and Hank; but while

Larry and Hank fight to forge a relationship that offers space for sexual freedom, Arthur and Perry see infidelity as a threat and a betrayal. Buzz and James are the resident queens, as Emory and Harold are in *The Boys in the Band*, but they also become a loving couple. The beautiful Ramon might be a sex object, like Crowley's cowboy, but he disdains that role and is actually a successful artist who will be the medium of Gregory's choreography. McNally's characters are functioning professionals capable of love. Their homosexuality does not cripple them. They also manifest some of the weaknesses of American consumer culture as it is manifested in gay culture, a worship of youth and an attendant fear of mortality.

Arthur's melancholy confession to Perry of his attraction to Gregory's beautiful young lover, Bobby—"Desire is a terrible thing. I'm sorry we're not young anymore" (p. 20)—sums up a crucial theme in McNally's play. Tennessee Williams's Blanche DuBois exclaims, "The opposite of death is desire," but what happens to desire as one grows older? For gay men, whose gayness has been tied to their sexuality and sexual attractiveness, this is particularly a problem. The evil genius, John, brings to this country gathering a beautiful, young Puerto Rican dancer who exults in his beauty and his independence. Ramon's physical beauty has a potent effect on all the men. It has also had an effect on the play's audiences and critics as column inches have been spent discussing the physical attributes of the actor who plays Ramon and who spends much of the play nude. That nudity is not (or not just) a cynical showbiz ploy. Ramon's body is a reminder to these men of what they feel they are losing. In the presence of his friends, John speaks of Ramon only as a sex object, a male bimbo, but alone, when Ramon is asleep, he declares his love. Gregory, a dancer-choreographer who is painfully aware that his body will no longer allow him to dance, realizes that he must let the talented Ramon dance his work for him: "Gregory was suddenly a 43 year old man whose body had begun to quit in places he'd never dreamed of looking at a 22 year old dancer who had his whole career ahead of him" (pp. 127–28). When Gregory's lover, the beautiful, young, blind Bobby compromises his relationship with Gregory by having sex with Ramon, Ramon blatantly tells Gregory what his presence has already made clear: "You're old and you're scared and you don't know what to do about it" (p. 118). Bobby, we discover, eventually leaves Gregory for someone younger.

Despite his love for Perry, Arthur becomes infatuated with Ramon as he had been with the sweet, young Bobby. Arthur knows, however, that he is not attractive to these young men, however, much Ramon may flirt and tease, as he knows what cheating can do to a relationship: ". . . it's never been the same. It's terrific, but it's not the same" (p. 19).

John Jeckyll, who has brought Ramon to the country house, tries to relive with Ramon his first adolescent sexual experience, one that involved no actual physical contact. But the story allows John a kind of eternal youth: "He will always be 17 years old and I will always be 19. Neither of us grows old in this story" (p. 95). John cannot regain his youth with his memory any-more than he can with Ramon.

Ramon has the self confidence and independence that comes with youth and beauty. When asked when he loves himself, he answers:

> I love myself when I'm making love with a really hot man. I love myself
> when I'm eating really good food. I love myself when I'm swimming naked.
> . . . But most of all I love myself when I'm dancing well and no one can
> touch me. (p. 55)

Ramon's open sensuality sets him apart from the older characters and links him with Bobby, with whom he has a passionate but brief encounter in the kitchen. The wild card for all the characters is sexual desire, but the older men opt for order and stability in their sex lives.

At the tense first dinner on Memorial Day weekend, Ramon has the naiveté to spout a truism that, as usual, happens to be true, however, trite:

> RAMON: I think the problem begins right here, the way we relate to one
> another as gay men.
> JOHN: This is tired, Ramon, very tired.
> RAMON: I don't think it is. We don't love one another because we don't
> love ourselves. (p. 54)

This could be a line out of *The Boys in the Band,* but McNally's characters are not the self-flagellants of Crowley's play. These men are functional, even successful. They may not be as self-loving as Ramon, but there is no doubt of their desire and capacity for love. *Lips Together, Teeth Apart* and *A Perfect Ganesh* showed that McNally believes that self-loathing is an American prob-lem, not a gay one. These men know their limitations and try to reach out to others constructively.

The self-hating boys in the band came together because they were gay and, therefore, misfits. They had nowhere else to go. The support they of-fered each other was at best tenuous. McNally's characters have forged a gay family:

> I want to write about family. To me a very important line is when Gregory
> says, "Are you going home to Texas?" Bobby says, "No, home is here.
> Texas is where my parents are." Gay people do create a society for them-
> selves, an extended family.[13]

This is a major difference between *Love! Valour! Compassion!* and *The Boys in the Band.* In Crowley's play, eight homosexuals come together for a social event, but one never understands what beside their homosexuality brings them to Michael's apartment to be vilified. The group may represent Crowley's idea of a microcosm, but it does not represent a community—or Crowley is dramatizing his notion that a gay community is impossible. Lanford Wilson's *5th of July* ultimately places its gay couple at the center of an extended biological family but outside any supportive gay community. For all their occasional squabbles, the men in McNally's play have forged strong bonds over a number of years.

Though some characters are happily coupled for various lengths of time, the most important bond is friendship:

> PERRY: No one for miles and miles. We could be the last eight people on earth.
> BUZZ: That's a frightening thought.
> PERRY: Not if you're with the right eight people. (p. 88).

These men form a family with all the attendant stresses and strains. McNally has written of his wish "to write about family." He sees the characters in *Love! Valour! Compassion!* as "an extended family with relatives you like more than others."[14] Such assertions raise the central question for gay men: How do we place ourselves within the discourse of family? An answer may be by retaining or reforging links with our own families, if those families have not rejected us. Another solution may be by forging our own intentional families, closely bound communities offering love, support, sometimes patronage. In her fine study, *Families We Choose: Lesbians, Gays, Kinship*, Kath Weston describes gay families she has known:

> In the Bay Area, families we choose resembled networks in the sense that they could cross household lines, and both were based on ties that radiated outward from individuals like spokes on a wheel. However, gay families differed from networks to the extent that they quite consciously incorporated symbolic demonstrations of love, shared history, material or emotional assistance, and other signs of enduring solidarity.[15]

This dynamic operates throughout McNally's play. Buzz tells the audience at the end of the first act, "All in all, there was a lot of love in Gregory and Bobby's house that first night of the first holiday weekend of the summer" (p. 62). Not merely warmth, friendship, or camaraderie, but love. Yet the family unit also expands during the course of the play. By the end, Ramon, who begins as a date John brings along, ends up being chosen by Gregory to replace him as a dancer. James Jeckyll has been accepted into the family as a friend and as Buzz's lover. Even John Jeckyll, however isolated, is still there, invited back time and again. His loneliness and sense of being unloved is greatly a product of his own imagination.

The family supports the illness and aging of its members. Bobby is blind, Buzz and James have AIDS, Gregory is depressed over the waning of his abilities as a dancer. Within the family unit all this is acknowledged and supported.

The most vivid visual image in the play is the sight of six gay men dancing the "Dance of the Little Swans" from *Swan Lake.* The dance takes teamwork and precision: the dancers must move as one. In one sense, the image is hilarious camp—six large men in tutus, ballet slippers, and the white, feathered headdresses of the little swans executing dainty choreography, a far cry from the powerful homoerotic imagery of Matthew Bourne's brilliant revision of the classic ballet. But McNally makes the image one of love and community in the face of mortality and AIDS. First James, the most ill of the group, collapses and has to return to bed. Then, as the five continue, one by one they step out of the dance and tell the audience how they are going to die. The dance becomes an absurd, defiant protest against mortality, but it is also an image of family.

The dancing is an extension of the group singing that begins the first two acts and ends the third, men's voices blending in nostalgic songs like Stephen Foster's "Beautiful Dreamer." Unity and harmony. Music as the sound of community.

In the play's final tableau, all the characters are skinny-dipping in the moonlight. The nudity is not erotically charged, as Ramon's is earlier in the play. It is nakedness, vulnerability, childlike innocence. The moment has been compared to Thomas Eakins' celebrated painting, "The Swimming Hole," an idyllic picture of naked men and boys unabashed in presenting themselves for the viewer's gaze.

Love! Valour! Compassion! dramatizes and celebrates a community of gay men in which we see a variety of forms of gay male intimacy: long-time lovers, former lovers who have become close friends, rivals who become collaborators, colleagues who have become friends. Singing together, dancing together, these men comprise an ensemble based on an intimacy idealized by some heterosexual men, but such intimacy is only possible when fear of homosexuality is removed.

In *Angels in America* illness, particularly AIDS, is the unmistakable sign of gayness. Like many closeted gay men, Roy Cohn was outed by AIDS. Prior's bravery and unselfishness in the face of AIDS is one of the signs of his sainthood, perhaps one of the reasons the angels choose him as their prophet of stasis. Joe's resistance to his sexual desire is manifested in vomiting blood, a corollary to Prior's shitting blood. Louis wants to bear the outward signs of his crime, wounds to match Prior's lesions. At the end, Prior has lived with AIDS for five years. AIDS is no longer a death sentence. McNally, generally more tied to the governing metaphors of disease and death, more obsessed with mortality, sees his diseased characters as doomed:

ARTHUR: Every time I look at Buzz, even when he's driving me crazy, or now James, I have to think, I have to say to myself, "Sooner or later, that

man, that human being is not going to be standing there washing the dishes
or tying his shoelace.
PERRY: None of us is. Are. Is. Are? (p. 121)

Love! Valour! Compassion! presents a complex picture of living with
AIDS. Both the comical Buzz and the sweet Englishman, James Jeckyll, have
full blown AIDS, but what we see is the development of a romance between
them. We discover that James goes back to London and commits suicide: "I
wasn't brave. I took pills. I went back home to Battersea and took pills"
(p. 137). But James's recounting of his death is placed in the context of each
character sharing how he is going to die. Death is inevitable. McNally does
not denigrate the horror of AIDS, but he does want to underscore that we all
die, that AIDS is only one of many causes of the inevitable. Moreover, contrary to the more homophobic depictions of AIDS, gay men not only die; they
also live and live happily.

Arthur feels survivor guilt, Gregory plans AIDS benefits. Everyone is
aware of and copes with the reality of AIDS, of how many men have been
lost and how callously AIDS has been treated by so many straight people.
Yet there is no sense of surrender. James claims that his favorite phrase is
Hamlet's "We defy augury." Even James's suicide can be seen as a refusal
to submit passively to AIDS. James takes control of his own death.

In his previous works, *Lips Together, Teeth Apart* and *A Perfect Ganesh* Terrence McNally has dramatized more vividly than any other playwright
the outer display and inner workings of homophobia, which is, after all, what
gay men most have in common. As many writers have pointed out, lesbians
and gay men are the only minority who do not share their minority status with
their parents—who are, in fact, usually educated by their parents to believe
that what they are is wrong and that it must be changed or at least denied.
McNally has shown us a mother who is haunted by her refusal to accept her
son and a sister who cannot deal with her dead brother's homosexuality.

Much of previous gay drama has shown us gay men who hate their own
homosexuality, who react in various ways to their internalized homophobia.
Even Louis and Joe in *Angels in America* are to some extent dysfunctional homosexuals, if not the sort of basket case we find in Larry Kramer's *The Destiny
of Me.* (pp. 233-6) Gayness is not a problem for any of the men in *Love! Valour! Compassion!* Finding what they want and need is.

In Act II, Bobby talks to the audience about why he believes in God:
"Other people are as imperfect and frightened as we are. We love, but not
unconditionally. Only God is unconditional love and we don't even have to
love Him back" (p. 87). Yet there is a lot of unconditional love sought and
received in the play. The unlikable John may not totally receive love, but he's
still there on Labor Day weekend, still accepted as part of the family. James
may not believe in love enough to stay with Buzz. Ironically, it is Bobby who

leaves his lover because he couldn't deal with the increasingly obvious signs that Gregory is aging and waning in physical strength. McNally commented in an interview:

> I've learned as I get older, without unconditional love we never reach our potential. I've had it in my life personally in the past couple of years, and I'm like, "Wake up and smell the coffee. You are so lucky, celebrate this and go, man. The sky's the limit. Why are you holding yourself back?" And this play is just the beginning.[16]

McNally prides himself on "the enormous amount of affection and tenderness between men" the play offers.[17] It is this sense of love and community that separates *Love! Valour! Compassion!* from other gay plays. One can quibble about the cast being basically white, or about the lack of women, straight or gay, in this world. But this is the only one of McNally's last four plays that does not focus on the strongest, most fascinating female characters in contemporary drama. One has to place *Love! Valour! Compassion!* in the context of *Frankie and Johnnie in the Clair de Lune, Lips Together, Teeth Apart, A Perfect Ganesh,* and *Master Class.*

Throughout our history, gay men have developed strong positive bonds that often are in sharp contrast with the bitchy, bickering stereotype of much homophobic drama and film. Nor are we the isolated figures of film and television—the queen without a life or society. That is the myth straights use to keep young gay men in the closet. There is a world elsewhere. One of the greatest and most unique virtues of *Love! Valour! Compassion!* is its depiction and celebration of the links of love, loyalty, and patronage that are forged in gay society. These men do not talk politics; they try to do something. Yes, it is a white, middle-class New York microcosm, but no more parochial than the world Kushner presents.

These two plays, *Angels in America* and *Love! Valour! Compassion!* represent differing but complementary views of how a class of urban gay men saw themselves at the beginning of the 1990s, when AIDS was still thought to be a death sentence and the central fact of gay experience.

THE MAN THAT GOT AWAY

> But I didn't love him. I can't help that, can I?
> —JOHN IN *My Night With Reg*

Like *Love! Valour! Compassion!, My Night With Reg*[18] is a comedy-drama informed by AIDS. McNally's play takes place over three summer holiday weekends, Kevin Elyot's play takes place over the course of three parties in

Guy's London flat, each one a few years after the previous one. Yet the parties blend into one another in this ninety minute one-act play as if they were one party. The same characters come and go in the same clothes. This false sense of continuity makes the audience question all the more what has changed and what has stayed the same.

In the first scene, Guy is preparing a little flatwarming dinner. The group is a small one because most of Guy's friends have either died or split up, leaving the awkwardness of deciding which half of the former couple to invite. The party will include Reg, the partner of Guy's best friend from Cambridge days, Daniel; two acquaintances from the local gay pub, Bernie and Benny, a bickering couple; and John, with whom Guy has had a secret infatuation since his university days. Also present is Eric, an eighteen-year-old working-class kid who works at the pub and has been painting Guy's flat. Like the young men in *Love! Valour! Compassion!,* Eric reminds these forty-something men of their age and their continued desire.

Before the guests actually gather for the party, the scene smoothly segues into another gathering a few years later, after Reg's funeral. During the course of the two scenes, everyone reveals to Guy that they have had affairs or one night stands with Reg. Guy and Daniel's old university friend, John, has been sleeping with Reg for a year. Bernie, Bennie, and Eric all had one night stands with him. If it weren't for AIDS, this situation would be the beginning of a typical British sex farce. Indeed the double entendre contained in the title could be the title of the typical West End romp. But Reg has died of AIDS and one cannot avoid thinking about the epidemiological conse-quences of Reg's promiscuity—has he infected anyone or everyone? The hor-rible irony is that the third scene takes place after the funeral of Guy, the only character who has not slept with Reg. Indeed, Guy has barely slept with anyone, except for one unfortunate, unpleasant incident of unprotected sex with a mortician from Swindon (a ghastly image of the grim reaper that be-comes more hilarious if one knows Swindon). There is a lot of gallows humor barely under the surface of *My Night With Reg,* yet sex is never far from anyone's mind throughout the play. Even young Eric, who has been the voice of moral conscience, betrays his lover by going to bed with John after Guy's funeral.

In *Love! Valour! Compassion!,* AIDS is treated with unabashed senti-ment in moments like Buzz's kissing of James's Kaposi's sarcoma lesion, or as part of a more pervasive sense of mortality. In Elyot's play, AIDS is a mordant joke. However, AIDS is not the only bleak element in the play. Like much British drama, Elyot's play is one of misunderstandings and missed connections. Though many critics described *Love! Valour! Compassion!* as Chekhovian, Elyot's is truly a Chekhovian play of solipsism and futility. Guy tries repeatedly to tell John he has loved him since their university days, but John, wrapped up in his own infatuation, never hears him. Nor would John be the best partner as he has already run through the family fortune and is as feckless as they come. Daniel tells Guy that John is "adorable, but completely irresponsible."[19] John never realizes Guy loves him until Guy leaves him his flat, which he does not know what to do with. Actually Eric should have been left the flat in which he takes a proprietary interest. John supposedly loves Reg, but Reg is his best friend's partner. Bernie and Bennie have been a couple for years, but break up when Bernie can put up with no more of Bennie's philandering. The unseen Reg is, from all reports, magnificent in bed, each man's wildest sexual dream come true, but totally without scruples (Reg, by the way, is American).

The connections between these men are more amorphous than those in McNally's play. Guy, John, and Daniel are university chums, but John only surfaces every few years. Eric has developed a friendship with Guy. Benny and Bernie used to go to the bar where Eric works. These men are not tied together by common interests. Though AIDS has touched their lives, they do not work for AIDS charities. They are all too self-absorbed for that.

My Night With Reg is a witty, well-written play, but what is Elyot's point of view toward the piquant happenings he has created? Is this a satire, a social corrective, or simply a picture of London gay life as he has experienced it, a world where friendships aren't really friendships and relationships aren't particularly loving? Or is this the dark side of human behavior that fascinates British audiences, a vision of people who operate outside the Victorian dicta of manners and sexual propriety? However witty, it is a dark vision more because of the lovelessness than because of the shadow of AIDS.

The play contains typical elements of gay drama, much camp behavior and a dose of nudity as well as a complex set of diversions from realism. Irony abounds, but Elyot finds little to celebrate. Is celebration possible within this kind of post-Beckett drama of non-connection and meaningless action? *My Night With Reg* presents a slice of gay society in which friendship and loyalty count for little and in which a loving relationship seems impossible. The absence of a loving relationship seems characteristic of British gay drama. There is a celebration of eroticism, of coming to terms with one's gayness, but no possibility of a loving commitment.

ARRESTED DEVELOPMENT

However problematic, *Love! Valour! Compassion!* and *My Night With Reg* have artistic virtues that, in performance, make us forget their more questionable assumptions. McNally's work assumes that these privileged white men (and one eroticized Latino) are a true cross-section of American gay men, while Elyot's assumes a nihilism and cynicism about the possibility of human connection. In 1998, both McNally and Elyot wrote plays in which the weaknesses of their earlier work predominate.

Elyot's *The Day I Stood Still* is written in three scenes spanning three decades. Horace, the central character, is a librarian who lives in a state of chaotic stasis. His life began and ended in the few non-sexual minutes he spent with his adolescent love, straight Jerry, in the sixties. Though Jerry was also with his girlfriend, Judy, that day, Horace remembers it as the only day he was alive:

> There was one day, one day we had . . . which was sort of complete. One
> of those moments when you realize, "Ah, that's what it's like to be happy."
> I hoped there'd be more days like that, but there weren't.[20]

Since that time, Horace has had virtually no life. His one social contact seems to be Jerry's widow, Judy, though it is only memories of Jerry that connect them and the fact that Horace is the godfather of Jerry and Judy's son, baptized with the very sixties name of Jimi. Three decades after this one moment of life, seventeen-year-old Jimi, the spitting image of Jerry on that one fine day, appears in Horace's apartment, seeking solace for a lost first love: "He's the only thing that's meant anything. If that is it, then I don't see the point" (p. 63). Horace is hardly the person to offer any constructive advice. After much booze and coke the middle-aged man and his godson are nestled on the floor, Jimi tentatively stroking Horace's hair, Horace gently resting his head against Jimi's thigh.

The three scenes are presented out of linear chronological order. The first scene, literally *in medias res,* takes place when Jimi is four. His mother and her current beau, a Frenchman with an obsession for cooking, make a surprise visit to Horace's flat. Horace is expecting a hustler he has hired, Terrence, who is also too lost in sad memories of his own to fulfill his contracted task. Terrence, a former soldier in Northern Ireland, is haunted by memories of a mate who was shot. Like Horace and Jerry, Terrence and his beloved friend exchanged necklaces. Terrence's grim worldview is a working-class version of Horace's elegantly worded description of his unpublished novel: "Obsessive desire. Bleeding humanity. The tragic inexplicability of existence. The usual" (60):

> You're shat into the world, find there's a load of other poor cunts who didn't
> ask to be here, work your bollocks off trying to get on with them, then
> realize you're on your tod. Fucking joke, isn't it? (p. 42).

The second scene, thirteen years later, is Horace's encounter with Jimi. The final scene shows us Horace's magical day at age seventeen, in which he, Jerry and Judy hang out in Horace's apartment. To us the day looks like one of those dreary teenage days of aimless hanging out. Horace's unrequited love for Jerry makes it much more for him. When Jimi and the very stoned Judy leave, planning to meet Horace later at the amusement park, Horace is accosted on his balcony by Terrence, offering him a "wank" for a pound.

The Day I Stood Still gives us a sequence of events that repeat themselves. The same chair collapses in each scene. A floorboard keeps caving in. Terrence moves through various stages of prostitution and bitterness. Horace's love for Jerry is transferred to Jimi. The patterns do not offer meaning or solace, they are merely repeated pratfalls and missed connections. Class twice keeps Terrence and Horace apart as sexuality keeps Jerry and Horace separate. Why can't Horace move on, get a life? The play suggests that there is no meaningful life to get. Elyot offers up existential despair rather than meaningful connections of any kind.

Watching and reading *The Day I Stood Still,* I found myself getting angry and frustrated, not with the inert Horace, but with Elyot himself. Why does Horace's not-so-gay homosexuality seem to justify an uninteresting inertia? In what way is this grim solipsism supposed to be interesting? Why does Horace remain indifferent to the unhappiness of his less fortunate companion Terrence? Why is he hung up on a seventeen-year-old? Why should I care? Elyot is a clever writer, but he is becoming the gay Simon Gray, offering up literate boulevard tragicomedies of unrequited lust and chic despair.[21] Gray, like Elyot, presented characters fixated on teenage homosexual crushes. *The Day I Stood Still*, inhabits a hermetic world of post-Pinter British drama, echoing plays rather than life, disconnected from the real problems facing gay men.

Terrence McNally's *Corpus Christi* is another case of arrested development—not the characters', but the playwright's. Rather than seeming remote from lived gay experience, as Elyot's play did, it reflects the worst assumptions of contemporary urban, upper middle-class gay men.

Corpus Christi created headlines months before it opened at the Manhattan Theatre Club. As soon as the media reported that McNally's new play was dramatizing the life and death of a gay Jesus Christ, the theater's administration folded under extreme threats from religious groups of damage to the theater, its personnel, and audiences and canceled the production. When writers, theater artists, and well-meaning organizations staged protests in favor of free artistic expression, the theater decided to produce *Corpus Christi* after all. This sort of drama of religious conservatism squaring off against defenders of the first amendment has been played out in smaller cities south of New York: Marietta, Georgia over a production of McNally's *Lips Together, Teeth Apart;* Charlotte, North Carolina over *Angels in America*; Greensboro and Raleigh, North Carolina over productions of *La Cage aux Folles*, of all things. Usually the right wins. Either the production is canceled or funding for the arts is cut off by the local government. Security was the issue at the relatively well-heeled Manhattan Theater Club, not money. New York City is not likely to cut off funding to the arts, one of the city's major tourist attractions. *Corpus Christi* went on with tighter security than we expect at airports. I had to check in my Swiss Army Knife. Across the street, ardent Catholic protesters picketed and prayed. Surely Christians have better things to do—feed the poor and help the sick, perhaps?

The week *Corpus Christi* opened, young Matthew Shepard was brutally beaten and left to die, hanging against a deer fence in Wyoming. The symbolism wasn't lost on ministers who used the Shepard story to preach against hate of difference in general and gay people in particular. Shepard quickly became a gay martyr. Candlelight vigils were held across America. Shepard's face appeared on *Time* as well as *The Advocate*. It was a gruesome story of a brutal act perpetrated by two young losers in the name of homophobia. Only the crazy, mean Rev. Fred Phelps of Wichita, the Captain Ahab of homophobia, saw Shepard's death as anything but evil. Matt Shepard's story made one think about the symbolic power of martyrdom in galvanizing a community.

Martyrdom can also be sexy. One has only to look at Renaissance paintings of the martyrdom of Saint Sebastian, particularly the one in the Uffizi Gallery in Florence painted by the artist known as Sodoma, to see that depictions of torture can be erotically charged. A semi-nude, beautiful young man is being penetrated by arrows. He is standing, but passive. The picture is one of pleasure, not pain. *Corpus Christi*'s picture of Christ as a beautiful young man, crucified in his white jockey briefs (the image adorns the cover of the published text of the play), is similarly erotically charged.

I do not agree with the New York critics who found *Corpus Christi* boring. McNally has written a contemporary mystery play with resonances of medieval cycle plays like the York Crucifixion. However, the play is disturbing and somewhat infuriating. I have no doubt McNally is aiming for a personal statement here, but the play raises serious questions about the youth worship, narcissism, and single issue politics that are rife in the gay community. After a matinee of *Corpus Christi,* I overheard two elderly Jewish women in the ladies' room line complaining that the play did not speak to them. But who does *Corpus Christi* speak to beyond beautiful young gay men and their older admirers?

When you enter the theater, the actors, all good-looking young men, all white except one Asian American, all graduates of universities and conservatories, are milling about the bare stage, chatting, warming up, talking with members of the audience. At the beginning of the play, as they are blessed in a New Age sort of ceremony and given their characters, they move upstage to lockers and change into their attire for the play, white shirts and khaki pants. Why are all the disciples handsome young men? Might a disciple or two be homely or over thirty? Why do we watch these cute young men strip down to their underwear and change? For the specular pleasure of it? Jesus isn't played by the best actor of the lot, but by the most conventionally good-looking. As the middle-aged men in *Love! Valour! Compassion!* are obsessed with the good looks of the young Ramon and Bobby, so McNally shows his erotic inclinations. Youth is sexy; age isn't. Youth is idealistic and optimistic; age is anxious and cynical. McNally, my age, is unquestioningly accepting the youth worship of American culture, particularly gay culture, and placing it onto the Christ story. At least these guys don't all have those gym-buffed bodies like the underwear ads. Are the actors all gay? Maybe none of them is, but they have no problem playing gay men, which in this play means saying one is gay and kissing other men (a playwright friend once said to me that if you want good male-male kissing scenes, get straight actors. They work harder at it).

McNally's self-identification is all over the place in *Corpus Christi*. A middleaged man's teen memories are grafted onto the Christ story. The title of the play comes from McNally's Texas hometown as well as from the Eucharist. Though the play seems contemporary, Joshua's (Jesus is Joshua here) birth, youth, and adolescence all transpired in 1950s Texas. High school is the site of homophobic violence and initiation into homosexuality through Judas, Joshua's first love, with whom he painted "JandJ4VR" on the water tower. What do we know about Judas? He doesn't like people and is proud of his "big dick." While I won't call this blasphemy, as the Christians pick-eting, chanting, and praying across the street from the theater do, I have to admit it cheapens a crucial myth of Western society.

This version of Christ's life and passion takes place in an all-male world in which our actors also play the few women in the story (Mary, Joshua's teachers, and his prom date). McNally's religious community is a male enclave. McNally never comments on this. The Son of God moves away from conventional female influences into a sexual male fraternity. Women teach him "feminine" things: poetry, dancing, musical theater, "sissy" things that are also stereotypical signs of gayness. A nun in parochial school teaches Joshua to sing "I'm in Love with a Wonderful Guy." Joshua is being taught signs of homosexuality that were part of McNally's (and my) generation. All male relations are either homosexual or homophobic.

Christ's passion is reduced to homophobia. He may be the son of God, but he's crucified because he's gay. When Pilate offers the crowd Barabbas instead of Christ, the crowd's reaction is simple homophobia:

> PILATE: Will you therefore that I release to you the queer or the thief, Barabbas?
> ALL: Not the queer, the thief. Barabbas! Barabbas! Barabbas!
> JUDAS: "And Barabbas was released to them."
> BARABBAS (*kneeling before Pilate*): God bless you, sir! I'll remember you for this. (*He Kisses the hem of Pilate's robe, then stands*) Then he got very drunk and went to a neighborhood they called Boy's Town and fucked his brains out—what was left of them.[22]

Even Barabbas is gay. *Corpus Christi* is filled with the wishful thinking that filled gay gossip a generation ago. We were comforted by the supposition that every guy, particularly homophobes and good-looking movie stars, was a closeted gay. We were just courageous enough to admit our sexuality, thus superior to them, or inept at hiding it. The play perpetuates the myth that homophobes are always stupid. The same high school bullies who terrorized Joshua in the school bathroom reappear to strip and scourge him at his passion. There are homophobic brutes like this—or like the boys who killed Matt Shepard—but there are also smart homophobes who can do far more harm, the Dick Armys, Colin Powells, Bill Buckleys, and Gary Bauers.

The problem with *Corpus Christi* is that it doesn't explore its own assumptions. It is a middle-aged man's idealization of youth, but only in the terms of his generation. I kept feeling that those handsome, talented young men on stage might have more interesting stories to tell about sexuality in the late 1990s and might find the sexual politics of the script they were enacting a bit naive. McNally is projecting onto the life of Christ his adolescent fears of forty years ago. A few nights before I saw *Corpus Christi,* I sat in a Manhattan restaurant with my best friend from high school who, after a martini or two, recounted the horrors of his 1950s high school experience as a somewhat effeminate young man bullied and threatened with sexual assault in a locker room. He has never gotten over those terrifying moments. At first I thought this was odd, but later considered how much my high school past still informs my life and work. My friend and I have vivid memories of those years, but we never remember things the same way. *Rashomon.* In his fifties, McNally has gone back to his adolescence, but without much ironic distance. Then there is the problem of identification. McNally seems to see himself as Joshua/Jesus.

Medieval biblical plays made the Christ story contemporary with the time and place of performance, combining the timeless with the contemporary. I am a Christian by birth, but not by theology. But even I, a secular humanist, was bothered by the notion that Christ was crucified primarily because he was gay and that the most revolutionary thing he did was perform a gay marriage ceremony. This is an extreme example of the selfighteousness and self-congratulation that is leading gay critics to turn their sights on gay culture. There are no social, economic, or political issues here beyond gayness. The disciples party and screw. They're there because they love Joshua. The fact that Joshua is the Son of God seems more an irritant than a reason for martyrdom. At the end this cute guy in his briefs is hanging on a cross. If one buys the erotics of the piece, and the charm and talent of the cast, one is won over for a time. Then you start thinking. Gayness does not make us inferior, but it sure as hell does not make us divine (not literally, anyway).

British writer Mark Simpson mocks the sense of superiority and religious mission of many contemporary gay men:

> Coming out is thus a moment of revelation and redemption: I was blind,
> but now I see; I was lost, but now I'm found. Just like the homos in the

Stonewall bar that night in Year Zero, from the nasty straight-acting grub emerges a fabulous gay butterfly with wings of lycra.[23]

For *Corpus Christi,* the moral superiority and sexiness of that butterfly are reinforced by an erotically charged martyrdom. Like the creator of the York Crucifixion play, McNally knows that Christ's martyrdom combines sex and violence. To top it all off, now we're the Sons of God. The poor, unhappy brutal heterosexuals, humping away in Texas motel rooms or stuck in unhappy marriages should want to kill us. We've got it all. *And we* can work miracles.

McNally, once one of our best satirists, seems to have read too many copies of *Out* Magazine. His next play should be about a middle-aged man who thinks the story of Jesus is a portrait of the artist as a young man, a cute gay guy from Texas.[24]

The Day I Stood Still and *Corpus Christi* are each in their own ways too hermetic. The former is trapped in the windowless, fictional world of British drama, living on its ironies and sense of futility. Like Beckett's tramps, its characters sigh, "Nothing to be done." It's an easy stance for audiences who step over homeless beggars on their way from Waterloo or Charing Cross stations to the Royal National Theatre to see the play. Nothing to be done, so we have no responsibility for other people, much less our own inertia. The latter allows us a smug self-righteousness without the social conscience that lives at the heart of Christ's teachings. Sell all you have and give to the poor wouldn't do much for the coffers of the Manhattan Theatre Club and wouldn't play too well to those of us who paid fifty bucks to see the play. It would also devastate our consumer economy. Embracing all people regardless of difference works both ways. Christians would have to embrace us, but we affluent gay men would have to embrace the poor, the old, and, (gag!), the homely. Even if Tony Kushner lets his audience off very easily at the end of *Angels in America*—playwrights, like actors, have a hunger to be liked by their audience—he at least gives us pieces of social critique and questions the assumptions of left and right wing ideologies. The problem is that only Kushner's Republican villains know how to tie ideology to action.

To some extent, McNally, whose plays have been produced in New York since 1963, and Elyot, whose first hit, *Coming Clean* premiered fifteen years ago, represent an older generation of gay playwrights. Rich from his libretti for the musicals *Kiss of the Spider Woman* and *Ragtime* and his New York hit play about Maria Callas, *Master Class* (which bombed in London), McNally has become mainstream. Elyot's *My Night with Reg* was a commercial and artistic success. *The Day I Stood Still* was produced by the prestigious Royal National Theatre where it remained in repertory for six months. Meanwhile, a younger generation of playwrights, working in smaller venues, are rethinking what it means to be gay as the century ends. The final chapter will be devoted to their work.

CHAPTER NINE

LOVE AND WAR: GAY DRAMA
AT THE TURN OF THE CENTURY

> In a state of war, as in a state of love, the familiar world is turned upside
> down, belief systems and values are put to the test, and the body becomes
> central, vulnerable. Whereas war is intent on destroying the body, love has
> the ability to reconstruct or rediscover the body's sensuality.
> —*Naomi Wallace*[1]

What do I want from contemporary gay theater? I have a menu, not one item.
I would like it to examine the assumptions of urban gay culture at this point
in time. I would like gay drama to show our awareness of our privileges as
much as our dwindling oppression. I would like to see an acknowledgment of
the spectrum of same-sex desire from two to six on the Kinsey scale, and not
reinforcement of the gay-straight binary. Not all men who occasionally have
sex with men are closeted gay men. Gayness is a class and cultural identification—a club not all men want to join, even if they desire other men. I would
like to see how homosexual desire and homophobia fit into other patterns in
American and/or British society, and how our notions of sexuality clash with
those of other cultures. I am interested in the ways in which our work and
social lives intersect with those of non-gay people. This may seem to contra-
dict my praise of *Love! Valour! Compassion!,* which does little of this sort of
work. I would rather say that McNally's play shows us where we are, but I
would like to see plays that point the way to where we should be going at
the turn of the century.

In some ways, film is now doing the job better; not commercial stuff
like *In and Out* or *The Object of My Affection* but independent film. Ang
Lee's *The Wedding Banquet* (1993) placed a middle-class, mixed race New

York gay couple against the notions of male roles and family in traditional Taiwanese society. It also questioned the exclusive homosexuality of its central character. Wong Kar-wai's *Happy Together* (1997), dramatized the cultural alienation of a Chinese gay couple in Argentina. Eric Mueller's *World and Time Enough* (1996), shows a gay couple dealing with the death of fathers, the encroachment of dehumanizing megamall culture, and what art might mean at the end of the twentieth century. The Cuban *Strawberries and Chocolate* (Tomás Gutierrez Alea, 1995), offers a Cuban intellectual's fraught relationship with a straight young man as a platform for issues of loyalty and cultural pride in contemporary Cuba. Richard Spence's *Different for Girls* (1996), shows us a romance between a straight man and a transsexual that plays on differences of class identification as it questions fixed notions of gender and sexuality. Recently, mainstream films have been offering probing views of gay experience. Alan Ball's screenplay for *American Beauty* makes repressed homosexuality the most destructive force in the film's sad suburban world in which the only happy couple is gay. Anthony Mingella's very personal adaptation of Patricia Highsmith's *The Talented Mr. Ripley* turns the novel about an amoral sociopath into a film about thwarted gay love and the closet in the late 1950s, in which the only productive, totally sympathetic character is a loving gay man. Even a fluffy comedy like Tony Vitale's *Kiss Me Guido* (1997), offers a satire on the relationship between ethnic and gay stereotypes and suggests, through "straight" Frankie, that sexuality may not be so easily defined. The most interesting irony of this film is that it is gay Warren who needs to categorize by sexuality, ethnicity, and class. I want to see plays that do this work of joining our identity with a larger cultural critique.

The focus of this chapter is on contemporary plays by a new generation of writers (most of these plays were written by artists in their twenties) that raise crucial questions about the links between sexuality and related issues—gender identity, particularly the politics of masculinity; ethnicity; and class. I divide the plays into two categories: love, which focusses on plays that explore the development and/or failure of male-male relationships; and war, which uses love or sex between men as a means of exploring larger issues of masculinity and violence.

The most interesting recent works about male-male relationships all have the specter of HIV hovering over the action, but they move from stories of death and memorial to stories that explore the possibility of life with AIDS. In the last five years, AIDS has moved from being a terminal illness to a chronic condition (for those who can afford treatment) which makes plays written only a few years ago seem like remote history. However, what makes these intimate, poetic plays—Andrew Alty's *Something About Us*, Samuel Adamson's *Clocks and Whistles*, Chay Yew's *A Language of Their Own*, and Joe Calarco's *Shakespeare's R & J*—so exciting is their exciting experimentation with the verbal and visual language of contemporary drama.

"A SERVICE OF REMEMBRANCE. A REALLY RUDE ONE."

Of all the British gay AIDS plays, Andrew Alty's *Something About Us* offers the most affirming vision of gay eroticism. The skepticism toward emotional connections beyond the erotic that one finds in much British gay drama is evident here, but Alty's play is radical in redefining the bonds of sex and friendship between men of different classes. AIDS may no longer be the death sentence it was when Alty wrote his play, but Alty points the way to a new affirmation of sex and the body lost in much of the AIDS discourse.

The central character of *Something About Us* is Michael, a thirty-ish gay bureaucrat. Detractors might call Michael anal. He is fastidious, organized, cautious. He is also singularly devoted to his best friend and alter ego, Peter, who now has AIDS. Peter is the opposite of Michael. A locomotive engineer traveling the same route everyday between London and the south coast, Peter has looked for excitement in his sex life: "I just wanted something exciting to happen! I wanted to have an *adventure*. That's all. Everything else was so—ordinary."[2] Now Peter has AIDS and Michael has become his primary caregiver. In the first act, subtitled "The Departure Lounge," Peter and Michael are ostensibly waiting at the airport for a plane to take them to a vacation in Malaga. Peter is making up games to pass the time while Michael tries to read Camus's *The Plague*. Through a medical miracle, Peter's AIDS related infections, including his KS lesions, seem to have disappeared and he seems to be able to look to a future he didn't think he would have. As their plane is delayed, Michael and Peter begin fighting over their significant differences and how those affected their response to Peter's illness. Michael resents Peter's irresponsibility—that he kept playing when he knew he was sick.

Peter resents Michael's caution and organization. Michael finally admits that his anger at Peter is really anger at himself:

> I'm angry because I'd walk out through those sliding glass doors. I'd feel the car-keys in my hand, feel the fresh air blowing in my face. And I'd look up at the sky and I'd say to myself, "Thank God it's him. Thank God it's not me" (p. 23).

It soon becomes clear that Peter is not miraculously cured. He loses control of his bladder. Michael has to help him change clothes. When their flight is finally called, Peter decides to go on alone to Malaga. Before he leaves, Peter tells Michael, who is absorbed in his book:

> Michael? Michael, can you hear me? (*Michael doesn't reply, doesn't look up.*) Michael, you know—you didn't let me down. I know you think that. I know you think you did. But you didn't. I wish I'd told you that. I wish I'd had the time. (p. 33)

By this time one realizes that what is really happening is quite different from what appears to be happening. Peter is moving in and out of a dream as he nears his final moments. His departure from the airport is his death. And Michael has loyally been sitting by his side, caring for him. What has come out in this real or imagined discussion is the depth of devotion and difference between these two dear friends—"best sisters"—who are joined by each having what the other lacks. At the end, Peter asks Michael to describe Camus's *The Plague* to him:

> Well. The people are quarantined. Many of them die. The rest endure almost intolerable hardship and loss. But they never lose their humanity . . . they never stop caring for each other I suppose (*Pause*) So far anyway. (p. 33)

As Michael reads, Peter leaves for his journey.

The beauty of this first act is that the "real" action is never spelled out. The audience becomes aware of it only toward the end, but the scene is always as Peter is dreaming it, weaving in and out of consciousness, occasionally making contact with Michael, loyally sitting by his side.

The second act, "Madagascar," is named after a game Peter invented while he was in the hospital: "You open the Atlas. Close your eyes. Stick your finger somewhere on the map. And. Wherever your finger lands. You have got to *promise* you'll go there" (p. 59). Michael's finger landed on Madagascar. In this powerful scene, Michael and an ex-lover of Peter's have a unique, Dionysian memorial service that transforms both of them.

Months after Peter's death, Michael has finally ventured beyond his routine of work and solitary nights at home and has picked up Dean, a good-looking, working-class man in a bar. Dean has even more of a one-track mind than Peter—sex is his only topic of conversation. As lonely and horny as Michael is, he can't perform. While Dean waits for the next night bus, he asks to see photographs of Michael's departed friend whom he recognizes:

> MICHAEL: Oh, God. Dean . . . Not *that* Dean . . .
> DEAN: Yeah.
> MICHAEL: You went out with him.
> DEAN: Yeah. (*Clears his throat*) A couple of years ago. (*silence. Dean is upset*)
> MICHAEL (*Looks at him*) Ohh Christ. . . . This is typical, isn't it? I go out on my own for the first time in months. A boy I fancy gutless virtually throws himself at me. And Peter's been there first. (p. 45)

Dean's response to the shock is an emotional and sexual challenge:

> DEAN: Come on, Michael. Let's do it. Let's have a wake. Fuck it. Let's have a funeral.

MICHAEL: I've already had one.
DEAN: Let's have another. I mean just you and me. A service of remembrance. A really rude one. (p. 46)

For the next two days, Michael and Dean have their service of remembrance, which is also Michael's liberation from Peter and, to an extent, from his own repression. The next morning, after two rounds of sex interspersed with conversation, while Dean is sleeping, Michael looks at a picture of himself in his photo album:

Who's that? (*Looks closer*) Who the hell is that?
I'm sure I've seen him before.
Wait a minute . . .
I remember him now.
Wasn't he the quiet one? The one that didn't say much.
The one who wouldn't have a drink because he was driving?
The one with the naff shorts—remember?
He stood outside the backroom all night trying to work up the courage to walk in.
And wasn't it him that wouldn't take his shirt off in the night club?
who got embarrassed if you caught him cruising?
the one who organized everything?
what's his name?
The sensible one.
The serious one.
The boring one.
Peter's friend . . .
Michael. (p. 52)

The next afternoon, Michael and Dean compare what Peter said about them to each other. Peter dumped Dean

"Because it's all about you, isn't it? Your fucking pleasure.
DEAN: That's all there is. What else is there? (p. 57)

For Dean as it was for Peter, sex is an antidote to the ugliness of life for poor, working class men: "Out there, pal, it's not clean. It's not tidy. Oh no. It's filthy. Fucking filthy" (p. 57). Yet Peter and Michael are right—Dean avoids any feeling above the neck. It's all escape for him. He, even more than Peter, is the opposite of Michael.

Dean lashes back by telling Michael how Peter used to mock his cautiousness and adds his own reading of what Michael really fears: "You might let go. You might forget who you are and what day it is, and—this is the really creepy part, isn't it—you might not care!" (p. 58).

By bringing Dean home, Michael has, in essence, stuck his finger on the map and must now visit his Madagascar, which Dean says is "Very hot. Sticky. Sweaty. Primitive" (p. 65). The journey will also be Peter's requiem. Communion is the sharing of LSD, Michael's first experience with drugs; the candlelight mass is the shaving of drugged Michael's backside. The epiphany is Michael's realization of Peter's death as sacrificial: "He did it for me. . . . He took *risks*. I just *watched* (p. 64). The "Libera Me" is Michael's first experience being fucked.

The two day ritual journey to "Madagascar" has made Michael understand and absorb the best of Peter, his love of a life that is senseless and unpredictable. Dean has discovered the mixed blessing of human connection:

> DEAN: It's hard, innit?
> MICHAEL: What?
> DEAN: . . . Giving a shit.—So much easier not to. (p. 68)

When the reality of Monday morning arrives, Dean and Michael vow to become "sisters."

In typical British style, *Something About Us* celebrates eroticism, physicality, but does not present the possibility of a loving partnership. Alty is giving his own spin on the British gay fantasy first codified by E. M. Forster in his classic novel, *Maurice*—the liberation of the repressed middle-class man by the ultra-physical working-class bloke. Here there is no problematization of gayness, only an education in point-of-view toward human experience. Alty's play manages to be polemic and liberating at the same time. The action, while seemingly realistic, is metaphorical. The characters are both realistically conceived and, at the same time, types—opposites that joined make a complete person. Alty believes that the joining must take place within the individual, not through a coupling. Above all, *Something about Us* is a celebration of the joys of the flesh that have become compromised by the poison of AIDS and AIDS discourse. The image of Peter is of a man who celebrated life, "threw himself at it," as Michael says, even with AIDS. Yet what Peter and Dean lack is the potential for the selfless devotion Michael can express, and which will be more valuable now that Michael is off the sidelines and in the game of gay life. In the original London production, Faure's gentle, elegant Requiem was the musical underscoring for this sacrament, a reminder that there is something ethereal and beautiful about the sacrament taking place.

Alty's play celebrates the Dionysian more than a play like McNally's *Love! Valour! Compassion!*. These nude bodies are doing more than swimming and being looked at. But his play is another eloquent response to the question of what it means to be gay in the age of AIDS. There are no victims here, only heroes. Anger at oppressive, homophobic society is at best marginal to the real issue of personal liberation and human connection that comes from within, not from social change. Individuality and a sense of spirituality infuse both plays. And there is always the reminder of the beauty of the body and the sacrament of sex. Above all, there is less interest in making peace with the straight people in the audience than in finding joy for gay people. The double meaning in Alty's title is a fitting definition for the best of contemporary gay drama: the plays celebrate "something about *us*," suggesting a bond with a gay audience, "something about *us*" that is different from *them* and special.

ROMANTIC QUARTETS

> Yeah, well, it's crap, i'n't? Words, words, words, words.
> —CLOCKS AND WHISTLES

My thesis from the beginning was that gay drama offered a chronicle of the impossibility, then possibility of male-male love, set against the social forces that made that love thorny, if not impossible. Now, at the turn of the twenty-first century, there seem to be fewer external obstacles to love, particularly for middle-class men in Europe, Canada, and the United States. This means that our difficulties are often the same as those for anyone in contemporary society. Our stories could, to some degree, be anyone's stories. Sexual orientation is only part of the picture. The best recent plays about male-male love are both intimate works that explore variations on the theme of communication within different types of love relationships.

Samuel Adamson's *Clocks and Whistles* (1996) begins as another wry British play about missed connections but, through the interweavings of its five characters, it offers an intriguing picture of class and ambiguous desire. The action centers on the development of a relationship between two unlikely partners: quiet, reflective Henry, an editor by profession and writer and observer by vocation, and Trevor, a country boy who has emigrated to London where he works in a factory. Trevor is an aspiring poet; Henry devotes a lot of time to his diary. The richness of Adamson's play is seen in the way it eludes or evades simple identity politics. Its central character, Henry, says at one point, "God, how I hate gay anthems," the only time the G word is used in the play. While some characters try unsuccessfully to define the sexual orientation of others, the words "gay," "bisexual," and "straight" seem either too rigid or too irrelevant to describe these characters, who also elude each others' definitions and emerge as complex and indefinable.

Like Kevin Elyot's protagonists, Adamson's Henry seems passive and indecisive about his emotional life. As best we can tell, his sex is rare and anonymous. He may fill his diary with descriptions of his feelings, but he doesn't verbalize them in conversation. Trevor, something of a Laurentian

working-class stereotype, is sexually voracious. His neighbor Caroline, an outspoken artist who is clearly smitten with Trevor, tells Henry: "We all see him
go out . . . he returns late at night with a stranger in tow, sometimes a woman,
sometimes a man. He thinks he's Joe Orton."³ It is just as likely that Trevor
doesn't know who Joe Orton is. Trevor is brutally honest about everything but
his feelings for Henry and yet, promiscuous Trevor is proud of the duration of
his friendship with Henry. Caroline tells Henry, "Apart from me, but I don't
count, you're the only person I've ever known who's put up with him for more
than six months" (p. 107). Henry can deal with Trevor's promiscuity with men
and women—he himself has occasional anonymous sex on Clapham Common
and has at least once called an escort service for an unsuccessful liaison with a
female prostitute. What Henry cannot stand is Trevor's relationship with his
best friend, Anne: "I was so jealous. He was mine. You were mine" (p. 102).

Trevor aptly compares Anne to Sally Bowles, a fictional diva attracted
to gay or bisexual men, who is played in the film version of *Cabaret* by a
favorite diva of gay men, Liza Minnelli. Anne is a wealthy aspiring actress
whose parents died when she was young. Her primary relationship since adolescence has been with a crass, Americanized entrepreneur, Alec, who supports her. Trevor is fascinated with Anne. Henry adores Anne, but has never
had sex with her, though the impulse has struck him: "The urge came over
me, but, but I didn't want to seduce her . . . I wanted to do it there in the
street" (p. 43). When Henry is evasive about Trevor, Anne rifles through
Henry's notes, finds Trevor's address, and arrives at Trevor's Paddington flat
with a picnic lunch to see what this new lover is like. Driving to Trevor's,
Anne runs over a sidewalk sculpture Caroline has created. This disaster is an
example of Anne's careless destructiveness. What does Anne want from Trevor? Does she see merely a working-class fling? ("He's a strange boy. Low.
A curious mixture. Very, very cute buns" [p. 50].)? Or is her intrusion in
Henry's love life a way to connect with Henry? Trevor would like the three
of them to become friends, perhaps a menage. Henry cannot see anything
positive in Anne's encroachment. As Trevor, Anne, and Henry walk to Hyde
Park with Anne's picnic lunch, Henry repeats to himself the word "snared."
His anger and jealousy make him bad company, but he cannot understand his
continuing attraction to Trevor. He tells Alec:

> He's a lout, you know. He writes bad, bad poetry and he comes all the way
> to Clapham just to show it off and I'm too kind to tell him the truth. It's
> pretentious and shallow. And he has sex with more people than I know. He
> doesn't care who they are, he just goes out and picks them up from these
> seedy places he goes to. He spends half his time in front of the mirror, and
> he listens to rotten music and well, Jesus, Alec, he's just a bloody drip.
> ALEC: But you like him a lot, don't you.
> HENRY: Yes. (p. 93)

Henry, the moralist, wants Trevor and Anne, each in their separate compartments, to be his. Anne, whose career, during the year the play takes place, moves from unemployed actress to Honey in a fringe production of *Who's Afraid of Virginia Woolf,* to a West End production, to a film contract in France, severs her relationships with Alec and Trevor and, finally, Henry, who has never realized how much she loved him. Alec is right when he tells Henry, "You think you're on the watch, but you never see" (p. 93).

In the penultimate scene, Trevor breaks down and cries in Henry's arms: "I'm a risk. I couldn't give blood. I'm a risk" (p. 108). This realization makes Trevor realize it's time to settle down—with Henry. In a moment typical of Adamson's subtlety, a potentially sad moment is turned into a positive one. When Henry tells Caroline that Trevor is moving in with him, she answers, "It won't last," not realizing that the specter of HIV has indeed made the relationship impermanent:

> *Beat. They all look at each other. Tension. Trevor bursts out laughing.*
> *Henry laughs too.*
> TREVOR: Nothing does, Caroline. Whatever lasts? (p. 111)

Characters in *Clocks and Whistles* are proud of their honesty. They seldom lie, but they often sin by omission. Anne is mistress of changing the subject when asked about the personal details of her life. Henry is only candid about his feelings with Alec, the character he despises. Trevor can talk about his sex life, but not his feelings. Yet Adamson can see in this network of deception the possibility of a relationship between Henry and Trevor.

Adamson is a careful observer of social types. Characters are defined in part by their neighborhoods. Henry shares a flat in Clapham, an artists' neighborhood of South London, with a man he barely knows. Trevor lives in seedy Paddington, a neighborhood of small flats and cheap tourist hotels. Anne lives in fashionable Chelsea, Alec in affluent Holland Park. Anne and Trevor would never meet were it not for their common bond with Henry. Trevor and Henry only meet through the classless society of gay pubs. Characters are also defined by their dialect. Though Anne is not university educated, she has the language of an aristocrat. She gives Henry one of those upper class nicknames, "Frappy," shops at the right King's Road stores, and speaks disdainfully of Trevor's class. Alec, who lived in the United States from the late seventies to the late eighties, tries to sound American, "Anything to keep others from the God-awful truth" that he's English and probably lower middle class. Trevor is articulate, but not refined. Adamson doesn't spell this out—he doesn't need to. An outsider himself—he's Australian—he is an excellent observer of contemporary London manners.

American audiences might be somewhat frustrated at Adamson's economy, at the extent to which characters don't articulate their feelings, but few

contemporary plays are as rich in presenting nuances of characters and relationships. Few plays present such a complex love story with such subtlety.

Chay Yew's *A Language of Their Own* (1995), an elegant chamber
piece for four actors, is the American counterpart to *Clocks and Whistles,* a
rich portrait of love in the nineties. Like *Clocks and Whistles* it is precise in
its presentation of character, locale, and idiom, while eschewing theatrical
realism. Like chamber music it works through counterpoint, repetition, and
development of motifs. The theme is the language of love; not romantic love
as much as the way lovers fail to communicate. Robert, the only non-Asian
character, offers the history of this language:

> In the beginning of our relationship, we learned each other's language
> Like overeager babies
> Mouthing unintelligible gaggles and sounds
> Unable to articulate
> Clumsily tripping on words
> Falling into abject frustration
> But once we found the common language
> Each action and deed, every word and sentence was a joy, and an
> excitement
> A tingling of senses
> A radiant discovery.[4]

The dwindling of a relationship can also be traced through its language:

> Then we tired of it [the common language]
> Lost interest
> Got lazy
> Became indifferent
> Words gradually lost their meaning and significance
> . . . .
> In the end, we spoke different languages. (p. 217)

Elegantly and economically, with a bare stage and four characters, Yew
presents the history of three couples. The first line of the play, repeated often
throughout the action, is "I can never forget what he said to me," a harbinger
of the power of language throughout the piece. Oscar, upon learning that he
is HIV-positive, tells his lover of four years, Ming, "I don't think we should
see each other anymore," that they will change from lovers to friends, "A
change of labels" (p. 123), none of which is accurate. The first act, entitled
"Learning Chinese," is a history of the relationship of Oscar and Ming from
meeting to "marriage" to breakup to their last conversation months after Ming
has moved out and both have found new lovers. Throughout, both are pain-

fully self-conscious about the language they use. To some extent, this self-consciousness is based on ethnic confusion. In his introduction to the anthology, *Aiiieeeee!,* Frank Chin writes:

> Language is the medium of culture and the people's sensibility, including the style of manhood. Language coheres the people into a community by organizing and codifying the symbols of the people's common experience. Stunt the tongue and you have lopped off the culture and sensibility. On the simplest level, a man in any culture speaks for himself. Without a language of his own, he is no longer a man. The concept of the dual personality deprives the Chinese-American and Japanese-American of the means to develop their own terms.[5]

As the Chinese American must deal with two conflicting cultures expressed in very different languages, so too must the gay man find a language for emotions forbidden by the culture in which he is raised. Oscar, perfectly bilingual, suffers from the reticence that is part of his culture. Ming, more confused about his culture, bearing a Chinese name he gave himself, but more Americanized than Oscar, suffers more emotional and cultural confusion. He calls himself "a banana," "Yellow on the outside. White on the inside." Like English, love is a new language. When Oscar and Ming meet for the first and last time after their breakup, Oscar notes, "All of a sudden, we've become two awkward strangers in a cold room. Wrestling with a new, unspeakable language that belongs only to old lovers" (p. 160). Yet at that crucial moment, the characters cannot say what they feel:

> OSCAR [to himself]: I'm still in love with you. Tell him. . . . Tell him or he'll go away. Again.
> MING [to himself]: He's being silent again. It's so annoying.
> OSCAR [to himself]: For once, express yourself. Tell him about your feelings. (p. 170)

When Oscar finally is able to say "Come back," Ming knows a return is impossible:

> It's like learning Chinese. Once I started speaking English, I stopped learning how to speak and write Chinese. I dropped one culture for another. And you can't go back. (p. 174)

Ming moves to Los Angeles with his new white lover Robert, a waiter, while Oscar establishes a more cautious relationship with Daniel, "a radical queer Asian who lives and breathes Sondheim" (p. 169). The second act, "Broken English," traces these relationships. As is often the case with new relationships, particularly those formed so soon after the breakup of a couple, Oscar and Ming maintain at least a psychic attachment that is not erased by their new loves.

Ming's new relationship with Robert is characterized by a lack of language:

> MING: I see us.
> ROBERT: Not saying a word. (p. 181)

That silence is read by Robert as peace, comfort; by Ming as unarticulated dissatisfaction:

> ROBERT: I see you.
> MING: Silent.
> ROBERT: Not saying a word.
> MING: Frowning. (p. 182).

The most ominous phrase in their silent relationship is: "We should—talk." With Robert, Ming is frustrated at his inability to respond articulately to Robert's expectations. While Robert dreams of a conventional lifelong marriage, of growing old together, Ming is restless and wants sexual variety. Ming finds sexual release at the baths while Robert, more emotionally needy and frustrated by Ming's infidelities, finds another Asian lover. Finding no language to express his confusion and frustration, Ming lashes out physically at Robert.

We have fewer direct conversations between Oscar and Daniel. They speak to us, the audience, more than to each other. Daniel loves Oscar, but knows "it's très difficult to live with someone who's HIV positive. Très, très très high maintenance" (p. 184). Oscar moves from fear of commitment (though the lovers live across the street from one another), to panic attacks at IKEA, to repeating *ad nauseam* the phrase, "I love you": "It's delightful. Nice. It's driving me insane" (p. 204). Ultimately, when Oscar can no longer deal with his illness, Daniel has to find sleeping pills for Oscar to kill himself.

Throughout the play, when the characters are feeling intensely, they become inarticulate:

> DANIEL: "I want to say—say—I don't know what I want to say—there are so many things—and I can't—so many things but—" (p. 219)

or

> MING: The things I want to say—
> ROBERT: Come out—
> MING: Yes. Like this. The words—thoughts—it's—(p. 206)

The most loving conversation Ming has is the one Oscar imagines as the sleeping pills take hold, yet Ming didn't bother going to the funeral:

> MING: I remember telling him regardless of what happened, I would be there for him. I promised him. I did. And I would have, you know. Really. Now all I've said—it's just words. Empty words. (p. 224)

And the only candid conversation Oscar has with Daniel is the one Daniel imagines after Oscar's death. At the end Ming and Robert stutter toward a reconciliation.

The beauty of *A Language of Their Own* is its universality presented within a specific social context—middle-class, Asian American gay men. There is an extent to which ethnicity and culture are important in understanding Ming and Oscar, but the history of the attempts at, failures at, finding a language to connect one to and separate oneself from a loved one resonates beyond the specifics. Yew's theatrical style—actors and words on a bare stage—emphasizes the language and removes those elements that particularize (except the race and gender of the actors).

ADDICTION

Like *Clocks and Whistles,* Steve Murray's *Rescue and Recovery* examines love and sexual morality in a time of relative amorality. Like *A Language of Their Own,* the play alternates narration and flashback enacted on an almost bare stage. *Rescue and Recovery* centers on the changing relationship of Cameron Trace and his wife, Janie, from the moment she discovers his sexual interest in men until the final emotional separation, which comes years after their legal separation. The central question asked through the gay and straight relationships in this dark satire is: What is marriage, straight or gay, at the end of the twentieth century?

At the opening of *Rescue and Recovery,* Cameron appears naked in front of the audience, "making the metaphor manifest."[6] In finally acting, at age thirty-something, on his desire for men, Cameron realizes that the body can be at war with the brain, in which he has tried to live: "Part of me is shy. This part [*pointing to head*] not this part [*pointing to crotch*] but this part [*the head*] usually wins."

The mind-body split is accompanied by another dangerous duality: "propriety and passion, those are two things that split you apart." Cameron is a recovering addict (to alcohol, cocaine, and Demerol), and, once unleashed, sexual passion becomes another addiction. While Janie, a lawyer, goes though a relatively graceful adjustment to losing her husband, trying to remain his "best friend" ("I was flawless"), Cameron, an intelligent physician, is blind to the hurt he causes her. Their greatest pride seems to be their ultra-civilized post-marital relationship.

JANIE: Honey, two people with our history—people would kill for a relationship like ours. No screaming arguments, no broken glass, the tiniest bit of child support, and you get Brian [their son] every Sunday.

For two years after their separation, Cameron and Janie still go out together to parties and cultural events. Cameron has thrown himself into his work, and Janie is still devoted to her ex-husband. The crisis comes in their modified relationship when they both meet Timothy, Jay, and Mark. Timothy and Jay, a thirty-something gay couple, are the somewhat mysterious engineers of Cameron's future. Timothy is an ultra-camp ex-actor with AIDS-related infections who works for the historical preservation society. Jay, seemingly meek, works for Exxon, and defends Exxon's endangering of the environment:

> Yeah yeah, the environmental stuff. It's bad. It happens. But to get what you want, some things have to go. Anyway, I'm corporate. It's a business like any other. It's all just business in the end. Strategy, patience and coming out on top. Like chess. You know what you want and you get it.

Timothy and Jay's professions reflect their ethics: Ailing Timothy wants to preserve traditional values like love and loyalty. Jay is all self-interest. He also is possessed of a large penis, which has a brutally uncomplicated relationship with his brain.

Timothy arranges for Janie to deal with his will and insurance, which will give Jay a healthy chunk of money, and he makes Cameron his physician. At Thanksgiving dinner, he asks Cameron to consider taking up with Jay when Timothy dies: "I want you to rescue him, Cameron." What Timothy fails to tell Cameron is that Jay is already in a sexual relationship with stunningly handsome young Mark, a bank teller:

> I invited Mark to dinner and told Jay, "Make your move." And prayed he would not make his move. I should have hated him for accepting my . . . offering. But instead, his weakness became adorable to me, because he didn't know it was weakness. Kid in a candy store. Gorging. And somehow I managed to transform his heartlessness into an amusing trait, like snoring or a cowlick. A thing you forgive and even love. That's marriage.

Timothy believes above all in an ideal of marriage, "This dream I have of rightness, where the people who should be together would be together."

At the Thanksgiving dinner, there is a long discussion of addiction, which becomes the play's central metaphor. When Timothy asks Cameron if he misses the drinking and drugs, Cameron responds:

> It never goes away. Wanting it. The thing about drugs, alcohol—any addiction. It's like—I know it's a false sensation, but they give you a sense of

beginning, middle, end. It's like an art form. Any kind of drug. It creates a sense of drama where there is no drama, a feeling that you're part of something. Very seductive. . . . It makes you feel like you're not alone.

Jay talks about drunkenly climbing a tree to try to save a drunken friend who had climbed to the top of the tree and could not get down: "You do things like that, fucked up. Try to rescue somebody when you yourself, you're in no condition." The ensuing action asks whether anyone is in a condition to rescue a loved one.

Mark is also at Timothy and Jay's Thanksgiving. Shortly afterward, in one of the most erotically charged scenes in gay drama, he appears in Cameron's office for a physical examination. Mark uses the physical as a means of seduction. When Cameron asks Mark to take off his clothes to complete the examinations, Mark asks Cameron to help him. While slowly undressing Mark, Cameron gives a lengthy description of the anatomical changes that take place during an orgasm. But he knows that the stimulus for these physical events is not scientific:

> CAMERON: It's perception. It's poetry, a thing that happens between two people, an invisible tug that translates into—
> MARK: Fuck me.
> CAMERON: Or words to that effect.

Cameron is a romantic in a world of pragmatists. The difference between Mark's response and his own signals trouble. Mark is a mess of contradictions, demanding total devotion, but feckless and unfaithful; decrying the fact that everyone sees him as a sex object, but sexually voracious; a proclaimed serial monogamist, but always unfaithful. When challenged, Mark reminds lovers that he is an orphan, as if that fact excuses all insensitivity. Mark can live with his contradictions because he is totally unreflective. As Janie aptly observes: "He never meant anything. That was his special charm."

Cameron, the recovering addict, becomes addicted to Mark, excited by his beauty and tantalized by his contradictions. He knows they have nothing in common except the sex, but Mark has become the center of Cameron's life. When Mark inevitably leaves Cameron to return to Jay, after Timothy, Jay's partner, has committed suicide rather than face further illness (or was it out of disillusionment with Jay?), he places all the blame on Cameron in a series of wan cliches, like "I love you with all my heart, Cameron, but a relationship is built on trust and openness,"—under the circumstances a textbook case of projection. Cameron goes into a kind of withdrawal, sick with anger and self-pity. When he finds out that Jay is not only having sex with Mark, but has had sex with Janie the night of Timothy's funeral, Cameron goes to Jay's house for a confrontation. Instead he gets fucked on Jay's kitchen floor: "I mean he was doing it to me every other way, why not make the metaphor manifest." To complete the metaphoric fucking, Jay gives the recovering alcoholic a double scotch, which sends him on a binge of drink and drugs. When Janie finds him lying on his coffee table, having missed days of work, Cameron exposes the insensitivity to his ex-wife and best friend that finally separates them:

> CAMERON: Oh, Janie, they tricked me.
> JANIE: Male duplicity? I could've taught you a few lessons.
> CAMERON: You don't know what it feels like.
> JANIE [with an edge]: Oh, yeah, how could I?

Janie decides that she cannot again help with his recovery:

> You have to decide, do you climb up that tree after them? . . . I didn't climb the tree. It was the first time I didn't. . . . And that is when your heart breaks. When you know, finally, know that this is not your story.

Cameron, the man of science who got trapped inside his heart, slowly recovers again from his addictions, including the one to Mark, but addictions remain in the system: "He's in my system. That most addictive drug. Love. That uncontrollable substance." Janie finds herself a wealthy real estate developer. Cameron moves in with Kyle, the nurse (now medical student) with whom he had the affair that broke up his marriage. But Cameron and Janie are still friends, though they cannot stand to be in the same room anymore, linked now not only by their son, but also by the hurt caused by love:

> CAMERON [about Mark]: God help me, but I was in love with him. And I was not enough.
> JANIE [about Cameron]: I was not enough. We are married now, more than ever, in our wanting.
> CAMERON: I can never forgive him—
> JANIE: I can never forgive him—
> CAMERON: For making me love him
> JANIE: Like he said.

Friendship is not enough, but love can take one over even if the object of love is totally unworthy. One never quite gets over the love of one's life, but one must move on. As Cameron says about recovery from his addictions, "Experience leads to loss."

Rescue and Recovery, set in contemporary Atlanta, is not specifically about gay or straight culture, but the culture all affluent, middle-class Americans share, dreaming of ideal, lasting attachments, but being unable to sustain them. Total pragmatists like Jay manage to survive intact, but playwright Steve Murray sides with the flawed romantics. One does learn from experience but never loses the urge to become addicted to an unworthy object.

Clocks and Whistles, A Language of Their Own, and *Rescue and Recovery* all focus on the possibility of negotiating relationships in a culture that has no moral code to support them. Terms like love, fidelity, and loyalty have no stable referents, but still stand as ideals for the central characters. Within the specific middle-class milieu the playwrights depict—London for young artists in their twenties, Boston for Asian American gay men, and Atlanta for affluent professionals, these plays offer critiques of contemporary mores that go beyond parochial gay issues. These plays disprove the old homophobic canard that universality and heterosexuality are synonymous and that gay issues are superficial and tangential. They prove that our drama is not just about being gay.

TRANSFORMATION AND LIBERATION

Joe Calarco's *Shakespeare's R & J* (1997), a counterpart to the Bard's tragedy of forbidden love in a violent society, is a paradigm of the self-examination, transformation, and celebration that defines gay drama.

Four young men, students at an austere Catholic boys' school, enter a room. They are wearing the uniform of their school—white shirt and tie, dark trousers, gray v-neck sweater with the school's insignia. Briefly we get a picture of their day as they march like automatons, reciting litanies of thou shalt nots, particularly "Thou shalt not lust" in the same emotionless bark with which they recite mathematical formulae. A bell sounds, signaling the end of the school day, and the boys gather in a room away from the eyes and ears of authorities. To the boys, this room is like the enchanted forest of *A Midsummer Night's Dream,*[7] a place of enchantment and erotic possibility. One young man takes a copy of Shakespeare's *Romeo and Juliet* out of a trunk. What follows, in Joe Calarco's *Shakespeare's R & J,* is a simultaneous presentation of two dramas, both using Shakespeare's words (a fair amount of *Romeo and Juliet* some sonnets, some sections of *A Midsummer Night's Dream*). One drama is a presentation of a condensed version of *Romeo and Juliet* with the four actors playing all the parts, but another drama unfolds as the boys act this play as a means of expressing their pent-up emotions, sexual urges, and chaotic drives. In acting out *Romeo and Juliet,* the boys can briefly drop their well-drilled inhibitions and touch each other, physically and emotionally.

On one level, we in the audience forget that Juliet, her mother, and her nurse are played by male actors. The actors are so good that, like Shakespeare's audience, we are willing to accept the conventions the production establishes. There are no costumes, so no drag. Acting does everything, and

Daniel J. Shore is simply the best Juliet I have ever seen, the most impassioned, mercurial, touching. When the boys first play Lady Capulet and the Nurse, there is a brief moment of confusion: How should the boys play women? At first, the boys talk in falsetto, but the boy playing Juliet begins his (her) first lines simply and honestly in his own voice. The other boys look surprised, then follow suit. The mimicry of women ends and the boys concentrate, as good actors do, on playing the emotions and intentions of characters regardless of gender. Juliet, after all, is the creation of a man to be played by a young man.

Homosocial and homoerotic energy are everywhere, as they are in many contemporary productions of Shakespeare's play. Mercutio suffers from the unrequited love he feels for Romeo. One of the most heartbreaking moments comes after the ball when Mercutio realizes that Romeo, whom he and Benvolio cannot find, must be with a woman. The look of heartbreak on his face reflects that moment every gay adolescent feels at some time when the object of his unrequited love finds a girlfriend. The horseplay between Romeo and his friends always has a sexual undertone. In their horseplay, Romeo and Mercutio unconsciously mimic sexual positions. Mercutio's death, which comes right before Romeo consummates his marriage to Juliet and thus loses his virginity, is the death of the possibility of homosexual love for Romeo. Is the actor playing Mercutio "acting gay" or acting love for another person regardless of gender?

On one level we believe this *Romeo and Juliet* sans scenery and costumes, sans women, sans many of the characters (Paris, Romeo's parents), because the acting is so committed. There is an honest merging with Shakespeare's words few contemporary productions of Shakespeare manage to find. Yet there is also another touching play being performed, that of high school boys experimenting with emotions they have been taught to repress. When the boys playing Romeo and Juliet kiss in the ball scene, the other two boys gasp in astonishment and horror. Shakespeare's play is not now about forbidden love between members of warring families in fourteenth century Verona, but about forbidden desire between two boys in the late twentieth century. Despite the gasps of their friends, the boys kiss again and again. Like Romeo and Juliet, these boys discover that they like the feeling of kissing each other. The kissing in this tiny theater reminds us again of the power of the male-male kiss I discuss in Chapter One. Who is kissing here—two schoolboys or Romeo and Juliet or two male actors? All three, of course. This *R & J* is, first and foremost, a testament of the power of theater to question, complicate, and liberate.

Shakespeare's play and the boys' experiences collide most forcefully in the wedding scene in Friar Laurence's cell. The boys playing Romeo and Juliet, kneeling facing each other, start to read their lines out of the script, but the other boys, suddenly fearful of the implications of this wedding of two young men, take the script away and start throwing it back and forth. One boy rips out the page with the text of the wedding scene. The boys playing

Romeo and Juliet have been robbed of their lines. After an awkward silence they start reciting one of Shakespeare's love sonnets as the other boys become more and more agitated. Finally the boy who plays Friar Laurence, in the only moment of real violence we see in the production, hits Romeo across the head with the script. This sends Romeo briefly to the floor, unconscious. Realizing the extremity and cruelty of his action, the boy playing Friar Laurence starts reciting another sonnet, "Let us not to the marriage of true minds admit impediment." The boys join hands and unite. Somehow the chanting of this sonnet, a contrast to their earlier chanting of prayers and dogma, ends the resistance to the signs of love and commits the boys more strongly to their performance. They no longer need the script. They strip off their sweaters and ties and fully commit to the rest of the play. There is no longer a separation of repressed schoolboy actor from character.

The voices of patriarchal authority—the Duke banishing Romeo, Lord Capulet—are played by the boys uniting and chanting like a many-headed, many-voiced monster—like the voices of authority they are briefly evading.

At the end of the performance of *Romeo and Juliet,* the church bells signal morning. The boys, except the boy who played Romeo, put their sweaters and ties back on and turn back into automatons. Romeo tries to bring them back into life, but cannot. For a night they were able, by speaking Shakespeare's words, to evade the restrictions imposed on them. They march off leaving Romeo alone in their charmed space, repeating Romeo's lines from act I, "I dreamt. I dreamt." Or is it Nick Bottom's line from *A Midsummer Night's Dream?* Or both?

The performance of *Romeo and Juliet* is framed by quotations from *A Midsummer Night's Dream.* The room in the school has been transformed into an enchanted space away from laws and "Thou Shalt Nots." At the end, the boys are briefly reconciled by Puck's epilogue, but the night and the dream are over. Entering the world of Shakespeare's love story is like entering the woods in one of Shakespeare's classic comedies. The restrictions of society do not rule and true love can be expressed. When the characters leave the green world and return to society, relationships have changed and true love is celebrated in marriage. Here there is no such liberation. The proscriptions the boys have been taught are too well ingrained.

Briefly two boys evaded the language that has been drilled into them and find through another language, the "approved" canonical voice of Shakespeare, a means of expression of adolescent love. Joe Calarco, who created this extraordinary performance says, "Personally I think all the boys are straight, but by acting out the play, they learn acceptance of all kinds of love." I have a feeling that Calarco concocted this statement out of fear that *R & J* might be perceived as a gay play, an assumption that may limit the audience. If not, Calarco has missed the point of the work he has created. *Shakespeare's R & J* expresses the idea that love has nothing to do with socially imposed notions of gender except that we are taught we may love some people and must not love others. Rigid notions of gay and straight are beside the point. Why must the boys be straight or gay? The play queers the labels: male/ female, masculine/feminine, gay/straight. We could end the matter by saying the boys are bisexual, but, in addition to being a silly word, that's a label that tries ineffectively to cover up the fact that the binary formulation of gay/ straight simply does not work.

The actors are not acting gay or straight. They're acting emotions, including love and sexual desire. While watching the love scenes of *Romeo and Juliet,* we simultaneously believe Shakespeare's play and believe the discovery of sexual feelings between two of the boys. The warring Capulets and Montagues do not end their feud until four kids are killed, but briefly four boys have overcome the homophobia that has shut them off from new possibilities of love. There is enormous exhilaration in the boys' encounter with Shakespeare and their exploration of new emotions. There is also danger. The play is, as great theater always is, subversive, particularly for those in the audience exposed to hitherto proscribed feelings and experiences.

In his program notes for *Shakespeare's R & J,* Joe Calarco writes: "This is a play about men. It is about how men interact with other men. Thus it deals with how men view women, sex, sexuality, and violence."[8] The same could be said for the less romantic, more violent plays of Naomi Wallace, Neal Bell, and Oliver Mayer.

WAR

Why is it that gay playwrights have recently been turning to plays set in times of war? The most obvious connection is the government's anti-gay policy, known as "Don't ask, don't tell," a last ditch attempt to enforce the closet in a society where, for many, the closet has been intolerable. "Don't ask, don't tell" would be ridiculous if it were not so destructive, sanctioning witch hunts, vicious hazing of personnel thought to be gay and, on occasion, brutal murder. Clearly the ironies and lunacy of "don't ask, don't tell" lie behind the action of D. M. W. Greer's *Burning Blue,* Naomi Wallace's *In the Heart of America,* and Neal Bell's *Somewhere in the Pacific.* The plays I shall discuss also see war and other violent territories, like the boxing ring, as crucial areas in which to critique American codes of masculinity. It is in the best of these plays about masculinity and violence that we also see the most daring theatrical experiments, extensions of the ground-breaking work Tony Kushner did in *Angels in America.*

The most commercially successful and most problematic of the war plays is D. M. W. Greer's *Burning Blue,* which opened at the King's Head, a fringe theater in London and eventually moved to the West End. Greer's play is far more prosaic than *In the Heart of America* and *Somewhere in the Pacific.* It's an odd combination of the gung ho silliness of *Top Gun* with 1950s realism, more made-for-television movie than post-Kushner drama. Greer, a naval officer's son and a former naval officer himself, is interested in how career officers, devoted to the military, deal with homosexuality.

The central characters in *Burning Blue* are four U.S. Navy pilots who are devoted to the military and, in a *Top Gun* buddy way, are devoted to each other. The play focusses on the outcome of a ludicrous, Draconian investigation of the alleged homosexuality of one of the men. Daniel, an admiral's son who is devoted to his military career, was seen dancing with one of his buddies, Matt, in a gay bar. This dancing episode is the only physical expression of their sexual attraction to each other. Though Matt is married to a passionately homophobic southern belle (presumably to keep him from straying), we know he is "sensitive" and potentially gay because he is a composer who keeps an electronic keyboard with him on the carrier (reminding us of the time "musical" was a code word for gay). Though Matt and Daniel are in love, they never have sex. Their most erotic moment is a brief admission of love and a rather chaste kiss, after which Matt crashes his plane and dies. A grief stricken Daniel is forced to leave the Navy.

Daniel and Matt's two straight buddies, Will and Boner, offer straight perspectives on Daniel and Matt's innocent "romance" and on the issue of gays in the military. Boner, the eternally horny farmboy does not mind in the least. He has tried every kind of sex with various humans and mammals and has decided he prefers women. Will, however, who thought Daniel was his best friend, explodes in a fit of jealousy. He has lost his best buddy—to another man—and has been thrown into an emotional tailspin.

Throughout, Greer is interested in the relationship of friendship to love; in the language of queer theorist Eve Sedgwick, the relationship of homosociality to homosexuality. Daniel has been irresponsibly protective of his best friend, Will, whose eyesight is beginning to fail. It is actually because of Will's failing eyesight that Matt is killed. It is not homosexuality that is a threat to military effectiveness, but homosocial loyalty.

The most powerful scene in the play is the final confrontation between Daniel, who has resigned from the military, and his former best friend, Will, who has refused to speak to him. Finally, Will explodes, not in the expected homophobic tirade, but out of betrayal and jealousy:

> When you told me you were in love with Matt I didn't know where I fit into your life. Why wasn't our friendship enough? I thought—I thought I was the man you loved the most. You can screw women . . . you can screw men . . . I don't give a damn who you fuck . . . it doesn't matter! *(He starts to crumble.)* But where do I fit in now? What happens to me?[9]

The final curtain suggests a reconciliation between Will and Dan, but during this tirade I wonder what Will's wife, who stands in the background, thinks. Are military wives inured to their position as secondary to their husband's best buddies? Throughout, Greer seems to fall into the sexism of his aging adolescent male characters. Matt's wife is a bitch and Will's the strong, silent, loyal type. Are there no other possibilities? Moreover, Greer doesn't seem the least bit critical of the ways in which the military supports the arrested development of his male characters. These are men in their thirties! Have Will and Matt never dealt with their homosexual feelings before this?

Greer does not seem to have any gay politics beyond a hatred for the military's anti-gay stance. But what does being gay mean to him? When the military investigator asks straight Boner why he went to a gay bar, Boner answers, "the music's better and the people are more fun."[10] Yet the gay people in *Burning Blue* aren't more fun. Straight Boner's nude, mocking flirtation with the investigator offers the only moment of humor and theatrical fun in the play, but even that moment would have made more sense and had more theatrical impact if a nude gay man had come on to the investigator. Greer's point seems to be that gay people and straight people are all equally dull. Moreover, the play is not clear about what type of response it wishes to evoke. Daniel doesn't get furious or defiant when he is expelled from the military. He remains the good boy scout.

Burning Blue tries, in an assimilationist move, to demonstrate an injustice to homosexuals and to win a over a straight audience by erasing all gay difference. What gets lost in the process is gayness. Is it only the desire to kiss other men that makes gay men different? Does unjust treatment have no effect on gay men? Did Daniel feel no kinship to the non-military men in the gay bar he went to—to the queens and drag queens, the leathermen and the clones? *Burning Blue*'s viewpoint is conservative. Heterosexuals should be tolerant of gay men, but gay people shouldn't threaten straight people with any signs of difference.

What would that difference be? Of course there is no universal, essentializing answer to that. Gay people are as diverse as heterosexuals, perhaps more so, and, like heterosexuals, gay people are not always tolerant of difference, even among our own ranks. What I find appealing about my gay friends might be considered by others to be outmoded stereotypes. One of my gay students was horrified by what he saw as a parade of negative stereotypes in the film of Paul Rudnick's *Jeffrey*. I didn't see the camp interior decorator, Sterling, as a negative stereotype. I saw him as a comically exaggerated version of people I know and love—even of myself. No depiction of gayness can please everybody, least of all gay men, who can be as frightened of any divergence from conventional masculinity as their straight neighbors. But gay drama has to begin with what we see in ourselves and each other without diluting that vision to accommodate the heterosexuals in the audience. If they happen to find a connection, a commonality, a way into the play, fine. Universality in drama comes from a specificity that other groups and cultures can read themselves into, not from accommodation and compromise. I said in the preface that gayness in drama is expressed through variations and elaborations on these five elements: *display,* of the male body and of queer theatricality; *polemic,* some assertion of where we will not compromise with the mainstream: *self-examination* of ourselves as individuals and members of what is called the gay community; *transformation* through theatricality and irony of the representational and narrative forms that maintain our oppression; and *celebration* of our courage, resistance, and difference. There is a fair amount of nudity and polemic, but little that is gay in *Burning Blue.*

A number of post-*Angels in America* plays, clearly influenced by Kushner's poetic style, defying linear notions of space and time, go farther in connecting homosexuality with larger issues. They critique gender politics and conventional notions of masculinity, examine race and class as crucial markers, and explore American domestic and foreign policy as a mirror of white, masculine, heterosexual attitudes. They also try to work within a more daring, transformative style that avoids the clichés and narrative traps of realism.

In the Heart of America (1994), by Naomi Wallace, is set in both specific and metaphorical territory. Literally, the play is set in Kentucky, Atlanta, Georgia, and Iraq during the Gulf War, but the title denotes another sort of quasi-anatomical location, a "heart" of America, not the heartland, but the emotional/spiritual center. What does America have to do with a heart? This is the crux of Wallace's concern, a state's domination of the bodies and, therefore, the "hearts" of its citizens. As she puts it:

> Theater can be a space for what Alan Sinfield calls "cultural dissidence": a place to disrupt the cultural amnesia that denies historical resonance and obscures interlocking oppressions, the foregrounding of which might help build a common core of resistance. The domination and destruction of the body are central to oppression. How do the body's sensuality and sexuality survive in the face of a system (be it the military or late capitalism) intent on destroying them? How do we continue to love and resist in the face of oppression?[11]

Like *Angels in America, In the Heart of America* is a fantasia. Tony Kushner is an obvious influence and has directed a production of Wallace's play at the Long Wharf Theatre in New Haven. This fantasia, set primarily during the Gulf War, is about various American identities and identifications: class, ethnicity, gender, sexuality, and how the American military mentality, an extension of American masculinist mystique, exploits difference. All of this is set within the traditional genre of murder mystery. During the Gulf War, a young soldier disappears, and his sister sets out to find what happened to him. It is also a love story, set within a culture that sanctions rape and genocide but doesn't know what to do with love, particularly same-sex love.

The play begins in a Kentucky motel room where Fairouz, the sister of the missing soldier, Remzi, has located someone she thinks can give her the answers she seeks. Fairouz is an Arab American woman who identifies with her Palestinian roots more than with her Atlanta home. She lives with and cares for her mother, who refuses to speak English, the language of the people who provide weapons to destroy the homes and lives of her people. Fairouz is crippled from a childhood attack of white schoolchildren who literally took a hammer to one of her feet. She has a deeply conflicted relationship with her brother Remzi, who as a child watched his sister be attacked without intervening. At the beginning of the play, Fairouz is speaking with Craver Perry, who is standing on his head, a deft if obvious visual metaphor for his mental state; guilty, grief-stricken, and confused. Craver was Remzi's lover. As Remzi watched Fairouz's be foot maimed by white schoolchildren, Craver watched Remzi be beaten to death by fellow soldiers. Craver is a dirt-poor Kentuckian, self-proclaimed white trash who joined the army because it was a way out of poverty. Remzi believed in the American dream of assimilation. He was not Arab American or Palestinian American. Joining the army was claiming his place in what the rabbi in *Angels in America* calls "the melting pot in which nothing is melted." He saw no contradiction in fighting Arabs.

When Fairouz asks Craver how he avoided getting spiritually lost during the war, he answers:

> Because I fell in love. In our bunkers at night, Remzi used to read the names [of missiles] out loud and it calmed us down. He must have read the weapons manual a hundred times. All those ways to kill the human body. Lullabies. It was like . . . they were always the same and always there and when we said them to ourselves, there was nothing else like it: Fishbeds, Floggers, and Fulcrums. Stingers, Frogs, Silkworms, Vulcans, Beehives, and Bouncing Bettys. (p. 449)

Remzi and Craver make erotic foreplay out of the names of killing machines. Later, they are sent out to pick up and bury body parts of Iraqis blown apart by these impersonal weapons. Love is possible in a state of war, but the language of love becomes perverted by the presence of violent death. When Remzi finally asks Craver, "Why are we here killing Arabs?" Craver answers:

> For love? Say it's for love. Don't say for oil. Don't say for freedom. Don't say for world power. I'm sick of that. I'm fucking sick of that. It's true isn't it? We're here for love. Say it just once. For me. (p. 458)

For Craver, love can transcend the grotesque circumstances. Remzi, however, is slowly becoming aware of his real nationality. He visits his parents' village in Palestine where he feels out of place, but realizes: "They live in poverty, and they're the enemies of the world" (p. 446). Craver and Remzi are caught having sex and are brought in for interrogation. When Remzi hears the officers

call an Iraqi prisoner the traditional racist epithets for the Arab enemy—
"Sandnigger, Indian. Gook"—he jumps up and attacks the officers and keeps
fighting until he is killed. In a war fought by missiles with no man-to-man
combat, Remzi has heroically lost a courageous battle against the racism that
justifies violence.

Even the love that has redeemed these soldiers is mired in language of
difference:

> Remzi said to me the first time he kissed me, "What are you now, Craver
> Perry? A White Trash River Boy Who Kisses Arabs and Likes It?" I said,
> "I'm a White-Trash-River-Boy-Arab-Kissing-Faggot." (p. 451)

Remzi and Craver cannot transcend the language they were educated to use,
but they find ways to invert it—like Craver's headstands—and turn it into a
language of love.

Two other characters move in and out of the action. One of them is
Boxler, the man once known as Lieutenant William Calley, the perpetrator of
the My Lai massacre during the Vietnam War. Boxler is a remnant of an
earlier type of war in which men, not missiles, did much of the killing, and
not always according to the rules of engagement. For many Calley was a hero.
Songs were written about him. He survived the bad press and a brief prison
sentence, but haunts the play as the man totally conditioned by the military
mentality: "I was born a human being, you know. But one can't stay that way
forever. One has to mature" (p. 463). Boxler is haunted by Lue Ming, a Viet-
namese woman whose baby Calley/Boxler shot. Lue Ming has come back to
find Calley/Boxler, but first mistakenly lands in the same Kentucky motel
room where Fairouz is interrogating Craver Perry. Calley's murder of Lue
Ming's baby was not a justifiable act of war; it was murder of an innocent by
a man trained to kill. The military lists Remzi's death as "friendly fire," the
accidental killing of a soldier by his own comrades.

At the end, Fairouz and Craver vow to tell the true story of Remzi's
death: "Talking about it might keep me alive." The story is of men conditioned
by a culture that allows them to feel anything but love. Craver says of his
fellow soldiers who arrested him and Remzi: "They were lower ranks. Just
kids. Like me. Kids who never got the summer jobs, who didn't own CD
players. They knocked us around" (p. 466). There's always something separating people: class, ethnicity, sexuality, gender. Even Fairouz, obsessed with
finding out what happened to Remzi, is really seeking a projection of herself
and a wish to be freed from being a woman in a male-dominated world: "I
don't want him to come back to me as him, but as a boy wearing my face"
(p. 467). Remzi says to Craver: "Love can make you feel so changed you
think the world has changed" (p. 466). Wallace reminds us the world still
needs changing.

In the Heart of America is funny, touching, and tough. It manages to offer an uncompromising vision of American culture and to be theatrically powerful at the same time. I don't agree with everything Wallace posits in the play, but I'm delighted to be drawn into the argument. Wallace is also developing an exciting new non-linear theatrical language that offers new possibilities for contemporary theater. It is one of a group of plays that set gay desire within the context of war.

BONK. KER-SPLUNK

Sounds keep echoing through Neal Bell's *Somewhere in the Pacific* (1999), which is, like *In the Heart of America,* part fantasy, but solidly grounded in history and current gay politics. The "bonk" of a baby being bounced on its head, the "ker-splunk" of flying fish hitting the water, the "splish" of stones being thrown into the skull of a dead Japanese soldier, the "splash" of potatoes hitting a pot of water imitating the sound of rocks against a skull, the "poosh poosh" of corpses colliding in the water. These are the sounds of violence to heads that obsess these marines and sailors. Desecrating a head is somehow destroying that which makes them human, individual. "Bonk" is the sound of sex as well as the sound of a bouncing head. How does one remain alive and human in war? What does love mean for men facing death?

The title, *Somewhere in the Pacific* (1997), sounds like one of those descriptive captions that appeared on the screen at the beginning of a classic war movie. It suggests and denies geographical specificity. It reflects the point of view of the marines and sailors on this old transport vessel sailing to an indefinite, but terrifying locale. If the men see anything ahead, it is their death.

> DUANE: I can see the beach where I guess we all die.

> CHOTKOWSKI: There is nothing out there. Not one gooddamn thing.[12]

The time is more precise. It is July 1945, and these men think they are an invasion force headed for Japan. Unbeknownst to them, two atom bombs will end the war they are fighting. What unites the men on this ship is the anguished familiarity with death their war experience has already given them. Obsessed with visions of death and grief from past loss, these men are all in an indefinite "somewhere" in place and time. Though the interactions of the marines and sailors on the nameless ship demonstrate a variety of forms of male-male love—the love of father for son, husband for wife, comrade for comrade—what separates the men is their response to the possibility of male-male desire, the wild card of homosexuality.

The men on the ship are also haunted by events from their past that combine love, loss, and betrayal. Captain Albers is in the throes of grief over the suicide of his son and is barely in control of himself or his ship. Albers is obsessed with a letter his son left behind, recounting how one member of his platoon would piss into the mouth of dead Japanese soldiers:

> McGuinness thinks it's funny, whenever he finds a dead Jap, to stand over the wretched creature and piss in its mouth. I was horrified at first, and then ashamed. And now I'm not. I'm not anything. Now I just watch. Now it just seems like war. I'm afraid of *myself.* (p. 15)

Throughout the play acts of desecration of the dead that parody male-male genital contact and penetration are contrasted with acts of love. Japanese soldiers cut off the penises of the men they kill and stuff them into the victim's mouth. Albers's son throws pieces of coral into the bullet hole in a dead Japanese soldier's head. Chotowski lobs rocks into the water-filled skull of a dead Japanese soldier.

The captain is horrified that his own son's body could be so desecrated. He believes he hears his son's voice over the ship's loud speakers, reading his suicide note. His obsession with his son makes him delay in ordering the usual evasive maneuvers needed to elude Japanese submarines. In Captain Queeg-like fashion he sets up an investigation to find who supposedly read his son's letter over the loud speaker system (actually, he imagined the voice, but dreams and hallucinations are presented in Bell's play as being as real as rational experiences). In the process, Albers finds McGuinness, the marine who was in his son's company and who pissed in the dead Japanese soldier's mouth. After a brutal interrogation, McGuinness spitefully tells Albers that his son killed himself out of grief at the death of his beloved friend: "Rusty cried a long time. We all knew what that meant" (p. 57). Albers cannot accept that his son might be a "faggot."

McGuinness has his own memory—of running in terror and deserting his friend Duane. He tried to return, but got lost. Only in a dream can McGuinness confess his feelings to Duane: "I loved you, you son of a bitch. Like my own brother" (p. 27), but in his dream Duane has been bayoneted and castrated by the Japanese.

McGuinness is the one marine on the ship who is bothered by the "clouds of fairies" he sees around him. Actually, the only "fairy" we see is the only sailor amongst the marines, Billy, a nineteen-year-old who joined the Navy when his beloved Johnny was killed:

> The only person I ever loved was Johnny.
> He was killed.
> So I enlisted.
> I wanted to kill somebody. (p. 76)

Billy is devoted to avenging Johnny's death and finding the feelings he lost when Johnny died. Early in the play, Billy explains how the flying fish the men see manage to suspend themselves in the air:

> They start to hump way down, is what I heard. And they buck and thrash
> all the way to the top, and their wings are pumping, faster and faster, and
> when they come—they come so hard—they go up. In the air. (p. 8)

Sex is the one way to raise oneself above the ugliness of war.

Billy finds himself in a ferocious embrace with Hobie, a young marine obsessed with the certainty of his imminent death and the thought that his wife has left him because she knew he was going to die. When Billy and Hobie make love on the deck of the ship, they take off, like flying fish. Such physical passion is the only escape from death. When they fall back to the deck, Hobie, guilty and confused, tries to distance himself from the man he just had sex with: "I am going to die. Next week. Maybe sooner. My wife knows that. Why don't you? (p. 33)" In the stage directions, Bell uses words like "ferocious" and "desperate urgency" to describe the fierce sexual acts of Billy and Hobie. They are directed toward each other and against the violence and death of war. Can there be love in such a fierce union of bodies? Hobie finds himself falling in love with Billy, but he does not have words for his feelings. When the two are together, Hobie speaks of his wife—heterosexual discourse expressing homosexual desire.

McGuinness tries to entrap Billy, but the captain, who is dealing with the knowledge of his own son's homosexuality, will not participate: "You remind me of the man who complains of a fly in his soup, and the waiter replies, " 'Would you keep it down or *everyone* will want one.' " Billy has his own plans for McGuinness:

> I was always afraid I would meet a man like you.
> I used to have a dream . . .
> In the dream I kill the man. (p. 40)

However, when Billy raises a stanchion over McGuinness's head, the marine slips on a banana peel and falls, saving his life but provoking the laughter of the rest of the men. Billy is saved a murder conviction and McGuinness, the homophobe, gets the humiliation he deserves.

Sex, loving sex, even among men who barely know each other, is the positive opposite to the killing and desecration of corpses. Bell ties these images together when Chotowski lobs potatoes into a bucket of water, mimicking his throwing stones into the skull, while telling Hobie: "I think you two [Hobie and Billy] should fuck each other's brains out. While you still got em—dicks, brains, arms, legs, faces . . . Then me" (p. 51). This is a violent image of sex as a means of reveling in the body in the face of imminent death.

When a torpedo hits the ship, Billy saves McGuinness from drowning and heroically tries to keep Hobie alive. With land in sight, one by one, Chotkowski, Duane,
and Albers, let go of the life raft and allow the sea to offer them escape from the war and from their own minds. When Hobie dies, Billy passionately kisses him, "in a fury." He deserves a silver star for trying to save the men, but since Lieutenant DeLucca has reported his sexual activity, Billy is arrested instead. DeLucca sees Billy's homosexuality as chaos and:

> There has to be order.
> Somewhere.
> Why were we fighting? (p. 82)

The reality is not only war, but the military's insistence on forbidding, or at least denying, the reality of love and sex between men. Billy will be stripped, humiliated, interrogated and thrown out of the military. For loving men, Billy is told he is not a man.

Bell has not written a simple-minded diatribe against the military's ridiculous anti-gay policy, one that is enacted and supported by a cowardly chief-of-state whose famous sexual acts are illegal in twenty states. *Somewhere in the Pacific* is a rich poetic play about men in a situation that intensifies all of their emotions. The "somewhere" suggests a place both specific and unknown. The ship is a purgatory. The play jumps backward and forward in time because the only important time for these men is either past or still to come. As the ship must zigzag to avoid detection by Japanese submarines, the play zigzags through time and space. The only straight lines lead to love or death.

"I NEED TO SWEAT THIS OUTTA ME."

Young boxer Pedro Quinn is explaining to his trainer why he is punching the air until he reaches the point of exhaustion. What he is trying to sweat out is the homosexual desire he cannot escape, though he inhabits a world in which *"maricon,"* the Spanish equivalent of "faggot," is the harshest epithet, one that denies one's manhood. Oliver Mayer's *Blade to the Heat* (1994) centers on the symbolic battle of the boxing ring. It is the 1950s and boxing is now dominated by poor Blacks and Latinos:

> Them Irishers and Jews got jobs. Regular work. They got no ambition no more. Only ones still here is the colored boys. . . . And the Spanish boys. 'Cause for them it's still tough outside. The boy who fights nowadays is either black or Porta Rican or roman'ic.[13]

Mayer focusses on Latinos and how boxing fails to affirm their masculinity. All the male characters in the play seem obsessed with homosexuality. It is the subject of their taunts and the cause of their insecurity. The action centers on two boxers, Irish-Latino Pedro Quinn and Cuban-born Mantequilla Decima. Early in the play, during a championship fight, Quinn endures Decima's killer punch: "then, inexplicably, he smiles. A mysterious, unsettling smile"(p. 10), which is an expression of the joy he feels boxing, even while being hurt in the ring: "You feel so alive. So alive in there" (p. 16). Quinn wins the fight and Mantequilla becomes haunted by Quinn's smile: "I gonna see that smile in my dreams" (p. 12). When another fighter, Vinal, publicly accuses Mantequilla of being a faggot, a *maricon* like Quinn, Mantequilla becomes insecure about his own masculinity and is humiliated by the thought of losing to a "faggot," to Quinn. Vinal accused Mantequilla to find his Achilles heel: "One look at him and I knew that macho crap would drive him crazy" (p. 30). Vinal also understands what makes Pedro Quinn smile when he takes a beating. Some boxers:

> They here cause they like the smell of men. They like the form, man. The
> way a dude looks when he throws a blow, his muscles all strained and
> sweaty, his ass all tight bearing down on the blow, his mouth all stopped
> up with a piece of rubber, and only a pair of soaking wet trunks between
> his johnson and yours. They like it. And they like to catch a whupping for
> liking it. (p. 29)

Quinn is attracted to his best friend Garnet, a young Black singer who has built a career on his imitation of Jackie Wilson and James Brown. When the two men finally kiss, Quinn panics and punches Garnet. Boxing has for so long been his means of repressing his homosexuality that his violent response is an automatic defense of his machismo. Pedro thought the championship belt "was supposed to protect me" from forbidden sexual desires: "You are what you were before. Just everybody knows" (p. 37).

The fears and conflicts of these men are reinforced by a two man Greek chorus of older boxers and hangers-on, Three Finger Jack and Alacran. Alacran thinks that the possibility that Quinn may be homosexual sullies the purity of the sport and that he should be shunned. Jack is loyal to the young boxer. Both older men use terms of love and endearment with the boxers they serve, as did the coaches in Clifford Odets's boxing classic *Golden Boy* (1937), which also explores the relationship between homoeroticism and boxing. In Odets' play, the homosexuality of gangster Eddie Fuseli, who loves and comes to own Joe Bonaparte, represents the corruption and materialism, endemic to American capitalism, that destroys his boxer hero. In Mayer's play, homosexual desire is the possibility of love Pedro's machismo has perverted into violence. As Pedro says, "I hurt people. This is all I know" (p. 39).

The finale of *Blade to the Heat* is a rematch between Quinn and Mantequilla. In the final round, Mantequilla, frustrated that Quinn won't collapse under the rain of punches he is receiving and still obsessed with the specter of homosexuality, kisses Quinn on the lips. Finally sinking to his knees after another of Mantequilla's killer punches, Pedro sees Garnet in the audience, rises, and literally punches his opponent to death. In the final moment, Pedro embraces Mantequilla and kisses him. Earlier Sarita, Mantequilla's girlfriend, says to Pedro:

> You want more, don't you? Outa life. Don't you? That closeness. That—
> thing—you get—in there? I swear I'd give anything to get that close. (p. 39)

The only closeness between two people that seems possible is the bizarre love scene Pedro and Mantequilla play out in the ring. The only kiss comes with a killer punch. *Blade to the Heat* is in one sense a history play, set at the moment of the Cuban revolution, showing Latino machismo as enacted through boxing. But *Blade to the Heat* also shows this machismo in crisis because of the ineradicable presence of homoeroticism. Garnet, who represents the new Black rhythm and blues that celebrates sensuality, though containing its own homophobia, cannot offer love as liberation. He can only appear at the end as an angel of death. Love requires a physical and emotional tenderness that stands opposite to the macho erotics of the ring.

Like Clifford Odets, Mayer has found a verbal poetry in the language of his characters, but the real power of the play is visual, in the contrast between the violence of the boxing scenes and the showbiz glitz of Garnet's rhythm and blues. Few recent plays exploit the visual possibilities of the theater as successfully as *Blade to the Heat*.

In the conflict between violence and homoeroticism, these plays examine the forces that turn love into tragedy—at least as much tragedy as *Romeo and Juliet*. What Wallace, Bell, and Mayer powerfully dramatize is that homophobia is intertwined with other negative social forces: myths of masculinity, racism, sexism, and the nationalism and xenophobia that lead to war. Within this world, the most powerful image is of a man passionately kissing a dead man. Until the forces the plays dramatize are reconfigured, love between men is fleeting and doomed.

BORDERS

Few contemporary plays fulfill my definition of the attributes of gay drama as well as Guillermo Reyes's *Deporting the Divas*. Using metatheater, drag, and camp, Reyes's play is a delightful, yet impassioned examination of the links between sexuality and ethnicity for a group of Latino men. The script tells us that the setting of the play is "San Diego: the border,"[14] but the border becomes not only a physical reality, but also a series of binary oppositions that collapse under investigation. As the play progresses, we see that borders exist between male-female, masculine-feminine, gay-straight, brown-white, Spanish-English, real-imaginary, real-theater. These borders can be policed, but ultimately they cannot be maintained.

While the central character is Michael, a "Mexican-American border patrolman who doesn't speak Spanish and is also in the closet" (p. 19), the ideal is the Diva, the female creature who defies binaries, the goddess for gay men:

> the Diva has been battered, trashed around, used and spat out, like a queer or like an illegal alien, or combinations thereof, and yet she has fought back with sweat, guts and tears and continues to occupy a space in our collective imagination. . . . She desires to be worshiped as the spiritual androgynous force of nature that she is. She is there to redeem our genders and to bless and to coalesce them and, at last, we are free to love and dance and taste forbidden fruit. (p. 43)

Michael has to learn to love divas and, ultimately, he has to become a diva to love himself. Yet now he, a Mexican American, tries to maintain the geographical border and the equally permeable borders of gender and sexuality. Michael is haunted by an embarrassing event. Looking for illegal aliens, he broke into a border shack and found himself in the middle of a Mexican American gay wedding: "female priest, multi-layered cake, no-host bar, practical gifts: toaster ovens and Mary Kay products" (p. 4). His colleagues see this as a joke, but Michael is haunted by the transgressive event, which reminds him of what he is missing: "I need something grand, and magnificent, almost unreal in my life—even if it just happens in my head" (p. 14). Yet he is frightened of the possibilities of liberation his imagination might arouse: "I'm often scared that what I'll see next brings me closer to madness—either that or personal fulfillment, whichever comes first" (p. 4). Was it coincidence that Michael happened upon the gay wedding the night his wife left him?

Michael fantasizes about a romance with Sirena, his ideal woman who, like all the women in Reyes's play, is performed by a man: "Sirena is, of course, played by a man, but she is not just a camp impersonation of womanhood, she *is* womanhood, at least in its 1940s incarnation of masochistic suffering heroine with a hidden past and tremendous destructive passion" (p. 29). The Sirena of Michael's daydreams is more controllable than Michael's new boyfriend, Sedicio, who wants Michael to "Leave behind your repressed fantasies, no matter how glamorous, and embrace the 'open border' lifestyle that I represent" (p. 37). Michael's relationship with Sedicio throws him into a full-fledged identity crisis, or what Reyes refers to as a "His-Panic Breakdown." Sedicio, whom Michael meets in a Beginning Spanish for Latinos class, is a diva out of drag, openly gay, clear on what he wants, and avowedly revolutionary. Michael tells Sedicio, "The border is still the law. You break it, you pay for it," to which Sedicio responds, "It's more complex than that, you oughta know, you're bisexual" (p. 46). Throughout *Deporting the Divas* the geographical border is analogous to the borders of sexuality. Aliens and gay men are mirror images. When Michael and Sedicio make out in a car near the border, Sedicio says:

> SEDICIO: Let's go before they think we're committing shocking, immoral acts that will destroy Western civilization.
> MICHAEL: Like sodomy?
> SEDICIO: Like immigrating. (p. 25)

At the end, Michael settles for his artificial borders, keeps his job, and goes back to his wife. Loving a gay man who is also an illegal immigrant is too much for the policeman inside Michael. He offers Sedicio "a discreet affair on the side," which Sedicio refuses. Michael will pass for straight. Sedicio, an illegal alien, has learned to pass for legal to stay in America, "Maybe I don't mind passing for something I'm not" (p. 70), but the question remains: Should he pass for straight when one needn't: "There are alternative families, there are other ways to live, and some of us don't belong anywhere other than the border" (p. 70).

Can borders be avoided? When Michael and Sedicio start seeing each other, Michael says: "I want to make love to you only within the boundaries that you have so wisely set up," but Michael ultimately sets up too many boundaries. Michael is not yet ready to become a Diva, the only person who can collapse borders. At the end of the play, Michael goes out to the empty shack where he saw the gay wedding and imagines himself surrounded by divas "standing tall, ready to transport me to that grand, fabulous world where I will arise, one day, ready and eager to face the music and sing along!" (p. 73).

Reyes's border cannot be shown on stage because it is a state of mind; rather a series of states of mind. Like Michael's Sirena, it is a potent product of the imagination, offering order to those who need it, but, like the doors of a French farce, trying to shut out what cannot be so easily controlled. *Deporting the Divas* also plays with the border between stage and audience, fantasy and reality. Consistently, playfully metatheatrical, it is constantly reminding us of its artifice. When Marge McCarthy, cousin to Joseph McCarthy and voice of the white, upper middle class in the play, calls the sheriff, Dean, to tell him she is coming to visit him during a scene, Dean reminds her, "Marge, we're played by the same actor, OK?" Characters fight over narration and curse flashbacks. As only the grand artifice of the diva can defy borders, so the diva playfulness of Reyes's metatheatricality can do justice to is celebration of divadom. This is grand, gay theater, defying the restrictive strictures of realism and honoring its past.

I ended previous editions of this book with some sort of Grand Statement. This seems less realistic now. Gay playwrights are considered major playwrights in the United States. The crucial issue now is not the contested place of gay men in our society, but what "gay" will mean in the twenty-first century, whether the term has outlived its historical moment, and how same-sex desire fits into a larger constellation of issues. For those of us invested in theater, the issue is also what theater will mean for gay men.

We're out onstage and off. Now what?

NOTES

PREFACE TO *STILL* ACTING GAY

1. Alan Sinfield, *Gay and After* (London: Serpent's Tail, 1998), p. 99.

2. Alan Sinfield, *Cultural Politics—Queer Reading* (Philadelphia: University of Pennsylvania Press, 1994), p. 71.

3. John Weir, "Going In," in Mark Simpson, ed., *Anti-gay* (London: Freedom. Edition, 1996), p. 30.

4. Quoted in Alan Sinfield, *Cultural Politics*, p. 74.

5. Sean O'Connor's *Straight Acting: Popular Gay Drama from Wilde to Rattigan* (London: Cassell, 1998), covers this material effectively.

6. Therese Jones, Introduction, *Sharing the Delirium: Second Generation AIDS Plays and Performances* (Portsmouth, NH: Heinemann, 1994), p. xi.

7. See my essays, "From *Summer and Smoke* to *Eccentricities of a Nightingale*: The Evolution of the Queer Alma," *Modern Drama*, Vol. XXIX, no. 1 (Spring, 1996), pp. 31–50, and "The Sacrificial Stud and the Fugitive Female in *Suddenly Last Summer, Orpheus Descending,* and *Sweet Bird of Youth*," in *The Cambridge Companion to Tennessee Williams,* ed. Matthew C. Roudané (Cambridge: Cambridge University Press, 1998), pp. 128–146.

INTRODUCTION

1. Quoted in an interview with Robert Massa, *Village Voice* (June 28, 1988), p. 38.

2. Alan Sinfield, *Out on Stage: Lesbian and Gay Theatre in the Twentieth Century* (New Haven: Yale University Press, 1999), p. 1.

3. For the most part, I choose to use the word *heterosexism* instead of the more common *homophobia.* Philosopher Richard Mohr's argument won me over:

    > It is worth noting the problems with the term's [homophobia] adoption. At a minimum, it is vague. If it just means "fear of gays," modeled, say, on "xenophobia," why not just say so and save two syllables? More important, the coinage is morally misleading. Its use makes it sound as though bigotry is a mental illness, like agoraphobia, or a physical illness, like hydrophobia. But the bigot's problem is not disease, whether mental or physical. The bigot is not sick; he is immoral. . . . If antigay bigotry needs an abstract noun, "heterosexism," though awkward, at least sets the concept in the correct moral constellation, by placing it alongside "racism" and "sexism." Richard Mohr, *Gays and Justice* (New York: Columbia University Press, 1988), p. 12.

    Joe Cable, in *South Pacific,* sings of bigotry, "You've got to be carefully taught," and one cannot totally blame the person who hates homosexuals without addressing the institutions that support such hatred. Thus the battle of gay people with religious conservatism, whether Christian, Jewish, or Muslim (though in the United States the Christian fundamentalists are the noisiest) and Republican leaders.

I will use *homophobia,* then, only when I literally mean a phobia (uncontrollable, irrational fear) about homosexuality (Brick's in Tennessee Williams's *Cat on a Hot Tin Roof,* for instance). Otherwise, I shall use *heterosexism.*

4. Sinfeld, *Out on Stage,* p. 4.

5. This is not the place to get into a full discussion of all the terms for us over the past fifty years, but I try to historicize somewhat. The polite term for us before the late sixties was "homosexual," a silly word in all sorts of ways. Yes, "gay" was used by us in our own discussions before then. So was "queer" in a less ironic, politicized way than it is now.

6. A word about my practice of dating plays. The date listed in parentheses is that of the New York or London production. *The Green Bay Tree* was produced in both cities in 1933. Contemporary American plays tend to have a number of productions in regional theaters or workshops before they are produced in New York. I will list the date of the New York production. Publication information will be found in the notes.

7. For discussions of Fitch and Kelly, see Robert A. Schanke and Kim Marra, *Staging Desire: Queer Reading of Playwrights, Critics, and Designers in American Theater History* (Ann Arbor: University of Michigan Press, forthcoming).

1: SEEING GAY

1. Martin Esslin, *The Field of Drama* (London: Methuen, 1987), 60.

2. Herbert Blau, *Take Up the Bodies: Theater at the Vanishing Point* (Urbana: University of Illinois Press, 1982), 289.

3. Don Shewey, "The Actor as Object of Desire," *American Theatre*(October 1990), 7:30.

4. Herbert Blau, *The Audience* (Baltimore: Johns Hopkins University Press, 1990), 26.

5. The production took place at the Shakespeare Memorial Theatre, Stratford-upon-Avon, 1987, and at the Barbican Center, London, 1988.

6. William Shakespeare, *The Merchant of Venice*, in Stanley Wells, Gary Taylor, John Jowett, and William Montgomery, eds., *William Shakespeare: The Complete Works* (Oxford, England: Clarendon Press, 1988), 448. Further references to this play are to this edition.

7. The "shadow" of the "Elizabethan sin of Sodom . . . was never far from the flower-strewn world of Elizabethan friendship and it could never wholly be distinguished from it." Alan Bray, "Homosexuality and the Signs of Male Friendship in Elizabethan England," *History Workshop Journal*, no. 29 (Spring 1990), 16. Bray's recent essay unravels the complex relationship of physical intimacy, romantic language, male friendship, and sodomy in Elizabethan England.

8. For the classic reading of the fraught complex of homosociality and homosexuality and their relationship to women, see Eve Kosofsky Sedgwick, *Between Men* (New York: Columbia University Press, 1985).

9. For the central work in this area, see Alan Bray, *Homosexuality in Renaissance England* (New York: Columbia University Press, 1995).

10. Blau, *The Audience*, 53.

11. My use (my colleague Stanley Fish might say misuse) of the term *interpretive community*, needs some explication. To Fish, the interpretive community is "made up of those who share interpretive strategies, not for reading but for writing texts, for constituting their properties." "The meanings and texts produced by an interpretive community are not subjective because they do not proceed from an isolated individual but from a public and conventional point of view." Stanley Fish, *Is There a Text in This Class: The Authority of Interpretive Communities* (Cambridge, Mass.: Harvard University Press, 1980), 14.

    Is there a gay interpretive community in Fish's sense of the term? I would have to answer yes and no. For much of the period covered in this study, the self-image of gay men was a text written by dominant culture. Dramas reflect this internalized homophobia. Post-Stonewall gay writers and performers defy, challenge, and reshape the middle-class American interpretive community that forms the audience for drama, but there is some question whether, in the process, they create another interpretive community.

On the other hand, many lesbians and gay men, from the time they knew they were "different," joined a shared pattern of rereading and writing that finds a space for their sexuality. When I speak of separate interpretive communities, I refer to the fact that a gay man is likely to read, say, a Tennessee Williams play differently from a heterosexual man. Moreover, gay writers are likely to be aware that they are writing for two audiences, gay and straight, with two different codes.

12. "The combination of themes—homosexuality and the horrors of Dachau—may be overwhelming." Lee A. Jacobus, Editor's Preface to Martin Sherman's *Bent*, in Jacobus, ed., *The Bedford Introduction to Drama* (New York: St. Martin's Press, 1989), 907. This syntactical equation of homosexuality and Dachau is classic, but it is particularly surprising from St. Martin's, a press that has been in the forefront of gay literature.

13. Martin Sherman, *Bent*, in Don Shewey, ed., *Out Front: Contemporary Gay and Lesbian Plays*, 127. Further references to *Bent* are to this text.

14. Simon Watney quotes an article in the *Sun*, a trashy London tabloid, about gay actor Michael Cashman's casting as the gay Colin on the hit soap opera "Eastenders": " 'There is no suggestion that actor Michael Cashman is gay in real life. He is simply playing a role.' " Watney comments on the "pathological insistence that the actor is distinct from the part he plays, as if to reassure readers that no actor who is gay in 'real life' could possibly appear on *Eastenders*." *Policing Desire: Pornography, AIDS, and the Media* (Minneapolis: University of Minnesota Press, 1987), 87.

The same sorts of assertions appeared in the American press about Jack Coleman and William Campbell, the lovers on "Dynasty." The *Sun* article about Michael Cashman was particularly silly since the actor is openly gay.

15. Proposed by the Conservative government in 1987 and passed by Parliament in 1988, Section 28 forbids any local government to "intentionally promote homosexuality or publish material with the intention of promoting homosexuality" or "promote the teaching in any maintained school of the acceptability of homosexuality as a pretended family relationship." Thus government-supported theaters like the Royal National Theatre, the Royal Shakespeare Company, the Royal Court, and smaller theaters throughout the United Kingdom receiving local government subsidies could be enjoined from presenting plays that offered positive gay images. The National Theatre 1990 production of Sherman's *Bent* provided a test case in the most highly visible arena. The production was so successful that it moved from the National to the West End for a run limited only by Ian McKellen's other commitments. See Jeffrey Weeks, *Coming Out: Homosexual Politics in Britain from the Nineteenth Century to the Present*, rev. ed. (London: Quartet Books, 1990), 237–248.

16. Martin Sherman's A *Madhouse in Goa* opened at the Lyric, in Hammersmith, March 1989, for a limited run, then moved to the West End for another limited run. It was directed by Robert Allan Ackerman. Rupert Graves played David; Ian Sears, Costos.

17. Martin Sherman, *A Madhouse in Goa* (Charlbury, England: Amber Lane Press, 1989), 28.

18. Richard Mohr, "Outing: A Problem in Gay Ethics" (unpublished draft), p. 10.

19. A word on the use of the term *gender*. In current theoretical writings, one's sex (male or female) relates to biological attributes. One's gender (masculine or feminine) is a social construction. Thus the gender order is not a natural hierarchy, but a socially constructed one that places heterosexual men above women and homosexual men.

This distinction gives another reason for the absurdity of the term *homosexual*. Homosexuality does relate to the act of sex and the same-sex object of desire, but definitions of homosexuality and discourse about homosexuality, being social constructions, are not stable descriptions of natural phenomena. They change from time to time and from society to society.

Moreover, a homosexual is not only different from a heterosexual by reason of the sex of the object of his desire, he is also shaped by his own history of oppression, marginalization, or rejection because of his homosexuality.

20. "Some men, of course, will resist kissing. This resistance is often a last holdout against a full commitment to homosexuality ('cowboys don't kiss'). Hustlers who think of themselves as straight don't kiss. When young adolescent boys start fooling around with each other, they also often draw the line at kissing. As long as their lips don't meet they can believe that what they are doing is not homosexual, but just a way of getting their rocks off." Charles Silverstein and Edmund White, *The Joy of Gay Sex* (New York: Crown Publishers, 1977), 133.

21. C. A. Tripp, *The Homosexual Matrix* (New York, New American Library, 1977), 226.

22. Arthur Miller, *A View from the Bridge* (New York: Viking, 1960), 44. Further references are to this edition. The Broadway premiere, directed by Martin Ritt (September 1955), featured Van Heflin as Eddie and Richard Davalos as Rodolfo.

23. Some colleagues have argued with this characterization of Miller's attitude toward sexual politics. Others see my reference to Miller's "brutal patriarchy" as unsupported name-calling. For both groups I offer this clarification.

   Arthur Miller sees wives as long-suffering creatures whose duty it is, not only to put up with their husbands' failures and cruelty but also to support staunchly their husbands' illusions or downright lies. In *Death of a Salesman* (1949), Linda Loman supports Willy even though he has consistently lied to her, bullied her, and cheated on her. That she should not only submit to this treatment but lionize the man who treats her this way is never questioned. Esther, at the beginning of *The Price* (1968), is rightfully dissatisfied with her guilt-ridden, self-pitying husband, but ultimately Miller has her uphold the very illusions about his mean-spirited father and his duty toward his father that have been the source of his (and her) unhappiness. In *The Crucible* (1953), Elizabeth Proctor takes the blame for her husband's adultery and thus the responsibility for the whole mess with Abigail. Ultimately Proctor takes his stand not because of his wife but for his three sons.

   Although the men are weak, the women are often presented as the cause of the problem the play depicts. In *The Crucible*, Abigail, after all, is the problem. It is not, as it was historically, a group of prepubescent girls who were empowered by their superstitious elders: it is a group of frustrated, unhappy adolescent girls, led by a girl who has slept with a man and developed what amounts to a "Fatal Attraction," evil, destructive infatuation for him. Female sexuality is as much the problem as male superstition. In *The Price*, the most violent image is of the mother vomiting on her husband's hands when he tells her all their money is lost.

24. Arthur Miller, *After the Fall* (New York: Viking, 1964), 98.

25. *The Boys in the Band*, by Mart Crowley, was first performed off Broadway at Theatre Four on April 14, 1968, under the direction of Robert Moore. Peter White was Alan, Robert La Tourneaux the hustler. The text was published in 1968 by Farrar, Straus & Giroux. The scene under discussion is on pages 81–83.

26. Lanford Wilson's *Fifth of July* opened at the Circle Repertory Theatre on April 27, 1978, under the direction of Marshall Mason. William Hurt was Ken Talley, Jeff Daniels his lover, Jed. It opened on Broadway, under Mason's direction, at the New Apollo Theatre, on November 5, 1980. Christopher Reeve (later succeeded by Richard Thomas) was Ken. Jeff Daniels (later John Dossett) was Jed. The original text was published by Hill and Wang, 1979 (the kiss is on page 11). The Broadway text, which is considerably revised, is available from Dramatists' Play Service, 1982 (the kiss is on page 8).

27. *Six Degrees of Separation*, by John Guare, opened at the Mitzi E. Newhouse Theater of Lincoln Center in New York, on May 19, 1990, under Jerry Zaks' direction. Stockard Channing was Ouisa; James McDaniel, Paul; David Eigenberg, the hustler. The play moved to the Vivian Beaumont Theater on October 28, with Courtney B. Vance in the role of Paul. The text was published by Vintage in New York, 1990. The scene under discussion is on pages 47–50, and further references are to this edition.

28. I cannot help but be curious about how blacks respond to Guare's play. It is clear from a white point of view why the dangerous stranger must be black, and from a heterosexual point of view why he is gay. But making him a gay black raises unanswered questions about the intense problems of black heterosexism.

29. Margaret Walters, *The Male Nude: A New Perspective* (Harmondsworth, England: Penguin, 1978), 17.

30. Barbara Freedman, *Staging the Gaze: Postmodernism, Psychoanalysis, and Shakespearean Comedy* (Ithaca: Cornell University Press, 1991), 1.

31. Walters, *The Male Nude*, 11.

32. Tennessee Williams, *A Streetcar Named Desire*, vol. 1, *The Theatre of Tennessee Williams* (New York: New Directions *Publishing*, 1971), 371.

33. Tennessee Williams, *Cat on a Hot Tin Roof,* vol. 3, *The Theatre of Tennessee Williams* (New York: New Directions Publishing, 1971), 30.

34. Robert Patrick, *T Shirts*, in William M. Hoffman, ed., *Gay Plays: The First Collection* (New York: Avon Books, 1979), 42. The play was first performed at the Out-and-About Theatre, Minneapolis, October 19, 1978, and directed by Richard E. Rehse. Further references are to the published text listed above.

35. Robert Patrick, *Mercy Drop and Other Plays* (New York: Calamus Books, 1979). The production was first performed at the WPA Theatre in New York in February 1973, under the direction of Hugh Gittens. Kevin Breslin played the boy, Johnny.

    Patrick notes that in the original production of *Mercy Drop*, one of the leading characters who was to appear nude had to keep his clothes on because he contracted warts on his penis. "Rather than give science-fiction overtones to what is, after all, essentially a love story, he was allowed to retain his jumpsuit" (p. 3). The published script contains more production photos than is usually the case, many featuring nude shots of the lead actor. Patrick's Author's Note, explaining why the other actor is clad, not only explains the discrepancy between written text and photos but also offers an apology for providing less nudity than the words promise. The "audience" for the published text was to receive the same view of nudity as the theater audience.

36. Patrick, *Mercy Drop*, 78.

37. I don't want to suggest that male nudity happened only in gay drama. The Broadway success of the rock musical *Hair* in the sixties proved its commercial viability. It was also a feature of such unsuccessful commercial countercultural dramas as the short lived *Che*, by Lennox Raphael. A nude scene provided the climax of the highly successful *Equus*, by Peter Shaffer. Though the scene was a heterosexual "sex" scene, the focus was on the male character, and the sexual attraction of the older narrator-character for the boy who appears nude is not too well hidden (see chapter 3 of this book).

38. Terrence McNally, *The Lisbon Traviata* (New York: The Fireside Theatre, 1990), 88. The first New York production opened at the Theatre Off Park on June 4, 1985, under John Tillinger's direction, with Benjamin Hendrickson as Stephen and Steven Culp as the unclad Paul. A revised version was produced at the Promenade Theatre in October 1989, under Tillinger's direction, with Anthony Heald and John Slattery as Stephen and Paul.

39. Ben Jonson, *Epicoene, or The Silent Woman*. The play was directed by Danny Boyle for the Royal Shakespeare Company, Swan Theatre, Stratford-upon-Avon, in the summer of 1989. Jared Harris was Clerimont, Liza Hayden his "ingle." John Hannah was Epicene.

40. For the most cogent, witty discussion of this subject, see Stephen Orgel, "Nobody's Perfect: Or Why Did the English Stage Take Boys for Women," in Ronald R. Butters, John M. Clum, and Michael Moon, eds., *Displacing Homophobia* (Durham, N.C.: Duke University Press, 1989), 7–30.

41. Simon Trussler, Introduction to Ben Jonson's *Epicoene* (The Programmetext for the Royal Shakespeare Company production) (London: Methuen, 1989), xiii.

42. Dyer notes how effeminate "queens" and mannish "dykes" are considered to be more like the opposite sex. "Yet they are not exactly masculine or feminine either. In gay usage, they may be an assertion of in-betweenism or more generally of a refusal of rigid sex role-playing; but in their use within the dominant culture they are more characteristically portrayed as people who in failing, because of not being heterosexual, to be real women or men, at the same time fail to be truly masculine or feminine in other ways." "Seen to Be Believed: Some Problems in the Representation of Gay People as Typical," *Studies in Visual Communication* (Spring 1983), 9:12.

43. Harvey Fierstein, *Torch Song Trilogy* (New York: Gay Presses of New York, 1980), 15. After the individual plays of the trilogy had their LaMama productions, *Torch Song Trilogy* was presented off off Broadway by The Glines on October, 16, 1981, in a production directed by Peter Pope and with Fierstein as Arnold. The production later moved off Broadway and then to a small Broadway house, the Helen Hayes Theatre.

44. Jerry Herman, "A Little More Mascara," in Fierstein's *La Cage aux Folles*. George Hearn played Albin/Zaza in the Broadway production, which opened at the Palace, under Arthur Laurents' direction, in August 1973.

45. It is interesting to note that the London production of *La Cage aux Folles* was not a success. Drag is much more a staple of British low comedy (see television shows like *Monty Python's Flying Circus or Benny Hill*) and is connected to the mockery and degradation of women. This celebration of American drag simply did not translate.

46. David Henry Hwang, *M. Butterfly* (New York: New American Library, 1988), 60. Further references are to this edition. *M. Butterfly* opened on Broadway in March 1988, in a production directed by John Dexter, with John Lithgow as Gallimard and B. D. Wong as Song. I write in chapter 3 about Dexter's ability, in production, to bring out the homosexual subtext in Peter Shaffer's plays, but in New York and London (with Anthony Hopkins), his production of Hwang's play assiduously avoided its subtext.

47. Charles Ludlam, *The Mystery of Irma Vep, in The Complete Plays of Charles Ludlam* (New York: Harper & Row, 1989), 795.

48. Derek D. Smith played Edgar, Jane, and Irma. Wil Love played the other characters in this production, which opened in May 1991.

49. "To interpret a text is not to give a (more or less justified, more or less free) meaning, but on the contrary to appreciate what *plural* constitutes it." Roland Barthes, S/Z, trans. Richard Miller (New York: Farrar, Straus, & Giroux, 1974), 5. While any theatrical adaptation limits the number of plural readings, and may add more, between the readings of adapter and audience member, the kind of reading Barthes describes is exactly what Bartlett gives the Balzac story. I have been interested to see that none of the interviews with Bartlett I have read cites Barthes' work. Perhaps Bartlett, who is a student and translator of French literature, did not want his work to appear too esoteric.

50. Neil Bartlett, *Sarrasine* (unpublished libretto), 1990. The musical score was composed by Nicholas Bloomfield. I am grateful to Neil Bartlett and *Sarrasine*'s producer, Simon Mellor, for letting me study the script and allowing me to quote from it.

51. Honoré de Balzac, *Sarrasine*, trans. Richard Miller, in Roland Barthes, S/Z (New York: Farrar, Straus, & Giroux, 1974), 252. In Balzac's story, Sarrasine is a sculptor, a perfect image for his rigid readings of those he wants to be his subjects.

52. Quoted in Gerard Raymond, "The Last Castrato: Neil Bartlett Adapts Balzac's Short Story, *Sarrasine,*" *Theatre Week* (September 2–8, 1991), 22.
    The protean nature of La Zambinella is effectively reflected in Nicholas Bloomfield's superb musical score, which veers from quotations from eighteenth-and-nineteenth-century opera to show tunes and Edith Piaf-like love songs. The instrumentalists who provide the background music and accompany the songs are onstage with the actors and, at times, interact with the characters.

53. Williams, *A Streetcar Named Desire*, 355.

2: AIDS DRAMA: DISPLACING *CAMILLE*

1. Paula A. Treichler, "AIDS, Homophobia, and Biomedical Discourse," *October* (Winter 1987), 43:42. See also Treichler's essay "AIDS, Gender, and Biomedical Discourse: Current Contests for Meaning," in Elizabeth Fee and Daniel M. Fox, eds., *AIDS and the Burdens of History* (Berkeley: University of California Press, 1988), 190–266.

2. Simon Watney, "The Spectacle of AIDS," *October* (Winter 1987), 43:78.

3. Robert Chesley, *Hold,* in *Hard Plays/Stiff Parts: The Homoerotic Plays of Robert Chesley* (San Francisco: Alamo Square Press, 1990), 154. Further references to *Hold* are to this edition.

4. Robert Chesley, *(Wild) Person, Tense (Dog),* in *Hard Plays/Stiff Parts,* 133.

5. Robert Chesley, *Night Sweat,* in *Hard Plays/Stiff Parts,* 66.

6. Lanford Wilson, *A Poster of the Cosmos,* in M. Elizabeth Osborn, ed., *The Way We Live Now: American Plays and the AIDS Crisis* (New York: Theatre Communications Group, 1990), 74.

7. Jean Claude van Itallie, *Ancient Boys,* in *Gay Plays: An International Anthology* (New York: Ubu Repertory Theater Publications, 1989) 393.

8. Terrence McNally, *Andre's Mother,* in Osborn, ed., *The Way We Live Now,* 191.

9. William M. Hoffman, *As Is,* in Don Shewey, ed., *Out Front: Contemporary Gay and Lesbian Plays* (New York: Grove Press, 1988), 547.

10. Richard Greenberg, *Eastern Standard* (New York: Grove Weidenfeld, 1989), 63.

11. Sander L. Gilman, *Disease and Representation: Images of Illness from Madness to AIDS* (Ithaca, N.Y.: Cornell University Press, 1988), 2.

12. Charles S. Rosenberg, "Disease and Social Order in America: Perceptions and Expectations," in Fee and Fox, eds., *AIDS and the Burdens of History,* 27.

13. Alan M. Brandt, "AIDS: From Social History to Social Policy," in *AIDS and the Burdens of History,* 155.

14. See Jeffrey Weeks, *Sexuality and Its Discontents: Meanings, Myths, and Modern Sexualities* (London: Routledge & Kegan Paul, 1985).

15. Brandt, "AIDS," in *AIDS and the Burdens of History,* 151.

16. For a fuller discussion of AIDS and morality, see Simon Watney, "The Spectacle of AIDS," *October, 43* (Winter 1987), 71–86.

17. Susan Sontag, *AIDS and Its Metaphors* (New York: Farrar, Straus & Giroux, 1989), 72–73.

18. For a study of the relation of AIDS literature to the past and to memory, see John M. Clum, " 'The Time Before the War': AIDS, Memory, and Desire," *American Literature* (December 1990), 62:648–667.

19. I am thinking particularly of the Marwoods of George Lillo's *The London Merchant (1731)* and Gotthold Lessing's *Miss Sara Sampson (1755).* This Marwood herself is a descendant of William Congreve's unhappy, destructive Marwood in *The Way of the World (1700).* The fallen woman, then, moves from seventeenth-century aristocratic comedy to eighteenth-century bourgeois "tragedy" to nineteenth-century romantic melodrama.

20. Alexandre Dumas, fils, *La Dame aux Camélias,* Edith Reynolds and Nigel Playfair, trans., in Stephen S. Stanton, ed., *Camille and Other Plays* (New York: Hill & Wang, 1957), 118. Further references to the play are to this text.

21. Alexandre Dumas, fils, *La Dame aux Camélias,* David Coward, trans. (Oxford, England: Oxford University Press, 1986), 11.

22. Dumas, fils, *La Dame aux Camélias* (the novel), 37–38.

23. Gilman, *Disease and Representation,* 256–257.

24.　Catherine Clément, *Opera, or the Undoing of Women*, Betsy Wing, trans. (Minneapolis: University of Minnesota Press, 1988), 62.

25.　In Nicholas Muni's 1991 contemporary staging of Verdi's *La Traviata* at the New York City Opera, Violetta, Verdi's version of Marguerite, dies of AIDS, not consumption. While reviewers noted that the audience giggled at the hospital ward death scene that had poor Violetta singing "Addio del Passato" with tubes in her nose, the production acknowledged the resemblance between the master narrative of *La Dame aux Camélias* and contemporary AIDS narratives.

26.　My focus in this book is on gay men, but the causality I describe in this section has been applied to other "risk groups" for HIV infection. Drug addicts too are seen as suffering the wages of sin or of excessive appetite, which is seen as the same thing. The distribution of clean needles, like the distribution of condoms or safe-sex information, is resisted because some feel that preventing or denying the "sin" is preferable to saving the "sinner." Thus the category of "innocent" People With AIDS as if there are guilty People With AIDS.

　　　Because there are a number of affluent gay men who support the theater, their experiences with AIDS are most often the stuff of drama. Even television drama tends to present AIDS as a disease of affluent men.

27.　Gilman, *Disease and Representation*, 258. Gilman notes that from the Enlightenment, the image of the syphilitic shifts from male to female, "but then only with the female as the image of the source of infection" (253–254).

28.　Watney, "The Spectacle of AIDS," 73.

29.　Charles Ludlam, "Observations on Acting," *American Theatre* (October 1990), 7:36.

30.　There were a number of such couples in 1985, the year of the gay on network television. The prototypes were Stephen Carrington and Luke Fuller on *Dynasty*, a couple that bore many resemblances to Michael and Peter, who appeared later the same year.

31.　*Our Sons* was written by William Hanley, directed by John Erman. It aired on ABC.

32.　John J. O'Connor, "Gay Images: TV's Mixed Signals," *New York Times* (May 19, 1991), sec. 2, p. 32.

33.　Larry Kramer, *The Normal Heart* (New York: New American Library, 1985), 71.

34.　The Gay Sweatshop is Britain's leading gay theater group. It began producing gay drama in London and on tour in 1974 and is still active. For a comprehensive history of this important group, see Philip Osment, "Finding Room on the Agenda for Love: A History of Gay Sweatshop," in *Gay Sweatshop: Four Plays and a Company* (London: Methuen, 1989).

35.　Andy Kirby, *Compromised Immunity*, in Osment, ed., *Gay Sweatshop: Four Plays and a Company* (London: Methuen, 1989), 57. Further references are to this edition.

36.　Richard Greenberg, *Eastern Standard* (New York: Grove Weidenfeld, 1989), 19. Further references are to this edition.

37.　van Itallie, *Ancient Boys*, in *Gay Plays*, 368.

38.　William M. Hoffman, *As Is*, in Shewey, ed., *Out Front*, 520. Further references are to this edition.

39.　Edmund White, "Esthetics and Loss," in John Preston, ed., *Personal Dispatches: Writers Confront AIDS* (New York: St. Martins Press, 1989), 149.

40.　Robert Chesley, *Jerker, or the Helping Hand*, in Shewey, ed., *Out Front*, 453. Further references are to this edition.

41.　Harvey Fierstein, *Safe Sex* (New York: Atheneum, 1988), 57–58. Further references are to this edition.

42.　Larry Kramer, *The Normal Heart*, 114. Further references are to this New American Library edition.

43. Larry Kramer, *Reports from the Holocaust: The Making of an AIDS Activist* (New York: St. Martins Press, 1989), 186.

44. Alisa Solomon, "AIDS Crusaders Act Up a Storm," *American Theatre* (October 1989), 6:39.

45. Stephen Chapot, "Liz Taylor, Live," in Preston, ed., *Personal Dispatches*, 95.

46. There have been a number of works based on the AIDS quilt. For those who have not seen the quilt, the HBO telefilm, available on video, *Common Threads: Stories From the Quilt*, is a superb introduction to the significance of the quilt. It is also a fine documentary of a chapter in gay life, to be seen in the context of other major documentaries, such as *Before Stonewall* and *The Times of Harvey Milk*. Also useful as an introduction is *The Quilt: Stories From the NAMES Project* (New York: Pocket Books, 1988). I was also instructed by the text of Richard Mohr's illustrated lecture, "TEXT(ile): Reading the NAMES Project AIDS Quilt."

47. This production, *Unnatural Acts*, was developed by Jeffrey Storer and Ed Hunt, artistic directors of the Manbites Dog Theater of Durham, North Carolina. The Durham production was transferred for a limited run to Joseph Papp's New York Shakespeare Festival at the Public Theater.

48. Solomon, "AIDS Crusaders," 40.

49. Bruce Nussbaum, *Good Intentions: How Big Business and the Medical Establishment Are Corrupting the Fight Against AIDS* (New York: Atlantic Monthly Press, 1990).

50. Burroughs-Wellcome, a pharmaceutical corporation whose American headquarters are in Research Triangle, between Raleigh and Durham, North Carolina, are the producers of AZT, until October 1991 the only antiviral drug approved for use against HIV. Burroughs-Wellcome was the first target of AIDS activists, in 1987, because of the exorbitantly high price of AZT. Bowing to demonstrations and press coverage of the protest, they lowered the price by 20 percent, but it is still high. For a full description of the controversy, see Bruce Nussbaum, *Good Intentions: How Big Business and the Medical Establishment Are Corrupting the Fight Against AIDS* (New York: Atlantic Monthly Press, 1990).

    Jesse Helms, former television commentator, is the ultraconservative senator from North Carolina. Characteristically, Helms began his 1990 run for reelection with an antigay speech. He has also been the strongest spokesman against the National Endowment for the Arts funding of projects with homoerotic content.

51. Douglas Crimp, *AIDS Demo Graphics* (Seattle, Wash.: Bay Press, 1990), 19.

3: CLOSET PEDERASTS

1. Their statement was reprinted in *American Theatre* (March 1991), 7:50.

2. Philip Brett, "Britten and Grimes," in Philip Brett, ed., *Benjamin Britten: Peter Grimes* (Cambridge, England: Cambridge University Press, 1983), 189.

3. Three arguments on outing are particularly forceful. Richard Goldstein, "The Art of Outing: When Is It Right to Name Names," *Village Voice* (May 1, 1990), 33–37; Gabriel Rotello, "Why I Oppose Outing," *Outweek* (May 29, 1991), 10–11, 64; Richard Mohr, "Outing: A Problem in Gay Ethics," draft of a chapter from a forthhcoming book (1991).

4. Eve Kosofsky Sedgwick, *Epistemology of the Closet* (Berkeley: University of California Press, 1990), 7.

5. African-Americans became truly uncloseted in 1917, when black actors played blacks for the first time on Broadway, but plays about the taboo of miscegenation had been salacious theatrical material since Dion Boucicault's nineteenth-century melodrama, *The Octoroon* (1859). Various forms of incest dominated American "serious drama" in the twenties and thirties. See Clum, *Ridgely Torrence* (New York Twayne, 1972).

6. While there are many fine histories of the development of the concept of the homosexual and the development of the language of homosexuality in the nineteenth century, two are landmark

works: Michel Foucault, *The History of Sexuality*, Robert Hurley, trans., vol. 1, *An Introduction* (New York: Pantheon, 1978); and Jeffrey Weeks, *Sexuality and Its Discontents: Meanings, Myths, and Modern Sexualities* (London: Longman, 1980).

7. Jonathan Katz, *Gay American History* (New York: Avon Books, 1976), 139.

8. Katz, *Gay American History*, 138.

9. George Chauncey, *Gay New York: Gender, Urban Culture, and the Making of the Gay Male World 1890–1940* (New York: Basic Books, 1994), p. 312.

10. Ramona Curry, *Too Much of a Good Thing: Mae West as Cultural Icon* (Minneapolis: University of Minnesota Press, 1996), pp. 17–18.

11. Mae West, *The Drag in Three Plays by Mae West*, ed. Lillian Schlissel (New York: Routledge, 1997), p. 108.

12. West, *The Drag*, p. 140.

13. Quoted in Ramona Curry, *Too Much of a Good Thing: Mae West as Cultural Icon*, p. 3.

14. In the published edition of Osborne's *A Patriot for Me* are printed the cuts and alterations requested by the Lord Chamberlain. Three entire scenes about Colonel Redl's homosexual activities are to be cut, as well as such minor details as references to "clap" and "crabs." Even a scene with Redl and a woman together in bed "must not be played with the couple both in bed." John Osborne, *A Patriot for Me* (London: Faber and Faber, 1965), 128. Since Osborne refused to agree to the cuts, the Royal Court Theatre was turned into a private club for the run of the play. Such "clubs" were not under the Lord Chamberlain's jurisdiction.

15. Richard Dyer, "Seen to Be Believed: Some Problems in the Representation of Gay People as Typical," *Studies in Visual Communication* (Spring 1983), 9:2.

16. Jeanie Forte, "Realism, Narrative, and the Feminist Playwright," *Modern Drama* (March 1989), 32:117.

17. Jill Dolan, "Lesbian Subjectivity in Realism: Dragging at the Margins of Structure and Ideology," in Sue-Ellen Case, ed., *Performing Feminisms: Feminist Critical theory and Theatre* (Baltimore: Johns Hopkins University Press, 1989), 46.

18. Alan Sinfield, "Closet Dramas: Homosexual Representation and Class in Postwar British Theater," *Genders* (Fall 1990), 9:115.

19. Kaier Curtin, *We Can Always Call Them Bulgarians* (Boston: Alyson, 1987), 178. Curtin quotes a *New York Times* interview with Shairp at the time of the New York opening of *The Green Bay Tree* (November 12, 1933): "The idea which grew into *The Green Bay Tree* came to Mr. Shairp one day when he was walking in Hampstead Heath, near his home, he saw a man and a boy driving together, and something in the boy's wistful expression suggested to him the theme which is the basis for the play. When he returned home he told his wife he had found a new subject and then went directly to work." In recent years, Hampstead Heath has been a famous cruising area.

20. Mordaunt Shairp, *The Green Bay Tree*, in Michael Wilcox, ed., *Gay Plays* (London: Methuen, 1984), 33. Further references to the play are to this edition.

21. "In some schools such as Harrow, where Terence Rattigan was a pupil, it became fashionable for boys in rebellion against school values 'to proclaim their genuine or affected homosexuality.' This pattern allowed the cultivation of leisureclass male homosexuality as a possible, unspecific, unavowed component within a general, Bohemian, artistic, and theatrical stance. It was these cultivated gentlemen who sought lower-class partners. And partly because they were the producers of books and plays and—eventually, hesitantly, and obliquely—alluded to the matter, this became the expected pattern of homosexual relations." Alan Sinfield, "Closet Dramas: Homosexual Representation and Class in Postwar British Theater," *Genders* (Fall 1990), 9:113.

22. Peter Burton, Introduction to Shairp, *The Green Bay Tree, Gay Plays*, 53.

23. Jed Harris cut this final flower-arranging from the Broadway production, as if the sight of a

man arranging flowers was too shocking. Julian sends Trump out for the flowers and sits alone onstage, smoking a cigarette, as the curtain falls.

24. Martin Gottfried, *Jed Harris: The Curse of Genius* (Boston: Little Brown, 1984), 142.

25. Gottfried, *Jed Harris*, 143.

26. Gottfried, *Jed Harris*, 143. The legendary animosity Laurence Olivier had for Jed Harris developed during rehearsals of *The Green Bay Tree*. Harris' brutal treatment of actors infuriated Olivier, who later claimed that he based his characterization of Shakespeare's *Richard III* on Harris. Olivier also claimed that he hated playing Julian: "He was weak, indecisive, despicably without backbone. I never felt comfortable playing him, and I began to despise myself for his disagreeable qualities" (quoted in Thomas Kiernan, *Sir Larry* [New York: Times Books, 1981], 101). Note that Olivier hates the character's weakness, not his sexuality.

27. Curtin, *We Can Always Call Them Bulgarians*, 186.

28. Noël Coward, *Design for Living* (Garden City, N.Y.: Doubleday, Doran & Co., 1933), 12. Further references to *Design for Living* are to this edition.

29. John Lahr, *Coward the Playwright* (London: Methuen, 1982), 83. Lahr's discussion of *Design for Living* is as disapproving of the central trio as Ernest is, and in 1982, he would still refer to the bisexuality of the play's heroes as "abnormal sexuality." Fortunately, Lahr was not in a position to do the disservice to Coward that he did to Joe Orton.

30. Noël Coward, Introduction to *Play Parade*, vol. 1 (London: Heinemann, 1934), xvii.

31. According to Leslie Halliwell, the film, directed by Ernst Lubitsch, with Gary Cooper (hardly one's idea of a sophisticated Coward leading man), Frederic March, and Miriam Hopkins had only one line left from Coward's play, thanks to pressure on Paramount from the Legion of Decency, the Catholic pressure group (*Halliwell's Film Guide: 7th Edition* [New York: Harper & Row, 1989], 265).

32. John Osborne, *Look Back in Anger* (New York: Penguin, 1982), 19. Further references are to this edition.

33. Peter Shaffer, *Five Finger Exercise* (New York: Samuel French, 1958).

34. Shelagh Delaney, *A Taste of Honey*, in Henry Popkin, ed., *The New British Drama* (New York: Grove Press, 1964), 97. Further references to the play are to this text.

35. Harry and Bill's meeting in *The Collection* is not the only Pinter meeting that has overtones of a homosexual pickup. The meeting of the protagonists on Hampstead Heath is an inside joke that got a laugh in the original London production of *No Man's Land* (1975). Aston's bringing Davies home in *The Caretaker* (1960) has similar overtones.

36. Simon Trussler, *The Plays of Harold Pinter* (London: Victor Gollancz, 1973), 111.

37. John Mortimer, Introduction to Georges Feydeau, *Three Boulevard Farces* (Harmondsworth, England: Penguin, 1985), 9.

38. C. W. E. Bigsby, *Joe Orton* (London: Methuen, 1982), 17.

39. Peter Shaffer, *Black Comedy and White Lies* (New York: Stein and Day, 1967).

40. In 1967 the British government decriminalized private consensual sex between men over the age of twenty-one, except prisoners and members of the military. In a kind of catch-22, the consensual act of sex, so long as it was private, was legal, but any invitation to have sex was not. Recently, Clause 25 of the Criminal Justice Bill listed among serious violent crimes that are to receive tougher prison sentences a number of consensual homosexual activities.

41. Quoted in John Lahr, *Prick Up Your Ears* (New York: Knopf, 1978), 156.

42. Lahr, *Prick Up Your Ears*, 35n.

43. Lahr, *Prick Up Your Ears*, 215.

44. Bigsby, *Joe Orton*, 67.

45.   Joe Orton, in John Lahr, ed., *The Orton Diaries* (New York: Harper & Row, 1986), 125.

46.   Lahr, ed., *The Orton Diaries*, 256.

47.   Lahr, *Prick Up Your Ears*, 276.

48.   Lahr, *Prick Up Your Ears*, 276.

49.   The film of Lahr's biography was directed by Stephen Frears and released in 1987.

50.   Alan Bennett, Introduction to *Prick Up Your Ears: The Screenplay* (London: Faber, 1987): "Dramatizing the act of writing is never easy: the paper ripped from the typewriter and flung into the wastepaper basket. . . . But how else do you do it?" (p. vii).

51.   Bennett, *The Screenplay*, ix.

52.   Orton, in Lahr, ed., *The Orton Diaries*, 125.

53.   Orton, in Lahr. ed., *The Orton Diaries*, 251.

54.   Orton, in Lahr, ed., *The Orton Diaries*, 251.

55.   Jonathan Dollimore, "The Challenge of Sexuality," in Alan Sinfield, ed., *Society and Literature*, 1945–1970 (New York: Holmes & Meier, 1983), 51.

56.   Joe Orton, *What the Butler Saw*, in *The Complete Plays* (New York: Grove Weidenfeld, 1976), 370. Further references to Joe Orton's plays are to this text.

57.   Dollimore, "The Challenge of Sexuality," 54–55.

58.   Lahr, *Prick Up Your Ears*, 205.

59.   Orton, in Lahr, ed., *The Orton Diaries*, 53. Williams obviously had more admiration for Orton than Orton had for him. According to Orton, Williams saw the New York production of *Entertaining Mr. Sloane* (1964) twice and "says it's the funniest play he's ever seen" (The Orton Diaries, 157). Williams dedicated a late play, "The Blonde Europeans," to Orton. In May 1967, Orton and Halliwell stayed in the Tangiers flat in which Williams had written *Suddenly Last Summer* (1958). For Orton, it was decorated in "the kind of taste I abhor" (*The Orton Diaries*, 157).

60.   Alan Sinfield, "Who Was Afraid of Joe Orton," *Textual Practice* (Summer 1990), 4:271.

61.   Lahr, *Prick Up Your Ears*, 156.

62.   Simon Shepherd, *Because We're Queers: The Life and Crimes of Kenneth Halliwell and Joe Orton* (London: Gay Men's Press, 1989). "In his plays Orton continually infiltrated the action with images of sexy boys. These images are carefully set up, created in front of us, and thus become fetishistic" (p. 102).

63.   Shepherd, *Because We're Queers*, 102–103.

64.   Orton, in Lahr, ed., *The Orton Diaries*, 45.

65.   Orton, in Lahr, ed., *The Orton Diaries*, 145.

66.   Lahr, *Prick Up Your Ears*, 134.

67.   Orton, in Lahr, ed., *The Orton Diaries*, 203.

68.   Lahr, *Prick Up Your Ears*, 130.

69.   John Lahr sees a good deal of Kenneth Halliwell, Orton's longtime companion, in Wilson (Lahr, *Prick Up Your Ears*, 128–138). According to Lahr's constantly negative reading of Halliwell, Wilson is the closest approximation to Halliwell's self-destructive personality, and the circumstances of Wilson and Frank's life, like their difference in age, seem autobiographical. *Ruffian on the Stair* began as an adaptation of a novel Orton and Halliwell coauthored, *The Boy Hairdresser*.

70.   Shepherd, *Because We're Queers*, 165.

71.   Shepherd, *Because We're Queers*, 165.

72. Sinfield, "Who Was Afraid of Joe Orton," 167.

73. Peter Shaffer, *Equus* (Harmondsworth, England: Penguin, 1977), 108.

74. For a more traditional reading of the religious dimension of these plays, see John M. Clum, "Religion and Five Contemporary Plays: The Search for God in a Godless World," *South Atlantic Quarterly* (Autumn 1978), 77:418–432.

75. One might say further that the relationship between the two women in Shaffer's *Lettice and Loveage* (1988) could be added to his catalog of closeted homosexual relationships.

4: AMERICAN DREAMS

1. Paula Treichler, "AIDS, Gender, and Biomedical Discourse: Current Contests for Meaning," in Elizabeth Fee and Daniel M. Fox, eds., *AIDS: The Burdens of History* (Berkeley: University of California Press, 1988), 205.

2. There is a study to be written on the relationship between the homosexuality of many of the male movie stars of the fifties (Clift, Dean, Mineo, Hunter, Hudson, to name just a few) and changing images of masculinity. The ménage à trois played out by James Dean, Sal Mineo, and Natalie Wood in *Rebel Without a Cause* (1955) had not only a potentially gay element (which is why Mineo/Plato had to be killed off) but also a really gay element. It also raises the issue of interpretive communities, for the homosexuality of these figures was "common knowledge" among gays, who then could provide their own subtext to films starring these actors (think of the turbulent relationship between Hudson and Dean in *Giant* (1956), for instance).

3. In the telefilm *Rock Hudson*, the star's agent, Henry Willson (played by Andrew Robinson), is the villain of the piece for destroying Rock's relationships with men to protect his stardom. Willson also arranges Rock's marriage when rumors start getting out of control. Hudson eventually fires Willson so that he can have a love life. In the telefilm, Hudson is the nice guy made unhappy by sharks. Marc Christian, the lover who sued Hudson's estate because Hudson did not tell him he had AIDS, is a selfless lover duped by Rock's evil secretary, who is devoted to protecting Rock's straight image.

4. Richard Mohr, "Outing: A Problem in Gay Ethics," draft of a chapter from a forthcoming book (1991), 17.

5. Robert Anderson, *Tea and Sympathy* (New York: Random House, 1953), 3. Further references to *Tea and Sympathy* are to this edition.

6. For example, in the 1982 film *Making Love*, the gay writer, played by Harry Hamlin, quotes Laura's final line to the married doctor he has just initiated into the joys of gay sex. It is the only camp line given to this homogenized character.

7. In the film adaptation, Hollywood "justice" prevailed, and Laura became a "fallen woman" because of her salvation of Tom. The film ends with Tom, ten years older and married, reading a letter from Laura in which she states that what they did was wrong. The film, of course, also removes any hints of homosexuality, overt or latent, from the teachers.

8. Mohr, "Outing," 20.

9. Loring Mandel, *Advise and Consent* (New York: Samuel French, 1961), 17.

10. Allan Berube, *Coming Out Under Fire: The History of Gay Men and Women in World War II* (New York: The Free Press, 1990).

11. This is also true to some extent of his short stories, in which furtive sex is treated in poignant, if elliptical language, but he still seemed more comfortable dealing candidly with homosexuality in the more private form of the short story and lyric poen than in the theater, where public disclosure became the object of terror. I deal with the relationship of the stories to the plays in an essay; see John M. Clum, " 'Something Cloudy, Something Clear': Homophobic Discourse in Tennessee Williams," in Ronald R. Butters, John M. Clum, and Michael Moon, eds., *Dis-*

placing Homophobia (Durham, N.C.: Duke University Press, 1989), 149–169. For a discussion of Williams' short stories, see also Claude J. Summers, *Gay Fictions: Wilde to Stonewall* (New York: Continuum, 1990), 133–155.

12.   Tennessee Williams, *A Streetcar Named Desire*, vol. 1, *The Theatre of Tennessee Williams* (New York: New Directions Publishing, 1971), 354. Further references to *A Streetcar Named Desire* are to this text.

13.   Richard Dyer, "Stereotyping," in Richard Dyer, ed., *Gays and Film* (New York: Zoetrope, 1984), 32.

14.   This may be why *A Streetcar Named Desire* is continually quoted in gay drama. A classic example is George's cry "Flores para los muertos" in Edward Albee's *Who's Afraid of Virginia Woolf?*, which seems to be there as an homage to Williams and a recognition of the closeted gay dimension of his own play. In early 1991, the gay male theater group, Bloolips, and the lesbian theater collective, Split Britches, presented *Belle Reprieve*, their cross-dressed version of *Streetcar* with Bette Bourne as Blanche.

15.   Tennessee Williams, as quoted in Michael Bronski, *Culture Clash: The Making of a Gay Sensibility* (Boston: South End Press, 1984), 115.

16.   The best recent discussion of the meaning and implications of camp, a sythesis and extension of previous definitions—one pertinent to my discussion of *Streetcar* and other gay drama—can be found in Jonathan Dollimore's *Sexual Dissidence: Augustine to Wilde, Freud to Foucault* (Oxford: Oxford University Press, 1991). Camp, for Dollimore, "renders gender into a question of aesthetics. Common in aesthetic invovement is the recognition that what seemed like mimetic realism is actually an effect of convention, form, or some other kind of artifice. . . . Camp comes to life around that recognition; it is situated at the point of emergence of the artificial from the real, culture from nature" (p. 311–312).

17.   Evidence suggests that the homosexual connotations of the words I cite here were part of American gay slang in 1947 and that Williams knew the "code." In the letters he wrote to Donald Windham before *Streetcar* was written (Donald Windham, ed., *Tennessee Williams' Letters to Donald Windham, 1940–1965* [New York: Holt, Rinehart, & Winston, 1976]), Williams refers to his young, casual sexual partners as "trade," another term appropriated into gay slang from the jargon of prostitution, and speaks often of his propensity for "chicken"—boys—a preference he clearly shares with Blanche. According to Harld Wentworth and Stuart B. Flexner's *Dictionary of American Slang* (2d supplemental ed. [New York: Thomas Crowell, 1975]), straight meant heterosexual as early as 1945. Eric Partridge's *A Dictionary of Slang and Unconventional English, Eighth Edition* (New York: Macmillian, 1984) claims that "quean" was used to identify an effeminate homosexual as early as the late nineteenth century. The term comes from "quean," a British term for a prostitute. According to Kaier Curtin (*We Can Always Call Them Bulgarians*, pp. 73–78), characters in Mae West's *The Drag* (1927) called themselves "queens" and spoke of their penchant for "rough trade." The evidence for "trick" and "turn the trick" is more circumstantial. Since by 1947 Williams had already written about male prostitutes, whose slang was surely that of their female counterparts, he would surely know their slang.

> He learned a great deal from the bold homosexuals. Like jazz musicians and dope addicts, they spoke in code. The words "fairy" and "pansy" were considered to be in bad taste. They preferred to say that a man was "gay" while someone quite effeminate was a "queen." As for the manly youths who offered themselves for seduction while proclaiming their heterosexuality, they were known as "trade," since they usually wanted money. Gore Vidal, *The City and the Pillar* (New York: E. P. Dutton & Co., 1948), 156.

18.   Harold Beaver, "Homosexual Signs (In Memory of Roland Barthes)," *Critical Inquiry* (Autumn 1981), 8:106.

19.   Beaver, "Homosexual Signs," 106.

20.   Tennessee Williams, *Suddenly Last Summer*, in vol. 3, *The Theatre of Tennessee Williams* (New York: New Directions Publishing, 1971), 351. Further references to *Suddenly Last Summer* are to this edition.

21. Tennessee Williams, *Cat on a Hot Tin Roof*, in vol. 3, *The Theatre of Tennessee Williams* (New York: New Directions Publishing, 1971), 15. Further references to *Cat on a Hot Tin Roof* are to this edition.

22. Recent productions, like Howard Davies' superb 1988 production at the National Theatre of Great Britain, which he recreated with a different cast for Broadway in 1990, have removed Williams' euphemistic obscenities and replaced them with their real counterparts.

23. In Richard Brooks' screenplay for the 1958 movie, direct references to homosexuality are removed, making Brick's problems alcoholism and arrested development.

24. Tennessee Williams, "The Critic Says Evasion; I Say Mystery," *New York Herald Tribune* (April 17, 1955), sec. 4, p. 2. Reprinted in Maria St. Just, ed., *Five O'clock Angel: Letters of Tennessee Williams to Maria St. Just, 1948–1982* (New York: Penguin, 1990), 110. Lady St. Just does not mention that the piece was published—only that Williams gave it to her for safe keeping.

> It is interesting to see that Williams would defend his "mystery" while candidly explaining his play. It is also interesting to note the use of the word *must* instead of the more neutral *will* in describing Brick's "heterosexual adjustment." Williams' dictum for Brick is in line with medical and moral thinking in the mid-1950s. How much did the playwright really buy into such attitudes?

25. Tennessee Williams, "Too Personal?," preface to *Small Craft Warnings*, in vol. 5, *The Theatre of Tennessee Williams* (New York: New Directions Publishing, 1976), 220. Further references to *Small Craft Warnings* are to this edition.

26. Quoted in Ronald Hayman, *Tennessee Williams: Everyone Else Is an Audience* (New Haven: Yale University Press, 1993), p. 215.

27. Tennessee Williams, *Vieux Carré*, in *The Theatre of Tennessee Williams, Volume 7* (New York: New Directions, 1980), 178.

28. Quoted in Donald Spoto, *The Kindness of Strangers: The Life of Tennessee Williams* (New York: Ballantine Books, 1985), 319.

29. Tennessee Williams, Introduction to William Inge, *The Dark at the Top of the Stairs* (New York: Random House, 1958), vii–viii.

30. The complex relationship between Williams and Inge is discussed in biographies of both writers. Williams was instrumental in getting Inge's early work produced, but in the 1950s Williams saw Inge as his antagonist in an intense rivalry that extended to comments on Inge's personal style. Williams was disturbed by Inge's success and despised his closeted, "gentlemanly" behavior: "Inge may be [agent] Audrey's [Wood's] gentleman playwright, but I prefer to remain her degenerate playwright" (Spoto, *The Kindness of Strangers*, 251).

31. William Inge, *Come Back, Little Sheba, in Four Plays* (New York: Grove Press, 1958), 23. The play was first presented on Broadway, February 1950.

32. William Inge, *Picnic, Four Plays*, 90. First produced on Broadway, February 1953. In Mart Crowley's *The Boys in the Band*, a character says of the hunky, vapid hustler who comes to the party to be Harold's birthday present: "He looks right out of a William Inge play to me." (New York: Farrar, Straus, & Giroux, 1968), 77.

33. "Such material could not have found wide public approval in the sexually reticent Eisenhower era when it was being composed, but the therapeutic value of writing it was probably very significant to Inge." Ralph F. Voss, *A Life of William Inge* (Lawrence, Kans.: University Press of Kansas, 1989), 144.

34. William Inge, *The Tiny Closet, in Summer Brave and Eleven Short Plays* (New York: Random House, 1962), 189. Further references to *The Tiny Closet* are to this edition.

35. William Inge, *The Boy in the Basement, in Summer Brave and Eleven Short Plays*, 163. Further references to *The Boy in the Basement* are to this edition.

36. Inge's dislike for actors burns through a number of his plays, particularly, *A Social Event*.

37. William Inge, *Where's Daddy* (New York: Random House, 1966), 31. The play was first produced on Broadway, March 1966.

38. Georges-Michel Sarotte, *Like a Brother, Like a Lover: Male Homosexuality in the American Novel and Theatre from Herman Melville to James Baldwin* (Garden City, N.Y.: Doubleday Anchor, 1978), 108.

39. Howard Taubman, "Modern Primer: Helpful Hints To Tell Appearances From Truth," *New York Times* (April 28, 1963), sec. 2, p. 1.

40. Tennessee Williams' *The Milk Train Doesn't Stop Here Anymore* (1963), in its first, less campy version, directed by Herbert Machiz, was first presented on Broadway in January 1963, with Hermione Baddely and Paul Roebling. (A revised, Kabuki-style howler with Tallulah Bankhead and Tab Hunter opened a year later. Later still came the film version, *Boom!* (1968), in which Liz Taylor camps it up, with Noel Coward playing the witch—on the stage a female part, in the film a bitchy queen—a rare case of film uncloseting a gay subtext.) While the *Times* mildly approved of the 1963 version, the play did contain, in the handsome young man as angel of death (if not in the cartoon women), one of Howard Taubman's telltale signs of homosexual drama: "The character who passes this miracle for her is one of those handsome, pallid young men with a dead heart who has become a fashionable symbol for some of our playwrights." (Review of *The Milk Train Doesn't Stop Here Anymore*, New York Times [January 18, 1963], p. 7). In his April article, cited in note 39, Taubman would make clear the homosexual subtext underneath this fashionable symbol.

41. Edward Albee, *Who's Afraid of Virginia Woolf?*, in *Selected Plays of Edward Albee* (New York: Nelson Doubleday, 1987), 120. Further references are to this edition.

42. Richard Schechner, "Who's Afraid of Edward Albee?," in C. W. E. Bigsby, ed., *Edward Albee: A Collection of Critical Essays* (Englewood Cliffs, N.J.: Prentice-Hall, 1975), 64. I am fascinated by Schechner's ability to ascertain not only the sexual orientation of Albee's audience but also their sexual potency.

43. Schechner, "Who's Afraid," in Bigsby, ed., *Edward Albee*, 65.

44. Philip Roth, "The Play That Dare Not Speak Its Name," in Bigsby, ed., *Edward Albee*, 105.

45. Roth, "The Play That Dare Not," Bigsby, ed., *Edward Albee*, 109.

46. Stanley Kauffmann, "Homosexual Drama and Its Disguises," *New York Times* (January 23, 1966), sec. 2, p. 1. The article was reprinted in Kauffmann, *Persons of the Drama* (New York: Harper & Row, 1976), 291–294.

47. Stanley Kauffman, "On the Acceptability of the Homosexual," *New York Times*, February 6, 1966, sec. 2, p. 1. The essay was reprinted in Kauffmann, *Persons of the Drama*, 295–298.

48. The review was reprinted in Stanley Kauffmann, *Theater Criticisms* (New York: Performing Arts Journal Publications, 1983), 98–100.

49. Kauffmann, *Theater Criticisms*, 150.

50. Georges-Michel Sarotte, *Like a Brother, Like a Lover* (Garden City, N.Y.: Doubleday Anchor, 1978), 142.

51. Sky Gilbert, "Closet Plays: An Exclusive Dramaturgy at Work," *Canadian Theatre Review* (1989), 59:55–58.

52. Gilbert, "Closet Plays," 57–58.

53. Gilbert, "Closet Plays," 58.

54. Foster Hirsch, "Evasions of Sex: The Closet Dramas," in Philip C. Kolin and J. Madison Davis, eds., *Critical Essays on Edward Albee* (Boston: G. K. Hall, 1986), 130.

55. The one play that transcends this sort of reading, though it doesn't completely escape it, is *A Delicate Balance* (1966). I might add here that the key to reading Albee is in the adaptations, particularly of Carson McCullers' *The Ballad of the Sad Cafe* (1963).

56. Edward Albee, *The Zoo Story*, in *Selected Plays*, 12.

57. Alan Sinfield, "Who Was Afraid of Joe Orton?" *Textual Practice* (Summer 1990), 4:273–274.

58. "I do know I felt I was Johnny while I was writing it. I identified with him completely. . . . About a year later I was watching a production of the play at the Mark Taper forum in Los Angeles when I realized I was Frankie." Introduction to *Three Plays by Terrence McNally* (New York: Penguin, 1990), xi.

59. Quoted in the frontispiece of *Three Plays by Terrence McNally*.

60. Frank Rich, "2 Terrence McNally Couples Struggle to Love, Against the Odds" (rev. of *Lips Together, Teeth Apart), New York Times* (June 26, 1991), sec. B, p. 3.

61. Otis Stuart, "Measuring the Times: Terrence McNally Straddles the Sexual Divide," p. 93.

62. Quoted in Otis Stuart, "Measuring the Times: Terrence McNally Straddles the Sexual Divide," *Village Voice* (September 3, 1991) p. 93.

63. Terrence McNally, Introduction to *Three Plays by Terrence McNally*, ix.

64. Craig Lucas, "A Gay Life in the Theater," *American Theater* (November 1990), 7:24–29, 68.

65. Craig Lucas, *Prelude to a Kiss* (New York: Dutton, 1990), 31.

66. Lucas, *Prelude to a Kiss*.

67. I have pluralized this catch-all term *the gay experience* to convey my understanding of the myriad, contradictory elements it inadequately names. There are only gay experiences. As for the gay sensibility, I am drawn to Jonathan Dollimore's argument: "I shall suggest that there is a sense in which the very notion of a homosexual sensibility is a contradiction in terms. I am interested in an aspect of it which exists, if at all, in terms of that contradiction—of a parodic critique of the essence of sensibility as conventionally understood." *Sexual Dissidence: Augustine to Wilde, Freud to Foucault* (Oxford: Oxford University Press, 1991), 308.

5: DRAMATIZING GAY MALE HISTORY

1. Robert Wallace, "To Become: The Ideological Function of Gay Theatre," *Canadian Theatre Review* (Summer 1989), 8.

2. Don Shewey, "Pride in the Name of Love: Notes on Contemporary Gay Theater," Introduction to *Out Front: Contemporary Gay and Lesbian Plays* (New York: Grove Press, 1988), xxv.

3. Philip Brett, Postscript to Philip Brett, ed., *Benjamin Britten: Peter Grimes* (Cambridge, England: Cambridge University Press, 1983), 191.

4. Eve Kosofsky Sedgwick, "Pedagogy in the Context of an Anti-Homophobic Project," *South Atlantic Quarterly* (1990), 89:142.

5. Christopher Marlowe, *Edward the Second* (New Mermaids Edition) (London: Ernest Benn, 1967), 34. Further references to *Edward II* are to this edition.

6. Larry Kramer, *The Normal Heart* (New York: New American Library, 1985), 114.

7. For an articulate argument for homosexuality as a social construction, see David Halperin, *One Hundred Years of Homosexuality and Other Essays on Greek Love* (New York: Routledge, Chapman & Hall, 1990).

8. Larry Kramer, *The Normal Heart*, 114.

9. This is a statement by director Nicholas Hytner in the program for the Royal Shakespeare Company production of *Edward II* in 1990.

10. Jonathan Goldberg, "Sodomy and Society: The Case of Christopher Marlowe," *Southwest Review* (Autumn 1984), 69:377.

11. This is Gerard Murphy as quoted in " 'Sweet Lies': Terrence Michael Stephenson Talks to Director Gerard Murphy and Actor Simon Russell Beale About the RSC's New Production of *Edward II*," *Gay Times* (August 1990), 36.

12. Alan Bray's *Homosexuality in Renaissance England* (London: Gay Men's Press, 1982), is the seminal work on this subject. His 1990 essay, "Homosexuality and the Signs of Male Friendship in Elizabethan England," *History Workshop Journal* (Spring 1990), 1–19, complicates a reading of *Edward II* by showing how expressions of love and affection between men were common signs of favor in the Elizabethan court and were not necessarily signs of sodomy: "Marlowe describes in this play what could be a sodomitical relationship, but he places it wholly within the incompatible conventions of Elizabethan friendship, in a tension which he never allows to be resolved" (p. 10).

13. Purvis E. Boyette, "Wanton Humor and Wanton Poets: Homosexuality in Marlowe's *Edward II*," *Tulane Studies in English* (1977), 22:36. A typical "traditional," "enlightened" view of homosexuality in *Edward II* can be found in Sharon Tyler, "Bedfellows Make Strange Politics: Christopher Marlowe's *Edward II*," in James Redmond, ed., *Themes in Drama, 7: Drama, Sex, and Politics* (Cambridge, England: Cambridge University Press, 1985), 55–68. For recent, classic homophobic criticism, see Ronald Huebert, "Tobacco, Boys and Marlowe," *Sewanee Review* (Spring 1984), 92:206–224, in which is found the following gem: "For Gaveston: showily dressed, ostentatiously vain, flirtatious or bitchy as the mood strikes him, eager to parade his coy submissiveness when the king is at his side, rapaciously greedy for power when he isn't. Gaveston, in short, is the stereotypical homosexual" (p. 214).

14. Stephen Orgel, "Nobody's Perfect: Or Why Did the English Stage Take Boys for Women?," in Ronald R. Butters, John M. Clum, and Michael Moon, eds., *Displacing Homophobia: Gay Male Perspectives in Literature and Culture* (Durham, N.C.: Duke University Press, 1989), 16.

15. Bray, "Homosexuality and the Signs of Male Friendship," 9.

16. Bruce R. Smith, *Homosexual Desire in Shakespeare's England: A Cultural Poetics* (Chicago: University of Chicago Press, 1991), 213.

17. Simon Shepherd, *Marlowe and the Politics of Elizabethan Theatre* (London: Harvester Press, 1986), 198.

18. In a number of recent productions, Lightborn has been played by the same actor who played Gaveston. This, I think, is appropriate. George L. Geckle, *Text and Performance: Tamburlaine and Edward II* (Atlantic Highlands, N.J.: Humanities Press International, 1988), 100. Though the stage directions are confusing, the sixteenth-century historian Holinshed tells us that Edward was murdered by having a hot poker inserted in his anus. The RSC production of 1990 enacted this graphically.

19. Claude J. Summers, "Sex, Politics, and Self-Realization in *Edward II*," in Kenneth Friedenreich, Roma Gill, and Constance B. Kuriyama, eds., *"A Poet and a Filthy Play-maker": New Essays on Christopher Marlowe* (New York: AMS Press, 1988), 236.

20. Bruce R. Smith sees Edward's martyrdom as his greatest performance: "Without doing a thing, Edward emerges as the Noble Sufferer. Thanks to all his practice in role-playing, the master rises to the occasion magnificently." *Homosexual Desire in Shakespeare's England: A Cultural Poetics*, 218.

21. Hugh Whitemore, *Breaking the Code* (New York: Fireside Theatre, 1987), 104.

22. Larry Kramer, *The Normal Heart*, 114.

23. Alan Bennett's double bill of plays about Guy Burgess and Anthony Blount, *An Englishman Abroad and A Question of Attribution*, were presented under the title *Single Spies* by the National Theatre of Great Britain in 1988 and published by Methuen in London the same year. The production was successful enough to be moved to the West End. I don't discuss the plays in this chapter because they do not deal with the relationship of the characters' sexuality to their treason.

24. See chapter 3, note 9 for a description of the cuts the Lord Chamberlain ordered.

25. Redl's story is also depicted in the 1984 Hungarian film *Colonel Redl*.

26. John Osborne, *A Patriot for Me* (London: Faber & Faber, 1965), 19. Further references to *A Patriot for Me* are to this edition.

27. Arnold P. Hinchcliffe, *John Osborne* (Boston: G. K. Hall, 1984), 80.

28. Julian Mitchell, *Another Country* (Ambergate, Derbyshire, England: Amber Lane Press, 1982), 24. Further references to *Another Country* are to this edition.

29. It is ironic that Julian Mitchell's screen version of *Another Country* plays up the teenage love between Guy and his beloved Harcourt (who is never seen in the play) but cuts most of the political discussion.

30. Some of my gay students tell me that many fraternities accept homosexual brothers but demand they protect the heterosexual image of the fraternity by staying away from campus gay groups and gay demonstrations.

31. David Rabe, *Streamers* (New York: Alfred A. Knopf, 1977), 59. Further references to *Streamers* are to this text.

32. Richard Hall, "The Elements of Gay Theater," in Richard Hall, *Three Plays for a Gay Theater* (San Francisco: Grey Fox Press, 1983), 153.

33. Noel Greig and Drew Grifiths, *As Time Goes By, in Two Gay Sweatshop Plays* (London: Gay Men's Press, 1981), 27–28. Further references to *As Time Goes By* are to this edition.

34. Philip Osment, *This Island's Mine*, in Philip Osment, ed., *Gay Sweatshop: Four Plays and a Company* (London: Methuen, 1989), 94.

35. Martin Sherman, *Bent*, in Don Shewey, ed., *Out Front: Contemporary Gay and Lesbian Plays* (New York: Grove Press, 1988), 85. Further references to Bent are to this edition.

36. William M. Hoffman, Introduction to William M. Hoffman, ed., *Gay Plays: The First Collection* (New York: Avon, 1979), xxix.

37. Doric Wilson, *Street Theater*, in Shewey, ed., *Out Front*, 7. Further references to *Street Theater* are to this edition.

38. Christopher Hampton, *Total Eclipse* (London: Faber, 1981), 9. Further references to *Total Eclipse* are to this edition.

39. Noel Greig, *The Dear Love of Comrades*, in *Two Gay Sweatshop Plays* (London: Gay Men's Press, 1981), 140. Further references are to this edition.

40. The concept of homosexual relationships bridging differences in age and class remains strong in England. The gay relationship depicted in 1987 and 1988 on the British TV soap opera "Eastenders" was between Colin's a fortyish middle-class outsider to the working-class neighborhood in which he lived, and Barry, an eighteen-year-old who sold records from a stall in a street market. Colin's flat was, stereotypically, much more contemporary in style than those of his neighbors. The relationship was quickly ended after howls of protest over a scene that showed Colin and Barry in bed together.

41. This is Noel Greig as quoted in Philip Osment, "Finding Room On the Agenda For Love': Introduction," in *Gay Sweatshop: Four Plays and a Company* (London: Methuen, 1989), xliii.

42. Lawrence Mass, "Homosexuality and Music: A Conversation with Philip Brett," *Christopher Street* (September 1987), 24. Thanks to my colleague, Michael Moon, for calling my attention to this article.

43. Philip Brett has written a number of articles on Benjamin Britten and compiled a collection of essays on *Peter Grimes*. Clifford Hindley has written several essays on gay themes in Britten's work, including: "Love and Salvation in Britten's *Billy Budd*," *Music and Letters* (1989), 70: 363–381 and "Contemplation and Reality: A Study in *Britten's Death in Venice*," *Music and Letters* (1990), 71:511–523.

44.   Paul Godfrey, Preface to *Once in a While the Odd Thing Happens* (London: Methuen, 1990), n.p. Further references to *Once in a While the Odd Thing Happens* are to this edition.

45.   Philip Brett, "Britten and Grimes," in Philip Brett, ed., *Benjamin Britten: Peter Grimes* (Cambridge, England: Cambridge University Press, 1983), 187.

6: FASHIONING A GAY SELF

1.   John Guare, *Six Degrees of Separation* (New York: Vintage, 1990), 34.

2.   Tennessee Williams, *A Streetcar Named Desire*, in vol. 1, *The Theatre of Tennessee Williams* (New York: New Directions Publishing, 1971), 398.

3.   Christopher Durang, *Sister Mary Ignatius Explains It All For You, in Christopher Durang Explains It All For You* (New York: Grove Weidenfeld, 1983), 195. Further references to the play are to this edition.

4.   Christopher Durang, *Beyond Therapy,* in *Christopher Durang Explains It All For You*, 272.

5.   Lanford Wilson, *The Madness of Lady Bright*, in William M. Hoffman, ed., *Gay Plays: The First Collection* (New York: Avon Books, 1979), 180. Further references to *The Madness of Lady Bright* are to this edition.

6.   Robert Patrick, Preface to *Untold Decades* (New York: St. Martin's Press, 1988), xiv.

7.   Robert Patrick, *The Haunted Host*, in Ed Berman, ed., *Homosexual Acts: A Volume of Gay Plays* (London: Inter-Action, 1975), 84. Further references to *The Haunted Host* are to this edition. The performance history of *The Haunted Host* is a minihistory of gay drama. The original production in 1964 was directed by Marshall W. Mason, who later became artistic director of the Circle Repertory Company and directed Lanford Wilson's plays and William M. Hoffman's *As Is* (1985). The two characters of *The Haunted Host* were played by Patrick and Hoffman. Ten years later, in 1974, it was one of the first plays coproduced by London's Gay Sweatshop. In 1991, a New York revival starred Harvey Fierstein, who had made his first nondrag appearance in a 1975 production of the play.

8.   Doric Wilson, *Street Theater*, in Don Shewey, ed., *Out Front: Contemporary Gay and Lesbian Plays* (New York: Grove Press, 1988), 58.

9.   Kaier Curtin, *We Can Always Call Them Bulgarians* (Boston: Alyson, 1987), 328.

10.   Judy Klemsrud, "You Don't Have to Be One to Play One," *New York Times* (September 29, 1968), sec. 2, p. 3.

11.   William M. Hoffman, Introduction to *Gay Plays: The First Collection* (New York: Avon, 1979), xxvii.

12.   Vito Russo, *The Celluloid Closet: Homosexuality in the Movies*, 2d ed. (New York: Harper & Row, 1987), 176.

13.   Mart Crowley, *The Boys in the Band* (New York: Farrar, Straus & Giroux, 1968), 13. Further references to *The Boys in the Band* are to this edition.

14.   Patrick, Preface to *Untold Decades*, xv.

15.   Terrence McNally, *The Lisbon Traviata*, in *Three Plays by Terrence McNally* (New York: Penguin Plume, 1990), 85. Further references to *The Lisbon Traviata* are to this edition.

16.   In an earlier version of the play, Stephen stabs Mike with a pair of scissors: "I'm surprised more people don't stab their lovers. Instead, they yak, yak, yak. Where does that get them? Nowhere. But look at us. The final duet." (Terrence McNally, *The Lisbon Traviata*, in Shewey, ed., *Out Front*, 417). This ending is in many ways more logical, if less "realistic." Stephen finally turns his life into an opera.

17.   Albert Innaurato, *Coming of Age in Soho*, in *Best Plays of Albert Innaurato* (New York: Gay

Presses of New York, 1987), 7. Further references to *Coming of Age in Soho* are to this edition. In its first incarnation, the central character was a woman, Gioconda. At producer Joseph Papp's suggestion, the leading female character was changed into a male character.

18. Harvey Fierstein, *Torch Song Trilogy* (New York: Gay Presses of New York, 1980), 15. Further references to *Torch Song Trilogy* are to this edition.

19. In the film, Arnold's relationship with Alan becomes central and is clearly a relationship built on mutual love.

20. William Finn, *In Trousers, The Marvin Songs* (New York: The Fireside Theater, 1991), 80. Further references to *The Marvin Songs* are to this edition.

7: CELEBRATING OUR GAZE

1. I am aware that a number of feminists, male and female, have been offended by what they see as the misogyny of *The Crying Game*. The only female character becomes more psychopathic as the film goes on and, ultimately, is killed by the transvestite. Some critics say the film suffers from the "Tootsie Syndrome"—that only men can play good women. No one can win in the sexual politics of film noir. Some one has to be the villain, but it could be said that being the villain is more empowering than being the victim.

2. On the telecast of the Awards ceremony, Mr. Davidson was barely shown, as if this openly, flamboyantly gay actor was unfit for television. All reports in the gay press indicated that Mr. Davidson was all that closeted Hollywood most fears.

3. Quoted in Guy Trebay, "Crossover Dreams," *The New Yorker* (March 22, 1993), 52.

4. Robert Tanich, "*Straight and Narrow* Within an Historical Context," *Plays and Players* (September, 1992), 17.

5. *Porcelain* opened at the Royal Court Upstairs on August 5, 1993, directed by Glen Goei, who played the transvestite, Song, opposite Anthony Hopkins in the London production of *M. Butterfly*.

6. My take on *M. Butterfly* has been, to some extent, revised by Marjorie Garber's convincing analysis in her superb study, *Vested Interests: Cross Dressing and Cultural Anxiety* (New York: Harper, 1993), 239–252. Garber's book is the best analysis yet of the symbiotic relationship of transvestism and theater and the crucial role of transvestism in exploding binary gender definitions.

7. John Byrne, *Colqu'houn and MacBryde* (London: Faber & Faber, 1992). Produced at the Royal Court under the direction of Lindsay Posner in September, 1992.

8. J. R. Ackerley, *The Prisoners of War in Gay Plays, Volume Three*, Ed. Michael Wilcox (London: Methuen, 1988), 105. The revival of *The Prisoners of War* opened at the New End Theatre on February 2, 1993. It was directed by Ken Butler. Conrad was played by Ashley Russell; Grayle by Neil Roberts.

    I read Ackerley's play in researching the first edition of this book, but found it too tortured, too closeted, to be worthy of discussion. Ken Butler's production showed me a more contemporary reading of the play that proved that it is a crucial part of the canon of gay drama. Further references are to this edition.

9. Conrad says of Grayle: "He's sincere, anyway, and . . . clean. I value that" (107). In Ackerley's autobiography, *My Father and Myself*, he describes his qualifications for the Ideal Friend he never found: "He should not be effeminate, indeed preferably normal; I did not exclude education but did not want it, I could supply all that myself and in the loved one it had always seemed to get in the way; he should admit me but no one else; he should be physically attractive to me and younger than myself, the younger the better, as closer to innocence; finally, he should be on the small side, lusty, circumcised, physically healthy and clean: no phimosis, halitosis, bromidrosis." *My Father and Myself* (London: Pimlico, 1992 [first pub. 1968]), 125. It is in-

teresting to note that, as Conrad, in his madness, ultimately switched his affections from Grayle to his azalea. Ackerley ultimately gave up the search for the Ideal Friend and lavished all his affection on his dog, Queenie: "Yet looking at her sometimes I used to think that the Ideal Friend, whom I no longer wanted, perhaps never had wanted, should have been an animal-man, the mind of my bitch, for instance, in the body of my sailor, the perfect human male body always at one's service through the devotion of a faithful and uncritical beast." (*My Father and Myself*, 218). Much of Conrad is an autobiographical projection of Ackerley.

10. The one weakness in this fine production was that budgetary factors led to the cutting of two characters, the doctor and Conrad's servant, who are crucial to the play's exposition. Both present the medical facts and past experience the audience needs to understand Conrad's condition. Without them, it can seem that Conrad breaks down solely because of Grayle's indifference.

11. This production of Ackerley's play brought to mind D. A. Miller's analysis of the problem about connotation as a means of suggesting homosexuality in a dramatic or cinematic text. For Miller, "the shadow kingdom of connotation" is "where insinuations could be at once developed and denied, where . . . one couldn't be sure whether homosexuality was being meant at all, but on the chance it was, one also learned, along with the codes that might be conveying it, the silence necessary to keep about their deployment." However, Miller is right in also seeing that, "if connotation, as the dominant signifying practice of homophobia, has the advantage of constructing an essentially insubstantial homosexuality, it has the corresponding inconvenience of tending to raise the ghost all over the place. For one received in all its uncertainly, the connotation instigates a project of confirmation." D. A. Miller, "Anal Rape," in Diana Fuss, ed., *Inside Out: Lesbian Theories, Gay Theories* (New York: Routledge, 1991), 125.

    Ackerley, as a homosexual who was certainly open in all his nondramatic works, had little stake in the codes operative in his day, yet he did manage to write a play that was, on paper, so seemingly discreet that the Lord Chamberlain and the first producers didn't even notice the homosexual content of the play.

12. After the production of *The Prisoners of War*, Ackerley wrote the scenario for a gay romance between a wealthy young man and a workman. He never wrote the play, perhaps because the scenario wasn't really dramatic, but it also would have been impossible to get the Lord Chamberlain's approval for a production. The scenario is printed in Ackerley's posthumously published memoir, *My Father and Myself* (1968). See my essay, " 'Myself of Course': J. R. Ackerley and Self-Dramatization," *Theatre* (Summer 1993).

13. Unlike American soap operas, which offer a fantasy version of society in which everyone is rich enough to act, dress, and live in surroundings just like those on the commercials, British soap opera builds on the tradition of working-class urban realism pioneered in the heyday of American television drama by Paddy Chayefsky. The keynotes are courage and loyalty.

14. Jonathan Harvey, *Beautiful Thing* (Bush Theatre Publications, 1993), 50–51. The play had its premier at the Bush Theatre in July 1993, under the direction of Hettie Macdonald. Mark Letheren and Jonny Lee Miller were Jamie and Ste. Patrician Kerrigan played Sandra.

15. Davidson and Tony Kushner were the subjects of GAP ads. Some will decry my correlation of the images of gay men battling the system and a commercial image of gay pride being used to sell clothing but, for better or for worse, commercial images are recognitions of empowerment in our society. One of the reasons commercial television shows precious few representations of lesbians and gay men (except occasionally on the news) is that the manufacturers of products and advertising agencies that market products are frightened to target gay audiences on television with gay characters. However, since public television, forever in an image crisis, is increasingly frightened of gay-related material (Lawrence Welk fans will be offended?), our faint hope is still the commercial media. Gay readership of books and magazines has been recognized by advertisers and publishers. Case in point is not only the raft of new magazines targeted at gay readers, but also *The New Yorker*, where the ad with Sullivan's picture appeared, which has become quite obviously gay-friendly under its new leadership. Can commercial television be far behind? From the looks of recent Levis commercials, clearly aimed at young women and gay men, the answer is a hopeful no.

16. *Falsettos* opened at the John Golden Theatre on April 29, 1992. It won the Tony award for Best Musical Score and Best Book for a Musical. Despite a rocky start, the show caught on and ran well into 1993.

    Unfortunately, the overly cautious production turned the script against itself. The male lovers barely touched, and the one kiss exchanged by the lesbian couple was turned into a laugh by the "take" of the actress playing the wife, Trina, who walks in on this kiss. The show was played totally from a heterosexual point of view.

17. *Kiss of the Spider Woman* has a book by Terrence McNally, music by John Kander and lyrics by Fred Ebb. The production was directed by Harold Prince. Brent Carver played the gay window dresser, Molina; Anthony Crivello, the revolutionary Valentin; Chita Rivera played the Spider Woman. Despite mixed reviews when it opened in London in September 1992, and generally negative response from gay members of the audience, the production, which began its life in Toronto, opened on Broadway in May 1993. The show, best seen as an unintentionally funny disaster would, if it were at all possible to take seriously, set gay representation in theater back decades. It is hard to believe that the man who gave us *The Lisbon Traviata* and *Lips Together, Teeth Apart* would participate in this farrago.

18. This battle is waged over specific issues like the right of openly gay men and women to be in the military, but also waged in more theatrical and ultimately more important ways. In Atlanta, Georgia, for instance, lesbian and gay men proudly display rainbow flag license plates and bumper stickers on their cars as a way of showing gay and straight drivers just how many lesbians and gay people there are (and there are a lot!). This performance is a highly effective way of making a gay presence known in an automobile culture.

19. *The Harvey Milk Show.* Book and lyrics by Dan Pruitt, music by Patrick Hutchison. Performed at Actor's Express, Atlanta. Directed by Stephen Petty. Chris Coleman played Harvey, Brian Barnett was Jamey. The show opened in Fall 1991 and was brought back for a three-month run in Fall 1992. I am grateful to Dan Pruitt for allowing me to quote from his script. References are to the unpublished script (Copyright 1991, Pruitt and Hutchison).

20. One of the strong points of the Atlanta production of *The Harvey Milk Show* was the electricity generated by the Harvey and Jamey, Chris Coleman and Brian Barnett. It is the first time I have seen a gay relationship in a musical played with such intensity.

21. The *Destiny of Me* opened on October 20, 1992, at the Lucille Lortel Theatre in New York. The production was directed by Marshall W. Mason. Jonathan Hadary played Ned. John Cameron Mitchell played Alexander. At the performance I saw, understudy Richard Jay Sullivan was a touching, funny Alexander.

    I am grateful to Larry Kramer and his assistant, Ben Pesner, for sending me a copy of the typescript of *The Destiny of Me* before its publication. Page references are to the published edition (New York: NAL Dutton, 1993).

    I have a more extended discussion of *The Destiny of Me* in "Kramer vs. Kramer, Ben and Alexander: Larry Kramer's Voices and His Audiences," in Lawrence D. Mass, ed., *We Must Love One Another or Die: The Life and Legacies of Larry Kramer* (New York: St. Martin's, 1997), pp. 200–214.

22. The low budget Off-Broadway production, in which there were no doctors or nurses in the National Institutes of Health except Della Vida and his wife, emphasized this sense of succumbing totally to the ministrations of a heterosexual couple. The idea that gay Persons With Aids put themselves into the hands of heterosexuals was not treated critically in the play, despite its clear link to the play's critique of the dysfunctional heterosexual, heterosexist home which is the source of Ned's strengths and weaknesses.

23. David Bergman, *Gaiety Transfigured: Gay Self-Representation in American Literature* (Madison: University of Wisconsin Press, 1991), 128–29.

24. Wayne Koestenbaum, *The Queen's Throat: Opera, Homosexuality, and the Mystery of Desire* (New York: Poseidon Press, 1993), 47.

25. Paul Rudnick, "Laughing at AIDS," *New York Times*, January 23, 1993, sec. 1, p. 21.

26. Paul Rudnick, *Jeffrey* (New York: Penguin Plume, 1994), p. 7. Further references are to this edition. *Jeffrey* opened at the WPA theater in New York in January, 1993, in a production directed by Christopher Ashley. John Michael Higgins played the title character. In March, 1993, *Jeffrey* moved to the larger Minetta Lane Theatre. A film version of *Jeffrey* was released in 1996.

27. One could say that Tennessee Williams and Edward Albee did this successfully in *A Streetcar Named Desire* and *Who's Afraid of Virginia Woolf*, but there was no positive space allowed to the homosexual in their critique except for the coded space of closet drama or the closet of exposition.

28. Note, for instance, how crucial the words "performance" and "performative" are to Eve Kosofsky Sedgwick's central work, *Epistemology of the Closet* (Berkeley: University of California Press, 1990): e.g., "Closetedness is itself a performance initiated as such by the speech act of silence" (3). Indeed, it is virtually impossible not to describe the closet in terms of performance. So is coming out a performance. Recent gay scholarship has pointed out the extent to which heterosexuality is also a performance: "Gender is a kind of imitation for which there is no original" [Judith Butler, "Imitation and Gender Insubordination," Diana Fuss, ed., *Inside/Outside: Lesbian Theories/Gay Theories* (New York: Routledge, 1991), 21.].

29. Diana Fuss, "Inside/Out," ibid., 1–2.

30. I agree with W. B. Worthen that: "The theater works to claim a certain kind of meaning for the drama by claiming—even legitimating—a certain kind of experience for the audience as significant. The rhetoric of theater, that is, frames a relationship between the drama, stage production, and audience interpretation, and it is within that relationship that our experience as an audience takes place." *Modern Drama and the Rhetoric of Theater* (Berkeley: University of California Press, 1992), 1.

 Yet, as critics, we must avoid seeing the audience as a homogenous group. While there are demographic observations to be made about audiences, they, too, resist essentializing (ask any actor!). Playwrights, however, are conscious of establishing a rapport with an audience, and the kind of codes which will maintain or threaten that rapport.

31. Thomas E. Yingling, *Hart Crane and the Homosexual Text: New Thresholds, New Anatomies* (Chicago: University of Chicago Press, 1990), 34.

32. At a student production at Duke University in 1992, Paul's monologue earned a nightly ovation. Not surprisingly, the actor who played Paul found the audience reward for his nightly display of shame disconcerting.

33. David Wojnarowicz, *Close to the Knives: A Memoir of Disintegration* (New York: Vintage, 1991), 114.

34. Paul Vogel, *The Baltimore Waltz* (Garden City, N.Y.: The Fireside Theatre, 1992). Further references to the play are to this edition.

35. Yingling, *Hart Crane and the Homosexual Text*, 34.

36. Terrence McNally, *Lips Together, Teeth Apart* (New York; New American Library, 1992), 30. Further references to the play are to this edition.

 The play opened at the Manhattan Theatre Club on May 28, 1991. The production, directed by John Tillinger, featured Swoozie Kurtz (Sally), Nathan Lane (Sam), Anthony Heald (John), and Christine Baranski (Chloe). It subsequently moved to the Lucille Lortel Theater for a long run.

37. It is interesting to note the stereotype that gay men are better looking than heterosexual men. During the 1992 presidential campaign, comedians joked about Ross Perot's assertion that if he were elected president, he would not allow homosexuals on his cabinet. Michael Feldman, on American Public Radio's "What Do Ya Know?" quipped "Ross Perot is so good looking I was sure he was gay."

38. Richard Dyer, "Believing in Fairies: the Author and the Homosexual," *Inside/Outside: Lesbian Theories/Gay Theories*, 188.

39. Judith Butler, "Imitation and Gender Insubordination," *Inside/Out: Lesbian Theories, Gay Theories*, 22–23.

40. David Savran: *Communists, Cowboys and Queers: The Politics of Masculinity in the Work of Arthur Miller and Tennessee Williams* (Minneapolis, University of Minnesota Press, 1992), 168. Savran's book contains a comprehensive, convincing treatment of Williams as a subversive gay author.

41. Tony Kushner, "Perestroika," Part II of *Angels in America*. I am deeply grateful to Tony Kushner for his generosity in letting me read and quote from the typescript of his play. Some more revisions may have ensued between the edition I read in April 1993, and the play that appears on Broadway and is published. Thanks, too, to Tony Kushner's agent, Joyce Ketay, and to Mr. Kushner's and my mutual friend, the ever generous Ariel Dorfman, for their assistance. Further references to this version of "Perestroika" will be indicated by P.

42. Tony Kushner, *Angels in America: A Gay Fantasia on National Themes, Part I: The Millennium Approaches* (London: Nick Hern Books, 1992), 1. Further references to this edition will be indicated by M. *The Millennium Approaches* was also published in two parts in *American Theatre*, in the June and the July/August 1992 editions. Both parts are published in book form in America by Theatre Communications Group.

43. Roy Cohn is also the subject of the first half of Ron Vawter's brilliant one-man show, *Roy Cohen/Jack Smith*. For the first half of this show, Gary Indiana has fabricated an anti-gay-rights speech Cohn is supposed to have given in 1978. Cohn took a male date to the speech.

44. Quoted in John Lahr, "Beyond Nelly" [review of the Los Angeles production of *Angels in America*], *The New Yorker* (November 23, 1992), 127–28.

45. Interview with Tony Kushner in *Royal National Theatre Platform Papers 2: On Angels in America* (London: Royal National Theatre Bookshop, 1992), 11.

46. Quoted in John Lahr, "Beyond Nelly," *The New Yorker* (November 23, 1992), 129.

8: LOVING COMMUNITIES?

1. James Collard, "Sex in the City," *Out*, Issue 73 (December, 1999), p. 60.

2. McNally, Terrence. *Love! Valour! Compassion!* and *A Perfect Ganesh* (New York: Plume, 1995), p. xii. Further references are to this text. The play opened at the Manhattan Theatre Club in November 1994, directed by Joe Mantello. In January 1995, it transferred to the Walter Kerr Theatre. The film, directed by Mantello and featuring most of the original cast (Jason Alexander replaced Nathan Lane), was released in 1997. An earlier version of this discussion was published as "Where We Are Now: *Love! Valour! Compassion!* and Contemporary Gay Drama," in *Terrence McNally: A Casebook,* ed. Toby Silverman Zinman (New York: Garland, 1997), pp. 95–166.

3. Some might say that Louis Ironson goes through equal conflict and crisis. Actually Louis makes his decision to leave Prior early in the play and spends the rest of it punishing himself and others for his decision. I am aware that my critique of *Angels in America* in this chapter contradicts what I said a few pages before. Five years have passed and I have seen and read the play many more times.

4. *Angels in America* is typical of many gay cultural productions in its demonizing of Republicans. While I await the Republican Party's disavowal on the gay bashing endemic to its right wing, I am increasingly skeptical of the Democratic Party's supposed monopoly on social justice.

5. Alexander Doty, *Making Things Perfectly Queer: Interpreting Mass Culture* (Minneapolis: University of Minnesota Press, 1993), p. xiv.

6. Eve Kosofsky Sedgwick, *Tendencies* (Durham, N.C.: Duke, 1993), p. 8.

7. Sedgwick, *Tendencies*, p. 9.

8.   Lee Siegel, "Literary License," *The New Republic* (November 9, 1998), p. 34.

9.   *A Place at the Table* is an eloquent argument for gay rights, but also an attack on the gay left. Bawer argues, in a rather prissy way, for assimilation into mainstream society. *The Advocate* is the national gay news magazine. *Out* is the leading glossy gay magazine. Totally consumer oriented, *Out* is one of those magazines in which you can't tell the difference between the copy and the ads.

10. Leo Bersani, *Homos* (Cambridge, MA: Harvard, 1995), p. 66.

11. *Homos,* p. 68.

12. John Weir, "Going In" in Mark Simpson, ed., *Anti-Gay* (London: Freedom Editions, 1996), pp. 32–33.

13. Carol Rosen, "Terrence McNally: The *TheaterWeek* Interview," *TheaterWeek* February 27 1995), pp. 12–24.

14. Rosen, p. 21.

15. Kath Weston, *Families We Choose: Lesbians, Gays, Kinship* (New York: Columbia, 1991), p. 109.

16. Quoted in Rosen, pp. 22–23.

17. Toby Silverman Zinman, "The Muses of Terrence McNally," *American Theatre* (March 1995), p. 15.

18. *My Night With Reg* opened at the Royal Court Theatre in London in March 1994, directed by Ian Rickson. It opened at the Criterion Theatre in November 1994 and was later transferred, with a new cast, to the Playhouse Theatre in June 1995.

19. Kevin Elyot, *My Night with Reg* (London: Nick Hern Books, 1994), p. 26.

20. Kevin Elyot, *The Day I Stood Still* (London: Nick Hern Books, 1998), pp. 56–57. Further references to this play are to this edition. The play opened at the Royal National Theatre Cottesloe Theatre in January 1998, directed by Ian Rickson, featuring Adrian Scarborough as Horace.

21. Gray is an ostensibly straight British playwright whose major work through the seventies and eighties tended to focus on unhappy middle-aged straight men who were obsessed with adolescent loving relationships with other men. His plays include *Butley* and *Otherwise Engaged.* See my essay " 'Being Took Queer': Homosexuality in Simon Gray's Plays," in *Simon Gray: A Casebook,* ed. Katherine Burkman (New York: Garland Press, 1992), pp. 61–84.

22. Terrence McNally, *Corpus Christi* (New York: Grove Press, 1999), p. 75. The play opened at the Manhattan Theatre Club in New York in October 1998, directed by Joe Mantello.

23. Mark Simpson, "Gay Dream Believer," in *Anti-gay,* p. 5.

24. Jim Grimsley's *The Lizard of Tarsus* (1990) is a more poetic, challenging play about Jesus, who has returned to earth in a mythical present and has been imprisoned by Paul. Like Dostoevsky's "Grand Inquisitor" chapter of *The Brothers Karantazov,* Grimsley's play is basically a dialogue between Jesus and a believer who also plans to crucify him again. The play acknowledges, but does not focus on Jesus's relationship with his beloved disciple John: "We were very close."

       Paul Rudnick's *The Most Fabulous Story Ever Told,* which opened at the New York Theatre Workshop in December 1998, is an hilarious burlesque of the Old Testament from a flamboyantly gay point of view.

9: LOVE AND WAR: GAY DRAMA AT THE TURN OF THE CENTURY

1. Naomi Wallace, Author's Introduction to *In the Heart of America,* in *Staging Gay Lives: An Anthology of Contemporary Gay Theater,* ed. John M. Clum (Boulder, CO.: Westview, 1996), p. 427.

2. Andrew Alty, *Something About Us.* Unpublished typescript courtesy of the playwright, p. 25. Further references are to this edition. The play opened at the Lyric Hammersmith Studio in June 1995.

3. Samuel Adamson, *Clocks and Whistles* (Charlbury, UK: Amber Lane Press, 1996), p. 30. Further references are to this text. *Clocks and Whistles* opened at the Bush Theatre, London in April 1996, directed by Dominic Dromgoole. The production featured John Light, Neil Stuke, Kate Beckinsale, and Michael Cashman as Henry, Trevor, Anne, and Alec.

4. Chay Yew, *Porcelain and A Language of Their Own: Two Plays by Chay Yew* (New York: Grove Press, 1997), p. 216. Further references are to this edition. *A Language of Their Own* opened at the New York Public Theatre in April 1995. The production was directed by Ong Keng Sen and featured Francis Jue, B. D. Wong, Alec Mapa, and David Drake as Oscar, Ming, Daniel, and Robert.

5. Frank Chin, Introduction to *Aiiieeeee!* (Garden City, N.Y.: Doubleday Anchor, 1975), pp. 35–36.

6. Steve Murray, *Rescue and Recovery* (unpublished mss., 1999). All further references are to this edition. Thanks to Steve Murray for providing the script. *Rescue and Recovery* had its premiere at Atlanta's Actors' Express in July 1999, and had an unprecedented five month sellout run. At the time of this writing, it is slated for an Off-Broadway production. The original production was directed by Chris Coleman.

7. Joe Calarco "adapted" and directed *A Midsummer Night's Dream* for the Shakespeare Theater in Washington, D.C. in November 1999. Unlike his *R & J,* the *Dream* used traditional gender casting. Nevertheless, Calarco queered the play by placing the audience's scopular focus on the bodies of Oberon, Demetrius, and Lysander. The young male lovers got progressively undressed during the production (their female counterparts remained dressed), and the audience was teased with the idea that Lysander would lose his designer briefs. Oberon appeared nude throughout the "ballet" that opened the second half while Titania remained fully clothed. This dream was a celebration of the male body.

8. Joe Calarco, *Shakespeare's R & J* (unpublished typescript, 1998). Thanks to Joe Calarco and his agent, Nicole Graham, for getting me this script. The play opened at Expanded Arts, Inc., New York City, in September 1997, with Greg Shamie and Daniel J. Shore as the star-crossed lovers. The production moved to the John Houseman Studio Theatre in January 1998, where it ran for a year.

9. D. M. W. Greer, *Burning Blue* (London: Oberon Books, 1995), p. 101. The original production, directed by John Hickok, opened at the Kings Head Theatre, London, in March 1995. It transferred to the Theatre Royal, Haymarket, London that July.

10. Greer, *Burning Blue,* p. 82.

11. Author's Introduction to *In the Heart of America,* in John M. Clum, ed., *Staging Gay Lives* (Boulder, CO.: Westview Press, 1996), pp. 427–28. References to the text of the play are to this edition. The premiere was at the Bush Theatre, London in August 1994, directed by Dominic Dromgoole and starring Zubin Varla and Richard Dormer.

12. Neal Bell, *Somewhere in the Pacific* (unpublished manuscript, 1999), p. 66. First produced at Manbites Dog Theatre, Durham, N.C., February 1999. Further references are to this version. The production was directed by Jody McAuliffe and featured Adam Saunders, Adam Smith, Peter Gail, Derrick Ivey, Eamonn Farrell, and David Ring. Thanks to Neal Bell for providing a copy of the script.

13. Oliver Mayer, *Blade to the Heat* (New York: Dramatists Play Service, 1994), p. 32. Further references are to this text. The production, directed by George C. Wolfe, opened at the New York Public Theatre in November 1994.

14. Guillermo Reyes, *Deporting the Divas* (unpublished mss., 1996, rev. 1998), p. 3. Thanks to the playwright for providing this script. Further references to this play are to this manuscript. *Deporting the Divas* had its 1996 premiere at the Celebration Theater, Los Angeles, directed by Jorge Huerta, with Julian Vicente as Michael.

ANNOTATED LIST OF RESOURCES

Rather than offering a bibliography that repeats information on primary and secondary material offered in the endnotes, I present below a selective, annotated reading list of published gay drama, as well as information on other bibliographical resources. An asterisk (*) denotes that the play is discussed in this book.

Anthologies

Berman, Ed. *Homosexual Acts: A Volume of Gay Plays.* London: Inter-Action Imprint, 1975.

Clum, John M. *Staging Gay Lives: An Anthology of Gay Drama.* Boulder, Colo.: Westview, 1996.

Feingold, Michael, ed. *Grove New American Theatre.* New York: Grove Press, 1993. The majority of plays in this anthology are gay plays.

Gay Plays: An International Anthology. New York: Ubu Repertory Theatre Publications, 1989.

Helbing, Terry, ed. *Gay and Lesbian Plays Today.* Portsmouth, N.H.: Heinemann, 1993.

Hoffman, William M. *Gay Plays: The First Collection.* New York: Avon, 1979.

Hughes, Holly, and Román, David. *O Solo Homo: The New Queer Performance.* New York: Grove Press, 1998.

Lane, Eric, and Shengold, Nina. *The Actor's Book of Gay and Lesbian Plays.* New York: Penguin, 1995.

Osborn, M. Elizabeth, ed. *The Way We Live Now: American Plays and the AIDS Crisis.* New York: Theatre Communications Group, 1990.

Osment, Philip. *Gay Sweatshop: Four Plays and a Company.* London: Methuen, 1989. Containing Osment's superb essay on the history of London's Gay Sweatshop.

Senelick, Laurence, *Lovesick: Modernist Plays of Same-sex Love.* London: Routledge, 1999.

Wallace, Robert, ed. *Making, Out: Plays by Gay Men.* Toronto: Coach House Press, 1992. Contemporary Canadian gay drama.

Wilcox, Michael, ed. *Gay Plays.* London: Methuen, 1984.

———. *Gay Plays: Volume Two.* London: Methuen, 1985.

———. *Gay Plays: Volume Three.* London: Methuen, 1988.

———. *Gay Plays: Volume Four.* London: Methuen, 1990.

Shewey, Don, ed. *Out Front: Contemporary Gay and Lesbian Plays.* New York: Grove Weidenfeld, 1988.

V = a film or television version is available on video.

unpub = unpublished at time of my writing. Thanks to the playwrights and their agents for providing me with a typescript.

Plays

A selective reading list of published plays which form a gay dramatic canon. Versions listed are those most easily obtainable (hard cover first editions of plays discussed in this text are listed in the endnotes). If the work appears in one or more of the anthologies listed above, the anthologized version is noted. I also note video versions of the plays listed.

Ackerley, J. R. *The Prisoners of War* (in Wilcox, vol. 3). Revived successfully in London in 1993, this 1925 play is the first modern English play to deal openly and positively with homosexuality. The setting is a Swiss hotel in which a group of wounded soldiers are interned during World War I.*

Adamson, Samuel. *Clocks and Whistles.* Charlbury, England: Amber Lane Press, 1996.*

———. *Grace Note.* Charlbury, England: Amber Lane Press, 1997. Two plays about monster mothers and their families opened in London the same month; Adamson's play at the Old Vic and David Hare's *Amy's View,* at the National. Both starred distinguished British actresses (Geraldine MacEwen in the Adamson and Judi Dench in the Hare). While Adamson's was the better play, the Hare opened first and had a more elaborate production and better promotion. Here a mother, suffering from the first stages of Alzheimer's, still reigns over her family, including a gay son.

Albee, Edward. *The American Dream, The Zoo Story, Who's Afraid of Virginia Woolf, Selected Plays of Edward Albee.* Garden City: Nelson Doubleday, 1987.*

———. *Three Tall Women.* New York: Dutton, 1994. Albee's first commercial success in three decades, this play about four stages in the experience of a woman (ages twenty-six, fifty-two, ninety-two, and at the moment of death) is a grand vehicle for actresses. Like many of Albee's earlier works, death is the focus. The only male role is the silent, gay son, the object of his mother's wrath.

———. *Tiny Alice.* New York: Atheneum, 1965.

Anderson, Robert. *Tea and Sympathy: Famous American Plays of the 1950s.* New York: Dell, 1962.*

Baraka, Imamu Amiri (LeRoi Jones). *The Baptism and The Toilet.* New York: Grove, 1967. Baraka's vision of racial hatred among young men set against homosexual desire.

Baron, Jeff, *Visiting Mr. Green.* New York: Stage and Screen, 1998. This could have been a formulaic play the sort of thing one might see on television, had it not been written by a gay writer who has much in common with his protagonist, a young gay, Jewish executive who, as court-decreed community service has to visit and care for the elderly Jewish man he almost runs over. A lovely play about intergenerational friendship.

Bartlett, Neil. *A Vision of Love Revealed in Sleep* (in Wilcox, vol. 4). Bartlett, distinguished translator, novelist, playwright, and director, creates—with the collaboration of composer Nicholas Bloomfield—unique, sophisticated musical theater pieces that are collages of high culture celebrating an old fashioned notion of the "gay sensibility." Detractors dismiss Bartlett/Broomfield collaborations as outdated high camp. Those of us who admire them find them powerful, stimulating theatrical extravaganzas, using elements of nineteenth-century culture to define contemporary gender and sexual identity. *A Vision . . .* is a theatrical version of a prose poem by Victorian painter Simeon Solomon. Bartlett and Bloomfield's *Sarrasine* (1990), is discussed in the text.

Beane, Douglas Carter, *As Bees in Honey Drown.* Garden City, NY: Stage & Screen, 1997. A terrifically entertaining play that is bound to be a movie. A grand con woman seduces, in every possible way, a callow, gay, would-be novelist. The grand Alexa Vere de Vere is one of the best roles for a young actress in years.

Bennett, Alan. *Single Spies and Talking Heads.* New York: Summit Books, 1990. *Single Spies* comprises two one-act plays offering bittersweet portraits of British spies Anthony Blount and Guy Burgess.

Bentley, Eric. *Round 2* (in Wilcox, vol. 4). A New York gay version of Viennese playwright Artur Schnitzler's comedy of sexual manners, *La Ronde.*

Bourne, Bette, Peggy Shaw, Paul Shaw, and Lois Weaver. *Belle Reprieve* (in Helbing). A collaboration of the lesbian group, Split Britches, and the gay troupe, Bloolips. An imaginative, gender-bent set of variations on the characters in *A Streetcar Named Desire.*

Bowne, Alan, *Forty Deuce.* New York: Sea Horse Press, 1981. A Grim, realistic picture of the life of teenage street hustlers around Times Square.

Brecht, Bertolt. *Baal* and *The Life of Edward the Second of England.* trans. William E. Smith and Ralph Manheim. *The Collected Plays of Bertolt Brecht*: Volume I. New York: Vintage, 1971.

Baal is an early play in which the anti-hero's homosexuality underscores his outsider status. Brecht's free adaptation of Marlowe's *Edward II* loses the eloquence of the original, but is a gritty, powerful variation. Gaveston is definitely the commoner the barons describe.

Bumbalo, Victor: *Adam and the Experts*. New York: Broadway Play Publishing, 1990.

———. *Niagara Falls and Other Plays*. New York: Calamus Books, 1984. *Niagara Falls* is a truly funny pair of one acters about an upstate New York Italian American family's response to the homosexuality of the son, from his father's disapproval to his newly married sister's envy of what strikes her as a charmed life.

———. *Tell* (in Helbing). In the spirit of Robert *Chesley's Jerker, Tell* consists of two masturbatory fantasies told to a hospitalized AIDS patient; the first by a male visitor, the second by a nurse. A celebration of the continued life of the erotic imagination.

Busch, Charles. *Four Plays*. Garden City: Fireside Theatre, 1990. Busch is a lover of camp low culture—fifties beach movies and B horror films—but his theater pieces are more than spoofs of what is already funny. They send up gender stereotypes in complex ways. The collection includes the long-running *Vampire Lesbians of Sodom*.

———. *Three Plays by Charles Busch*. New York: Fireside Theatre, 1993. Three extravaganzas Busch wrote for the Limbo Lounge.

———. *You Should Be So Lucky*. New York: Fireside Theatre, 1994. A more conventional play than Busch's usual cross-dressing extravaganzas, a vehicle for Busch to play the male lead. Christopher is a Greenwich Village electrologist who finds himself with an a fairy godmother in the person of an elderly Jewish businessman. This is a gay version of the kind of commercial comedy that was the meat and potatoes of Broadway fifty years ago, now as archaic a form as the Hollywood B movies Busch usually celebrates.

Chesley, Robert. *Hard Plays/ Stiff Parts: The Homoerotic Plays of Robert Chesley (Night Sweat, Jerker, Dog Plays)*. San Francisco: Alamo Square Press, 1990.*

———. *Jerker, or the Helping Hand*. (in Shewey).*

———. *Stray Dog Story*. New York: JH Press, 1984.

Churchill, Caryl. *Cloud Nine* (New York version). New York: Methuen, 1984. An important mixture of feminism and gay politics often performed in professional and university theaters, though now its politics have been dated by AIDS. An American version, directed by Tommy Tune, was a long run Off-Broadway success.

Clum. John M. *Randy's House* (in Clum). A response to the 1993 Cobb County, Georgia, anti-gay referendum. A gay household and conservative Southern household are brought together by the relationship of two teenage boys.

Coward, Noel. *Design for Living, Coward Plays: Three*. London: Methuen, 1979.*

Cristofer, Michael. *The Shadow Box*. New York: Avon, 1977. An often produced story of inmates of a cancer hospice and their loved ones, featuring a gay writer, his dreary male lover and his lively, feckless ex-wife. Soap opera drivel, which merely switches the stereotypes of flighty gay male and devoted wife.

Crowley, Mart: *The Boys in the Band*. New York: Farrar, Straus, and Giroux, 1968. The film version is still available on video.*

Demchuk, David. *Touch: A Play for Two* (in Wallace). Two nude men discuss pornography. An interesting dramatic conflict between active erotic imagination and commitment to a relationship.

Dietz, Stephen, *Lonely Planet* (in Lane and Shengold). A lovely, poetic play about the effects of AIDS on two friends, but the play's virtue is in its indirection. It's a contemporary version of Ionesco's *The Chairs*.

Drake, David. *The Night Larry Kramer Kissed Me*. New York: Doubleday Anchor, 1994. The text of Drake's solo show, a series of monologues on aspects of gay life from gay bashing to gym culture.

Durang, Christopher. *Christopher Durang Explains It All For You*. New York: Grove Weidenfeld, 1983. A collection of Durang's early plays, including *Beyond Therapy* and *Sister Mary Ignatius Explains It All For You*. Brilliant satires on the forces of heterosexism. There is an awful film version of *Beyond Therapy* available on video.

———. *Laughing Wild*, in *Baby With the Bathwater* and *Laughing Wild*. New York: Grove Weidenfeld, 1988. Two of Durang's funniest plays. *Laughing Wild* contains a highly personal monologue that offers Durang's takes on homophobia and the idea of AIDS as God's retribution. The final essays explain why this gifted playwright hasn't written much recently.

———. *Complete Full-Length Plays, 1975–1995.* Lyme, NH: Smith & Kraus, 1997.

———. *Twenty-seven Short Plays.* Lyme, NH: Smith and Kraus, 1995.

Durang hasn't been writing as much in recent years, but these volumes attests to his talent as a satirist. The plays remain hilarious, particularly *Beyond Therapy* and *Laughing Wild* in the volume of full-length plays and his classic send up of *The Glass Menagerie,* "For Whom the Southern Belle Tolls" in the collection of short pieces. The volume of short pieces is often the basis of evenings of Durang one-acts.

Eagleton, Terry. *Saint Oscar.* London: Field Day, 1989. The most recent Oscar Wilde play, by a famous literary critic. Eagleton is less interested in seeing Wilde as a martyr than in understanding the connections between Wilde's politics and his behavior.

Elyot, Kevin. *Coming Clean.* London: Faber, 1984. British comedy about what happens when a gay couple hires a houseboy.

Fierstein, Harvey. *Forget Him* (in Shewey)

———. *Safe Sex.* New York: Atheneum, 1987.* There is a video of the third, weakest play of the trilogy, "On Tidy Endings," with Fierstein and Stockard Channing.

———. *Torch Song Trilogy.* New York: Gay Presses of New York, 1980.* The film version is available on video.

Finn, William. *The Marvin Songs* ("In Trousers," "March of the Falsettos," "Falsettoland"). Garden City: Fireside Theatre, 1991.* The original cast albums of "March of the Falsettos" and "Falsettoland" are available on CD.

Fraser, Brad. *Poor Superman.* Edmonton, NEWest Press, 1995. Another dark Fraser play, this time with projected captions like the Superman comics the male characters love. An artist who is going through a fallow period finds his muse in a young, married restaurateur. Such a simple recounting belies the power of Fraser's play about people on the outside of conventional society.

———. *Unidentified Human Remains and the True Nature of Love.* Winnipeg: Blizzard Publishing, 1988. One of the most produced Canadian plays. Written by a gay Albertan, this provocative dramatic meditation on love and violence has inspired critical controversy. (V)

Gellert, Roger. *Quaint Honor* (in Wilcox 2). 1958 pioneering English play about schoolboy romance.

Genet, Jean. *The Maids and Deathwatch.* Translated by Bernard Frechtman. New York: Grove, 1954. *Deathwatch* is Genet's only play with gay characters.

Gide, Andrew. *Saul in My Theatre: Five Plays and an Essay.* New York: Knopf, 1952. Written in 1896, first published in 1906 and produced in 1923, this is one of the first modern plays to deal openly with homosexual love. Beautifully, sensually written, *Saul* dramatizes a triangle of the ill-fated King Saul; his son, Jonathan; and the heroic future King, David, who must choose his destiny over his love for the frail Jonathan.

Gilbert, Sky. *Capote at Yaddo: A Very Gay Little Musical* (in Wallace). Sky Gilbert, drag artist and playwright, is one of the luminaries of the Toronto gay theater community. This is a musical depiction of life among the semi-closeted gay literati in the 1940s, focussing on the brief relationship of young Capote and a distinguished American critic, Newton Arvin (who would later be a victim of anti-gay witchhunts).

Gill, Peter. *Certain Young Men,* London: Faber & Faber, 1999. Produced at London's prestigious Almeida Theatre with a starry cast, Gill's play is an extension of his early one act, *In the Blue,* Like much of Gill's work, this is an elegant, beautifully written interweaving series of non-connections. Like many of his British peers. Gill does not seem to believe in the possibility of gay relationships. His editorializing sounds like a number of "post-gay British writers": "That's gay culture. That's about the size of it. Don't laugh. The make of your underpants" (p. 53).

———. *Mean Tears and In the Blue.* Birmingham, England: Oberon, 1987. *Mean Tears* is a powerful depiction of a gay version of co-dependency. The one-act *In the Blue* is a celebrated series of variations on the beginning and end of a gay relationship.

Godfrey, Paul. *Once in a While the Odd Thing Happens.* London: Methuen, 1990.*(V)

Gray, Simon. *Butley, Plays: One.* London: Methuen, 1986. The witty depiction of an English professor who cannot cope with homo- or heterosexual relationships. Most of Gray's plays involve at least one homosexual character, reflecting Gray's mixed feelings about homosexuality.

Green, Julian. *South.* New York: Marion Boyars, 1991. Produced in France in 1953, this is a modern Racinian tragedy of fate and disastrous love, in this case the sudden, unrequited passion a young Polish-born Union army officer feels for a puritanical Confederate officer on the eve of the Civil War. Born in 1900 in Paris of American parents and educated at the University of Virginia, Green returned to Paris and became one of France's most celebrated novelists. He was a close friend of Andre Gide and, like Gide, wrote volumes of candid memoirs. This translation, by Green, was produced in London in 1955 under the direction of the young Peter Hall with Denholm Elliott in the cast.

Greenberg, Richard. *The American Plan* (in Feingold). Underrated by the New York critics, this is a Jamesean (Feingold says Chekhovian, and he's right too) picture of a complex network of characters: a very American young man visiting a posh northeastern lakeside resort in the 1950s, the deeply neurotic young woman he meets and thinks he loves, her worldly, dominating mother, and his opportunistic male lover. A complex picture of innocence and experience, sincerity and deceit.

———. *Eastern Standard.* New York: Grove Weidenfeld, 1989.*

Greenspan, David. *Dead Mother, Or Shirley Not All in Vain* (in Feingold). It begins with a character concerned about the plethora of gay characters on the stage and moves from there into a bizarre theatrical foray in which six actors play a range of characters from Jewish mothers embodied in their gay sons to Prometheus and Alice B. Toklas.

Greer, D. M. W. *Burning Blue.* London: Oberon Books, 1995.*

Greig, Noel. *The Dear Love of Comrades: Two Gay Sweatshop Plays.* London: Gay Men's Press, 1981 (also in Osment).*

———. and Griffiths, Drew. *As Time Goes By: Two Gay Sweatshop Plays.* London: Gay Men's Press, 1981.*

Grimsley, Jim. *Mr. Universe and Other Plays.* Chapel Hill, N.C.: Algonquin Books, 1998. Jim Grimsley is writer in residence at Steve Stages in Atlanta and a distinguished novelist. His plays are *sui generis*, surreal, constantly surprising, but always provocative. *Math and Aftermath,* for instance, takes place in 1943 on the Bikini Atoll in the Pacific the day before the United States sets off a test blast of a hydrogen bomb. There, a gay porn film is being made. In typical Grimsley fashion "distortions in the fabric of space-time" have the action going backward and forward, sometimes simultaneously. The clearest influence on Grimsley's work seems to be the young work of Sam Shepard, but with more intellectual sophistication.

Guare, John. *Six Degrees of Separation.* New York: Vintage, 1990.* (V)

Hall, Richard. *Three Plays for a Gay Theater.* San Francisco: Grey Fox Press, 1983. Contains Hall's important essays on gay drama.

Hamilton, Godfrey, *Kissing Marianne,* In Clum

———. *Road Movie.* (unpublished) Godfrey Hamilton is the writer half of Starving Artists Theatre Company. He writes plays for his artistic and life partner, actor Mark Pinkosh. Though they are now based in Los Angeles, Londoner Hamilton and American Pinkosh have had more success in England and Scotland. Hamilton's plays are poetic, elegiac works of love and loss. *Kissing Marianne,* which depicts the reunion of two brothers after thirteen years, asks how the metaphor of brotherhood, or, more specifically, incest, defines the emotional and spiritual intensity of gay relationships. *Road Movie,* in which the virtuosic Pinkosh plays all the parts, depicts a young gay man's travels across America and his love for a free-spirited Californian.

Hampton, Christopher. *Total Eclipse.* London: Faber, 1969.*

Hare, David. *The Judas Kiss.* New York: Grove Press, 1998. Both Tom Stoppard and David Hare, distinguished middle-aged heterosexual British playwrights, took on Victorian homosexual love in 1998. The first act of Hare's play about the relationship of Oscar Wilde to his beloved Bosie takes place in the hour before the police arrive to arrest Wilde for gross indecency. Hare offers a sensible, convincing interpretation of why Wilde did not leave for France: "If I run now, my story is finished. For as long as I stay it is not at an end. I prefer my story unfinished." The second act depicts Bosie leaving Wilde in 1897 to return to his family and their fortune. Hare's Wilde is devotedly in love with a most unworthy object and Bosie's aristocracy seems to be the reason for his many faults.

Harvey, Jonathan. I like the way Harvey sets his gay characters in a wider social context. His straight folk are as lonely, eccentric, and randy as his gay men. The plays show the commonality of straights and gays in carefully observed urban environments, from council estates to Kentish Town flats. The plays vary wildly in quality, but are always entertaining.

——, *Babies*. London: Methuen/Royal Court, 1994. Former schoolteacher Harvey writes of a young schoolteacher who goes to a student's birthday party and finds himself chased by her mother and tied up by her uncle. Sweet, funny, lightweight.

——, *Rupert Street Lonely Hearts Club and Boom Bang-a-Bang*. London: Methuen, 1995. Two parties from hell. *Boom Bang-a Bang,* the better of the two plays, take place when friends gather for the televising of the Eurovision song contest, as camp a spectacle as television offers. By the end even the television has exploded

——, *Hushabye Mountain*. London: Methuen, 1999. *Hushabye Mountain* is Harvey's AIDS fantasia and coming to terms with grief over losing a loved one with the help of family, friends, drugs, Judy Garland, and Mary Poppins.

Herbert, John. *Fortune and Men's Eyes*. New York: Grove 1967. Sex and power among teenagers in prison. A much performed play (even made into a poorish film, available on video) by a major Canadian playwright.

Hoffman, William M. *As Is* (in Shewey and Osborn).* There is a lugubrious video version, well acted but directed too heavily.

——. and Holland, Anthony. *Cornbury: The Queen's Governor* (in Hoffman). A mix of history and theatrical fantasy centering on the transvestite colonial governor of New York.

Inge, William. *The Boy in the Basement*, and *The Tiny Closet, Summer Brave and Eleven Short Plays*. New York: Random House, 1962.*

Innaurato, Albert. *Best Plays of Albert Innaurato*. New York: Gay Presses of New York, 1987. Contains *Gemini*, Innaurato's long-run play about a Harvard graduate in the throes of homosexual panic, and *Coming of Age in Soho*.*

Jonson, Ben. *Epicoene, or The Silent Woman*.* Available in a number of editions of Jonson's plays. The RSC text, published by Methuen (1989), contains Simon Trussler's insightful essays.

Katz, Jonathan. *Coming Out*. New York: ARNO, 1975. A docudrama of gay and lesbian history and historical figures by the author/compiler of the essential reference volume, *Gay American History*.

Kaufman, Moises. *Gross Indecency: The Three Trails of Oscar Wilde*. New York: Vintage, 1998. Another play about Oscar Wilde, but this one, particularly in Kaufman's New York production, is an original work of theater. Kaufman is a disciple of the German director Erwin Piscator, the precursor of Brecht's epic theater and the agitprop pieces the Federal Theatre produced in the 1930s. Each act is presented in a different style, from docudrama in Act I to something verging on expressionism in Act III. Here Wilde's significance as the first public figure to be defined by his homosexual acts is explored.

Kearns, Michael. *Intimacies/More Intimacies* (in Helbing). Monologues of a varied group of people with AIDS.

Killingworth, Gerald. *Days of Cavafy* (in Wilcox 4). A presentation of scenes from the everyday life of the great poet.

Kirby, Andy. *Compromised Immunity* (in Osment).*

Kondoleon, Harry. *The Fairy Garden* (in Shewey). Kondoleon is something of a surrealist, building gentle, dream-like fantasies out of domestic situations. A playwright who cannot be properly appreciated without seeing his work.

——. *Zero Positive* (in *The Way We Live Now*). Kondoleon's whimsical comedy about AIDS and death manages to stay this side of cloying and to be genuinely affirming.

Kramer, Larry. *The Destiny of Me*. New York: NAL Dutton, 1993.*

——. *Just Say No*. New York: St. Martins, 1989.*

——. *The Normal Heart*. New York: New American Library, 1985.*

Kushner, Tony. *Angels in America, Part One: The Millennium Approaches*. New York: Theatre Communication Group, 1993.*

———. *Angels in America, Part Two: Perestroika*. New York: Theatre Communications Group, 1993.*

Lorca, Federico Garcia. *The Public and Play Without a Title*. New York: New Directions, 1983. *The Public* is Lorca's only gay play.

Lucas, Craig. *Prelude to a Kiss*. New York: Dutton, 1990. The hit comedy by the openly gay playwright-filmmaker (*Longtime Companions*). An example of contemporary "closet drama," the fantasy depicts a body switch of a bride and elderly man at a wedding reception, and the ensuing problems for the groom. Made into a film which is available on video. (V)

———. *What I Meant Was: New Plays and Selected One Acts*. New York: Theatre Communications Group, 1999. Lucas gets more and more interesting, now combining his theatrical experimentation with dark satire (though the darkness was already there in work like *Reckless*.) Includes *The Dying Gaul,* Lucas's most powerful, angry play thus far, part satire on Hollywood, part sex triangle. A young writer is seduced by a powerful, bisexual Hollywood producer, who sums up Hollywood's attitude about gay sex: "You can do anything you want. As long as you don't call it what it is." The producer's wife, as amoral in her own way as is her husband, finds a unique way to get close to her husband's new lover—she contacts him on the Internet, posing as his deceased lover. The ending loses credibility, but the first three-quarters of the work are scathing Jonsonian satire. Lucas dedicates his play to Tony Kushner, but he is less compromising than his dedicatee.

Ludlam, Charles. *The Complete Plays*. New York: Harper and Row, 1989. Ludlam's plays, like those of Charles Busch, must be seen to be appreciated, but the volume at least is a record of his many scripts.

MacDonald, Robert David. *Chinchilla and Webster, Three Plays by Robert David MacDonald*. London: Oberon Books, 1991. Two backstage dramas about sexual and theatrical politics. *Chinchilla* depicts a Diaghalev-like impressario. *Webster* is a rather fantastic, but vibrant, portrait of the great Jacobean dramatist who, in MacDonald's play, had a craving for boy actors (the boys make Eve Harrington seem self-sacrificing). A vivid conjectural picture of backstage life in a Jacobean playhouse.

Mann, Emily. *The Execution of Justice* (in Shewey). Docudrama about trial of Dan White for murdering Harvey Milk and Mayor George Moscone. One wishes for a bit more imagination. Overshadowed by the film documentary *The Times of Harvey Milk*.

Mason, Timothy. *Bearclaw* (in Wilcox 2). Well-crafted play about the relationship of a gay Native American nursing home orderly with "difficult" senior citizen.

———. *Levitation* (in Wilcox 3). Begins as a classic American back-porch drama, but gently and effectively becomes more poetic. What Thornton Wilder might have written if he could deal with his homosexuality.

McGuiness, Frank. *The Carthaginians*. London: Faber, 1989. Five people, including a flamboyant queen, occupy a Derry graveyard.

———. *Innocence: The Life and Death of Michelangelo Merisi, Caravaggio*. London: Faber, 1987.

McPherson, Scott. *Marvin's Room*. New York: NAL Plume, 1992. A funny, touching, humane play about a dysfunctional family coming together in the face of illness. Not on the surface a gay play or an AIDS play, the published script is converted into an AIDS text by the morbid, graphic introduction by Larry Kramer and foreword by the late Scott McPherson.

McNally, Terrence. "Andre's Mother" (in *The Way We Live Now*).* Has been presented on television.

———. *Corpus Christi*. New York: Grove/Atlantic, 1999.*

———. *Lips Together, Teeth Apart*. New York: New American Library, 1992.*

———. *The Ritz and Other Plays*. McNally's bathhouse farce in a volume with his early plays. Though it is a bit slow, Richard Lester's film of *The Ritz* (available on video) does have the original cast and gives a better sense of the play than reading the script will.

———. *Three Plays*. New York: New American Library, 1990. Includes the revised version of *The Lisbon Traviata** (original version in Shewey) and McNally's hit play, *Frankie and Johnny in the Claire de Lune*.

———. *Love! Valour! Compassion!* (V) and *A Perfect Ganesh* New York: Plume, 1995.* *A Perfect Ganesh* is one of my favorites of McNally's plays. Two older women travel together to India. One is haunted by the violent, gay-bashing death of her son, whom she rejected. I see this, *Lips Together, Teeth Apart,* and *Love! Valour! Compassion!* as a trilogy. This play focusses on compassion and shares the theme of mortality with the others. The play is narrated by the Hindu god, Ganesha.

Mitchell, Julian. *Another Country*. Ambergate, Derbyshire: Amber Lane Press, 1982.* The film version, available on video is an enjoyable romance—quite different from the play. (V)

Morris, Sidney. *If This Isn't Love*. New York: JH Press, 1982. Popular romantic comedy about the vicissitudes of a gay couple over twenty-five years.

Morse, Carl. *Annunciation* (in Helbing). A clever playlet in which a gay angel, Michael, appears to a pregnant woman to announce that her son will be the one in ten to be gay. Mother-to-be isn't pleased.

Moss, Simon. *Cock-Ups*. London: Faber, 1984. An imaginative dramatization of the last days of Joe Orton and Kenneth Halliwell.

O'Hara, Robert, *Insurrection: Holding History*. Printed in *American Theatre* Volume 15, no. 2 (February, 1998). The play began as O'Hara's M. A. thesis project at Columbia and has since been produced by the Mark Taper Forum, the New York Public Theatre, and the American Conservatory Theatre. A contemporary gay black man travels back in time to a slave insurrection. A brilliant historical fantasia.

Orton, Joe. *The Complete Plays*. New York: Grove Weidenfeld, 1976.* *Entertaining Mr. Sloane* is included in Hoffman, but one should read all of Orton's plays. There are videos of the film versions of *Entertaining Mr. Sloane* and *Loot*.

Osborne, John. *A Patriot for Me*. London: Faber, 1965.*

Osment, Philip. *This Island's Mine*. A panoramic theater piece in Gay Sweatshop style. Scenes of gay life in England in the 1980s.

Pagan, Adrian, *The Backroom*. London: Bush Theatre Scripts, 1999. One of the few gay plays in London this past year, *The Backroom* depicts the "behind the scenes" conversations of a group of sex workers in an Earl's Court gay brothel. It's more sitcom than slice of life, but totally absorbing.

Patrick, Robert. *The Haunted Host*, (in *Homosexual Acts*).*

———. *Mercy Drop and Other Plays*. New York: Calamus, 1979.* A satire of tv's "This Is Your Life" turns into a dark satire on American values.

———. *T Shirts* (in Hoffman).* A biting satire on the emptiness of gay nonrelationships in the 1970s.

———. *Untold Decades: Seven Comedies of Gay Romance*. New York: St. Martins, 1988.

Pintauro, Joe. *Plays by Joe Pintauro*. New York: Broadway Play Publishing Company, 1989. The gay playlets in this collection also appear in Wilcox 4.

Pomo Afro Homos, *Dark fruit* (In Clum). Recently, the boundaries between performance and drama have become blurred, and some of the best gay writers and performers are doing performance work (lower budget, easier to tour). The comic or serious monologue was, in my youth, a staple of commercial theatrical fare in the hands of artists like Ruth Draper or Joyce Grenfell. Now, in a more politicized form, it's called "performance art." Pomo Afro Homos (postmodern African American homosexuals) was a superb trio of who toured the country offering their satiric scenes of African American gay life. Their material and performances were sharp, uncompromising, funny and often touching. *Dark Fruit,* the group's second collaboration, is a collection of eight brilliant sketches.

Rabe, David. *Streamers*. New York: Knopf, 1977.* Robert Altman's fine film version is available on video.

Ravenhill, Mark. *Shopping and Fucking*. London: Methuen, 1997. Ravenhill's play was a smash hit in London, where young people will fill a theater for a play that connects to their lives, but a total fizzle in New York. I felt that Ravenhill had written a better play than I saw in the inept London production. *Shopping and Fucking* is one of a number of dark, violent plays written by young British playwrights (Jez Butterworth's *Mojo* and the overrated works of the late Sarah Kane, the dramatic equivalent of obscene graffiti, are other examples). Ravenhill's world is one of self-hating young people whose relationships and fantasies are all of buying and selling. The central character, Mark, tells a fourteen-year-old hustler, "Because I thought if I pay then it won't mean anything." Meaning is not only lost; it is feared.

Reyes, Guillermo. *Men on the Verge of an His-panic Breakdown*. (In Clum).

———. *Deporting the Divas.** (unpublished) Born in Chile, educated in Washington, D.C., and now a Professor in Arizona, Reyes is the dramatic voice of Latino gays. *Men on the Verge . . . ,* a hit on both coasts, is a series of monologues about gay Latino men in America caught in a cultural and sexual nervous breakdown. From hustlers to restaurateurs to gay Republicans, his characters are survivors, but always confused, always in what Reyes calls "transcultural shock."

Shaffer, Peter. White Liars. New York: Stein and Day, 1967. Shaffer's only truly uncloseted gay-friendly play is the curtain raiser to the one-act *Black Comedy*, discussed in chapter 3. In *White Liars*, a young man, Frank, pays an old fortuneteller to give his flatmate and friend, Tom, a handsome rock singer, information that will scare him away from Frank's girlfriend. While it seems at first that Frank is worried about alienating his girlfriend's affections, he really is frightened of losing Tom, who, it turns out, has been sharing Frank's bed as well as that of Frank's supposed girlfriend. The fortune-teller is horrified at the web of white lies the two men have woven, which remind her of the lies she herself has lived. She knows the only hope for Frank is to free himself from the callous, bogus, heterosexual taker," Tom, and find a man worthy of his love. The 1993 revival of the two plays at New York's Roundabout Theater, directed by Gerald Gutierrez and starring in *White Liars* Peter Mac-Nichol, David Aaron Baker, and Nancy Marchand, demonstrated that *White Liars* is the paradigm for all the thwarted homosexual desire in Shaffer's plays and the only play in which the desire is acknowledged openly and somewhat supportively.

The Roundabout Playbill listed *White Liars* and *Black Comedy* as "Two Plays of the Sixties," probably as a way of distancing the producers from any gay anger at the dated depictions of the gay characters. Yet in Gutierrez's production, even *Black Comedy* emerged as a gay-friendly play. What was stunning was that some of the elderly ladies in the Wednesday matinee audience audibly expressed shock and consternation at Frank's agonized confession of love for Tom. It was like watching the play in the mid-sixties with all the melodramatic shock value Shaffer built into the play undimmed by time and greater enlightenment about homosexuality. Any gay or gay-friendly audience member in the supposedly gay nineties could see Frank's confession coming from his first entrance.

Shairp, Mordaunt. *The Green Bay Tree* (in Wilcox I).*

Sherman, Martin. *Bent.* (in Shewey).*

———. A *Madhouse in Goa*. Ambergate, Derbyshire: Amber Lane Press, 1989.* A powerful double bill, produced successfully in London with Vanessa Redgrave and Rupert Graves, about personal, political, artistic, and ecological betrayal.

———. *Passing By* (in Wilcox 1). Lovers contract hepatitis together. A Pre-AIDS romantic comedy.

———. *When She Danced*. Ambergate, Derbyshire: Amber Lane Press, 1988. Loved by British critics in its three London productions (most recently, in 1991, with Vanessa Redgrave and Michael Sheen as the gay Greek pianist), but dismissed by New York critics. A depiction of one of the last days of Isadora Duncan. The gay character has the last word on Isadora.

Silver, Nicky. *Etiquette and Vitriol: The Food Chain and Other Plays*. New York: Theatre Communications Group, 1996.

———. *Raised in Captivity* New York: Theatre Communications Group, 1995.

Nicky Silver is a major voice in contemporary gay theater. His characters seem always to be on the verge of hysteria, willing to commit desperate acts, like stealing a young man who plays an angel in the Radio City Music Hall Christmas show or eating oneself to death. His gay characters are as demented as their straight counterparts. What almost all of his characters share is a need to talk loudly, constantly. His plays are a series of hilarious verbal explosions. *Raised in Captivity* is the best of Silver's works thus far. Typically, it is a family saga. Everyone feels too much or not enough; no one feels worthy of life. Violence is everywhere. The brother and sister discover they are products of a violent rape. Brother is obsessed with a murderer with whom he carries on an epistolary relationship. In the midst of this violence and self hatred, some kind of love is the only happiness. The play is simultaneously hilarious and profoundly sad.

Stevens, David. *The Sum of Us*. New York: Fireside Theatre, 1991. A recent hit Off-Broadway as well as in Australia. Discussed in chapter 4.

Stoppard, Tom. *The Invention of Love*. New York: Grove Press, 1998. Stoppard's fantasia on gay themes centers on Victorian poet-classicist A. E. Housman, who repressed his homosexual desire through his poetic and scholarly work. The final scene is a fantasy argument between

Housman and his opposite, Oscar Wilde, who tells the poet "Your 'honour' is all shame and timidity and compliance."

Swados, Robin. *A Quiet End* (in Helbing). A touching play about a group of men with AIDS who live together.

"The Madness of Lady Bright" (in Hoffman).*

Thomas, Colin. *Flesh and Blood* (in Wallace). A troubled teenage boy has problems dealing with the gayness and illness of his older brother. Written for teen-age audiences, it is a powerful play about family ties.

Tolans, Jonathan. *The Twilight of the Golds.* (V) Tolins tries to make a Wagnerian epic out of a simple domestic drama. A gay man's pregnant sister learns through genetic testing that her son will be gay. David, the gay man, sees this as a rejection of him and severs relations with his family. The parallels between this saga and *The Ring of the Nibelung* take a leap of faith that the viewer is not willing to make. The strength of the piece is Tolin's creation of smothering Jewish parents who are both loving and judgmental. In some ways the television movie, co-written by Tolins and featuring a stellar cast led by Faye Dunaway and Brendan Fraser, by playing out the big confrontations in the style of domestic realism, gives them more power, though I don't quite buy David's mini-Ring production or the final reconciliation engineered by David's lover. The film gives sister Suzanne and her husband more of a voice and a terrific bathroom confrontation.

Tremblay, Michel. *Hosanna*, trans. John Van Burek and Bill Glassco. Vancouver: Talonbooks, 1974. An early play by the highly talented gay Quebecois author. An aging drag queen and her paunchy, aging stud lover realize that times have changed and that their stereotypical gender identifications are out of date.

van Itallie, Jean Claude. *Ancient Boys* (in Ubu anthology)*

Vogel, Paula. *The Baltimore Waltz.* New York: The Fireside Theatre, 1992.*

Wasserstein, Wendy. *The Heidi Chronicles and Other Plays.* New York: Penguin, 1990. Heidi's best friend is a gay pediatrician.

Wellman, Mac. *Sincerity Forever* (in Feingold). Wellman has become the dramatic thorn in the side of the far right. His satire of American conservatism and homophobia is purposely outrageous and right on target, but his plays often lack something in form and polish—they are often more like extended revue sketches. *Sincerity Forever* is his best written piece, a satire of middle American mores in which the small minds of Klan-attired townspeople are taken over by diabolical furballs. Only Jesus, a foul-mouthed Black woman, can save the townspeople.

West, Mae. *The Drag*, in *Three Plays by Mae West*, ed. Lillian Schlissel. New York: Routledge, 1997.* Finally West's banned 1927 play of gay life has been published. It's not great art, but is most valuable in offering a picture of urban gay slang at the time. Class has always been important in understanding gay culture, and West offers a prurient view of one tier of urban gay life.

Whitemore, Hugh. *Breaking the Code.* New York: Fireside Theatre, 1987.*

Wilcox, Michael. *Lent.* London: Methuen, 1983. A reminiscence of adolescence by one of Britain's leading gay playwrights.

———. *Massage and Other Plays.* A paedophile and a rent boy.

———. *Rents.* Wilcox's celebrated depiction of Edinburgh rent boys (hustlers).

Wilson, Doric. *Forever After.* The muses of comedy and tragedy, played by drag queens, interfere in a gay romance.

———. *A Perfect Relationship.* Wilson is one of the most pungent satirists of the pre-AIDS gay scene, both loving and understanding its absurdities.

———. *Street Theater* (in Shewey)*

Wilson, Lanford. *Burn This.* New York: Hill and Wang, 1987. Heterosexual passion and homosexual caution. A romance for the late twentieth century.

———. *5th of July.* New York: Hill and Wang, 1978. Revised "Broadway" version, New York: Dramatists Play Service, 1982.*

———. "A Poster of the Cosmos" (in *The Way We Live Now*).*

Yew, Chay. *Porcelain and A Language of their Own.* New York: Grove Press, 1997.* *Porcelain* is also in Clum. Los Angeles based Singapore native Chay Yew is the leading Asian gay playwright. His first play, *Porcelain,* had its first successful production in London in 1992. Five actors sit in chairs on a bare stage decorated only with red origami birds. Four of the actors provide a chorus and play the supporting roles as the play examines the implications of a murder in a London public toilet. A nineteen-year-old Chinese boy has killed a man with whom he had an affair. Loneliness, racism, internalized homophobia, and "cottaging" (sex in public toilets) are explored in a simple but powerful poetic drama.

Criticism

The following major studies of gay drama have been published since *Acting Gay* was first published.

Clum, John M. " 'And Once I Had It All': AIDS Narratives and Memories of an American Dream." In Timothy F. Murphy and Suzanne Poirier, eds. *Writing AIDS: Gay Literature, Language and Analysis.* New York: Columbia University Press, 1993.

———. " 'Myself of Course': J. R. Ackerley and Self-Dramatization." *Theatre* (July 1993).

———. *Something for the Boys: Musical Theater and Gay Culture.* New York: St. Martin's, 1999.

DeJongh, Nicholas. *Not In Front of the Audience: Homosexuality on Stage.* London: Rutledge, 1992.

Garber, Marjorie. *Vested Interests: Cross-Dressing and Cultural Anxiety.* New York: Harper Perennial, 1993. The best book on the subject with a considerable amount of material on theatrical transvestism.

Goldberg, Jonathan. *Sodometries: Renaissance Texts, Modern Sexualities.* Stanford: Stanford University Press, 1992. A fascinating section on Marlowe and "The Transvestite Stage."

Koestenbaum, Wayne. *The Queen's Throat: Opera, Homosexuality, and the Mystery of Desire.* New York: Poseidon, 1993. Highly personal and provocative, this brilliant book is the best discussion yet of the attraction opera holds for many gay men.

Miller, Carl. *Stages of Desire: Gay Theatre's Hidden History.* London: Cassell, 1996.

Miller, D. A. *Place for Us: Essay on the Broadway Musical.* Cambridge, MA: Harvard University Press, 1998.

O'Connor, Sean. *Straight Acting: Popular Gay Drama from Wilde to Rattigan.* London: Cassell, 1998.

Savran, David. *Communists, Cowboys, and Queers: The Politics of Masculinity in the Work of Arthur Miller and Tennessee Williams.* Minneapolis: University of Minnesota Press, 1992.

Sinfield, Alan. *Out on Stage: Lesbian and Gay Theatre in the Twentieth Century.* New Haven: Yale University Press, 1999.

Bibliographies of Gay Drama

Gay Theatre Alliance Directory of Gay Plays. Terry Helbing, ed. New York: JH Press, 1980. Descriptive list of plays to 1980.

Loeffler, Donald L. *An Analysis of the Treatment of the Homosexual Character in Dramas Produced in the New York Theatre from 1950 to 1968.* New York: Arno Press, 1975, 188–201.

Shewey, Don. *Out Front: Contemporary Gay and Lesbian Plays.* New York: Grove Weidenfeld, 1988. List of produced and published gay drama listing publisher or, for unpublished plays, producing theater.

Publications

The following periodicals offer regular coverage of gay drama.

American Theatre is the best periodical on our theatre, with solid articles on gay drama and dramatists. Many issues contain a full-length play.

The *Village Voice* contains coverage of New York theater, including gay drama and performance art.

Many gay newspapers and magazines contain theater coverage. *The Advocate* is the national gay magazine. There is some theater coverage, which tends to focus on the West Coast. Local gay newspapers such as the *New York Native,* and the *Washington Blade* contain area theater coverage.

In England, the weekly magazine, *Time Out* is the best record of gay drama. The *Gay Times* has some arts coverage.

Canadian Theatre Journal and *Canadian Drama* have offered solid coverage of Canadian gay drama. Both often print playscripts.

INDEX OF NAMES AND TITLES